JUST CARING

JUST CARING

Health Care Rationing and
Democratic Deliberation

Leonard M. Fleck

UNIVERSITY PRESS
2009

OXFORD
UNIVERSITY PRESS

Oxford University Press, Inc., publishes works that further
Oxford University's objective of excellence
in research, scholarship, and education.

Oxford New York
Auckland Cape Town Dar es Salaam Hong Kong Karachi
Kuala Lumpur Madrid Melbourne Mexico City Nairobi
New Delhi Shanghai Taipei Toronto

With offices in
Argentina Austria Brazil Chile Czech Republic France Greece
Guatemala Hungary Italy Japan Poland Portugal Singapore
South Korea Switzerland Thailand Turkey Ukraine Vietnam

Copyright © 2009 by Oxford University Press, Inc.

Published by Oxford University Press, Inc.
198 Madison Avenue, New York, New York 10016
www.oup.com

Oxford is a registered trademark of Oxford University Press.

All rights reserved. No part of this publication may be reproduced,
stored in a retrieval system, or transmitted, in any form or by any means,
electronic, mechanical, photocopying, recording, or otherwise,
without the prior permission of Oxford University Press.

Library of Congress Cataloging-in-Publication Data

Fleck, Leonard M.
Just caring : health care rationing and democratic deliberation /
Leonard M. Fleck.
p. ; cm.
Includes bibliographical references.
ISBN 978-0-19-512804-8
1. Health care rationing—Moral and ethical aspects—United States.
2. Public health—Moral and ethical aspects—United States.
3. Health services accessibility—United States.
4. Right to health care—United States. 5. Health care reform—United States. 6. Social
justice—United States. I. Title.
[DNLM: 1. Health Care Rationing—United States.
2. Democracy—United States. 3. Health Care Reform—United States.
4. Health Priorities—United States. 5. Healthcare Disparities—United States.
6. Insurance, Health—United States. WA 540 AA1 F593j 2009]
RA410.53.F62 2009
362.1'0425—dc22
2008040396

9 8 7 6 5 4 3 2 1
Printed in the United States of America
on acid-free paper

To Jean, My Partner
In Life
In Love
In Labor

PREFACE

For the past 25 years I have written about what I refer to as the "Just Caring" problem. In brief, what does it mean to be a "just" and "caring" society when we have only limited resources to meet virtually unlimited health care needs? From a moral point of view, the problem of health care rationing is *the* problem of contemporary health care. If we cannot adequately meet all the health needs of patients in our health care system, how can we selectively meet health needs in ways that are congruent with our sense of what a just and caring society ought to be?

The word "rationing" calls up in the minds of most people a shortage of resources. But we are not short of physicians or hospital beds or MRI scanners; in that regard we have the capacity to meet the health needs of all our citizens. Our real shortage is fiscal. We are unwilling to allocate the money that is needed to meet the health needs of all our citizens. We are faced with what some writers (Enthoven and Kronick, 1989) refer to as "a paradox of excess and deprivation" in our health care system. Medicaid patients often have great difficulty finding physicians who are willing to provide care for them at reduced compensation levels. We have, in addition, 47 million uninsured in the United States who have no assured access to needed health care. That is the deprivation part of the paradox. On the excess side of the paradox we have these extremely expensive cancer drugs ($50,000–$100,000 for a course of treatment) that yield only extra weeks or months of life.

The Institute of Medicine (2002) reports that about 20,000 of those uninsured Americans die each year *for reasons directly connected to their lack of insurance.*

That is, they lack affordable access to primary care. Consequently, these individuals eventually present to the health care system with advanced disease that is now beyond cure. They die prematurely. How can a society as wealthy as our own that wishes to think of itself as a "just and caring" society tolerate that unnecessary loss of life? In particular, how can we spend so much money on health care interventions that do so little good, yet fail to spend money on timely, relatively inexpensive interventions that could have saved decades of life for each of those 20,000 individuals? The story of Douglas Schmidt at the beginning of Chapter 1 is perfectly illustrative of this point.

What is also paradoxical is that our society publicly affirms in thousands of ways that human life is "priceless." In practice, the lives that are priceless are the lives of paytients [sic]—individuals who are very well insured, permitting them access to many very expensive, marginally beneficial medical interventions. Thus, even though many of our politicians deny that there is any rationing in our health care system, the fact is that we do ration by the ability to pay. We cover up this fact by shedding crocodile tears that threaten to flood a number of major media outlets when a tragic case draws media attention. In late 2007 that was the case of Nataline Sarkisyan. Nataline was 17 years old; she had been battling leukemia for three years. The first two medical efforts had failed to defeat her cancer. On November 21 she received a bone marrow transplant followed with high-dose chemotherapy in Los Angeles, the cost of which is normally $250,000. Her brother was the source of the donated bone marrow. That donation may well have triggered the medical complications that were the immediate cause of her death. Those complications included multi-organ failure (at least her kidneys and liver) and severe neurological complications resulting in a coma. These latter complications diminished significantly the likelihood of survival. Her surgeons wanted to do a liver transplant, which offered a small chance of several extra months of life. The insurance company, however, refused to approve coverage for that surgery (likely in excess of $300,000). Outrage erupted and tears flowed after many media markets across the United States began covering the story.

What is disturbing and disingenuous is that none of the 20,000 premature deaths associated with lack of insurance elicited any media attention, much less copious tears. Nataline was unfortunately doomed to die; no amount of money would change that. Some amount of money, however, would have saved the lives of those other 20,000 individuals.

We are too quick too blame overzealous lawyers, overpaid CEOs of health care institutions, and greedy insurance companies for the fiscal shortfalls in our health care system. Each of us should be "looking within" instead. We are very much of a divided mind in regard to our health care system. We want for our future possible selves as patients everything contemporary medical technology can offer that will improve the length or quality of our lives. But as presently healthy taxpayers/insurance premium payers we want health care costs controlled. We tell Congress that; we tell Aetna that. We do not want "others" to be spending "our money" on these extremely expensive cancer drugs or other "last-chance therapies." We expect these "others" to be good citizens and good patients, accept their deaths with equanimity, and die cheaply. These "others" have no right to waste "our money." Of course, what we avoid giving any thought to is the fact that we are just another one of those "others" from the point of view of our fellow citizens. This captures in a nutshell the "Just Caring" problem: Why should anyone else pay attention to my demands for justice in meeting my health care needs when I refuse to pay attention to their demands for justice in meeting their health care needs?

Where do all these health needs come from? Why have health care costs in the United States escalated from $26 billion per year (5.2% of GDP in 1960) to $2.3 trillion per year (16.5% of GDP in 2007) (Borger et al., 2006)? One primary answer can be given to both these questions. Emerging medical technologies over the past 40 years have been the primary drivers of health care costs. These same medical technologies have dramatically expanded what we regard as the domain of "health care needs." Daniel Callahan (1990) has been the most correct and most consistent advocate for this point. How many coronary angioplasties did we "need" in the United States in 1970? The correct answer is that we needed none because the technique had not yet been invented. How many of these procedures did we "need" in 2006 in the United States? We apparently needed about 1.2 million of them at a cost of about $35,000 each. There have been thousands of these examples in our health care system over the past 40 years.

Another health policy analyst (Wildavsky, 1977) has introduced another memorable phrase into the literature: We are "doing better and feeling worse." We are "doing better" because we have reduced by more than 50% over the past 30 years the number of people who die each year of heart disease. This is due to both multiple advances in cardiac medicine and surgery, as well as successful public health programs aimed at smoking and diet changes. But we are "feeling worse" because these prolonged lives are now afflicted with a greater, prolonged burden of more costly chronic degenerative illnesses, such as cancer, joint problems, and Alzheimer's disease. We are also seeing a large increase in patients in their eighties and nineties seeking major and costly cardiac surgery (Bachetta et al., 2003) that would have been unthinkable 15 years ago (because of great improvements in the skill and technique of these surgeons). We have to wonder, from the perspective of what a just and caring society ought to be, how we can fund through Medicare these life-prolonging technologies for patients in their nineties while allowing tens of thousands of the uninsured to die prematurely, far short of age 70, often by decades. This, too, is part of "feeling worse."

If we fail to address directly that "care gap" by having frank public discussions of the "Just Caring" problem, the consequence will be that the care gap will get worse. As things are now, about 35% of that $2.3 trillion (roughly $800 billion) is spent on the 13% of our population over age 65 (Freund and Smeeding, 2002). But the aging-out of the "baby boom" generation will see a doubling of the size of that population group (from 39 million to about 78 million) by the year 2030, which will be about 21% of the total population then. If current medical technology does not improve a bit over the next 20 years, we would have a serious moral and political problem so far as the fair allocation of health resources in our society is concerned. But that is clearly a false assumption. Rather, we are very likely to see the full deployment of the totally implantable artificial heart during that time (now in clinical testing). That device will have costs of about $300,000 per implantation. Who should have a just claim at public expense to that device? Should all Medicare patients be eligible, including patients in their eighties and nineties? Should all Medicare patients with cancer have access to those expensive cancer drugs? Think about the other costs of medications needed by the elderly.

These are the sorts of facts that make the need for health care rationing inescapable. The full support for this claim and the many dimensions of this problem are laid out in the first two chapters of this volume. If the need for health care rationing cannot be avoided, then how ought it be accomplished? There are three critical characteristics to a fair approach to health care rationing: it must be (1) public or visible, (2) self-imposed, and (3) justified by public reasons, the sorts of reasons that citizens in a liberal pluralistic democratic society must be prepared to give each other to legitimate any public policy. What we reject are all rationing practices that are effected secretly or invisibly, so that patients are unaware of the health care they need that is being denied to them. What we reject for the most part are rationing practices based upon individual ability to pay for needed health care. What we reject are rationing practices and protocols that are a product of interest group conflict and relative interest group power. What we reject are rationing protocols that are a product of pure individual medical judgment uninformed by publicly legitimated considerations of health care justice.

What we explain and endorse as the basis for a fair approach to the health care rationing problem in the middle chapters of this volume are processes of rational, democratic deliberation. It is through these *public* conversations that we collectively articulate and construct our shared sense of health care justice and a complex set of rationing practices and protocols that we judge to be congruent with that sense of health care justice. All who could be affected by the outcome of this deliberative process are welcome as participants in the deliberative process.

What this process is intended to yield are "just enough" (not perfectly "just") rationing protocols that we are collectively willing to impose upon our future possible selves (perhaps needing what we will have judged to be excessively costly marginally beneficial health care). These rationing protocols are justified both by our considered judgments of health care justice and by our reciprocal willingness to impose these limitations on our future possible selves. In effect, what we say to one another is this: "I am unwilling to pay for an artificial heart (or these expensive cancer drugs) for your future possible 80-year-old self because there are too many other health care needs that we are currently failing to meet at earlier stages in life where we can do more health good for less money. Or, even if we cannot do "more good for less money earlier in life," we sometimes have a moral obligation as a matter of justice to spend substantial sums of money for effective medical interventions that will help someone come closer to attaining a normal life expectancy. I understand that if I am unwilling to spend that money for you for an artificial heart or expensive cancer drugs at age 80, then you also have the right to refuse to spend your money for an artificial heart or those cancer drugs for me at that age." This is reciprocal justice. This is *freely self-imposed* rationing.

To be effective and fair, this deliberative process requires that we all be part of the same health care system, not the thousands of health care systems we now find in the United States We need a system that is "leakproof." We need a system in which we can say that the savings we achieve by imposing a specific rationing protocol on your future possible elderly self and my future possible elderly self will be "captured" and used for what we collectively judge are higher priority, more costworthy, and more beneficial health care services. What would be morally objectionable would be having those savings leak out to shareholders or higher CEO salaries or increased physician income.

I have spoken here of health care rationing in connection with future health care needs of the elderly as if they alone are the focus of rationing decisions. That is not my intent. I have to use examples such as that because an overwhelmingly disproportionate share of health care spending is directed at meeting the health care needs of the elderly. In practice, however, just rationing decisions will need to be made at all stages of life with regard to most disease processes and most medical interventions in some range of clinical circumstances. Some writers will argue that rationing is avoidable, that massive resource savings can be achieved simply with painless gains in efficiency and elimination of wasteful medical practices. But we will show that too often one person's waste and inefficiency is another's life-sustaining medical care. This is certainly the case with patients in a persistent vegetative state.

The "Just Caring" problem is extraordinarily complex because of the heterogeneity of health care needs, because of clinical uncertainty, because of great variation in the effectiveness of different health care interventions (sometimes related to patients' physiological differences, sometimes related to behavioral choices), because of styles of medical practice, because of uncertain criteria for judging the costworthiness of various interventions, and because of a conflicting understanding of what should count as a *just* distribution of health care resources. Consequently, there are no economic formulas, no practice guidelines, no evidence-based medical protocols, no moral theory, no managerial rule books, no legal understandings, and no prescient experts that can yield fair, reasonable, and legitimate resolutions to the "Just Caring" problem. What we need instead are the processes of rational democratic deliberation guided by public reason (Rawls, 1993) and infused with democratic social intelligence (John Dewey, 1916, 1935) to achieve the social agreements (shared understandings of health care justice and specific rationing protocols/health care priorities) necessary to begin to resolve the "Just Caring" problem. This volume is intended to provide the resources needed to initiate that conversation.

ACKNOWLEDGMENTS

I must first thank my partner in life and love and labor, Jean Edmunds, for her endless energy, outstanding research skills, and soothing emotional support throughout this project. Jean has the patience of Job, the wisdom of Solomon, and the wit of the Irish—I needed all of that! I must also thank my academic colleagues (broadly construed), whose diligent work made my own work possible. I have in mind Norm Daniels, Daniel Callahan, Dan Brock, Allen Buchanan, Dan Wikler, Ezekiel Emanuel, Paul Menzel, Rosamond Rhodes, Anita Silvers, Adrienne Asch, Peter Ubel, Margaret Battin, Leslie Francis, Haavi Morreim, Frances Kamm, Tristram Engelhardt, Erik Parens, Arthur Caplan, Tom Murray, Marion Danis, Larry Gostin, Jim Childress, Chris Hackler, Tim Murphy, Dan Sulmasy, Reidar Lie, Mary Mahowald, Dorothy Vawter, and Niall Maclean. These are all individuals whom I know personally who have produced important work related to issues of health care justice or democratic deliberation—work that I have found to be insightful or provocative or both. I hope my own work is worthy of their respect.

I also need to thank my colleagues at the Center for Ethics and Humanities in the Life Sciences at Michigan State University, who are the most supportive colleagues any academic could ever hope for. I need to mention by name those who tolerated me the longest—Howard Brody, Tom Tomlinson, and Judith Andre. I have been blessed. I offer a special word of thanks to Peggy Anderson, who resolved a number of technical "Word" glitches associated with linking separate chapters with endnotes into a single document. Jan Holmes also deserves credit for rescuing, expediting, or retrieving assorted documents and manuscripts over the years.

I must also thank colleagues in my other academic home, the Philosophy Department at Michigan State University; especially Martin Benjamin, Bruce Miller, Jim Nelson, Hilde Lindemann, Steve Esquith, Marilyn Frye, and Richard Peterson. They have offered numerous helpful comments at colloquia at which I have participated. I am especially grateful to Martin Benjamin for the summer reading groups he organized in his home on topics in social and political philosophy. I thank Marsha Rappley, Dean of the College of Human Medicine, for a reasonable level of committee work, which has allowed me the time to complete this volume. She has been a pillar of support for the entire Center for Ethics.

I thank my graduate students in the Philosophy Department, who have contributed in numerous ways to the quality of the seminar I offer on "health care justice." They will enrich and renew this field. I mention in particular Susan Goold, MD, whose own work on democratic deliberation has been part of that renewal. I thank my medical students for their patience and good humor. I am confident they will be just and caring physicians who will help to reform our health care system.

I am enormously grateful to all my former professors who taught me to write well, read voraciously, and think critically. It is not their fault that I have an unmanageable proclivity for pleonastic prose. I thank Michigan State University for the sabbatical in 2002 at Northeastern University that allowed me to generate first drafts of several important chapters in this volume. And I thank the Philosophy Department at Northeastern University for a warm reception and a nurturing intellectual atmosphere.

Finally, I thank my parents and my siblings for a lifetime of emotional support that included lots of laughs, a few tears, and many wonderful meals. Our own children (Jonathan, Eileen, and Matthew) have been heroically tolerant of my philosophic idiosyncrasies, especially my expectation that they struggle with the "trolley problem" at the beach during the summer when they were eight, ten, and twelve years old. I tried to mollify them by saying that I could have made them work through Kant's Transcendental Deduction, but that was a poor tactic. My daughter Eileen gets the last bit of praise. She is a long-distance runner who has been state champion in Michigan for cross-country. Throughout the writing of this volume I kept next to my desk a large poster of her running. The reader can readily appreciate the need for that inspiration.

Chapter 13 was originally published as "Just Caring: The Challenges of Priority Setting in Public Health," in *The Blackwell Guide to Medical Ethics*, edited by Rosamond Rhodes, Leslie Francis, and Anita Silvers (Oxford, UK: Blackwell Publishing, 2007, pp. 323–40). My thanks to Wiley-Blackwell for permission to reprint this essay. Chapter 10 was originally published as "Just Caring: Do Future Possible Children Have a Just Claim to a Sufficiently Healthy Genome?" in *Medicine and Social Justice: Essays on the Distribution of Health Care*, edited by Rosamond Rhodes, Margaret Battin and Anita Silvers (Oxford, UK: Oxford University Press, 2002, pp. 446–58).

Leonard M. Fleck, Ph.D.
March 20, 2008

CONTENTS

1	JUST CARING: AN INTRODUCTION	3
	The "Just Caring" Problem: Core Argument	5
	Rationing Justly: The Moral Challenge	11
	Applications of the Deliberative Model	20
2	THE ETHICAL CHALLENGES OF HEALTH CARE RATIONING	34
	The Story of Coby Howard and Its Lessons	35
	Why Health Care Rationing Is Inescapable	39
	Renal Dialysis and the Medicare End-Stage Renal Disease (ESRD) Amendments	44
	The Totally Implantable Artificial Heart (TIAH)	55
3	PRICING HUMAN LIFE: GETTING BEYOND TRAGIC CHOICES	71
	Is Human Life Priceless?	74
	Tragic Choices or Tragic Disingenuousness? Invisible Rationing	81
	Invisible Rationing and the Publicity Condition	88
	Managed Care and Health Care Rationing	95

4	ELEMENTS OF HEALTH CARE JUSTICE	100
	Is Health Care Morally Special?	103
	Non-ideal Justice: A Moral Analysis and Defense	112
	Pluralism, Justice, and Rational Democratic Deliberation	124
5	RATIONAL DEMOCRATIC DELIBERATION: SCOPE AND STRUCTURE	140
	The Scope of Rational Democratic Deliberation	141
	Fair Health Care Rationing: Not Markets, Not Physicians, Not Bureaucrats	148
	Rational Democratic Deliberation: Taking Seriously the Tragedy of the Commons	151
	Rational Democratic Deliberation: Key Structural Features	160
	Rational Democratic Deliberation and Fair Health Care Rationing	164
	Wide Reflective Equilibrium and Just Health Care Rationing	171
	Priority Setting, Wide Reflective Equilibrium, and Rational Democratic Deliberation: Addressing the Stability Problem	177
	Facts, Wide Reflective Equilibrium, and Democratic Deliberation	181
	Constitutional Principles of Health Care Justice and Rational Democratic Deliberation	184
	Evaluating the Deliberative Process	195
	Objections and Responses	199
6	SETTING LIMITS FOR EFFECTIVE COSTLY THERAPIES	202
	Problem Introduction	202
	Setting Limits: Options in the ESRD Program	205
	Setting Limits: Options for HIV+/AIDS Patients	208
	Setting Limits: The Case of Artificial Hearts	219
	Setting Limits: Concluding Comments	227
7	LAST-CHANCE THERAPIES	229
	Introduction: Scope of the Problem	229
	Why Last-Chance Therapies? Weak Moral Arguments	231
	Last-Chance Therapies and Rational Democratic Deliberation	242
	Futility and Last-Chance Therapies	249
8	RATIONING, CATASTROPHIC ILLNESS, AND DISABLED PATIENTS	254
	Introduction: The Scope of the Problem	254
	Needs Are Not Enough; Effectiveness Must Matter	256

	The Oregon Plan and the Disability Critique	259
	Health Care Justice and the Disability Critique	263
	Defining the Disabled: Ethical Implications	268
	Conclusions	273
9	IS AGE-BASED RATIONING EVER "JUST ENOUGH"?	276
	Defining the Problem: Can We Accept Natural Limits to Life?	276
	Justice and Age-Based Rationing: Fair Innings	279
	The Prudential Life Span Account	285
	Age-Based Rationing: Major Objections	290
	Age-Based Rationing: Responses to Objections	291
	Age-Based Rationing and the Duty to Rescue	294
	Conclusions	299
10	DO FUTURE POSSIBLE CHILDREN HAVE A JUST CLAIM TO A SUFFICIENTLY HEALTHY GENOME?	300
	Framing the Issue	303
	Preimplantation Genetic Diagnosis (PGD): A Historical Side Note	306
	Does Justice Require Public Funding for Limited PGD?	308
	Concluding Comments: Justice and Genetic Enhancement	316
11	ORGAN TRANSPLANTATION: WHEN IS ENOUGH ENOUGH?	318
	Scope of the Issue	318
	The Maximization Argument: A Critical Moral Analysis	320
	The Pittsburgh Protocol: How Dead Must Donors Be?	324
	Organ Procurement and Financial Incentives: A Critical Assessment	327
	Presumed Consent/Duty to Donate: Critical Remarks	331
	Justice and Multi-Organ Transplants or Retransplants	333
	Concluding Comments	341
12	THE LIBERALISM PROBLEM	342
	Justice, Health Care Needs, and Morally Controversial Interventions	342
	Liberal Communitarianism: Is It Just Enough? Is It Liberal Enough?	347
	Resolving the Liberalism Problem: Public Reason and Public Interests	352
	Concluding Reflections	359

13	THE ETHICAL CHALLENGES OF PRIORITY SETTING IN PUBLIC HEALTH	362
	Defining the Problem	362
	The Scope of Public Health: Challenges and Choices	365
	Health Care Justice and Public Health: When Is Enough Enough?	368
	Setting Public Health Priorities Justly: The Limits of Moral Theory	375
14	FINANCING HEALTH CARE FAIRLY	379
	Why National Health Insurance?	379
	Why Health Reform?	383
	Assessing Competing Proposals for Health Reform	384
	Health Savings Accounts: A Critical Assessment	385
	Health Care Vouchers: A Critical Assessment	388
	Single-Payer Reform: A Constructive Proposal	394
	Summary and Reflective Conclusions	399
	NOTES	403
	REFERENCES	427
	INDEX	447

JUST CARING

1

JUST CARING

An Introduction

Angel Diaz is 69 years old and in the very advanced stages of Alzheimer's Disease (AD). He had been a machine operator and part-time minister in Philadelphia (Anand, 2003). The first signs of AD were in the early 1990s. His brother cared for him until May of 2002 when Angel choked on some food and required emergency hospitalization. He emerged ventilator-dependent with a feeding tube, and was discharged to a nursing home. In February 2003 Angel developed pneumonia and intestinal bleeding. Since then he has spent 140 days in the hospital at a cost of $280,000, less than half of which was covered by insurance. This represents a very large drain on the charity care resources of this hospital. Is a just and caring hospital (or Medicare/Medicaid) morally obligated to provide these resources to sustain Angel's life in this extremely debilitated state? If an abnormal rhythm had been detected in Angel's heart that could possibly become a fatal arrhythmia, would a just and caring hospital be morally obligated to install an Implantable Cardiac Defibrillator at a cost of more than $40,000 (Goldberger and Lampert, 2006; Pauker et al.; 2005; Petersen, 2003)? If Angel went into heart failure, would we be morally obligated to provide him with a Left Ventricular Assist Device (LVAD) at a cost of about $200,000? Could failure to provide such care be rightly construed as unjust discrimination against individuals with disabilities?

In March of 2003 Douglas Schmidt, 37 years old, from Portland, Oregon, collapsed as a result of a very serious epileptic seizure. He sustained very severe brain damage that left him in a ventilator-dependent comatose state. After seven months and a series of other medical crises that included kidney failure and multi-drug resistant pneumonia his partner and a court-appointed guardian asked a judge that his ventilator be removed and that he be allowed to die (Associated Press, 2003; Colburn, 2003). How should we think of this death from a moral point of view? Is it sufficient to describe it as an unfortunate tragedy because he had died in the prime of his life? Ordinarily, that would be a true and adequate description. However, Mr. Schmidt was uninsured. He needed two expensive medications (Celexa for obsessive-compulsive disorder, and Lamictal, an antiseizure medication) to prevent these major seizures for which he was at risk. He lost his prescription drug benefit because of budget cuts at the state level. Lamictal cost $13 per day. His drug costs for a year would have been about $5,500. Given these additional facts, would we (citizens who aspire to have a just and caring society) still conclude that his death was "merely unfortunate," a matter of "bad medical luck"? That description no longer seems quite accurate. There seems to be something wrong here. At the very least we are motivated to say that this should not have happened. It looks uncaring, and it might be unjust as well.[1]

At the end of 2005 Dr. Michael DeBakey suffered what would later be diagnosed as a dissecting aortic aneurysm (Altman, 2006). He was 97 years old at the time; he is unquestionably among the most preeminent of heart surgeons in the world. He was very uncertain that he wanted anything other than palliative care, in part because he feared being left with serious cognitive deficits as a result of the surgery. But his wife and colleagues partially persuaded him to accept surgery, though the local anesthetists refused to participate in the surgery because they judged it excessively risky and his consent uncertain.[2] The surgery did go forward and was successful, though there were numerous complications that required an eight-month hospitalization whose costs exceeded one million dollars. Altman reports that these costs were "absorbed" by the hospital, as opposed to being charged to Medicare or any other insurer. The question I want to raise is whether Dr. DeBakey had a just claim to the million dollars worth of medical and hospital care he received (recognizing the enormity of his contributions to medicine). If we had a socially legitimated rationing protocol that would deny such surgery to anyone over age 80 because of the costs of the intervention, and with the greater likelihood of a bad outcome (death or survival with a serious disability) and the judgment that higher priority health needs would otherwise go unmet, would Dr. DeBakey have been treated unjustly had he been denied this procedure in accord with this social rule?

I am asking the reader to engage in a little thought experiment just now. Pretend as if I gave you a "money wand," which has magical powers. It cannot create money from nothing. That is contrary to the fundamental laws of economics. But it can "magically move" money from one budget to another, just as you can move text in your word processing program from one document to another. It is February of 2003. Would you use your money wand to move money from Mr. Diaz to Mr. Schmidt? If you do, Mr. Diaz will die from his intestinal bleeding within days of being hospitalized. Mr. Schmidt will have his drugs paid for and will not suffer the epileptic seizure that ultimately resulted in his premature death. You may not feel completely good about this. You might really want money for both men.

But the money wand is not that magical. All you can do is move money. Would you judge (however regretfully) that you had made a better choice, morally speaking, by saving Mr. Schmidt's life and allowing Mr. Diaz to die? Likewise, pretend that Dr. DeBakey's medical problem occurred in February 2003 as well. You could also use your money wand to move money from Dr. DeBakey to Mr. Schmidt. Would you use your money wand in that way as well? That sort of question, ultimately, is the focus of this book.

THE "JUST CARING" PROBLEM: CORE ARGUMENT

We are going to be discussing the problem of health care rationing throughout this book. As we will quickly see, it is a complex and multidimensional moral and political problem that is ultimately inescapable. One dimension of that problem is the task of just priority setting. This is what I was asking you to think about in connection with the three earlier stories. If we had unlimited sums of money for meeting health care needs, then there would be no need for priority setting. But no magic wand exists that creates money from nothing. This is what I have referred to since 1980 as the "Just Caring" problem: What does it mean to be a just and caring society when we have only limited resources to meet virtually unlimited health care needs? In 2006 we in the United States spent about $2.16 trillion on health care, which represented about 16.3% of our Gross Domestic Product (GDP) (Catlin et al., 2007). This is an astounding sum of money. No other country in the world spends as much per capita for health care as we do (just under $7,000 in 2006), or as large a fraction of their GDP.[3] But we still have 47 million individuals who are without health insurance and without assured access to needed health care, as in the case of Mr. Schmidt. Reasonable projections to 2014 put us at $4.08 trillion for health spending, or 19.5% of GDP (Heffler et al., 2005).

Limited Resources and Unlimited Needs

Why do we say that we have only "limited resources" to meet health care needs? One answer is that there are many other legitimate compelling social needs that command resources, not to mention all manner of legitimate private wants.[4] Another answer is that taxpayers and insurance premium-payers are very unwilling to spend much more money on health care. Roughly 45% ($903 billion) of that $2 trillion (in 2005) represents public funds, mostly Medicare and Medicaid (Catlin et al., 2007). For the past several years Congress and the vast majority of state legislatures have passed numerous tax cuts, which must necessarily have consequences for health care since health spending is the second largest budget category at the federal level, and sometimes the largest at the state level. Most of the rest of that $2.0 trillion comes from health insurance premiums paid directly by employers (but ultimately by employees). Up until 1995 most employees did not directly feel those health insurance costs because those costs were part of a "benefit package." However, as health care costs have risen more and more precipitously, employers are either dropping health insurance altogether or requiring all manner of cost-sharing by employees as a way of instilling more cost-conscious health choices by them, including premium-sharing, co-payments for specific services, and various deductibles (Enthoven and Fuchs, 2006, Galvin and Delbanco, 2006; Matthews, 2003; Strom, 2003; Terhune, 2003).

How much have health care costs escalated in recent decades in the U.S.? Why have they escalated? Is it just hyperbolic rhetoric when we refer in our "Just Caring" question to "virtually unlimited health care needs"? In 1960 we spent only $26 billion on health care in the U.S., which was 5.2% of GDP at the time. That rose to $73 billion by 1970 as a result of average 10.6% annual increases in health expenditures during that decade (Catlin et al., 2007). More than half of those escalating costs are explained by emerging medical technologies over the past forty years; everything from the creation of the ICU to respirators to advanced diagnostic technologies (MRI, CT, and PET scanning); exquisitely engineered (very costly) drugs that yield many extra life-years (the protease inhibitors for HIV+ patients), to extremely complex surgical interventions (all manner of organ transplants and cardiac interventions) that also yield many extra years of life; elegant prosthetic equipment that permits functional restoration for individuals who have suffered devastating injuries, to the potential for genetic intervention in eight-cell embryos as well as adults in all areas of medicine. If we consider the three earlier scenarios, we will immediately realize that none of these individuals would have been alive to generate all the costs they did but for the expensive medical technologies that have been deployed over the past forty years. Further, we would not have had the moral or political problem associated with the premature death of Mr. Schmidt but for the invention of the drugs Lamictal and Celexa. To be sure, Mr. Schmidt would have died prematurely, but that death would then have been correctly described as being merely "unfortunate." Further, there would have been no need for a state-funded prescription drug program for the uninsured because the uninsured could easily have afforded whatever drugs were available from their personal funds.[5]

The other point that needs emphasis is that the volume of health needs and emerging medical technologies are correlative with one another, not independent of each other. As Daniel Callahan has masterfully demonstrated (1990), and as we will show again in detail in Chapter 2, what we regard as the domain of health needs (that make important moral claims on society) expands in tandem with these emerging medical technologies. Prior to 1970 there was no need for coronary bypass surgery or coronary angioplasty because they had not been invented as yet (though, of course there were coronary arteries closing off and causing heart attacks). But in 2004 there was an apparent "need" for 1.7 million of these two procedures. For 2007 it is estimated that there will be more than 7 million inpatient cardiovascular operations and procedures with a total direct cost of $283 billion (American Heart Association, 2007, p. 37). There is a projected annual need for 600,000 implantable cardiac defibrillators (ICDs) by 2012 at a cost of $40,000 each ($24 billion annually); 200,000 left ventricular assist devices (LVADs) annually for patients in end-stage congestive heart failure at $150,000 each ($30 billion) annually (*Heart Disease Weekly* editors [published by News RX], 2003); and a potential annual market of

350,000 totally implantable artificial hearts (TIAHs) at a cost of $200,000 each ($70 billion annually). In 2003 there were 13 million Americans on statins (cholesterol-lowering drugs) at a cost to consumers of $20 billion (Mitka, 2003); but some medical experts maintain that 65 million Americans ought to be on statins, which would represent a potential annual cost of $100 billion.[6] About 400,000 Americans currently have been diagnosed with multiple sclerosis, with annual costs per patient of about $40,000 and projected lifetime costs per patient of $2.2 million (Whetten-Goldstein et al., 1998). Presently (2007) more than 470,000 individuals in kidney failure have their lives sustained through the End-Stage Renal Disease Program of Medicare at a cost of about $57,000 each, or $23 billion annually (U.S. Renal Data System, 2006). This program is growing by about 25,000 patients per year. Projections are that 660,000 patients will have their lives sustained by that program by the year 2012, and 2.24 million by 2030 (when much of the "baby boom" generation will have aged out).

We should also keep in mind the very high costs associated with treating medical conditions that are not life-threatening. It is estimated that by 2030 the demand for total hip arthroplasties will grow by 174% to 572,000 cases per year, at a cost of $25,000–$30,000 per case (in 2007 dollars), or about $17 billion per year (Kurtz et al., 2007). More startling still are the projections for total knee arthroplasties, which are projected to increase by 673% by 2030 to 3.48 million procedures per year—$29,000 per case (in 2007 dollars), or $102 billion per year (Kurtz et al., 2007). In 2003 health expenditures for adults with arthritis or other rheumatic conditions in the U.S. totaled $321.8 billion (Yellin et al., 2007).

If we wished, we could generate a very long list here by discussing the needs of patients with various forms of cancer, the needs of patients with hemophilia or COPD, or various forms of liver disease, cystic fibrosis, or AIDS. We could discuss the needs of patients who have suffered various severe impairments as a result of accident and what the capacities of rehabilitative medicine are. We could talk about the need for expanded long-term care, especially for the very rapidly growing population of patients with Alzheimer's disease (projected to reach 16 million in the U.S. by 2030, from 4.5 million in 2006). These are for the most part extremely old patients who were able to attain these very long lives as a result of the successes in the other areas of medicine we have been surveying.

The point I am reinforcing is that health needs are virtually limitless because the development of novel and costly medical technologies shows no sign of abating. If health needs continue to expand as they have for the past forty years, health costs will continue to expand as well unless we deliberately intervene to control costs. If we deliberately intervene, then we must be prepared as a society to deal with what Uwe Reinhardt (1982) has called the two Great Equations in health care.[7] They are that COST CONTROL = CARE CONTROL and that COST CONTROL = INCOME CONTROL. The latter equation is fundamentally a political problem. I do not intend to discuss that at any length, though as a society we would ignore that political fact at our peril. The other great equation represents, what I will argue, a moral problem. That is our central problem. That is the "Just Caring" problem. That is the problem of health care rationing.

Rationing Is Inescapable

The need for health care rationing is inescapable. I need to postpone to Chapter 2 providing more fully the argument and evidence that will justify that claim. However, there is one misconception that needs to be dispelled immediately, namely that health care rationing is a problem we will need to address in the near future. The implication is that rationing is not part of our health care system at present. That is simply false—Mr. Schmidt was a victim of a rationing decision. The bureaucrats who cut funding for the prescription drug program for the uninsured working poor did not see themselves as making a rationing decision; they were merely cutting health care costs for the state of Oregon. That is, they did not see themselves as "denying needed care" to Mr. Schmidt. But that is what they did, and that is a good rough definition of what rationing is about. This is why that first Great Equation says that cost containment in health care means care containment.

Very few individuals who have responsibility for health care budgets ever see themselves as being responsible for making rationing decisions. They see themselves instead as setting health care priorities, making allocation decisions across health programs, increasing efficiency in the delivery of health services, identifying more cost-effective medications for a formulary, and educating patients to make wiser (less costly) decisions about their own care through the use of co-pays and other financial incentives. When I was a member of the White House Task Force on Health Care Reform in 1993 for the Clinton Administration we were informed that we were to abstain from use of the language of rationing (Fleck, 1994b). Any of the locutions introduced earlier in this paragraph were acceptable, but not the word 'rationing.' If we went to an authoritative dictionary to discover why the word 'rationing' elicits such a strong aversive reaction we would find nothing that would enlighten us; we have to look instead to our own political culture. What rationing implies in a health care context is that someone with a genuine health need is denied the health care intervention that they need and want for primarily monetary reasons (as opposed to reasons related to the absolute scarcity of that health care intervention, such as a transplantable liver). Rationing means that someone who is healthy (and in a position of political power) denies an individual who is sick and powerless the health care which they need. On the face of it, rationing appears to be illiberal, inhumane, and immoral. These connotations are very firmly attached to the concept of rationing in our political culture (Ubel, 2000, chap. 2).[8] To be clear, I am only stating this as a cultural fact, not as a normative conclusion I would endorse.

If we return to the case of Mr. Diaz, and if we imagine at the beginning of his hospital admission that his attending physician and the hospital administrator made a careful assessment of his medical circumstances, and if they concluded that Mr. Diaz was likely to have a very long, very expensive stay that would result in his not being cured and their not being paid, and if they decided not to provide him that care and "allow him to die," then this would be a paradigm case of rationing with all the negative connotations I outlined above. Mr. Diaz (or his relatives) would not have freely consented to this denial of care. From a sociocultural perspective Mr. Diaz is a politically powerless member of our society. And Mr. Diaz would have been denied this care and condemned to death for primarily monetary reasons. If this is what rationing "really" is, then we can see why no respectable person would want to be associated with such a practice. In reality, however, Mr. Diaz was offered everything medicine had available that offered any chance at all of reversing his medical problems, no matter what the cost. What our society wants to profess is an absolute respect for the value of human life. We sometimes capture this sentiment by saying that human life is priceless (Ubel, 2000), that we have a "duty to rescue" (Hadorn, 1991; McKie and Richardson, 2003) when we have the medical capacity to save or prolong a life, and that we are morally obligated to make that effort no matter what the financial cost. If we are really committed as a society to these values, however, then how do we explain the rationing decisions that resulted in the death of Mr. Schmidt? Was this just a moral lapse of some sort?

Mr. Schmidt did not die as a result of any rationing decision; on the contrary, more than a million dollars was spent trying to save his life after that epileptic seizure occurred. Mr. Schmidt only died when he did because his partner asked that his ventilator be withdrawn since she believed that was in his best interest, all things considered. That difficult and thoughtful decision by her was one that the medical staff and the courts agreed needed to be respected because we are a liberal society that endorses the practice of respect for patient autonomy. This is essentially the moral logic that justified hospice programs. Again, to be clear, I most certainly endorse this latter bit of moral logic. But I reject the view of those who would deny that any rationing decision had been made here.

The Problem of Invisible Rationing

A distinction needs to be introduced here that will be critical to the overall argument of this book. This distinction will help to explain the view of those who deny that Mr. Schmidt's death was related to any rationing decision. The distinction is between "visible" and "invisible" forms of health care rationing, sometimes discussed in the literature as the distinction between "explicit" and "implicit" rationing (Fleck, 1987; Fleck, 1990a, 1990b; Hall, 1997, chap. 6; Mechanic, 2006; Mechanic and Schlesinger, 1996). I need to reserve until Chapter 3 a careful and critical analysis of this distinction, but some introductory comments are in order for the sake of conveying the core argument of this book.

There are two key claims that I will want to defend. First, the vast majority of rationing decisions that occur in our society occur in the invisible or implicit mode. That means the decisions themselves are effectively hidden from public scrutiny, and that the political actors who enact these decisions do not see themselves as being morally accountable for any of the bad health outcomes for individuals affected by these decisions. As I explain below, this is what happened in the case of Mr. Schmidt. Second, invisible or implicit health care rationing is presumptively unjust. This is because such decisions violate an absolutely central element of our shared conception of justice, what the political philosopher John Rawls has referred to as the "publicity condition" (Rawls, 1993, pp. 66–71). In brief, when we have just social policies and practices nothing is hidden, and nothing needs to be hidden. This is why our legislative bodies must deliberate publicly and why judicial proceedings (with rare exceptions) must be conducted publicly as well.

A perplexed reader might reasonably ask at this point, "How could it be correct to say that an invisible rationing decision was made with respect to Mr. Schmidt? After all, this was a public policy or public budget decision—nothing was hidden." True, the budget decision was not hidden. But the responsible legislators and bureaucrats would have described the decision to themselves and to the public as an allocation decision, not as a rationing decision. They would have argued that they did not deny Mr. Schmidt access to the medications he needed to avert his seizures; they merely denied funding to the program that paid for those medications. Further, they will argue, it is not as if they had sole or primary responsibility for providing the funding needed to purchase those medications. What about Mr. Schmidt's family or friends, or his church or neighbors? They could have helped, but they did not. More generally, the taxpayers of Oregon were in a stingy mood and expected legislators to do something to control health care costs borne publicly. Further still, they can argue, it was an unfortunate medical accident that Mr. Schmidt had this seizure; no one should be held morally blameworthy for that. After all, there were hundreds or thousands of other patients who obtained needed medications through this prescription coverage program, such as drugs to lower their cholesterol or to control their blood pressure. None of them dropped dead (we will hypothesize) as a result of the program no longer being funded.

I will accept as descriptively accurate everything said in the prior paragraph. What the description illustrates, however, is that the rationing decision itself that is implicit in this budgetary shift is almost completely invisible. That is, none of those involved in making or executing this policy decision sees a moral problem, a matter of health care justice that ought to be assessed explicitly. Nor do they see themselves as having any moral responsibility for Mr. Schmidt's fate. This is seriously morally problematic, as I shall argue more fully in Chapter 3. No doubt there are political and psychological advantages to keeping rationing decisions implicit and invisible, as Calabresi and Bobbitt (1978) have argued. But from a moral point of view such efforts are fundamentally dishonest and *can* conceal what are real injustices from both recognition and correction. Thus, for the time being I am simply agnostic on the issue of whether or not Mr. Schmidt has been treated unjustly.

The Need for Explicit Rationing

What would I need to know in order to move off this agnostic stance? What would render this budgetary decision visible and explicit as a rationing decision? The first thing I would want to know was where the money saved by closing down this prescription drug program was reallocated. Ideally (I will argue), those responsible for this decision would say they were faced with immoveable limits on total available dollars for meeting health care needs through public budgets. Consequently, they went through a careful and deliberate process aimed at establishing health care priorities from the perspective of health care justice (which we need to leave unanalyzed and undefended until Chapter 3). Their best judgment was, as a result of these deliberative efforts, that there were too many serious, unmet health needs among the very poor in the state, and hence, that the dollars saved by closing down this prescription drug program should be redirected toward those other higher priority health needs of those who were clearly a lot worse off. Nothing guarantees that this conclusion is free from either empirical or normative error. If the reasoning is public, however, then others will have the opportunity to correct such errors.

Mr. Schmidt would still have died under this scenario, but his death would have a very different moral character attached to it. It would be correctly described as being regrettable and unfortunate, but not unjust. What the decision-makers in this case could say honestly to themselves, to Mr. Schmidt's friends and family, and to all the citizens of Oregon was that they had anticipated the possibility that deaths such as this would occur. They could explain that they had constructed a powerful computer model that permitted them to know statistically that an outcome such as this was likely. However, that same computer model predicted that many more lives would be put at risk among those who were much less well-off than Mr. Schmidt; consequently, they judged themselves obligated to redirect resources to that other program. Further, they could explain that they realize Mr. Schmidt is certainly not among those who are very well-off or even somewhat well-off. But neither is Mr. Schmidt among those who are least well-off.[9] In a more just world, resources would be redirected from less urgent needs of those already well-off to the prescription drug program that had helped Mr. Schmidt. However, there are no social mechanisms in our financially fragmented health care system as it is now to permit that transfer of resources in a short period of time. Finally, with slight changes in social and financial circumstances Mr. Schmidt could have been among those who were least well-off, in which case he would have been a beneficiary of the redirected funding rather than a victim. From this other point of view he presumably would have approved the budgetary switch in funds. This would be a morally significant fact.

RATIONING JUSTLY: THE MORAL CHALLENGE

The scenario I sketched above can become real only if our putative decision-makers first admit they are faced with a rationing problem, and then admit that this is primarily a moral problem that ought to be resolved in accord with the norms of justice. Much in our social and political life conspires against any such admission. On the contrary, the assertions I would realistically expect to hear from our decision-makers would be these: (1) We are not making a rationing decision; there is no need for health care rationing. (2) There is no moral problem here at all; this is simply an economic and budgetary issue. (3) If anyone insists that a moral issue exists here, then we believe this is not a matter of justice. Rather, it is a matter of charity or beneficence, which can be freely given or freely taken away. That is, we have not done anything for which we could be judged morally blameworthy. I believe that all three of these assertions are morally incorrect. A thorough discussion of my reasons for concluding this must wait until Chapters 3 and 4. However, for the sake of presenting a complete overview of the argument of this volume I need to offer some preliminary and suggestive considerations.

My claim is that the problem of health care rationing must be seen primarily (not exclusively) as a problem of health care justice. I reject the view that health care can be distributed in a morally acceptable manner through some combination of individual ability to pay and charitable impulse. I also reject the view that there are charitable obligations in health care that are dominated by the need to save or sustain human life no matter what the cost and no matter what the quality of the life-years saved. We can return to the cases of Mr. Diaz and Mr. Schmidt to illustrate more sharply the preliminary points I wish to make.

Recall the magic wand I gave you at the beginning of this essay. You could use it to move all the money that would otherwise be spent on Mr. Diaz and spend it instead on the prescription drug needs of a still reasonably healthy Mr. Schmidt. Actually, Mr. Schmidt himself would only need $5,500 of that for the year. So we could really imagine helping fifty other individuals, just like Mr. Schmidt, with paying for their very expensive prescription drug needs. I also said that if you used the magic wand in this way you would likely not feel completely comfortable about what you had done. You would feel this discomfort because you would know that Mr. Diaz's death a few days later came about as a result of your decision. Further, you would know this connection with near certainty. In contrast, you would not know that you had saved Mr. Schmidt's life (or that of any of the other fifty individuals whose prescription drug needs you filled through the use of your magic wand). In all those cases the drugs were needed to control a medical condition that "might," given the right collocation of circumstances, otherwise result in death or some other permanent medical disability. But the chance of such bad outcomes in the space of a year was probably relatively small. Mr. Schmidt might well have gone the entire year without a seizure or with only a minor seizure at worst. Filling out the background picture in this way should cause us to reflect. Ultimately, however, I would contend that this was a morally appropriate use of the magic wand best explained and justified by an appeal to specific considerations of health care justice.

To accept this conclusion we have to begin by taking very seriously the premise that we have only limited resources to meet unlimited health needs. We concretize that premise in this case by saying we have only one pot of $270,000. We cannot save both Mr. Diaz and our fifty uninsured individuals like Mr. Schmidt. No doubt we are torn because we *know* we are sacrificing Mr. Diaz's life. We are tempted by what appears to be a very powerful moral imperative: If we have the capacity to save a life, then we are morally obligated to save that life no matter what the cost. We have a duty to rescue that life. Those other fifty lives are not imminently imperiled.[10]

At this point we need to consider my hypothetical additions to Mr. Diaz's case. We detect a cardiac arrhythmia or even more serious cardiac problems requiring either the implantable cardiac defibrillator or the left ventricular assist device. Both of these are very expensive, life-prolonging interventions that will do nothing to improve the quality of Mr. Diaz's life. If we insist that the "duty to rescue" and the "pricelessness of human life" ought to be the dominant ethical considerations in this case, then in effect what we are doing is taking money from the prescription drug coverage for the uninsured and giving it to Mr. Diaz, thereby putting another fifty individuals "at risk" for serious adverse health outcomes. Is that fair? This seems like a natural and reasonable question to raise.

Why Justice? Why Not Beneficence?

Speaking very generally, issues of fairness arise when we have a cooperative enterprise involving many individuals, and there are risks/costs and benefits associated with that enterprise. We have to imagine that this enterprise will endure for many years, perhaps many decades. If certain groups of individuals bear virtually all the risks or costs of that enterprise while others enjoy virtually all the benefits, then this will strike all reasonable persons as paradigmatically unfair. Our health care system is reasonably construed as a cooperative enterprise whose tremendous success is owed to the huge public investments that have been made in generating the knowledge and technology that constitute contemporary health care.

Imagine the director of a very large transplant program who wants to build a "world-class" transplant program. He wants to recruit the absolute best transplant surgeons. To generate the resources needed to accomplish that he secretly cultivates a very large base of potential organ recipients who are all multimillionaires. They may be in good health now, but they worry about their vulnerability to future major organ failure. All who are part of this database understand that needed organs will go to the highest bidder so that extraordinarily high salaries can be paid to the surgeons and the transplant director. Since transplantable organs are absolutely scarce (fewer than 10,000 non-kidneys being available in the U.S. each year), the obvious implication is that non-millionaires would have a substantially reduced chance of receiving an organ transplant if they had the need. This will strike most of us as being very unfair because all of us would have contributed through taxes to funding the research that developed the knowledge and technology associated with organ transplant programs. The fact that someone must serve as the director of such programs does not give that person the right to use those programs for the personal enrichment or aggrandizement of themselves and their colleagues. It is unfair that the relatively less well-off should bear virtually all the costs associated with building transplant capacity so that mostly the very rich would enjoy the benefits. We understand that there is an absolute scarcity of transplantable organs relative to need. Still, what all can reasonably insist upon is that there is a fair and transparent process for making these allocation decisions such that all who have contributed to this cooperative social enterprise would have a fair chance to benefit.

Someone might read this scenario and think that what is "really" morally wrong here is that this common good has been appropriated for purely selfish ends. I agree that such selfish behavior is clearly morally wrong, but that would distract us from the point I wish to emphasize. If that transplant director had been a "closet Marxist" who used his role as transplant director to make certain that no wealthy individuals received organ transplants and that a disproportionate share of transplantable organs went to relatively poor individuals (even if those individuals might have a substantially lower prior probability of a successful transplant), then that individual too would be open to justified criticism from the perspective of health care justice. Essentially the same analysis as in our first scenario would explain the wrongness of his actions, even though personal gain is not a dominant motivating factor.

If the CEO of a very large medical center were personally committed to the view that human life is priceless, and if that CEO used 90% of the charity care dollars of that hospital to sustain the lives of patients in a persistent vegetative state (or other equally debilitated states which were medically irreversible) at the expense of thousands of other poor and uninsured patients in that hospital service area whose medical needs were not imminently life-threatening, then that CEO would justifiably be open to moral criticism from the perspective of health care justice. No doubt he is "doing good for others" with these charitable resources and those others that are at risk of death, and his efforts are not tainted by selfish desires. Still, these dollars represent a social good cooperatively generated whose disposition needs to be governed by norms of justice.

If this CEO had a personal fortune that he chose to disperse as charity in this way, then he would not be open to moral criticism. If he created a charitable foundation with this exclusive objective in mind and attracted large donations from like-minded individuals, then too this charitable dispersal of resources would be morally permissible. But the charity care dollars of a hospital are not like that—their dispersal must not violate widely shared norms of health care justice. Lavishing more than a million charity care dollars on Mr. Schmidt or Mr. Diaz are not obviously morally defensible allocations of *limited charity care dollars* if the only moral justification for that allocation is an appeal to the claim that human life is priceless or that we have a "duty to rescue" in these circumstances.

We may justifiably invoke as sufficient justification the duty to rescue when we are dealing with rare rescue situations that involve extraordinarily high costs, such as the rescue of individuals in Antarctica who are faced with potentially life-threatening medical problems. But the whole point of our discussion so far has been to show that opportunity for extremely expensive rescues from death in our contemporary health care system are anything but rare; they are ubiquitous. And they are increasing in frequency and cost with all the expansions of life-prolonging medical technologies we have alluded to above. If our fundamental premise is correct that we have only limited resources to meet virtually unlimited health care needs, and if the bulk of these resources are rightly thought of as social resources (such as Medicare, Medicaid, or those hospital charity budgets), then choices need to be made about how those resources are best allocated. The primary deficiency, both rational and moral (with the moral appeal to either the pricelessness of human life or the duty to rescue) is that they provide us with no specific guidance as to how such choices ought to be made. It is as if any choice at all that is made that has as the primary source of its justification either the duty to rescue or the infinite value of human life is thereby immunized from moral criticism. Some extremely arbitrary allocation decisions, as illustrated above, would thereby be given unmerited moral legitimacy. But, as I shall argue in Chapters 4 and 5, a well developed conception of health care justice can provide a framework for making such difficult rationing and allocation decisions on grounds that are rationally defensible and that do not suffer from the risk of arbitrariness associated with these alternate appeals.

An obvious objection might be raised at this point—namely, that there is no widely shared conception of health care justice in our society, which could serve as a legitimate basis for making fair rationing decisions. What we find instead is that there are libertarian (Engelhardt, 1996), utilitarian (Eddy, 1996; Gibbard, 1983), moderately egalitarian (Dworkin, 1993; 2000, chaps. 7–8), strictly egalitarian (Veatch, 1986), and fair equality of opportunity (Daniels, 1985) accounts of health care justice. Further, I shall argue in Chapter 4 that none of these theoretical accounts of health care justice is really adequate by itself to address well all the very complex problems of health care justice associated with the need to make rationing and priority-setting decisions. In some circumstances a libertarian account may yield a morally reasonable response to a particular rationing problem. In other circumstances some version of either utilitarian or egalitarian accounts will yield a reasonable response. In still other circumstances several of these theoretical accounts might yield responses that from a moral point of view would have to be judged to be "not unreasonable"—not morally objectionable from a (pluralistic) perspective of health care justice. This outcome is not ultimately acceptable, either from a moral or a practical point of view, especially when we are in circumstances where we need an impartially authoritative judgment of what would be a just outcome. The concern is that one or another party in a resource rationing dispute would have more social or political power and simply use that power to impose its decision on the other, citing a preferred account of health care justice to provide a cover of moral legitimacy.

Justice and Rational Democratic Deliberation: Self-Imposed Rationing

I will argue in Chapter 5 that there is a way around this theoretical indeterminacy that will preserve a just outcome that has thorough moral legitimacy, as opposed to a thin cover of moral legitimacy. This will be accomplished through an appeal to a certain conception of the role of rational democratic deliberation in addressing a broad range of problems of health care justice.

There are three core moral considerations that are brought together through the rational democratic deliberative practices I imagine. First, rationing decisions, to be fair, must be *rationally justified* to those who are most likely to be affected (adversely from their point of view) by them. Individuals affected by these rationing decisions must be offered reasons for these decisions that they cannot reasonably reject. Ideally, the reasons referred to would be reasons that these individuals themselves could rationally affirm.

Second, the deliberative process itself must be *public, visible, and transparent* so that individuals who might see themselves adversely affected in the future by some rationing decision could see that there was nothing unfair about the deliberative process itself. Also, what we have in mind here is an actual deliberative process, not simply a hypothetical deliberative process that we could imagine occurring in a certain way.

Third, the primary virtue of this deliberative democratic model (when properly construed) is that all rationing decisions would be *self-imposed* in a very morally substantive sense. Individuals could not reasonably judge that more powerful "others" in our society were imposing rationing decisions upon them.

Let me briefly illustrate what this self-imposed model of rationing through a deliberative process is about. First, we have to imagine a factory that employs a thousand individuals just like Mr. Diaz, except that they are thirty years younger than him.[11]

Second, these factory workers are capable of imagining several hundred future possible health problems that they or members of their families might experience. They also understand what sorts of therapeutic or palliative interventions contemporary medicine has available as responses to these problems, the cost of these interventions, and the probability that such interventions will be successful. Third, they understand that they cannot afford to purchase all that medicine has to offer for all possible medical problems. They have a budget of 14% of their total wages with which to purchase an insurance package for themselves and their families.[12] Fourth, they realize that they must consider their choices from a comprehensive relational perspective. That is, they cannot determine the choice-worthiness of individual health interventions as such. Each option needs to be understood as involving a trade-off; something must be given up in order to secure access to something else. Each option needs to fit somewhere on an overall prioritizing scheme, which will imply that interventions at the lowest level of priority are always at risk of dropping off as part of the health insurance package that would be purchased.

Fifth, all these workers recognize themselves as free and equal participants in the rational deliberations aimed at defining this health benefit package, as well as the interventions/medical circumstances that will be outside this package. That is, inclusionary and exclusionary choices will be made only on the basis of morally relevant rational considerations that can command the free assent of participants. No one has authority to simply impose their will in these matters on others.

Sixth, the workers understand that what they are ultimately doing is making potential rationing decisions for future possible versions of themselves. They are capable of imagining themselves as being in the medical circumstances of Mr. Diaz at the beginning of this essay. They might see such circumstances as tragic and regrettable, but they would fully appreciate the fact that these were not medically reversible circumstances. Specifically, they would know that contemporary medicine has no capacity to reverse Alzheimer's dementia. They would also understand the difference in the quality of life of a person in the mild or moderate stages of Alzheimer's dementia as opposed to the advanced stages of the disease. That is, they would know that the quality of that life is very marginal and that functional distinctively human capacities are virtually nonexistent. Given this understanding, they could conclude that if an individual such as Mr. Diaz in the advanced stages of dementia is faced with a life-threatening medical problem of another sort (such as intestinal bleeding, a life-threatening cardiac arrhythmia, or kidney failure), then nothing other than palliative care ought to be provided. In other words, he ought to be allowed to die.

Mr. Diaz's death, at that particular time, would have come about as a result of a rationing decision. But it would have been a decision (ideally) that Mr. Diaz himself would have freely and rationally endorsed as one of these thousand factory workers. He did not know at the time the insurance package was ratified that this would be his fate, though he would have known that this was a possible fate for him. What he would have judged at the time with his coworkers was that there were neither good moral or economic reasons for wanting to sustain a marginal life such as that indefinitely. He would have judged that there were much higher priority health needs that deserved the funds that were saved by denying expensive life-pronging care to that future possible version of his own self. He might have imagined at the time that he could have had a major heart attack at age forty, that he would then want access to either an implantable cardiac defibrillator or a left ventricular assist device, either of which would have sustained his life at a relatively high level of functioning for a significant period of time.

The scenario I have sketched here may have something of an imaginative and hypothetical quality to it, but it is a scenario (I shall argue later) that is realizable. This is not in the same league as John Rawls' "original position" argument, though a suitably constructed democratic deliberative process can have in the real world the fundamental moral virtue of impartiality that is seen in Rawls' disembodied spirits stripped of all personal identifying features. The opportunity to test this claim empirically is very much at hand as I write. And there is a matter of moral necessity as well—I have in mind the roughly 76 million members of the post-World War II "baby boom" generation, whose numbers will bring about at least a doubling of the U.S. population over age 65 by the year 2030. Though the elderly comprised only 13% of the U.S. population in 2006, they accounted for roughly 35% of all health expenditures in that year, roughly $756 billion. Per capita health expenditures in the U.S. in 2006 were about $6,800. If we remove those over age sixty-five from the population, then per capita health expenditures were about $4,000. That raises the per capita health expenditures for the elderly in 2006 to about $18,500. To appreciate what this portends (morally speaking), over the next couple decades we need to realize that health expenditures for the elderly at that point in the future would be $1.55 trillion per year *in constant dollars that would purchase no more health care technology than the current generation of the elderly.* That assumption is extremely unrealistic and greatly underestimates those future health expenditures, given many of the extremely costly life-prolonging technological developments that are only now beginning to be more widely disseminated, especially in the direction of the elderly.

The bottom line is that one inescapable focal point for making rationing decisions will be in relation to the elderly. The generation that will cause these problems is largely in very good health at present. More importantly, morally speaking, they remain largely ignorant as individuals regarding what their very specific future health care needs might be. That means they are well positioned to make fair-minded rationing decisions for their future possible selves, many of which will be variations of Mr. Diaz. Some individuals in that generation have already experienced heart disease and cancer, which might suggest that they will be incapable of being suitably impartial in the democratic deliberative process. We might imagine that they would become lobbyists for their own special health interests. However, the deliberative process is one of mutual education. Individuals with specific current diseases will be reminded that they are vulnerable to many other health disorders, and hence, that they would be at least imprudent not to give serious consideration to those possibilities. Further, they will have complex bonds of attachment to friends and family who are elderly, who may well have very different health needs. Also, they will be reminded that the goal of the deliberative process is to achieve agreement about a range of more or less specific rationing decisions, policies, practices, and priorities. That will require each and every deliberator, no matter what their current health status, to take a more balanced and comprehensive view of the possible options than what narrow self-interest might suggest. In other words, the deliberative process I imagine need not be just a philosopher's fantasy; it is quite capable of realization among relatively ordinary human beings willing to engage in serious reflection.

Daniels and Sabin (2002) remind us that there is no necessary connection between political legitimacy and political justice. If a democratic deliberative process is properly conducted (procedurally speaking), then the policies and priorities that emerge from that process will have democratic legitimacy. However, that does not yield a guarantee that the results will be just as well; other factors need to be brought into play. Further, these other factors need to be an integral part of the democratic deliberative process itself if we are to avoid what Daniels refers to as "the democracy problem."

The "democracy problem" begins with the question, "Can the democratic deliberative process yield an outcome that is unjust?" If so, what gives us the capacity to recognize that fact about the outcome? If we have a moral theory, or some other rational source of moral insight, that gives us the capacity to recognize an unjust outcome, then we do not need the democratic deliberative process to figure out what is the just choice to make. But if we have no such moral theory, then we have no moral grounds for objecting to the outcomes of a legitimate democratic process. In effect, justice is reduced to legitimacy. To my mind, neither of these possibilities is acceptable.

The Nature of Public Justification

In Chapter 5 I describe and defend three factors in the democratic deliberative process that are justice-promoting in their orientation. The first is one that Daniels and Sabin (1997; 1998a, 1998b; 2002—among many others) emphasize greatly, the process of reason-giving. We have to imagine that participants in the deliberative process have differing perspectives on the justness of some specific rationing problem, but they are willing to be persuaded to change their mind, if suitable and powerful moral reasons can be given why they should change their mind. Not any sort of reason will achieve this result. What is needed are what Rawls (1993, chap. 6) refers to as "public reasons," which for now may be minimally characterized as reasons that are divorced from any comprehensive philosophic or religious vision. Both atheists and fundamentalists can agree on some range of reasons why murder is wrong, and this agreement can be achieved without requiring either to convert to the other's world view. We shall argue that such public reasons can be articulated as well for purposes of addressing some range of issues related to health care justice.

Second, the "public space" within which democratic deliberation occurs is not completely unbounded. Metaphorically speaking, there are "constitutional principles of health care justice" that create boundaries regarding the sort of proposals that may be justly deliberated. Any health care rationing or priority-setting proposal that violated one of these constitutional principles would be off the conversational agenda. So this is another way in which the justice-promoting characteristics of the deliberative process are protected. One of the social responsibilities of contemporary philosophers is to use their skills to articulate, refine, and critically assess these constitutional principles of health care justice (as I shall try to do in Chapter 5). This might strike some, at least on first appearance, as elitist and subversive of the *democratic* quality of these deliberative efforts. But I will argue that the precise opposite is true, that these philosophic efforts are needed to protect the integrity and justness of the democratic deliberative process.

Third, public reasons and attentiveness to conversational boundaries demarcated by constitutional principles of health care justice will do much to assure the justness of the outcomes of the deliberative process. But there must also be a *sufficient* degree of coherence among the considered judgments of health care justice that emerge from these deliberative processes (and among the constitutional principles of health care justice) to assure that our overall approach to health care rationing and priority setting is "just enough." The mechanism for achieving this sort of deliberative coherence is what Rawls and Daniels have referred to as "wide reflective equilibrium" (Daniels, 1996; Rawls, 1971).

That phrase has something of an academic and technical ring to it; it may seem to be far removed from our actual moral experience. But it is not. To give a quick and simple illustration, we currently (2006) spend about $57,000 per person per year through the End-Stage Renal Disease (ESRD) program to sustain the lives of individuals in kidney failure. These are public dollars expended through a special addition to Medicare in 1972. The program was motivated primarily by the fact that about 20,000 people per year would otherwise die of kidney failure because they could not afford to pay for the technology that would sustain their lives. In effect, what we are saying today is that it is not unreasonable to spend $57,000 per year to sustain each of about 430,000 lives in 2006. HIV+ patients are in similar circumstances since 1996 when the first of the protease inhibitors were introduced into medical practice. These drugs have proven to be exceptionally effective in protecting and partially reinvigorating the immune systems of HIV+ individuals whose CD4 count has decreased to the point where they are vulnerable to the opportunistic infections that define AIDS. These drugs dramatically reduce the viral load of these individuals and forestall their vulnerability to life-threatening opportunistic infections. But the combination of drugs needed to achieve these therapeutic results has costs in the range of $15,000–$20,000 per year. AIDS activists have been successful in securing public dollars from many state and federal programs to underwrite the costs of these drugs for the majority of individuals who had no insurance and little ability to pay. But a public reaction to this funding has appealed to the language of "special treatment" to undercut this funding. That is, the argument has been made that it is "unfair" to use public dollars in this way (Casarett and Lantos, 1998).[13] However, from the perspective of wide reflective equilibrium, such a funding decision does "cohere with" the decision we made regarding dialysis patients. In morally relevant respects, the two population groups would seem to be very much alike; that is, both population groups are relatively young and the relevant treatments are effective in achieving reasonable therapeutic objectives. Consequently, the burden of proof would fall to those who asserted that a distinction needed to be made and that this distinction was morally justified. Otherwise, it would appear that some of the social stigma associated with AIDS was being permitted to shape our health care priority-setting decisions.

We need to reserve until Chapter 5 a fuller discussion of the role of wide reflective equilibrium in the democratic deliberative process. For now I simply want to reinforce a point made earlier—we need the practices of public reason-giving, respect for the constitutional principles of health care justice, and use of wide reflective equilibrium to preserve the justness of the rationing and priority-setting judgments that emerge from the deliberative process. These practices represent morally necessary conversational constraints on the deliberative process,[14] but they are rarely so constraining in their effects that for any one rationing or priority-setting problem only one morally right answer can be given. Typically, multiple "just enough" options will exist. This implies that the deliberative process serves a practical purpose. That practical purpose will be both choosing a particular option and conferring moral and political legitimacy on it.

APPLICATIONS OF THE DELIBERATIVE MODEL

Chapter 5 is clearly the most central theoretical chapter in this volume. Of necessity, this chapter will have a general and schematic character to it. My primary goal will be to provide a moral and philosophic defense for a certain conception of rational democratic deliberation and its role in addressing a range of health care rationing and priority-setting problems. That general defense will be inadequate—the value of this model needs to be proven by its practical ability to address a range of health care rationing and priority-setting problems, which will be the task of the last nine chapters of this volume. Those chapters will have a predominantly analytic and argumentative quality to them.

The goal in each chapter will be to define as fairly and as reasonably as possible a certain rationing problem, and the factual and moral context around that problem. In the real world, defining such a problem is itself a legitimate subject for democratic deliberation. Philosophers can do much to facilitate that task, which is what I will be modeling in each chapter. But philosophers have no special moral authority to be the ultimate arbiters of how such problems get articulated. Problems can be formulated in ways that are fundamentally flawed, either morally speaking or factually speaking. Problems can be formulated in ways that are not defensible on the basis of public reasons or in ways that are calculated to violate one or another constitutional principle of health care justice. Philosophers can "remind" deliberative participants of these commitments in order to motivate their rejection of such flawed formulations. But, again, deliberative space is such that there will typically be multiple morally legitimate ways in which a particular problem of health care rationing might be formulated.

Philosophers who have addressed problems of clinical medical ethics are generally sensitive to the way in which case facts can alter the moral judgments that are or are not warranted in those circumstances. Problems of health care justice will also be fact-sensitive in many complex ways. Medical facts, scientific facts, technological facts, economic facts, epidemiological facts, religious and cultural facts—all of these can have a bearing on the sorts of judgments of health care justice that might be warranted in specific circumstances. Hence, as I articulate each of the problems of health care justice in the chapters that follow I shall try to portray the relevant facts as accurately as possible. I am certain I will fail on occasion in that regard, but the virtue of a public and open deliberative process, as in the scientific enterprise, is that the opportunity will be there for others to make the necessary corrections. Complicating all of this in the real world is that many of the facts we need to consider will be inherently probabilistic.

Given the specific formulation of a rationing problem that will define each chapter, the primary goal of each chapter will be to articulate and defend a series of considered judgments of health care justice that will either limn more precisely the space of that particular deliberative effort (what we might regard as contextual reflective equilibrium) or possible outcomes of that deliberative effort. None of these chapters begins as the proverbial blank slate; all of the problems I will discuss in later individual chapters have been the focus of much moral and political discussion already, though not from the perspective I am recommending. Ultimately, the reader should think of the end of each chapter as the starting point for a specific deliberative dialogue in the real world.

Individual chapters can be read profitably, but there are complex relationships among the chapters, which reflect features of the real world. Patients, their health care needs, and their just claims to have those needs met will not sort themselves neatly into the individual chapters. To illustrate, the just claims to have health care needs met for persons with disabilities is a focal point of intense social discussion (Wasserman et al., 2005). We think of individuals who have suffered spinal cord injuries, or children born with various physically handicapping conditions, or children with various developmental disabilities. Advocates for persons with serious disabilities have expressed strong moral objections to the use of certain tools for priority setting in health care that they see as having objectionable discriminatory consequences for persons with disabilities. Specifically, the use of Quality-Adjusted Life-Years (QALYs) as an outcome measure is seen as systematically disadvantaging persons with disabilities, since the life-years gained by them from any health intervention will be discounted by whatever standard is used to measure the quality of the life-years gained (Hadorn, 1992; Harris, 1987, 1995, 1996; Hope, 1996; McKie et al., 1996; Menzel, 1992a; Nord, 1999; Orentlicher, 1994, 1996; Singer et al., 1995).

For the sake of argument let us accept the moral legitimacy of this objection. Now I ask the reader to imagine a 92-year-old woman in the advanced stages of Alzheimer's with a heart arrhythmia. First, should we think of her as a person with disabilities? That is, is she among those who would be wrongfully discriminated against if we considered her quality of life in deciding whether it was worth it from a social point of view to provide her with a $40,000 implantable defibrillator? From a functional point of view she would display functional losses similar to someone with very serious developmental disabilities. Second, as a very old person she is among those who represent only 13% of the population but consume 35% of all health resources in any given year. If the need for health care rationing is inescapable, then a single locus for health spending that is that large will have to be carefully assessed from the perspective of health care justice. Third, if we do think of this woman as properly belonging to the class of disabled persons, then all others like her must be thought of in these terms as well. This will result in a huge increase in the category of persons with disabilities because a very substantial proportion of the elderly with serious chronic disabilities of many sorts would gain admission to the disability category (and the moral/political protections offered by that category). Fourth, if we accept this outcome, then we have made all the more difficult the challenges of health care rationing, since it would appear that we would have created internal competition between the elderly with disabilities and the non-elderly with disabilities. If we reject all quality of life considerations as morally relevant for making just rationing decisions, then what considerations should provide the norms for making just rationing decisions? We are not going to try to answer any of these questions just now; our goal was only to warn the reader of the overlapping complexity among rationing problems in the real world.

The Challenge of Priority Setting: Are All Health Needs Equal?

How ought health care priority setting be justly accomplished? That question too will be part of the focus of Chapter 5. We will start with the recognition that the term "priority setting" is largely a more politically palatable way of talking about rationing. Oregon is often seen as a model of how priority setting might be accomplished. A large critical literature emerged around that effort which we will not review in any depth (Hadorn, 1991; Kitzhaber, 1993; Strosberg et al., 1992). What the term "priority setting" was intended to convey in Oregon was the need to make rationing decisions explicitly, rationally, and systematically. What Oregon wanted to reject were approaches to rationing that were arbitrary, ad hoc, a product of political power, or a result of special pleading. That very general orientation is one I endorse as well, but that will not take us very far in addressing any real rationing problems.

What we need to move toward is what I will describe as mid-level principles for achieving fair rationing outcomes. We will start with the obvious: Health needs count. Health needs have presumptive moral relevance and weight (Butler, 1999, pp. 45–55; Daniels, 1985, chap. 2). Health-related desires do not count, at least so far as the problem of just priority setting is concerned. The obvious becomes murky as we move away from the central instances of health need. How should we (citizens in a just and caring society) think of the "need" of infertile couples for access to the new reproductive technologies, most of which are relatively expensive (Warren, 2002)? Are such asserted needs on a moral par with various sorts of cosmetic surgeries? Or what sorts of needs are there for the very heavily advertised "fast CT scans" for heart disease or cancer that cost $300–$400 each? These are promoted as preventive health care for asymptomatic individuals, and they do on occasion turn up early signs of treatable serious disease. The vast majority of the time they either show no disease (psychological relief) or false positives (eventual psychological relief after more invasive and costly follow-up tests) (Grann, Neugut, 2003; Greenland, 2003; Hunink, Gazelle, 2003). The obvious next question is, "How often might we imagine that individuals have a "need" for these fast CT scans, given that cancer might appear at any time?" Cancers are often fatal; infertility is never fatal. Does that suggest that these fast CT scans deserve to be thought of as representing a higher priority need than medical interventions for infertility?[15]

The other murky aspect of needs concerns their relative weight in relation to each other. What morally relevant considerations should be used to determine that weight? Oregon again provides us with an obvious and general response to that question. In short, needs only matter for priority-setting purposes if medically effective therapies exist that will address those needs. Again, this general response will not take us nearly far enough by itself for addressing the priority-setting problem. Imagine a 61-year-old patient with rheumatoid arthritis and another 61-year-old patient with early stage coronary artery disease. I assume all would agree that these are genuine health needs. Further, in both cases drugs can be used to address these needs effectively, though in neither case will these drugs result in a cure. What would we imagine might be reasonable grounds for saying that one need should be given higher priority over the other?

This question has an odd quality about it. It sounds "philosophical," in the pejorative sense of that term. What we really want is a practical reason for needing to answer it. So we imagine next a 61-year-old with a very inflamed appendix, very near to bursting. This too is a health need with an effective surgical response. What sort of priority ought to be awarded to meeting this need relative to our other two needs? Are we as tempted to dismiss this question as "philosophical" as we were above? I can think of two reasons why we would not do that. First, the surgical intervention in this case is curative; the health threat is completely addressed. Second, failure to intervene would result in a burst appendix, peritonitis, and death (premature and avoidable). This might cause us to propose as a general priority-setting rule that we ought to give very high priority to (fully fund) health interventions that effectively save lives or that save numerous life-years that would otherwise be lost. This certainly looks like a just and reasonable principle that would command wide support. However, the world will again resist earnestly the neat categories that moral philosophers would hope to apply.

Ultimate Needs? Last-Chance Therapies

What we likely find most morally salient in the scenario with the badly inflamed appendix is the *urgency* of the need, the *lack of effective alternatives,* and the likelihood of *imminent death*. The problem, however, is that these very same morally relevant characteristics are shared by what have come to be called "last-chance" therapies (Daniels and Sabin, 1997; 1998a; Fleck, 2002a), which will be the focus of Chapter 7. The left ventricular assist device (LVAD) and the totally implantable artificial heart (TIAH) would be two quick examples of such therapies. The difference between these interventions and surgery to address a burst appendix is that these interventions are not curative; they do nothing to alter the underlying terminal disease process other than prolong the life of an individual for a relatively brief period of time. This is not an inconsequential outcome, especially from the perspective of someone otherwise faced with imminent death. But typically there are very high costs associated with these interventions, both at the level of individual patients and (more worrisome) at the aggregate level, where costs mount into the tens of billions of dollars annually. Those factors would suggest (given limited resources to meet virtually unlimited health needs) that some distinctions must be made among needs (even urgent needs), and that the cost of meeting those needs has some moral salience. But cost considerations alone will yield neither morally perspicuous nor morally defensible distinctions among these urgent needs. Many other factors must be taken into account as well.

Prioritizing Health Needs: Should Age Matter?

If we have an 85-year-old in end-stage heart failure, should he have just as much a right to a $150,000 left ventricular assist device as a 62-year-old with exactly the same degree of heart failure and the same prognosis (roughly a gain in life expectancy of 12–24 months)? In both cases individuals may be faced with the prospect of death within three months; again, these are clearly urgent needs. Must we see them as *morally equal* needs such that we would be rightly accused of being unjust if we were to provide the LVAD to the younger individual only? This is the question of age-based health care rationing, the focus of Chapter 9. Given the aging out of the post-World War II "baby boom" generation, this question is of enormous moral and political urgency.

Currently about 70,000 individuals in the U.S. are over the age of 100. The predictions are that there might be 850,000 such individuals in the U.S. in the year 2050 (Dominus, 2004; Krach and Velkoff, 1999). The problems of justice might be more manageable with respect to this cohort if some pattern of debilitating and costly health problems afflicted members of this cohort from some specific age forward; then we could rely upon some form of moral consistency to generate outcomes that were just enough. But demographers tell us that it is extremely improbable such a pattern would emerge. A likely pattern is that many will die in their 70s and early 80s from cancer, heart disease, and stroke, though they will have had many extra years of life as a result of very costly interventions. The longer-lived portion of the cohort is likely to have enjoyed remarkably healthy lives into their late 80s and 90s, but then they are likely to face many of the same medical problems as the "less fortunate" part of the cohort that will have already died. From the perspective of health care justice will they then be just as entitled to all the expensive life-prolonging medical care as those other cohort members who already died? Does the fact that these hyper-elderly individuals have "the same urgent health needs" as those deceased individuals mean they also have the "same just claims" to resources needed to meet those needs? This will be one of the central issues in the age-rationing debate that will have to be invigorated again.

Prioritizing Health Needs: Fair Aggregation Issues

One of the frustrating features of the problem of health care justice is that health needs are so heterogeneous and so unevenly distributed—both across individuals and across time in the lives of individuals. Some individuals need a million dollars worth of health care just to get through the first year of life. Other individuals live to age 100 having used no more than several thousand dollars worth of health care. We try to neutralize these moral distracters by focusing all our attention on health needs. Whatever one has in the way of health needs will make a presumptive moral claim. It will be morally irrelevant that some health needs cluster more heavily on some individuals rather than others. However, we then remind ourselves that we have only limited resources to meet virtually unlimited health needs. That draws our attention to two sorts of "aggregation" problems, which will be the focus of Chapter 8.

One class of problems pertains to patients labeled as "bottomless pits" (an admittedly uncharitable phrase) (Wikler, 1983). These are patients who seem to have never-ending health needs that are extremely costly to manage. It is not as if we are wasting resources trying one ineffective intervention after another. The problem is that our interventions do "work" in that they are effective in sustaining life and ameliorating symptoms to some degree, but our interventions are never so effective that the needs go away. And the needs command extraordinary quantities of costly health resources—so much so that we are tempted to assert that no one could possibly have a just claim to *that much* in the way of health care resources. Maybe that is true. If so, what are the morally relevant considerations that would justify our drawing that conclusion in individual cases? What must give us pause is the Rawlsian consideration that such individuals are clearly among the "worst off" in our society. Still, will that warrant anyone possessing unlimited rights to health care?

The second sort of "aggregation" problem we need to consider in this chapter is whether just claims to have health needs met must always be considered from a "slice-of-time" perspective rather than a "course-of-life" perspective (Veatch, 1988). From a "slice-of-time" perspective an individual who has an urgent health need (for which we have a very costly, effective, but non-curative intervention) has a strong just claim to have that health need met *no matter how much prior use he has made of the health care system*. Past use is entirely morally irrelevant. However, in an increasing number of circumstances that moral directive appears to be unreasonable and prima facie unjust, given overall limited resources for meeting health needs.

To give one quick example, in the early 1990s individuals who were HIV+ who had progressed to AIDS were faced with a two-year life expectancy, multiple opportunistic infections, and last year-of-life costs in excess of $100,000. But protease inhibitors were discovered in 1996, and so-called "triple therapy" proved a life-prolonging intervention for the vast majority of these patients who have gained a number of extra years of life at a cost of $20,000 per year (Bartlett, 1997). Now the virus is mutating around these drugs and threatening the lives of these individuals again. However, fusion inhibitors have now been introduced into the medical armamentarium, again prolonging these lives by attacking HIV in a different way (Cervia, Smith, 2003; Lalezeri et al., 2003). This has raised the cost of each life-year saved to about $35,000. Yet other drugs are in development that will attack HIV in other ways. Individuals may gain twenty or more years of life that would never have been possible just a few years ago, but the aggregate costs will be several hundred thousand dollars per person to achieve this result. The critical justice question is this: If we eventually run out of ways to attack and control HIV, then these individuals will be faced with the same life-threatening opportunistic infections that could be managed for last year-of-life costs of about $100,000, as before. If a prior generation had a just claim to those last year-of-life resources, would the generation that had benefited from all these costly advances have an equally just claim to those same resources? Or would it be morally permissible in this and similar circumstances to reassess such claims from a course-of-life perspective? If we did consider this a legitimate option, what would be the morally relevant considerations that would legitimate the course-of-life perspective in some circumstances and the slice-of-time perspective in others?

Prioritizing Health Needs: Should Personal Responsibility Matter?

Chapter 6 will analyze two other sets of issues associated with using health care needs as a starting point for health care priority setting. These are issues of personal responsibility and access to very effective (but very costly) health care interventions. Ordinarily we think of health needs as arising from bad luck; that would put them all on a moral par with one another. That is what justifies having those needs (often costly) medically addressed by drawing from a common pool of resources. But if individuals are in some substantial sense *responsible* for having particular costly health needs (lung cancer associated with a thirty-year history of smoking; heart disease or diabetes associated with obesity), then a question naturally arises about whether they have a just claim to have those needs met from common resources (Stell, 2002; Wikler, 1987). The core moral argument would seem to be that those needs were avoidable if that individual had only made different choices. Consequently, why should the rest of us (saintly individuals) have to bear those excess health costs? However, as our later analysis will show, the picture of personal responsibility suggested here is much too simple to withstand moral scrutiny. The causal strands associated with most health needs are very complex mixtures of personal, economic, familial, genetic, cultural, and political factors. What I shall argue in this chapter is that it will be extremely rare that we will be morally justified in failing to meet some specific health need because that individual has some personal responsibility for having that need.

Another complex issue we need to discuss is the "liberalism" problem, which will be in Chapter 12. This has multiple dimensions, which we can only allude to for now. Lomasky (1980), for example, has argued that any form of national health insurance will be unjust because it will require everyone to pay through taxes or premiums for health care "needs" that are deeply morally objectionable to some in our society. The abortion issue springs readily to mind, but there are dozens of other issues today. Many will object to all forms of Assisted Reproductive Technologies, many forms of genetic interventions aimed at sorting out eight-cell embryos, the use of embryos for developing our capacity to do embryonic stem cell research, the results of that embryonic stem cell research in the emerging field of regenerative medicine, genetic manipulation of embryos for either therapeutic or enhancement purposes, the use of animal organs to increase the supply of transplantable organs for humans, and so on. This all comes under the rubric of the "liberalism" problem because political liberals are supposed to refrain from using the coercive powers of government to impose any particular vision of a "good life" on those who would not embrace that vision unless a genuine public interest requires such an imposition (Emanuel, 1991). One way of dodging the liberalism problem is to exclude from any national health insurance package any health service that would elicit conscientious objections from one or another religious or cultural group in our society. However, it is easy to imagine that serious health care injustices could be legitimated that way. Consider, for example, some group of fundamentalists who objected to providing all AIDS-related drugs to AIDS patients on the grounds that this permitted them to continue their "sinful ways" at the expense of the righteous and God-fearing. So we will need to explore more carefully ways in which we could reconcile our liberal commitments with the demands of health care justice.

The flip side of this first version of the "liberalism" problem involves health care needs that might be religiously generated. I first encountered this problem in connection with a Jehovah's Witness patient with an ectopic pregnancy, which I wrote about for *The Hastings Center Report* (Fleck, 1995). This patient absolutely refused any blood transfusion in keeping with her religious beliefs. There then was substantial blood loss and she was faced with imminent death. But the surgeon put her in a paralytic coma and transfused her with Epogen, a very expensive drug that would rebuild her red blood cells without an actual transfusion. She needed two weeks in the ICU at a cost of about $100,000. This cost had to be absorbed by the hospital since she had no health insurance. Did she in fact have a just claim to these health care resources because of her religious beliefs? This particular patient never asked for this care. At the time, the intervention was very novel. The real issue today would be whether each and every Jehovah's Witness patient faced with major surgery and the possibility of blood loss threatening death would have a just claim to such an expensive intervention in order to protect their "desire" to live *and* the integrity of their religious commitments. If we had a national health insurance program of some sort, or even just Medicare and Medicaid, would we as a matter of justice be morally obligated to cover such alternative interventions, most especially when they are very costly? Consider the case of individuals who have quasi-religious beliefs about the possibility of being brought back to life and "cured" if they are quickly cryopreserved at the time of their "death." May such individuals be justly denied coverage for these health care needs?

Preventive Health Needs: Do Future Possible Children Have a Need for a Healthy Genome?

We ordinarily think of health needs as being attached to individuals whose fears and anxieties are visible to all sensitive individuals. But there are at least two major exceptions to this understanding. These are health needs attached to the genetic endowment of future possible children and preventive health needs, often discussed under the rubric of public health. These topics will be the focus of Chapters 11 and 13. One key question would be: How high a priority, from the perspective of health care justice, ought we to give various preventive health interventions? Imagine that an extra billion dollars was added to the health care budget of the nation. Should those extra billion dollars be used to fund "lung reduction" surgery (about $70,000 per case) for individuals in the end-stages of COPD, which would give them on average an extra year of life? Or should that money be used to fund some range of programs aimed at preventing young people from starting to smoke or helping those who already smoke to quit? What should we take as the justice-related criteria that would help us answer these questions? Our very large question is this: How important are public health needs (as a matter of health care justice) relative to acute and chronic health needs?

Much of the discussion up to this point will have been about health needs attached to individuals. However, there are also health needs that transcend individuals and that require health care resources, such as public health needs and public funding priorities with respect to health care research. Chapter 13 will address a number of these issues from the perspective of health care justice. The large questions we must consider are these: What justice-relevant criteria should be used for establishing priorities among public health care needs? Are utilitarian considerations by themselves morally sufficient? In any overall priority-setting process how do we imagine public health needs relating to the health needs attached to individuals? These same sorts of questions need to be raised with respect to public funding for health care research (Callahan, 2003). There are morally distinctive features of the research enterprise, the most important being that the primary goal of the research enterprise is the development of medical knowledge that will prove beneficial to future generations of patients. This necessarily implies that funds that could have been used to meet current health needs of individuals are used instead to advance research goals that can only benefit future possible patients. How should a just and caring society determine what fraction of total health spending should be invested in health care research when there are serious unmet health needs that could in principle be met if resources were redirected?

In Chapter 11 our large question to be addressed is: To what extent is a just and caring society morally obligated to provide an adequate genetic endowment to future possible children (Buchanan et al., 2000; Fleck, 2002b; Mehlman and Botkin, 1998)? And, how high a priority ought these health needs attached to future possible children be accorded relative to the urgent needs associated with either costly life-saving interventions or interventions under the rubric of "last-chance" therapies? A range of issues will need to be considered. There are relatively remote issues associated with genetic testing. To what extent ought we, a just and caring society, underwrite the costs of genetic testing for individuals who know from family history that they are at risk of having a child with a genetic disorder that would very adversely affect either the length of life or quality of life of a future possible child? If a couple already knows they are at risk of having a child with a serious genetic disorder that will manifest itself from very near birth on, and if they very much want to have a child that is "genetically their own," then is a just and caring society morally obligated to underwrite the $40,000 cost of preimplantation genetic diagnosis, which will allow them to have a child that is genetically their own and saved from a premature death and unnecessary suffering? Our moral intuitions might tug us in very different directions in this matter.

On the one hand, this preventive effort is very effective, unlike many preventive efforts that might have 20% success in helping individuals to quit smoking or abusing alcohol. Further, a child is given a normal life expectancy and normal life opportunities as opposed to being afflicted with a genetic disorder that severely diminishes length of life as well as life opportunities. But, on the other hand, some will argue that such public funding represents public support for overt discrimination against persons with disabilities. The couple is saying (in effect) that they do not wish to have a disabled child, and society is giving them the resources to attain that goal. Further, the moral reality is that with preimplantation genetic diagnosis, the parents are choosing which future possible child will be born by choosing between affected and unaffected embryos. We are not talking about an embryonic defect that is therapeutically corrected; affected embryos are simply discarded. An additional implication of this criticism is that democratic legitimation of a program that would fund such choices does nothing to alter the invidiously discriminatory character of these choices as far as disability advocates are concerned.

Prioritizing Health Needs: QALYfying Disabilities

Chapter 8 will address in considerable detail a number of health care justice issues related to persons with a broad range of disabling conditions and chronic health needs. The core moral challenge will be this: In making rationing decisions and establishing priorities among health care needs, should all needs of a particular sort be regarded as being morally equal so long as there are effective and costworthy interventions available to address those needs? Or, alternatively, should it be morally permissible to take into account the quality of the life-years that are being saved or ameliorated in particular medical circumstances? In other words, if we are doing bypass surgery for clogged coronary arteries, then the life-years saved or ameliorated will be of a lower quality if they are attached to individuals with Down's syndrome or that were born blind or that are quadriplegics as a result of an automobile accident some number of years ago, or that are suffering serious mental illness. The ultimate implication is that meeting these latter needs would justifiably be thought of as having a lower priority from the perspective of health care justice. If we were in a situation where resources were very scarce (or absolutely scarce as would be the case with natural hearts or livers for transplantation), then we would be morally justified in first allocating those resources to meeting the relevant health needs of those without any of these disabilities before meeting the same health needs of those with these disabilities. An outcome such as this would be judged to be clearly discriminatory in a morally objectionable sense; and I would strongly concur with that judgment. However, there are other sorts of cases that raise more troubling implications for this conclusion.

We think all the way back to the cases at the beginning of this chapter, the cases of Mr. Diaz and Mr. Schmidt. Clearly they can be properly described as disabled individuals, as would also be true for patients in the end stages of Alzheimer's disease. But are we morally obligated to conclude that all these individuals have just as strong a just claim to expensive life-prolonging medical care as individuals with the same medical problems (arrhythmias that are potentially fatal without the $40,000 defibrillator) who otherwise have minimal disabilities, and hence, saved life-years of substantially higher quality? In these latter cases I do not believe that the obligations of justice are the same as in the earlier cases. If that is true, then what are the morally relevant considerations that would allow us to make defensible moral judgments across a broad range of disabling medical conditions? Answering that question will be the major challenge of this chapter.

Several other fundamental questions will need to be addressed in this chapter as well. First, who are the disabled (Brock, 1995a, 1995b; Callahan, 1995; Mehlman et al., 1997; Peters, 1995)? How expansive or restrictive should our use of that term be? Political advantages may accrue from a more expansive use of the term, which would include virtually everyone with a serious chronic disorder. However, that might have the effect of rendering more difficult the discussion of the justice-related issues. We noted above the moral importance of being able to say honestly that just rationing decisions are self-imposed as a result of a certain rational, democratic, and deliberative process. It is easy to imagine that many advocates for persons with disabilities would vigorously insist that this be the case. In other words, they would not want currently "abled" citizens (who too often have a much distorted sense of the quality of the lives of persons with disabilities) to make rationing decisions that would be imposed upon those with disabilities. But one of the virtues of a very broad deliberative process is that the vast majority of participants would be quite healthy and quite ignorant of their future possible health needs. That means they could achieve more closely in practice the sort of impartiality that is generally seen as morally desirable. By way of contrast, a deliberative process that only included persons with various disabilities would lack an effectively impartial perspective.

The potential would exist for endless irresolvable argument among those with various physical disabilities, those with various cognitive impairments, those with various psychiatric disorders, and so on.

Physicians and Rationing: Just Incentives for Cost Control

We can imagine that the prior chapters will have resulted in morally cogent conclusions about how health care rationing and priority-setting decisions ought to be made. We can imagine that the substantive considered judgments of health care justice we articulate in regard to the challenges of health care rationing are in fact "more just" than the practices we currently have in place. However, none of this will matter, practically speaking, unless we also have in place professional habits and social policies that faithfully translate into practice the justice-promoting features of these considered judgments. Chapter 14 will address this challenge with respect to physicians.

The medical reality is that medical care is always delivered to individual patients. Further, the medical circumstances and medical needs of many individual patients will be quite complex and require astute individualized judgment to protect the best medical interests of those patients. Evidence-based medicine does not yield recipes to be followed mechanically in caring for a specific patient; the same will be true with respect to the application of just rationing protocols that are the outcome of democratic deliberations. Because there is an inescapable need for medical judgment, and because medical judgment will have consequences with respect to the cost of care, we have seen since the late 1980s the proliferation of all manner of incentives and disincentives (financial and otherwise) to shape medical judgment in ways aimed at reducing costs for payers. Such schemes represent a potential threat to both the well-being and the fair treatment of individual patients (Bodenheimer and Grumbach, 2005, chap. 13).

We might be tempted to think that cost control mechanisms and rationing protocols ought to be implemented somewhere above the clinical encounter, thereby permitting physicians to make pure medical judgments of what is in the best interests of their patients uncorrupted by financial considerations (Sulmasy, 2007). However, such a hope is largely illusory. Medicare DRGs (diagnosis-related groupings) were introduced in 1984 as a prospective payment mechanism aimed at reducing expensive and marginally beneficial hospital days. Hospitals received a flat payment from the federal government for a patient who "fit" under a particular DRG. Physician income was unaffected by the DRG payment. Nevertheless, physicians understood that their staff privileges were at risk if they failed to alter their medical practice in a way that would result in the quicker hospital discharges that both the hospital and the federal government expected.

In theory, physicians retained the legal and moral right to keep their patients in the hospital for as long as they deemed medically necessary, no matter how much of a financial loss the hospital might endure. In fact, they had to alter their style of practice to fit these economic constraints. The overall outcome of the DRG payment mechanism may have been "just enough," though there is little evidence that considerations of health care justice played any role at all in the construction of the system (Fleck, 1987). We can confidently say that no one has a strong just claim to expensive, marginally beneficial hospital days. But that very general moral judgment hides some very gray circumstances at the level of individual patients. Individual physicians would have to make judgments about those "days" and the degree to which they were medically necessary. What we want to know is whether the actual incentives in the system as a whole (as actually implemented) might have tilted medical judgment a little strongly in the gray areas in the direction of denial of hospital days to which specific patients had a "just enough" claim. We can also ask, "Did anyone want to know the answer to that question? Did anyone make an effort to find out an answer to that question?" In the first part of this chapter we shall critically assess several of the more common cost-containment mechanisms that are designed to control physician judgments that have cost consequences for third-party payers.

Creating a Just Health Care System

The second part of Chapter 14 will focus on the issue of health reform. The large question we need to answer is this: What sort of system for financing and delivering health services do we need in order to implement and preserve the considered judgments of health care justice regarding rationing and priority setting that we will have endorsed in the earlier chapters? As we will have emphasized throughout this book, the most we can hope to achieve is some reasonable, non-ideal "just enough" health care system. There is no such thing as a "most just" health care system (Brennan, 1993; Brock and Daniels, 1994; Daniels et al., 1996; Menzel, 1992b). Instead, we will find that there are a number of health care systems we can choose that will be "just enough." Trade-offs will be inescapable; details will matter. Consequences, actual and projected, will matter when it comes to assessing the relative justness of options. Should we permit for-profit health care enterprises to be part of any "just enough" health care system (Gray, 1991; Mahar, 2006)? Ideologues on either side of this question will have quick and certain answers, but I will argue that such answers are almost certainly wrong. Consequences matter. In some circumstances the existence of for-profit options may not threaten the justness of the system or specific parts of the system. If such options yield socially desirable efficiencies and expanded services, they should be permitted. On the other hand, if they threaten the capacity of the system to preserve the justness of the system, they must be excluded. Of late a number of physician-owned specialty hospitals have sprung up in various parts of the U.S. They threaten to take the most profitable patients with cardiac, orthopedic, or oncologic problems away from community hospitals, thereby undermining the capacity of those hospitals to provide high-quality care and charity care for less well-off segments of the community. Prima facie, that seems to raise obvious questions about the justice of such enterprises (Manning, 2003; Reilly, 2002, 2003).

We cannot get into all the details of how the financing and delivery of health services might get organized. But we can identify the features of current systems that are clearly unjust, so much so that reasonable deliberators would not wish to design any system of health care with those features. Accomplishing that much yields useful guidelines for the design of more just health care systems. Norman Daniels (1986) identified almost two decades ago one such essential guideline with respect to health care rationing issues. To put it in terms a bit more vivid than he chose, a fair rationing system must be "leakproof." The resources saved by denying individuals non-costworthy, marginally beneficial care must be redeployed within the health care system to meet other higher priority health needs (as determined by a democratic deliberative process), as opposed to allowing those savings to seep out into investors' pockets or inflated salaries. Our goal in this concluding chapter will be to identify the most fundamental of those guidelines for the design of more just health care systems.

2

THE ETHICAL CHALLENGES OF HEALTH CARE RATIONING

What does it mean to be a just and caring society when we (societal decisionmakers) have only limited resources to meet virtually unlimited health care needs? What does it mean to be a just and caring hospital or managed care organization (MCO) when administrators have only limited resources to meet the virtually unlimited health needs of the patient population for which they are responsible? What does it mean to be a just and caring physician or other health professional when only limited resources are available to meet the disproportionate health needs of the patient before that professional now? These three questions are all variants at different social levels of the problem of health care rationing, which is the central focus of this volume. This is what I refer to as the "Just Caring" problem, whose scope and complexity I will sketch below as the primary task of this chapter.

There are two preliminary claims embedded in the "Just Caring" problem, which need to be explicit. First, the problem of health care rationing is fundamentally a *moral* problem and must be addressed as such. There are economic and political and organizational/administrative aspects to the problem, but it would be fundamentally wrongheaded to believe that the problem could be resolved through the magic of the market, administrative acuity, or political power and pandering. What we are faced with is essentially a problem of justice, not simply misfortune (as I shall argue below). If we do not have enough in the way of resources to save all lives at risk from serious illness, or to restore normal functioning impaired by disease or accident, or to prevent the occurrence of serious illness, then which among these health needs ought to be met as a matter of justice, as a matter of the fair allocation of limited resources, as opposed to charity or social beneficence?

Second, the need for health care rationing is inescapable. There is no avoiding the need to deny individuals what from a social point of view is judged to be noncost worthy, marginally beneficial health care. This is a complicated point that requires substantial argument and evidence. For now we may simply illustrate it with a case from Oregon that gained considerable media attention—the case of Coby Howard.

THE STORY OF COBY HOWARD AND ITS LESSONS

Coby was a seven-year-old boy in 1987 with lymphocytic leukemia. His parents were poor and, consequently, his health care was provided through Medicaid. He did receive what was standard treatment for his leukemia initially; however, that failed to bring about a remission. The only intervention that could potentially save or prolong his life was a bone marrow transplant; the cost of that was $100,000. Medicaid was unwilling to cover that cost. This was a consequence of a newly adopted policy by Oregon Medicaid that it would no longer cover transplants in general (Thorne, 1992, p. 27).

Readers will recall the economic malaise of the 1980s, a consequence of which was that many states were starved for tax revenue. In general, Medicaid represents the second most expensive item in state budgets, behind only education. In addition, at that time (and for most of the intervening years to the present) Medicaid costs were growing at annual rates in the 10–15% range, which forced state administrators to seek ways to reduce those costs (Thomas, 1993).[1] It was noted at the time that the same funds that Medicaid expended for thirty transplants would be able to provide 5,700 other Medicaid recipients with basic health care (Thomas, 1993); that is, more medical good for more people could be done with this reallocation. Media attention helped with a private fund-raising effort for Coby Howard, but only $70,000 had been raised when Coby died (Klevit et al., 1991).

It is fair to say that Coby Howard's death came about in part as a result of an explicit rationing decision. We are using this case to illustrate the point that the need for health care rationing is inescapable.[2] Some readers will vehemently object that this case illustrates precisely the opposite of what was intended. They will pointedly ask: "How can state bureaucrats claim honestly that they cannot find $100,000 to underwrite the cost of this surgery? This is a young boy. His life is at stake. There are no other medical options that might save his life. Even if we had been in the middle of a recession, the state could surely find those resources in a society as wealthy as our own." This response, however, is very wide of the mark. To see why this is so, consider the following points.

Imagine that the state did find that "extra" $100,000—is there any morally cogent reason why that money would have to be allocated to meet the needs of Coby Howard? Imagine that there was another boy, whom we will call Bobby, same age as Coby, afflicted with a life-threatening cancer, and needing a very expensive intervention to save his life. The difference between the two, so far as prognosis is concerned, is this: If Bobby receives the $100,000 intervention, then he has an 80% chance of cure and a normal life expectancy. Coby, in actual fact, was not a good candidate for the bone marrow transplant because he was not in remission. We will stipulate (for the sake of argument) that if Coby had gotten the bone marrow transplant, the most optimistic scenario would have been a 10% chance of a three-year survival. Given these facts, would it not be reasonable and *not unjust* (to avoid the need for complex argument at this point) that the $100,000 be used for Bobby's sake? If this seems agreeable, then a rationing decision would have been made. That is, we would have judged that too little benefit at too great a cost would have been realized had we invested that money in Coby rather than Bobby (and so we would be denying Coby that benefit).

We need to carry the argument one step further. If we could come up with that first $100,000, then surely we could find a second and a third and a fourth chunk of $100,000 in the nooks and crannies of these multibillion dollar state budgets, each representing the opportunity to prolong Coby's life. However, I would counter by conjuring up life stories of Annie and Donald and Edward, all of whom needed very expensive life-saving interventions, all of whom were much more likely to benefit from having access to these resources, as in the case of Bobby. Eventually, of course, after enough of these $100,000 discoveries, we would get to the story of Zoe. Her medical circumstances and needs would be such that the most fair-minded and reasonable of decision-makers would be evenly divided as to whether she or Coby ought to receive this $100,000 grant. We can imagine that Coby finally receives the $100,000—what follows from that? Zoe is then left in the position that Coby had occupied; we have still made a rationing decision.

Some readers will be impatient with this sort of (apparently) contrived moral and philosophic argument. As noted already, what really happened in Oregon was that funding for thirty Medicaid transplants were given up so that Medicaid benefits could be extended to 5,700 more individuals. *Was that a morally permissible trade-off to make? To personalize that a bit, would it be morally permissible to trade off Coby's transplant so that two hundred more individuals could receive Medicaid benefits for a year?* And, to sharpen the point, the reader should assume that none of those two hundred individuals were likely to have any medical needs that year that were remotely life-threatening. I will assert for the sake of argument that it is morally permissible to deny Coby the transplant so that two hundred more individuals could be added to Medicaid and have their health needs securely met. My primary reason for this judgment would be that there was too small a chance and too little good that could be done for Coby as opposed to the additional Medicaid recipients.

The response I would imagine receiving from many people is that I was guilty of sacrificing the life of a little boy for some social or moral abstraction, the imagined health good of some collection of two hundred individuals without names or faces or identifiable concrete medical needs. That, they would contend, is an unconscionable trade-off. The one thing that is morally certain and morally real is that Coby Howard will die if he is denied the bone marrow transplant. That, they argue, is the only moral consideration that should serve as a shining beacon to guide my decision. However, I would argue that if I were guilty of mistakenly giving moral weight to what is no more than an abstraction, then Coby's defenders are equally guilty of that mistake. What they would have us believe is that Coby's life is of absolute moral value, that there are no other competing moral considerations relevant to this decision, and consequently, that our clear and unequivocal moral obligation is to pay for the bone marrow transplant. That, however, is plainly false, as I will argue in Chapter 2.

In brief, if Coby Howard's life is of absolute value, then the life of each and every individual faced with a life-threatening medical problem is of absolute value. In practice, that means that if there is any medical intervention for prolonging an individual's life—no matter what that intervention costs and no matter how small the good that is actually achieved—we would be morally obligated as a society to assure that individual access to that intervention. Given the enormous proliferation of life-prolonging technologies in the past thirty years (which we sketched in Chapter 1), and given that the vast majority of Americans are likely to have the need for such interventions (often several times in the face of several life-threatening illnesses), the potential exists for literally spending our entire gross domestic product on such interventions.[3] This is an obvious moral and political impossibility. Consequently, the need for health care rationing is inescapable.

An additional moral and historical point must be made. Coby Howard elicited a strong social reaction for two reasons. First, he was a child with a name and a face. Second, there was a deliberate and visible public decision to deny him the life-prolonging care that he needed. The obvious consequence of the latter point is that our society (through Medicaid) is causally and morally responsible for the fact that Coby Howard died when he did and as he did. We (self-proclaimed caring citizens of this society) would like to avoid having to accept that sort of responsibility. But we (taxpayers of this society) are less than enthusiastic supporters of the Medicaid program. The practical political result of this latter stance is that Medicaid is inadequately funded in every state.[4]

Though we think of Medicaid as providing access to needed health care for the poor in our society, the reality is that on average only 40% of the poor (those below the federal poverty level) are eligible for Medicaid. This varies dramatically from state to state, depending upon political will and fiscal resources. Oregon in 1987 was actually doing better than average, since 58% of those below the poverty level in Oregon received Medicaid. In general, however, when state budgets are under pressure, Medicaid will be trimmed by raising eligibility standards so that a smaller fraction of the poor are covered. A consequence of such decisions will often be that the serious health needs of the newly ineligible poor will be unmet, the results sometimes being the same as for Coby Howard—premature death. But the political difference is that such deaths are morally hidden and politically invisible. No social decision is made to deny an identifiable individual life-sustaining health care, which allows society the moral illusion that these deaths are merely a product of medical misfortune for which no one is morally responsible.[5]

One additional observation needs to be made with regard to the Coby Howard case. A critic might fairly ask, "How do we know that Coby Howard was most deserving of being denied expensive life-prolonging medical care? Do we really know that of all the care that Medicaid was providing that year, the care required by Coby was the least cost-worthy and the least beneficial?" I believe that an honest answer to that question would be that we had no such knowledge. This answer ought to elicit some degree of moral discomfort, given that the life of a young boy was at stake. If such momentous rationing decisions are inescapable, then we ought to be able to justify them clearly and confidently.

No doubt this lack of confident moral justification bothered John Kitzhaber (1991), then President of the Oregon Senate (and an emergency room physician). He was certain that the need for health care rationing was inescapable. He was equally certain that rationing was already part of Medicaid, and that the way it was done there was both irrational and unfair (Thorne, 1992). As noted already, if state budgets were under pressure, then savings were achieved in Medicaid by altering eligibility thresholds. It did not matter how urgent or crucial were the health needs of an individual now excluded from Medicaid. Nor did it matter how trivial were many of the health needs of persons that were covered within Medicaid. Nor did it matter that many interventions covered by Medicaid were marginally effective at best and not at all costworthy. To put it starkly, Medicaid patients with common colds could command the time of physicians, while patients such as Coby Howard were allowed to die. This seems neither right nor rational.

To correct this situation Kitzhaber pushed a package of bills through the legislature. The goal of the package was to make certain Medicaid would cover all the poor (as defined by the federal government). In addition, cost savings would be achieved through a comprehensive priority-setting process. A commission was created to carry out this priority-setting process and to solicit broad public input into the process. The primary public input pertained to the social values that the public wanted exemplified in the health priorities that were chosen. The ultimate result was a list of 709 condition–treatment pairs that were prioritized from those judged most effective to those judged least effective. The legislation did not permit the legislature itself to alter this priority list, the concern being that powerful health-related interest groups would use their political power to reshape the list at the expense of the fairness that was achieved by the more impartial commission. The sole responsibility of the legislature was to establish a level of funding for the Medicaid program, which would determine how far down that list treatments would be covered.[6] That approach had the desired effect of eliciting more funding from the legislature so that they were able to fund all the way down to condition–treatment number 587.

Clearly, funding down to only number 587 meant that rationing was legitimated for services below that level. But the virtue of this approach, as opposed to the prior approach, is that it is substantially more rational and fairer. That is, a morally and politically reasonable account could be given regarding why someone might be denied a form of health care they desired, including Coby Howard-like cases where life itself was at stake. Further, *the account was public and explicit*. No one had to fear that they were victimized by the arbitrary judgment of a particular caregiver or health manager, or by the political clout of some interest group. A medically and morally informed judgment had been made that certain medical interventions were too unlikely to yield enough medical good to justify the expenditure of limited social resources. Further, this approach had the moral virtue of expanding the access of the poor to health care that was judged to be most likely very beneficial and worthy of social investment (Fleck, 1990a).

I have made several controversial claims thus far for which I ask the reader's patience in providing the needed justification. One such claim is that the need for health care rationing is inescapable. The story of Coby Howard illustrates the point but falls far short of justifying the global claim; we turn to that task first. Subsequent to that we will offer a long series of rationing scenarios whose goal is to illustrate the scope, complexity, and magnitude of the "Just Caring" problem. We will often tell stories about individuals, for whom (or with whom) a rationing decision must be made. Every rationing decision comes down to this level, even if affected individuals are not aware of the fact that such decisions have been made. This is the level at which patients and families and caregivers face the painful consequences of rationing decisions. This is a perspective that is always morally salient. Equally salient (prima facie), however, is the aggregated social perspective associated with rationing or allocation decisions made as a matter of social or institutional policy. Often these two perspectives will be in moral tension with one another, as we shall see when we discuss our experience with renal dialysis and the Totally Implantable Artificial Heart (TIAH).

WHY HEALTH CARE RATIONING IS INESCAPABLE

I start with the assumption that therapeutically effective health care is morally special. Access to effective medically needed care *today* often makes the difference between life and premature death. It often makes functional recovery from otherwise permanently disabling injury possible. It often relieves symptomatic suffering associated with acute or chronic disease that would otherwise grossly interfere with our ability to work (earn a living) or simply enjoy the ordinary pleasures of life. These facts alone attach some degree of moral significance to health care that cannot be meaningfully attached to the vast majority of other products and services generated by our economy.[7]

Further, it is also morally significant that the technologically advanced and therapeutically effective health care system we have today is a product of *public investment* in medical research (the NIH budget is presently [2007] at about $31 billion), in training physicians and other health professionals, and in the buildings and infrastructure needed to deliver patient care. It is difficult to imagine what the moral argument would be for extracting tax dollars from the poor and working poor and uninsured in our society to create a health care system for the insured middle class that would be inaccessible or only sporadically accessible for the poor and uninsured. This looks unjust. Likewise, exempting from taxation the value of health insurance benefits for the middle class (a $200 billion tax subsidy in 2006 to the middle class) also has the appearance of injustice since this subsidy is not provided to those who are least well-off (health-wise and wealth-wise) for the most part. Worse still (as noted by many economists), this subsidy has the unjust effect of promoting health care inflation with the consequence that workers at the economic margin are pushed off the rolls of those covered by health insurance.

The point of the preceding paragraph is that the health care rationing issue would not be an issue deserving public attention unless there was something morally special about access to needed health care. If someone is denied access to a new refrigerator or new iPod or new television because they are unable to pay for these products, no one sees this sort of rationing as being morally problematic. But being denied access to a hospital emergency room (in great pain) because one's blocked small intestine (due to cancer) is not imminently life-threatening (and one has no money or health insurance to cover the cost) will strike most of us as being morally criticizable (both unkind and unjust).

Some readers may conclude that the point of the argument is to motivate health reform in the direction of a universal health care system. I endorse that conclusion, but nevertheless that will not obviate the need for health care rationing within that system (which is my real point). Health care needs (not wants) far exceed our capacity to provide the financial resources needed to meet those needs—this is essentially why health care rationing is inescapable, and why it must be seen as a moral problem.

Some number of writers and policy analysts deny that health care rationing would really be necessary if some number of other health reforms were put in place. Often the appeal is to getting rid of all the waste and inefficiency in our health care system by committing ourselves to evidence-based medicine, and the use of electronic medical records, and the abolition of for-profit aspects of our health care system, and providing more consumer-friendly information about various features of our system, and reducing medical error, and improving health care quality, and reducing excessive incomes for medical specialists, and eliminating duplication of hospital facilities precipitated by costly technological competition among those facilities, and failure to use less expensive health care providers for tasks now done by more expensive providers, and providing more palliative care at the end of life instead of futile high-cost life-prolonging care, et cetera. Bodenheimer and Grumbach (2005) would be among those advocating what I will dub an "efficiency first" approach to the problem of health care rationing. This approach has an obvious appeal: Why would we want all the moral anguish and social divisiveness associated with health care rationing if we can achieve our health care cost containment objectives "painlessly" through simply making more efficient use of the resources we already have? However, this hope is to a large extent unrealistic if we give the matter some critical attention.

One succinct way of expressing our core criticism is that one person's "waste and inefficiency" is another person's only hope for staving off death or a strongly desired "margin of safety" aimed at minimizing the risk of a preventable death. For example, the reader is asked to think about patients in a persistent vegetative state (PVS). There may be as many as 25,000 such patients in the U.S. at any point in time; the annual cost of their care (feeding tubes and long term care facilities) is somewhere in excess of $3 billion per year. However, nothing that we do will improve their prognosis or add to the quality of their lives. In fact, their lives are entirely without quality, without any type of experience at all. Given this, it is easy to see how many people might see this as "wasteful and inefficient," though advocates associated with either Right to Life or various disability groups clearly have an entirely different perspective on the matter (as events around the *Cruzan* and *Schiavo* cases demonstrate). Denying those individuals life-sustaining care (once confidently judged to be in PVS) is definitely not considered by these advocates to be a form of "painless cost control" aimed at finding uncontroversial better uses for those health care resources. Rather, they would see this as painful, compassionless rationing.

Another example would be associated with the introduction of DRGs under Medicare in 1984. At the time, standard practice dictated a ten-day hospitalization for a relatively uncomplicated heart attack. The DRG that covered that event reimbursed for only a four-day stay, which almost instantly altered medical practice. The judgment was that those extra six days did very little for recuperation that could not be accomplished at home. This looks like a paradigmatic case of painless cost control and increased efficiency. However, one of the things we know statistically is that some small fraction of those discharged patients will have a second heart attack between days five and ten. Some of those patients will live a short distance from the hospital; EMTs will quickly arrive and save them. Others will live twenty miles away in a lovely isolated suburban cove with similar-sounding street names that consistently confuse EMTs. Those patients will die of that second heart attack, though they could have been saved if their hospital stay had been prolonged. This feels a little more painful. A casual observer might not see rationing. After all, the cause of death will be listed as "heart attack," not "stingy DRG." And the truth of the matter is that the patient *might have died anyway*, even in the safety of the hospital ICU. That takes some sting out of the pain. But that sting (I argue) ought to be there since this is properly described as a rationing decision. We (our legislators) collectively decided that the likelihood of benefit from those six extra days was too low and the cost to taxpayers too high to justify paying for those days (and preventing those "statistical" deaths). This is what rationing often looks like in practice—well disguised, uncontroversial, no worse than a flu shot, essentially painless.

A very large portion of what primary care physicians do on any given day is very mundane, simple health care, far below their level of training. Enormous potential exists for saving money by having these procedures done by physician assistants (PAs) or nurse practitioners (NPs); this strikes me as a reasonable thing to do. However, we ought not ignore the fact that some number of very subtle symptoms of more serious medical problems might be missed by these PAs or NPs, the consequence of which might be either irreversible injury or premature death for these patients (likely small in number). Some physicians might have missed these symptoms as well—we should readily admit that. Still, if such a broad change were introduced into our health care system for the sake of efficiency, we would have been making a rationing decision at the same time. That is, we would have been accepting these "excess deaths and health damage" as a reasonable trade-off for the cost savings. This is not something that is readily admitted because it is painful to recognize and easy to overlook. To be clear, I am not saying that such rationing is intrinsically morally objectionable. It is not, especially if the vast majority of our population were subjected to such random risks because this change of practice was so widespread. But it is incorrect to describe such a change as merely a matter of greater efficiency that raises no potential moral problems.

Hospitals compete with one another to protect their patient base by over-investing in expensive technologies, such as MRI or PET scanners.[8] This certainly contributes to health care cost escalation and would be described as being inefficient by health care economists. What happens in practice is that these technologies are overused for (insured) patients who can benefit (at most) only marginally in order to recoup investment costs. Under ideal circumstances we would only use these technologies for patients who had a clear medical need as determined by the best medical evidence currently available. We might imagine a national health planning agency responsible for determining the most efficient number and distribution of any of these technologies. This looks like "painless" cost control, and it is at that decision making level, but the consequence would then be that individual physicians, knowing that only so many "slots" were available for genuinely needy patients, would have to deny patients who were *unlikely* to benefit at all (or benefit only marginally) access to these technologies. In the vast majority of cases these would be reasonable and morally inconsequential choices. But in a small number of cases something will be missed (a treatable tumor or more complicated fracture) that will have disastrous consequences for that patient. This means we really made a rationing decision for the sake of greater efficiency. Again, this is not an outcome that is necessarily morally problematic, especially if the vast majority of the population is subject to this random allocation of risks. The alternative is what is genuinely morally problematic—namely, the promiscuous proliferation of these technologies for the exclusive benefit of paytients (sic).[9] This contributes significantly to generalized health cost inflation and motivates marginal employers to dump health insurance for their employees, thereby increasing the ranks of the uninsured who would then have at best random access to this technology, even when they had clear medical need. That outcome is presumptively unjust.

Finally, there is the very large literature that has grown around the "futile end-of-life" care debate. The general claim by policy analysts (and physicians in practice) is that tens of billions of dollars are wasted on providing "futile" medical care at the end of life that does nothing more than inhumanely prolong the process of dying when (for a fraction of that cost) compassionate palliative care could be provided instead. Surely (the argument goes), denying individuals futile inhumane care and offering humane palliative care instead could hardly be tarred as "rationing" medical care. This is admirably *humane and efficient* cost control. Again, however, I will contend that the clinical and social reality is more complex than this simple description would suggest.

To begin with, much debate has occurred in the relevant literature regarding how to define "futile" care (Rubin, 1998; Rubin, 2007; Tonelli, 2007). If we adopt a very restrictive definition (Tomlinson and Brody, 1990), then expected savings will be minimal at best. If we adopt a more liberal definition, then the potential savings will be large and the moral challenges even larger (Jecker, 2007). Much will depend upon what we (citizen–patients and physicians) regard as "reasonable medical goals" relative to which we judge whether a particular intervention is futile or not. The vast majority of oncologists seem to believe that spending $300,000 per patient for a few extra months of life through providing these extraordinarily expensive cancer drugs is a reasonable medical goal (Nadler et al., 2006). That is, they would not see this as an instance of "futile" medical care since the goal is some prolongation of life acceptable to the patient or family, as opposed to the goal of curing their cancer (relative to which these drugs would be futile).

I reject the idea that such extraordinarily expensive care is a reasonable goal (from the perspective of health care justice), but I endorse the claim that it is morally disingenuous to characterize such care as being futile (Lantos et al., 1989). For the very same reason, I would endorse the claim that providing feeding tubes to patients in a persistent vegetative state is not futile care, either. The feeding tubes are effective in sustaining the lives of such patients as are the cancer drugs. Health plan managers who are responsible for budgets may endorse that more expansive definition of futility because (in clinical practice) this can be presented to patient families as an incontrovertible medical judgment, as opposed to what is in fact a rationing decision disguised as a medical judgment. This is a disingenuous conversation-stopper; this is not morally honest. It is primarily for this reason I contend that more expansive invocations of futility to reduce the use of expensive health care resources at the end of life only hides the rationing problem as opposed to resolving or minimizing it.

The other issue that demands comment is appealing to the compassionate cost savings that are possible with more expansive uses of palliative care at the end of life. This too has proven to be more elusive and illusionary, and another of those instances where we are "doing better and feeling worse." Few will dispute the claim that we have been extraordinarily successful in improving the quality of palliative care at the end of life over the past fifteen years. However, some forms of palliative care are themselves quite expensive. That should force us to consider the question as to whether patients are entitled as a matter of justice to all forms of palliative care, no matter what the cost, no matter how marginal the palliative benefits. Put another way, is it reasonable to believe that all patients in need of palliative care have an unlimited just claim to such care? The moral challenge implicit in this last question becomes clearer when we consider a frequent assumption made in palliative medicine at the end of life, namely that patients will either elect aggressive life-sustaining care or palliative care. However, the very success of palliative care at the end of life (especially in regard to the worst effects of cancer therapy) has caused many patients to want **both** aggressive cancer care and palliative care (because the palliative care has made aggressive cancer care more bearable and acceptance of death less desirable). The obvious net effect of this is to boost aggregate health costs and to make the rationing problem more painful, not less so (Wright and Katz, 2007).[10]

Our conclusion again is that the need for health care rationing is not going to be obviated by greater efficiency, by more astute health care management, or by finding the right incentives to shape either patient or physician behavior. There are moral issues here that must be addressed as moral issues. How did we get to this point?

RENAL DIALYSIS AND THE MEDICARE END-STAGE RENAL DISEASE (ESRD) AMENDMENTS

ESRD: Historical Background

One of the earliest problems of health care rationing pertained to renal dialysis, which was perfected in the 1960s. Kidney failure without dialysis is a death sentence. In 1968 only one dialysis "slot" was available in the United States for every ten people who needed access to dialysis to avoid dying. At the time, the cost of dialysis was about $35,000 per person per year—equal to almost $90,000 in 2006 dollars. The actual average annual cost of dialysis in 2006 was about $57,000 per person. Few people could afford access to dialysis then. Morally speaking, this meant that thousands of people were dying each year whose lives could have been prolonged indefinitely if they had access to dialysis. Money alone was preventing their access to this very effective technology that was capable of prolonging life by twenty years or more (Gojgic, 2000). This struck many as morally intolerable in a society as wealthy as our own. They believed that making rationing decisions by ability to pay (or by any other criteria) for a technology that was this effective in prolonging meaningful life was not morally defensible.

In 1972 a bill was proposed in Congress (Public Law 92–603) that would provide public funding for both renal dialysis and renal transplants for anyone with kidney failure. This bill has been characterized as national health insurance for kidney failure.[11] Everyone with kidney failure would have the relevant expenses covered by the program, no matter their insurance status, work status, age, or income.[12] Lobbyists for the bill arranged to have one of their members dialyzed before Congress to emphasize the urgency of their message; this tactic led to the quick passage of the bill. Most Americans may have seen this as a matter of moral obligation. That might be an obligation of social beneficence or of social justice; for now we can pass over that point. Analysts of the bill projected that the cost of the ESRD program would reach its peak twenty years out at about $250 million per year (Eggers, 2000b). In fact, in 2006 there were about 470,000 individuals whose lives were sustained by the program at a cost to Medicare of about $23 billion per year (U.S. Renal Data System, 2006). Roughly 25,000 more individuals (net) are added to the program each year.

At the level of the individual patients whose lives have been sustained, this program appears to be clearly morally commendable. More than one million people have had their lives prolonged over the first thirty years of the program (Eggers, 2000b). Still, at a broader social level the program appears open to moral criticism. Shortly after the passage of the ESRD Medicare amendments, hemophiliacs requested the same level of public support for essentially the same reason. They needed factor VIII to prevent potentially fatal episodes of bleeding. Again, this was a very expensive and effective life-prolonging intervention. For any individual in any year the cost of this drug would vary from a few thousand dollars to $100,000; it all depended upon the number and severity of bleeding episodes with which they might be afflicted. But Congress turned a deaf ear to their request for public funding comparable to the ESRD program. *Were the hemophiliacs treated unjustly? Could they justifiably complain that their health needs were just as urgent, and the technology for addressing those needs just as effective and unaffordable, as was the case with renal patients?*

A similar problem arose in 1979 when the antirejection drug cyclosporine became available. Major organ transplants were first attempted in the late 1960s, but their success was limited because of the medical problems of managing the immune system's rejection mechanisms. Cyclosporine changed that (Eggers, 2000a)—the result was five-year survival rates of 75% or more for heart and liver and pancreas transplants. These were certainly results that could be justly described as being effective, much more than marginally beneficial. But cost was an issue. Heart transplants in 2006 had costs of $300,000; pancreas transplants were $150,000, and liver transplants could exceed $200,000. Kidney transplants cost about $90,000, and the ESRD program paid for them. For many this fact raised an obvious problem of equity. *Why should individuals with failing hearts have to pay taxes to underwrite the costs of kidney transplants when they could expect no comparable social benefit for themselves? What would morally justify making funding distinctions among these transplantable organs such that it would be fair to fund kidney transplants but not heart transplants, especially when the technologies are equally effective and life itself is at stake in all these cases?*

Historically, an answer is available to this latter question, but it might not be a morally compelling answer. Paying for dialysis for two years is roughly equal to the cost of a kidney transplant. The alternative is that an individual is on dialysis for ten years or longer; the aggregate costs at ten years would be $570,000 (in constant dollars). It clearly makes economic sense to fund the kidney transplants; and it can be argued that it makes moral sense as well since patients will have a greatly improved quality of life with the transplant as opposed to dialysis.[13] No such trade-off is available with the other transplants. However, the individual with the failing heart can make the reasonable claim that if the government is willing to spend $570,000 to prolong the lives of some individuals in kidney failure, then it ought to be willing to spend $300,000 to prolong the life of someone with heart failure. We should all be thought of equally as citizens. Equal concern and respect for each and every citizen would seem to speak in favor of public funding for heart and other major organ transplants.

The Larger Ethical Challenges Raised by the Dialysis Program

Yet another moral perspective on this matter requires our attention. The empirical fact is that there are presently only about 2,500 hearts that become available each year for transplantation. If we cast the widest possible medical net for transplant candidates, there could be 350,000 potential candidates for these hearts each year in the U.S. Obviously, all but a tiny fraction of them die now from their heart disease. If there is no public funding for heart transplants, and if most people cannot hope to elicit $300,000 worth of charitable support from their local communities, then the vast majority of these transplantable hearts will go to those who are economically very well-off. Many in our society will find this morally offensive—whether one lives or dies should not be determined by an individual's ability to pay for the technology needed to sustain one's life. This moral sentiment is what prompted the creation of the ESRD program. However, we can produce as many dialysis machines as we wish; but transplantable human hearts are absolutely scarce. There are only 2,500 available because that is roughly the number of individuals in our society who are declared brain dead each year (most often as a result of traumatic head injury), and whose families are willing to donate their organs to save the lives of others. It is this fact that adds a perplexing moral dimension to these transplants, especially if they were to be publicly funded. Such funding would enable individuals of very modest means with failing hearts to compete successfully with individuals of very substantial means. These latter individuals will have paid taxes to support such a public program, a consequence of which might be that they are denied access to the heart transplant needed to save their lives. *Can they justifiably claim that they are treated unjustly under such circumstances, that access to such expensive life-prolonging medical resources ought to be determined by an individual's ability to pay without government subsidy?*[14]

In the early 1990s there were proposals for increasing the supply of transplantable organs via xenotransplantation (and those efforts continue [Cooper, 2003; Tai et al., 2007]). At the time the proposal had something of a science fiction quality to it. But in the intervening years there has been clear progress in developing a breed of pigs that have been genetically engineered so that their organs would not be instantly rejected when transplanted into humans (Chadwick, 2003). However, this does add yet another layer of moral complexity to the rationing debate. Recall that a relevant and reasonable excuse for our society declining to pay for the costs of heart transplants is that in so doing we would not increase the number of lives saved thereby; we would merely alter who the recipients of the heart transplants might be. But if we are successful in developing genetically engineered non-rejectable pig organs for humans (including kidneys), then the moral salience of that excuse evaporates. As things are now, the best results for kidney transplants come from living-related donors. Those donors, of course, take some medical risk in undergoing what is major surgery. There are also familial psychological pressures to contribute a kidney if one is in fact a "good match" for the family member needing a donated kidney. The option of compatible animal organs would obviate those risks and pressures, but it would also exacerbate the social justice problem.[15] *What would be the moral justification under such future possible circumstances for not funding heart and pancreas and liver transplants from such genetically engineered animals if we were using their kidneys and underwriting those costs with public funds?* Alternatively, if societal decision-makers anticipate this sort of divisive and morally problematic implication *from successful genetic engineering of pigs (or other animals), would such decision-makers be open to moral criticism if they chose to close down this line of research? That is, could such a decision be correctly characterized as being either unjust or uncaring, especially if such research demonstrated genuine scientific promise, as opposed to being no more than a theoretical scientific possibility?*

Yet another issue of justice has been raised in the past ten years regarding the ESRD program. Readers need to appreciate that dialysis is a very demanding medical intervention that significantly compromises the quality of life of individuals. Two features in particular are most relevant. Dialysis typically occurs three times each week for four hours or so each time. Individuals can take in only very tiny quantities of liquid between dialysis treatments, the result being a very intensely felt perpetual thirst. Individuals often have been left in a lethargic state after dialysis because of the way in which their red blood cells are "beaten up" by the therapy itself. In the late 1980s a genetically engineered drug called Epogen (erythropoeitin) became available that effectively addressed this latter problem (Eggers, 2000b), but the cost of this drug was in the range of $8,000–$10,000 per patient per year (Pollack, 2000). Medicare chose to cover that cost, which has added annual costs to the program of about $1.5 billion (Pollack, 2000). Our questions would be these: *Would Medicare be open to moral criticism if they had decided not to provide public funding for the drug, leaving it entirely up to an individual's ability to pay? That is, would such a decision be justifiably described as being either unjust or uncaring? Alternatively, is Medicare open to moral criticism for choosing to fund this drug, the argument being that Medicare in general has not funded (prior to 2005) prescription drugs for the elderly (unless those drugs are integral to hospital care)?*

Clearly there are very substantial costs associated with Epogen. Two sorts of justifications would seem to support Medicare absorbing those costs. The first is that the quality of life of dialysis patients was significantly improved with the drug. The second is that the need for hospitalization has been reduced as a result of this drug. Some critics may wonder how we can justify spending such large sums of public money to improve the "quality of life" of these patients when there appears to be so many more urgent and more compelling health needs in our society. However, there is a "suicide rate" among dialysis patients that is seven times greater than would be predicted for a comparable population of otherwise healthy individuals. That is, individuals elect to stop dialysis, thereby bringing about their deaths from renal failure, because they find their quality of life to be so diminished by the therapy. But Epogen has clearly contributed to a 17% reduction in mortality among dialysis patients for the period 1989–97 (Nissenson and Rettig, 1999, p. 170). There are no acceptable statistics on the reduced costs associated with reduced hospitalization and mortality; for our purposes we will simply stipulate that there is a reasonable balance between these hospitalization savings and the costs of Epogen. Still, we are left with a disturbing and increasingly common phenomenon in contemporary health care, which Wildavsky (1977) has aptly captured in the phrase "doing better and feeling worse." We feel better because we have reduced mortality associated with dialysis, but each of those extra life-years gained costs Medicare $57,000 for the continuing need for dialysis for these patients. Should an economic fact such as that be accorded any *moral weight* when we are trying to determine whether a just and caring society ought to underwrite the costs of Epogen?

Just Caring for "Similar" Health Care Needs

I have said little up to this point regarding what might motivate or justify this appeal to the language of justice. Two commonsense moral considerations seem to be at work in our discussion thus far. First, like cases should be treated alike. Obviously there can be argument about the correct application of this principle. Are Coby and Bobby alike enough that a lottery should be used to determine which would receive the $100,000 for their medical therapy if only one such sum of money were available? Or is the fact that Bobby has so much better a prognosis determinative of a morally relevant dissimilarity? Second, medical need creates presumptive just claims to health resources. The concept of "need" does not have clear and obvious boundaries. For now all we require is a shared understanding of what virtually all would agree is a clear medical need. When life itself is at risk (unless one has access to some medical therapy), that would be a clear case of medical need. Health care providers and managers who are appropriately situated relative to individuals with such needs would seem to be open to moral criticism if they were simply to ignore such needs. This is just a rough moral intuition that I ask the reader to consider as we continue our discussion of the dialysis case.

We noted already that the ESRD program pays the cost of a kidney transplant for individuals who would otherwise need dialysis. These individuals will also need to be on antirejection drugs (such as cyclosporine) for the rest of their lives. The ESRD program will pay those costs of $10,000–$12,000 per year for the first three years after transplant. Beyond that, an individual is responsible for bearing those costs. *Is it unjust that individuals are denied public funding for their antirejection medications?* Like cases ought to be treated alike. The ESRD program pays for the Epogen that combats the serious lethargy dialysis patients otherwise must tolerate. So what would justify not paying the costs of the antirejection medications? Further, if need is a morally relevant consideration, then it seems as if more is at stake, health-wise, with the risk of organ rejection than with the lethargy. Gordon (2006) makes precisely this point. She notes that, as things are now with the three-year limit, "one patient in thirteen, who would have otherwise died earlier, would be alive twenty years later" (p. 1062) if the ESRD program paid for antirejection medications without limit.

There is still another dimension of this scenario we should consider. Dialysis can be accomplished in several different ways. At first, all dialysis was done in a hospital setting; today there are 3,500 dialysis centers that do much of this work. More importantly, home dialysis is an option. From the perspective of the ESRD program it is a preferred option since the costs of dialysis are reduced by more than half in the home. These savings are achieved both because the method of dialysis is different and because the patient is trained to perform the tasks in the home that would otherwise be performed by a paid technician in a dialysis center.

We would like to believe that all medical decisions would be made on the basis of what is in the best interests of each individual patient, and that patients have a genuine opportunity to participate in the making of that best interest judgment. We would also like to believe that money would generally not be a determining factor in making therapeutic decisions—but it is. Only about 15% of dialysis patients in the U.S. are on home peritoneal dialysis, whereas other countries have much higher rates (Nissenson and Rettig, 1999, p. 164). It is not clear that this distribution reflects patients' own choices based on their judgment of their best interest. There is some reason to suspect otherwise. About 65% of these dialysis centers are for-profit enterprises. Though payment rates have remained flat for the past ten years (without even adjusting for inflation), these centers have remained profitable to investors. They have been forced to achieve efficiencies, such as the creation of large chains of these centers comprised of hundreds of facilities. A noteworthy fact is that if an independent center is forced by economics to cease operations, they can usually sell their patient lists for $25,000 to $40,000 per patient (Nissenson and Rettig, 1999, p. 173). Each of those patients represents a ten-year revenue stream of more than a half-million dollars. If physicians are among the investors in these facilities, that would create an incentive to steer patients in that direction.

No doubt some patients *need* these facilities; home dialysis is not a medical option for them; others, however, ought to have a choice. Certainly from the perspective of the wise use of public resources it would be desirable that more of these patients choose home peritoneal dialysis. That suggests this question: *Could a just and caring society justifiably alter its dialysis reimbursement policy so that all individuals for whom home peritoneal dialysis was a reasonable medical option would be expected to take that option?* To enforce that expectation, individuals who chose otherwise (who were reasonable candidates for peritoneal dialysis) would be expected to cover the costs above those of peritoneal dialysis. The moral argument might be: You do have a medical need for dialysis. A just and caring society must provide this to you to sustain your life. But you do not have a need for *dialysis provided through a center*. If you make this choice, you must bear those additional costs.

We value in our society giving patients medical options, but that value can come into conflict with considerations of justice in the fair allocation of limited resources. Is what we have described here one such instance of that? We value in medicine not just choice, but *informed* choice. What information do patients have a right to know related to center-provided dialysis? As noted already, federal reimbursements have been flat and capitated to centers for at least one ten-year period (1992–2002); this creates incentives for economizing, which might compromise the best interests of patients. Rarely do patients know of these incentives or the changes in the provision of care that come about as a result of these incentives. But these can be correctly described as another way in which rationing is accomplished in our society. More specifically, many dialysis centers reduced their costs by laying off nurses and hiring less costly technicians to do their work. They have also reduced a bit the length of dialysis sessions, ignored nutritional status issues, and reused dialysis filters, all of which can *on occasion* result in health outcomes for patients that will require a hospitalization (Nissenson and Rettig, 1999, pp. 168–70).

Hospitalization itself represents a risk to health because of nosocomial infections. The costs of these outcomes, of course, are not borne by these dialysis centers.

The reader will notice I emphasized that these outcomes happen "on occasion." This adds to the difficulty of making careful and accurate moral judgments. Some patients will have a need for hospitalization related to dialysis that cannot easily or fairly be attributed to any of the cost-constraining measures listed above. In other cases the hospitalization would not have occurred but for the cost-constraining measures. It will most often be the case that we have no reliable way of judging which it is at the individual level. That by itself makes moral accountability very difficult to assess.

Assume for the sake of argument that in a particular instance we know that inadequate dialysis time caused a patient to need hospitalization. Who should be held blameworthy for that? Can the dialysis center claim justifiably that reimbursements were so stingy that it was impossible to provide good patient care and pay reasonable competitive salaries to staff and provide a reasonable rate of return to investors? In other words, a stingy Congress or Health and Human Services should really be held accountable for making a morally questionable rationing decision that only became evident at the level of the dialysis center. Some readers will be very critical of this response, perhaps seeing this as the worst sort of rationalization for protecting profits at the expense of patients. No doubt this is sometimes true, but we must avoid the temptation to think that the whole rationing problem would go away if the profit motive in medicine were eliminated. We can easily imagine federalizing the whole dialysis program, then the program would be publicly funded, and professionals employed by the state would deliver services. In other words, no for-profit entities would be involved. If payment levels remained essentially the same, then rationing decisions would still have to be made. Further, the temptation would be to accomplish that in a way that was largely hidden from both patients and the larger public, as is done now.

Finally, yet another facet of the broad problem of health care rationing can be illustrated by the ESRD program. The fastest growing cohort of dialysis patients is comprised of those over age 75. About 20% of all new dialysis patients are over age 75 (Nissenson and Rettig, 1999, p. 163). Half of all new patients were over age 65 in 1998, compared to 1978 when only 25% were over age 65. Kurella et al. (2007) points out that between 1996 and 2003 "78,419 octogenerians and 5,577 nonagenerians initiated dialysis in the United States." The annual rate of dialysis initiation for these two cohorts nearly doubled during that period of time; median survival for this combined cohort was one year. More importantly, in 1978 only 10% of dialysis patients had kidney failure attributable to diabetes, while 45% had kidney failure attributable to diabetes in 1998 (Eggers, 2000b, p. 521). These statistics may not strike most readers as being especially significant. After all, many will argue, the age of someone with failing kidneys should be morally irrelevant when it comes to determining their access to therapy; the fact that they have a life-threatening medical problem is what gives them a presumptive claim on the therapy. However, the historical fact is that moral support for the ESRD program was very forceful because the vast majority of individuals with failing kidneys were middle-aged or younger. That is, these individuals were going to die very prematurely. Further, the perception was that these individuals were essentially healthy, except for this one life-threatening but ameliorable medical problem, their failing kidneys. Losing such salvageable life-years "merely because of money" seemed especially unconscionable.

As noted above, however, the medical and demographic realities related to dialysis have changed dramatically over the past thirty years. Today we have a substantially older and sicker dialysis population, and something needs to be done to control the escalating costs of the program.[16] Daniel Callahan (1987) made an extremely controversial proposal in the late 1980s, namely that we ought to embrace age-based health care rationing, especially when life-prolonging technologies are very expensive; and in older individuals, provide extra life-years of somewhat diminished quality (or worse). Callahan sees dialysis as precisely the sort of technology he had in mind in offering this proposal. He never picked a very definite age beyond which such a denial would take effect; instead, he would usually say that this should occur in the late 70s or early 80s because by then, individuals would have had the opportunity to live a full life. The implication is that such individuals do not have a strong moral right to "yet more" life at substantial public expense, especially when it is the case that there are more compelling unmet health care needs for expensive and effective life-prolonging technologies among much younger individuals in our society.

Still, the obvious problem, which Callahan himself acknowledges (and which explains his reluctance to identify a very definite cutoff age for denial of these technologies) is that there are a lot of very vigorous older people in our society. Very likely, a majority of those beyond age 70 in our society would correctly describe themselves as being in very good health (Lubitz et al., 2003). The implication of this for our discussion of rationing and ESRD seems clear. We are not, in good conscience, going to deny dialysis to a vigorous individual beyond age 80 whose only serious medical problem is kidney failure.[17] Whatever the moral considerations were that prompted us to provide dialysis to the forty-year-old will be equally applicable to this eighty-year-old. But there is another argument in the background that would also be a source of moral discomfort if we adopted some definite age as a cutoff.

Imagine Albert and Bonnie, age 79 and 82 respectively, both in reasonably good health except that each has recently developed end-stage kidney failure. Albert gets dialysis but Bonnie does not. Albert remains on dialysis until age 84, when he has a fatal heart attack. If we had some really compelling moral reasons for choosing age 80 as a cutoff, then it would appear that Albert ought to get dialysis for a year, after which he would be removed. But there are powerful moral intuitions that would speak against that idea. What would be morally compelling reasons for choosing age 80 as a cutoff? A short answer would be to point out all those very high-quality, much younger life-years that we could save at very great expense if we were willing to redeploy the resources now being spent on those over age 80 for dialysis. But my strong suspicion is that if we were each to consult our own "sense of justice" in this regard, we would conclude that it was *unfortunate* (but not unjust) that those younger life-years were lost. However, saving those life-years by literally taking away life-sustaining dialysis from those who were dependent upon it at age 80 would be both cruel and unjust. Again, this is not intended as a conclusive moral judgment; we are at this stage of our inquiry merely mapping the moral terrain associated with health care rationing, using dialysis as a rich and fruitful source of justice-related moral issues.

Ragged Edges and Health Care Justice

Our next step is to explore a recurrent theme in the rationing debates, what Callahan (1990, chap. 2) has felicitously labeled the "ragged edge" problem. It pertains to the fact that rarely do bright lines exist "in nature" that provide us with clear boundaries regarding where rationing decisions are made most fairly. Imagine Albert and Bonnie again, same ages as above. But this time, Albert has advanced diabetes and advanced heart disease associated with his renal failure. His predicted life expectancy is no more than two years. Bonnie, on the other hand, is in reasonably good health except for the renal failure. *Would it be morally permissible (not unjust) to provide dialysis to Bonnie under the ESRD program, but deny it to Albert?* If pressed for a moral justification for such a proposal, I imagine it would be twofold. Albert has lived a long life already; he is almost eighty. Others should have the opportunity to achieve a comparable lifespan, especially if they are at risk from premature death because they (or society) cannot afford the costs of some effective but expensive life-prolonging intervention. Further, the quality of Albert's life is very substantially diminished by the confluence of these disorders. If there are younger, higher-quality life-years that can be saved by an alternate deployment of those resources, then saving those lives and life-years ought to have higher moral priority.

We can now change Bonnie's life story slightly. She has some very painful arthritis, which clearly diminishes the quality of her life. In addition, she has had to deal with depressive episodes every now and then due to her inability to get over the death of her husband. Does she too have a diminished moral claim to dialysis as a result of these factors diminishing somewhat the quality of her life? That is one illustration of the ragged edge problem. We would like to have bright lines illuminate our moral judgment in these matters, but what we most often find in reality are poorly lit, frayed, tattered, and irregular margins around disease processes with uncertain outcomes.

Then there is the story of Charles who is 60 years old, but whose medical circumstances are the same as Albert's. So he has advanced diabetes and heart disease with a predicted life expectancy of no more than two years. Does the fact that he is "only" 60 give him more of a just claim to dialysis? Would it be unjust to deny him access to dialysis on grounds of consistency? That is, the quality of his remaining life is the same as Albert's. If we deny Albert those extra years at social expense, then we ought to deny Charles as well. This is another one of those ragged edges.

Some sort of decision needs to be made, but it looks as if any decision will have a very arbitrary character to it. Many social policy decisions involve arbitrariness, such as an age at which alcohol may be legally consumed. But in the case of dialysis, the life or death of individuals is what is at stake—none of us can be morally comfortable with the thought that a decision such as that would be made arbitrarily, without a compelling and consistent moral justification. Dr. Norman Levinsky (2001), a very prominent nephrologist, vigorously opposes denying individuals dialysis on the grounds that they have comorbid conditions likely to result in their deaths within two years (see Lowance, 1993). He sees such a judgment as being entirely arbitrary. He writes, "Most people no doubt would value one added year of life highly if it is of reasonable quality in their own judgment" (2001, p. 101). Levinsky also takes to task the SUPPORT (study to understand prognoses and preferences for outcomes and risks of treatment) investigators (Hamel et al., 1997) who argued that dialysis was not cost-effective, and should not be offered to patients with terminal conditions with less than a 50% chance of six-month survival.[18] Likewise, he rejects the contention of Moss (1995) that it is inappropriate for physicians to offer dialysis to patients who have less than two months to live. It would appear that Levinsky wants to avoid the moral hazards associated with the ragged edge. His view (in this range of cases) is that if decisions need to be made, let patients make them themselves in the light of their own goals and values. No doubt this is often a commendable moral view to adopt; however, the critical moral issue before us now is a matter of justice primarily, not respect for patient autonomy.

The very large question is this: Do ALL patients in kidney failure have an equally strong just claim to access dialysis at public expense? This is not a question that can be *justly* answered through an appeal to respect for patient autonomy. The autonomous choices of patients to accept or decline medical treatment ought to be respected when they have a just claim to those resources. Otherwise their preferences are justifiably set aside (as I shall argue below). Levinsky (2001) offers three other sorts of patients for our consideration who might be faced with renal failure and the need for dialysis. These are patients in a persistent vegetative state (PVS), or in advanced stages of dementia, or with AIDS (as defined by the Centers for Disease Control). It would be reasonable to say that all three types of these patients have profoundly diminished quality of life; though with AIDS patients, that judgment would be much more complex and variegated at the individual level. *Does that provide a morally sufficient reason for concluding that these patients have either no just claim, or an extremely low priority claim, to renal dialysis to further prolong their lives?*

Levinsky himself has serious reservations in all three cases. His concern with respect to both PVS patients and patients in the advanced stages of dementia is that this will start us down a morally slippery slope. That is, if we think of these individuals as being mentally disabled, then we will be tempted to withdraw or not provide life-sustaining care to individuals who are profoundly retarded, then moderately retarded, and so on. Levinsky also notes the medical reality that an extremely small number of patients "confidently diagnosed" as being in PVS regain (somehow) some degree of consciousness (usually quite impaired). If all PVS patients with kidney failure were denied dialysis, then that tiny number who might experience that marginal degree of recovery would be denied that opportunity for extended life. Levinsky also worries that relatives or staff responsible for caring for these patients might be worn out by the burden of caring for them. Consequently, they might be tempted to withdraw dialysis as a way to alleviate their own burden under the guise of ending the suffering associated with a life not worth living. Further still, many in our society might be tempted to deny or withdraw expensive life-prolonging care from patients who are judged to have brought their medical problems upon themselves through bad choices. AIDS patients are often judged in this way, but the 45% of patients with kidney failure due to diabetes (poorly managed) might be judged in this way as well. Levinsky sees all such judgments as contrary to the spirit of compassion that must be the moral center of medical practice.

Still, Levinsky will acknowledge that dialysis for PVS "does raise the question whether it is a justifiable use of limited societal resources" (2001, p. 103). And he will consider the same point with regard to patients with advanced dementia (though he worries about how a line can be drawn between moderate and advanced dementia). Levinsky is willing to accept a societal consensus in these matters, so long as that decision is arrived at openly. That is, he would reject as unethical the covert rationing practices that characterized the British approach to rationing dialysis in the 1980s (Aaron and Schwartz, 1984). He is also saying that he does not want individual physicians to have responsibility for these decisions. He wants to avoid two sorts of ethical risks: (1) the arbitrariness and inconsistency associated with individual judgments, and (2) an unwarranted compromise of the duty of loyalty that each physician owes her patients.

Levinsky's moral judgments here have a presumptive moral attractiveness about them, but we do need to ask some critical questions. He wants a societal "consensus" to determine whether or not we would provide dialysis to PVS patients with kidney failure. *What should count as a "consensus" in this context?* Would a simple majority be morally adequate? Or would we need something in excess of 95% social agreement? Then there is the question of how we would achieve and apply such a consensus. The political reality is that we do not have a single system for health care financing and delivery. To be sure, there is only one ESRD program, but that is something politically unique. Apart from that, we have the fifty different Medicaid programs, at least 1,500 different health insurance/managed care entities, the Medicare program (now itself effectively fragmented with the privatization of the Part D prescription drug benefit), and so on. Should it be up to each of these different programs to determine whether there is a consensus relevant to their constituencies regarding a PVS rationing protocol, for example, with respect to $40,000 implanted cardiac defibrillators? If so, we could reasonably expect that there would be variation from one Medicaid program or managed care plan to another. *Should that sort of diversity be regarded as ethically unacceptable, given that life and death decisions are at stake?* If individuals could easily move from one managed care plan to another, or if poor individuals could easily move from one Medicaid program to another, then this might reduce the ethically worrisome aspects of these decisions. But the large majority of American workers have no choice with regard to the health plan that is chosen for them by their employer.

Levinsky wants to protect the moral integrity of physicians by isolating them from the need to make rationing decisions. His essential position seems to be: If rationing decisions must be made, and if there is always something morally impure about these decisions, then we ought to isolate physicians from having any involvement in these decisions by having these decisions made at some societal level. However, this seems unrealistic for two reasons. First, physicians will often necessarily have to make medical judgments that will result in patients being subjected to (or exempted from) a rationing protocol. For example, if patients with advanced dementia are to be denied dialysis, then a physician will have to judge when a patient has progressed from moderate to advanced dementia. But, as Levinsky himself emphasizes, there are no medically sharp criteria that will cleanly yield these distinctions. Second, physicians today generally have contracts with several managed care plans. This means that they could be caring for patients with the same medical condition, but from different managed care plans, one of which has in place a rationing protocol with regard to that condition, the other of which does not. Should a just and caring and loyal doctor alter his/her medical practice with each of these patients to reflect limitations imposed by these plans?

We might imagine that a physician could manage this moral challenge by informing a patient of these limitations, thereby giving them the option of paying out of pocket for what a physician judges is a medically necessary service. However, this strategy would not be available to a physician if the relevant medical service was especially expensive and was covered by a capitation arrangement. In that situation the cost of that intervention would come from what that physician would regard as anticipated income. Physicians could refrain from mentioning such options to patients under such financing terms, but then physicians themselves are making rationing judgments very directly (but covertly). For now, our point is simply that it is virtually impossible in practice for physicians to divorce themselves from some level of moral responsibility for rationing decisions in health care today.

We have expended significant effort in explaining and illustrating the problem of health care rationing as that applies to access to kidney dialysis for patients with renal failure. The dialysis problem is historically important, morally complex, and of ongoing relevance. It would be morally challenging if the dialysis problem were the whole of the problem of health care rationing—but it is not. In the remainder of this chapter I want to introduce other health care interventions that raise in various ways the problem of health care rationing. My goal is to make evident the heterogeneity and the complexity of the problem of health care rationing. The practical moral conclusion will be that no appeal to some relatively simple principle of health care justice, whether utilitarian or libertarian or egalitarian, will be sufficient to address adequately the heterogeneity of health care rationing problems our society will need to face.

THE TOTALLY IMPLANTABLE ARTIFICIAL HEART (TIAH)

We start with the case of the TIAH. As I write, eleven patients have actually received this device; two have survived for a year (but died shortly beyond that). All received the AbioCor version of this device. It has had some problems with causing clot formation, but it is now believed those problems have been remedied (Dowling et al., 2003). I have every reason to believe that this device will be at least as successful as bypass surgery once we get beyond this experimental phase. The predictions associated with the use of this device are that in the U.S. we could implant 350,000 of these devices per year at a cost per implantation of about $300,000 (in 2006 dollars). The expectation is that this device will yield on average five extra years of life expectancy, not a morally insignificant gain. If we did implant that many devices, this would add about $70 billion per year to the cost of health care in the U.S. Is a just and caring society morally obligated to make sure that all who have the relevant medical need for this device (end-stage heart disease) have access to it, if they want it? The assumption we make (for the sake of argument) is that all the moral considerations that prompted the formation of the ESRD program would equally justify (and morally require) the creation of an End-Stage Heart Disease program.

It will be helpful to put our TIAH case, along with our other cases, into a larger economic context so that we might better appreciate the challenges to health care justice. In 2006 we in the U.S. spent about $2.16 trillion on health care, which represents about 16.3% of our GDP. In 1970 we spent $70 billion on health care, which represented 7.0% of GDP at the time. In a little over 30 years we have more than doubled the fraction of GDP that we allocate to health care. Further, nothing in the foreseeable future suggests a significant alteration of this trend line. While there are many factors that conspire to produce these escalating health care costs, more than half of the annual total increase is explained by advancing medical technology. The artificial heart is a perfect example of this.

In the relatively near future, the "aging out" of the post–World War II "baby boom" generation will very much exacerbate those escalating cost problems. In 2005 there were about 39 million individuals over age 65 in the U.S.; this represents about 13% of the population. Current projections are that figure will reach 78 million by the year 2025, which will then be about 21% of the total population. This statistic is very significant, morally and economically and politically, because roughly 35% of total health expenditures in the U.S. are for that 13% of the population over age 65. In 2006 Medicare spent about $420 billion on meeting the health needs of the elderly (Centers for Medicare and Medicaid Services, 2004, table 3).[19] This is only about half of the total health expenditures for the elderly, which were about $800 billion in 2006. These statistics might suggest that the elderly are a very moribund lot, but that is in fact not true (Lubitz et al., 2003). Cutler (2003, p. 1084) writes, "Only one third of the years lived after age 70 are lived with a disability, but the costs of care in those years account for two thirds of lifetime medical spending." One of the practical implications of this latter point is that virtually any significant effort to control health care costs will have a disproportionate impact on the quantity and quality of health care received by the elderly, which will at least have the appearance of being unjustly discriminatory. With this in mind, we can return to our TIAH scenario.

Of the 350,000 potential candidates each year for a TIAH, roughly 70% of them would be over age 65 and eligible for Medicare. If all of them did in fact receive the TIAH, that would add $72 billion per year to the cost of Medicare. *Is a just and caring society morally obligated to make this option available at Medicare's expense to all who have the relevant medical need?* In December of 2003 Congress passed a Medicare prescription drug benefit after a prolonged, rancorous debate. The ten-year costs of this benefit to Medicare (2006–2015) are projected at $800 billion, with a tenth-year cost in excess of $140 billion that would rapidly escalate thereafter as "baby boomers" continued to join the ranks of Medicare. What needs to be emphasized, however, is that $800 billion represents only a fraction of total prescription drug costs for the elderly for that period. Total costs are projected at $2 trillion. This suggests yet another problem of health care justice.

If we cannot afford to meet all the health care needs of the elderly through public funding, ought we cover more of those prescription drugs, especially for low-income elderly, before we pay anything at all for artificial hearts? Some readers might find this an easy question to answer. More than twenty million of the elderly would benefit from an enhanced prescription drug benefit, compared to a couple hundred thousand who would be the beneficiaries of an artificial heart. This looks like a powerful utilitarian argument. However, the dialysis problem is lurking here, though on a much larger scale. The artificial heart would be clinically available to those under age 65, and presumably health insurance would cover that expense for most. This would be an effective life-prolonging therapy, promising on average five extra years of life *for individuals who would be faced with death in the very near future.* These would all be identifiable individuals. Further, their numbers in Medicare would be very socially significant, about 240,000 individuals "condemned to death" each year by being denied the technology that could prolong their lives. When we had only natural hearts for transplantation we were faced with absolute limits—we could alter who the recipients of these transplants would be, but we could not alter the total available. That provided a reasonable and acceptable moral explanation for why we could not do more. But there is no absolute limit on the number of artificial hearts we could produce. Consequently, no convenient excuse exists for failing to save all who can be saved, except the sheer cost of it.

As we have already noted, plain appeals to the "sheer cost" of anything will not do much by way of resolving the moral question of what we ought or ought not to do. The obvious follow-up question always exists, "If we took the money from elsewhere (in health care/outside health care), would we not then be able to pay for these artificial hearts?" However, if we were to do that, we would have to provide some sort of justification for such a fund transfer. Remember, we are talking about $72billion.

What Norms Should Govern Allocating Artificial Hearts?

Several possible justifications exist to which we might appeal. We might say that *more lives will be saved* by spending this money for artificial hearts as opposed to wherever the money was taken from. But this prompts the follow-up inquiry as to whether all those lives saved are equally worthy of being saved. More precisely, some of those lives saved will go on for ten years or longer; others might last only a year. No doubt each and every one of those lives is equally worthy of moral respect.

However, that does not obviously imply that each and every life at stake has an equally just claim to an artificial heart at a cost of $300,000. The sort of situation we have in mind involves various possible comorbidities. If a patient will die from their heart disease in two months without an artificial heart, but they also have metastatic cancer, which will almost certainly cause their death within two years, do they have as strong a just claim to an artificial heart as a patient without any such comorbidities and a projected lifespan of ten more years? This raises the "ragged edge" problem again.

The moral urgency associated with creating the ESRD program derived largely from the fact that the lives at risk from kidney failure were middle-aged or younger. But once the program was created, no one could offer cogent enough reasons for denying access to dialysis to anyone with kidney failure, no matter what their age, no matter what their comorbidities, no matter how short their projected life expectancy, even with dialysis. Consequently, program costs increased dramatically because of the number of "lives saved" by the program, the fastest growth being in the oldest cohort during the 1990s and beyond. If Medicare were to fund access to the artificial heart, such a scenario would be equally likely there, unless a strong case could be made for an alternate justificatory norm.

An obvious alternative norm would be to look at *life-years saved* as opposed to lives saved. In practice this would mean looking at some range of life-saving medical alternatives and judging which interventions saved more life-years. This would be a more complicated and morally problematic effort than might appear at first. Would we, for example, make comparisons among these interventions from the perspective of their *average predicted outcome*? This is obviously a figure that can be manipulated depending upon where we would choose to create boundaries for "appropriate" use of the intervention. We noted that we could do 350,000 artificial heart transplants in the U.S. with an average gain in life expectancy of five years. That average can be raised by deciding that we will not offer the artificial heart as an option to patients who have a predicted life expectancy of two years or less. Some will see this as a just and reasonable choice to make, perhaps arguing that applying this logic across a range of life-prolonging technologies will result in our maximizing the number of life-years saved within the limits of some budget. Others will see such a choice as unjust and unreasonable, perhaps calling particular attention to the potential for arbitrary decisions all along the clinically fuzzy and ragged edges in the vicinity of that two-year criterion.

Another problem with the unqualified life-years criterion is that many will argue it is unreasonable not to take into account the *overall quality* of the life-years that are saved. The critical question might be put this way: *Is a just and caring society really morally obligated to save life-years at very substantial cost no matter what the quality of life for the individual whose life is prolonged? More concretely, if we did gain ten life-years by providing an artificial heart to a physically vigorous individual in the advanced stages of Alzheimer's, should we really believe that those ten years are just as morally important from the perspective of health care justice as ten years gained for a 65-year-old who needs a heart transplant but otherwise is in very good overall health?*

Over the past twenty years a very large amount of literature has grown up around the moral legitimacy or illegitimacy of employing quality-adjusted life-year (QALY) criteria for purposes of making rationing and allocation decisions in health care. We cannot review that literature just now, but we can raise some critical questions to focus attention. I will begin by confessing my judgment in this matter—it seems obvious to me that we have no moral obligation to sustain the life of an individual in the end-stages of Alzheimer's (AD) with an artificial heart transplant. That is, we have not treated that individual unjustly by denying them the transplant. I would make the same judgment with respect to patients who are confidently judged to be in a persistent vegetative state, even if they are relatively young, such as Terry Schiavo in Florida.

But I am also mindful of the very strong moral objections that have been raised by advocates for persons with disabilities to the use of QALYs. Those advocates see the use of QALYs as invidiously discriminatory with respect to all who have any sort of disability whatsoever (Hirskyj, 2007; Peters, 1995). If QALYs are regarded as a morally legitimate consideration in making rationing decisions, then individuals with disabilities will consistently be denied costly life-sustaining medical care because their lower-quality life-years will be judged to be less worthy of being saved or sustained.

An obvious question to pose is whose perspective is used to assign assorted weights to differing degrees of disability. Disability advocates note that most often, individuals without disabilities are the source of these judgments. An individual who has enjoyed his sight all his life might be asked to assign a value (from 0–1) to a year of life in which he would have lost his sight. If the average response from one hundred sighted individuals is 0.7, then that number is the value of a QALY for someone who is blind. But individuals who have been born blind or lost their sight as a result of accident or disease will most often provide a radically different answer to such researchers. Very often they will value a current life-year at 1. That is, they will judge themselves to have high-quality lives. They see judgments coming from the sighted as reflecting prejudice and ignorance. They contend that if they are faced with heart failure and are in need of a heart transplant they ought to have as strong a just claim to an artificial heart as anyone who is sighted.

I am again going to insert my own perspective here and affirm the moral judgment of those advocating on behalf of the blind; however, this hardly settles very much. The blind can speak for themselves, as can the hearing impaired, and those with various disabilities linked to mobility. But patients in the advanced stages of Alzheimer's or in a persistent vegetative state cannot speak for themselves. Further, if "experience counts," morally speaking (if actual experience gives legitimacy to certain judgments about one's quality of life), then no one really has any moral authority when it comes to either advanced AD or PVS. So what should we conclude from that so far as these issues of health care justice are concerned?

Further still, there are numerous forms and degrees of disability that can be arrayed (partially) along a continuum from being blind to being in PVS. Can some kinds and degrees of disability (at some place on the continuum) legitimately be taken into account in making rationing decisions? That is, individuals in those more severely disabled states would be judged as having less just claims (or no claims at all) to expensive life-prolonging medical interventions, such as the artificial heart. Who do we imagine would have the moral right to make such judgments? And what do we imagine would be the morally legitimate criteria that would justify such judgments? In particular, how do we imagine managing in a morally defensible way the very large, very complicated ragged edge that would be associated with making such judgments in practice?

Another criterion we must assess as a source of justification for possible rationing and allocation decisions regarding the artificial heart is *cost-effectiveness*. The core idea behind cost-effectiveness analysis is easy enough to understand—if we have only limited resources to meet virtually unlimited health care needs, then neither ethics nor economics would regard as either rational or fair purchasing more expensive QALYs before we had purchased all available less expensive QALYs.[20] For example, if the cost per life-year saved of an average patient receiving the artificial heart is $60,000, and if the average cost per life-year saved of providing clotting factor to an individual with severe hemophilia is $100,000, then we ought to save all the cardiac QALYs we can before we start saving any hemophiliac QALYs.

The first question we want to ask ourselves is whether we want to endorse this approach in general from a moral point of view. Is using cost data in this way too crude, too morally insensitive, too likely to violate one or another important consideration of health care justice? This is essentially a utilitarian approach to thinking about distributive justice issues in health care. Utilitarianism has been criticized sharply and repeatedly from a deontological perspective, most effectively with the work of John Rawls (1971), as a basic approach to distributive justice issues in society. The most common criticism of utilitarianism is that its single metric of moral success is maximization (in this case, cost-effective QALYs), which can have as a consequence the violation of basic rights of individuals to life-saving needed health care. If hemophiliacs with more severe forms of the disease were denied access to the $100,000 needed each year for a sufficient quantity of the clotting factor so that artificial heart transplants were funded instead, would they have been treated unjustly? The moral issue here can be sharpened up with the following perspective in mind.

Hemophilia is a disease that afflicts children from birth on, though the more severe and costly versions of the disease might not manifest themselves until later in the first decade of life. Heart disease, and the need for heart transplantation, is generally a need much later in life. Is this a fact of great moral salience? Does it matter that the life-years we would seek to save in the case of hemophiliacs are attached to very young individuals who would have had little opportunity to enjoy a life, whereas the life-years saved through a heart transplant are generally attached to older individuals who have had ample opportunity to enjoy most of a life? There seems to be an important matter of distributive justice here that is not adequately respected if our sole criterion of health care justice is maximizing the quantity of some health good purchased for a fixed sum of money.

Other moral anomalies in this context also seem to require our attention. Our general question may be framed this way: What counts as the just aggregation of health need for purposes of making fair allocation and rationing decisions? Some individuals have serious heart disease and need a heart transplant to survive. The cost of saving each of their expected life-years might be $60,000 each. Other individuals have that same heart disease, and are in renal failure as well. They may already have been in renal failure for five years at a cost of $57,000 per life-year saved (which for the sake of argument we will regard as still a reasonable cost for saving this life-year, though perhaps just barely so). If these patients now need both these interventions, then the actual cost of saving each of their remaining life-years is at least $117,000 each. *Should a just and caring society aggregate such health care costs at the individual level, thereby denying this individual the needed heart transplant on the grounds that each of his future life-years are now excessively costly from the perspective of health care justice? Or should we judge instead that the morally correct perspective for making such judgments is a disaggregated perspective? That is, is it morally irrelevant how many different expensive life-prolonging interventions an individual might need, as long as each one is below some societally acceptable cost level and is effective enough in achieving the health objectives for which it was designed?*

Another morally intriguing fact worth noting is this: If this individual is denied the heart transplant and dies from his heart disease a few months later, then the costs of five years worth of dialysis would be saved (about $280,000). From a moral point of view this looks like an unseemly bonus attached to making such a rationing decision. Seeking some sort of compromise would appear to be morally desirable. Norman Daniels (1985) has noted with a very vivid phrase, however, that the distribution of health care often has a "lumpy" quality to it. We cannot just come to a compromise with such a patient to divide things evenly. We cannot give him the heart transplant for two and a half years and then remove it from him. If he gets the heart transplant, he gets five extra years of life; if he is denied the heart transplant, he gets no extra years of life.

My suspicion is that most of us would be very morally uncomfortable with the idea of denying an individual (faced with imminent death) a heart transplant because he would also need five more costly years of dialysis (in addition to the five he already had). If we were pressed for reasons for our judgment in such a case, we would most likely call attention to the urgency of the needs of this patient (life itself is at stake) and the fact that we had an effective medical intervention that would forestall death for a significant period of time. However, the case can be made more morally difficult in incremental steps. It is not uncommon for patients with poorly managed diabetes to be faced with renal failure and heart disease. And some of them will be HIV+ as well, which will mean they will need "triple therapy" (protease inhibitors as well) to sustain their lives at a cost of about $20,000 for each life-year gained. For the sake of argument, we will estimate that the new cost of each year of life gained for this patient is $150,000. Is that number now high enough that the balance of reasons should shift against providing this individual with the heart transplant he now needs?

I can easily imagine many resisting accepting that shift for essentially the same reasons as before: A life is at stake and the technology is effective. In effect, those who take that view are saying that it is morally unacceptable to aggregate health care costs in this way as a basis for making a rationing decision, either with respect to an individual or some class of individuals. If this view is asserted strongly enough and consistently enough, then some rather radical implications become clear.

We suggested earlier (given the very high up-front costs associated with the artificial heart) that a recipient of the device ought to have a predicted survival of at least two years, which would mean a cost per life-year saved of about $150,000. But from the perspective of the deontological view we are assessing here, that would not be acceptable. In fact, if predicted survival with the artificial heart were only six months, proponents of this view would logically insist that it be provided to such patients. More generally, these proponents seem committed to the view that no amount of money is too much to spend if the prolongation of a human life is at stake. In other words, human life is priceless. Protecting human life from death must be awarded an absolute priority in any rationing scheme from this perspective, which then has as a consequence drawing away enormous sums of health care dollars from all other health needs that do not involve a risk of death, such as spending money on the treatment of arthritis in the elderly. I shall argue in Chapter 3 that this is not a morally defensible position. Numerous circumstances exist in which a just and caring society will be morally justified in accepting the loss of life-years that in theory would be medically salvageable.

Another dimension in the artificial heart problem is the role of physicians in making these rationing decisions. Many readers will have imagined up to this point that policymakers or bureaucrats were putting in place various possible rules and criteria for determining who would have legitimate access to an artificial heart. But several possibilities we have considered clearly required making some sort of quality of life judgment or likely length of life judgment; physicians who are responsible for the care of these patients must make these judgments. As Levinsky (1984) has argued, these physicians seem to be placed in a morally untenable position. They are expected by all of us to be loyal and uncompromising advocates for the best interests of each of their patients. At the same time, society has imposed upon them responsibility for making honest clinical judgments that will in many cases result in their patients being denied access to the expensive care that represents their only hope for additional life. Levinsky wants physicians to have nothing to do with making rationing decisions of any sort. I am not at all confident that this is a realistic hope. This issue certainly deserves further discussion and analysis, which we must defer until Chapter 14.

We can imagine some possible ways around this "loyal physician" problem, at least with respect to the artificial heart. We might say that we should simply allow free markets and "ability to pay" determine how many artificial hearts are produced and how they are distributed. This does effectively dissolve the "loyal physician" problem, at least with respect to artificial hearts. If this were a satisfactory response, however, then we would have no reason for putting in place or maintaining the ESRD program for patients in renal failure. If distributing access to needed health care is to be determined by the ability to pay of individuals, then there is no moral issue associated with health care rationing, just as there is no moral issue associated with how DVDs or iPods are distributed by the market. This is a view that libertarians will embrace, at least in healthy theoretical moments in the isolation of a study. But few people on reflection in the real world will want to live with the consequences of this view. This observation is hardly a refutation of the libertarian perspective. A more detailed critical assessment will be offered in Chapter 4.

I will concede, however, that some circumstances exist in which it would not be unjust to allow individual ability to pay determine whether or not someone has access to a health care intervention, even what might be described as a life-prolonging intervention. A very general way of characterizing those circumstances would be to say that they involve what morally legitimate social actors have judged to be marginally beneficial, non-costworthy health care. Imagine, for example, a life-prolonging intervention that has costs in excess of $100,000. If, in particular circumstances for a particular patient, that intervention had only a 1–2% chance of achieving the normally expected result, then this would be described as marginally beneficial and non-costworthy from the perspective of a social institution that had only limited resources to meet virtually unlimited health needs.[21] From a moral point of view the wealthy can be justly allowed to purchase such interventions for themselves so long as no one is made worse off as a result. Again, this is a quick point deserving of more careful argument and analysis.

For now I do not believe that anyone could reasonably argue that this characterization would apply to all possible uses of a future safe and effective version of the artificial heart, which implies that it would be presumptively unjust to restrict access to the artificial heart to those with individual ability to pay. Too many relatively young individuals are too likely to benefit significantly from this device to permit their lives to be lost because they were unable to pay for it. Still, rationing decisions will need to be made with respect to the artificial heart, and those decisions will need to be made justly and in ways that do not threaten the integrity of physicians as loyal patient advocates.

Should a just and caring society choose age 70 as a cutoff for publicly supported access to the artificial heart, which would mean these devices would be publicly funded for all those with the relevant medical need below that age? Quite clearly this represents age-based rationing, which was the focus of an intense public debate in the late 1980s. Again, our only goal at this point is to tease out some of the key moral issues along with the complexity that surrounds them. The moral virtue associated with a specific age is that it is a bright line rather than a ragged edge, vulnerable to arbitrary and subjective judgments. Further, as Callahan (1987) argued at the beginning of this debate, individuals by that age will have had an opportunity to live a full life. We can ask rhetorically, "Does society owe anyone more life than that?" Though this question is supposed to elicit a negative answer, Callahan's critics asserted a strong affirmative answer instead. They claimed that his proposal represented an invidious form of age discrimination, that a society that embraced this proposal would be telling the elderly that they no longer have worth in that society, that they are like a worn-out piece of machinery that needs to be discarded to make room for more productive machinery. Apart from that, the medical facts are that a substantial majority of individuals in their 70s and 80s in our society are in vigorous health. If any of them have a devastating heart attack which will result in their "premature death" without an artificial heart, then it appears as if it would be indecent and inhumane to deny them that intervention simply because they were beyond age 70. This argument has considerable force if we imagine that the life-years we are expecting to save for these older individuals are as numerous and as high in quality as those we hoped to save for those in their 50s and 60s. Very often this will be the case (Lubitz et al., 2003).

Another perspective also needs to be considered, which might threaten the moral validity of that bright line at age 70; this is a "desert" argument. Individuals who were careless with their health in earlier stages of their life (smoking, high-fat diet, lack of exercise) would very likely have heart attacks before age 70 rather than after age seventy. If they receive an artificial heart at social expense, that has the appearance of being rewarded for bad health behavior. By way of contrast, individuals with lifelong excellent health habits will still be vulnerable to heart attacks, though these will occur later in life (sometime beyond age 70). Denying them access to an artificial heart and the extra life it promises looks like punishment for good health behavior. This, the critic of age-based rationing contends, is unjust. Is there an alternative? Someone will surely suggest that individuals whose heart disease is a product of consistently bad health choices should be denied access to an artificial heart at social expense. The logic behind this argument is clear, but our capacity to translate this logic into fair and practical criteria for separating the "worthy" from the "unworthy" is certainly lacking. How many lifetime cheeseburgers or French fries or pounds of bacon or sweet rolls or pounds of Cheetos (and so on) would be necessary to justify being denied an artificial heart at age 65? Would some amount of exercise "correct for" some degree of excess consumption of fatty food? And who would keep track of this sort of data? Would patients have Fifth Amendment rights not to incriminate themselves in matters of health behavior? Would physicians be dragooned into the role of food and health police? What would that do to social expectations that physicians be loyal patient advocates? How could we possibly deal with the incredibly ragged edge that would result from pursuing this path for making rationing decisions with regard to the artificial heart?

Allocating Artificial Hearts: Priorities, Probabilities, and Patient Profiles

I introduced the example of the artificial heart into this discussion of rationing because it challenges many of our deepest moral commitments. Further, it has the pedagogical and philosophical virtue of being "real enough," since we have effective working experimental models; but at the same time it has not been widely deployed, which means there is opportunity for thoughtful public and professional conversation about how that deployment might be brought about justly and in accord with a number of other basic moral commitments. Still, our discussion thus far has been very one-dimensional. We have thought about the artificial heart as if it is unequivocally effective for all with the relevant need, that it satisfies an urgent need, and that it unquestionably belongs in the category of highest-priority health needs. However, that represents a very distorted and simplistic understanding of the medical and social circumstances around the artificial heart. Three other dimensions need to be introduced: (1) the health care interventions that precede any decision about an artificial heart, (2) the problem of probabilities associated with most complex health interventions, and (3) the problem of priorities in relation to a broad range of expensive life-prolonging interventions outside cardiology, not to mention other expensive health care interventions that do not have individual life-prolongation as their goal.

Very few healthy people have a sudden cardiac problem, survive, and then are told that they need a heart transplant or they will be dead in a matter of months. The overwhelmingly common scenario is one in which a primary care physician informs a patient that his blood pressure or cholesterol is elevated, and that he is setting himself up for a future heart attack or stroke. He will then be told that he needs to lose some weight, alter his diet, get more exercise, and reduce the major sources of stress in his life. Most Americans will not do well when it comes to following these directives. As a consequence, they will be offered medications aimed at lowering their blood pressure or lowering their cholesterol, or both. These latter drugs are known as statins, and Lipitor would be a well-known example. In 2003 there were 13 million Americans on these statins, which represented $15 billion in income for the pharmaceutical companies that produce them. (That represents a wholesale figure; the cost to consumers would be about $20 billion.)

A recent report suggested that the criteria for putting patients on statins have been set too high. The conclusion was that 65 million Americans "need" to be on statins now (National Heart, Lung, and Blood Institute, 2002). If this were interpreted as a moral imperative of some sort, then consumers would be expected to spend $100 billion per year on this class of drugs alone. *If we had in place some form of national health insurance, would a just and caring society be morally obligated to underwrite the costs of statins for 65 million Americans?*

The very asking of this question has something of a ridiculous quality to it. In 2007 the total direct costs of cardiovascular disease in the U.S. was estimated at about $283 billion (American Heart Association, 2007, p. 39). If statins reduced the incidence of those disease processes by 80%, then their cost and enhanced use would be clearly warranted—but statins offer only a fraction of that degree of effectiveness.[22] There is considerable dispute among medical researchers on this point, which we do not need to review in any detail just now. What is germane is that statins in Europe are "straining the fixed budgets of national health care systems" (Mitka, 2003, p. 2243).

The core problem seems to be that statins offer some degree of benefit (perhaps only marginal) for virtually all patient groups for whom statins represent a relevant medical option, and virtually no harm is associated with their use (Mitka, 2003). Age seems to be irrelevant, as well as whether patients are with or without symptomatic cardiovascular disease. Nevertheless, from the perspective of incremental cost-effectiveness analysis there are substantial differences associated with different subgroups of patients who are at risk for a coronary event. To illustrate, using the work of Marshall (2003), if patient "A" has a 5% chance over the next five years of a coronary event, then the cost of preventing that event by putting them on simvastatin is about $360,000. If patient "B" has a 10% chance over the next five years of a coronary event, the cost of preventing that event with simvastatin is about $180,000. If patient "C" has a 20% chance over the next five years of a coronary event, the cost of preventing that event with simvastatin is about $90,000. And if patient "D" has a 30% chance of a coronary event in the next five years, the cost of preventing that event with simvastatin is about $60,000. From the perspective of cost-effectiveness analysis, only this last option makes economic sense. However, as Mitka (2003, p. 2244) observes, relying upon this sort of economic data "creates a situation in which a government is telling citizens who are susceptible for heart disease that they have to wait for a proven therapy until their projected risk increases." Of course what we know statistically, and what will be a source of great anxiety for knowledgeable patients, is that some number of patients in those lower risk strata will have a coronary event (sometimes fatal) before they have the opportunity to move into those upper risk strata. *How, then, should a just and caring society decide who should have access to statins at social expense through, for example, Medicare and Medicaid?*

Several of these statins are coming off patent as I write, which means their costs will be reduced to the consumer by about 66%. However, at the very same time "super-statins" are being developed that promise to create this very same problem again. These developments raise some interesting rationing questions. Ordinarily, price reductions at the 66% level would be most welcome in health care, but the reduced price could increase pressure from consumers for greater access. If, as noted earlier, the potential is there to quintuple the market for statins in the U.S., and if that potential is actualized by the price reduction suggested, then the net result would be an annual aggregated increase in health care costs for statins from $20 billion to $33 billion. Is a just and caring society morally obligated to acquiesce to that net increase in health care costs, given that tens of millions more individuals would have access to these statins?

There are alternatives. If we assume (for the sake of argument) that the current distribution of access to statins is "just enough," if we assume that statins are "needed" in a morally strong enough sense only by those patients who are identified as being at a 30% five-year risk of a cardiac event, then will a society remain "just enough" if those limitations are kept in place as the price of statins is dramatically reduced? In other words, under our scenario aggregate costs for statins would drop in the U.S. from $20 billion to $7 billion annually. Actual savings would then result which could be used to cover other high-priority health needs. We need to follow out this thought experiment one step further.

Under this latter scenario, 52 million individuals with cardiovascular disease (elevated cholesterol levels and/or hypertension, for the most part) would be denied access to statins at social expense—this would mean these individuals would have access to these drugs on the basis of ability to pay. Would such a limitation of access be morally objectionable from the perspective of health care justice? Two variables ought to be considered in trying to answer this question. Some of these individuals will be solidly in the middle class and able to afford these drugs if they see them as medically important. Other individuals will be in a much weaker financial position and unable to afford these drugs, no matter how they feel about their need for them. The other variable to be noted is the different risk strata that these individuals could occupy. They could be at 5% or 10% or 20% or 25% five-year risk of a cardiac event. Is there anything morally objectionable about lumping together for distributional purposes all these different risk strata? After all, someone in the 25% risk category might argue they have five times the risk of a cardiac event as someone in the 5% risk category.

Another factor that needs to be assessed is the predicted effectiveness of these statins at different risk levels. Being on these statins at any risk level does not reduce to zero the probability of a cardiac event during those five years; on the contrary, if one is at the 10% risk level for a cardiac event over five years, then being on those statins will reduce that risk to 7% over those five years. That is, seven individuals out of every 100 at that risk level will still have a cardiac event during that five-year period. In absolute terms, three individuals will have been spared that cardiac event during that period. Should this way of presenting the relevant medical facts alter what we see as the requirements of health care justice in this regard?

Finally, what sort of moral weight should be attached to the fact that, in principle, individuals have considerable control over the factors that would place them in these elevated risk categories where the issue of statins gets raised as a medical option? Individuals can alter their diets, lose weight, engage in more exercise, and so on, thereby obviating any need for these statins. Granted these are not easy things to do, and social situational factors may make this extremely difficult for some individuals. Nevertheless, are these facts such that the problem of justice with respect to statins is greatly attenuated or entirely eliminated?

Let us step back for a bit and look at the larger picture again. David Cutler (2003) notes that since 1950 in the U.S. there has been roughly a 50% decline in death from cardiovascular disease. We have gone from an annual death rate for cardiovascular disease of about 400 per 100,000 in 1950 to about 200 per 100,000 in 2002. One practical implication of this is that a 45-year-old man today will live 4.5 years longer than in 1950 as a result of medical interventions related to cardiovascular disease. Another implication is that each year now (as in 2003) there are 600,000 persons alive who would have died as a result of heart disease if we had only the medicine today that we had in 1950 for addressing heart disease. Cutler estimates that about a third of these additional lives and life-years are attributable to primary prevention (diet, exercise, drugs such as the statins, and antihypertensives), another third to secondary prevention (drugs used to protect and improve cardiac function after a cardiac event), and another third to high-technology interventions (bypass surgery, angioplasty, stenting, implantable cardiac defibrillators, left ventricular assist devices [LVADs], and so on).

At one level, statistics such as this represent a magnificent tribute to the effectiveness of contemporary medicine. At another level, they represent the painful political reality associated with the economic distortions caused by the problem of escalating health care costs. In 2001 there were 13.4 million Americans living with coronary heart disease at a cost then of a little more than $200 billion for that year (American Heart Association, 2004, p. 42), and increasing annually. Costs in 1950 would have been negligible. Five million of those 13 million were living with congestive heart failure. In 2004 we did 427,000 bypass surgeries at a cost of about $63,000 each, and 1.3 million angioplasties and stenting procedures at an average cost of $38,000 each. We also did 1.3 million diagnostic cardiac catheterizations (American Heart Association, 2007, p. 37). We installed more than 200,000 implantable cardiac defibrillators at a cost of $40,000 each in 2006, but it is expected that we will be installing about 400,000–600,000 of these devices per year starting in 2012 (due to improvements in their functioning), which would represent an annual cost of $16–$24 billion.

We must expect all these numbers to increase very significantly over the next two decades as the "baby boom" generation ages out. We also note another example of the ragged edge phenomenon—specifically, the increasing number of individuals in the ninth decade of life who are undergoing these very invasive cardiac surgeries, both because they are judged to be medically capable of enduring the surgery and because improvement in surgical technique makes this possible. This is the same phenomenon we saw playing out with respect to end-stage renal disease. The difference, of course, is that the numbers are much larger in the case of patients with cardiac problems, roughly 30 times greater at present.

To appreciate the economic and moral magnitude of what all this portends for the year 2025 we need to have in mind the following points. First, we will see a doubling of the Medicare population during that period to about 78 million individuals, if we assume an essentially unaltered rate of death for that population. But, secondly, we have no right to make that assumption because that would require our also assuming that there would no improvements or additions to current cardiac technology, much less expanded demand for what already exists. This would be an extremely unrealistic assumption. Consequently, a more realistic assumption for 2025 would be that there will be significantly more than 78 million individuals over age 65, that a much larger proportion of them will be over age 85, that the lives of a greater proportion of them will be sustained by various forms of cardiac technology, and that at least 12 million of them will have Alzheimer's disease to some degree (compared to the four million Americans currently diagnosed with Alzheimer's). All of this would suggest dramatically increased cardiac costs, both in the aggregate and in terms of the average cost per life-year saved. To illustrate the problem, we offer the following examples.

Some makers of implantable cardiac defibrillators (ICDs) maintain that we ought to be implanting 600,000 of these devices each year in the U.S. (Petersen, 2003). These devices are intended to prevent fatal cardiac arrhythmias by shocking the heart back into a normal rhythm when an abnormal rhythm is detected—roughly 250,000 Americans die suddenly each year as a result of one of these arrhythmias. Medicare has sought to control the deployment of these devices (and costs to Medicare) by requiring that they be available only to patients in whom disturbed heart rhythms have been detected. The manufacturers of these devices want that eligible patient pool expanded to include individuals who may be at risk of developing these arrhythmias (because they have suffered a heart attack and were in early stages of heart failure) but have not as yet demonstrated the sort of disturbed rhythm that would meet Medicare's criteria for an ICD.

In one clinical trial sponsored by Guidant (one of the manufacturers), it was found that after 20 months 19.8% of patients on average who did not have these devices died, while only 14.2% of those with the ICD died during this same period (Petersen, 2003). This represents a saving of five extra lives from sudden death out of every 100 who had already suffered a heart attack and were in the early stages of heart failure. But in order to achieve this "extra good," it would cost $4 million per group of 100, or $800,000 per life saved. *Is a just and caring society morally obligated to underwrite the cost of this expanded deployment of these ICDs?* How important, from a moral point of view, is this use of limited health care dollars, as opposed to any number of other uses? It looks as if a true health need is being met; deaths are being prevented. But the problem is, there is only a 5% chance of achieving that result in a 20-month period for this class of patients. It is not as if we can say that, for every patient in this class, we are giving them five extra years of life by giving them an ICD. The vast majority of the patients in this class will get those five extra years of life with or without the ICD.

One of the other things we know about ICDs and their current patterns of implantation is that 81% of these patients have not had their ICD fire in the past five years (Gehi et al., 2005). That means these devices have yielded nothing more in the way of medical effectiveness for that 81% other than some degree of anxiety relief. One recent cost-effectiveness analysis (Pauker et al., 2005) suggests that we should be implanting no more than 50,000 of these devices per year, which would yield a cost per QALY of about $37,000. As things are now, we purchase many of these QALYs at about $367,000 each (Al-Khatib et al., 2005). In 2006 the T-wave alternans test was introduced into our medical armamentarium (Bloomfield et al., 2006; Heuser, 2006). This test has the ability to reduce by 30% the number of individuals who would be judged as suitable candidates for an ICD. At current (2006) implantation levels, more than 60,000 individuals would be denied these devices, thereby achieving a savings of $2.4 billion. A major virtue of the T-wave alternans test is that it is 98.7% accurate; that is, it correctly identifies almost 99% of the time whose ICD will not fire over the next two years to prevent a sudden cardiac death. Of course, that also means it gets it wrong 1.3% of the time—from a cohort of 60,000, that represents about 800 lives that will likely be lost as a result of a fatal arrhythmia that would likely have been reversed if that individual had an ICD. But the cost of saving those 800 lives each year would be $2.4 billion. *Is a just and caring society morally obligated to ignore these nattering nabobs of economic negativism and save these lives because we have the technological capacity to do so? Alternatively, if we acquiesced to their analysis, what would be the moral justification for accepting 800 preventable deaths?*[23]

Our goal in this chapter has been to sketch a portion of the moral complexity and heterogeneity of the problem of health care rationing. Some of that complexity is related to the extraordinarily fragmented way in which we finance and deliver health care services in the United States. But substantially more of the complexity is related to emerging medical technologies and the internal complexity of clinical medical practice. Consequently, the problem of health care rationing is as real and urgent in Europe as it is in the U.S. The additional practical and theoretical claim we now make (and defend later) is that no single substantive theory of health care justice will be sufficiently sensitive and nuanced to address satisfactorily the full range and complexity of the problem of health care rationing. What will be required instead is a pluralistic conception of health care justice, in addition to a procedural approach to resolving many very concrete problems of health care rationing for which there might otherwise be multiple morally reasonable resolutions.

3

PRICING HUMAN LIFE

Getting Beyond Tragic Choices

Many philosophers are familiar with what has come to be known as the "trolley" problem, introduced into the literature by Philippa Foot (1967), but made famous by Judith Jarvis Thomson (1986). There are many possible variations of it; here is one.

The conductor of a trolley has suddenly dropped over dead and the brakes have failed. You are one of a few passengers on the trolley, and you are nearest to the conductor. The trolley is running downhill. You can see far enough ahead that you know the trolley will stop safely eventually. However, you also see five workers on the track ahead. If you simply allow the trolley to follow its present course, those five workers will be killed. You have a choice—you can grab the steering mechanism and direct the trolley down a spur where it will again come to a safe stop—but a small child is playing on the tracks. That child will be killed if you choose to steer the trolley down that spur. What should you do?

The case is filled with moral land mines. Maybe "the best" thing to do is to keep your seat and stay calm and let the course of events play out. Five men will be killed, but this will be the result of an "unfortunate accident." It is not as if you tampered with the brakes; your hands are clean. But you have the technology (the steering mechanism) to prevent those deaths. However, choosing to use that technology would mean that you would be choosing to "deliberately kill" that small child on the track. By way of contrast, if you leave the steering mechanism alone, then you are merely "allowing to die" those five workers. But if lives must be lost, should not the numbers matter? Saving five lives ought to be a stronger moral obligation than saving just one life. But those five workers know that repairing railroad tracks can be dangerous work; they understand those risks and they have to accept those consequences. Then again, why should these workers have to pay with their lives for the negligence of a parent who allowed their child to play on the tracks? That child had no right to be there. But how could anyone justify killing this child for the neglect or indifference of a parent? Further, this child might well represent many more potential saved life-years than the potential for saved life-years represented by the five workers. Then again, it is mistaken to claim that turning the steering mechanism represents the "deliberate killing" of this child— the death of the child is a "foreseen but unintended consequence" of making that decision. The child's death would be unfortunate and regrettable, but it would not be correctly described as a violation of that child's "right to life."

Philosophers have gotten quite engaged by the many issues raised by this case. Most laypeople dismiss the case as weird and unrealistic, a perfect illustration of philosophic silliness. However, I will want to show that this case does represent quite well at least one major dimension of the problem of health care rationing— namely, the inescapability of the need to make such rationing decisions with life and death consequences for different individuals or different groups of individuals. Benefit managers for private companies, executives with managed care plans, bureaucrats or legislators with state government, all have to work with fixed budgets so far as health care is concerned, with the consequence that their decisions regarding the allocation of health care resources can have life and death consequences for one or another category of patients. They "steer" resources one way rather than another. In that respect, the trolley problem is very much with us today.

We can begin with the case of Mr. H (a sadly real case disguised to protect privacy). The case occurred at a major urban university medical center. Mr. H was 20 years old at the time and afflicted with severe hemophilia A. He had developed an inhibitor problem when he was very young, which meant he could not tolerate the factor VIII that was necessary to clot his blood when he experienced a bleeding problem. This is an immune system reaction, an inhibitor problem that will arise for about 15% of hemophiliacs. Other drugs were used to control the bleeding in his case, though they were less effective. Mr. H became increasingly disabled as a result of disease progression. This was connected with bleeding into his joints. Hospitalizations were becoming more frequent and the need for intense rehabilitation thereafter was becoming more prolonged. Mr. H did have an experimental option—an attempt could be made to overwhelm his immune system with very high daily doses of factor VIII over a period of eight months. The cost of this effort would be about $5 million (because of the cost of an eight-month hospitalization as well as the cost of factor VIII). In very young children this intervention has a success rate of about 70–80%. But the predicted likelihood of success for Mr. H was no more than 30% because he was so much older. Further, even a successful intervention would not represent a cure of the underlying disease process. Mr. H would still need $100,000 worth of factor VIII every year for the rest of his life. Is this hospital morally obligated to take $5 million from its charity care budget to meet the health needs of Mr. H?

There is an alternative use for the $5 million. Many working poor, uninsured individuals live within the service area of this hospital. Among these we would find 150 AIDS patients who have failed various versions of "triple therapy." Their only hope now for keeping HIV in check would be access to fusion inhibitors in conjunction with some variant of triple therapy. The cost of that would be $35,000 per patient per year. That means the lives of these 150 AIDS patients (working uninsured) could be extended for one year with that same $5 million. Should the hospital ethics committee (to whom the case of Mr. H had been brought) take the $5 million and direct it toward Mr. H, or direct it instead toward those 150 AIDS patients? Stated in this way we have a situation that looks very much like our trolley problem, except that there is nothing unrealistic here.[1]

I want to put aside most of the moral issues that philosophers would typically raise in connection with the trolley problem—in other words, issues related to the "killing/letting die" distinction (Steinbock and Norcross, 1994). Those issues are not usually raised in public discussions about health care rationing. But the issue that is raised is the pricelessness of human life. This is clearly what motivated Congress in 1972 to pass the ESRD amendments to Medicare, thereby guaranteeing that no one would die of kidney failure simply because they could not afford the technology that would sustain their life (Menzel, 1983, p. 40; Rettig, 1976). Likewise, this is what seemed to spark public outrage in the case of Coby Howard in Oregon, or Child B in Great Britain (Ham, 1999). And at least some ethics committee members appealed to this consideration in the case of Mr. H. In all these cases the thought seems to have been that it is seriously morally wrong to allow individuals to die of their medical problems when we have the therapeutic intervention needed to save their lives, and all that prevents the actual use of that intervention is the cost of employing it. Further, the notion that human life is priceless is not just *a* morally relevant consideration in these sorts of circumstances—it is *determinative* of the right thing to do (in the minds of those ethics committee members). No other morally relevant considerations are weightier. I believe, however, that the assertions contained in these last three sentences are morally wrong and must be rejected as moral generalizations.

In this chapter my goal will be to defend the following constellation of propositions. First, human life is not literally priceless in any morally significant sense. Put more positively, there are morally legitimate limits to what any society or any individual must spend to save or sustain the life of another person. Second, holding the pricelessness of human life as a fundamental moral value (or worse, a supreme value) is misguided, incoherent, and morally pernicious. Third, if the assertion of the pricelessness of human life is permitted into specific health care rationing debates, then the typical consequence will be that the rationing decision will be driven underground, rendered invisible, and therefore hidden from critical moral scrutiny. That consequence itself is seriously morally objectionable. Fourth, there are profound moral issues that need to be addressed with respect to the many complexities of the problem of health care rationing. But these issues are best addressed from the perspective of health care justice. In other words, if appeal to the pricelessness of human life were banned from all discussions of health care rationing, nothing of moral consequence would have been lost, and much in the way of moral clarity would have been gained.

IS HUMAN LIFE PRICELESS?

We should start with the recognition that several different things might be meant when the claim is made that human life is priceless. We will dismiss very quickly some very self-serving invocations of this language. Genentech was challenged in 2006 regarding the $100,000 price tag they had attached to their drug Avastin (bevacizumab) when used to treat breast or lung cancer (as opposed to the $50,000 price attached to that drug for treating colorectal cancer). Their justification was "the inherent value of these life-sustaining technologies" (Berenson, 2006). Instead of making the usual appeal of high-tech research costs, the company cited the pricelessness of human life as a justification for their pricing decision. Likewise, a survey of oncologists (Nadler et al., 2006) showed that the vast majority of them did not think spending $300,000 per QALY for cancer drugs was excessive. Needless to say, these self-serving attitudes severely tarnish any moral luster attached to the pricelessness of human life as a moral value.

Not all interpretations of the pricelessness of human life are going to be morally objectionable (Fleck, 2006). For example, someone may mean by that notion that the social worth of an individual (their social status or contribution to the national economy) should be completely irrelevant when it comes to determining how much society should spend to save or prolong that individual's life in the face of a life-threatening illness or accident. This is a worthy moral principle. If a physician and a philosopher and a philandering philatelist all have the same medical problem and are in need of the same very costly medical intervention, then (other things being equal) all should have an equal right to access that intervention. In other words, it would be morally objectionable for some societal representative to deny access to that intervention to the stamp collector (who engaged in philandering as a hobby) simply because neither stamp collecting nor philandering were seen as sufficiently worthy social activities.[2] We can refer to this as the "equal moral worth" interpretation of the pricelessness claim.

Another version of the pricelessness claim would be the nonutilitarian view that the cost of saving either a life or a life-year should not determine *by itself* what will count as a just allocation of limited health care resources when we (as a society) cannot afford to save all the life-years that medical technology could potentially salvage. In other words, it will often be the case that multiple morally relevant considerations will need to be assessed for purposes of determining whether someone has a just claim to some very expensive life-prolonging medical intervention, as opposed to saying that cost-effectiveness is the single criterion that will yield a morally correct answer all the time. If cost-effectiveness alone determined the just allocation of health care dollars for saving lives, then we would never be morally obligated to spend $300,000 to save a life-year. However, the drug imiglucerase has precisely those costs for someone who has symptomatic type 1 Gaucher disease and can only benefit from enzyme replacement therapy. These will be younger individuals (roughly 4,500 in the U.S.)—children and young adults who would not achieve a normal life expectancy if symptomatic and without this drug. This by itself (I contend) will be a morally compelling reason for providing access to this treatment.[2] By way of contrast, if Gaucher's afflicted primarily individuals beyond age 80 (otherwise in reasonably good health), I would be prepared to argue that health care justice (as I delineate this concept in Chapter 4) would not require that this drug be provided to them. That would not be because these individuals had only marginal social worth; that rationale would violate the "equal moral worth" construal of the pricelessness principle. Rather, the primary reason would be that these individuals already had an adequate opportunity to lead a full life, and others would be denied that opportunity if the $300,000 went to the 80-year-old. This is what is known in the literature as the "fair innings" argument (Harris, 1985).

That brings us to our third construal of the claim that human life is priceless, namely, that society has a moral obligation to spend any amount of money to save all lives and life-years that medical technology permits. This is the view that clearly needs to be rejected because if it were adopted, the result would be a gross distortion of societal priorities that would not be just, compassionate, or prudent. We can begin our discussion by calling to mind several cases.

First, Baby K was born anencephalic in Virginia. This is a well-known case (Annas, 1994) in bioethics. Anencephalic infants have a functioning brain stem that will sustain heart and lung activity, but most of the rest of their brain matter is missing. Such infants may survive for a period of several days to a month, though aggressive life-sustaining care can be provided that would sustain life for a longer period of time. The mother of Baby K insisted on such care, which resulted in survival for 2.75 years at a cost of more than a million dollars to either Medicaid in Virginia or the hospital where this infant was born. Our question is this: Does Baby K have a moral right to all that care because "human life is priceless"? Would it be morally wrong if our society were to put in place a rationing protocol that would deny all such infants life-sustaining care?[3] There are four hundred such infants born each year in the U.S. (Mathews, 2007). If all such infants in a cohort were given such care, that would represent an aggregate cost of $400 million per year.

There are about 4,000 infants born each year in the U.S. with necrotic small bowel syndrome; generally infants born very prematurely. They do not have a functioning gut, and consequently they cannot take food by mouth. Without medical intervention they will starve to death. What we can provide them is total parenteral nutrition (TPN)—an extraordinarily expensive way of feeding these children, with costs of about $250,000 per infant per year. A first response to this type of case might be that we are clearly morally obligated to provide such life-sustaining care, especially if (as has been suggested) we ought to be providing care at this cost level to children with symptomatic type I Gaucher disease. However, there is this medical difference: After four years, TPN has the very unfortunate effect of destroying the liver of the child. A liver transplant can save the life of the child at a cost of $250,000 for only an additional two years, and then a multi-organ transplant would be required at a cost of about $600,000. Survival rates would be slightly less than

20% at 5 years, and slightly more than 5% at 7 years (Intestinal Transplant Registry, 2003). The cost for each cohort of these children for four-year survival would be $4 billion. If we gave them two extra years of life, the cost for getting each cohort to age six would be about $8 billion.

The questions that I believe we ought to be asking are the following: Are we morally obligated as a just and caring society with limited resources to spend that $8 billion to assist each cohort to reach age six? From the perspective of health care justice should we give higher priority to using these resources to save and sustain the lives of children with either Gaucher disease or hemophilia, in part because they will be able to come much closer to a normal life expectancy and appreciate the qualities of human life more so than a child below age six? Would it be morally permissible to put in place a rationing protocol as public policy that would deny life-prolonging care to infants born with necrotic small bowel syndrome in order to provide a range of medical benefits for children with better long-term prognoses? But none of these questions can be asked meaningfully if we are committed to the belief that human life is priceless in that third sense.

We introduced in Chapter 2 the Lakeberg conjoined twins case. It would cost more than one million dollars for the surgery to separate the twins and surgically reconstruct the six-chambered heart to be a functional normal heart. There was less than a 1% chance that either twin would survive a year with the surgery. Loyola University Medical Center refused to do the surgery because those uncompensated care costs would have reduced the capacity of that hospital to meet the health care needs of the uninsured working poor living near that hospital. What I ask the reader to assume for the sake of argument is that all the health needs met with the dollars denied the Lakeberg twins would be *non-life-threatening* health needs. Should we conclude that such an allocation represented a huge moral mistake because the principle of the pricelessness of human life in this third sense was violated?

The case of Nancy Cruzan garnered substantial public attention in the late 1980s, as did the case of Terri Schiavo in 2005. Both individuals ended up in a persistent vegetative state (PVS) that lasted for seven and fifteen years, respectively. Both cases were the focus of intense litigation fueled by both personal and political motives (of which I shall pass over). I want to focus instead on the cost of care in each case. Nancy Cruzan's care cost about $800,000 (1990 dollars), paid for by the Medicaid program in Missouri. What some might find morally troubling is that Missouri Medicaid covered only those who were at or below 35% of the federal poverty level. Terri Schiavo's care cost somewhere in excess of a million dollars for those fifteen years, and Florida Medicaid covered a substantial portion of that; again, Florida covers with Medicaid less than 50% of those below the poverty level. The question that needs to be asked is this: If either of these states refused Medicaid funding for patients in PVS and redirected those dollars toward expanding access (a bit) to needed medical care for those below the poverty level, would such a policy decision be open to justified moral criticism? That is, would such a decision be a violation of the value of the pricelessness of human life because both Nancy and Terri would have died soon after their accidents without that costly medical support? And if this latter question is answered affirmatively, does it then imply that if a cancer were found in either patient or a heart arrhythmia were detected, would we then be morally obligated to spend an additional $100,000 or more to address such medical problems in order to prevent their "premature" deaths? Again, to put this last question in a proper context, there may be as many as 25,000 patients in PVS at present (Hirsch, 2005) whose annual care costs would be about $4 billion.

At one level, asserting that human life is priceless has a certain moral attractiveness. One person cannot rightly own another person because persons are not property. Parents may speak of "having children," but that simply means that they have responsibility for those children, not that those children belong to them as their property to do with as they wish. Kant is usually seen as the classic source of this view; he makes a distinction between things with a value (price) and things with dignity (Kant, 1785/1958, p. 102). Things with a value can always be exchanged for other things with an equivalent value. But Kant sees human beings as being "beyond value" because they have an "intrinsic dignity," sometimes construed as "infinite worth." I fundamentally agree with Kant on this point, but at the same time I do not see his assertion here as having much relevance to the issues at the focus of our attention. Persons are always to be treated as ends in themselves; they are never to be used as mere means to achieving the purposes of another individual. When individuals are used in that way, the moral implication is that those individuals are worth less than the goal achieved by so using those individuals. The implication is that those individuals are not beings with intrinsic worth, that they are not autonomous moral agents. Kant's point is that others are reducing those individuals to mere objects of manipulation. This, however, has very little to do with our concerns about the pricelessness of human life in this third sense. What Kant's point will pertain to (which we discuss in our next section) is the practice of invisible rationing; in other words, hiding rationing decisions from individuals who are directly and adversely affected by those decisions. That practice does violate the moral rights of individuals because it involves treating them as mere things to be used for achieving someone else's cost-containing purposes.

I first started thinking about the problem of pricing human life in the late 1970s when I stumbled on an article about the collapsing state of bridges in the U.S. The article pointed out that fifty people die each year in the U.S. as a result of bridge collapses. Two members of Congress were asked to comment. They were told it would cost $26 billion (then) to repair these decaying bridges, to which they responded that human life was priceless (and consequently Congress ought to appropriate the needed funds immediately). If no more bridges collapsed for the next ten years, that would mean 500 lives would have been saved at an average cost of $52 million each. But if the pricelessness of human life is seen as a supreme moral value or dominant social categorical imperative, then fixing those bridges and saving those lives is precisely what we would be morally obligated to do. It did not take years of research to realize that none of these individuals were granted immunity from death for these expenditures; on the contrary, they were now vulnerable to being killed at grade-level railroad crossings. About 800 individuals each year in the U.S. die at these crossings, often because they drive around crossing gates that have already been lowered. These deaths too are preventable if we separate all such crossings, either by creating overpasses or underpasses, the cost of which would be somewhere in excess of $400 billion. If we are absolutely committed to the pricelessness of human life, then it seems as if we would be obligated to commit to that expenditure.

I suspect few readers would readily endorse this last conclusion. I imagine instead the thought that there must be less expensive ways to save human lives. There are. We can reduce the national speed limit on all roads to thirty miles per hour—that would likely save 25,000 lives per year for the very modest cost of repainting all of our speed limit signs. I expect even fewer readers would endorse this last proposal. The very last persons I would imagine endorsing this proposal would be any member of Congress, despite their avowed commitment to the pricelessness of human life. A proposal such as this is not just unreasonable, it is fanatical in affirming that only one value really counts (in that it trumps all other values when there is a conflict).

Fanaticism with respect to any moral value is a genuine evil, because in practice it results violating countless other moral values clearly deserving of due regard. Imagine that 10,000 individuals each year in the U.S. suffer devastating spinal cord injuries along with other life-threatening injuries. We might easily spend $200,000 on each of them to bring them back from the brink of death. Having "saved their lives" in accord with our commitment to the pricelessness of human life, we then leave them on their own. That is, we offer nothing in the way of rehabilitation or palliative care services because there are always more places where those same dollars can be spent that will involve saving or prolonging other lives, such as installing totally implantable artificial hearts in end-stage Alzheimer's patients or patients in PVS. Surely we ought to wonder whether the values of either compassion or justice regarding the spinal cord injury patients are being reasonably respected when these "life-saving" dollars are redeployed to these other patients. But if the pricelessness of human life is a supreme value, then these other moral values are reduced to worthlessness.

Two other critical points need to be made. If we reflect carefully, we shall see that the pricelessness of human life (in our third sense) is both morally vacuous and morally insidious. Its vacuity may be brought out this way: If the pricelessness of human life means anything, then it must mean that each and every human life is equally priceless, equally worthy of unlimited lifesaving investment. But then what is that supposed to mean in practice in a world in which resources are always scarce relative to wants and needs? Our primary focus in this essay is on lifesaving health care resources, but numerous ways of saving and prolonging lives can be identified outside the domain of health care, as was illustrated by our collapsing bridges, dangerous railroad crossings and highway safety examples. If we do not have unlimited dollars for saving lives in all these domains (where we have opportunities for reducing the risk of death), then what guidance does the pricelessness principle offer regarding how we ought to prioritize our lifesaving investment decisions among these domains?

Does the pricelessness principle warrant, for example, allocating scarce medical resources on the basis of the relative number of people who are afflicted with a particular terminal illness? Or does it warrant our taking into account when making allocation decisions for research and therapy for various terminal illnesses whether these diseases affect primarily the very young, the middle-aged, or the very old? Does it allow us to make allocation decisions with respect to various terminal illnesses on the basis of whether a particular illness allows for a relatively long and fruitful period of life after initial diagnosis with only minor suffering, as opposed to a long and pain-filled period of life, as opposed to a short and pain-filled period of life? Given limited resources, should the primary goal of the pricelessness principle be to maximize the number of lives saved or the number of life-years saved? Given limited resources, what precisely would the pricelessness principle counsel regarding very large differential costs associated with saving this life or life-year rather than any others? Are we supposed to first save the least expensive life-years, then move smoothly up the supply curve?

Does the pricelessness principle allow us to put *any money at all* into research aimed at finding cures for terminal illnesses if it is the case that these funds would not be available to forestall preventable deaths in the present? In other words, if we were relatively confident of the success of this research in the next ten years, and if such success would mean that fifty times more lives would be saved than compared to those that would be lost in the interval, would the pricelessness principle then endorse our allocating those funds to this research (and allowing those current and near-future lives to be lost)? Alternatively, if our level of confidence regarding the success of this research were much reduced, then what would the pricelessness principle require that our allocation decision be? Does the pricelessness principle warrant putting more of our lifesaving dollars into consumer education or other preventive measures, as opposed to spending that money to find cures for otherwise fatal medical problems that are the product of poor consumer choices? Again, particular efforts at consumer education may be more or less successful in achieving their lifesaving objectives. Is there any particular percentage of success below which the pricelessness principle would forbid investment? Or, even if these educational efforts were 100% successful in altering consumer behavior (e.g., quitting smoking or adopting a significantly healthier diet), would the saving of these lives be too abstract, too statistical, too far into the future to justify not using these same resources to save lives that are imminently at risk from some current health threat?

My conclusion is that the pricelessness principle offers no rational moral guidance at all for addressing any of the above questions, and consequently, it is morally vacuous. A defender of the principle might respond that we can invoke principles of egalitarian or utilitarian or libertarian conceptions of justice to address any of the questions posed above (and, no doubt, some other range of morally relevant considerations might be invoked as well). However, that response would only reinforce my conclusion: any substantive moral work that needs to be done will have to be accomplished by considerations other than the pricelessness principle. That principle is vacuous and inept for purposes of rationally addressing any of the very real allocation decisions we must address in our world today.

If invoking the pricelessness principle were no more than sanctimonious or symbolic social rhetoric, then it could be safely ignored for purposes of real world social policymaking. However, the rhetoric is not just innocent and sanctimonious; it is insidious and morally dangerous. Consider any of the scenarios above in which we are supposed to decide which lives to save (as we must do in the real world). What happens in practice is that we can stand condemned by the pricelessness principle since we will always be saving some lives at the expense of other lives that will have been sacrificed. But if we stand condemned no matter what we do, then that seems to undermine the point of the moral enterprise. For why should we strive to make an intelligent morally defensible decision if no matter what we do we are open to the charge of having acted wrongly? This opens the door for political expediency, economic efficiency, and a host of other nonmoral considerations to be the dominant factors shaping health care policy regarding resource allocation. To wit, it was recently reported that candy manufacturers heavily lobbied Congress to alter daylight savings time in the fall by one week so that Halloween would fall inside that window (Lee, 2007). They believed this would give children more time to gather candy in daylight and thereby increase candy sales. But the rationale offered to Congress was that this would result in fewer children's deaths as a result of being struck by cars in the dark (while embracing total silence on the matter of future fatalities from diabetes and heart disease for these sweeter children).

There is an alternative way of looking at the pricelessness principle, but it results in what some might regard as an even more morally insidious outcome. Specifically, if we always make policy choices and allocation decisions that result in saving or prolonging some number of lives, then we can always praise ourselves (morally speaking) for acting in accord with the pricelessness principle. But then the pricelessness principle can become moral camouflage that prevents us from making any deeper moral inquiries into whether any specific allocations were just or congruent with other important moral considerations that ought to be taken into account. The dialysis program we mentioned in Chapter 2 is a good example of what we have in mind. When the 1972 amendments to Medicare were passed that provided funding for this program, advocates for persons with hemophilia were seeking comparable levels of public support to underwrite the very high costs of factor VIII. But their pleas were effectively hidden from public perception because what was emphasized to the public was that this large commitment had been made to saving the lives of patients in kidney failure. To be clear, I am not suggesting that this allocation decision was obviously unjust or otherwise morally flawed, but then neither do we know that the decision was made justly, that due consideration was given to the health needs and prima facie just claims of hemophiliacs but those claims were not found to be weighty enough to warrant actual funding. In that respect appeals to the pricelessness principle can provide superficial moral legitimacy for decisions that required much more critical moral thought.

Again, imagine an alternative version of the Lakeberg conjoined twin case. Imagine that Loyola University Medical Center decided to do the separation surgery, and that those costs were covered by their charity care dollars. No thought at all is given to what that would mean for the local uninsured poor whose medical needs would go unmet as a result of this decision. Instead, Loyola's advertising department emphasizes the excellent publicity doing this surgery is likely to garner for the medical center, perhaps attracting a larger middle class clientele. Again, those uninsured poor in the neighborhood are just statistical lives and hypothetical patients who might show up at the hospital sometime in the future with something other than imminently life-threatening needs. But the Lakeberg twins would be real and photogenic and at risk of death (though they probably could have survived a year, maybe two, without the surgery). The point is that a spokesperson for the hospital could announce that they were going to undertake the surgery because these lives were priceless and it was cruel (morally unthinkable) that we would allow these children to die when we had the medical technology that offered them the only chance for life available. The net effect of offering this rationale would be to provide legitimacy (moral camouflage) for this intervention that would cut off any further moral inquiry aimed at determining whether this was a "just" or even "just enough" choice. This is morally insidious. This point will become even clearer in the next section as we examine the practice of invisible health care rationing.

TRAGIC CHOICES OR TRAGIC DISINGENUOUSNESS? INVISIBLE RATIONING

I may be able to take credit for having introduced into the literature the language of "invisible rationing" (Baker, 1992). But the phenomenon itself was called to public attention by Aaron and Schwartz in their book *The Painful Prescription* (1984). They were curious about how the British through the National Health Service (NHS) were able to make rationing decisions regarding access to dialysis without provoking a huge public backlash (and demands that the NHS follow the lead of the U.S. and assure access to dialysis for all who have the relevant need). What they discovered was that these decisions were made by individual primary care physicians in ways that were effectively hidden from the patients who were directly affected by these choices (1984, pp. 34–40). Many in the U.S. believed that a rule in the NHS barred those over age fifty-five from being candidates for dialysis. But there was no such rule. If there had been such a rule, it would have been easier to imagine that backlash being generated. Instead, an informal "understanding" came to be among primary care physicians that patients over age 65 would not be given access to dialysis, and patients whose kidney failure was related to heart disease and diabetes would be denied dialysis if they were over age 55. Their belief (well-founded) was that the government was intransigent in the matter of controlling health care costs, especially for very high-cost technologies that would only prolong life of greatly compromised quality. The government was not going to invest more money in creating more dialysis slots. Primary care physicians could have sent all these patients up to the specialists, but that would have only made the problem worse (and more visible). So primary care physicians would "explain" to patients denied access to dialysis that they were sorry but there was nothing more that medicine could offer them. What patients "heard" was that their kidney failure was beyond medicine's capacity to treat, not that they were being denied access to dialysis in the interest of controlling health care costs. In this sense, the rationing decision was "invisible" to those who were directly affected by it.

Some might be prepared to argue that making these decisions invisibly was a morally decent and compassionate thing to do, all things considered. Many of those primary care physicians might have felt precisely this way since they had no power to create more dialysis slots, but under these circumstances the potential for serious injustices was clearly a risk. For example, physicians themselves are as vulnerable as anyone else to renal failure. But it is difficult to imagine a 57-year-old British physician in renal failure with heart disease and diabetes meekly accepting denial of access to dialysis on the grounds that medicine could do nothing more for him. He would clearly know that medicine could do more, that dialysis was an option, and that as a physician he "deserved" an exception to the usual "merely informal" understanding of who should or should not have access to dialysis. Likewise, a physician who had a cranky, difficult 63-year-old patient in renal failure could just as easily deny that patient access to dialysis in this invisible way without fear of having such a decision challenged by a patient who would be ignorant of these informal understandings. This denial would be arbitrary and self-serving in a clearly morally objectionable sense, but it would very likely succeed because there was no public rule or criteria that would permit the patient to appeal this denial. This is clearly unjust. Physicians have no moral authority to give or withhold health care services in accord with whatever personal values they embrace because physicians have been granted that authority by the state to serve *public* purposes (and to do so justly).

I am very confident of my conclusion that invisible rationing techniques are presumptively unjust. They violate the most central element of our shared conception of justice, what Rawls (1971, p. 16) refers to as the "publicity condition." When our public policies and practices are just—in other words, when they are a product of uncoerced agreement among free and equal citizens seeking fair terms of cooperation—then "nothing need be hidden" (Rawls, 1993, p. 68).[4] Others, however, would dispute the validity of my conclusion. That is, they would be strong defenders of the moral permissibility of invisible rationing decisions, especially in situations comparable to the NHS and dialysis. Calabresi and Bobbitt (1978) would be my strongest critics in their book *Tragic Choices*. This will take us back to the problem of the pricelessness of human life. They do not believe that that particular value commitment should be regarded as a supreme value of any sort; they simply take it as a social and political fact that it is one among a number of more or less equal fundamental values. In operational terms, a fundamental value is one that never ought to be violated. But if there are multiple fundamental values, then it will often be the case that these values will come into conflict with one another in specific concrete circumstances. That is, it will not be possible to avoid violating one or another fundamental value. This is what Calabresi and Bobbitt regard as a tragic choice.

Tragic choices for Calabresi and Bobbitt are not just difficult or painful choices. They are choices that are profoundly morally flawed no matter what we do because basic or ultimate values are at stake, such as the need to affirm both the absolute value of human life while at the same time justly distributing limited health care resources that have as a consequence the loss of some human lives that in theory could have been saved. If we deny patients in renal failure over age 65 access to dialysis in order to have sufficient resources to save children from premature death from treatable leukemic conditions, then we have made a tragic choice. We may believe that this is a difficult but reasonable choice—we are saving the lives of these young children who have not had the opportunity to live a life, and who can look forward to a life of high quality once they get through this health crisis. The lives we are failing to save belong to individuals who have had ample opportunity to live a full life. But Calabresi and Bobbitt would not be satisfied with this justificatory explanation. One of our other fundamental moral values is the *equal value* of all human lives. We are (they would argue) clearly devaluing the lives of older citizens by sacrificing them for the sake of the young in this case. Indeed, any instance of sacrificing some lives in order to save others (effected by third parties, as opposed to being some form of heroic self-sacrifice) will also violate a fundamental moral norm. These choices are not morally acceptable, all things considered. They are intrinsically morally flawed so far as Calabresi and Bobbitt are concerned. But this is not their ultimate moral conclusion.

For Calabresi and Bobbitt the fundamental moral task is to "preserve the moral foundations of social collaboration" (1978, p. 18). Those foundations are what are repeatedly threatened by these tragic choices they call to our attention. From their perspective the virtue of invisible rationing is that this allows for the preservation of those moral foundations. If we can find ways of hiding from social awareness the making of these choices, then we will better preserve the moral foundations of social collaboration. They recognize that such mechanisms violate our societal sense of honesty, and that honesty and openness are themselves fundamental social values, but the alternative for them would be *visible* tragic choices, which is to say "an exposed inegalitarianism" and "exposed decisions against life" (1978, p. 37). Their claim is that these tragic choices are not amenable to rational moral resolution. Consequently, the most we can do is "cope" with such choices. And one such coping mechanism would be to mask in various ways the making of these choices to minimize the risk of social scrutiny and the consequent risk of intense irresolvable social divisiveness.

Two critical comments are in order. First, why did Calabresi and Bobbitt write their book? Their reply is that this would "allow us, as citizens, to accept responsibility for tragic choices decided in our names." We could better see ourselves "acting to save ultimate values from necessary desolation" (1978, p. 27). Does this mean they really want *all of us* to have a clear reflective awareness of these tragic choices and of the invisible decision mechanisms we employ to mask these choices? If so, what is the point of *invisible* decision mechanisms? From whom are we seeking to hide some tragic truth? From ourselves? Then why be reflective about the matter? From someone else? This last question suggests a serious moral problem.

The passages cited call to mind images of tragic moral heroes committed to ennobling moral ideals, but knowing they are destined to be defeated. Are we, the educated elite readers of this volume, likely to be the moral heroes called for by Calabresi and Bobbitt? Not likely. What is more likely is that it is *others*, such as working class Britons, who are expected to be the (unknowing) moral heroes. The language of necessary tragic choices makes it easy for comfortable societal power holders to rationalize the imposition of injustices *on others*. Worse still, these "others" do not even know they have been the victims of injustice, or that this has been justified under the guise of protecting from corrosion the moral bonds that link us with them in a moral community. Who would knowingly want to be part of a moral community like that? No wonder invisible rationing mechanisms are needed.

My second criticism is that the language of "tragic choices" tends to insulate the consciences of societal decision makers from critical moral self-reflection, for the implication of the phrase itself is that the injustices are necessary and inescapable. I grant that we cannot expect to achieve perfect justice; maybe the most we can reasonably expect in complex social systems is "rough justice," which will often include our having to tolerate minor injustices.[5] This outcome is not morally objectionable so long as these injustices are distributed in something of a random fashion across the population as a whole. But if these injustices tend to fall disproportionately on members of groups that are already socially disadvantaged, then we ought not be so morally complacent about the inevitable unjust outcomes from the "tragic choices" that we must make in anguish. The problem is that the language of tragic choices makes it easy to be complacent, since it is easy to confuse the necessity of some injustices *in general* with the necessity of this particular pattern of injustices. Thus, a large literature has accumulated over the past few years around the topic of health disparities in the U.S., especially with regard to racial/ethnic groups (Satcher and Pamies, 2006). I am reasonably confident that some of these disparities have little or no moral significance. But I would be open to justified moral criticism if I casually dismissed all of these health disparities as being no more morally consequential than differences in height throughout our population, especially if I offered that conclusion without any basis in empirical inquiry or moral analysis. Worse still, if I argued that the need for health care rationing is inescapable (because resources are always scarce relative to needs), and consequently, we have to make these tragic choices that result in some health needs being unmet (thereby generating these disparities), and hence, these disparities are morally inconsequential, then this would be precisely the use of the language of tragic choices that would be morally insidious.

The use of invisible rationing mechanisms is much more widespread than most people would recognize. As I write, Rudy Giuliani (former mayor of New York City and 2008 Republican candidate for president of the U.S.) has announced he is glad he had his prostate cancer in the U.S., where he will have an 82% chance of survival, as opposed to Great Britain, where his chance of survival would only be 44%. Apart from the inaccuracy and disingenuousness of these statistics (Krugman, 2007), Giuliani claimed that this is what we could expect if Hillary Clinton's health reform plans were enacted. That is, we would have low-quality socialized medicine and health care rationing. The implication that the listener was supposed to draw from this claim was that what we now have is high-quality health care for almost everyone in the U.S. and no rationing. What we actually have is high-quality health care for well insured paytients (sic) and widespread use of invisible rationing mechanisms (something like the "dark matter" of our health care system).

A considerable number of health policy analysts and researchers are advocates for the use of invisible rationing mechanisms, essentially because it is easier to make painful rationing decisions without predictable patient confrontations if patients knew such decisions were being made. Blumstein is one policy analyst who is a strong advocate for the use of these invisible rationing mechanisms. His major conclusion is that we "should seek to distance the government from nitty-gritty micro-allocation matters to the greatest extent possible by developing macro-allocation policies and leaving their implementation to nongovernmental units where appropriate" (Blumstein, 1983, p. 394). More specifically, he advocates with Calabresi and Bobbitt the use of "aresponsible" agencies to make micro-allocation decisions (agencies such as juries), because their character "disguises the weight being assigned to different variables and blurs the hierarchy of values chosen" (Blumstein, 1983, p. 372).[6]

Blumstein does not cite any particular rationing mechanisms that might be used in this way in the health care system, but it is easy to make the case that Medicare/Medicaid DRGs (diagnostic-related groupings) and Medicare HMOs would readily fit what he has in mind. DRGs represent a fixed sum of money that the federal government agrees to pay a hospital prospectively for a particular hospitalization for a particular diagnosis; there are now about 745 distinct DRGs. Each sum of money attached to a given DRG is supposed to represent the average sum needed to treat a Medicare patient with that diagnosis, and is paid prospectively. It represents all that Medicare will pay for that episode of hospitalization (with a few exceptions for patients who are major outliers). If a hospital is able to treat a given patient more quickly and more efficiently than normal (thereby saving resources), then the hospital makes a profit. If a patient requires a longer hospitalization and more resources, then the hospital will take a loss on that patient. What we wish to emphasize is that under this system physicians and hospital administrators become the real allocators of health care resources (as opposed to any government bureaucrats).

What might be regarded as the virtue of this approach to rationing and health care cost containment is that the Medicare program (the federal government) is not interfering in the practice of medicine; Medicare is allowing physicians to practice the best medicine possible. Physicians, of course, have been under constant pressure by hospital administrators to discharge these patients as quickly as possible, (i.e., as soon as these patients no longer have a clear need for hospital care). The federal government counts on the commitment of physicians to the core values of medicine (and the threat of malpractice) to prevent gross exploitation of these patients for the sake of enhancing the bottom line of the hospital. By and large that reliance is rationally justified, but there are always these gray areas in patient care where a reasonable case can be made either for saying that this patient needs another couple days in the hospital or they might be equally safe finishing their recuperation at home.

The incentives under DRGs clearly tilt in the direction of sending such patients home. If that patient has competent and caring and attentive caregivers at home, all is likely to go well. If those caregivers are careless (but well-meaning) or indifferent or inattentive (distracted by other responsibilities), then things might go badly for that patient. This is where invisible rationing comes in. Physicians are not going to have conversations with patients or their families to assess whether it is really safe enough to send that patient home to that environment. If there is a bad outcome for that patient, then clearly Medicare cannot be held responsible for that outcome. Medicare cannot be accused of making an unjust rationing decision. Medicare never saw that patient; Medicare never made the judgment that patients in that DRG deserved only so many days in the hospital, Medicare simply paid the hospital to provide good care to that patient. Likewise, on the assumption that the physician's medical judgment was not corrupted or mistaken, it will be difficult to justify the claim that the physician or hospital administrator was responsible for the bad outcome in the patient. In short, there is enormous moral obscurity here. It would be very difficult to judge confidently that the outcome in any case such as this was unjust as opposed to being merely unfortunate (not morally blameworthy). In these circumstances there is no way of knowing what the hierarchy of values was that shaped any of the decisions made here. It permits all the relevant political actors to even deny that any rationing decision was made (hence, Giuliani and other such politicians are off the hook when they assert that rationing is not part of the American health care system). That ensures that these invisible rationing decisions are never subject to critical moral scrutiny by either social authorities or health professionals who carry them out. Worse still, patients themselves (who potentially might be unjustly adversely affected) are in even a less effective position for raising any protest.

Loren Lomasky, a libertarian political philosopher, will agree with Blumstein on the political utility of aresponsible agencies. He is a critic of any form of national health insurance, especially if it would involve government defining a package of health care benefits that would be guaranteed to all (and by silent implication, denying other potential benefits to all by virtue of noncoverage in that benefit package, perhaps because these other potentially beneficial services yielded too little benefit at too high a cost). As a libertarian, Lomasky's primary objection will be that some *single value scheme* would be employed by government either to include or exclude services from this benefit package, which would be coercively imposed on the populace. What Lomasky wants to preserve is the opportunity for individuals as individuals to decide what they judge for their own reasons to be either costworthy or non-costworthy health care. But he realizes that if we must have insurance schemes of some sort in health care, then rationing and cost-containment decisions will have to be made by some sort of board representing those insurance schemes. He sees as a political virtue that such boards would be private (and that there are about 1,500 insurance plans/managed care plans in the U.S.). As he notes, "nonpublic boards [are] not constrained by obligations of equal protection to an entire citizenry. Flexibility is enhanced, and the implications of unsavory choices are localized" (Lomasky, 1980, p. 83).

To be fair to Lomasky we must emphasize that the article quoted was published in 1980. But the case I am about to cite ten years later does illustrate (painfully) his point. John McGann was an employee of H & H Music Company in Texas who discovered in December of 1987 that he had AIDS. At the time he was diagnosed, his company offered health insurance with a lifetime limit of one million dollars. Six months after he discussed his health problems with his employer, the company sent a notice to all employees announcing that health care benefits for AIDS and all related medical problems would have a lifetime limit of $5,000. No limitation was placed on any other catastrophic illness (*McGann v. H & H Music*, 1991). The various courts that heard or reviewed this case upheld the right of the company to impose this limitation, because the limitation applied to all employees whether or not they were currently HIV+; that is, this was not discriminatory in a legally objectionable sense. What we have to wonder is whether Mr. McGann (after losing his lawsuit) took comfort in the fact that flexibility had been enhanced for H & H Music and that the implications of this unsavory choice had been localized.

How should we think about the McGann case? It might not appear to be a good example of invisible rationing because it was formally adjudicated (and received considerable media attention at the time). But what were significantly invisible were the specific values that precipitated this rationing decision. Having to pay for the care that an AIDS patient would need would be very expensive—directly for the employer, indirectly for all the employees. Surely there is nothing morally objectionable about trying to protect the incomes of all these employees. Imagine that H & H Music took a poll of all its employees, and 95% of them agreed that reduction of AIDS coverage was a reasonable choice to make since they did not see their heterosexual selves as being especially vulnerable to AIDS. Surely (many will wish to argue) we ought to respect individual and majoritarian liberty in this regard. Further, Mr. McGann should have been more responsible for his own health. Why should his fellow employees have to pay for the consequences of his "indulgent and irresponsible" sexual lifestyle? Also, health care coverage is a *benefit* that was freely given by H & H Music, which means it can be just as freely taken away, in whole or in part. Might one or another employee have had a discriminatory attitude toward homosexuals that motivated their acceptance of the reduction of AIDS coverage? Of course that could have been true, but that has nothing to do with the rationing issue since all these other value considerations (allegedly) justify that reduction.

Our point in the above paragraph is that this is a perfect illustration of what the blurring of the hierarchy of values is about. For the sake of argument we can say that there is no perfectly general right to health care (which both Blumstein and Lomasky would assert). Still, there may well be specific rights that specific individuals have to specific forms of health care in specific circumstances. Why would anyone buy into Medicare (and the DRG mechanism) or any other health plan unless they had some assurance that they were contracting for some level of health care to which they were now justly entitled? If this is the case, then Blumstein's invisible rationing mechanisms that "blur the hierarchy of values chosen" are open to serious moral criticism. For what they blur from public scrutiny (especially those most directly affected) are possibly substantial rights-claims that will end up being ignored or violated. Further, as Katz and Capron have observed, obscuring the bases of these decisions leads to fear and misunderstanding, and, more importantly, "abuse, particularly of those groups within society who are traditionally the objects of neglect and mistreatment" (Katz and Capron, 1975, p. 3). This is precisely what seems to have happened in the McGann case. With invisible rationing mechanisms it is easy to disguise injustices as randomized and localized misfortune (or a sound business decision).

Blumstein's response is that "some overtly inegalitarian values will of necessity appear in official allocative criteria," as we saw in the case of dialysis, which would mean favoring some illnesses over others, which "would constitute a significant breach of the societal myth of egalitarianism" (Blumstein, 1983, p. 371). But if egalitarianism is really a mythic moral ideal, then Blumstein is saying we should preserve the myth because it will allow us to employ these invisible mechanisms that will effect inegalitarian injustices, while publicly proclaiming our commitment to egalitarian ideals. That makes our moral ideals convenient devices of oppression. Myths like that deserve to be exposed. That brings us back to the moral importance of the publicity condition in matters of health care justice, most especially in regard to the creation of just health care rationing policies and practices and protocols.

INVISIBLE RATIONING AND THE PUBLICITY CONDITION

What I need to justify is the claim that the publicity condition is at the core of our shared conception of justice, and hence, that violating the publicity condition is prima facie unjust. Seven considerations will support this claim. First, following Rawls (1971, 1993), adherence to the publicity condition is necessary for creating a well-ordered society that will fulfill a notion of fair terms of cooperation and mutual advantage. I take it that fair terms of cooperation are a product of agreements entered into by free and informed cooperating parties. For what would it mean to call something an "agreement" if several of the key provisions were hidden from some of the contracting parties, especially if some could use those hidden provisions to gain special advantages over others? This is more properly labeled exploitation rather than cooperation. The publicity condition reduces opportunities for exploitation under the guise of fair cooperation arrangements.

Second, the publicity condition increases the likelihood of *mutual* advantage in cooperative arrangements. The publicity condition itself does not impose any particular conception of "the good" upon cooperating parties, nor does it allow cooperating parties to impose their conception of the good on others. Instead, it creates an environmental condition in which cooperating parties can assess for themselves whether the benefits and burdens of a specific cooperative venture are sufficiently advantageous from their own point of view to warrant their joining that venture.

Third, what follows from our first two points is that the publicity condition protects the basic autonomy of all the cooperating parties by encouraging the free and full exploration of alternative forms of cooperation. That is, the publicity condition protects the equal rights of all parties in a cooperative arrangement, thereby promoting moral respect.

Fourth, the publicity condition fosters *stable* social arrangements because they are a product of free and informed agreements which participants view as mutually advantageous. Such stability is essential if we are to have justice over the life of a society (or our lives as individuals), as opposed to merely discrete occasions of justice within the life of a society.

Fifth, the publicity condition promotes truth (critical rationality) and honesty, both of which are essential for just social arrangements. A well-ordered society does not require for its stability "institutionalized delusions" or "some form of false consciousness," for in such a society "nothing is or need be hidden" (Rawls, 1980). What the publicity condition demands, in effect, is that a certain kind of social conversation is essential to a stable, just society. It is a conversation that is honest; it does not require social delusions. (Here, of course, is where I find the major flaw in the "tragic choices" arguments of Calabresi and Bobbitt with regard to the notion of the pricelessness of human life. If their argument is taken seriously, then enormous opportunities exist for all manner of injustices to be perpetrated, mostly against those who are less well-off, under the guise of moral necessity.) It is a conversation that permits and facilitates the participation of *all* (the publicity condition is a strong antidote to elitist justice) because the conversation is about the policies and practices that will fundamentally shape the lives of all in that society. It is a conversation in which citizens "fully account" and plainly account for their beliefs and conduct, because there is no justification for "blurring the hierarchy of values chosen"—at least where matters of justice are concerned. What are constructed through this conversation are shared understandings. In the case of health care rationing, that shared understanding will be about rationing protocols that will apply to all and the public reasons, considered judgments of health care justice, that will justify those particular protocols.

We need to note that Rawls himself does not see this conversation resulting in a perfectly egalitarian society. Rawls recognizes that not all inequalities are inequities. This is why Rawls would not be troubled by Blumstein's concern regarding "overtly inegalitarian values" appearing in official allocative criteria. The whole point of a social conversation governed by the full publicity condition is that through it a society would sort out morally tolerable from morally intolerable inequalities. Such a conversation advances because public problems are publicly discussed. The major flaw of the invisible rationing mechanisms advocated by Blumstein and Lomasky is that they undermine our capacity to engage in these social conversations.

To give one quick illustration of the full publicity condition, we (in the U.S.) currently spend about three and a half times as much for health care for the elderly (over age 65) as opposed to the non-elderly. In 2004 we spent $14,797 per elderly person for health care compared to $4,511 for the non-elderly (Schmid, 2007). These are very large inequalities, but these are not generally seen as intrinsically unjust inequities. What we can explain to one another through this social conversation is that the elderly generally have much greater health needs, which generate presumptively stronger just claims to health resources for both the elderly and non-elderly. That is, health *needs* are not distributed equally, so neither should resources to meet those needs. Also, on the assumption that our social understandings and commitments in this matter remain stable, the non-elderly confidently expect that they will have comparable access to this same level of resources to meet their future health needs as elderly individuals. Given this sort of transparency, and given the reasonableness of the *public reasons* invoked as justification for these inequalities, it is difficult to understand why these inequalities would need to be hidden. By way of contrast, if there are significant inequalities in health status and access to needed health care related to race or socioeconomic status (as appears to be the case), then it is "understandable" why dominant interest groups would wish to keep that hidden, but that hardly makes it justifiable. What would we imagine would be the sorts of *public reasons* that these dominant interest groups (healthier and wealthier) would give to these less favored groups to convince them that these inequalities were not really inequities that required remediation? That brings us to our sixth consideration that justifies seeing the publicity condition at the core of our shared sense of justice.

The publicity condition promotes the criticism of rules or social arrangements in need of change due to changing socioeconomic or technological circumstances (such as racially-linked health disparities), thereby promoting *stable* social change through which justice may be preserved as well. By way of contrast, informal policies and rules that are hidden from public scrutiny (such as the informal understandings regarding dialysis among British physicians) provide a safe haven for unjust practices. Then, when such practices are exposed (as they usually are), that has a pronounced destabilizing effect on the larger set of social arrangements and a corrosive effect on the bonds of trust in a society. A painful illustration of that may be found in what is popularly referred to as the "Tuskegee syphilis experiments" from the 1930s in which poor rural black men were allowed to go untreated for syphilis for forty years in order to see the natural course of syphilis. In 1972 that shameful episode in medical history was exposed by a *New York Times* reporter. The social distrust that was generated among African Americans, both of our health care system and of the intentions of physicians caring for them, reverberates all the way to the present.

Lastly, due process is protected by the publicity condition. As Winslow puts it, "knowledge of the rules not only generates legitimate expectations, it also provides a basis for complaint if those expectations are unfairly abrogated" (Winslow, 1986, p. 203). Individuals are effectively denied a basis for appeal when hidden policies adversely affect their rights.

We can illustrate our points regarding the virtue of the publicity condition with an example taken from David Eddy (1996, pp. 102–09). He asks us to imagine a factory that employs 1,000 women. These women would know their lifetime risk of breast cancer. The owner of the factory understands their concern about breast cancer and offers them $1.5 million over 10 years to be spent however they wished to address that concern. At the time Eddy proposed this thought experiment, there was intense interest in autologous bone marrow transplants with high-dose chemotherapy (ABMT-HDC) as a "last-chance" therapy for women with metastatic disease. The cost of this intervention was about $150,000, and was believed that it offered a 10% chance of three-year survival. The other relevant statistics would be these: If the money had not been made available, then 36 of these women would die of breast cancer after 10 years. If the money was used to buy ABMT-HDC for

10 women, then 35 of these women would be dead from breast cancer after 10 years. If the money were used to buy 10 years of annual screening mammograms, then 29 of these women would be dead of breast cancer after 10 years.

What is morally significant is that none of these women would know what their own personal risk of death from breast cancer during this period would be. In that respect they are all behind a practical Rawlsian veil of ignorance—that is, they are capable of being suitably impartial. We imagine their having a conversation among themselves with regard to their options. If their goal is to maximize the likelihood of their survival for the next 10 years, then prudent rationality would dictate choosing the screening mammogram option. If the conversation is reflective enough, then all will be mindful that choosing the mammogram option means there will be no money for the ABMT option. In turn, that will mean that 29 women over the next 10 years might make a desperation plea to all the others to reconsider their decision so that they might have access to this one therapy that promises some life prolongation they will otherwise be denied. These are women who will have names and faces, and who will elicit powerful emotions (unlike the 29 who can only be abstractly conceived right now). Still, the most likely scenario would be near unanimity for choosing the screening mammogram option. Such a choice would be free, fully informed, prudent, and fair.[7]

Nothing would have been hidden or misrepresented to these women; all the conditions for full publicity would have been satisfied. Still, we can reasonably predict that some number of these 29 women will make a desperate plea to these other women after their disease has metastasized for taking a portion of the remaining funds and using them for ABMT rather than more screening mammograms. Such women would certainly deserve our empathy, but they would not have been treated unjustly if their pleas were compassionately turned down. This is what all freely agreed to when all could be suitably impartial, mutually respectful. Acquiescing to their pleas could only make others worse off who had a right not to be made worse off. The temptation to acquiesce is powerfully there because "others" who would be made worse off would be nameless and faceless, unlikely to elicit feelings of compassion.

Here are a couple of scenarios we can imagine, both of which would generate justified moral criticism. After five years (and the deaths of several women from breast cancer) two women find themselves with metastatic disease. They are very good friends with the owner of the factory who provided the $1.5 million in funding, and ask him to do something so that they can gain access to ABMT. He announces that screening mammograms will not be covered for the next two years so that these women can get ABMT. This would be unjust for several reasons. He promised these resources for ten years. An additional woman will likely die as a result of noncoverage of the screening mammograms for two years. Some women have already died who respected their agreements and did not make any special efforts to circumvent those agreements. The publicity condition is violated because no one agreed ahead of time that these monies could be taken back and used to provide ABMT to individuals who were special friends of the factory owner. That these women are special friends of his provides no moral justification for breaking the agreements. He is free to treat them as friends by using $300,000 of his own money to purchase ABMT for them; no one could reasonably claim that represented an injustice to anyone.

In an alternative scenario we can imagine that these two women with metastatic cancer are extraordinarily friendly with a large fraction of women in this factory, 51% to be exact. A group of their friends suggest (out of a sense of friendship and compassion) that a vote be taken to modify the original agreement so that ABMT can be provided to these two women. They get the vote and they get 51% agreement. I would contend that such a change was unjust for the same reasons as with the factory owner above. Agreements can be modified by the contracting parties *for good reason*; in this case, fair reasons. But it is not obvious that there are any justice-relevant considerations that would justify this alteration (and there are justice-relevant considerations that would speak against this alteration). We might imagine that a fair process (majority vote) makes this outcome just. However, if the original agreement had been endorsed by 95% of the women at the factory, then fairness would seem to require a comparable level of endorsement for a modification (especially because at least one additional woman would die as a result of this change). There is an alternative that permits these considerations of friendship to be respected without violating justice, namely that the 51% who would approve this change give up *four years* of screening mammograms that they alone would otherwise get. But the cost of that would be the predictable deaths of two additional women (which they are free to accept for the sake of friendship).

Our example with the factory workers is simplified for analytic purposes. My purposes diverge from David Eddy's purposes. Eddy is using this example to trumpet the virtues of cost-effectiveness analysis as a method for addressing rationing problems. I agree with him that cost-effectiveness matters, but I do not agree that cost-effectiveness matters decisively, that this is *the* rationally relevant consideration that should dictate the correct outcome in matters of health care rationing. Eddy (it seems) is a straightforward utilitarian in these matters. I will argue later that a number of nonutilitarian considerations often must be taken into account in assessing the justness of various rationing decisions. If cost-effectiveness considerations correctly generated were sufficient by themselves to yield just rationing decisions, then the publicity condition would be of greatly diminished relevance. Paying attention to publicity would provide some assurance that no mistakes were made in making technical calculations, but essentially the publicity condition would be met if these technical matters were accessible to the relevant experts (as opposed to the broad public affected by a particular rationing decision). Though Eddy introduced the factory worker example into the literature, he did not seem to attach any moral importance to the fact that these women made this rationing decision for their future possible selves, that this represented *self-imposed* rationing as opposed to a rationing decision imposed by businessmen or bureaucrats for their reasons, not the reasons that these women might give one another. But when the publicity condition is fully realized, then this sort of democratic deliberative autonomy is possible. More importantly (I shall argue), this sort of democratic deliberative autonomy is morally necessary in order to construct and legitimate just health care rationing decisions.

If we return for a moment to our earlier discussion of DRGs and HMOs (more broadly, managed care plans), then we should notice that neither of these cost control mechanisms encourages democratic deliberation regarding the justness of their structure or consequences. Of course it is legitimate to ask why there should be such conversation at all. That is, why should we not be satisfied with saying that both DRGs and HMOs represent complex policy mechanisms designed by various experts for purposes of better controlling health care costs? As long as these technical devices for controlling costs apply impartially to everyone (either in Medicare or a particular managed care plan), is that not fair enough? So why would democratic deliberation be necessary to protect justice?

We can answer this last question if we focus on the essential nature of DRGs and HMOs as prospective payment mechanisms that have cost control as a primary goal—a conflict of incentives is central to both. Physicians and plan administrators have been paid all that they will be paid for health care services for a specific disease episode or period of time; hence, they are motivated to do less for a patient. On the other hand, the patient has paid all that is required to be paid already; hence, the patient is motivated to demand more, and the "more" will often take the form of expensive, marginal benefits. Is it unjust if patients are denied these marginal benefits? If patients have already paid for those benefits, or have been led to believe they have paid for those benefits through ambiguous or deceptive advertising, and then are denied them, that is unjust. Or if some patients are denied these benefits and those savings are then used to provide marginal benefits for other patients who are similarly situated, that is unjust. Or if all patients are denied those benefits and the savings achieved provide significant discretionary income to physicians and administrators, then that is unjust. But if, for example, all Medicare patients, while in good health and having adopted the perspective of fair-minded rational moral and economic deliberators, were to agree that some types of health services that yielded only expensive and marginal benefits were not a good buy, and if that meant lower Medicare premiums so that all Medicare recipients could use those savings for other purchases that were more important to them, then there would be nothing unjust about foregoing those benefits since all had agreed.

Thus, a recent report in the journal *Cancer* on lung cancer in the elderly (Woodward et al., 2007) indicated that the incremental cost-effectiveness ratio of treating metastatic lung cancer would be about $1.2 million for an additional year of life (because the actual average gain was a few weeks). It is easy to imagine that there would be both "better buys" and "more just claims" that could be satisfied by a redistribution of the resources otherwise expended on these patients with metastatic lung cancer. As things are now, however, no effective opportunity exists for such a democratic deliberative conversation to occur.

In the case of DRGs, proponents will say that incentives are built into DRGs to reward the most efficient use of the funds attached to each DRG. But that improved efficiency says nothing at all about the justness of the outcome. Who precisely is rewarded? As noted earlier, a conflict of incentives exist—hospitals and physicians are the immediate beneficiaries of any efficiency savings achieved. They might well direct those resources away from very marginally beneficial uses of health resources (which may or may not be unjust) and redirect those resources to what they judge to be more cost-effective health care interventions for the elderly (which may or may not be unjust). Alternatively, they may allow those resources to leak out of the care system and improve hospital amenities, or provide administrative or medical bonuses. This last prospect is clearly unjust, as Daniels (1986) has correctly argued.[8] But the prior alternative is morally flawed as well because the burdens of rationing or the benefits of reallocation of achieved savings are simply imposed on patients by (presumably) well-intentioned physicians or administrators without those patients having an opportunity for deliberative input, even though they are the ones whose just claims to needed health care might be most at risk. Worse still, it is not as if these physicians and administrators have had any conversations among themselves to articulate their own sense of justice and how that might apply to the overall administration of DRGs for the elderly. The reality is, there are literally millions of uncoordinated disaggregated nonsystematic decisions unilaterally made by these individual physicians as individuals that would only be randomly just at best.

I want to reiterate a point I have already made: DRGs are not intended to encourage conversation about their justice-relevant consequences, either among physicians or between physicians and their patients. Further, even if such conversations were somehow encouraged between individual physicians and individual patients, this would hardly speak to the problem of health care justice as that applies to DRGs. If anything, that would only make the problem worse, as patients would seek to enlist the help of their physicians to advance what they judged as their own health interests, potentially at the expense of both fairer and more cost-effective allocations of limited resources. The point I wish to emphasize is that justice requires broad public conversations that have something of a systemic character to them for purposes of assessing DRGs overall and the way they are applied in actual clinical practice. In this way, broad public understandings would be constructed regarding what would count as fair and reasonable rationing decisions—either for DRGs in general or specific DRGs. Such understandings would help to create public trust in the system by guiding medical judgment in practice so that the outcome reflects at least "rough justice."

Critics of this conclusion will again appeal to the *complexity* of medical problems as they afflict an individual, the need for *flexibility* in being responsive to those problems, and the inability of either bureaucrats or justice-minded democratic deliberators to respond in either a compassionate or medically appropriate way to those problems. Thus, Blumstein concedes that rules and regulations are certain; in that way they promote fairness, but they are inflexible. "The flexibility, possibly increased precision, and the opportunity for the exercise of compassion in individualized decision-making counterbalances the benefits of objectivity and limits on arbitrariness in formal standards" (Blumstein, 1983, p. 370).

No doubt it is a virtue of DRGs that they encourage flexibility, but that flexibility accrues mostly on the side of physicians and administrators. If patients are able to take advantage of that flexibility, the legitimate concern is that the rationing outcomes may still fail to be just enough. What about compassion? Again, DRGs permit as much compassion as a hospital will tolerate in its staff physicians. If specific physicians choose to provide expensive marginal benefits to some of their Medicare patients, what happens? We really do not know precisely. It may simply mean a slight reduction in the "profit margin" for Medicare patients, or stingier care for other patients in other DRGs, or less indigent care. An indefinite number of adjustments are possible, some of which might be morally neutral, others seriously unjust, but all of which would be mostly hidden from public scrutiny. Certainly all these effects will be invisible to the physician acting compassionately, who, consequently, will not be motivated to examine whether in acting compassionately he is also acting justly.

The capacity for compassion varies enormously from one person to another, as do the sorts of persons who can elicit compassion from each of us. No one is (ordinarily) *entitled* to compassion, but all of us are entitled to just treatment by our health care system. Compassion may be freely given, but justice is properly demanded. Invisible allocative mechanisms may permit compassion in response to individual circumstances, but first the demands for justice for all must be satisfied. It is precisely these latter demands that are too easily ignored or subverted by invisible allocative mechanisms. Justice does not necessarily exclude flexibility so far as clinical decisions are concerned, but it does put some presumptive boundaries on the scope of that decision-making and require clear, explicit justice-relevant justifications for any claim of a need to breach those boundaries. Thus, democratic deliberators would not be so imprudent as to attempt to collectively practice "just medicine." But democratic deliberators could agree that these extraordinarily expensive cancer drugs (such as Avastin) would not be provided to them if their future possible self had metastatic lung cancer. Or they could agree to forego those six extra hospital days that had been part of routine care for first-time, uncomplicated heart attack patients.

MANAGED CARE AND HEALTH CARE RATIONING

We now need to briefly consider some similar issues with regard to HMOs and, more generally, all sorts of managed care plans. David Mechanic defends managed care plans as the best approach available for achieving cost-effective health care. He takes as one of the virtues of managed care plans that it relies upon a system of "implicit rationing," which he defines as "a system that establishes constraints but allows patients and professionals to work out accommodations that fit the variety of their needs, inclinations, and preferences" (Mechanic, 1986, p. 208). Mechanic does recognize the need for society to set "realistic limitations" on how much health care is consumed; consequently, he is comfortable with having explicit limits set at that societal level. But at the clinical level he believes "every effort should be made to retain choices and options for patients and their doctors to do what best fits the contingencies of the specific situation" (p. 208). In a later paper, Mechanic writes, "I strongly share the values inherent in fair allocation and evidence-based practice and sympathize with the concerns that argue for shifting the rationing balance toward more visible approaches. . . . But I also believe that the call for explicit allocation, while seductive, is misleading and has the potential for mischief" (Mechanic, 1997, pp. 84–85). He goes on to give five reasons for his concerns about explicit rationing at the clinical level. Those reasons include the resistance to change of rules or understandings once in place because of constituencies that develop around them, the need for process (discovery and negotiation) in delivering medical care, differences among patients regarding their value commitments (how aggressive care should be, trade-offs between length and quality of life, preservation of bodily integrity), all the contingencies of medical care that relate to comorbidities and life situations, and concerns about acrimony in the public square as various interest groups seek to preserve their interests. "The fact of the matter is that despite the call by many ethicists for rationing to be explicit and transparent, this is in fact extremely difficult to carry out, since it mobilizes disease advocates and professional interest groups and results in considerable political conflict" (Mechanic, 2006, p. 139).

How should we assess Mechanic's defense of implicit rationing (critique of explicit rationing)? Is he a hard-nosed realist or a starry-eyed idealist? He is actually a bit of both—what he describes are very realistic challenges associated with explicit rationing protocols in the clinic. But he is vulnerable to the charge of excessive idealism in believing that implicit rationing can work (justly) with a modicum of good will and some sensitive communication between patients and physicians. Mechanic writes, "Enrolment in an HMO is really an agreement between the enrollee and the plan to accept a situation of 'constructive rationing,' although plans are not typically described to consumers in this way" (Mechanic, 1986, p. 214). This is idealism.

Readers will recall the intensely competitive advertising campaigns that characterized HMO relationships to one another during the 1990s. None of the advertising slogans were built around the themes of "quality constructive rationing," or "twice the rationing for half the price." On the contrary, the emphasis was on how much more care members as patients would receive because of the efficiencies achieved by these organizations. Patients had no reason to believe they would be denied any care they judged to be medically desirable. With that kind of initial misunderstanding, what would we imagine a "constructive rationing" conversation would be like between a patient and a physician? Who would be motivated to initiate such a conversation? Physicians would have little reason for promoting such conversations since such conversations (given their starting point) would be awkward at best, painfully confrontational at worst. Medically sophisticated patients might initiate these conversations, and, if they are strident enough and persistent enough, they might actually get the added medical care they would otherwise have been denied. But this could hardly be seen as a clear moral triumph since other medically similarly situated patients would have been quietly denied the same care, either because they were not sufficiently medically sophisticated to know what they had been denied, or because they were excessively timid in the face of medical authority and power. This looks like an injustice with regard to both the assertive and the timid patients. But if there are no explicit shared understandings of what would count as just or unjust denials of health services, then how could the conversation rationally proceed?

Mechanic again writes, "Internal review processes are also needed to ensure that patients who feel they were denied care inappropriately can have their concerns considered. The consequences of implicit rationing processes should be as open as possible, should be reviewed routinely by medical peers and through outside audit, and should be an important topic for discussion within health care institutions" (Mechanic, 1997, p. 91). But if rationing is accomplished implicitly without clear rules and criteria, then how does an internal review process know what to assess? This is again utopian. Mechanic refers to patients who feel they were denied care inappropriately. What exactly is meant by "inappropriate"? Our concern is with matters of justice. An internal review might identify care that should have been provided because it was "medically necessary" in a strong sense of that phrase. That speaks to the matter of good medical care; it does not speak to the justice issue.

To illustrate, if a patient has a CT scan and they must be injected with a contrast agent, and if they are injected with HOCA (the less expensive contrast agent at $10 compared to LOCA at $180), and if HOCA carries a one in a thousand risk of a severe reaction compared to the one in thirty thousand risk of such a reaction with LOCA, and if a patient becomes aware of the fact that they received the less expensive agent (but experience no side effects), do they have a just cause for complaint because they were exposed to this risk? The same sort of problem arises in connection with the use of clot-dissolving drugs after a heart attack. The older, cheaper drug (streptokinase at $200 per dose) carries a slightly greater risk of a potential fatal second heart attack within thirty days compared to tPA (at $2,400 per dose). Is it "bad medicine" to use either HOCA or streptokinase? My understanding is that these options are perfectly reasonable and acceptable *medical options*. But that says nothing about the implicit value question—in other words, whether patients are unjustly treated by being exposed to this additional risk. This is precisely the sort of thing that is central to implicit rationing *and that is outside the practice of medicine as such*. This is something that only patients/future possible patients can collectively decide. But that requires a collective explicit conversation if we are going to have a fair rationing protocol, as opposed to the random (possibly excessive) expectations of individual patients.

Finally, we turn to the work of Mark Hall (1997) who is sensitive to the moral risks associated with implicit or invisible rationing, but who wants a simple and practical approach to explicit rationing. He thinks about this as an informed consent problem, though he calls it a matter of economic informed consent. He imagines (in something of a libertarian mode) that there ought to be many kinds of managed care plans offering a range of insurance products that reflect more or less comprehensive coverage, more or less willingness to accept various risk–benefit trade-offs in exchange for a more affordable or a more risk-averse insurance package. Hall recognizes that his preferences in this regard are not well reflected in the real world at present; less than half of all workers have a choice of more than one health plan, and only about 10% of workers have a choice of more than two health plans. (This, of course, reflects the fact that most companies are not large enough to place their workers in more than two plans if they would hope to gain reduced plan costs by minimizing the economic risks to that insurance company.) Hall also notes that virtually all these plans emphasize in their literature their supreme dedication to optimal health care for all plan subscribers; few (if any) say anything about rationing to their potential subscribers. But Hall believes, morally and legally, that potential plan members must have the opportunity to consent in a sufficiently informed way to whatever rationing approach characterizes a particular plan—that means this must be divulged to individuals at the time of enrollment.

There is a limit to how far Hall will go in honoring the publicity condition. He does not believe that such disclosure is required in an actual clinical encounter (at the proverbial bedside). Nor does he believe potential plan members must be apprised of all the grimy details of specific rationing or cost-control or incentivizing approaches that might be used in the plan. Instead, he believes it is sufficient to inform these potential plan members that they are buying a constrained insurance plan committed to an economizing style of medical practice in exchange for lower premiums or more comprehensive coverage. He writes that "when patients make informed decisions to purchase more economical forms of health insurance, they consent in advance to a bundle of unspecified refusals of marginally beneficial care" (Hall, 1997, p. 194). He refers to this as "bundled" informed consent. He sees this as being analogous to the sort of consent a patient gives on admission to a hospital. Patients consent to a very broad range of routine medical tests and procedures without anyone having to obtain specific informed consent for each of these events. But my judgment is that this is a very inadequate bow in the direction of both the publicity condition and economic informed consent.

Bundled consent is reasonable in the case of hospital admission because the tests are very routine and very much part of good medical practice. But the domain of "marginally beneficial non-costworthy health care" is very large, very diffuse, very heterogeneous in terms of potential consequences for patients, and very much the focus of controversy among physicians, economists, ethicists and policymakers. What this means in practice is that there is enormous opportunity for subjective, idiosyncratic clinical/economic judgments to be used to deny individual patients this or that therapeutic or diagnostic intervention. If this is a fair description of what patients will often enough encounter, then what would merit our saying a patient had given "informed" consent to being denied some specific intervention? Further, how could anyone judge in an "informed" enough way that this particular denial was just or unjust? This approach still looks like it has most of the deficiencies we have already identified with invisible rationing.

Hall says that potential members of these managed care plans must give "free" consent. But the only matter about which there is freedom of choice is whether or not to join that plan. The actual rationing protocols as they work out in actual clinical practice across all the physicians in the plan are something that potential subscribers have no say in determining. (For that matter, current plan members would not have had a say, either.) Even if the plan had very detailed, very elaborate rationing protocols that were presented in just that way to potential plan members, the basic problem would remain, namely that those plan members were faced with a "take it or leave it" decision whose quality (from the perspective of health care justice) was a complete mystery.

While it is true that there might be many morally uncontroversial rationing/cost-control decisions with respect to which economic informed consent would be unnecessary (perhaps many of the trade-offs of name brand drugs for generic versions), it is just as true that many other rationing/cost-control opportunities would be open to reasonable controversy, and consequently, should not be left to the uncritical and unexplained judgment of plan managers or individual clinicians. Whether statins ought to be offered to patients at plan expense with total cholesterol of 200 or 220 or 240 would be one example. Other examples would include which clot-dissolving drugs were used for a heart attack, which contrast agent was used for a CT scan, when MRIs were appropriate as a diagnostic tool, and whether cholinesterase inhibitors would be a plan benefit for patients with some degree of Alzheimer's. All of these prior examples might be regarded as "low visibility" items because the vast majority of patients would never have occasion to think about these things if they were not brought to their attention (which, I would emphasize, is not a legitimate excuse for failing to bring such matters to the attention of patients).

Then there are the more "high visibility" items, which have in fact garnered considerable media attention because of their high cost and the public perception that these interventions could make the difference between life and death. This category would include all those extraordinarily costly "last-chance" cancer drugs, access to ICDs, lung reduction surgery for end-stage COPD, and LVADs for end-stage heart disease. Among analysts, near universal agreement prevails that these are clearly marginally beneficial interventions that are not worth the cost. Nevertheless (I will argue), this does not justify "bundling" all these items under some nonspecific economic informed consent process. This still represents a morally problematic form of invisible rationing—what is necessary from the perspective of health care justice is something that approximates "full publicity." What full publicity requires is that all these rationing options (to the extent that they are justice-relevant) be the subject of rational democratic deliberation that includes the opportunity to participate for all who could potentially be affected by these decisions. Rationing is more likely to be just if rationing decisions are autonomously self-imposed through the deliberative process in accord with deliberatively endorsed, considered judgments of health care justice. The substance of the deliberative process involves the giving of public reasons and the critical assessment of public reasons for one or another rationing protocol. This is how in practice fair terms of cooperation come to be articulated, understood, and publicly legitimated; this is what our fundamental moral norms of reciprocity and mutual respect require of us. In the next two chapters we turn to a fuller explanation and defense of these claims.

4

ELEMENTS OF HEALTH CARE JUSTICE

If an individual has advanced colorectal cancer, and if current chemotherapeutic regimens are no longer capable of stopping tumor progression, and if cetuximab (Erbitux) is the only remaining intervention that has proven effective in stopping tumor progression for an additional period of time, and if that individual's insurance company refuses to pay the $12,000 per month cost of the drug because it only increases median survival by 1.5 months (compared to palliative care only [Jonker et al., 2007]), then has that individual been treated unjustly? If an individual has total cholesterol of 200 but he wishes to achieve an additional margin of safe health by driving that number down to 160 through the use of statins, and if his insurance company refuses to cover the $1,100 per year cost of that drug because their judgment is that the additional gains are too marginal relative to cost, has that individual been treated unjustly? Should our answer to our questions matter whether we are talking about a working-class individual earning $35,000 per year or an upper middle-class individual earning $200,000 per year?

If a 58-year-old individual has moderate atherosclerotic heart disease, and if electrophysiological studies indicate an occasional abnormal rhythm, and if that individual has a T-wave alternans test indicating that there is no more than a 1% chance of a fatal arrhythmia over the next two years (which means he will be denied an implantable cardiac defibrillator [ICD] that costs $40,000 by his managed care plan), has that individual been treated unjustly? Imagine an alternate version of this scenario in which we have an 83-year-old individual whose heart disease is such that he has a 10% chance of a fatal arrhythmia in the next two years. Pretend that Medicare has introduced for cost-saving purposes a rule that would deny an ICD to anyone over age 80. Would such a rule be unjust? If such a rule existed, would it be unjust if more affluent elderly individuals were able to purchase this device with their own money? Consider another variation. The Medicare rule does not have any age limit; instead, the rule would deny an ICD to any Medicare patient with moderate to more advanced symptoms of Alzheimer's, essentially saying that for current or future quality of life reasons it was not worth it to implant ICDs in these individuals. Would that rule be just? What if there was no rule? What if instead a tacit understanding emerged among physicians that ICDs would not be offered to late-stage Alzheimer's patients? Would that be unjust? What if the tacit understanding was that in such patients physicians would not look for diagnostic indicators suggestive of cardiac disturbances that might otherwise merit an ICD? Would that be unjust?

All of our above questions need to be answered as a moral and practical matter. One answer might be that there are no obvious moral issues to be addressed in any of the scenarios above—these are all just economic transactions having to do with the purchase of services. If no fraud was involved, if prices for various insurance products reflected prevailing market conditions and considerations, if rules (tacit or explicit) denying individuals certain desired forms of medical care were applied uniformly to all who were in the same medical circumstances and had purchased the same insurance product, then no justice issues exist for discussion. A defender of a libertarian conception of health care justice would defend this view. I reject it, at least as an adequate conception of health care justice. What I need to show instead is that health care is "morally special," that it is properly thought of as a presumptive subject of justice. However, I also need to show that not *all* health care in all medical circumstances is correctly thought of as a matter of justice. If that were the case, then all forms of health care rationing would be presumptively unjust (and the point of our first two chapters was to show this was not true). This will be the first task of this chapter.

We need to identify and defend a reasonable theoretical perspective that will allow us to fairly distinguish just from unjust health care rationing protocols and practices. Daniels (1985) offers us an initial theoretical perspective that is very helpful in this regard, which he refers to as the "fair equality of opportunity" account of health care justice. This account has its limitations, but so will every other theoretical account of health care justice. Consequently, the view I will ultimately defend in that regard is that no single conception of justice can adequately address the very complex heterogeneous problems of health care rationing that are integral to our health care system in the United States.[1] What we need to commit to is a pluralistic conception of health care justice that will have an overall moderately egalitarian cast to it. The task of the latter parts of this chapter will be to defend that claim.

But even that pluralistic conception of health care justice will not have the internal resources needed to yield objective considered judgments of health care justice with regard to a very large number of concrete rationing problems in our health care system. What we will be faced with is what Rawls refers to as the "burdens of judgment" (1993). Some moral problems are too complex, involve too much factual uncertainty, are open to reasonable (but conflicting) conceptual characterizations, or call into play conflicting moral judgments rooted in distinct analogies that seem relevant to the issue at hand; consequently, our theories cannot yield an objectively dominant, reasonable, moral judgment in such matters that all reasonable moral agents in that specific moral conflict rationally ought to accept. This creates "moral space" that I will refer to as the domain of non-ideal justice. In that space, and with regard to any particular problem of health care justice, there may be several practical moral judgments that may all be viewed as being "just enough"—not perfectly just, but not fairly characterized as being "unjust." The task of the second part of this chapter will be to limn the boundaries of the domain of non-ideal injustice so that cleverly disguised unjust options are not accorded presumptive moral legitimacy in this domain. Why would that be important?

The short answer to our question is that the domain of non-ideal justice is also the domain of rational democratic deliberation. In some sense the starting point for the most common form of the deliberative process would be several "just enough" practical judgments with respect to some very specific rationing problem. The virtue of having that as a starting point is that this provides significant assurance that the outcome of the deliberative process will be "just enough" as well (in a substantive sense of justice), assuming that the deliberative process is not flawed in justice-relevant respects *as a process*.

A number of philosophers and political scientists have called attention to what they call "the democracy problem" (Daniels, 1993) in connection with the role of rational democratic deliberation in our moral and political life. In brief, they argue, we are faced with a sort of dilemma: If the deliberative process itself confers "rightness" or "justness" on the outcome of the process (pure procedural justice), then it seems as if the deliberative process could never "get it wrong." That is, the outcome of the deliberative process is supposed to be immune to substantive moral criticism so long as the process itself was not morally flawed. But that conclusion seems very contrary to our political experience—it seems we often do appeal to a range of substantive moral and political norms for purposes of identifying a substantively flawed outcome from the deliberative process. However, if we can legitimately do just that, then it seems that the deliberative process is entirely otiose. In other words, we could have gotten to that outcome through carefully crafted moral argument without the cost, complexity, inefficiency, and flaws of the deliberative process.

The task of Chapter 5 will be to address that apparent dilemma. This will require spelling out in considerable detail my understanding of the structure and process of a morally defensible and politically legitimate form of rational democratic deliberation. Essentially what I will argue is that there are (metaphorically) constitutional principles of health care justice that broadly define what are "just enough" health care rationing protocols and practices. These principles serve as one sort of substantive moral constraint on the deliberative process. The deliberative process is also constrained by the need to maintain wide reflective equilibrium, a kind of conversational coherence and consistency over long stretches of time. This will involve the use of public reason and the construction or reconstruction of considered judgments of health care justice pertinent to the issue being addressed. This will be a dynamic equilibrium since it must be responsive to constantly changing features of our health care system that may be justice-relevant, such as the introduction of costly new medical technologies or new types of health care financing schemes (such as medical savings accounts). We will also lay out the criteria for judging the fairness and reasonableness of the *process* aspects of rational democratic deliberation. And we will conclude that chapter with responses to the major criticisms of rational democratic deliberation as a source for just rationing protocols and policies and practices.

IS HEALTH CARE MORALLY SPECIAL?

When the question is raised as to whether or not health care resources are morally special, the intent is to suggest that health care ought to be distributed in accord with norms of justice as opposed to market norms (i.e., ability to pay). Two preliminary considerations would suggest that health care ought to be distributed in accord with norms of justice: its effectiveness in matters of life and death, and the massive public investments that yielded that effectiveness.

Health care today is often very effective in reversing or substantially ameliorating the effects of illness or accident. That is, needed health care can often make the difference between life and a very premature death, or between a serious temporary injury and a serious permanently disabling injury. These are morally significant outcomes. It is hard to imagine any consumer good or service distributed on the basis of ability to pay that has comparable consequences. Further, what would seem to be a related and relevant moral norm would be a "duty to rescue."

We would never accept as a moral excuse for failing to rescue a drowning individual that the life preserver was owned by me and that he (the drowning man) had no right to the use of it. Our health care system is very much like that life preserver, and our hospital emergency rooms are a close analogy. Rescue is (relatively speaking) easy—even high-cost rescues are affordable from a broad social perspective. We must also note that we are not talking about absolutely scarce goods ordinarily; hence, failing to provide rescue opens our society to justified moral criticism. Of course, in some circumstances we are faced with absolute scarcity, as in the case of transplantable organs or sometimes ICU beds. But again it is instructive that in those circumstances we do not auction these scarce lifesaving medical interventions to the highest bidder. Instead, we try to articulate justice-relevant criteria for awarding access to that intervention to one patient rather than another. This suggests there are shared moral understandings in this matter which we may not ignore.[2]

One of the limitations of our life preserver analogy as a basis for determining just claims to needed health care is that it would seem to restrict the justice issue to health resources linked to matters of life and death or risk of serious permanent disability. This seems too narrow, but a second consideration might yield a useful corrective. Our health care system is essentially a product of massive social investments by virtually everyone in our society. What we have in mind is the building of major health care facilities, investing in basic fruitful medical research, and training a broad array of highly skilled health professionals. The investment dollars come from private health insurance (linked to employment and the sweat of workers' brows, who are vulnerable to being laid off for reasons entirely beyond their control), from public taxes that support Medicare/Medicaid and NIH, and community charitable giving. It is difficult to imagine what the moral argument would be that would justify extracting resources from the near poor and working poor now uninsured to create this health care system primarily for the use of those who were already very well-off; this looks like it is exploitation. The obvious implication is that this can be corrected by providing assured access to needed health care for everyone, since virtually everyone has contributed to the creation of this common resource. But then this seems to generate the opposite implication of our first problem—it seems to be excessively expansive. Everyone would seem to have an unlimited just claim to everything the health care system has to offer that satisfies a health need. This is clearly a denial of the reality and the legitimacy of the rationing problem.

What we need is a moral perspective that justifies the claim that health care is morally special, that there are legitimate justice issues that must be addressed. In addition, that perspective must both identify a comprehensive set of health care services to which all would have an equal presumptive just claim, and facilitate the articulation of just rationing protocols and practices used to limit the domain of just health care claims. I believe Norman Daniels (1985) offers us a reasonable approximation of that perspective with his fair equality of opportunity account of health care justice.

We start with the moral intuition that health care justice should be linked with health care needs. But that concept by itself will yield too expansive and unregulated a form of access to health care services under the banner of justice. We can hardly expect to have a just distribution of health care resources if a subjective sense of health need is permitted to generate just claims to health care. Think of the food "needs" of the gourmet cook compared to the food needs of that American icon, Joe Sixpack. But some objective reference points for identifying health needs can also be excessively expansive. Callahan (1990, chap. 2) has astutely observed that in our culture every form of emerging medical technology generates a corresponding "need" for that technology. Again, this is hardly helpful if we have to take seriously the problem of health care rationing.

The helpful concepts that Daniels hit on were the notions of "normal species functioning" and a culturally relative "normal opportunity range." The additional concept to which he linked these two notions was the Rawlsian notion of "fair equality of opportunity." Health needs are given some objective constraints because they are linked to deficiencies in normal species functioning due to illness or accident. A broken leg clearly interferes with normal species functioning; it is a paradigmatic health need. Facial wrinkles associated with aging have no functional consequences; hence, no one can claim Botox is a therapy for that health "need."

Daniels' additional point was that health needs that make presumptively just claims on societal health care resources are those needs associated with protecting fair equality of opportunity. How expansive ought we to imagine that opportunity range to be? The answer to that question will be relativized to a society, and, to some extent, relativized to an individual as well. As we shall see, this is helpful for addressing both the "fair access" and "fair rationing" problems. Before explaining this further, let us back up one step.

Why should we not simply give everyone in our society "equal resources" that they can use as they wish to address whatever they regard as their health care needs? Just to pick a number, this could be a lifetime sum of one million dollars. We might see this as satisfying some sort of an egalitarian criterion of justice (same amount of money for each person) as well as a libertarian criterion (no one other than that individual is judging what should or should not be regarded as a legitimate health need). The problem, however, is that health needs (defined more objectively) are spread very unevenly across the population and across the lifetimes of individuals. Some individuals could easily use up that entire million dollars just to get through the first few years of life, while others are so genetically and environmentally favored that they barely use 5% of that sum to reach age 80, at which point they begin to use thousands of dollars to purchase daily doses of Viagra for their erectile dysfunction and minoxidal for their hair loss. If we perform a Rawlsian mental experiment behind a veil of ignorance, it is difficult to imagine that reasonable persons (not knowing their future possible health needs) would endorse a social policy that permitted the very premature deaths of some individuals (whose lives could have been substantially prolonged with access to costly therapies) so that other individuals could continue to experience sexual ecstasy beyond age 80 with a full head of youthfully dyed hair. So an "equal resources" approach to meeting health care needs will not yield consistently just outcomes.

Why is health care morally special? The answer Daniels gives is that it is very closely tied to protecting fair equality of opportunity, in much the same way that education is closely tied *in our society* to protecting fair equality of opportunity. If the U.S. were still the agrarian society it was at our founding, then providing free public education through grade 12 and heavily subsidized education beyond that would be pointless. Instead, we are this information-based, advanced post-industrial economy. Having access to free or heavily subsidized public education is essential to protecting fair equality of opportunity for all in our society. Not everyone will have the native intellectual endowment that would permit them to earn a doctoral degree; not everyone will have a social support system and a natural drive and energy that will permit them to take full advantage of the educational opportunities our society offers. Those factors are largely beyond reasonable and respectful social control; consequently, our society is not open to justified moral criticism for the social and economic stratification that results *as long as we have made reasonable efforts to assure fair access to those educational resources that allow individuals to compete fairly for available jobs and offices.*[1] Alternatively, if entrenched racism or an unfair distribution of tax dollars to resource-poor school districts effectively denies numerous individuals access to the educational resources needed to acquire socially valuable skills, then to that extent a society is open to moral criticism for failing to protect fair equality of opportunity.

Daniels argues that access to needed and effective health care is just as essential to protecting fair equality of opportunity in our society as is education. Imagine that an individual has a headache that would rate a '9' on a '10' scale. This is not a brain tumor; this is not a life-threatening medical problem of any kind. It is just a persistent intense headache. It does, however, have a distinctive etiology which makes it impervious to the usual headache remedies. But there is a new drug that costs $10,000 per year that effectively controls that headache, almost making it completely disappear. Is a just and caring society morally obligated to assure access to that drug for all who have the relevant need? Daniels (and I) would give a clear affirmative answer to this question. He would ask us to imagine what the life of this individual would be like with this headache. How could they function at the most menial of jobs, much less a professional position that required much energy and concentration? How could they interact in socially acceptable ways with friends and coworkers? Something as simple as an intense headache can be extraordinarily disruptive of our ordinary lives, and if that headache is persistent and recurrent, then we are going to be denied fair and effective equality of opportunity. If the hypothetical drug I mentioned above is nonexistent, then it is unfortunate that this individual will be denied access to the normal opportunity range of our society. But this is not an unjust outcome. On the other hand, if the individual is denied access to this very effective drug because they cannot pay for the drug, then in a society with a 12-trillion-dollar economy this is unjust. They have effectively been denied access to the normal opportunity range in our society.

Let me spell out a bit more fully some of the strengths and weaknesses of Daniels' account. I may have an intense love of music, and I may aspire to be an internationally acclaimed concert pianist, but my fingers are not as long or as supple as they would need to be to achieve that goal. Imagine there is a type of surgery that would give me the improved fingering skills I would need to achieve this goal, but the surgery costs $100,000. Would a just and caring society that embraced Daniels' fair equality of opportunity account of health care justice be morally obligated to provide me with those funds? No. This aspiration is far outside the normal opportunity range of our society. Our society would still provide me with access to a very fine musical education that would allow me to compete for musical positions that were within the normal opportunity range of our society. But what if my hands were such that I could never achieve a skill level at playing the piano beyond entertaining myself and a few friends? My hands are not arthritic or damaged by any other form of disease; they are just undistinguished. Then again, I would have no just claim to that surgery since all the rest of the normal opportunity range in our society would be open to me since I had no other limitations due to illness or accident. I would have to alter early on in life my career aspirations, but there is nothing uncommon or unjust about this phenomenon. Alternatively, nothing forbids my borrowing the money for the surgery that would allow me to pursue that dream.

To put this in personal terms, I have one leg that is an inch shorter than the other. Two years after I was born our family physician noticed the growth difference.

If nothing at all had been done surgically, I would likely have ended up with one leg about eight inches shorter than the other; that would have been a significant disability. I did in fact have three surgeries that prevented that from happening, but there is still a one-inch difference. From the perspective of Daniels' fair equality of opportunity account I would be certain I had a just claim to those surgeries. That is, it would have been unjust if I had been denied those surgeries because my father was unable to afford them. But now imagine there is a new surgery that for $100,000 could close that one-inch gap that remains (and requires that I wear a lift on my shoe). Would I have a just claim to that? No. There is no life activity of any consequence that I can think of that I was denied because of my short leg (other than the right to fight in the Viet Nam war)—I have complete access to the normal opportunity range of our society. Surgery to eliminate that difference would be more like cosmetic surgery (morally speaking) than any need linked to protecting fair equality of opportunity.

We said earlier that we need an account of why health care is morally special, that makes clear the sorts of health interventions in particular circumstances to which individuals have just claims (the access issue), as well as circumstances in which individuals can be justly denied access to certain health interventions (the rationing issue). The fair equality of opportunity account of health care justice goes far in achieving those objectives. Health care interventions that are largely enhancements will mostly be outside the domain of health care justice because they do nothing to protect access to the *normal* opportunity range. But we can also say that health care interventions which are only successful in sustaining bare biological life will also be outside the domain of health care justice.

We recall, for example, patients in PVS. Many of these patients are relatively young. We imagined signs of an irregular heartbeat in such a patient suggestive of vulnerability to a fatal arrhythmia. Would such a patient have a just claim to a $40,000 ICD that would save them from a "premature death"? From the perspective of a fair equality of opportunity account, a negative answer is warranted. Such a patient unfortunately has no capacity at all to access any portion of a normal opportunity range; they are completely incapable of doing or experiencing anything. Consequently, they have no just claim to an ICD or an LVAD or feeding tubes or any other life-sustaining care at social expense. Individual families are free to underwrite these costs for whatever social or religious reasons that might motivate them, so long as these efforts do not undermine the just claims of other patients who are clearly capable of benefiting from resources used by a PVS patient. We do not have a serious shortage of feeding tubes or nursing home beds in our society. But it would be unjust for a PVS patient to continue to use an absolutely scarce good, such as a ventilator or ICU bed, if a consequence of their use would be denying that resource to another patient who could clearly benefit (or who would be at risk of premature death if denied access to that resource).

We note that one of the strengths of the fair equality of opportunity account is that it does not create an automatic just claim to have any objective health need met. Nor does it say that some specific health intervention is something to which everyone would have a just claim. All such claims are context-dependent—they must be closely linked to protecting *fair and effective* equality of opportunity in practice, not just in theory. We can imagine a fairly vigorous 65-year-old with a suspicious heart rhythm suggesting a need for an ICD, and another 65-year-old in PVS with that same suspicious rhythm. The first would have a presumptively just claim to the ICD, but no such presumption would be warranted in the latter case. I would suggest that a similar sort of argument might be made in the case of end-stage Alzheimer's patients, though there are more controversial aspects to this case, and hence, we will reserve that discussion for later.

Another virtue of the fair equality of opportunity account is that it warrants being responsive justly to gradations in health need, and ability to benefit from having that need met in specific circumstances by a specific medical intervention. If social economic resources were unlimited, then expensive interventions could be provided to meet any objective medical need—even if the benefits in a specific case were likely to be very marginal. But this is contrary to fact; resources are always limited relative to need. Thus, if it were to cost $100,000 to eliminate that one-inch shortage in my leg, I would have at best a very marginal gain in access to the opportunity range in our society (I could fight in the Iraq war). If that $100,000 were taken from a 15-year-old who needed that money to address a leukemia with a bone marrow transplant that had a 50% chance of yielding a complete cure for that child, then that would be unjust because so much more opportunity was at risk (or could be saved) by that intervention.

This comparison has been deliberately constructed to illustrate a large gap between the two examples. I am reasonably confident that the fair equality of opportunity principle justifies the judgment I have made. But we could give a number of other examples where the gap would be much smaller and where it would be difficult to make the case that the fair equality of opportunity account would necessarily tilt the balance one way rather than the other. That is the sort of circumstance in which we would have to bring in rational democratic deliberation. The fair, effective equality of opportunity account cannot tell us at what level of total cholesterol individuals would have a just claim to statins paid at plan expense. Nor can it tell us whether a just society is morally obligated to fund the more expensive clot-dissolving drug rather than the less expensive drug in order to save one extra life per hundred patients who have a heart attack. And the same will be true with regard to the use of contrast agents for CT scans. All of these latter interventions are suitable subject matter for rational democratic deliberation because they reflect a need for judgment and trade-offs and priority setting, which are beyond the capacity for refinement of this principle.

One of the major criticisms of Daniels' fair equality of opportunity account (which he himself acknowledges) is the inability of the principle to deal effectively with the problem of patients who are described as being "bottomless pits."[2] These are patients with extremely complicated medical problems that require vast amounts of costly medical resources over very long periods of time. These are not Mr. Diaz-like patients where we can confidently judge the benefits being provided the patient are very minimal (no matter what the cost is). Virtually no effective equality of opportunity is being protected in the case of Mr. Diaz, which would then warrant the judgment that he has no just claim to those resources. But in the case of patients labeled "bottomless pits," many of the interventions with which they are provided are sustaining functional life by somewhat successfully addressing one medical problem or another. But each treatment might have very substantial side effects that require further intensive medical management. While many of these patients may have medical problems that will ultimately have a terminal outcome, that outcome might be several years into the future if aggressive medical care is continued. Many of these patients may be in a state of medical dependency for months or years at a time, mostly confined to a health care institution, but they may be very cognitively intact and capable of participating in a significant variety of life activities within a confined geographic area. These are not your paradigmatic nursing home patients, but these are patients who will never recover from all the medical problems that afflict them (though they will have intermittent minor medical successes).

We can take our story of Mr. H (factor VIII-resistant hemophilia) as one example of the sort of patient we have in mind. Another example is the case of Ed Van Houten, 45 years old, who has spent all of the past two years (1989–91) in a hospital (Dorschner, 1991). He spends most of his time in bed, watching television when he can. He is missing his left hand, and is blind in one eye and deaf in one ear. His kidneys failed ten years ago; he is diabetic and has heart disease. He has a rare lung disease that cannot be cured. His bones are so brittle that a recent coughing fit broke his hip. He has high blood pressure. His gall bladder and parathyroid gland have been removed. He has calcium deposits over large portions of his body, and horrific acne that causes an intense itch he cannot scratch. He has a brain disorder of unknown origin that often leaves him in a fog. He is depressed. His doctors describe him as a "difficult" and "manipulative" patient. The cost of his care in 1991 had exceeded one million dollars, which would be equal to about two-million 2007 dollars.

These patients are regarded as a critical challenge to Daniels' fair equality of opportunity account for two reasons. First, if these patients are provided with all the health care that they need and from which they can functionally benefit *as a matter of justice*, that yields an extraordinarily expansive set of health care services to which all in our society would have a just claim. We would come very close to regenerating the problem of the pricelessness of human life and denying the legitimacy of the "Just Caring" problem. We need a morally defensible conception of health care justice that does not do that; we need a conception of health care justice that yields *just* rationing decisions. So what are the resources of the fair equality of opportunity account that will yield that outcome with regard to these patients? This seems to be its second critical deficiency—if we seek to constrain the scope of "opportunity" to mean "economically productive" or capable of "socially useful" functionings, then we risk unjustly discriminating against persons with disabilities. That is, we would end up denying such individuals much very expensive rehabilitation services they would need. This is not a consequence that either Daniels or I would embrace. Further, patients who might be characterized as being "bottomless pits" will often elicit strong feelings of compassion. We are supposed to be a just *and caring* society. If we strive too mightily to be "just rationers" with regard to these patients, we are likely to be judged "uncaring rationers" as well.

For now I will not try to offer a reasoned response to the justice problem connected to patients characterized as being "bottomless pits." But I will sharpen the problem up just a bit. The first-year cost of providing medical and rehabilitation care for an individual who has suffered a high spinal cord injury (C1–C4) that leaves him a quadriplegic will be about $710,000; predicted lifetime medical costs for that patient will be about $2.8 million if the injury occurred around age 25. Low quadriplegia costs at age 25 will be $458,000 for the first year and $1.5 million for a lifetime (University of Alabama–Birmingham, spinal cord injury system website, 2006). I will simply assert for now that such individuals have a just claim to that level of medical care, and I believe Daniels' fair equality of opportunity account warrants that judgment. We earlier called attention to individuals who have Gaucher's disease, a metabolic disorder whose serious clinical manifestations might become evident in the late teens or early twenties. Imiglucerase is a drug that costs $300,000 per year. Individuals would have to take this drug for the rest of their life to prevent a premature death. If that permitted 30-year survival, this would be $9 million worth of care for that patient. I will again assert for now that such individuals have a just claim to that level of care, and I believe Daniels' fair equality of opportunity account would warrant that judgment as well. Should we regard these patients as being "bottomless pits"? If so, what would warrant my confident judgment about their just claims but only a very uncertain judgment in the case of Mr. H or Mr. Van Houten? We again leave this for later discussion.

We need to consider one other objection to Daniels' fair equality of opportunity account of health care justice. Segall (2007) calls attention to the fact that in the Medicare program almost 30% of total expenditures occur in the last six months of life. Medicare expenditures in 2006 were about $420 billion, which means about $130 billion for that last six months of life. What she contends is that if we take Daniels' fair equality of opportunity account seriously, we ought to deny those individuals the vast majority of that money *because there no longer are opportunities available to them that generate just claims to health care resources.* This conclusion will strike almost everyone as abhorrent, and consequently, serve as a reason for rejecting this principle as the moral justification for the claim that health care is morally special.[3] However, this objection is rooted in what (to my mind) is an ungenerous reading of Daniels.

As noted earlier, Daniels appropriated the fair equality of opportunity principle from Rawls, who uses it in connection with competition for jobs and offices. Daniels has good reason for not wanting that limited an understanding of the scope of that principle—access to needed health care is important for permitting individuals to pursue their *life plans*, whatever they might be. From the perspective of political liberalism, Daniels does not want to judge that one or another life plan is more or less worthy of health care that might be needed to pursue that life plan. One's life plan might be to be a "stay-at-home" mother, or a ski bum/surf bum, or a petty criminal, or a philosopher. Faced with a terminal illness, one's life plan might be to construct a fitting end to one's life, achieve reconciliation where needed, have final meals with friends, write letters to one's great grandchildren, et cetera. All these ordinary life activities are reasonably regarded as the sort of life opportunities that can generate presumptively just claims to needed health care if some sort of serious health problem would otherwise prevent my engaging in those activities. We should hastily add that this argument does not generate the conclusion that all $130 billion of those end-of-life Medicare dollars represent just claims. Patients who are like our case of Mr. Diaz would be justly denied access to expensive life-sustaining care by the fair equality of opportunity principle because they no longer have the capacity to carry out any life plan.

Segall (2007) raises another objection to Daniels' account as a basis for saying that health care is morally special. She calls attention to a growing literature regarding the "social determinants" of health. The central claim in that literature is that health inequalities among different population groups are more a product of income, social discrimination, education, environmental quality, job stress, and so on, than lack of access to health care services. Another way to put the point is that health care makes less of a difference in one's health status than these social determinants of health; consequently, if one wants to correct for health inequalities, then one must make broad social policy changes aimed at correcting these social determinants (Sreenivasan, 2007). The conclusion that Segall and Sreenivasan want to reach is that health care is not as morally special as Daniels and I would want to claim (nor does Daniels' fair equality of opportunity account give us the moral basis for making the policy choices that are the needed corrective). But that conclusion is too broad and too inadequately supported (Daniels, 2007).

A few quick illustrative statistics will make my point. There are 450,000 people whose lives are sustained by dialysis in the U.S. today. Over the past 30 years the death rate from cardiovascular disease has been reduced by 50%, which means *each year* in the U.S. about 700,000 people are alive today who would have been dead had cardiac medicine remained where it was in 1970. About 250,000 individuals with serious spinal cord injuries are alive today because of major advances in rehabilitation medicine that would otherwise be dead. There are several million Americans who are alive today because their cancers were detected early and treated effectively. Over the past 30 years the life expectancy of patients born with cystic fibrosis has increased on average from age 20 to age 50. Each year about 20,000 Americans die prematurely as a result of being uninsured; that is, they deny themselves or are denied by others access to what would otherwise have been timely and effective medical care. Then there are all the advances in noninvasive diagnostic technologies (CT, MRI, PET scans) that spare millions of patients each year more invasive diagnostic interventions with their risks of infection and death. These are the sorts of medical interventions Daniels and I have in mind when we assert that health care ought to be thought of as morally special, as generating issues of justice. I remind the reader that this claim does nothing more than get the discussion going about the scope of health care justice; it does not warrant the conclusion that these $100,000 cancer drugs that yield a few extra months of life are something to which every end-stage cancer patient has a just claim.

Our key conclusion from this section is that Daniels' fair equality of opportunity principle provides a reasonable basis for regarding health care in general as being morally special. In addition, when properly interpreted it identifies a comprehensive range of health care interventions to which all individuals with specific health needs would have a presumptive just claim. It also identifies some range of health services in some range of clinical circumstances that may be justly denied individuals. While this principle is useful in addressing *many* issues of health care justice related to access or limits, it does not have the capacity to address *all* the problems of health care justice endemic to our current health care system, such as the problem of justice in relation to patients characterized as being "bottomless pits." This is not a flaw in the principle that would give us reason to reject it; it is merely a limit in its utility. Its usefulness is increased when it is used in combination with other considered judgments of health care justice, generated either through careful moral argument and analysis or though legitimate processes of rational democratic deliberation. More specifically, we should regard this fair equality of opportunity principle as one of our constitutional principles of health care justice that help to demarcate the domain of non-ideal justice, the domain of rational democratic deliberation.

NON-IDEAL JUSTICE: A MORAL ANALYSIS AND DEFENSE

Moral philosophers have often been guilty of utopian thinking. Plato probably set a bad example in writing the *Republic*. Having philosophers as kings or presidents (or even mayors) is likely not a good idea—policymakers need to solve complex social problems in the real world that typically involve conflicts among multiple reasonable moral values, including conflicting concepts of justice. A capacity to compromise is essential for success in solving such problems. Many philosophers and nonphilosophers will be ill at ease, often disdainful, regarding compromise related to moral values. The thought will be that individuals willing to compromise their moral values will compromise anything. That is, they are fundamentally untrustworthy because they have no moral anchors in their lives; they are too willing to drift with the tides of values in fashion or the currents of self-serving passions. However, this is too unrealistic and too pessimistic a view of our moral capacities and our moral practices.

Martin Benjamin (1990) has persuasively argued for the notion of "integrity-preserving compromise." The premise behind this concept is that in a world of reasonable moral pluralism where there is no one dominant value that orders all other values into a single hierarchy, the capacity for moral compromise is a practical moral necessity.[4] This is the world of political liberalism, but it is also the world interior to each of us as moral agents in a morally complex world. We each wish to be able to live our lives in accord with a set of values that make our lives meaningful and meritorious. But we also recognize that we must live with others who may wish to live their lives in accord with a different set of values, or the same values prioritized differently. If we are to live peacefully with one another, then we must be mutually respectful. If we are to live at peace within ourselves when we are faced with deep moral conflict of the sort that characterizes much of health care ethics, then we are going to have to develop the capacity to be creative in balancing and accommodating and re-prioritizing such values in conflict. If we are to work with others in resolving morally complex social problems (such as our health care rationing issues)—the resolutions to which we all have to accept—then we will have to be creative in fashioning these integrity-preserving compromises. What gives such compromises *moral* integrity is that no moral values are being made subservient to purely selfish ends; rather, compromises of some values are worked out in order to protect a larger set of moral values important to the parties engaged in the compromise (and this is not accomplished at the expense of the rights of others who may not be parties to this project or this compromise).

Rawls sees himself as articulating an *ideal* theory of justice (1971) intended to be used as a critical tool for assessing the *basic structure of society*. But Rawls is very much aware of the limits of ideal theory. For purposes of assessing from a moral point of view social policies that have economic, political, organizational, technological and cultural dimensions, we will have to rely upon *non-ideal* moral theory. Rawls writes,

> In practice, we must usually choose between several unjust, or second best, arrangements; and then we look to non-ideal theory to find the least unjust scheme. Sometimes this scheme will include measures and policies that a perfectly just system would reject. Two wrongs can make a right in the sense that the best available arrangement may contain a balance of imperfections, an adjustment of compensating injustices." (1971, p. 279)

This is what I sometimes refer to as the domain of "interstitial justice" (Fleck, 1987). This phrase is intended as a contrast to the "basic structure of society."

Interstitial justice refers to all the nooks and crannies, all the intricate social spaces, in which the mundane problems of micro-justice occur. To illustrate, when Congress passed legislation that established the ESRD program for patients in kidney failure, could hemophiliacs justly complain that something comparable should have been done for them as well? We might be tempted to give this question an affirmative answer, but then that just generates the additional question of whether the uninsured had an even stronger just claim for assured access to needed health care than either renal patients or hemophiliacs. After all, the argument would go, they have *no assured access to needed health care*, whereas the hemophiliacs and renal patients might well have health insurance that covers most of their other medical needs. But then renal patients have a persistent, ongoing, life-threatening medical problem that must be treated with expensive dialysis every three days, whereas the vast majority of those without health insurance will be perfectly healthy for years at a stretch (and have no practical need for health insurance). Hence, justice would require protecting renal patients first. As for hemophiliacs, their medical problems are episodic (but chronic); in theory they can often exercise some control over their actual health risks, whereas patients in renal failure no longer have that option.

My goal is not to bring any resolution to this problem; it is simply illustrative of the kinds of justice issues that are pervasive in the interstices of our health care system. These issues are real; they do need to be addressed. But ideal moral theory will not yield any rationally compelling resolutions to these questions. Again, if we simply consider Rawls' theory of justice in its ideal form and attempt to apply it to some range of health care justice problems, we will find ourselves stymied and confused. Rawls wants to give moral priority to those who are "least well-off," but he also wants to protect fair equality of opportunity (as Daniels has interpreted this principle in a health care context). Mr. H and Mr. Van Houten would certainly be among those who are least well-off health-wise. A familiar statistic is that 52% of all health dollars spent in the U.S. (about $1.1 trillion in 2006) was spent on the 5% of patients who were the sickest, the least well-off as far as health care was concerned. But a clear consequence of that pattern of expenditures is a steady increase in the number of uninsured (about 47 million individuals in 2007) due primarily to low-wage employers dropping health care as a benefit as a result of steep increasing costs. If we were to undertake major health reform in the U.S. aimed at covering everyone with a reasonably comprehensive package of health benefits, it is doubtful we could continue to spend 52% of our health care dollars on that 5% of patients who are least well-off health-wise. We would have undertaken such reform in order to better meet our obligations under the fair equality of opportunity principle. Would that outcome be unjust, or is the current state of affairs unjust? Is it possible for us to fairly compare these two states of affairs? We obviously would not cut off access to needed health care entirely for those 5% who are least well-off. We might readily imagine identifying multiple subcategories of patients who were least well-off with the intention of continuing to provide care to some but denying it to others. What would be the resources of Rawls' ideal theory of justice that would allow us to make any of these decisions fairly? The short answer is that those resources are not there; we have to settle for outcomes that are non-ideally just or "just enough."

A word of caution is in order at this point. If the best we can realistically hope for is "rough justice," then it must nevertheless be rationally justified "rough justice." If we borrow a phrase from Martin Benjamin (2001), then it must be "integrity-preserving" rough justice. Otherwise we might be tempted to think that if ideal justice is unattainable, then any sort of rough justice at all would be as morally defensible as any other sort of rough justice in specific circumstances. A belief such as that would permit professional or societal power-holders to impose their arbitrary or self-serving will on others under the morally respectable guise of rough justice.

To illustrate our key point above, imagine a 10-bed ICU that is filled with patients. Two more patients are "at the door" after surgery for major trauma; both clearly need an ICU bed to assure their survival. Any patient discharged will be at substantially increased risk of premature death; none of these patients would be expected to die if they had access to the ICU for as long as their medical conditions required. We can imagine a broad age range (31–76 years old), and a complex range of medical circumstances that got them there in the first place, including one drunk driver and one smoker with a 30-year history. The ICU director must discharge two patients. What should we regard as a "just enough" procedure for discharging those patients?

I can think of a half-dozen options very quickly. Our ICU director decides to discharge the drunk driver because he cannot imagine more socially irresponsible behavior. He imagines that if that individual were to survive, he would likely end up killing someone else. He also discharges the 44-year-old patient with no health insurance and no likely capacity to pay for his care. His thought in that case is that paying patients yield the resources the hospital needs to compete for patients with neighboring hospitals, and since another patient needs to be discharged, it might as well be a nonpaying patient. This is a perfect example of what is *not* a matter of integrity-preserving rough justice—the reasons motivating this choice are arbitrary and self-serving; they are not justice-relevant. The two patients selected for discharge could "reasonably reject" (Scanlon, 1998) these reasons as being unfair and insufficiently justifying their being chosen for discharge.[5]

The ICU director could have chosen to use a lottery instead to remove those two patients, which would be respectful of the equal moral worth of each of the twelve patients. The ICU director could have discharged the two oldest patients, judging that they already had had the opportunity to live a full life. Or the ICU director could have discharged the two patients about whom we were most medically confident that they would have the shortest life expectancies, even if they had the opportunity for a maximal stay in the ICU (the moral appeal being to a utilitarian rule of saving the most life-years). I want to assume for the sake of argument that all three of these proposals have sufficient moral reasonableness about them that any one of them could yield an outcome that was "roughly just." This may look like the end of our discussion, but I will argue it is not.

Imagine that the ICU "day" director would be inclined to resolve the issue via a lottery, whereas the ICU "night" director would be more inclined to rely upon the age criteria. If there is conflict between them on such matters—say, when shifts are changing—then the medical director of the entire hospital intervenes and employs our utilitarian method. From the point of view of patients in this ICU, should they regard this as an acceptable form of rough justice, the outcome of which they could not reasonably reject (because we had stipulated that each of these principles could yield a roughly just outcome)?

I am inclined to view this situation as lacking "justice-preserving integrity," and consequently, these patients (assuming they were aware of the entire situation) would have good reason to reject the outcome of the application of any one of these principles. What is needed as a moral corrective to this situation would be a process of rational democratic deliberation, accessible to the future possible patients in the catchments area of this hospital. The deliberative process would be aimed at identifying the justice-relevant principles and criteria that these future possible patients would regard as being "just enough" bases for removing excess patients prematurely from the ICU.

What I want to call special attention to is that these deliberators could choose *any one* of the three principles we proposed above, and *now* that principle would yield an outcome that was "just enough" and that no longer was "reasonably rejectable" by any patients who might see themselves as being adversely affected by it in the future. The deliberators might also come up with a more creative and more complex and "more just" resolution (as judged by themselves) than anything I have offered here. Assuming the deliberative process has not been manipulated in some way to yield a predetermined selfish end, what makes this process an example of integrity-preserving justice is that (1) it is public; (2) participants are there as uncoerced free and equal deliberators; (3) participants can effectively deliberate in a suitably impartial spirit because they are all roughly ignorant of their future possible circumstances in an ICU; (4) participants can restrict themselves to giving only *public reasons* for their advocating one resolution rather than another; and (5) participants can recognize that they are imposing these rationing protocols on their future possible selves, which they can regard as being preferable to having these protocols imposed in arbitrary ways by others as described above.

What precisely is it that would give this deliberative process some presumptive moral legitimacy and moral preferability to alternative ways of achieving a resolution? First, there are several moral decision procedures (rules) that could be reasonably used to remove excess patients from the ICU. None of these decision procedures are deeply morally flawed; that is, none of them violate a moral rule that ought virtually never to be violated.[6]

Second, these decision rules are not morally ideal in that reasonable objections could be raised about the justness of the outcomes (actual or likely) of any one of these decision procedures. Thus, if we embrace the use of a lottery to convey equal moral respect for each patient, then the murderer/rapist patient might be saved and the crusading social activist might be put at risk of premature death.

But, third, we have no alternative realistic decision procedure that would yield a perfectly just outcome each and every time we were faced with the excess patients in the ICU problem. And, fourth, we cannot randomly choose among the non-ideal available decision procedures because they do yield very different predictable outcomes. But, fifth, no moral or philosophic argument can be made that would demonstrate that one or another of these decision procedures was unequivocally morally superior to the others. Still, sixth, future possible patients would not judge it fair or reasonable that the particular decision procedure invoked when faced with an actual shortage of ICU beds would be determined by the whims or biases of a particular ICU director, hospital medical director, or hospital administrator. Protecting fairness would generally require stability and predictability with regard to the application of a rule, especially if that rule could have life or death consequences.

Seventh, if a fair and rational democratic deliberative process were used to choose one of these decision procedures, then the outcome would have the legitimacy and justness and stability that would be required. What would justify our confidence in obtaining this outcome?

First, the participants in the deliberative process would be future possible patients in an ICU. They would be behind an effective "veil of ignorance" which would assure their *impartiality* in the deliberative process. They would not know their age as future possible ICU patients; they would not know the medical circumstances that required ICU care; they would not know how much ICU care they might need, what the probability of success of that care might be, or what the length of their survival might be after discharge from the ICU. But, like Rawlsian deliberators, they would have considerable knowledge about the range of medical possibilities that could be their fate.

Second, under these circumstances it is difficult to imagine what sorts of ideological biases or matters of self-interest could corrupt the deliberative process.

Reflective deliberators would realize that such considerations were likely contrary to their rational best interests. Imagine, for example, a Roman Catholic right-to-life deliberator faced with the question of whether a PVS patient in the ICU with a serious cardiac problem ought to be first discharged from the ICU. He might imagine himself as that patient; and he might initially believe, for ideological reasons, that such patients had an equal right to life best protected by using a lottery to discharge excess patients from the ICU. But he would be reminded that he also ought to imagine himself as a 48-year-old patient (with four young children) in that ICU with a life-threatening cardiac problem likely ameliorable with a future life expectancy of 20 years. Does he *really* want to give those two versions of his self an equal chance of surviving that ICU stay? And what if the PVS patient in one of those scenarios is a committed atheist?

That brings us to our third point: The deliberative process would proceed through the giving of relevant public reasons for choosing one decision procedure rather than another. Deliberators would be motivated to choose (construct) whatever decision procedure would protect their rational best interests. They might be initially strongly inclined to favor one decision procedure over another, but they would realize that it would be imprudent not to consider fair-mindedly what they might learn from others regarding their reasons for favoring an alternate decision procedure. The goal of the deliberative process is to get an outcome that is reasonably fair. No outcome will be perfectly fair; no outcome is likely to command unanimous support. But if an outcome is not open to reasonable rejection by anyone, then that outcome will be "just enough."

To illustrate this last point, imagine that some of the deliberators are strong egalitarians by philosophic disposition; they believe a lottery is the fairest way of removing excess patients from the ICU. But 80% of the deliberators have agreed to a decision procedure that reflects more of a utilitarian perspective than anything else. What they have agreed is that the individuals who have the highest probability of only very short survival outside the ICU are the individuals who should be discharged from the ICU. In other words, these are individuals for whom ICU care is providing no more than a marginal benefit. Is this an outcome that strong egalitarians can reasonably reject? My short answer is that they cannot. In another deliberative context with another rationing problem, that strong egalitarian perspective might well prevail. In *this* context it did not prevail. The practical question that needs to be asked is whether the substantive rights or interests of these strong egalitarians (or others in the deliberative group whose interests they hoped to protect) would be harmed by the decision procedure that was affirmed through the deliberative process. If that were true, then that outcome would be reasonably rejectable by them.

However, the strong egalitarians would have just as much a chance of being dismissed from the ICU as any of those deliberators who supported the utilitarian decision procedure, and they would have just as much a chance of benefiting from that decision procedure. By hypothesis (and in the real world as well the vast majority of time), all are more or less equally ignorant of their future possible health needs regarding ICU care. The strong egalitarians might have special concerns about persons with disabilities; they may be concerned that those individuals would be strongly disadvantaged (discriminated against) by this decision procedure. However, it is not as if it is the case that deliberators would have failed to consider that any of themselves might suffer some accident or illness that would leave them in a permanently disabled condition, and that disability might increase the probability that they would be among those discharged from the ICU. If all among the deliberators are more or less vulnerable to that happening, then an outcome such as that would be unfortunate, but not unjust. Consequently, this too would not yield a reasonable basis for rejecting the outcome of the deliberative process.

Another objection might be raised, very different from this first. A deliberator might say that the "real problem" is the shortage of ICU beds. If this is a recurring problem, then more ICU beds need to be constructed as opposed to throwing needy patients out of the ICU and putting them at risk of dying prematurely. The objection might continue that the "real injustice" is this shortage of beds, and further, that a deliberative process aimed at adapting to this bed shortage is perpetuating this unjust state of affairs. A couple responses might be offered to this latter objection which will help to further delineate the domain of non-ideal justice.

The concept we need to introduce is that of a "problem/decision sphere." This is a pragmatic, highly relativized notion. A problem/decision sphere will be defined by what is manageable, given a host of political, economic, organizational, normative, and technological constraints peculiar to that problem. Problem/decision spheres are not metaphysical parts of the world in the way that atoms are part of the world; problem/decision spheres need to have their boundaries fashioned by social and political actors sensitive to both pragmatic and normative considerations.

What I want to emphasize for our purposes is that these problem/decision spheres and the justice issues attached to them are *highly localized and very practical in nature*. The demand for ICU beds can vary considerably from day to day. Maybe we ought to have more ICU beds built in our region; maybe physicians need to make more discriminating judgments with regard to which patients *really need* an ICU bed and which patients are just marginally safer if they have an ICU bed. Maybe physicians need to be more directive with families who have very unrealistic hopes for recovery of their loved ones in the ICU, where aggressive life-sustaining care may be doing more harm than good by prolonging a process of dying. Maybe that lack of physician courage is fueling the demand for extra ICU beds. Maybe ICU beds are very profitable beds from the perspective of a hospital administrator, as long as those beds can be filled with paying patients. Maybe from the perspective of that administrator additional ICU beds make life easier for both pusillanimous physicians and persistently petulant families. But if those additional ICU beds primarily support extraordinarily expensive marginal benefits for those patients (or worse, painful prolongations of life beneficial only to others besides the patient), then there are serious problems of justice (and compassion) with having what are really excess ICU beds.

Having said all that, I need to bring the reader back to our original problem: too many patients and too few ICU beds. That is the localized, practical problem of justice we are faced with today (and that we [local hospitals] are likely to be faced with multiple times over the course of a year). There may or may not be a larger problem of justice associated with these ICU beds that deserves our attention as well. There may be very large system problems that are generating excess demands for ICU beds and creating serious problems of justice (maybe an excess number of medical specialists who are demanding ICU beds for their patients, thereby skewing inappropriately the allocation of limited medical resources). These larger problems may need to be bracketed for purposes of addressing fairly the immediate practical justice issue of having too few beds for too many ICU patients.

Non-ideal justice theory presupposes that it is reasonable and morally permissible to do this bracketing for purposes of direct action, in order to achieve an incremental improvement in the justness of the social practices that constitute the problem sphere under consideration. In other words, if current ICU practice is to allow individual ICU directors to decide which patients must exit the ICU when there is a bed shortage, and if those directors have only their own very vague criteria as a basis for those decisions, then patients would have little reason to believe they are being treated fairly; worse, they would have no clear public reference points for challenging the fairness of any such decision. Having a democratic deliberative process among future possible ICU patients that generates rationing criteria for those limited ICU beds that those patients would find to be "just enough" looks like a morally preferable state of affairs compared to that prior state of affairs. That outcome can be achieved for that problem/decision sphere without necessarily having to address the much larger problems of justice that might be there in the background, that might well have "a bearing" on the current justice issue, but that may be beyond our capacity to address effectively in anything less than a multiyear period of time.

We assume (though this is a defeasible presumption) that these incremental, contextual improvements are not brought about at the cost of increased injustice elsewhere in the social system. That is, we assume in this contextual mode that we are not just adapting to (and rendering more stable) injustices in the larger health care system that ought to be resisted and reformed; this is something to which we must always be sensitive. Still, it will often be the case that these incremental contextual improvements are all that is practically attainable, given constraints that (for the present) are too deeply entrenched.

We should emphasize that it would be utopian (badly misguided) if we were to risk giving up non-ideal justice theory. What we would be risking is being without any moral guidance at all in these interstitial situations that require justice judgments. There is nothing morally compelling about that possibility. The only alternative is to appeal to some sort of ideal theory of justice. But such theories tend to be gross instruments for dealing sensitively with micro-social issues. If we take seriously the demands of ideal justice theory, then we risk always having to advocate for revolutionary change in order to solve "justly enough" any social problem. This would make moral heroism morally obligatory. The alternative to moral heroism is an ineffective pseudo-heroism—better known as pious posturing—maintaining clean hands and a clean conscience by failing to engage in the difficult moral struggles and moral compromises required by the problems of our complex social life and a complex health care system. I find little that is morally commendable in that alternative.

Let me now make explicit another essential feature of interstitial justice, what I shall refer to as the "moral worth of meliorism" thesis. What meliorism amounts to is the claim that we have done something morally commendable if, in any given problem/decision sphere, we can bring about a more just state of affairs, all things considered, even though this state of affairs will fall far short of what might be required by ideal justice theory. This provides us with an internal reference point, relative to which we can measure internal socio-moral progress. This has considerable practical utility in that it prevents deliberate backsliding in matters of health care justice that might otherwise be excused by arguing that we still have an outcome that is "roughly just." It is also useful in prodding reformers not to settle prematurely and lackadaisically for very minor improvements with regard to specific health care injustices, when greater gains are reasonable and achievable with extra effort.

Meliorism implies that it makes sense to speak of states of affairs as being "more just" or "less just" relative to one another. In this regard I find myself dissatisfied a bit with a passage I earlier quoted from Rawls aimed at characterizing the circumstances of non-ideal justice, when he says that in practice we are usually confronted with having to choose among several "unjust" options. I am certain the practices of slavery as well as the Nazi's treatment of the Jews and other ethnic groups are unqualifiedly unjust. But if we were to put in place a universal health care plan in the U.S., and if (to control total costs) we put in place a rationing protocol that limited access to statins at public expense to those with total cholesterol above 240, or that limited access to ICDs to those patients whose T-wave alternans test results indicated a relative need for an ICD, then would those who had been denied these resources at plan expense be justified in saying they had been treated unjustly because they were going to be bearing some (small) additional risk of premature death that these other patients were spared?

We can imagine that these particular rationing protocols were a product of a fair process of rational democratic deliberation that all could participate in who might be potentially affected by the outcome. If so, these rationing protocols would seem to be "just enough." Still, we can imagine individuals with a cholesterol level of 200 saying they had paid scrupulous attention to diet and exercise, that they had a genotype that left them stuck at this higher cholesterol level, and that lots of other individuals were indolent and irresponsible in matters of diet and exercise, which is why they had high cholesterol levels. Now they were being "rewarded" for their irresponsible behavior with free access to statins, and *this was unfair*. Again, for now we ignore the substance of this claim simply to call attention to the fact that there can be in matters of health care justice several conflicting (but reasonable) concepts of justice that prevent us from asserting with absolute confidence that a particular rationing decision is just or unjust (in the way we can in assessing the behavior of the Nazis).

In the domain of non-ideal justice there are two tendencies that need to be assiduously monitored: complacency and instability. If we consider the situation described in the prior paragraph again, do we have the moral right to be complacent and to ignore the complaints of citizens with cholesterol levels of 200 (our contention being that the rationing protocols we have put in place are "just enough")? Or must we take seriously their complaints about the irresponsible health behaviors of other citizens/plan members and substantially revise the relevant rationing protocols to somehow take into account the relative degree to which individuals have been responsible managers of their own health? The large problem is this: If outcomes in the domain of non-ideal justice are always less than perfectly just, always inclusive of elements that might be regarded as unjust in some respects, then we have reason for wanting to reform that state of affairs. But "constant reform" would suggest "constant instability"—justice requires stability over reasonable periods of time, especially if specific rationing protocols now require sacrifices on my part with the expectation that there will be compensating benefits some number of years in the future.

In the final analysis, the problem of instability in a non-ideal context may be more manageable than this abstract presentation of the issue suggests. For any *one* rationing protocol approved through a fair, democratic, deliberative process it might appear that there are some clear "winners" and some clear "losers" (individuals who seem to have secured some benefits and others who secured more burdens and risks). But the larger system of rationing protocols (if fairly constructed through the deliberative process) may distribute those risks and benefits in a more balanced way.

What needs to be kept vividly in mind is that the outcome of a fair, democratic, deliberative process will be rational protocols with a *hypothetical* mix of risks and benefits for any particular individual. The deliberators are to a large extent behind a veil of ignorance so far as their future health needs and vulnerabilities are concerned. They agreed to the rationing protocols they did on the basis of largely statistical information about a general distribution of risks regarding any particular medical circumstance. So in the early stages of implementing those rationing protocols, virtually no one would have a strong rational basis for objecting to the entire set of rationing protocols.

As time passes and individuals are afflicted with different illnesses or are victims of accidents, the practical implications of specific rationing protocols will be actualized for them. A likely common pattern (assuming a universal health plan in the U.S.) is that in the early stages of a chronic degenerative disorder, individuals will have maximal access to a broad range of effective interventions that will allow individuals to cope effectively with what otherwise might have been debilitating symptoms of their chronic illness. (This would be in marked contrast to the current haphazard and uncertain access that most individuals currently have through private health plans.) In the mid-stages of that chronic disease process, individuals would continue to enjoy the now more costly benefits of a technologically advanced health care system. These interventions would continue to sustain to a large extent the functionality and quality of life of individuals with this disorder (though there will obviously be some variation due to biological differences among individuals). What is most morally noteworthy is that all individuals with this specific disorder would have access to all these ameliorative interventions; what all will have given up is secure access to the most costly and least beneficial interventions aimed primarily at prolonging life in the end stages of that disease process. That is, all will have given up those interventions at public expense, though some might have the private capacity to afford those interventions.

That some might be able to afford these marginal interventions might well generate "feelings of injustice" on the part of those who cannot afford those interventions, but those feelings do not amount to "just claims" that would justify calls for "reform" of the rationing protocols that put those limitations in place. It would be unfortunate under these circumstances that some of these individuals would have failed to achieve a normal life expectancy, but it would not be unjust. They in fact benefited to a much greater degree than would otherwise have been the case under the prior health care system; they also benefited in part because other plan members (who have already died from this disease) respected the cooperative agreements regarding these rationing protocols that permitted the reallocation of resources more generously to earlier stages in the disease process (where much more health good could be accomplished for all those patients). Given this background, individuals now faced with the harsher consequences of these rationing protocols would have no justification for demanding the revising of these rationing protocols. In this respect, the overall stability and fairness of the system is preserved.

We discuss below a number of other structural and methodological features of rational democratic deliberation in this non-ideal domain that preserve the stability of the internal morality (fairness) of the process. But the other threat to the stability of the process is from without. This requires some brief introductory comment, mostly to identify the nature and scope of the problem.

As noted already, emerging medical technologies (more than anything else) contribute to the problem of escalating health care costs and the moral problem of creating and sustaining just rationing protocols. This is going to create an especially painful problem when combined with the demographic challenges posed by the post–World War II "baby bulge." Our problem begins with the creation of the Medicare program in 1965. No doubt this program represented a more just response to the health needs of the elderly than reliance on families and private insurance to meet their needs. The elderly were at a stage in their lives where they had multiple health needs. Insurers at the time were either unwilling to offer them insurance at all or to offer them insurance they could not afford; creating Medicare provided a fair and effective way of meeting those health needs. The technology boom was barely a flicker at the time; no one had serious concerns about the ultimate affordability of the program.

But as the new technologies were disseminated—often with the goal of preventing premature death and disability in relatively younger portions of the population—nothing could prevent these technologies from being accessed by the elderly, where a proportionally greater degree of the burden of disease was concentrated. Further, with the Medicare program they had the financial means for affording these new technologies. Further still, compelling moral considerations required their having this access; the elderly were entitled to as much in the way of equal concern and respect as the non-elderly in our society. Heart disease is heart disease is heart disease, whether in the elderly or non-elderly. If the non-elderly are entitled to $3,000 drug-eluting stents as part of their angioplasty to open clogged arteries, then so are the elderly. This goes a long way to explaining how we managed to do 1.2 million angioplasties in the U.S. in 2006 at an average cost of about $35,000 (or $40 billion in the aggregate).

As noted already, roughly 3.5 times more dollars are spent per person for health care for the elderly as opposed to the non-elderly. In 1987 the cost of the Medicare program to the federal government was about $82 billion; that cost increased by 500% to $420 billion in 2006 (Borger et al., 2006). We justify (accept as reasonable) these costs because the elderly have so many more health needs compared to the non-elderly. However, as Callahan (1990) reminds us, there is that very intimate connection between what we come to regard as health needs and whatever new medical technologies have emerged in the marketplace. Callahan also reminds us of the "ragged edge" problem: Few medical interventions are *equally effective* for all who have the same medical problem. Thus, we are confident of the reasonableness (moral and medical) of an intervention that costs $100,000 but yields five extra years of life for a majority of patients. But that confidence gets wobbly when a significant minority of patients gains only five extra months of life for that same $100,000 intervention (and this is predictable at the time the intervention is offered). And there are multiple degrees of effectiveness in-between, often (not always) related to advanced age and comorbidities. Yet we are pulled in the direction of funding this intervention for all who can benefit to any degree at all, primarily because we believe fair treatment requires equal treatment for all with the same medical problem.

This last paragraph suggests that the elderly benefit only marginally from many costly life-prolonging technologies. That is a small truth at best. The larger (and more morally problematic) truth is that the elderly have benefited substantially from these technologies with increased life expectancy. But none of these interventions are curative—elderly individuals are living longer with their heart disease and their cancer and their diabetes and their lung disease. Consequently, the aggregate burden of chronic illness has increased dramatically among the elderly, which means greatly prolonged periods of costly medical dependency (still of reasonable quality), but giving rise to later much debilitated periods of medical dependency. Thus, current predictions are that we will see in the U.S. a quadrupling of the Alzheimer's population between now and 2030, from roughly 4 million to 16 million individuals.

Here is the problem to which I need to draw the reader's attention: If we think about all the costly new medical technologies introduced into the health care system over the past 40 years *one at a time,* we would find in each case that the elderly had a presumptively just claim to access that technology (and they had the resources for effective access because they had the Medicare program). But the consequence of adding up each of these just claims is an aggregate outcome that may be seriously unjust (because of the injustices that it produces elsewhere in our health care system).[7] To be more precise, Medicare is competing for federal dollars with the Medicaid program. The competition is intense because of the pressures for cost control exerted by the federal deficit and taxpayers (who do not want to pay more taxes). Medicare is in a politically much stronger position to capture those dollars than Medicaid. (The elderly are effective and well organized as a special interest group compared to the poor.) Though a significant portion of the elderly are relatively poor, a large majority are relatively financially well-off. The elderly clearly have greater health needs as a group, which establishes a presumptive just claim to the needed resources, but the poor who depend upon Medicaid have considerable unmet health needs that ought to generate just claims to the needed resources. On average, they are a lot less well-off (in many respects) than the elderly; the same will be largely true for the uninsured working poor.

From the perspective of a moderately egalitarian theory of health care justice (which would include Daniels' fair equality of opportunity account), there are some serious injustices here. More resources ought to be reallocated to meeting the health care needs of the poor and uninsured, but one practical obstacle is the fact that health insurance is tied to employment in the U.S., which means employers deny any responsibility for meeting the health care needs of the poor and uninsured. Maybe a case could be made for saying that fewer health care resources should be flowing into the Medicare program. But that would require taking resources away from Medicare beneficiaries to which they had just claims. What would we imagine the justice-based arguments would be that would yield this outcome? This situation has the appearance of requiring that we perpetrate injustices on the elderly in order to correct injustices currently endured by the poor and uninsured. Is this a trade-off that ought to be warranted by fair procedures of non-ideal justice? How would we avoid the charge of ageism—unjust discrimination against the elderly?

We cannot address these challenges just now. We simply wanted to illustrate how nonmoral factors in combination with reasonable considered judgments of health care justice can destabilize a non-ideally just moral equilibrium. Again, this is not a situation that will be rectified simply through more careful moral argument and analysis, or through a more studious application of well recognized principles of health care justice. Instead, resolution will require the skillful use of a process of rational democratic deliberation.

PLURALISM, JUSTICE, AND RATIONAL DEMOCRATIC DELIBERATION

I need to begin with an argument that justifies my claim that we need a pluralistic account of health care justice to address effectively the very complex problems of health care justice in our health care system. This will be a practical argument rather than a theoretical argument. It would take us too far afield (and ultimately lack persuasive power) to try to justify or critically undermine one or another theory of health care justice. I take it that one reason why these competing theories have some degree of staying power is that they do provide reasonable moral guidance with respect to *some range* of practical problems (as we shall see). But their philosophic advocates tend not to be satisfied with these modest pragmatic accomplishments, and, having excessively consumed intoxicating Hegelian spirits from the nineteenth century, now believe their favored theory has the capacity to conquer and rule the entire domain of morality. What we will show, however, is that all these competing theories fail to address well some range of practical moral problems that are better addressed by a competitor theory—this is why we should embrace a respectful pluralism regarding our concept of health care justice.

If we wish, we might imagine that each of these theories has "its territory" where it yields morally reliable and reasonable judgments. But there will be contested boundaries, primarily where novel moral problems erupt as a result of changing social, political, economic, or technological forces. It made no sense in 1960 to ask whether it was morally permissible for one individual to pay another to sell a kidney or a portion of their liver in order for that first individual to avoid imminent death—we did not have the medical technology that would make such a transaction possible, but we do have that technology today. And the question has both urgency and saliency today because of the shortage of major organs for transplants available from donors. Should such transactions be protected as a matter of just liberty by the state? Or should they be forbidden by law as unjust exploitation of the less well-off for the benefit of those already very well-off? There are boundary issues that must be addressed *as a practical matter*, which is to suggest that waiting for a theoretical resolution to be reached by philosophers several decades from now is not an option.

Those who are likely to be my staunchest critics will be libertarians, such as Engelhardt (1996), who are opposed to any conception of health care justice that they see as being foisted upon individuals through public policy. Engelhardt, who is a master of rhetorical excess, writes:

> The imposition of a single-tier, all-encompassing health care system is morally unjustifiable. It is a coercive act of totalitarian ideological zeal, which fails to recognize the diversity of moral visions that frame interests in health care, the secular moral limits of state authority, and the authority of individuals over themselves and their own property. It is an act of secular immorality. (Engelhardt, 1996, p. 375)

Though Engelhardt refers in this passage to a "single-tier, all-encompassing" health care system, he makes clear in later passages that no one in our society has a just claim to even minimally decent health care unless they can pay for it or unless it is given to them as a matter of pure charity. Engelhardt is a strong defender of the minimalist state, which means that the role of the state is essentially restricted to its police powers in preventing individuals from using violence or fraud against one another, to protect persons and their property from unconsented interference by others. For Engelhardt there are no positive rights or welfare rights to anything that must be provided by the state. One might acquire a right to something only through contracts that are freely entered into. Thus, for Engelhardt it would be unjust for the state to require physicians to provide their services to the poor or the elderly for fees that were below whatever a free market might permit them to charge for their services. He would see this as an unjust seizure of their property (medical skills).

The philosophic underpinnings of Engelhardt's view are what he refers to as the limits of state authority and the limits of reason. He writes that

> it does not appear possible by sound rational argument to choose among the numerous competing accounts of morality, justice, and fairness without begging

the question, arguing in a circle, or engaging in an infinite regress. The ground for this state of affairs lies in the circumstance that the disputants are usually separated by different basic moral premises and rules of moral evidence. (2007, p. 260).

The practical implication of this view is that the state would have no right to incorporate any of these contested conceptions of justice into public policies that the state could coercively enforce. Engelhardt concludes, "Given the limits of human moral rationality, one will start with persons and their property as givens" (2007, p. 262). In other words, it is legitimate for the state to protect persons and their property. We note in passing that this last quoted passage includes a long footnote reference appealing to the authority (and rational brilliance) of Hegel as support for this view.

Engelhardt's view may be fairly characterized as a type of philosophic skepticism—that is what the "limits of reason" thesis is about. But it is philosophically odd that Engelhardt should be so skeptical about the rational foundations of the views of others, but so rationally confident about the foundations of his own views. How is it that reason would be so inept in the hands of others but so powerful in his hands? Engelhardt clearly judges that the views regarding justice of Rawls, Scanlon and Dworkin (to name a few defenders of moderately egalitarians conceptions of social justice) are not rationally well-founded. He dismisses them all because they all permit to some degree redistributive policies that violate (in his mind) the liberty rights/property rights of wealthier members of society, as if those property rights were sacred, divinely ordained rights that only the impious and arrogant would dare to tamper with. He mocks philosophers, who appeal to the Divine Will as the foundation for their moral norms, while at the same time asserting that property and property rights are "given" (apparently through the magisterium of the Absolute Spirit, since no further argument is offered for this foundational claim).

However, the fact of the matter is that there is no "property" in nature (as a given), nor are there health care systems in nature—property is created through the state and through public policy. Our concept of property has evolved considerably over the past 200 years, largely in response to changing social, economic, and technological circumstances. Engelhardt (and other libertarians) see property as an extension of the person and that person's liberty. Possessing property (land and tools) in the eighteenth century meant that individuals could be self-reliant and could express their liberty as they wished with regard to their property. If their property could be seized by others (including the state), then this was a direct violation of the person. This represented a taking of the liberties that made that person a person. This involved treating that person as a thing who could be used for the purposes of another. The Industrial Revolution and Agricultural Revolution changed all that; productive property became increasingly concentrated in the hands of a few, so that the vast majority of individuals had only their own labor to sell. They had little bargaining power, and consequently, they became wage slaves, to use Marx's phrase. Their effective liberty was profoundly diminished, yet libertarians would staunchly defend the liberty rights of capitalists, all the while failing to protect the lost liberty rights of workers.

A comparable revolution occurred in medicine. In that case, however, the liberty right to practice medicine on whomever freely agreed to be a patient for that individual was taken away from all. Monopolistic control to practice medicine was invested by the state in the medical profession. What justified (at least pragmatically) this restriction of individual liberty was a public interest in preventing harm to individuals who would not be able to assess the knowledge or skill levels of individuals who claimed to be medical practitioners. More generally, a public interest is an interest that each and every one of us has, but that we as individuals (or as groups of individuals) could not adequately protect or advance without the coercive and coordinating powers of the state. Thus, through the use of fair and open democratic procedures we invest the state with the authority to create public policies that will protect those public interests.

A large number of regulatory policies imposed by the state are justified through an appeal to such public interests; this would include policies outlawing child labor, fair labor standards, a broad range of environmental policies, and the work of the Food and Drug Administration. In all these cases the liberty rights/property rights of some individuals are constrained in order to protect these public interests. No doubt Engelhardt would object to these state-imposed restraints. But does he have any good reasons for objecting, as opposed to ideological zeal? No.

We return to Engelhardt's insistence on the limits of reason. Those limits are supposed to restrain the ideological totalizing impulses of reason by supporting a skeptical attitude toward all such efforts. But Engelhardt's libertarianism is just as much a matter of ideological totalizing as any other comprehensive philosophic theory, and consequently, ought to be subjected to the same skeptical appraisal. The value of individual liberty is given a place of moral and political supremacy over all other values. Engelhardt might insist that this is the precise opposite of what he has in mind when he rejects totalizing theories; everyone is free from unconsented interference by others. But that is a pure *theoretical* belief. In reality, individuals who have amassed substantial wealth and property have been able to effectively impose their will on others, thereby rendering their liberty no more than a theoretical abstraction. Ideological zeal is what blinds individuals to certain moral and political and economic facts.

As noted already, we have made huge public investments in creating our health care system, most especially in the training of physicians. These investments were justified because they satisfied a public interest that otherwise would have languished. For individuals to appropriate those public investments and treat them as pure private property, which they are entirely free to use as they please for their own private benefit, is to exploit the working poor and uninsured who contributed through their taxes to the creation of this system. The working poor and uninsured that are denied effective access to needed health care because they lack the ability to pay for that care have been denied effective equality of opportunity—that is, they have been denied effective liberty. If they suffer permanent disability or the risk of premature death as a result of being denied access to needed health care, it is doubtful they will take comfort in being told by Engelhardt that they are indeed fortunate because they have been spared "a coercive act of totalitarian ideological zeal" associated with the imposition upon them of a single-tier, all-encompassing health care system (as in Canada).[8]

We can take seriously Engelhardt's "limits of reason" thesis. What follows from that? Must we be libertarians? Must we be entirely without a moral rudder in our political life? The Rawls of *Political Liberalism* (1993) would give a negative answer to both these questions (and so do I). Rawls has more confidence in what he refers to as "public reason." Rawls writes,

> Public reason is characteristic of a democratic people: it is the reason of its citizens, of those sharing the status of equal citizenship. The subject of their reason is the good of the public: what the political conception of justice requires of society's basic structure of institutions, and of the purposes and ends they are to serve. (1993, at 213)

What public reason avoids is any commitment to any particular comprehensive philosophic doctrine. Public reason makes no appeal for justificatory purposes to any ultimate truths, whether moral or metaphysical. Public reason deals with retail truths, fallible truths, always subject to revision in the light of future evidence. Public reason deals with only retail moral judgments, considered moral judgments that are typically contextually bound. Public reason is fundamentally pluralistic in the matter of public values. No single value will be supreme, nor will there be some single hierarchy of rationally preferred values. Values will constantly have to be balanced in relation to one another and in relation to the reasonable goals of a specific public policy. This balancing process will be both rational and reasonable, relying upon both the method of wide reflective equilibrium and processes of rational democratic deliberation among free and equal citizens. Through such processes, public reason itself will be refined and enhanced (contrary to the moral pessimism of Engelhardt).

I now want to turn to assessing succinctly the moral strengths and moral limitations of these major conceptions of health care justice; the focus will be more practical than theoretical. The goal will be to justify the claim that we ought to embrace a pluralistic conception of health care justice, especially with reference to rational democratic deliberation in a non-ideal context. What we want to show is that each of the major conceptions of health care justice has fruitful applicability. But each of them, if used exclusively to address the *entire* range of problems of justice in our health care system, will yield outcomes that all but the ideologically blinkered will recognize as being unreasonable or unjust.

Libertarians will resist any claim that there are justice-based social obligations to assure access to needed health care for anyone. I will posit for the sake of argument that this position can be consistently defended (nothing internally inconsistent about this view). Nevertheless, it is impossible to imagine any libertarian who is not a pure intellect accepting the *practical* consequences of this view for themselves or anyone they care about. How many libertarians would accept the risk of death for their children when they (as parents) lose health insurance because they lost their job as a result of an enterprising capitalist shipping those jobs to another country? Think of all the childhood illnesses that are not preventable but that are treatable at great expense, such as serious asthma, or cystic fibrosis, or congenital heart defects, or childhood cancers, and so forth. Or imagine a well-insured middle-class libertarian in the earliest stages of recovery in an ICU for a massive heart attack. But ICU beds are scarce at the moment, and a wealthy libertarian with a serious heart attack offers the hospital ten times the normal rate for that ICU bed now occupied by the middle-class libertarian. From a libertarian perspective the hospital is free to take that offer and transfer the middle-class libertarian to a regular hospital bed where his risk of non-survival will be quadrupled. One might desperately hope for reputational reasons that a hospital would never do such a thing, but from the perspective of libertarian theory nothing prevents the hospital from so acting. The patient does not own the bed; the patient does not even have a contract to "rent" the bed for any specific period of time. Everything depends upon the free choices of the doctors and the hospital. Would middle-class libertarians chose a libertarian basic structure for society from behind the veil of ignorance if the above states of affairs would have to be accepted as just outcomes?[9]

Apropos to this scenario, Allen Buchanan (1998) has made an interesting argument. He notes the frequency with which middle-class patients in managed care organizations in the U.S. get extremely angry because they are "unjustly" denied the care they have a right to. He asks these patients what conception of justice they are appealing to as the basis for these claims. He then points out that there seems to be no shared social understanding of what health care justice requires in the way of assured access to needed health care. Instead, there are only contractual generalities which these managed care organizations are free to interpret as they wish (since they wrote the contracts and have the lawyers to enforce their interpretation). Consequently, these middle-class patients are only spouting empty rhetoric when they cry "unjust." Buchanan is not an anti-justice philosopher; on the contrary, his actual point is that the insured middle class has been indifferent to the plight of the uninsured in the U.S., in effect saying their plight is unfortunate but not unjust. If that is what they truly believe, however, then Buchanan is saying to the insured middle class that they too are merely unfortunate when economically powerful insurers deny them needed health care on the basis of their reading of these contracts. Buchanan's real take-home message is that Americans need to engage in public conversations aimed at articulating and legitimating a shared understanding of health care justice. That shared understanding is very unlikely to be a predominantly libertarian understanding because of the risks of exploitation or abandonment to which sicker, poorer patients would be vulnerable. Though I cannot fully argue the point just now, I will contend that a moderately egalitarian conception of health care justice will yield a more expansive, secure, and effective set of liberties for all with regard to access to needed health care than a classical libertarian position.

One aspect of the moral and political appeal of libertarianism is that individuals make rationing decisions for themselves.[10] However, the moral and political reality is that such *effective* liberty is limited to those who are healthy, well-insured, and economically well-off. Few will voluntarily invite into their health plans those with costly chronic illnesses, which means those who are least well-off healthwise are also least likely to have secure access to the care they need. They have no effective liberty in this regard. Engelhardt (1996) will see fair negotiation and agreement as the key mechanism for the just distribution of goods in a respectful libertarian society. Fair negotiation is supposed to be uncoerced negotiation—what should "uncoerced" mean?

Imagine a health care world divided into two radically distinct systems: a superior health care system for the healthy and wealthy, and a much inferior system for the poor and chronically ill. Imagine a wealthy individual, Mr. Tromp, in the early stages of heart failure. He needs a heart transplant. He finds a poor individual, Mr. Bill, with failing kidneys faced with imminent death because he cannot afford dialysis. He negotiates. He will pay for dialysis for three years for Mr. Bill if he in turn agrees to surrender his heart for transplantation in three years. Mr. Bill can refuse the offer and die next month, thereby exercising his liberty and showing he has not been coerced. Then Mr. Tromp moves on to Mr. Will. This looks like exploitation, even if it technically does not involve coercion. What reasonable libertarian (at risk of kidney failure due to diabetes) would want to embrace this as an acceptable outcome of a libertarian conception of health care justice? Are there moral resources within libertarianism that would prevent such outcomes? I cannot find them. This suggests that our libertarian intuitions need to be constrained, most likely by some sort of egalitarian considerations. Daniels' fair equality of opportunity account of health care justice is one reasonable effort in that direction; it does involve a balancing of libertarian and egalitarian considerations.

Still, in the most universal and egalitarian (all are assured a thick package of health benefits) health care system that is feasible, health care costs will need to be controlled. There will be limits; some health care needs will not be met. Recall our introducing the problem of artificial hearts, the TIAH. In the U.S. we could in theory implant 350,000 of these devices per year at a cost of $300,000 each. Now imagine that we wish to embrace a universal health care system with a reasonably comprehensive benefit package. Given the costs of the TIAH, we decide to only fund artificial hearts for those below age 70, or those who had a confident predicted life expectancy of three years or more. Or we can imagine funding only 100,000 implantable defibrillators per year at $40,000 each. In both cases the core moral justification would be that such expenditures yielded too little benefit at too great a social cost (the appeal here is utilitarian), and other higher-priority health needs would go unmet if those dollars were diverted to these other goals.

Under such circumstances wealthier individuals denied these interventions at social expense could nevertheless purchase them with their own resources *and this would not be unjust*. This is radically different from our Mr. Tromp example. No one would be made less well-off in a justice-relevant sense as a result of permitting such wealth-related purchases, as long as everyone has had the opportunity to have their health sustained earlier in life by a thick package of guaranteed health services. Neither artificial hearts nor ICDs are absolutely scarce items, so the poor are not denied them because the rich outbid them. Also, we have a considered societal judgment that these interventions in these medical circumstances are cost-ineffective. Libertarianism offers a reasonable moral justification for permitting such purchases. To this extent, such libertarian moral judgments are justifiably included in a comprehensive conception of health care justice.

We cannot at this point spell out what we see as all the moral virtues or defects in the libertarian position so far as health care goes; justice and liberty bound one another, and that is morally important. We would not want to live in a world where all our behavior was assessed from the perspective of social justice. Americans should be free to spend $4 billion per year on potato chips or $65 billion per year on beer without being scolded for failing to buy more statins or more cancer drugs with those same dollars. Likewise, if we were to have some form of national health insurance, and if we were to exclude from coverage some of these extraordinarily expensive cancer drugs that did too little good for too great a cost, we still ought to allow families or private groups to organize charity drives to buy those drugs for some individuals. We need to permit a domain of health beneficence beyond the domain of health care justice so long as decisions in that domain did not adversely affect the just claims of others within the domain of health care justice.

It might seem that another virtue of libertarianism is that it gives us an escape route from the problem of liberalism and health care justice. This is less obvious and more complex. The core problem is this: If we have some form of national health insurance for social justice reasons, then should that insurance package include or exclude all manner of health care services that some in our society find objectionable for religious or cultural reasons of some kind? Examples would include abortion, physician-assisted suicide, contraceptives, RU-486, Viagra, preimplantation genetic diagnosis, prenatal testing, all forms of alternative reproductive technologies, all genetic testing aimed at altering reproductive decisions, organ transplants, blood transfusions, and so forth—this list can get very long. The argument is that individuals who are deeply morally opposed to one or more of these interventions are being coerced by government to pay for these interventions for others through their taxes. This is a violation of their moral integrity and religious freedom by a supposedly liberal government. Libertarians see this as a reason for rejecting all forms of national health insurance that involve providing a single benefit package that is the same for all. They will push instead for health care vouchers with some socially determined value that individuals as individuals can use to purchase health services with which they are fiscally and religiously comfortable. The problem with that approach, however, is that individuals are left in a weak bargaining position relative to insurers, most especially individuals with costly preexisting medical conditions. Those insurers will insist that they have liberty rights too, most especially the right to set prices and to set coverage limits. If this is taken as a given, then their liberty rights will always trump the liberty rights of sick individuals. This is a substantial cost to social justice, social compassion, protecting equality of opportunity, and protecting effective, equal, and basic liberties. As we shall see in a later chapter, there are ways of addressing these benefit package issues that are congruent with our liberal political commitments, protective of social justice, and respectful of different religious/cultural commitments.

Utilitarian considerations will also necessarily have to be part of a comprehensive pluralistic conception of health care justice, but I will argue that they cannot be dominant. When health care resources are scarce relative to need, it is not unreasonable to maximize the health good obtained for each dollar spent. However, an unfettered maximization principle yields familiar injustices. If our goal with artificial hearts is to maximize the number of life-years saved at the lowest cost, then we will often be giving these devices to otherwise vigorous 90-year-olds who were already genetically favored for long life, thus giving them a yet longer life (another ten years, say) while we deny the artificial heart to a 50-year-old with a prospect of only three more years due to bad luck in the genetic lottery. If our society can only afford so many artificial hearts, most people would be morally troubled that a 90-year-old would be favored over a 50-year-old. The seven extra life-years saved would just not be seen as such a weighty moral factor; it is not obvious that most people would see even flipping a coin here as a morally reasonable option. Still, the virtue of utilitarianism is that effectiveness matters. We are forced to ask ourselves whether a cancer drug that costs $70,000 for a course of treatment and an average gain in life expectancy of 5.5 months represents a wise and just social investment. Likewise, we are forced to ask ourselves whether we should be implanting more than 100,000 ICDs annually at a cost of $40,000 each, given the remote and diminishing likelihood of benefit as we move above the 100,000 level.

Cost matters (for social justice). Effectiveness matters (for social justice). But many other factors matter as well, in order to get outcomes that are socially just, all things considered. David Eddy (1996) is a strong advocate for the role of cost-effectiveness analysis in determining which healthcare services should be regarded as "essential" to a comprehensive package of health benefits we would want to guarantee to all in our society. Often this will give us helpful guidance. Prescribing statins at a cost of about $1,100 per person per year may make a lot of sense for patients with very high cholesterol, especially if other mechanisms for bringing those levels down have failed. What we may reduce or postpone for long periods of time are heart attacks, strokes, and other major health disorders linked to high cholesterol levels. Statins can also have "some" beneficial effects for patients with total cholesterol of 180, though those effects will be very marginal and the costs per life-year gained or heart attack averted might range from several hundred thousand dollars each to a few million each. Individuals who are extraordinarily risk averse might still wish to purchase those marginal benefits. A society respectful of individual liberty ought to permit that (though obviously we should not subsidize such purchases with tax deduction benefits). But clearly, considerations of justice would not require such coverage as essential to our societal benefit package.

Then we have to consider items such as imiglucerase for patients with Gaucher's disease. These are young patients. This drug costs $300,000 per patient per year, but it makes the difference between life and death. This is a drug that patients will have to take every year to sustain their lives, which means lifetime costs of several million dollars. The annual cost of sustaining the life of a patient on dialysis (2006) is about $57,000. Some see this as the outer limit of what society ought to pay per life-year saved. If we are absolutely morally comfortable with this as a limit, then we will not pay for imiglucerase; clearly, a hard-nosed utilitarianism would require this decision. What will leave many ill at ease with that conclusion is that these are very young patients and the drug is very effective. The drug does not prolong life in a profoundly debilitated state. It may not allow individuals to achieve a normal life expectancy, but that will be all the more reason why a just and caring society ought to fund it, so that individuals can have as much of a life of reasonable quality as possible. If we endorse funding imiglucerase, then are we morally obligated to fund all those extraordinarily expensive cancer drugs that yield only marginal gains in life expectancy? If we want to give a negative answer to this last question by appealing to utilitarian considerations, then why should those same considerations not speak against imiglucerase? This suggests that the sort of consistency enforced by utilitarianism may not be as morally desirable, all things considered, as we would like.

Other examples are likely to be equally problematic for exclusive reliance on a utilitarian conception of health care justice. Coal miners do very dangerous work for relatively low wages, and are vulnerable to a number of medical problems that will cause premature death, such as black lung disease. Imagine that there is a new treatment for that disorder that can yield three extra years of life of reasonable quality for those men at a cost of $100,000 for each of those years. Again, this will fail the kidney dialysis standard, but it should be morally bothersome that these men accept these health risks to provide all in our society with a cheap source of energy. Arguing that they chose this line of work freely is disingenuous at best—relatively speaking, few other jobs pay as well in the impoverished areas where coal is mined. Non-utilitarian considerations of health care justice will have to be invoked to justify our providing these men with these life-prolonging resources.

A strict egalitarianism (Veatch, 1986) will also necessarily have to be part of a comprehensive pluralistic conception of health care justice. There are of course arguments among egalitarians regarding what it is we are morally obligated to equalize. Should that be equal respect, or equal resources, or equal opportunity, or equal outcomes as determined by some measure of welfare? What motivates Veatch is concern about the just claims of persons with major disabilities, either mental or physical.

Veatch is a strong critic of utilitarianism. He sees persons with disabilities as being seriously (and unjustly) disadvantaged by social policies rooted in utilitarian moral commitments. We noted earlier that young individuals suffering a high-up spinal cord injury will have lifetime medical costs of about $2.8 million, and first-year costs that will approach one million dollars. From a utilitarian perspective it will be difficult to construct an argument that will justify that level of social support *as a matter of justice*. Veatch's perspective helps us to understand why there is something morally deficient about the utilitarian conclusion. With sufficient societal investment these are individuals who can be functionally restored (given advances in rehabilitative medicine) to a reasonably fulfilling life. For Veatch, what we owe these individuals as a matter of justice is the opportunity for "equality of outcome determined as the net welfare considered over a lifetime" (1986, p. 131). I will note in passing that we can get this same result from Daniels' fair equality of opportunity account. Why should this point matter?

Imagine another scenario in which an individual has suffered a traumatic brain injury (TBI). The injury is such that the individual is cognitively reduced to the status of a baby six months old. Under the most optimistic recovery scenario realistically imaginable, an investment of a million dollars worth of specialist rehab care over a period of five years might be able to raise that level of cognitive functioning by an additional six months. Is a just and caring society morally obligated to provide that care? If I have read Veatch correctly, then Veatch and Daniels would give very different answers. Daniels could reasonably conclude that the functional gain achieved for a million dollars is so slight that providing resources for that purpose would be of very low priority, especially in relation to what those same resources could provide for patients who have suffered high-up spinal cord injuries. Veatch's view (as captured in the quoted passage) is that we are morally obligated to protect the opportunity for that patient to achieve a level of net welfare "over a lifetime" equal to what others in our society can achieve. This will strike many as having strongly counterintuitive moral implications.

Consider the following implications. It will mean that if we have only a limited sum of money for providing rehabilitative care for a broad range of patients who have suffered devastating medical injuries, our TBI patient would be very near the top of the list for resources because his net welfare over a lifetime would be so low relative to everyone else in that pool. It would mean that if our spinal cord injury patient (now a high-functioning quadriplegic for the past 20 years) and our TBI patient both had the same serious life-threatening injury at the same time, and there was only one ICU bed available, then the TBI patient would have to get that bed because his lifetime welfare would have been so low. This looks very unreasonable; this does not look like some form of morally objectionable discrimination against persons with disabilities.

Veatch's broad egalitarian intuition is quite reasonable. If our quadriplegic patient at age 55 has a life-threatening medical crisis, and another individual (non-disabled) at age 55 has a very similar life-threatening medical crisis, and there is only one ICU bed, then a flip of the coin ought to determine who would gain access to that bed. This is a reasonable egalitarian commitment. If we alter this scenario slightly and add that the predicted life expectancy of our quadriplegic is five years (if he has access to the ICU) but the predicted life expectancy of our other patient is 10 years (if he has access to the ICU), then a reasonable egalitarian view would still require a flip of the coin to determine who got the ICU bed. However, if Veatch were to invoke that "net welfare over a lifetime" clause and give automatic priority to our quadriplegic patient, then I suspect many would judge that to be an unreasonable egalitarian conclusion.

The large questions to which Veatch draws our attention are these: If there are just limits with regard to the quantity of health care resources that persons with disabilities are entitled, then what criteria ought to be used to establish those just limits? If those just limits will be determined at times through processes of rational democratic deliberation, how do we avoid a democratic majority enacting rationing protocols that reflect biases and stereotypes adversely affecting the legitimate health interests of persons with disabilities? If we are going to be committed to some more stringent form of egalitarianism, then would that form of egalitarianism permit prioritization among persons with a broad range of disabilities? If so, then what more specific criteria can be used to do that prioritizing that will be congruent with a more stringent form of egalitarianism? If no prioritizing is permitted, then will this imply that persons with disabilities who have the potential to make unlimited demands on health care resources have unlimited just claims to those resources? How expansive or inclusive ought the category of "persons with disabilities" be? Should it include everyone in various stages of Alzheimer's dementia? All patients in PVS? All individuals who are profoundly developmentally delayed? All individuals with serious psychiatric disorders? I will argue that these are very challenging moral problems that cannot be satisfactorily addressed as health care justice issues if we were to rely exclusively upon a strict egalitarian theory of health care justice.

Let us retreat for a moment to firmer moral ground. Individuals with the same medical condition (a life-threatening but treatable form of cancer or heart disease) ought to have equal access to the same medical care (the additional assumption being that the treatment is likely to have similar efficacy). That individuals have suffered a spinal cord injury or a brain injury or are developmentally delayed should be irrelevant in determining fair access for having health care needs met unrelated to that disability. Equal concern and respect requires meeting the health care needs of persons with disabilities to the same degree as we meet comparable needs of persons without disabilities. This intuition was essential to the ESRD program for patients in kidney failure. It was very much a rebuke of the Swedish Covenant committee in Seattle in the late 1960s that used social worth criteria to determine who would have access to a dialysis slot. These are the intuitions to which we appeal when we criticize the fragmentation of the U.S. health care system that results in extraordinarily unequal treatment for patients with essentially the same medical problems. However, these same intuitions leave us without the moral resources needed to address fairly and effectively the health care cost-containment problem.

Strict egalitarians would seem to require that we provide ICDs to end-stage Alzheimer patients, and that we either implant 600,000 ICDs annually in the U.S. or else no ICDs. Their reasoning would be that we are otherwise making invidious quality of life judgments about end-stage Alzheimer's patients.[11] That is, we are denying their equal worth as persons; we are saying that it is not worth it to society to save those lives from a premature death. As for ICDs in the aggregate, there is no invidious social worth judgment in implanting none or implanting 600,000. However, both those options seem unreasonable. Utilitarian and moderate egalitarian considerations would likely yield a more reasonable social judgment regarding ICDs, but a strict egalitarian would resist such a compromise. Likewise, I would contend that the strict egalitarian has few moral resources for putting limits on the care that Mr. Diaz receives, as well as most other cases where we need decisions regarding "last-chance therapies" (Fleck, 2002a).

A moderate egalitarianism would seem to provide a more promising and reasonable approach to our rationing problems. One of its moral virtues is the Rawlsian bias of choosing health policies for cost control and rationing that favor, to some degree, the "medically least well-off." A moderate egalitarianism will require that a just and caring society provide dialysis to patients in end-stage kidney failure (otherwise faced with premature death). The same will be true for AIDS patients needing expensive protease inhibitors, and later, fusion inhibitors (Fleck, 1999). But a moderate egalitarian will stumble when having to deal with the "last-chance therapy" problem in all its complexity. All those patients would seem to be among the "medically least well-off" because they are faced with a terminal outcome unless they are given access to some very expensive medical intervention that will marginally prolong their lives (as with the very expensive cancer drugs mentioned earlier). Note that "all those patients" would include Mr. Diaz. No doubt a strong justice argument could be made for providing last-chance therapies to *some* of these patients, but which ones would have the strongest just claims? What precisely would be the moral resources within a moderate egalitarianism that would allow such distinctions to be made justly *and cost-effectively*? How precisely would moderate egalitarians judge who the "medically least well-off" were? Would such a phrase always include reference to life-threatening medical problems? Could someone with a very severe form of arthritis relievable only by some very expensive medication be included among the "least well-off"? And would a moderate egalitarian judge that if there were a conflict between meeting the needs of severe arthritis sufferers and the needs of patients like Mr. Diaz, the arthritis sufferers had the stronger just claim?

One other form of egalitarianism briefly requires our attention; this is what is known as "resource egalitarianism." Ronald Dworkin (2000) would be a strong proponent of this perspective in a health care context. He writes that a just distribution of health care resources "is one that well-informed people create for themselves by individual choices, provided that the economic system and the distribution of wealth in the community in which these choices are made are themselves just" (2000, p. 313). Dworkin is asking us to engage in a thought experiment—for that purpose, we would need only a rough sense of what a fair distribution of wealth might be. We could simplify things a lot by choosing 15% of gross income for all as our national health care budget (and we could adjust the share of actual individual income taxed for this purpose in accord with some reasonable proportion). Dworkin then advocates a "prudent insurance approach" to determining a package of health benefits guaranteed to all in our society. This means we accept limits on universal coverage "and we would accept these not as compromises with justice but as required by it" (2000, p. 315).

Dworkin is confident that prudent individuals would not want insurance for expensive, marginally beneficial, life-prolonging interventions in PVS, the advanced stages of dementia, or when faced with a terminal prognosis in the next six months. That means all of these interventions could be excluded from a basic universal health plan in the U.S. without fear of doing something unjust. Beyond that, things get fuzzy and uncertain. Will very effective but extraordinarily expensive drugs such as imiglucerase be covered for Gaucher's patients (a very rare disorder)? Will protease inhibitors and fusion inhibitors for AIDS patients be part of the benefit package at $35,000 per patient per year? Will the artificial heart be a covered benefit for all, or for some, or for no one? Will any alternative reproductive methods be covered for couples (individuals?) facing problems with infertility? IVF currently has a cost of eight to ten thousand dollars per cycle.

Dworkin recognizes that there are not easy and obvious trade-offs to be made among all these therapeutic and diagnostic interventions. What he imagines (2000, p. 317) is that some sort of representative citizen board would be responsible for making these decisions. Medical experts and other relevant disciplinary experts would be part of the board, as would many ordinary citizens of various ages, socioeconomic, and cultural backgrounds. At this point Dworkin is faced with a critical problem (which he does not seem to recognize)—what is supposed to govern the deliberations of this representative group as they make their choices regarding what is or is not covered in the national insurance package? Are their choices automatically "right and just" because they have been decided through this deliberative process? Are there unjust choices that they might endorse?

As nearly as I can judge, this deliberative process is something like a black box for Dworkin. It resembles in some respects the jury process. That is, Dworkin would want fair-minded experts to present the deliberators with all the relevant information about the therapeutic potential, side effects, long-term consequences, and so on of various health care interventions in various clinical circumstances; cost information and epidemiologic information would be presented as well. After that, the deliberators process this information and offer their recommendations. But what if there are widely prevalent societal stereotypes or prejudices that could have a decisive impact on some of these recommendations? It is easy to imagine this happening in the case of those very expensive AIDS drugs we mentioned above.

Very religious individuals with a certain leaning would condemn the behavior that resulted in these individuals becoming HIV+ in the first place, and they would see the health care system as a mechanism for punishing that behavior. Maybe a sufficient number of respectable liberals in the group would persuade the majority to reject such religiously based influences in the deliberative process. Still, the larger problem would be that a very large segment of the American population would be critical of individuals whose costly life-threatening health problems were the product of what they regarded as irresponsible behavior. They would argue that it was unjust that they who had been scrupulously attentive to protecting their own health should have to pay for the "irresponsible choices" of these AIDS patients. Consequently, they would refuse to include coverage for protease inhibitors and fusion inhibitors in the basic health care benefit package—they would expect instead that individuals cover these costs on their own or by attempting to purchase some sort of "topping out" insurance. As we will see in the next chapter, the model I propose will minimize the risk of those sorts of deliberative outcomes because the conversation is constrained by both constitutional principles of health care justice and the requirements of wide, reflective equilibrium.[12]

Again, our major point is that other strands of a comprehensive conception of health care justice would be needed to address these issues. But our additional point is that very often all these strands together will not provide the intellectual resources needed to yield a morally compelling answer to a specific rationing problem. Imagine the case of Alice and Betty, 42 and 44 years old, each with terminal liver failure and a two-month life expectancy. We have one liver that becomes available for transplant purposes. Who should get it? The two are similar to one another in all morally relevant respects, except that Alice would have only a two-year predicted life expectancy because of other medical problems, while Betty would have a predicted life expectancy of 20 years. From a utilitarian perspective we clearly maximize cost-effectiveness by giving the liver to Betty, but such a decision would seem contrary to our societal egalitarian commitments. Each individual has a right to "the rest of her life," no matter how long or short that might be. So the egalitarian might insist that the only fair way of resolving this problem is through the use of a lottery mechanism.

To my mind neither resolution seems unreasonable or unjust. I would add that neither argument seems so morally compelling that it clearly trumps the other. But we need a decision, and we need a stable and consistent decision to protect fairness at least within a health plan. That implies that we ought to reject the idea of simply allowing each transplant surgeon to go with her own moral intuitions. Even though neither choice in itself would be open to moral criticism, this method would certainly cause rejected patients to wonder whether some morally questionable factor tipped the balance one way rather than the other in the case of their transplant surgeon. A better and fairer approach, I argue, would be a process of rational democratic deliberation that yielded a societal rule for addressing such questions.

I have in fact posed the Alice/Betty problem to dozens of audiences of health professionals and laypeople whom I have equipped with audience response devices that permit anonymous responding. I remind them that all of us are vulnerable to liver failure for many possible medical reasons, and that a future possible version of ourselves might be either Alice-like or Betty-like. We have no way of knowing now who we might be; we are as a practical matter behind a Rawlsian veil of ignorance in this regard. What should our social rule be? Virtually without exception, 80% or more of every audience to whom I have posed this question will choose to maximize life-years saved in this situation. (If Betty's predicted life expectancy is reduced to the 4–6 year range, then the audience will shift toward a more egalitarian choice.) Morally speaking, it really does not matter which choice prevails through this deliberative process, since there are sound justice-relevant considerations to support both. Still, the deliberative process itself is morally and politically necessary.

Flipping a coin to get a decision would not have the same moral or political value as the deliberative process. The deliberative process itself contributes to the development of what Rawls calls "public reason" (Rawls, 1993). These are the moral capacities essential to peaceful problem-solving in any liberal, pluralistic, democratic society. Public reason requires that we give reasons to one another, especially with regard to "constitutional essentials," that are independent of commitment to some comprehensive religious or philosophic doctrine, since all of us (with our very different deep commitments) must still live with one another under a single set of basic rules. The deliberative process also contributes to the articulation of a richer pool of shared considered moral judgments (in a way analogous to the way in which scientific knowledge is generated and tested), available in this case for addressing more thoughtfully and confidently emerging problems of health care rationing in the future. In the short term, the moral virtue of the deliberative process is that it is public, contrary to the hidden and invisible approaches to health care rationing that dominate in both the U.S. and UK (Aaron and Schwartz, 2005; Fleck, 1987). The deliberative process is also rational in that *morally relevant reasons* need to be given to one another for legitimating one rationing decision rather than another (see Daniels and Sabin, 2002). It is not political or economic power that shapes decisions, nor interest group politics. Finally, the deliberative process yields an outcome correctly described as self-imposed rationing—all will have to live with the implications of the rationing decisions they have legitimated.

Someone may argue that it is misleading to describe the outcome as self-imposed rationing, when, as in our example of Alice and Betty, 20% reject the outcome. However, our primary concern has to be the question of whether those 20% are being treated unjustly, as when the healthy and wealthy impose rationing protocols upon the sick and the poor as a way of protecting their own advantages. This is clearly not the case. At least some portion of that 20% will end up benefiting as a result of this rule. That is, they will be in the position of Betty when their livers fail. Some, of course, will be in Alice's position and see themselves as being harmed. However, the same will be true for the same proportion of the 80% who approved the rule. In both cases the harm is correctly described, morally speaking, as unfortunate, and not unjust. Further, it is not as if the rule was an outcome of a tyrannical democratic majority; the members of the majority had nothing in common other than the fact that they individually came to endorse a set of reasons supporting the maximizing option. Neither did they manipulate or distort the deliberative process in order to arrive at a prearranged outcome. We might be tempted to say that a liberty-respecting society ought to give the 20% an opt-out option, as when we said it was not unjust for the wealthy to purchase their own ICDs if a rationing protocol would otherwise deny them one at public expense. But livers are absolutely scarce—if any of the 20% obtained a liver outside the maximizing rule, the necessary implication would be that someone acting under the rule would end up dying for lack of a liver transplant. That would be unjust.

We turn in the next chapter to a fuller explication and defense of my conception of rational democratic deliberation and its role in bringing about a more just allocation of limited health care resources, whether fiscal or non-fiscal.

5

RATIONAL DEMOCRATIC DELIBERATION
Scope and Structure

The take-home message from the last chapter was that our theories of justice have their limits; some problems of health care justice are too complex, too ambiguous, or too open to reasonable but conflicting responses for any one theory to yield *the* clearly rationally dominant response. So we argued that this created space for an important role for rational democratic deliberation. We suggested—even if we failed to make the point with perfect clarity—that this was not democratic politics as usual; (i.e., interest group conflict mediated by a legislative body that sought to craft a policy satisfactory to the most powerful of those conflicting groups). That process typically has little to recommend it from a moral point of view. We want a form of democratic deliberation that is impartial (deliberators that are not ideological zealots), that is a conversation among undominated equals (power relationships that do not constrain individuals from effectively voicing their views), that is honest and transparent (no presenting of positions for merely strategic reasons), that is mutually respectful (relies upon methods of rational persuasion rather than rhetorical manipulation), and that is committed to giving good reasons as the primary mechanism for moving the conversation toward resolution. The goal of the conversation is to create rules or policies or practices (in response to the specific problems that precipitated that conversation) that all will have to live with and that are fair and reasonable; that is, not reasonably rejectable by participants.

The following questions are the central issues addressed in this chapter. What is the scope and structure of rational democratic deliberation? Are there some sorts of allocation/rationing issues that ought not to be addressed through processes of rational democratic deliberation? What precisely is it that assures both the justness and the legitimacy of these deliberative processes? And how do errors or biases or other judgment-distorting factors get identified and corrected in the deliberative process? How can any deliberative process achieve anything like a fair or reasonable resolution, when controversy around so many of these issues is so pervasive and so deep-seated and so longstanding?

THE SCOPE OF RATIONAL DEMOCRATIC DELIBERATION

Should we trust to rational democratic deliberation the question of whether the costs of life-saving care for extremely low birth weight infants (under 26 weeks; less than 750 grams) should be covered as part of a national health insurance plan (or as part of some particular managed care plan)? Or is a just and caring society (with the relevant technological availability) morally obligated to provide such care? This issue gets raised because the cost of caring for each of these infants in the NICU will be several hundred thousand dollars. About 12,000 of these infants are born each year in the U.S. If that investment of medical and monetary resources resulted in an intact infant who could look forward to a normal life expectancy, then an answer might be easy and obvious. But the morally distressing fact is that about 60% of these infants will not survive the NICU; another 30% will survive with moderate to severe mental and physical disabilities (that are a side effect of medicine's best efforts to save these infants); and about 10% will survive with no more than minor disabilities. The cost of each of those intact survivors will be about $1.4 million. These are not staggering costs for the U.S., but they are significant. Still, $2–$3 billion per year could be saved if only palliative care were provided to these infants. The question we need to ask ourselves is whether there is a moral principle (reasonable and liberally neutral) that would obligate our society to provide such care, as opposed to permitting the matter to be decided through this deliberative process. If there is such a principle, then we would have a compelling reason for placing the matter beyond the deliberative process. Likewise, if there had already been sustained deliberation about the matter and a well considered judgment reached (widely regarded as reasonable), then the matter would again be beyond deliberation (unless a specific case had morally distinctive features about it that warranted a new and limited deliberative effort). On the other hand, if there are liberally reasonable justice-pertinent considerations that pull us in opposite directions (both within ourselves and among ourselves), then we would have presumptive justification for submitting this decision to democratic deliberation.

Here are some other issues that will raise essentially the same generic questions. May we submit to the deliberative process a proposal for withholding all life-sustaining care from anencephalic infants? Ordinarily these infants will die within a matter of days to a few short weeks after birth if they are not provided with the most aggressive life-sustaining care available. But there have been cases, such as the Baby K case in Virginia, where such infants have had their lives sustained for almost three years at a cost in excess of one million dollars; this was at the insistence of the mother. Did she have a just claim to those medical resources, given that medicine could do nothing to restore the missing brain matter and the complete lack of functional developmental capacity? Or could a society's failure to provide such care be rightly construed as a kind of discrimination against an infant with substantial disabilities, and therefore unjust?

We can raise the same issues in the case of infants with necrotic small bowel syndrome. If a rationing protocol for infants with necrotic small bowel syndrome were approved through a process of rational democratic deliberation, would such a protocol be just and justified? More specifically, the protocol would provide funding for palliative terminal care for such infants, but would not provide funding for the total parenteral nutrition (TPN) needed to sustain their lives (about $250,000 per year) nor the liver transplants they would need around age four required as a result of damage from the TPN. This protocol would not deny parents or physicians the right to provide aggressive life-sustaining care, but the costs of that care would not be covered through social resources. Parents would be free to cover these costs from their own pockets or to seek charitable assistance for that purpose.

To elaborate just a bit more, the justice issues seem more complicated than in the case of anencephalic infants, maybe more complicated than in Coby Howard-like cases as well. In these latter cases, these children are fated to die in a short period of time no matter what medicine attempts. Anencephalic infants have as close as we can imagine a quality of life that is at zero; nothing can change that. Coby Howard-like cases (end-stage childhood cancers) are more difficult because these are children who are in the early stages of a life that would be worth living but for the cancer. Still, a reasonable argument could be made to justify the denial of further aggressive, expensive, life-sustaining care that society did initially provide. Those resources for such care were apt in earlier stages of the disease process when there was a reasonable hope that the disease might be defeated. In the case of children with necrotic small bowel syndrome, some numbers of years of life of not unreasonable quality are available to these children if we are willing to provide the social resources; that is, TPN represents an effective medical therapy. It does accomplish the job of replacing what the gut is supposed to do by way of providing nutritional support for life, but these children are still doomed to a very premature death if a liver transplant is not done at age four, and more significant medical suffering with the necessary antirejection medications.

Here are some other rationing/resource allocation issues that could, in theory, be the focus of a decision arrived at through a process of rational democratic deliberation. Casarett and Lantos (1998) have raised the question of whether we have treated AIDS "too well." They call attention to the fact that all manner of governmentally funded programs have been put in place to help underwrite the costs of these extraordinarily expensive (but effective) medications that keep HIV at bay, and provide individuals with many extra years of life they would otherwise be denied. This is what they refer to as "AIDS exceptionalism." They acknowledge the fact that many HIV+ individuals have been stigmatized and unjustly discriminated against. They know that many private insurance plans have in various ways denied these individuals the coverage that was needed to underwrite the costs of the drugs needed to sustain their lives; they regard such denials as unjust. But they are bothered by the corresponding injustices that are created as a result of these government programs that fund access to these AIDS medications. They call our attention to the fact that lots of other people have terminal disorders requiring expensive medications they cannot afford because they too have been denied coverage by their insurance companies, but government has done nothing to redress those apparent injustices. Just to be clear, Casarett and Lantos are not demanding that all these funding programs be shut down; ideally, they believe we need major reform of our health care system so that there is fair financing/fair access to needed health care across the entire spectrum of treatable medical disorders. Special funding programs that appear to be the product of more effective lobbying by more powerful interest groups only increases the real and socially perceived injustice of funding decisions within our health care system.

So, what we want to imagine is that Casarett and Lantos have gotten their wish, that we have put in place in the U.S. some comprehensive form of national health insurance that includes covering the cost of these protease inhibitors and fusion inhibitors for HIV. The virus will likely mutate around the various combinations of drugs that are clinically effective at present. If we assume, however, that we are successful in giving these patients 20 extra years of life with these drugs, perhaps at an aggregate cost of $700,000 for each of those patients, then could we put in place through a process of democratic deliberation what I will call a "last year of life" rationing protocol? In brief, if the cost of the last year of life for AIDS patients is $127,000 (primarily because of very aggressive efforts to defeat one or another opportunistic infection), then we would be asking AIDS patients to give up that last year of life (defined as medical circumstances in which there is less than a 10% chance of one-year survival) in exchange for funding all the prior years of life gained with these drugs. Would there be anything intrinsically unjust about such a rationing protocol (which is to say it would be wrong for such a protocol to be approved through a democratic deliberative process)?

We mentioned earlier the artificial heart (TIAH), now in clinical testing—there is a very large potential cost issue there. Each of those devices would have costs (including implantation) of about $300,000. Computer modeling suggests that we could implant as many as 350,000 of these devices each year in the U.S., which would add $105 billion per year to the cost of health care. The substantial majority of those devices would go to individuals eligible for Medicare, which means the core justice issues would be inescapable. The potential would be there for $50–$55 billion more per year in Medicare expenditures, unless some set of rationing protocols were put in place.

Of the following options, which should we regard as being potentially "just enough" outcomes from a democratic deliberative process? Could we deliberatively choose an age limit (70, 75, 80) beyond which individuals would not be a candidate for an artificial heart? Or would this necessarily be a form of ageism; that is, unjust discrimination on a moral par with racism or sexism? We should add (as with our other proposals) that individuals who were wealthy enough or who had been able to purchase additional private insurance could receive these devices beyond whatever age would be set as a limit through the deliberative process. Would allowing this libertarian option be unjust?

A variation on our first option would provide partial social support beyond age 70 (or whatever age cutoff we adopted). That could be 50% of the cost of the artificial heart and implantation up to some absolute cutoff age. If that is $150,000, that amount is likely to be beyond the means of at least 90% of retired Americans. In theory, that figure could be made proportional to income. If someone has an income of $50,000 per year, they might only have to pay $20,000, but that would likely undermine substantially the cost-containment objectives of such rationing protocols in the first place. Alternatively, can it be argued that a $150,000 co-pay is intrinsically unjust since so few people would be able to afford that—or is that no worse (morally speaking) than an age cutoff with the option of paying the full costs out of pocket?

Another variation might need to be considered. We might be able to defend the libertarian option mentioned above, but one consequence of that option would be that these individuals would gain some number of extra life-years that others would have been denied. Those extra life-years are likely to involve some other costly medical problems; perhaps a cancer of some sort, perhaps Alzheimer's. The point is that if we do nothing to change current practice, then those costs would be covered by the Medicare program. Those costs might be seen, however, as being attached to the exercise of the libertarian option. If that is true, then could we put in place through the deliberative process an additional rationing protocol that would require all those exercising the libertarian option to pay for all their subsequent medical care from their own pockets or a private health insurance policy? Would there be anything unjust about such a rationing protocol?

Computer modeling of the benefits of the artificial heart suggests an average gain in life expectancy of five years. That outcome is what makes the device cost-effective from a social point of view; it is less than the cost per year of dialysis at present. If we are morally wary of using any age as a cutoff for access to an artificial heart, this suggests we might use effectiveness criteria instead. One proposal for democratic deliberation might be that we would deny access to an artificial heart for anyone who did not have at least a two-year predicted life expectancy with the device. In other words, if individuals had other life-threatening comorbidities, then they would be excluded as candidates for an artificial heart. Could this criterion be "just enough" for generating a rationing protocol approved through the deliberative process? To be clear about this protocol, what it implies is that individuals would die of their heart failure in the next few months as opposed to some comorbidity that would take their life in a couple years.

We might also consider a quality-of-life rationing protocol in connection with the artificial heart. We could raise again the issue of end-stage Alzheimer's patients with end-stage heart disease. But the more challenging issue would be patients in the moderate stages of Alzheimer's (a stage with fuzzy edges). If such patients with advanced heart disease are presumptive candidates for the artificial heart, then this is likely to get them well into the advanced stages of Alzheimer's. That generates additional health costs of about $60,000 per year for long-term care (very often a Medicaid expense), and that, in turn, generates some extraordinarily complex moral problems. The basic justice question is whether such patients were treated unjustly if such a rationing protocol were deliberatively adopted (and here I remind the reader that the deliberative process I have in mind is always about making decisions for our future possible selves). Still, the claim can be advanced that such a rationing protocol would be intrinsically unjust because it represented discrimination against persons with disabilities, even if that person was a future version of me.

Another possible social response would be socially tolerated medical silence. That is, physicians would simply not offer the artificial heart as an option when a patient was identified with advanced heart disease and moderate Alzheimer's disease. That option, however, looks very much like the sort of invisible rationing that has been the focus of serious moral criticism in Great Britain. Another option would be to "let families decide" on behalf of these incompetent patients. In theory, all these patients would have as much right to an artificial heart as any other Medicare patient, thereby avoiding the critique by disability groups of an obnoxious social policy. In practice, if families saw themselves at financial risk for long-term care expenses for these patients, many/most might choose to forego an artificial heart as being contrary to the "best interests" of these patients. If this outcome is a foreseen effect of this policy (which we [policymakers] vigorously contend is "unintended"), then is this really just a more sophisticated self-deceptive form of invisible rationing?

We need to consider one more example—age-related macular degeneration (AMD). More specifically, we want to focus on neo-vascular AMD (NV-AMD). This is primarily a disease process in the elderly, robbing older individuals of their central vision. This is a disease process that affects one eye at a time; a progressive disorder that typically results in legal blindness in an eye after two years. About 200,000 new cases are diagnosed in the U.S. each year. If one eye is affected, there is a 43% chance that within five years the other eye will be affected as well. This disease does adversely affect the quality of life for older individuals. It results in significantly increased feelings of anxiety and depression; it results in the increased risk of falls (and the significant consequences of such) in the elderly (Soubrane et al., 2007). A new drug has become available that can be used to treat AMD, a monoclonal antibody, ranibizumab (trade name Lucentis). This drug costs about $2,000 per injection, and a course of treatment is for two years at monthly intervals. The cost of a course of treatment, then, is about $50,000. Clinical trials have only recently concluded. Those trials showed stabilization or visual improvement for 35–40% of the patients given this drug (Epstein, 2007). We need to note that stabilization means in this context a loss of less than three additional lines of vision. (These are Snellen lines of vision; there are ten lines on the standard chart.) Some patients actually gained two additional lines of vision. Visual improvement is measurable after just seven days; what is unknown at this time is for how long the visual gains or stabilization can be maintained beyond the two-year course of therapy without additional injections. Needless to say, the cost of this intervention is extraordinarily high and the long-range effectiveness is very uncertain. If this intervention is approved as a Medicare-covered benefit, it would add $10 billion per year to the cost of the Medicare program. Are we morally obligated as a just and caring society to cover this drug for AMD?

This particular example came to mind because NICE (National Institute for Clinical Excellence) in the UK refused to approve coverage for this drug within the NHS in the early part of 2007 because it was judged to yield too little benefit relative to its cost (and all the other high-priority health needs of the elderly). But 13,000 "letters" arrived from angry elderly individuals demanding that NICE reverse this judgment (BBC News, December 14, 2007). NICE did in fact reverse its judgment in late 2007, but NICE still maintained a significant restriction on access. Initially, NICE required that an individual could have access to this drug only *after* the second eye had begun to be affected by AMD. To be clear, this means that an elderly individual must accept blindness in one eye as part of the price of access to this drug; and then there is no more than a 35–40% chance that the drug will prevent blindness in that other eye for two years (maybe longer). This restriction would reduce by more than half the potential costs to the NHS, since only 43% of individuals with AMD in one eye will go on to face AMD in the other eye over the next five years. Still, the loss of vision in one eye is a significant functional loss, especially in the elderly. (The skeptical younger reader should cover one eye for a day and go about their normal routine, taking great care if that day includes driving.) In its more recent announcement, NICE lifted its requirement that one eye had to be affected first, but it would fund only fourteen injections of the drug since it is believed this level of treatment would be adequate for *most patients*.

Our question is this: Could we justly approve the original NICE rationing protocol in the U.S. either for Medicare (or for some form of national health insurance) through a democratic deliberative process? Or would such a protocol be intrinsically morally flawed? Would it be unjust or uncaring (violative of obligations of either justice or social beneficence) if we denied the elderly assured economic access to this drug?

There are obvious additional hypothetical rationing scenarios we might consider. Could we agree to fund coverage for the first affected eye with the understanding that if treatment failed in that eye, then no treatment would be available at social expense for the other eye (the medical assumption being that the probability of failure in that other eye was very high as well)? Given the extraordinarily high cost of this treatment, it is problematic that there is a 60–65% failure rate. It would be reasonable to identify medical criteria that would screen out such candidates before the treatment was attempted. However, it is relatively rare in medicine that we find a sharp division between therapeutic responders and nonresponders. The more common scenario involves the "ragged edge" to which Callahan (1990) has called our attention. So we might imagine a scenario in which individuals with a specific genotype were much less likely to be responders to this drug, ranibizumab. To be precise, let us say that the likelihood of a therapeutic response from individuals with this genotype would be no more than 5–10%. Could we then have a just rationing protocol approved through democratic deliberation that would deny these individuals access to this drug at social expense?

One other scenario might go like this: For those individuals who did respond therapeutically with stabilized or somewhat improved vision in one eye, we can imagine that the improvement lasts for a year beyond the last injection, then visual degradation begins. Since we (through the deliberative process) agreed that this first round was required as a matter of justice, would we now be morally obligated to fund a second round for two years at $50,000 (assuming we had good medical reason to believe that a second round would be just as effective as the first round)? Or could we judge that those additional resources needed to be reserved for what we collectively judged were other higher-priority health needs for the elderly? A variation on this last scenario might be one in which it appears that the therapeutic effect is indefinite; at least five years out. But now the second eye of one of these therapeutically successful individuals is affected, and we have a reasonable medical basis for believing that this therapy would be equally successful in their other eye. Would we be morally obligated to provide this therapy again at social expense? Or could we (through the deliberative process) adopt a rationing protocol denying coverage for that second eye on the grounds that we could find higher-priority health needs for the elderly that made a stronger just claim on those resources? Or would such a rationing protocol be intrinsically unjust (one argument being that it failed to treat like cases alike, especially when we had judged in the first case that the therapy was effective and costworthy)?

This AMD scenario is important to our discussion for several reasons. First, this is clearly a therapeutic intervention that is about quality of life, as opposed to saving life. This raises the question of where in a prioritization scheme such interventions ought to be situated. More specifically, is it more important to restrict access to implantable cardiac defibrillators (ICD) for those with cardiac problems who are most likely to be at risk of an arrhythmic event in order to fund access to ranibizumab for all those who are at risk of losing vision in one eye due to AMD? Or are there weighty moral considerations that would require sacrificing vision in order to avoid the annual loss of eight hundred lives per year in connection with more restricted access to the ICD? Or is this a matter that can be justifiably decided through a rational democratic deliberative process, either way?

The other reason why this scenario is important is that we are very uncertain about the long-term medical consequences of ranibizumab—we do not know how sustained the therapeutic effect might be beyond two years, nor do we know whether we can better identify patients with AMD who are *most likely* to benefit from access to this therapy, nor do we know that we can achieve the same level of therapeutic effectiveness in a general older population with AMD in the real clinical world (as opposed to the world of carefully constructed trials with rigorous patient selection criteria). Though an intellectually reasonable response might be that we simply ought to wait until these issues are more clearly resolved with sound clinical evidence, the practical political fact is that there is enormous public pressure to get this drug into clinical practice, as we saw happened with NICE in the UK. If some dreadful side effects had shown up in the clinical trials, that might dissipate the public pressure. But the fact in this case is that side effects seem to be very minimal. So how should a just and caring society respond in the face of such pressure? Would the democratic deliberative process be untrustworthy because of the strength of public sentiment in this matter? That is, might justice be subverted? Does this imply that this sort of decision must be made outside the deliberative process? (We may add parenthetically that NICE was faced with a very similar problem in connection with the cholinesterase inhibitors and Alzheimer's patients.)

FAIR HEALTH CARE RATIONING: NOT MARKETS, NOT PHYSICIANS, NOT BUREAUCRATS

We turn now to exploring more fully the scope and structure of the democratic deliberative process. How should we imagine the relationship between a democratic deliberative approach to health care rationing and reliance on markets, or expertise, or health bureaucrats, or a legislative process to make fair rationing judgments? Do we imagine that we only turn to the deliberative process when these other mechanisms for accomplishing health care rationing fail? Or do we believe that the deliberative process (properly structured) is fundamental to achieving just rationing outcomes, and that these other mechanisms have their proper boundaries determined through the deliberative process? This latter view is the one I will defend.

The moral virtue of markets is that they are impersonal and impartial (in the sense that they do not make deliberate invidious discriminations). However, markets do reflect rather than correct broader societal inequities and discriminations; hence, in that respect they are not morally neutral distributional instruments. Moreover, markets fail to distinguish between health desires (tummy tucks, whole-body CT scans every year) and health needs (cancer chemotherapy), which is a moral failing if we believe health needs ought to be met before health desires (especially in the context of making rationing decisions). Markets are also supposed to be paradigmatically efficient, and this is generally true *outside the field of health care*. However, the health insurance mechanism in the U.S. has promoted an extraordinarily inefficient and wasteful form of competition among medical groups and among health care institutions. In short, markets in health care fail to control escalating health care costs, fail to establish morally defensible priorities for health spending or priority setting, tend to be entirely unresponsive to meeting the health needs of the financially and medically least well-off, and tend to generate wasteful and inequitable inefficiencies of their own (Gladwell, 2005; Powers and Faden, 2006, chap. 5). Unless individual ability to pay is seen as a primary source of just allocational outcomes, markets have no intrinsic capacity to yield just rationing protocols, because markets in themselves are entirely neutral among competing social values.

What this last point might suggest to some is that we can get just outcomes from markets if we have just inputs. If every individual is given their fair share of social resources for health care, then each individual is free to establish their own health priorities and their own health limits. They can decide for themselves what is or is not costworthy health care, such as whether they would want assured access to an implantable cardiac defibrillator while in the end stages of Alzheimer's disease. The implication is that a democratic deliberative process would be otiose. However, the very large unanswered question here is how and who would determine the dollar size of that fair share of social resources for health care, especially if our twin social objective must be to control health care costs?

A libertarian might feel that society had no right to dictate to an individual what should be regarded as a health desire as opposed to a health need. But unless society were to grant unlimited access to an individual for satisfying health preferences (whatever they were), some criteria would be needed to determine the size of the share of social resources an individual might receive. Further, as we noted earlier, we would not get a just outcome if the same dollar amount of social resources were awarded to each individual (either per year or over an entire lifetime), because the health needs (or wants) of individuals would vary so tremendously. That suggests that our fair social allocation of health resources would have to be tailored in some way to each individual. What additionally complicates this entire matter is the evolution of medical technologies, which create the potential to satisfy more needs or wants, such as the artificial heart or these new drugs for AMD. Is society supposed to factor in automatically these additional costs in determining the size of a just allocation of health resources for an individual? And should it matter at the level of the individual that some of these interventions are especially effective for some individuals, while only marginally effective for others (as in our AMD scenario)? (I will concede to the reader that this whole process is impossible to imagine as a practical matter, but I will ask you to bear with me, nevertheless.)

If society believes that fairness requires being completely responsive to the health preferences of individuals, then there is no rationing and no cost control. But if some limits must be set on the size of the resource grant to each individual (for reasons of both fairness and cost control), this will have to be accomplished apart from the individual and apart from the mechanism of the markets.[1] This could involve appeal to expertise of some sort, or health care administrators, or our democratic deliberative process.

Medical expertise would seem to have some obvious relevance to our problem. Physicians could serve as frontline rationers and identify what should count as justice-relevant health care needs. The general idea is that the likelihood of significant health benefit is a morally defensible basis for establishing health priorities and making rationing decisions. Physicians are the only ones in our society who have the relevant professional expertise and knowledge of individual patient circumstances to make such judgments well. To assist physicians in making these judgments knowledgeably, we need to invest in a major effort aimed at technology assessment and the development of practice guidelines that are based on sound clinical research. However, there is a twofold difficulty with this approach. First, whether we are talking about practice guidelines, cost–benefit analyses, cost-effectiveness analyses, or technology assessment, the judgment must ultimately be made that some therapeutic or diagnostic intervention does or does not produce enough benefit reliably (from some societal point of view) to warrant the cost. That is, at bottom there is a value judgment that needs to be made, and no amount of empirical clinical research will yield that value judgment as such. From whence comes that value? In a liberal democratic pluralistic society, patients may legitimately ask why they should accept that value when it is not their value. If they want a 5% chance of a year or two of life that might be represented by that autologous bone marrow transplant for breast cancer that will cost their insurance company (or Medicare) $150,000, then why should they be denied it because "society" thinks that is a bad buy? Secondly, why should they be denied it *by their physician*, who is supposed to be a loyal and uncompromised advocate of her patients' best medical interests (Levinsky, 1984)?

We can, of course, mute the force of this last critical comment by appealing to some panel of physician experts, but that does not respond to our first point, which is that a value judgment would have been made by this panel, and patients can legitimately complain that the values of that panel are not *their* values. In moral terms, their complaint might be that they are being used by these societal experts to achieve the cost-control objectives of society. They may well see themselves as suffering needlessly and dying prematurely for the sake of these societal objectives, which they themselves have not endorsed. Further, they might see physicians taking on this role as rationing experts and agents, as contrary to the core ideals of the medical profession.

A third approach to health care rationing would be relying upon bureaucratically or legislatively generated rationing protocols. This is supposed to extricate physicians from the moral dilemma above. The general idea would be that these rationing protocols come from some legitimate and authoritative "outside" source that imposes these protocols upon the physician so that the physician has no real choice to make, and hence, is supposed to be morally blameless. However, how could a morally conscientious physician allow herself to be used like that? Furthermore, rationing protocols that are bureaucratically generated can never be fine-grained enough to apply without judgment or adjustment to the very unique clinical circumstances of individual patients, which is to say that clinicians cannot really escape moral (or medical) responsibility for interpreting or applying these rationing protocols to individual patients (Morreim, 1991, pp. 45–70).

Someone might argue that rationing protocols generated in the public sector have some moral legitimacy because the values they reflect are public values or public interests. But this would be very naïve, politically speaking, for the reality seems to be that competing interest groups significantly shape the outcomes of the legislative process, and hence, the values of more powerful health interest groups would be reflected in any rationing protocols. If this is true (even if only some of the time), then what is the moral justification for physicians being the agents of these more powerful interest groups against the interests of their patients (or at least some portion of their patients)?

A good illustration of this point is what happened in the UK with regard to some of these extraordinarily expensive cancer drugs. NICE had initially recommended against including Herceptin and Avastin (trade names) under NHS coverage because they were so costly and offered only very marginal gains in life prolongation. But Genentech employed a clever "grass roots" campaign to get these recommendations overturned, which was successful (Boseley, 2006).[2] But the government did not add any funds to the budgets of local health authorities to reflect the additional costs they would bear to provide these drugs. Consequently, local health authorities had to make their own rationing decisions in the matter, largely hidden from public scrutiny. They might have made decisions that were fair and reasonable, but there was no effective way to judge this. Further, there was no assured consistency across the several hundred health authorities in the UK, though all citizens in the UK were supposedly entitled to the same set of benefits through the NHS. Moreover, whatever value perspectives were used to make these rationing decisions were not necessarily those of the patients affected by these decisions. Some patients (end-stage cancer) might have felt good that they would be the beneficiaries of having access to these drugs; these patients were visible and grateful. Other patients might have been denied health care that might have provided them with significant medical benefit, and to which they would have had a stronger just claim. But they would be invisible and not visibly aggrieved because they might not know they had been denied anything.

This very same situation prevails in the U.S. as well. We do not have NICE; in fact, as noted earlier, we generally avoid any explicit rationing protocols because they are extremely divisive and controversial, which is why they are politically unattractive. Instead, our bureaucrats and legislators use budgets as rationing tools. This is essentially what DRGs are: micro-budgets for an episode of illness. While the rhetoric is that this avoids legislators mucking about in the practice of medicine, the reality is that this permits legislators and bureaucrats to be indifferent regarding the fairness or the justness of the inevitable, invisible rationing outcomes. Depending upon the financial pressures that particular physicians face in particular institutional settings (particularly Medicare), patients under the same DRG can be treated very differently. In such a situation there is no overall consistency (even within an institution); instead, opportunity exists for arbitrary and discriminatory judgments for which no one will be held accountable. More generally, to the extent that rationing is accomplished through bureaucratic or legislative budgets, there is no assured rational relationship between medical need or likelihood of medical benefit and the diagnostic or therapeutic care that is actually provided. Further, there is no assured connection between the values that drive these rationing decisions and the values of the patients who will be most affected by these rationing decisions. Finally, there is a tendency for bureaucratic rationing to perpetuate inefficient processes of cost shifting rather than effective cost containment. As David Eddy has observed, the ultimate cost shift is to future generations who are unable to defend their interests through the political process (1996, chap. 15). An outcome such as that has nothing to recommend it, either morally or politically.

RATIONAL DEMOCRATIC DELIBERATION: TAKING SERIOUSLY THE TRAGEDY OF THE COMMONS

This brings us back to the role of rational democratic deliberation as a primary approach to health care rationing. If we want effective cost containment/rationing in health care (no cost shifting), then we have to find a way to link cost and value through patients, since they have the most to gain or lose—wealth-wise (as taxpayers/premium payers) and health-wise (as patients). And if we want a fair approach to health care cost containment and rationing, then rationing protocols will have to be public or explicit, rationally justifiable, autonomously imposed, and impartially generated and applied (as opposed to being a product of interest group politics and power). These are conditions that can best be met through processes of rational democratic deliberation.

Both David Eddy (1996, chap. 12) and Norman Daniels (1998a) have identified the essential moral insight that makes rational democratic deliberation fair and feasible: Any fair approach to health care rationing must be a product of patient choice, freely and rationally self-imposed, not simply at an instant of time but over the course of a life, and not simply from the point of view of my actual health-needy self (I am having a heart attack), but from the point of view of an indefinitely large number of possible healthy/unhealthy selves I might become (which will overlap in complex ways with numerous other selves that comprise our society). The distinction Eddy makes is between patients with a small "p" (who have health problems at the moment) and "Patients" in that all-inclusive sense that embraces both the currently well and currently ill. When we are engaged in deliberative efforts aimed at articulating fair and cost-effective rationing protocols, then we must occupy both those perspectives simultaneously. We must have the capacity to empathize both with the sick and anxious in our midst (patients with a small 'p' who really represent future possible versions of myself) as well as the mostly healthy (Patients) who are presently responsible for covering the vast majority of those health care costs in the form of taxes or insurance premiums (foregone wages). In this latter frame of mind, the thought will intrude repeatedly that perhaps some of these very expensive health interventions might not be worth it, at least from the collective point of view of those who must pay those costs.

Interlude for a Somewhat Reflective Health Care Blog

If, in the middle of a heart attack, I have the thought (as only a philosopher could) that it would be unjust and uncaring for society to deny me access to the lifesaving medical interventions I needed simply because I had no current ability to pay for those interventions (because I had reached my credit card limits as a result of a wild Christmas spending spree on myself), then in making that appeal to these moral norms I am implicitly saying that a just and caring and responsible society ought (morally) to have a budget available that would underwrite the costs of providing those lifesaving resources to me. Of course, the obvious question is why "society" ought to be responsive to my health needs (and imprudence) unless I am part of that society, which means I would be obligated to endorse for all (in similar circumstances) the norms I would now invoke for my own benefit. That endorsement cannot simply be an intellectual affirmation of these norms and practical expectations; it must be a real commitment of financial resources, my resources, to creating that budget in the first place. Further, I have no good reason to believe that I am in any way morally special, that my health needs deserve special or extraordinary treatment. Consequently, if I have what I regard as the reasonable moral expectation that the rest of society must come to my rescue (medically and financially) when faced with any serious threat to my health that can be defeated through a timely health intervention, then I must be prepared to do the same for any other member of society in similar medical circumstances, including any annoying (loud and obnoxious) neighbors I have who are poor parents and indifferent to the esthetic deficiencies of their property.

I also know that many people are vulnerable to many forms of cancer; I know I am at least as vulnerable as the average American. This is a scary thought. If there is some medical intervention that can defeat that cancer, then I certainly want to know I will have assured access to that intervention, and that I will not be denied that intervention for lack of ability to pay. If that cancer metastasizes, and if that means I will be faced with a premature death (before age 80; *I believe I have a right to live to age eighty*), then I expect that I will have assured access to these exceptionally expensive cancer drugs that might give me an extra year of life because my society would be neither just nor caring if I were denied those drugs (and forced to die a year before my time). Again, I understand that I am no more "morally special" than any other member of my society, including some of my arrogant hyper-opinionated professorial colleagues; consequently, if any of them were faced with cancer in any of the circumstances I feared, I would have to endorse expending social resources to rescue them as well. (I suppose some of my hyper-sensitive professorial colleagues believe I have some personality defects as well.) Those resources are obviously aggregated from the taxes or insurance premiums we all must pay.

One of my other neighbors is a true hypochondriac. He was all irate the other day because he had this intense headache which he believed (of course) was caused by a brain tumor. He demanded an MRI scan to rule out such brain tumor. That was going to cost his insurance company $1,000. Let me correct that last statement—it was going to cost me something more in the way of taxes or insurance premiums to rule out his hypochondria. That is unreasonable and irresponsible. That is an absolute waste of money and health care resources. There is nothing there in his brain but anxiety; an MRI does not cure anxiety.

By way of contrast, the reader should know that I have consulted the Internet about what to do (and demand) if I were to have a heart attack. Some of these hospitals will try to get away with giving me this older clot-dissolving drug called streptokinase because it costs only one-tenth what this newer clot dissolving drug (tPA) costs. But that newer drug increases by 1% my chance of not dying of a second heart attack during the next thirty days after my initial heart attack. It would be irrational (and clearly indicate a serious problem with lack of self-esteem) if I were not to demand tPA as my clot-dissolving drug.

I have seen some serious automobile accidents; it is worrisome that two million people each year in the U.S. are injured in those accidents. Many of these individuals end up as paraplegics or quadriplegics. This sounds awful, but I am amazed about what rehabilitative medicine has done for these individuals. These folks seem to have productive and fulfilling lives in spite of these very serious functional limitations. It costs a lot of money to achieve these results, maybe $700,000 for the first year of rehabilitation for someone faced with quadriplegia. But if I had to deal with this, I would not want to die prematurely for lack of needed and effective medical care, nor would I want to languish in some nursing home for the remainder of my life if these other options are available. A just and caring society must provide those resources.

Going back to my concerns (not anxieties) about having a heart attack, most Americans survive that first attack—but it is "just the first." There are always others. Those heart attacks damage heart muscle, and after a couple more you can be pretty certain you will be faced with heart failure. This is pretty scary, especially if you have not reached age 80. Thankfully the artificial heart is in the process of being clinically tested now—if I needed a new heart I could count on one of those; I would not have to compete with younger individuals for one of those very scarce natural heart transplants. This is what I would expect a just and caring society to do. But these artificial hearts are very expensive, roughly $300,000 in total costs. I read that we could be implanting as many as 350,000 of those devices per year in the U.S.; that would be $105 billion. That number really got my attention. Most of those devices would go to individuals eligible for Medicare, maybe $50 billion worth. I did a little calculating on the back of a napkin: If there are 40 million recipients of Medicare right now, then every one of them would have to pay $1,200 more per year in taxes or premiums in order to cover that cost. Of course, Medicare is mostly funded by America's workers, such as me; there are 160 million of us. Still, if that $105 billion total cost had to be covered by all of us, that would amount to almost $700 per worker in additional taxes or premiums we would have to pay each year (and that number might grow substantially with the aging out of the WWII "baby boom" generation). That $700 represents a lot of discretionary spending I would be denied.

I have some serious doubts about whether all 350,000 of those individuals would be deserving of an artificial heart. I eat a lot of broccoli and other green vegetables; I do not smoke; I have only a small gut. I should not have to pay for the excesses and indulgences of my fellow Americans. No one over 250 pounds should be allowed to be a candidate for an artificial heart, at least at social expense. Nor should individuals who have been long-time smokers be allowed an artificial heart at social expense. If I think about it a little more, individuals with Alzheimer's disease should not be candidates for an artificial heart, either. Something needs to be done to bring these costs down; this seems fair to me.

I was reading in the *Wall Street Journal* (Carreyrou, 2007) the other day about this guy (Mr. Dawson) who had a lifetime cap on his health insurance of $1.5 million. I cannot imagine wanting to use that much health care. He was only 61 years old. Halfway through his hospital stay he was told he had reached that cap; the hospital wanted to know how he intended to pay for the next million. You might think that this guy must have a zillion health problems and that he very much wishes he was dead instead. But what he had was a "staph infection" that should have been caught earlier by his physicians. By the time it was correctly identified, the infection was everywhere in his body. He was septic. Amazingly, he did survive, and he is happy to be alive. This is what I would expect of a just and caring society. I would also expect that he would not be faced with medical bills in excess of a million dollars. We are a wealthy society—we can clearly afford to save lives that are imperiled in this way. I would expect to have my life saved if I were in his situation. It would be morally wrong for only the wealthy to have access to the effective and needed medical care required in these circumstances.

I suppose I am assuming this is an extremely rare situation in the U.S. If there were a thousand such patients in a year, that would only amount to $2 billion (which we can afford). But in reading the article a little more closely, I noted that it is becoming much more common for individuals to reach that million dollar cap. Then I recalled reading that 54% of all health care dollars we spend in a year are spent on just 5% of the patients that year (Berk and Monheit, 2001)[3]—that would be about $1.1 trillion for 2006. This was startling. Still, if this money was well spent, if the outcomes from spending all this money were comparable to the outcomes from Mr. Dawson, then I would remain committed to the view that a just and caring society was morally obligated to make those funds available to save these lives. Unfortunately, I did a little bit of additional research.

At present (2007) there are about 750,000 cases of sepsis per year in the U.S.; roughly half that number represent cases of septic shock; roughly 150,000 of those cases will result in the death of the patient. The average cost of treating these patients may be about $50,000, and the aggregate cost might be about $35 billion per year. The vast majority of these patients are elderly, which means the incidence and costs of sepsis for the next 30 years can be expected to increase steadily. I am confident that if we could expect outcomes such as that in the Mr. Dawson case, we would be morally obligated to provide the care that would achieve those outcomes. But I wonder if we really would be morally obligated to provide such expensive care if we could identify with a very high level of confidence those patients who had less than a 20% chance of surviving this septic shock ICU stay. We could save several billion dollars per year that way.

My understanding is that health care costs have been increasing in the U.S. at the rate of about 7% per year for the past forty years. That would mean an increase of about $140 billion in 2007—about $900 more in health care costs/taxes/premiums for every working American. I readily admit that I am very internally conflicted about this whole matter. I am not comfortable with the thought of allowing individuals to die in the ICU if there is something we might do that might give them some chance of prolonged survival. But I am really thinking about Mr. Dawson. He is not *that* old, and he still has a lot of vigorous life in him. I also remember reading about Mr. Diaz in the *Wall Street Journal*. About $140,000 was spent on his care in the hospital for a bleeding problem. He was in the advanced stages of dementia. That was a complete waste of money, my money. Maybe what we should consider is that patients who are in septic shock who have been already seriously disabled by stroke or some form of serious dementia should be allowed to die. That is, no efforts to save their lives aggressively ought to be attempted.

I know this might sound cold or crass but if I was in end-stage heart failure (sure to be dead within a year) and I still had a number of good years ahead of me if I could get an artificial heart, then I think the dollars saved by making serious rationing decisions regarding these older cognitively incapacitated patients in septic shock should be used to provide me with an artificial heart. At the risk of repeating myself, I also think my hypochondriacal neighbor who is demanding MRI scans for his imaginary brain tumors must be denied such demands by physicians with some common sense and backbone. Again, I was shocked to discover that we are spending $200 billion per year on radiologic services in the U.S., and I have a strong suspicion that more than a small fraction of those scans are more wasteful than necessary. Again, one thing I know for certain is that I will be much more judicious in the use of CT or MRI scans for my health problems; I wish that everyone else in our society could be equally judicious.

I am aware of the fact that MRI and CT scans can be used to quickly rule out serious health concerns that patients might have—no doubt a lot of anxiety is relieved that way. I for one, however, believe that those anxiety-relieving dollars would be better used to provide cancer treatments that might save lives (and I strongly believe the vast majority of my fellow citizens agree with that thought). Again, I will be the first to admit that I am intensely internally conflicted about this entire matter. I am not at all comfortable with the thought of being stingy when it comes to health care, and lives, and functioning, and well-being are at stake. I want assured access to needed and effective health care, even if it is somewhat costly, but I do not want other people to waste my money on health care that is extraordinarily expensive and does little or no good. What do the rest of you think?

End of Somewhat Reflective Health Blog

Though it might not be obvious to every reader, this blog is really the beginning of a democratic deliberative process. Democratic deliberation must begin with a politically shared problem.[4] I want to emphasize that we are talking about a *problem*, not a conflict. Conflicts (in a law-abiding society) are resolved in court. But courts represent an adversarial system—there will be winners and losers. The point of recognizing something as a social problem is that we all need to work together to find a practical solution. It is not just *my* problem or *your* problem; it is *our* problem; we have a common interest in solving that problem. If my inability to pay for the bypass surgery I need is a matter of poor budgeting on my part, then it is my problem. If tens of millions of individuals find themselves unable to pay for the health care that they need because they lost the health insurance they thought was securely tied to their job (and this is a risk faced by more than a hundred million workers in the U.S.), then it is *our* problem. Virtually any of us can imagine a set of social and economic circumstances beyond our control that would result in our loss of health insurance.

The health care problem we are addressing in this book (and that our society is faced with) is not simply an access problem. It is much more complex than that. Escalating health costs—primarily related to the emergence of new and expensive health technologies—has made the access problem worse; but escalating health costs would be a major social problem even if they had no adverse effects on access. I want secure access to needed health; I do not want financial barriers to deny me that access. I also want health care that is affordable, that will not be excessively costly annually so far as taxes or premiums are concerned. And I want high quality health care; I want to know my cardiac surgeon is competent, well trained, and professional in every respect (always acting to protect my best interests). These are common interests; these are interests we all have.

Some might think of these "common interests" as just intellectual or theoretical interests. But they are very practical interests when we are all part of a common insurance pool (which the costs and risks associated with illness today require as a practical matter). That insurance pool is a perfect example of what the environmentalist Garret Hardin (1968) referred to as the "tragedy of the commons" several decades ago. Each of us (everyone in Michigan or Massachusetts), let us say, contributes $7,000 to creating that pool of resources to be used to cover necessary medical care for this year. That money can only be used for medical care, and that must be medically necessary care (however that gets defined). We are frustrated and angry that the cost of being part of that pool has increased by (on average) 7% for each of the past twenty years, though we realize we are getting a more expansive set of services for those extra dollars each year as well. To be more precise, "someone" has been a beneficiary of those more expansive services; many of us have been consistently abstemious in the use of health care over the past twenty years. Further, we are certain that a lot of people are taking more than their fair share of resources from that pool each year. We ask ourselves, "How can it be fair that someone puts in $7,000 and takes out $100,000?" Of course, we realize that that is the whole point of insurance—it protects us from financial disaster associated with high health care costs.

Still, I think of my anxiety-ridden neighbor (and lots of others like him) who demand $1,000 MRI scans for their phantom "brain tumor" headaches; certainly it is not fair or reasonable that he should be allowed to waste resources like that. But then this is precisely what the "tragedy of the commons" is about. We all have "a right" to use the commons because we have helped to create it. We all understand that the commons can be destroyed if we overuse it, but we have failed to articulate clear rules or understandings regarding what counts as appropriate or excessive use of the commons. The consequence is that the commons is overused and the cost of the commons is persistently pushed upward, despite the fact that virtually no one wants to bear those increased costs.

The human psychology at work here is not that difficult to discern. It is a very mundane mix of economic self-interest and a little self-deception. It is the sort of thing that happens routinely when twenty people are having a meal at a restaurant and agree at the beginning of the meal to divide the bill evenly. Everyone is motivated to believe that they can order a more expensive meal because nineteen other people are helping to pay for that meal. At the end of the evening, everyone is surprised that the cost of the meal is twice what they expected to pay. If anyone at that meal does exercise restraint, then they end up being "losers" in that they have a more ordinary meal than everyone else and they pay twice as much as that meal was really worth to them.

What also should be noted is that everyone is making their meal choices in the privacy of their own minds; no discussion occurs among all the participants of what their potential meal choices might be so that someone might be motivated to speak up and remind everyone of what the consequences of their unrestrained choices might be. Likewise, the thought may occur to several at the table that one or another individual is being excessively extravagant in their choice of a meal at group expense, but all will be silent on the matter, either out of a sense of social politeness or with the expectation that someone else ought to speak up (and accept the risk of being thought rude by everyone else at the table). Of course, once someone has announced their extravagant choice of a meal, then everyone else feels they have a right to upgrade their choices as well to just below the extravagant level legitimated by that one diner. This is where the self-deception comes in, since we convince ourselves that we are being abstemious by not exceeding the extravagant level achieved by our colleague.

If we want to make this analogy as close as possible to what is happening in the health care system, we have to imagine that throughout the meal the waiter is bringing additional unbidden appealing dishes (new creations by the chef/new and appealing health technologies). No one is obligated to sample those dishes, but if we do indulge then we will have to pay for them. Again, once one person indulges, all are equally motivated to indulge as well since the cost of the whole dish will be shared by all. The waiter (physician) is clearly motivated to bring these unbidden experimental dishes to the table since that increases the size of the tip he will receive. The same is true for the other waiter (the insurance company). Both are servants of our needs and wishes. To complete the analogy, we need to imagine everyone grumbling at the end of the meal about increased taxes being used to fund an expanded Food Stamp program.

What is the role of rational democratic deliberation with regard to the tragedy of the health commons? Its first role is to break the silence and to begin to allow all to talk about what all privately regard as a problem; not all will initially see the problem in the same way. In my health blog I was inclined to blame others for excessive and inappropriate use of the health care system. As long as that is a private conversation in the privacy of my brain, it is unlikely that I will be very self-critical. But in a deliberative group, others will politely remind me that I might not be as honest with myself as I ought to be. I am *certain* that my neighbor's headaches are not the result of a brain tumor, but I am reminded by my co-deliberators that *some (very small number)* of headaches are caused by brain tumors. Then I am also confronted with the fact that I want tPA (at $2,400 a dose) as my clot-dissolving drug of choice when I have a heart attack in order to gain a very small survival advantage that will have to be paid for by everyone else in the plan. What I am forced to consider is whether I am being fair and consistent when I would deny my neighbor his MRI at the same time that I indulge my desire for tPA. Maybe we are both a bit overanxious. If I think it is unfair for the health plan to pay for the relief of his anxiety, then what would justify me in expecting that the health plan should be willing to pay for the relief of my anxiety? Is there some way in which *we* could formulate a rule in this matter so that we will have a clear understanding of what will count as inappropriate use of health care resources? I emphasize the word "we" because this is the beginning of substantive problem-solving through the deliberative process.

I want to emphasize again that the deliberative process is not an adversarial process, though there may be times when superficial appearances suggest that it is. Consider the following recent story of a 17-year-old girl, Nataline Sarkisyan, who died after her insurance company refused to pay for a liver transplant that was needed to save her life. Reading that last sentence will almost certainly evoke in most readers a sense of instant outrage. But we need to consider the rest of the story. She had been suffering from leukemia. Her disease was not responding to first-line or second-line therapies. Her brother served as a donor for a bone marrow transplant, which generally costs more than $250,000. Unfortunately, she developed a complication from the transplant, likely graft-versus-host disease that caused her liver to fail. She also suffered brain damage that left her in a deep coma for several weeks before she died (Hennessey-Fiske, 2007). CIGNA HealthCare was her insurance company. Protestors outside their office caused CIGNA to reverse its original decision and agree to pay for the transplant, but the patient died the next day. Whose side are you on: this young girl or the insurance company?

That question makes this look like an adversarial issue. But if we reflect a bit, what we will find is that we are *internally conflicted*, virtually all of us. We feel enormous empathy for this young girl afflicted with cancer; we feel that we ought to be willing to spend whatever it takes to save this girl's life, or to at least give her a reasonable chance of being saved. But that surgery would cost at least another $250,000. What is really troubling, however, is that the likelihood of long-term survival for her is minimal. Her own surgeon (who was very optimistic) put her chances of survival for six months at 65%; other surgeons were much more pessimistic. A liver transplant will not alter the deadly, unavoidable outcome from her leukemia, even if it successfully "sustained her life" for a very brief time. Given all the other unmet health needs out there for life-saving medical care, it would be unjust to use these resources in this way.[5] If we individually and collectively experience this as an internal conflict about how to respond justly and compassionately, then there is no adversarial conflict. Instead, we will have to struggle collectively to fashion a reasonable response to this situation.

It would not require much democratic deliberation to realize that if we were to fund a liver transplant for this patient, we would be committed to virtually unlimited health care spending for every patient whose life was threatened by some medical problem—no matter how remote the chance of success, no matter how minimal the quality of life that was saved. That is, justice would require our making that commitment. It would be very difficult to imagine what the moral argument would be that would permit us to make a justifiable exception for this patient, but, for example, to deny artificial heart transplants to anyone (including PVS patients or patients in the advanced stages of Alzheimer's disease). If we collectively approved this transplant for this patient, then we would have to be prepared to pay for 350,000 artificial hearts per year in the U.S. We could not deny that device to anyone who wanted one who had the relevant medical need, even if it only provided months of extra life. This illustrates another important feature of the deliberative process—it is an *educative* process. Participants educate one another; in effect, improving the quality of our judgment individually and collectively.

Many democratic theorists will argue that the sole purpose of our democratic practices and mechanisms is to *aggregate* fairly the preferences of our citizens, no matter how well-informed or uninformed they might be. The claim is that it would be illiberal to promote practices that claimed to be both democratic and educative. No doubt some numbers of democratic judgments that need to be made are relatively trivial in their import. However, the judgments that are at the focus of our discussion are matters of health care justice; these are matters that can have life or death consequences for some members of our society. These are judgments that need to be stable, that need to be made in a way that is as fully informed as is reasonable. These are judgments that have the potential to affect the well-being of virtually all in our society in substantial ways. A *deliberative* democratic process takes seriously the need for educating citizens appropriately so that our considered judgments of health care justice are in fact a product of diligent *sustained comprehensive* consideration (Bohman, 1996; Gutmann and Thompson, 2003; Gutmann and Thompson, 2004).

RATIONAL DEMOCRATIC DELIBERATION: KEY STRUCTURAL FEATURES

Why do we imagine that this deliberative conversation must be *comprehensive and sustained*? We have already said that the Nataline Sarkisyan case seems justly resolvable with recognition of only a few clear points. Further, something like the Nataline case must be a very rare phenomenon. This is true, but it is a small and distracting sort of truth—a much larger picture requires our social attention. We can imagine a simple variation of the Nataline case: What if she were not in a comatose state? Instead, we imagine her perfectly conscious and faced with imminent death without a liver transplant. The complicating factor is that, even with the transplant, there is no more than a 5–10% chance she will survive another year because of the aggressiveness of the leukemia. Is a just and caring society still morally obligated to provide her with the transplant at social cost? What if we raise the one-year survival number to 20% and give her a 5% chance of indefinite survival? At this point we would need to put this case in a much larger context.

In the early half of the twentieth century, rescue from death by medicine would have been a relatively rare event. In the early part of this century, rescue by medicine from death is ubiquitous. In fact, the likelihood is that many of us will be rescued from death several times by contemporary medicine, and most of these rescues will be very costly. We will be rescued from both our first and second heart attacks; we will be rescued from two bouts of cancer; we will be rescued from a significant stroke; we might be rescued from kidney failure as well. I have just picked in this list some of the more common deadly medical threats to which we are all vulnerable. Of course, in medicine the word "rescue" is a highly relativized term; it is not like being rescued from a mountaintop after which I go on to live a full and normal life. Each of these life-threatening events leaves an individual somewhat more debilitated. Most often, the first event is the beginning of a chronic, downhill course that might be extraordinarily prolonged because the rescue effort itself is ongoing (as in the thrice-weekly dialysis sessions), or the multiple drugs that need to be taken daily to manage heart disease, and so on. The obvious question to ask is whether all of us are justly entitled to every rescue effort that is medically possible, no matter what it costs, no matter what the probability of success. The one thing that is absolutely obvious to all at this point (despite appearances) is that "someone else" is not paying for all these rescue efforts—each and every one of us is paying for these rescue efforts. Further, we all want to "do something" to control these costs. We want choices to be made that are just, compassionate, and cost-effective.

What we have actually done (as is illustrated by the Nataline case) is handed off responsibility for making these hard choices to insurance companies; they are the managers of the health care commons. But when they deny us something we desperately want for ourselves or our loved ones, we are outraged. We are certain that we are being treated unjustly; we are certain that these insurance companies are putting their own economic self-interest ahead of the rights and welfare of ill and anxious and vulnerable patients. But this is where Buchanan's point (1998) needs to be reiterated. What precisely is the understanding of justice to which all these aggrieved individuals are appealing? Have we had a social conversation in which we have come to a rich, nuanced, and comprehensive social understanding of the conception of health care justice that we want to govern these very difficult situations where rationing and cost-control decisions must be made? The truth of the matter is, we have had no such conversations. Worse, we have scrupulously avoided having such conversations, often threatening politicians who suggest that we ought to have these conversations. Nevertheless, decisions have to be made. It is not as if these are academic issues that can be pushed off into the future without any decision being made in the present. The consequence is that insurers have become the decision-makers in practice.

We object that decisions by insurance companies are often arbitrary and discriminatory and uncaring and unfair. But this is, at least in part, disingenuous since we (citizens/future possible patients) have taken no responsibility for providing them with any guidance regarding how we would like to see these decisions made. And, of course, *we* cannot provide that guidance if *we ourselves* have failed to engage in the deliberative conversations that would provide just and legitimate guidance to those insurance companies.

In the Nataline case, CIGNA reversed its original decision in the face of media attention generated by the protestors outside their office. *That* was clearly the wrong decision to make, since it was a response to mindless (and unjust) social pressure made to protect corporate self-interest (the public image of the company). In addition, this response from the insurance company reinforces the worst sort of public behavior and the most misguided of public beliefs. What the response of the insurance company encourages is using the media to generate public sympathy and public pressure. The story line is very common: A weak and oppressed underdog is going up against a brutal and oppressive institutional monster. This same story played out repeatedly in the 1990s regarding autologous bone marrow transplants in connection with breast cancer. At the time, this experimental intervention cost

$150,000 per case; the belief was that this intervention might offer women a 10% chance of three-year survival. Insurance companies would deny these women coverage because the procedure was experimental (and the hoped-for gain was very marginal). Women who were well educated and assertive threatened to bring in the media through their lawyers to embarrass these insurance companies. The tactic worked.[6] But the outcome was hundreds of millions of dollars in wasted resources and multiple injustices. Women who were more passive and less well educated simply accepted their fate. Should a just and caring society tolerate that outcome? Should the media be proud of itself for being the champion (only) of educated and assertive women?

One of the other consequences of the success of these women is that clinical trials aimed at definitively establishing the therapeutic value of these bone marrow transplants took extraordinarily long to complete because it was so hard to recruit women into trials where they would have only a 50% chance of getting the experimental therapy (which researchers and the media had been hyping). When the trials were completed and reported in 2001, the outcome was that this intervention was no better than conventional, less-costly therapies that had been available for a while. We would have hoped that this would have proven to be a valuable public lesson, but that lesson has gotten little attention outside academic circles. Consequently, there is little public appreciation of the need for a comprehensive, deliberative conversation about health care justice, as opposed to isolated incidents that elicit media attention and (misguided) public sympathy.

Before moving on, a summary of where we have been would be helpful. Bohman (1996) offers a useful summative characterization of what he refers to as "public deliberation." It is "a dialogical process of exchanging reasons for the purpose of resolving problematic situations that cannot be settled without interpersonal coordination and cooperation" (p. 27). The first key idea is that this is a *dialogical* process. It is a process of democratic (public) inquiry focused on what is judged to be a public problem. It is a public problem because a *public interest* or common interest is at stake. To speak of a public interest is to speak of something we all value and that we realize we cannot adequately advance or protect *unless we cooperate with one another to fashion a common resolution*.

That is our second key idea: All must work together to achieve a reasonable resolution. This means it is not an adversarial process with winners and losers. Ultimately, it is a *practical* task that must be accomplished, as opposed to an intellectual task. In the deliberative process we are not seeking truth, *we are seeking to construct a resolution to a public problem*. Often there will be multiple possible resolutions for such problems, but each possible resolution represents a different mix of different values with a different set of consequences for different groups of individuals. Assessing these alternative options will typically become the substantive focus of this deliberative process. But one of the key characteristics of liberal democratic societies is value pluralism; there is no single dominant value that orders all other values nor is there some dominant ordering of values that is *the* politically preferred ordering of values. That value pluralism is seen as a major virtue of liberal societies because of the range of possible satisfying lives that become options to individuals.

However, when faced with a public problem that requires a cooperative resolution, individuals must find or create public values that *all can rationally endorse* as relevant for resolving public problems, even if those values are not regarded as being especially important in the private lives of some individuals.

That brings us to the third key element characteristic of public deliberation. The deliberative process advances *through giving one another reasons* for preferring one resolution over another to a specific public problem. Giving reasons to one another is essential to a deliberative process that is mutually respectful of our status as moral agents, as free and equal persons (Daniels and Sabin, 1997, 1998a, 1998b, 2002; Fleck, 1992, 1994a; Gutmann and Thompson, 2003, 2004). This is the very opposite of a political process that is about using political power to impose one's will on another. Instead, this is about mutual education, mutual persuasion, and shared social problem-solving.

The reasons we must be able to give one another must be *public reasons* rooted in reasonable public values or public interests. The perspective we need to adopt as participants in this conversation is the perspective of citizens committed to preserving and enhancing a liberal pluralistic society in which we are all cooperative, mutually respectful members. If I am committed to a right-to-life position on the matter of abortion, then I can hardly give my fellow citizens as a reason for supporting a constitutional amendment outlawing abortion that the Pope expects that of me. Even if 90% of the country were Roman Catholic, if we still wanted to maintain the liberal pluralistic political character of our society, we could not allow Papal expectations to be among the reasons that could offer legitimate reasonable support for or against any specific public policy.[7] Only public reasons can offer public justification for public policies aimed at resolving public problems.

What is characteristic of public reasons is that they can be endorsed as reasonable and legitimate from the perspective of multiple reasonable comprehensive doctrines (religious and philosophic points of view). This phenomenon is what Rawls (1993) refers to as an "overlapping consensus." Such a consensus is the essence of public reason; it is essential to the stability of a liberal pluralistic society. This is not something that is "given"; rather, it is something that needs to be constructed through sustained rational democratic deliberation (in a way that is analogous to the construction of science and scientific reason over the past 300 years, as well as law and legal reason). What an overlapping consensus means is that adherents of diverse comprehensive doctrines can find reasons within their own comprehensive doctrines for supporting a broad range of public values that transcend all comprehensive doctrines (i.e., are neutral or agnostic with respect to the truth claims of those doctrines). This is what makes possible the creation of a political framework that is respectful of all reasonable comprehensive doctrines, where "reasonable" captures the idea that these comprehensive doctrines are respectful of other "reasonable" comprehensive doctrines, all of which endorse the social values and social practices that are integral to sustaining a liberal pluralistic democratic society.[8]

What this means in political practice is that justification of specific public policies, such as policies we will consider regarding health care rationing, occurs at two levels. The first level is the level of the social values endorsed in that overlapping consensus. The second level is that of specific comprehensive doctrines. No doubt it will often enough be the case that specific public policies will not be endorsable from the perspective of a specific comprehensive doctrine (i.e., orthodox Roman Catholics will not likely support public funding for preimplantation genetic diagnosis aimed at identifying embryos harboring genetic mutations that would severely reduce length of life or quality of life for those future possible children, as would be the case for Duchenne's muscular dystrophy). Still, Roman Catholics could respect such a policy as reasonable and legitimate from the point of view of social values that were part of the overlapping consensus integral to the character of a liberal pluralistic society (as we discuss in Chapter 11).[9]

RATIONAL DEMOCRATIC DELIBERATION AND FAIR HEALTH CARE RATIONING

What we have summarized above is a general model of public deliberation. We now want to consider what this model would look like in practice with reference to the problem of health care rationing. As noted already, the problematic situation that demands public attention has two major dimensions: the access dimension and the cost control dimension. As just and caring citizens we do not want ourselves or other citizens to die prematurely or to suffer needlessly when we have costworthy and effective medical technologies that can cure or ameliorate their medical problems—we want assured access to needed and effective medical care for all. But we also want to exercise reasonable control over total social health care costs so that we can satisfy other social needs as well as private desires. Given the generally unpredictable nature of health care needs and the very high costs of meeting some of those needs when they occur, we have to create a shared pool of social resources. That in turn generates our central justice issue: How do we know what counts as just access to that pool of resources? That is, when do individuals have just claims to access that pool? And when may society justly limit access to that pool? This is the social coordination problem that needs to be resolved, which we illustrated with our restaurant analogy. In Rawlsian terms, what will count as fair terms of cooperation with respect to our health care system and its resources? This is what provokes the need for public deliberation.

What we need to articulate through the deliberative process are shared considered judgments of health care justice that would justify either specific claims to specific health care resources in specific circumstances, or rationing protocols that would deny individuals access to specific health care resources in specific circumstances. Those considered judgments of health care justice are the reasons we give one another to justify a specific access protocol or a specific rationing protocol. Those reasons, however, will have legitimate persuasive power only if they are public reasons, only if they can be part of an overlapping consensus, only if they are sufficiently detached from any comprehensive doctrine. We remind ourselves that as citizen deliberators we are free and equal persons who must be mutually respectful in order to sustain in practice fair terms of cooperation. Mutual respect is about reciprocity; if a particular social rule that is constitutive of fair terms of cooperation binds you to behave in a certain way in certain circumstances, then I am equally bound by that rule in those circumstances.

Reason-Giving and Public Reason

Schauer (1995) gives a concise and insightful characterization of what the process of reason-giving is about in these deliberative contexts. He writes, "Just as making a promise induces reasonable reliance, giving a reason creates a prima facie commitment" (p. 649). If I assert that it would be unjust and uncaring for you (my fellow citizens) to allow me to die from an inflamed appendix at risk of rupturing (when the medical technology is readily available for effectively intervening), then I am making the implicit claim that it would be unjust and uncaring for our society to allow *anyone* to die under those circumstances. More specifically, I am promising that I will pay my fair share of the costs of providing these health care services for everyone in our society who has appendicitis and is at risk of dying prematurely from its consequences, even Estonian atheistic Republicans for whom I have great personal antipathy. Here we can again see the value of the deliberative process as a public, educational, reflective process, since other deliberators will remind me that they harbor great disdain for liberal Austrian Democrats (me), but they would still affirm my just claim to needed health care in the face of life-threatening appendicitis. Likewise, if I object to providing life-sustaining medical care to an 83-year-old individual who has a terminal cancer and who has just suffered a massive stroke because I regard a likely expenditure of more than $100,000 to sustain his life for two months in this grossly debilitated condition as wasteful and unjust (given numerous other higher-priority health needs that could be satisfied with those same resources), then what I am proposing to my fellow deliberators is a rationing protocol that would be applied to all similarly situated patients, including some version of my future possible self. Again, this is what reason-giving and public reason are all about in a deliberative context among free and equal citizens.

At this point we need to expand substantially our description of this deliberative process, with special attention to the reasons why a suitably conducted deliberative process can yield outcomes (access and rationing protocols) that are just and legitimate. We can begin with the question of how expansive a set of health benefits would be that would be guaranteed to all in our society as a matter of justice. We started with the example of treatment for appendicitis—under a normal range of circumstances it is virtually impossible to imagine any sort of morally relevant plausible public reason that could be given for denying anyone in our society access to that needed treatment. Further, there is nothing absolutely unique about that intervention such that no generalization would be warranted from our endorsement of that intervention; on the contrary, justice would require such generalization. A possible generalization might look like this: If anyone's life is threatened by a curable or ameliorable medical condition, and we have available an effective and costworthy medical intervention that can save that person's life with an acceptable level of functioning, then justice requires that we assure access to such medical interventions in such circumstances for all in our society.

Someone could argue that this generalization ought to be endorsed, but an even more expansive generalization would be warranted as well. That more expansive generalization would be some version of Daniels' fair equality of opportunity account of health care justice (1985). In effect, the point would be that "bare life" (as in PVS) would not be judged by most of us as being worthy of special moral status. What counts, morally speaking, is protecting our capacity to function effectively in all the numerous ways that make life interesting and rich and worth living. So the more general principle we ought to endorse would be: If practically significant functional abilities are threatened by a curable or ameliorable medical condition, and we have available an effective and costworthy medical intervention that can save or restore those functional abilities at something close to their former functional level, then justice requires that we assure access to such medical interventions in such circumstances for all in our society.

What we need to note with regard to both the generalizations we have offered here is that both will have fuzzy and controversial edges—what would be the minimal gain in life expectancy or functional capacity that would reasonably justify providing this life-saving or function-restoring technology, especially if it is very costly? Think of our Herceptin example in connection with metastatic breast cancer where the gain in life expectancy is (on average) five and a half months at a cost of $70,000. Or think of the $700,000 first-year rehabilitative costs associated with aiding someone who has become quadriplegic as a result of an accident. What would be the degree of effectiveness below 100% that would be the minimum necessary to reasonably justify our commitment to providing this technology? Think about the Lakeberg conjoined twin case, where the cost was in excess of one million dollars for a 1% chance of saving the life of one of the twins through surgical reconstruction of a six-chamber heart. Or think of the gain in subtle effectiveness achieved through a $70,000 myoelectric arm for someone whose arm was severed in an accident as opposed to the more common prosthetic arm that would cost less than 20% of the myoelectric arm (Boseley, 2007). Is there some cost beyond which it would be unreasonable (beyond the requirements of justice) for us to assure access to that technology, even if we have great reason to believe it will be very effective? Think about providing access to imiglucerase for Gaucher's disease at $300,000 per patient per year for an indefinite number of years. This is precisely the sort of stuff that would be appropriate subject matter for the deliberative process. There are no experts to whom we can appeal who can tell us the right thing to do with medical interventions in these fuzzy areas. Nor will there generally be empirical data that will make clear what the right social choices ought to be. Lots of possible choices within these fuzzy areas would become "just enough" if there is sufficient, reasonable, democratic agreement about those choices.

This last sentence might trigger the thought that the conception of justice with which we are operating in this deliberative context is purely procedural. In other words, as long as the deliberative body is sufficiently inclusive or sufficiently representative, as long as no voices have been inappropriately squelched, as long as there has been no fraud or coercion or deception aimed at subverting the informed deliberative character of the conversation, then whatever result has been agreed upon will be "just enough" simply by virtue of the agreement being fairly achieved. However, that is not the position I am endorsing. On the contrary, substantive justice-relevant considerations constrain the conversation in various ways. This is another of the implications of the fact that the conversation is a reason-giving exercise.

Sometimes our reasons and reasoning have no implications beyond a very specific limited context; at other times, our reasons and reasoning have spillover effects in a range of contexts, the boundaries of which might not be very clear. Let me illustrate each of those possibilities. The reader will recall our Alice and Betty example—they are roughly the same age (early 40s) and they both need a liver transplant within the next two months or they will die. We have only one liver to transplant. Alice has other medical problems and will survive only two years with the liver transplant; Betty may survive 20 years with a liver transplant. Should we be maximizers or egalitarians in deciding who gets the liver? Should we flip a coin to determine who gets the liver, thereby demonstrating equal respect for the right to life of each? Or should we seek to maximize the medical good achieved for a social investment of $250,000, thereby giving the liver to Betty?

As mentioned earlier, I have been unable to come up with any overwhelmingly powerful arguments for going either way. There are good justice-appropriate reasons for going either way. But the one thing that is perfectly clear is that we cannot allow in practice a flip-flop back and forth between these rationales since that would permit all manner of morally irrelevant features of individuals to be determinative of an outcome, thereby masking injustices with a justice-relevant rationale. So we need a social rule that says we will be either consistent maximizers or consistent egalitarians in such circumstances.[10] But the main point I wish to make right now is that the choice we make *in this very limited context* does not seem to have obvious implications for other medical contexts in which we need to make distributional judgments that have life-sustaining consequences. In other words, if we had to make judgments about allocating the "last bed in the ICU" justly, then we could again construct an allocation rule that had more of a maximizing lean or more of an egalitarian lean. In either case, we would not be morally obligated for consistency reasons to be maximizers if we had followed the maximizing route in allocating livers to Betty-like patients.

Genotypes, Health Care Justice, and Public Reason

By way of contrast, consider the following scenario: imagine that we discovered that patients with certain genotypes were extraordinarily positive responders to very costly drugs such as Avastin for colorectal cancer (while others were very poor responders). Then imagine that the same is true with respect to certain very expensive cardiac drugs (comparable in cost to the cancer drugs we have in mind).[11] Then imagine that the vast majority of patients with the favored genotype for those cancer drugs have the disfavored genotype for the cardiac drugs. In the deliberative process, the individuals with the favored genotype for the cancer drugs argue vigorously for coverage of these drugs in the national benefit package for those individuals with the favored genotype because the cost and effectiveness data are well within the range of many other interventions covered in the package so far as cost and effectiveness are concerned. In addition, they argue vigorously against coverage of these drugs for individuals whose genotype predicts only minimal responsiveness. Their key claim is that for those individuals, the costs are excessive and the likelihood of sustained health gain too low (less than 5%) to justify that use of resources. What they also argue against, however, is any coverage at all for those cardiac drugs because they know that they are very unlikely beneficiaries of those drugs, but they would have to pay for those drugs for others who would be the prime beneficiaries.

The point I want to make is that this particular set of inclusions and exclusions could not be justly approved through the deliberative process; at the very least, there are consistency requirements that must be respected. I have to believe that in any vigorous deliberative process, this point would be made and accepted (even by those who initially proposed this idea). To be explicit, the deliberative process could endorse a coverage protocol for both drugs for individuals with the favored genotypes, and a rationing protocol for both drugs for individuals with the disfavored genotypes—such a protocol would be "just enough." Presumably, it would be consistent enough with other rationing judgments endorsed for reasons related to very poor cost-effectiveness ratios; consequently, no powerful justice-relevant considerations would speak against such a protocol. Likewise, the discriminating judgment made in this case would not be discriminatory in that morally objectionable sense. Individuals endorsing this protocol might well know the relevant facts about their own genotypes, but what they would not know with any high degree of certainty was whether their future possible selves would be cardiac disease selves, or colorectal cancer selves, or selves that suffered from both diseases, or selves that suffered from neither disease. In other words, their endorsing such a protocol would occur from a largely morally impartial point of view, behind a proverbial veil of ignorance regarding their future possible disease states.

Another option that could be endorsed through the deliberative process would be a noncoverage decision for both drugs, no matter what genotype patients with either disease might have. This option might initially strike many as either irrational or unfair or both, but I can imagine persuasive, reasonable considerations that would speak against these criticisms. Here are some additional "facts" I would introduce for this discussion. For those individuals who had these favored genotypes (about 20% of the total patient population), the gain in life expectancy would be in the two- or three-year range; in other words, none of the drugs we have in mind are curative of either the cancer or the heart disease. Next, roughly another 20% of this patient group would have the disfavored genotype. The middle 60% would have genotypes with degrees of responsiveness all over the large middle range, but this is only a global description—we lack the genetic knowledge to predict with any level of confidence how anyone in this middle range will respond to these drugs. Finally, the drugs we have in mind have a cost of about $50,000 for a course of treatment. Each year there would be about 200,000 cancer patients who would be candidates for one of these drugs (if medical criteria alone determined who counted as a candidate) and about 800,000 cardiac patients. What this means in practice is that if every medically suitable candidate received one of these drugs, these two drugs would add $50 billion to total health care costs in the U.S.

That aggregate sum is what is seen in the deliberative context as being morally and economically problematic. That is, when a very global and comprehensive view of the entire range of health care needs and therapies is called to reflective attention, the judgment of deliberators is that there are too many other health care needs and corresponding interventions that make stronger just claims to that $50 billion in resources. In a very comprehensive prioritization scheme, the judgment of our deliberators is that these drugs in this context would be somewhere in the lowest third of that priority scheme. If we expanded substantially what we were willing to invest in our societal health care budget, then these drugs could be covered for these uses. Apart from that option, access to these drugs would be left to individuals and their personal health budgets. That is, individuals would either buy insurance products (if available) relatively early in life to protect against these risks in the future, or they would save their own money for this purpose. How individuals would respond would depend upon what might be called their risk budgets and their financial ability.

The claim I want to defend is that an outcome such as this, from the deliberative process, is not obviously unjust. If we return for a moment to our restaurant analogy, we might think of coverage for this sort of health good as being the moral equivalent of filet mignon or lobster. A just and caring society will not allow its citizens to starve to death or even to suffer with minimally adequate diets, but neither will such a society socialize the expense of whatever extravagant food tastes some of its citizens might have, especially if satisfying those tastes meant some substantial portion of the population was denied even minimally decent and minimally adequate food. If the analogy of these drugs with lobster or filet mignon is a fair analogy, then there would be nothing unjust about the fact that these drugs for these purposes were not part of a national health benefit package.

At this point one of the deliberators might remind us that 20% of the relevant patient populations can benefit significantly from having access to these drugs. For those patients, the cost–effectiveness ratio (cost per QALY gained) was well within the range of what was regarded as a reasonable expenditure. So, the argument goes, wouldn't consistency require coverage of these drugs for that 20% with the favored genotypes? The problem, however, is that there is a larger context that would have to be considered. It is true that the $10 billion annual cost of providing these drugs to these genetically favored patients is socially affordable and might not result in some unjust skewing of our overall health priorities. But there is that large 60% middle range of patients whose responsiveness to these drugs would be better than the lowest 20% group, but lower than the upper 20% group. We would have no reliable rational basis for making more fine-grained medical discriminations among members of this large middle group. As a practical matter and as a moral matter, we would either have to make these drugs available to all of them or deny these drugs to all of them.

If we made these drugs available to all, then we would be looking at aggregate annual costs for these drugs of about $40 billion. That would have significant justice-relevant consequences for our overall health care priorities, which our democratic deliberators might be reluctant to endorse. That in turn might cause our deliberators to think seriously about our steak and lobster analogy in connection with that genetically favored 20%. They might imagine that 80% of our population is genetically constituted in such a way that steak and lobster have no gustatory appeal, or else cause gastrointestinal distress. So why should we think that nutritional justice required that these 80% should underwrite the cost of providing steak and lobster for the 20% who would derive substantial satisfaction from these foods? The upshot of this analogy is that it would be neither irrational nor unjust for the deliberative process to endorse a rationing protocol that would deny these very expensive drugs to all who had the relevant medical need, including those whose genotypes would permit a more effective response to these drugs.

I am going to assume that some readers will still not see the reasonableness of this conclusion, so we need to add some additional explanation and justification. It is easy to imagine in this context that this group of genetically favored individuals is somehow being treated unjustly, as if some form of unseemly medical envy were at work here that was the real source of this rationing protocol. If medical envy were the real source of this rationing protocol, then this rationing protocol would be presumptively unjust. However, imagining this possibility requires a picture of the medical world that is not true—it requires us to believe that there is something like a tribe of these individuals with the favorable genotype who are seeking to take more than their fair share from the medical commons. But no such tribe exists.

What we can imagine, given likely future capacity to identify numerous medically significant genotypes in individuals, is that we have identified this favored genotype in the context we have been discussing. Further, these individuals set up a website that allows easy communication among themselves, thereby creating some sort of group identity. What practically might follow from that so far as their participation in the deliberative process is concerned? Do they all have good reason (even if self-interested reason) for wanting to see these cancer and cardiac drugs funded? The short answer is "No"! What we need to keep in mind is that the vast majority of these individuals with the favored genotypes will never have either the variant of cardiac disease or the colorectal cancer that would permit them to be superior responders to these drugs. These genotypes have nothing at all to do with their susceptibility to the disease processes we have in mind; they are (a priori) no more and no less susceptible to these disease processes than anyone else in the population. By hypothesis all these individuals know they have this favored genotype, but this knowledge will have minimal practical relevance for them in the deliberative process so long as they are disease-free in these two respects. The same will hold true for those who have the unfavorable genotype we hypothesized—as long as they are disease-free, having this particular genotype will have no practical relevance. Considerations of both prudence and justice will push in the direction of this conclusion.

Democratic Deliberation and Priority Setting

To better see why this is so, we need to take the proverbial "helicopter view" of the democratic deliberative priority-setting process. I realize that I have introduced in serial fashion one rationing scenario after another, as if we make a decision about each of these cases in complete isolation from every other rationing scenario we need to consider. But that approach in practice would be both rationally and morally unacceptable, especially if it is the case that there are real financial limits we must respect. If there were no financial limits, then the priority-setting exercise would be pointless. Those financial limits can be democratically adjusted; there is nothing obviously objectionable about that. But what will require careful moral justification are the relative places of different health care interventions on that prioritization list. Oregon, for example, created a list of 709 "condition–treatment" pairs that were ranked from 1 to 709. If we were to ask, "How confident are we that it would be clearly wrong to reverse the positions of items number 182 and number 184 on that list?" the correct answer would be that we had little confidence that such a reversal would be wrong. The fact of the matter is that we do not have the acuity of moral judgment necessary to "correctly rank" 709 items.[12] Having said that, however, we must quickly add that we would be absolutely confident we could not consider reversing in position items number 10 and number 331. This would be the equivalent of saying that it might be morally more important to fix a broken finger than to surgically intervene to prevent an appendix from bursting. Nevertheless, once a ranking scheme has been thoroughly vetted through the democratic deliberative process, those rankings are "just enough" and "legitimate enough" that future alterations would require substantial moral justification (perhaps motivated by changes in medical knowledge, medical technology, and medical practice) to legitimate those changes. This understanding is necessary to prevent premature (sometimes manufactured) public exuberance which lacked a substantial evidential foundation for some new medical technology distorting unjustly the prioritization scheme (recall the autologous bone marrow transplants for metastatic breast cancer).

WIDE REFLECTIVE EQUILIBRIUM AND JUST HEALTH CARE RATIONING

Our prioritization scheme must have a certain degree of stability in order to assure the justness of distributional outcomes over significant periods of time. But our prioritization scheme must also be responsive to changing medical knowledge, medical technology, and organizational options in order to maximize the health status of all our citizens. In that respect, everything in our prioritization scheme has a certain provisional quality to it. What prevents the provisional character of our prioritization judgments from becoming chaotic is the requirement that all changes will require that we have very good reasons for making those changes—that these are justice-based considerations capable of eliciting a sufficient degree of democratic consensus through the deliberative process to assure all that such changes are just and reasonable. The outcome we are seeking in this regard (morally speaking) is what philosophers refer to as "wide reflective equilibrium" (Daniels, 1996; Rawls, 1971, 1993). That the equilibrium is "reflective" means that the deliberative process is guided by justice-relevant considerations. That "equilibrium" is sought means that competing considerations of health care justice are balanced in a reasonable way relative to one another, and in relation to other morally significant considerations as well. This is what moral pluralism requires of us, and that pluralism is true with regard to our shared sense of health care justice as well. That the process is ongoing means the equilibrium is dynamic and responsive to changing medical practice.

Wide reflective equilibrium is seen as a coherence methodology so far as moral theory is concerned. What this represents is a rejection of ethical deductivism and ethical foundationalism. There are no self-evident foundational moral truths from which we can build up the whole of moral knowledge, nor are there clear and distinct moral principles from which we can deduce the true moral system. What we find instead are social conflict problems that have a moral dimension to them. That is, they elicit what we might call pre-reflective or marginally reflective moral judgments. This is very much a Deweyan perspective on the origin of what will become (through the deliberative process) our shared considered moral judgments. Solving those problems through a mutually respectful conversation among free and equal persons is what generates the complex moral norms that we gradually come to agree upon. This is the perspective that Rawls (1999 ["Kantian Constructivism in Moral Theory," 1980]) draws upon, and that we draw upon as well with Rawls.

Rawls is seeking to express more perspicuously the conception of justice that is embedded in our political tradition. That conception is very far from being a finished or complete conception of justice, because the very large historical political problem at the heart of our conception of justice is the question of how to balance freedom and equality. This is a problem that has a huge number of practical manifestations in virtually every conceivable public policy area, including health care policy. Rawls writes:

> An immediate consequence of taking our inquiry as focused on the apparent conflict between freedom and equality in a democratic society is that we are not trying to find a conception of justice suitable for all societies regardless of their particular social and historical circumstances. We want to settle a fundamental disagreement over the just form of basic institutions within a democratic society under modern conditions. We look to ourselves and to our future, and reflect upon our disputes.... Hence, we should like to achieve among ourselves a practicable and working understanding on first principles of justice. Our hope is that there is a common desire for agreement, as well as a sufficient sharing of certain underlying notions and implicitly held principles, so that the effort to reach an understanding has some foothold. (Rawls, 1999, pp. 305–06)

The main point I want to draw from this long passage is that our conception of health care justice in wide reflective equilibrium is essentially a practical or pragmatic conception. Rawls says that we reflect on "our disputes" regarding the balance of freedom and equality. I say (for our purposes) that we reflect upon "our disputes" regarding health care rationing, how that can be accomplished in ways that are socially just and socially caring. Our hope (following Rawls) is that there is "a common desire for agreement." What we have found is that we at least have social agreement that we must find a way of balancing adequate access to needed health care for all, with the goal of constraining health care costs fairly (and in accord with other relevant basic moral norms as well).

We also hope that there is a "sufficient sharing" of certain "underlying notions and implicitly held principles." We sought to exemplify that with our example of the inflamed appendix in danger of bursting—no reasonable person in our society will endorse the idea of allowing someone in those circumstances to die for lack of medical attention because they did not have the capacity to pay for the health care that was needed. This same sort of agreement is exemplified in the End-Stage Renal Disease program introduced in an earlier chapter. Once dialysis was invented and proved to be a very effective life-sustaining medical technology, we were not going to allow 20,000 or more people per year to die prematurely because they could not afford the medical care that would save their lives for many years. If space permitted, we would provide a very long list of such considered moral judgments on which there is nearly unanimous agreement in our society. These are the shared social understandings that permit the deliberative process to begin productively. It is most certainly not the case that all our judgments in these matters are controversial.

Deliberative Stability and Considered Judgments of Health Care Justice

What we struggle with, and what prompts the need for sustained and comprehensive democratic deliberation about these matters, is that we are unsure about how these considered judgments of health care justice apply in novel and complex situations where we must also balance against one another our access and cost-control objectives fairly. The dialysis example can easily generate and justify the idea that human life is priceless; we should be prepared to spend whatever it might take to save or sustain a human life of whatever quality so long as we have the medical technology that might accomplish that. But we have already argued that if we attempted to follow out that idea completely, the outcome we would get would be imprudent and unjust and uncaring. That is, we would virtually exhaust the entire health care budget on life-prolonging medical interventions, many of which would be extraordinarily expensive and would yield prolongation of lives of very minimal quality. Readers will recall the Baby K case, the anencephalic infant in Virginia sustained for 2.75 years at a cost of more than a million dollars. If every anencephalic infant were provided with this level of aggressive life-sustaining care we would have annual costs of more than one billion dollars. Then there are the issues I raised earlier in connection with 25,000 PVS cases or roughly one million Alzheimer's patients who are in the late stages of that disease process.

The point I am making is that if saving or prolonging human lives of whatever quality for any cost is seen as an absolute justice imperative, the consequence will be that there will be no money for palliative care, for reducing or eliminating human suffering that is medically ameliorable. It is impossible to imagine anyone with any degree of moral sensitivity shrugging their shoulders and passively accepting as unfortunate but not unjust the excruciating pain of cancer metastasized to bone that a patient was forced to endure because there were neither social nor personal resources for effective palliative measures. It is as morally unthinkable as allowing middle-aged patients in renal failure to die because they had no financial means to pay for dialysis. What this suggests is that providing palliative care as part of a comprehensive social insurance package would be very high up on any prioritization scheme that would win rational, democratic endorsement. That is, it would be very far above the theoretical option we would have of prolonging the extremely marginal lives I identified above. What the deliberative process then needs to tease out is the rationale behind these very firm, considered judgments of health care justice that are widely agreed upon, to see what rational insight they can provide in addressing somewhat more complex and less clear rationing cases.

Let me offer a somewhat complex string of examples to illustrate what this process might look like. We (just and caring democratic citizens) are morally confident that no considerations of health care justice would require sustaining the life of an anencephalic infant at a cost of a million dollars, or even a cost of $100,000. I believe we (just and caring democratic citizens) are equally morally confident that if we were to list a large number of childhood life-threatening medical problems for which we have very costly but effective medical interventions (meaning that these interventions have a high probability of saving a child from premature death or serious suffering and disability), we would collectively agree that all these interventions ought to be high on our prioritization scheme. The dominant moral justification might be that of protecting fair equality of opportunity. Further, our judgment would be that justice would require *all children in the relevant medical circumstances* to have access to these costly but effective medical interventions. We would reject as unjust children in these circumstances having differential access because of the vagaries of the insurance market and the judgments of private employers, especially if those vagaries resulted in premature death or otherwise avoidable permanent disabilities for these children.

In this essay I cannot list all the medical circumstances I have in mind here, or what the annual aggregate social costs would be of meeting these medical needs. But we have every reason to believe that, in the deliberative context I imagine, we would be able to draw up such a list and calculate those social costs. I am reasonably confident we would continue to endorse funding for cystic fibrosis, which affects about 35,000 individuals in the U.S., with an annual aggregate medical cost of about $1.5 billion. Average life expectancy for these individuals is age 30, and lifetime medical expenses will be in the vicinity of $1.5 million on average. There are mild to severe forms of the disease, with severe forms having annual medical costs of $140,000.

I would expect that children with hemophilia would also have their medical costs covered, and this would be seen as a requirement for a just and caring society. For the more severe forms of that disease, costs would average more than $100,000 per child. The reader will recall the case of Mr. H, who is a factor VIII-resistant hemophiliac. He was (at the time) 20 years old. The cost of attempting to defeat his factor VIII resistance would be about $5 million, and there was only a 30% chance this would work in his case. Cases such as this are tragic and unfortunate, but we could argue that it would not be unjust to deny him this treatment (given all the other childhood health needs that could be met with those same dollars). That is, we should imagine that funding for his case would be given very low priority in our prioritization scheme. The reader needs to keep in mind that this intervention would not cure his severe hemophilia; it would (if successful) reduce the suffering and growing disability his factor VIII resistance caused (and it might yield several extra years of life). This therapy is much more effective (70–80%) in young children, but the cost of this intervention is still about $1.5 million per case. How high a priority ought a just and caring society award this intervention?

We also noted earlier a recent research proposal that suggested (at least in the case of children with more severe forms of hemophilia) that they receive massive doses of factor VIII prophylactically in order to reduce the frequency of bleeding episodes and the crippling joint damage done by each episode. But that would raise the average cost of treating each of these children from $100,000 per year to $300,000 per year. Is a just and caring society obligated as a matter of justice to fund this intervention? How high a priority ought this intervention to receive in our overall scheme for meeting and funding health care needs in our society?

These last two examples could be the focus of some rather intense rational democratic deliberation. Here is my proposal for how we might attempt to move that conversation forward. Some children are born with severe brain malformations that are incompatible with developing any functional cognitive capacity. These children would be doomed to a very brief life unless very costly aggressive life-sustaining care was provided to them, as in the Baby K case. The question we ought to ask ourselves is this: "If we have only limited resources to meet all the health needs of children in our society, would it be more important, as a matter of justice, to fund these very costly hemophilia therapies as opposed to the life-prolonging options for these infants with gross brain malformations?" Again, the answer that I see emerging from a reasonable deliberative process is that we would award much higher priority to funding the costly hemophilia therapies—those children have significant functional capacities and life opportunities that could be effectively protected by their having access to these therapies. The infants with the gross brain malformations have no such opportunities. This is a scientific fact, a tragic fact, and a morally relevant fact. These sorts of morally relevant medical and scientific facts are an essential part of reflective equilibrium.

Two harder cases for this discussion would be infants born with necrotic bowel syndrome and extremely premature infants born at less than 25 weeks gestation and less than 750 grams. About 60% of these infants will die in the NICU after much suffering and great expense. Only 10% are likely to survive physically and cognitively intact (nothing more than minor disabilities). The least costly response to both our sets of cases would be to provide palliative care alone and allow these infants to die; this would save several billion dollars per year in first-year-of-life costs. Many would find this proposal morally troubling.

The low birth weight infants who survive the NICU survive with a range of disabilities, but few would conclude that the disabilities are such that these children do not have a life worth living. Further, with proper care and social support many of these infants are likely to come close to achieving a normal life expectancy. While their first-year-of-life costs will be very high (close to a half million dollars), their annual health care costs thereafter will be moderate (relative to the annual costs for children with either cystic fibrosis or hemophilia). (We should not forget that part of the moral cost for creating these survivors is the suffering in the NICU of the non-survivors, most of which is medically induced suffering.) Still, the question we would have to ask ourselves in a deliberative context is whether, from the perspective of health care justice, it was more important to save these very premature infants or to provide funds for those very costly interventions for children with severe hemophilia.

Maybe we think of these cases as being very close to one another in our prioritization scheme such that it would not be morally important which way we went collectively in determining priority. Then we need to consider our necrotic small bowel syndrome cases, about 4,000 per year in the U.S. These children will be largely cognitively intact, but they are doomed to die by age four because the TPN needed to save their lives in the present will destroy their livers by that age. The annual cost of TPN will be about $250,000 per child; a liver transplant can be done for $250,000 and yield two extra years of life. From the perspective of protecting fair equality of opportunity and the equal rights of all, do we conclude that justice requires that we give these children these six years of life? Each of these years has an extraordinarily high cost, but I suggested earlier that justice might require our providing access to imiglucerase for Gaucher's, even though the cost of that drug would be $300,000 per patient per year. Patients with Gaucher's are likely to live much longer than six additional years if they have access to this drug, but pretend for the sake of argument that they would only get six additional years. Then would moral consistency require that we make the same judgment in both cases? Or might it be fairly argued that those six adult years with Gaucher's would be so much richer as human life-years (invested as they would be with decades of meaningful memories and experiences) than the six years available to those children with necrotic small bowel syndrome, that justice would require (or permit) awarding much higher priority to saving the adult years than very early childhood years? I am not going to try to answer these questions.

My suspicion is that this case is close in some respects to our Alice and Betty case, that there are again utilitarian and egalitarian intuitions in conflict, and that it is not obvious that either of those intuitions has overwhelming moral support in its favor. So, another question we would have to ask is whether, in our justice-based priority scheme, we would see assured funding for these children as having higher or lower priority compared to the health care needs of those children with severe hemophilia who could benefit from those two very costly hemophilia interventions. Again, I will offer my own judgment that for a mix of utilitarian and fair equality of opportunity reasons, the health needs of these children with necrotic small bowel syndrome would be lower in the priority scheme than the other childhood needs just listed. And, as noted earlier, all of these needs we have been discussing would be significantly further down the prioritization list relative to those other costly childhood interventions that are very likely to yield many more life-years of high quality for children who are afflicted with a broad range of childhood medical problems, including cancers that are much more responsive to therapy today.

Still, I can imagine that many of my fellow deliberators would be extremely sensitive to the health needs of children, especially those who were tragically doomed to survive for only a small number of years. They might well insist that the dollars be available to meet those needs, which means in practice that they would insist on somewhat higher priority for what I see as controversial and marginal (from a justice perspective) childhood health needs. So the conversation might then evolve in another direction.

Comparative Justice Judgments and Democratic Deliberation

If we were strongly opposed to taking dollars away from childhood health needs (except in the most extreme cases—anencephaly and comparable disorders), then what adult medical needs would we give lower priority to in order to generate the dollars needed to fund these "costly" extraordinary childhood health needs? We introduced earlier the issue of implantable cardiac defibrillators (ICDs) at a cost of $40,000 each. And we noted research showing that 81% of those devices never fire over a five-year period of time (when $20,000 batteries would be replaced). And we suggested that a T-wave alternans test could be used to determine who was least likely to have that device fire over the next two years. Such a test could save more than $2 billion per year by reducing by 60,000 the number of these devices implanted per year. But the moral cost of doing this is that about 800 individuals from among that 60,000 would die of heart failure that otherwise would have been saved; these, of course, are generally older individuals. So the question for our deliberators is whether providing ICDs for these individuals who are *least likely* to benefit from them should be of lower priority than providing the medical resources needed by our more controversial childhood cases.

I think these sorts of pair-wise comparisons are rationally manageable and facilitate the creation of a fair and feasible prioritization scheme. I realize that literally hundreds of these pair-wise comparisons would have to be made and judged through the deliberative process. Many will be easy and obvious, and will not require much in the way of formal deliberation; others will require substantial deliberative effort, and might not be reliably resolvable in the somewhat earlier stages of a very prolonged deliberative process. That is, we might see ourselves as learning important things in later stages of the deliberative prioritization process that give us the tools and perspectives we need to fruitfully address earlier comparisons we found we had to table temporarily.

PRIORITY SETTING, WIDE REFLECTIVE EQUILIBRIUM, AND RATIONAL DEMOCRATIC DELIBERATION: ADDRESSING THE STABILITY PROBLEM

There are two sorts of outcomes that are important from a methodological perspective so far as these pair-wise comparisons are concerned. We want to elicit "considered judgments of health care justice" of suitable specificity that represent a sort of rule that would be used to fairly prioritize similar sorts of health care needs and treatment options. We also want to capture for future use the reasons and reasoning that were most successful in providing reasonable justification for awarding higher priority to one condition–treatment over another. This is what we need to maintain a reasonable reflective equilibrium over many years and decades with respect to our prioritization scheme. What will happen in practice is that our earlier collective deliberative judgments will be further refined and specified by what we learn in later deliberative efforts. This is essentially how we contribute to the creation of "public reason" as Rawls (1993) uses that term. That is, this is how we develop public reasons and public methods of reasoning that are suitable for citizens solving public problems in a liberal, pluralistic society.

To return briefly to our last example, we might conclude that those very expensive hemophilia treatments deserve higher priority for funding than those marginally beneficial defibrillators. We might initially formulate our considered judgment of health care justice in this way: "Children faced with imminent death from some life-threatening disease process have a just claim to whatever medical interventions offer any chance of saving their lives, even if the costs of that intervention are substantially higher than what we might spend for an adult in comparable medical circumstances." We might judge that the major justice-relevant reason for supporting this considered judgment is protecting fair equality of opportunity. These are not children who have virtually no effective opportunity to achieve or experience anything in life because of gross brain deformations; these are children who can, in theory, experience a considerable portion of the normal opportunity range in our society if we provide the medical resources they need in a timely way.

But then we call to mind the Child B (Jaymee Bowen) case in Great Britain (Butler, 1999). This was a young girl with a cancer that was not defeated by any of the usual cancer therapies. In addition, she had had a bone marrow transplant that had failed. She was now seeking a second bone marrow transplant at a cost of about $150,000 that would have virtually no chance of defeating her cancer or even giving her much additional disease-free life. The National Health Service denied her that funding. But if we follow the implications of the considered judgment we articulated above, then we would be forced to conclude that the NHS had made a serious moral mistake; that is, they acted unjustly in denying this bone marrow transplant. However, if the prior probabilities of success for this therapy are as dismal as the medical evidence seems to suggest, then it is far from obvious that the considered moral judgment of health care justice we framed above ought to be interpreted so inclusively that Child B (and other comparable near-hopeless childhood medical circumstances) ought to be covered by that judgment. The benefits are very marginal and the costs are extraordinarily high. This would suggest that Child B (and comparable cases) would be placed in the lowest of the 17 prioritization mega-categories used by Oregon (Dougherty, 1991), whereas the needs of children with severe hemophilia or our very low birth weight infants would be placed significantly higher up in our prioritization scheme. This would also suggest that we would refine our considered judgment of justice above by narrowing the scope of medically imperiled children covered by it. And we would articulate a new considered judgment expressing the claim that it would not be unjust to withhold funding for therapies for children threatened by imminent death, when those therapies promised little medical gain in terms of either length of life or quality of life relative to alternative uses of those resources. This is a concise example of how reflective equilibrium protects the fairness and the reasonableness of the deliberative process.

Some readers may see the reference to reflective equilibrium as something that sounds more like a philosophy seminar session than a deliberative process with which ordinary citizens can become fully engaged (Young, 2003). But the concept refers to a process of consistent reflective justification in the face of changing morally relevant considerations that are very much part of our lives as individual moral agents or as citizens struggling with complex policy issues as a community. To give a quick example, if someone contends that justice does not require funding protease inhibitors and fusion inhibitors for individuals whose immune systems have been seriously compromised by the AIDS virus (even though these drugs represent 10 to 20 extra years of life for such individuals at a cost of $35,000 per life-year gained), but that person also contends that justice requires funding these extraordinarily expensive cancer drugs at a cost of $50,000–$100,000 for a course of therapy that might offer only extra months of life, then we would demand from that individual some coherent explanation of how those two moral judgments were compatible with one another. The AIDS drugs cost much less than the cancer drugs and are medically much more effective in prolonging life and protecting quality of life than any of these cancer drugs. What exactly would be the rationale that would justify the claim that both these moral judgments were right and just, without at the same time disrupting massively what we might have regarded as fair, reasonable, and settled judgments of health care justice related to numerous rationing situations?

There is nothing esoteric or academic about raising such a question. Our judgments of health care justice are related to one another in complex ways, which is best captured by speaking of a dynamic equilibrium among them. Any explanation offered to make morally compatible our two propositions above would necessarily be disruptive of a large number of other justice judgments, which would have to be revised or deleted until that equilibrium was reestablished. We have already noted that a *dynamic* reflective equilibrium in matters of health care justice is inescapable because of the effects of emerging medical technologies, changing organizational structures, and changing economic relationships. But we are generally capable of explaining to one another in ways regarded as fair and reasonable the refinements and rebalancings we collectively craft in our judgments of health care justice in response to these external pressures.

Our legal system (or at least a somewhat idealized version of it) provides a good analogy for understanding how wide reflective equilibrium, in the context of rational democratic deliberation, works (and why it is needed). We raised the question earlier of whether the deliberative process could "get it wrong." That is, could the outcome of the deliberative process be a rationing protocol that was unjust? If we affirm that this can happen and that we can recognize when this has happened, then we must have a substantive standard of justice external to the deliberative process that permits us to make that judgment—but if that is true, then it seems as if the deliberative process is otiose. We (societal decision makers) should just look directly to that standard to make a just decision and not bother with the messy inefficiency associated with democratic deliberation. On the other hand, if we deny that there is such an outside standard (discoverable by pure reason), then it seems as if we must accept the outcome of a properly conducted deliberative process as just or "just enough." But few will be comfortable with that as a conclusion.

Our legal system is a social construction, but it is not an arbitrary construction, either in its structure or its workings. It is a system of checks and balances aimed at maintaining a kind of equilibrium. The most "reflective" part of that system would be our courts—ideally above the fray of narrow partisan interests. Courts have to resolve interpretive disagreements regarding how the laws apply to a particular social dispute brought into court. The laws themselves (somewhat ideally) represent shared social understandings about the scope and limits of the behavior of each of us in specific social and economic contexts. Our basic moral norms and judgments are also essentially shared social understandings about the scope and limits of the behavior of each of us in specific social contexts. Those shared ethical understandings may not be as formally formulated as are laws, but they are quite real features of our lives, as my earlier examples of confident judgments of health care justice were intended to illustrate. But then new social facts, such as new medical technologies that are costly and marginally beneficial, may disrupt what had been easy and obvious applications of one of these widely shared ethical judgments. The same sort of thing happens in our legal system with emerging technologies (i.e., the question of whether or not genes can be patented). A panel of judges in such matters would be the analogue of our deliberators: free and equal, mutually respectful.

Though conservative legal commentators will insist that judges may never "make laws," the social and political fact of the matter is that judges are often forced (by the nature of a particular legal dispute and the "open" nature of the laws that apply to that dispute) to render a decision that will create a novel precedent with the future force of law. Judges are expected to offer some sort of legally reasonable resolution of every case brought before them because the problem is real and it must be resolved. Judges have "deliberative space" for creative work with the law to fashion novel resolutions when required. But that deliberative space is not "wide open." It is rationally constrained in multiple ways. A fair and reasonable and legitimate resolution will require that judges must be attentive to (1) the legally relevant case facts, (2) scientific information relevant to the case, (3) precedents that apply to the case (with reasons and reasonings that offer potential legal justification for resolving a case one way rather than another), (4) relevant laws whose ambiguity may have helped to precipitate the legal dispute in the first place, and (5) constitutional considerations that might require that one or another law pertinent to the case be invalidated, but that always establish very firm boundaries for the deliberative space within which judges must work. These are the sorts of factors that require that a dynamic legal equilibrium be maintained.

Note that the equilibrium is not simply a matter of logical or interpretive coherence among legal concepts and other legal materials; that equilibrium is closely tied to our social/political/economic world in all its complexity. The pragmatic test of the justness and the reasonableness of any particular judicial resolution is that it does not trigger a number of other legal disputes. If it is a somewhat novel judgment that is rendered and it unsettles significant areas of what had been thought settled law without offering a legal explanation that can resettle those areas of law, then that judgment *might be* flawed. We are unlikely to be able to say with certainty that that judgment *is flawed* because that might take considerable additional deliberation to make that case.[13] The reader will recall civil rights legislation from the 1960s and the very widespread effects in terms of changed policy and practice it had, not to mention uncertainty and disputes about innumerable specific applications (such as all the issues around affirmative action). This same kind of equilibrium is what needs to be sustained in the deliberative conversations about issues of just health care rationing.

We saw above how someone who proposed severe restrictions on funding protease inhibitors for HIV but expansive access to these extraordinarily expensive cancer drugs would cause an unreasonable and irresolvable sort of moral disequilibrium. This represents a legitimate constraint on the deliberative process to minimize the risk of moral error. I offered this as an easy and obvious illustration of my point—I could have used something that would have been less obvious, more controversial, more likely to require sustained subsequent deliberation. For example, for individuals whose health problems are a very clear outcome of behavioral choices they have made (lung cancer from smoking; heart disease linked to major obesity), should they be penalized by being denied access at social expense to very expensive life-prolonging interventions that would have been unnecessary if they had been more responsible for their own health?

If we considered a very wide range of cases that fit this generic rubric of personal responsibility for health, we might find the reflective equilibrium shifting a bit in response to this or that specific example.[14] Some of that shift might be required by some of our more settled considered judgments of justice relevant to a specific case, but other portions of the shift would be precipitated by outcomes from the deliberative conversation. Some members of the deliberative group might make novel, morally convincing distinctions, or offer insightful moral analogies that cause a shift in thinking. What this makes perfectly clear is that the outcome of the deliberative process is not predetermined (as a matter of excellent moral argument and analysis) to one legitimate outcome, relative to which all other proposals are erroneous. All the morally relevant considerations pertinent to some of the more complex rationing and justice issues we must address will still often be insufficient to yield a single *just and legitimate* considered moral judgment. The work of judges will often require legal creativity, and the work of our democratic deliberators will likewise often require (constrained) moral creativity.

FACTS, WIDE REFLECTIVE EQUILIBRIUM, AND DEMOCRATIC DELIBERATION

Two other types of constraints shape the dynamic equilibrium of a rational democratic deliberative process: facts (medical, social, scientific) and constitutional principles of health care justice. While the moral maxim is true that you cannot derive an "ought" from an "is," it is equally true that many sorts of facts are morally relevant for making justified judgments of health care justice for rationing and priority-setting purposes. That is, it would be morally irresponsible to ignore such facts. We have no medical or scientific basis for believing we can grow a brain for an anencephalic infant. If a primary reference point for determining a fair distribution of health care resources is protecting fair equality of opportunity, then anencephalic infants can justly make only minimal demands for health care resources. The same unfortunate facts will be true for patients in PVS and patients in the end stages of Alzheimer's disease.

Other facts will make other differences in the deliberative process about rationing and priority setting. Currently, about 13 million Americans are on statins to lower their cholesterol. Those drugs cost about $1,100 per person per year, which was about $15 billion per year in 2007. Some researchers believe that more than 60 million Americans ought to be on these drugs—at current prices, that would raise aggregate costs to about $65 billion per year. We will assume for now that these drugs make a significant difference so far as morbidity and mortality are concerned for individuals with very high cholesterol levels or very bad ratios of HDL to LDL. But no evidence exists at present for saying those same differences would hold true for that entire cohort of 60 million Americans;[15] on the contrary, the likelihood is that those differences would become very marginal as cholesterol levels and ratios drifted in the direction of being slightly or somewhat elevated. It is a fact that $1,100 for a medical intervention today is a very reasonable price, generally speaking. But if tens of millions of people per year are judged to be in need of that intervention, the aggregate costs look less than reasonable. On the contrary, costs at that level would have the potential to greatly distort (from a health care justice perspective) the priority-setting process. If we have a relatively fixed health care budget (as I have argued is necessary), then we would need to ask what $50 billion worth of health care we would give up to fully fund these statins. If the cost of protease inhibitors and fusion inhibitors for HIV+ patients at $35,000 per patient per year is at about $25 billion in the aggregate at present, could we justifiably give that up in order to provide expanded funding for the statins? I cannot imagine the justice-based argument that would warrant that trade-off. Likewise, even though I have argued that these extraordinarily expensive cancer drugs are very marginally beneficial and far from being costworthy, I am inclined to believe an easy case could be made for awarding higher priority for funding to those drugs over the hugely expanded funding for statins we are discussing.

Some researchers have suggested that statins might have a very positive preventive effect with regard to Alzheimer's—the "factual" argument being suggested is that tens of billions of dollars per year would be saved in the form of reduced long-term care costs by this preventive intervention. However, all we have here are "speculative facts" as opposed to well supported scientific facts. We could not possibly justify using public resources *now*—very real billions of dollars in the present—to purchase optimistically imagined health care benefits very far into the future. Serious democratic deliberation about that matter would be justified only if the relevant scientific evidence has been well documented by reliable scientific research. Likewise, one physician is reported to have tried combining Avastin and Herceptin for a patient's breast cancer at a cost of $160,000 for one year's treatment *without any scientific evidence at all that this represented a reasonable experimental treatment option* (Culliton, 2008c, p. W44). This complete "lack of facts" would most certainly justify as a matter of justice not funding such arbitrary "innovative" interventions.

Facts have a certain stubborn quality about them—they are public. The facts I have in mind are warranted facts, scientifically reliable facts. Such facts are always open to revision in the light of future experience (as in plate tectonic theory), but those revisions will have to be rationally and scientifically well supported. Such facts constrain in morally important ways our deliberative conversations about specific issues of justice related to specific rationing problems. We may desperately wish that autologous bone marrow transplants with high-dose chemotherapy could save the lives of women with advanced breast cancer (especially when a significant number of women die even sooner from the deadly effects of the therapy itself). But the harsh facts are that this intervention yielded nothing for these women in terms of therapeutic benefit relative to the less-expensive cancer therapies already available.

Facts are not always harsh, and facts are not self-interpreting (especially from a moral point of view). To return to our example of the extremely premature infants, more than half of them will die in the NICU after substantial medically induced suffering. That is a harsh fact. But 10% will emerge essentially intact and another 30% will emerge with various degrees of impairment and disability. Those are facts, too. What represents a morally reasonable response to those more optimistic facts? Is the suffering and death of 60% of these infants a morally tolerable price to pay to save the other 40%? And whose choice should that be? Should this be a social choice; perhaps a paternalistic choice? Or should we respect the liberty rights of parents to make whatever decisions they (and their physicians) jointly judge to be in the best interests of their infant children/patients? Those individual parental decisions command very substantial societal resources, which is what generates a prima facie justice issue. Are the medical outcomes such that we could affirm through the deliberative process that these expenditures are reasonable and fair because they protect fair equality of opportunity for the 40% of these infants who survive the NICU? Here, facts are certainly pertinent but hardly determinative.

Again, a series of pair-wise comparisons might be helpful in the deliberative process in getting to a reasonable moral equilibrium. Relative to saving these extremely low birth weight infants, is it more or less important, from a health care justice perspective, to fund these extremely expensive cancer drugs (Herceptin, Avastin, Iressa, Gleevec) that might yield extra months of life for $50,000–$100,000? To fund protease inhibitors and fusion inhibitors for AIDS patients? To fund very expensive "last-chance" cancer therapies for children who have exhausted all other options? To fund Lucentis (ranivizumab) for macular degeneration in the elderly? To fund left ventricular assist devices (LVADs) for individuals in end-stage heart failure for $200,000 to gain an extra year of life or so? How important is it, morally speaking, to provide all the life-sustaining resources these infants need relative to the needs for major costly rehabilitation efforts of individuals who have suffered spinal cord injuries (or other comparably devastating but rehabilitable injuries)? How would we imagine formulating the decision rule/considered judgment of health care justice that would warrant one or another response to the health needs of these infants that would yield a stable enough overall reflective equilibrium?

Finally, as regards to facts, there are all manner of elusive, controversial, unreal, and poorly conceptualized "facts" that populate the world of health care, and that will add to the challenges of democratic deliberation. Is there really a disease called fibromyalgia? Is "social anxiety disorder" a true health need in the morally significant sense of that word? Is the incidence of thyroid cancer really seven times higher in the U.S. than in rest of the world (even though death rates are the same)? Or is this a sort of epiphenomenon related to the very high rates of screening we do for this (and a number of other) diseases?

CONSTITUTIONAL PRINCIPLES OF HEALTH CARE JUSTICE AND RATIONAL DEMOCRATIC DELIBERATION

We now turn to the final structural element in our understanding of the process of rational democratic deliberation and wide reflective equilibrium; these are what I have referred to as constitutional principles of health care justice. This is obviously a metaphorical use of the phrase, but it does point to a social phenomenon or social understandings that are quite real. One of the key functions of these principles is to define the legitimate space of democratic deliberation. There can be some rationing proposals that do not warrant deliberation because they violate in an obvious way one or another of these constitutional constraints. Some might see this as illiberal or elitist, but such concerns would be very wide of the mark. Imagine someone proposing that we give serious thought to reinstituting slavery as a way of regaining our competitive edge in world labor markets. Such a proposal would be morally and constitutionally outrageous—there are no reasonable moral or legal justifications that can even be imagined by perverse philosophic minds to support such a proposal. Rejecting it out of hand is the only reasonable and liberally appropriate response. This is what Cohen (1993) and Rawls (1993) defend as a "reasonable pluralism." Likewise, if someone were to propose that AIDS patients should receive no health care at social expense that was related to any disease condition linked to their being HIV+, this too would just as readily be justifiably rejected as an option for democratic deliberation.

What we imagine being expressed by these constitutional principles of health care justice are the most fundamental conditions that must be respected in order to have a well-ordered deliberative democracy capable of articulating and legitimating through the deliberative process a fully adequate pluralistic conception of health care justice congruent with public reason. I would identify the following constitutional principles of health care justice: A principle of Equality, a principle of Liberty, a principle of Fair Equality of Opportunity, a Publicity principle, a principle of Respect for Persons, a principle of Liberal Neutrality, and a principle of Reciprocity. I make no claim that this list is complete, only that these principles seem necessary to sustain the effort to articulate a fully adequate pluralistic conception of health care justice. I will briefly explicate and illustrate each of these principles. Philosophic readers will readily appreciate the fact that volumes have been written on each of these principles; I can only say enough about them to make clear their application in a deliberative process about health care justice and the problem of health care rationing.

We can begin with the Publicity principle. This principle requires that our rationing policies and practices be the product of a public, visible decision-making process. It is not sufficient that the outcomes of the deliberative process be public; it must also be the case that the reasons and reasoning behind a specific rationing or priority-setting decision be public, transparent. This is what builds trust and stability. This is what assures all that the process is fair and worthy of respect and acceptance, even when a particular decision is seen as adversely affecting the self-interests of an individual. This is what assures all that favoritism has not infected the process. This is what permits mutual education through the deliberative process and a broad sharing of critical perspectives, all of which is aimed at producing as fair and as informed an outcome as is reasonable.

We saw in Chapter 3 that there are many advocates for the "virtues" of invisible rationing. But on closer inspection we found those are virtues only Ayn Rand (fully insured) could love. Mechanic (1997) argued for the view that physicians should not have to disclose to patients specific cost-control incentives that might shape their medical judgments as they address the health needs of a specific patient (such as income-related penalties for doing "excessive" diagnostic testing). This has the "virtue" of avoiding difficult conversations with patients that might potentially undermine the patient's belief that his physician is loyal and trustworthy regarding the patient's best interests. Such denials of potentially beneficial care are easily accomplished because the mechanism of denial is silence—a patient has nothing to assess, much less respond to. Worse still, no reasons are given to the patient, so the patient cannot be educated about the limits of contemporary medicine and resource allocation. Worst of all, the patient has no ability to appeal a decision that might have been unfair. These are the sorts of practices that the publicity principle would identify as presumptively objectionable.

A recent research article on cancer and nursing home patients reported the following conclusion: "Very few cancer services are provided to Medicaid-insured nursing home patients, despite the fact that many of these patients likely experienced cancer-related symptoms and marked physical decline before diagnosis and death" (Bradley et al., 2008, p. 21). What is noteworthy about these practices is that there might well be reasonable considerations of health care justice that would justify these practices and these outcomes. Most of these patients are in moderate to advanced stages of dementia; most have other significant comorbidities that would cause many physicians to wonder whether it was either compassionate or just to institute treatment. We might also ask what would be the strong considerations of health care justice that would *speak in favor* of saying such patients had a just claim to costly life-prolonging health care resources, or that these health needs should be somewhat high up on a priority-setting list. My judgment is that it might be difficult to find such considerations.

Nevertheless, my other judgment is that these practices in any nursing home are presumptively unjust because they are clear violations of the Publicity principle. I am certain these nursing homes are not informing future possible patients or their family members that these are the practices of the nursing home, and that these practices are primarily motivated by the desire to save money. Further, from the perspective of a justice-based public justification, it would not be morally sufficient for such nursing homes to simply publicize their cancer-care denial practices. The deliberative process itself is essential to justifying these nursing home rationing practices; this is what "full publicity" would require. The primary virtue of the deliberative process itself is that it permits all of us to articulate and legitimate rationing protocols for our future possible selves. That is, the deliberative process permits us to make fully informed, self-imposed rationing decisions. We can imagine a poll being done of all 50-year-olds in the U.S., 90% of whom would endorse the cancer-related rationing practices for their future possible demented selves. Such a poll, however, would be morally inadequate because it would not give individuals the opportunity to learn from those who disagreed with them what their reasons were for disagreeing. The deliberative process permits a kind of mutual education that can result in more informed judgments by all.

This brings us to the second of our constitutional principles, the Autonomy principle. Individuals must have a reasonable and effective opportunity to decide for themselves as citizens which rationing/cost-control/priority-setting policies and practices are reasonable and just. What we need to be reminded of is that our health care system is a very complex, cooperative enterprise to which virtually all in our society have contributed in multiple ways; it is a public interest and a shared social good. Our health care system is a *public interest* because it is essential to protecting the health of each and every one of us (certainly when our lives are threatened by serious illness), and it is an interest we cannot adequately protect for ourselves simply *as individuals*. Consequently, complex cooperative behavior with all in our society is necessary to protect that interest. What this means in relation to our Autonomy principle is that autonomy *cannot* mean that individuals have the right to take whatever they want from the health care system for any reason whatsoever; that yields the tragedy of the commons. Likewise, autonomy does *not* mean that individuals are free to not contribute to sustaining the health care system because they feel perfectly healthy and do not see themselves as having any present need for the system; that generates the "free riding" familiar to all political scientists. What we have in mind is the conception of autonomy that Rawls has articulated.

Rawls distinguishes "rational autonomy" from "full autonomy." Both are part of his overall conception of autonomy. Rational autonomy is about "having the moral power to form, to revise, and rationally to pursue a conception of the good," and "to deliberate in accordance with it" (1993, p. 72). Full autonomy "is realized by citizens when they act from principles of justice that specify the fair terms of cooperation they would give themselves when fairly represented as free and equal citizens" (p. 77). Rawls goes on to say that full autonomy is something realized by citizens in public life—it is "realized by participating in society's public affairs and sharing in its collective self-determination over time" (p. 78). This is the very opposite of the individualism that is central to American culture, and potentially corrosive of the full autonomy Rawls regards as politically necessary to preserve just social institutions and policies. The fullest realization of autonomy requires the fullest realization of social justice. Full autonomy and social justice are synergistic—not antagonistic—values.[16]

Rawls' "original position" description is intended to model what *rational* autonomy is, and the conception of justice he argues would emerge from that position. We are suggesting that a comparable model in connection with contemporary health care will yield a comparable conception of health care justice. As we have already noted, the original position involves the use of a veil of ignorance. For Rawls, that veil is very opaque in order to model the degree of impartiality that is required for a reasonable conception of justice to emerge from the deliberations. That degree of opaqueness is not achievable in the real world, but that degree of opaqueness is not required in order for us to articulate (through the deliberative process in the actual world) a shared conception of health care justice. The vast majority of us are truly and naturally ignorant of our future health needs because so many potential health needs are a product of accident and arbitrary collocation of circumstances (i.e., flying in a plane with a passenger with TB). It would be imprudent (irrational) if there was a strong history of heart disease in someone's family, and consequently, he bought health insurance only for heart disease (believing he was somehow magically immune to cancer or arthritis or liver disease, and so forth).

To appreciate the point of our saying that Autonomy is a constitutional principle of health care justice, imagine our individual above being diagnosed with cancer and having insurance only for heart disease. He realizes how foolish he has been (since he now knows he does not have the resources needed to purchase the health care that would significantly increase his life expectancy), so he now seeks to purchase a more expansive health insurance plan, but is turned down by all insurers. He feels that this represents an unjust restriction on his autonomy. But it is explained to him that what he is proposing would really be an unjust violation of the autonomy of everyone else who has invested in the insurance program for the past forty years. He was not barred from joining this insurance plan forty years ago; he chose not to join since he believed (wrongly) that this would be a foolish waste of his resources. But if he were permitted to join now, then he would be seeking to enjoy the benefits of this insurance plan without having borne his fair share of the costs. Further, if he were allowed to make such a choice (as a matter of respect for individual liberty), then all others would have the same right; if all those others chose to exercise that right, then there would be no insurance plan at all. All would be at the mercy of their health fates. All would have expressed their individual autonomy initially, only to find later that they had sacrificed both their individual autonomy as well as their chance for full autonomy.

What full autonomy requires is the sacrifice of purely self-interested individual autonomy that seeks to gain personal advantage at unjust cost to others. Consequently, in matters of health insurance and health care rationing, full autonomy requires that we come to agreement on a package of health care benefits that is just and prudent for all, where "all" includes all those future possible versions of myself that might come to be as a result of the health-related contingencies of the world. No socially affordable health insurance benefit package can maximize the likelihood that all citizens in our society will achieve a maximally medically possible life expectancy. But a reasonable and just health insurance benefit package that is a product of a fair deliberative process will maximize the opportunity for all citizens to achieve a reasonable life expectancy by having assured access to needed, effective, and costworthy health care. That would represent full autonomy. The principle of Autonomy is designed to exclude—as a deliberative option—health care policies and protocols that would be obstacles to full autonomy.

Our third constitutional principle would be a Liberty principle—this is what we would expect in a liberal society. Individuals should be free to choose their health care providers so long as those choices do not threaten to undermine or violate our shared understanding of health care justice. To illustrate this point and its limitations, if we had agreed for some range of very mundane medical problems primary care providers would be nurse practitioners and physician assistants (as a way of making more efficient use of the medical talents of physicians), then an individual who insisted on seeing a physician instead would have to pay the difference in cost for exercising this liberty right. This is not an unjust constraint on the liberty rights of anyone, including the working poor who might not be able to afford to exercise this liberty right. Likewise, without being able to go into a lot of detail, individuals would always have the liberty right to buy their way out of any rationing protocol *so long as their exercise of that right did not undermine or threaten the just claims of others to needed health care.* As noted elsewhere, a rich person could not "outbid" a poorer individual for the last bed in the ICU or for a needed transplantable organ. Access to such (contextually) absolutely scarce medical resources would have to be determined in accord with other justice-relevant criteria articulated through the democratic deliberative process. Our Liberty principle protects the right of citizens to purchase whatever they want in the way of alternative health care services, but those purchases would again have to be with private resources if justice-relevant considerations rightly excluded such services from a societal health benefit package.

The Liberty principle would also protect some specific range of liberty rights of health care providers; again, so long as the actual exercise of those rights did not threaten the justice commitments legitimated through the deliberative process. Thus, it is not obvious to me that we would be justified in outlawing all for-profit aspects of medicine as presumptively unjust. We must, in each case or each kind of case, consider the empirical evidence available to make a reasonable judgment. Should we permit physicians to own for-profit labs or imaging equipment or other such medically relevant services? There may not be an easy answer to this question, and there might well be deliberative compromises that can be worked out. Regulatory efforts might be effective in controlling overuse of such facilities and excess costs that might represent less than just claims on social resources.

Physician-owned for-profit specialty hospitals might be an easier call; these hospitals do generally represent a threat to the just distribution of health care resources. This is because they generally take the most well-insured and most profitable patients from community hospitals without accepting any responsibility for meeting comparable medical needs of patients with little or no ability to pay for needed care. In community hospitals, profitable patients help to underwrite the costs of needed care for unprofitable patients. Hence, the capacity of community hospitals to continue to provide high-quality care to all their patients (care that is clearly within the scope of health care justice) is very much threatened by these for-profit physician-owned hospitals.

Insurers may demand the liberty right to turn away customers with potentially costly medical problems, but these are the sort of unjust practices that the Liberty principle cannot possibly warrant. If such patients cannot (as a practical matter) be fairly spread across insurance plans, then for-profit insurance plans can be justly outlawed. What they would most clearly undermine is the protection of fair equality of opportunity for those who are medically least well-off but clearly capable of benefiting from what medicine has to offer. Insurance companies may justifiably claim that they are not charitable institutions, that investors expect them to make profit-maximizing decisions. The justice-relevant implication of that assertion is that a society that aspires to be just and caring in meeting the health needs of all its citizens does not need that type of business, since it interferes with our social capacity to be justly responsive to all our citizens' health needs.

The Equality principle is the fourth of our constitutional principles of health care justice. This again will be a complex principle in practice. The simple formal expression of the principle is that like cases should be treated alike. If we take the perspective of some physicians at the clinical level for purposes of determining the applicability of this principle, they will assert that no two patients are clinically alike; the medical circumstances of every patient are unique. But if we take that as an absolute medical truth, we would risk never having any rules or guidelines that would assure the fair and stable implementation of any rationing protocols. So we should really take that medical judgment as a global practical exaggeration.

There are very many *kinds of medical cases* sufficiently alike to warrant a similar medical response. Hence, what our Equality principle will mean in practice is that if we have a rationing protocol regarding access to implantable cardiac defibrillators ($40,000 each) that limits them to those with specific results from a T-wave alternans test, then exceptions will not be made (at social expense) for individuals who are excessively anxious or especially demanding or affectionately ingratiating (offering delicious baked goods to their physicians). If exceptions are to be made to any just rationing protocol that has been deliberatively legitimated, then that exception must be made for explicit justice-warranted reasons available for review by some impartial party in a health plan.

Again, the primary reason (from a structural perspective) why the deliberative process can yield just rationing protocols is that deliberators are making these decisions for their own future possible selves. All are subject to the same rationing protocols in the same (roughly) clinical circumstances. This is how we respect one another as moral equals. There cannot be blue-collar and white-collar and gold-collar rationing protocols that correlate with socioeconomic status (or any other accidental social characteristic) if we are to have just rationing protocols and policies that are seen as fair by all to whom they apply. Medicine is complex and medical problems are complex—there will be legitimate exceptions to many rationing protocols, but those exceptions themselves must be clearly warranted by the relevant scientific evidence and clear, considered judgments of health care justice. Being a powerful politician or prominent CEO or lovable sports star or hugely famous rock star or quirky philosopher are all irrelevant characteristics that would warrant any exception to any rationing protocol.

The objection will be raised that, very often, rich individuals will be able to buy their way out of the potential consequences of any particular rationing protocol. That seems to threaten the fairness and stability of any system of health care rationing we collectively endorse. My response, however, is that if we have created a fair and reasonable set of rationing protocols congruent with a reasonable level of social resources we are willing to dedicate to the meeting of health care needs in our society, then no one among our democratic deliberators is made worse off by allowing the wealthy to buy these exemptions for themselves. What we would remind everyone of is that the vast majority of likely rationing protocols constructed through the deliberative process would be aimed at denying our future possible selves what we rationally judged to be very marginally beneficial, excessively costly health care. That is, we have, in effect, said to ourselves that we would not use our own money to buy such health care for ourselves because there are too many other uses for that money we value more highly. And, from a justice perspective, if I regard such marginal care as a bad buy with my money, then I have no moral or political right to commandeer the money of others to buy such care for myself. If other individuals still choose to make that purchase for themselves, then I am not morally harmed by that choice. We are a free society. There are lots of ridiculous things that wealthy people choose to spend their money on—if they wish to spend that same money instead on cancer drugs that cost $100,000 and that might give them several extra months of life, then that should not be objectionable as long as it is a wholly private expenditure (no tax breaks).

I can imagine some potential complications that might have to be resolved through the deliberative process. I cannot fully discuss these now, but I will identify the problem with an example. If someone has purchased one of those expensive cancer drugs, and then suffers complications associated with that therapy which we would ordinarily regard as covered health care services in the national benefit package, does justice then require that we cover those expenses from social resources or would justice require that individuals be responsible for those additional costs as well (the argument being that but for their purchase of that marginal therapy it was unlikely they would have been faced with these additional costly medical consequences)?

Our fifth constitutional principle would be that of protecting fair and effective equality of opportunity. Here I call attention to the work of Norman Daniels (1985), which is quite insightful in this regard. Our core moral intuition is that we ought to be responsive to health care needs. But the language of needs in social practice is open to wide and morally unmanageable interpretation. The health needs that matter (as far as justice is concerned) are those that are linked to protecting fair and effective equality of opportunity. Daniels uses the notion of equality of opportunity broadly; it is not limited to the notion of jobs open to talent. The "opportunity" he has in mind would be the normal range of human experiences that make life interesting and meaningful and fulfilling. Among the major moral advantages of this broad a conception of opportunity is that older individuals who are out of the work force or persons with a wide range of disabilities are not at risk of having their health needs ignored because they may not be economically productive members of society. So far as health care justice is concerned in protecting fair and effective equality of opportunity, the opportunities associated with being the CEO at Microsoft are no more and no less valuable than the opportunities available to the Executive Director of Not Dead Yet (a prominent disability organization) or the experiential opportunities available to a 91-year-old grandmother in an assisted living facility.

What I have just explicated is the "fair" part of equality of opportunity. But we need to take equally seriously (as a matter of justice) the "effective" part. Effectiveness can fail at either end of the medical encounter. Effectiveness may fail because the technology itself in the range of clinical circumstances for which it was designed may yield little in the way of objective clinical benefit. If an antidepressant lifts the experience of depression by only 20% in only 10% of patients who are given the drug, then that drug is not very effective in increasing or protecting the experiential opportunities of depressed patients who take that drug.

Effectiveness can also fail at the patient end of the clinical encounter. That is, a particular medical intervention may very often have dramatic life-prolonging or quality-of-life ameliorating effects. But in particular types of patients who are in particular types of clinical circumstances, its effectiveness may be barely detectable in terms of protecting or enhancing the experiential opportunities of those patients. An ICD can yield for some patients many valuable, fulfilling, extra years of life that they otherwise would have been denied by a reversible but otherwise fatal arrhythmic event. But if that patient is in the advanced stages of dementia, the device might work magnificently but it will have virtually no effect so far as protecting effective equality of opportunity. The capacity to enjoy a satisfying or meaningful life may have been completely lost in such a person—or worse, the life they actually experience might be terrifying, frighteningly confusing.

Another type of patient-centered failure might be related to the genotype of a patient—this is likely to be an increasingly common phenomenon over the next couple of decades. Some patients may have genotypes that are either especially responsive or especially nonresponsive to certain drugs. If we focus our attention for now on patients who are poorly responsive to a certain drug because of their genotype, this may be *unfortunate* (especially if this means their lives might be significantly shortened) but it is not obviously unjust if we have a rationing protocol that would deny them access to that drug at social expense. This challenge might be most socially distressing when the drugs we are talking about are regarded as "last-chance" therapies that are extraordinarily costly. But that social distress is not equivalent to justified moral distress.

As we saw above in our cardiac/cancer genotype example, it would be especially distressing when such drugs work especially well for some segment of this patient population but barely work at all in some larger portion of that patient population. It feels psychologically uncomfortable that we would provide social resources to a portion of this patient group and deny them to another portion of the group where the likelihood of a positive response was very low. Despite these psychological feelings, it would not be unjust if such a rationing/distributional protocol were adopted and legitimated through the democratic deliberative process. We can say that the "same patients with the same medical condition" were not treated equally. But there were these morally relevant differences between the groups; our principle of protecting fair and effective equality of opportunity would provide a presumptive moral warrant for such a choice. Again, we remind the reader that the deliberative process is taking place (generally) when the vast majority of deliberators are ignorant of their future possible medical circumstances. Thus, in this case deliberators could be in either the genetically favored group or the genetically disfavored group (should their medical circumstances develop that way). Consequently, whatever their judgment might be, it will not be flawed so far as impartiality is concerned; the protocol would be fair and legitimate. It would not violate any of our constitutional principles of health care justice nor would it be especially disruptive so far as reflective equilibrium was concerned.

Our sixth constitutional principle of health care justice is a principle of Respect for Persons. There are two major aspects to this principle: (1) respect for cultural and religious differences among patients related to health care needs, and (2) respect for patients as ends in themselves who should not be used by others for their ends. With regard to our first point, our general social rule (as a liberal, pluralistic society) ought to be seeking to accommodate special health care needs related to the cultural or religious commitments of patients *so long as the accommodation of those needs does not threaten the just claims of other patients to have their health needs met.* Thus, we respect the rights of Jehovah's Witness patients to refuse blood transfusions for surgery, and we will often modify surgical procedures in ways designed to minimize blood loss in order to maximally protect their lives while respecting their religious commitments.

By way of contrast, one of our newer drugs is a genetically engineered version of factor VII, which is very effective in achieving rapid blood clotting. This is an extraordinarily expensive drug that can cost $100,000 for an episode of bleeding. Some hemophiliacs will have a clear (no alternative) need for this drug to save their lives; they will have a presumptive just claim to that resource at social expense. If a Jehovah's Witness patient is aware of this drug, is undergoing major surgery with a substantial risk of bleeding out, but does not want to die and does not want a blood transfusion either, then (I argue) they would have no just claim to factor VII at social expense. Our unwillingness to provide this drug to them does not represent any disrespect for their religious beliefs; it represents instead the flip side of our liberal commitments to respect diverse religious views by insisting that we will not provide public subsidies for the support of an individual's religious beliefs (especially if those subsidies were provided at the expense of other just health care claims). Thus, we would provide this drug to these patients if they are able to pay for it, either through some form of supplemental insurance or through a charitable appeal to their community. But if no insurance company were willing to offer such a product, or if an individual Jehovah's Witness patient had been unable or unwilling to purchase that insurance, we would not be acting unjustly in denying them factor VII.

The other aspect of our principle of Respect for Persons is that patients not be used as means to satisfy the objectives of others. We cannot permit any coerced health care bargains. We cannot permit any cost-control protocols or practices that would threaten the integrity of the commitment of physicians to the just medical interests of their patients. We cannot permit cost-control mechanisms aimed at patients that motivate patients to deny themselves needed beneficial health care, especially if such cost control mechanisms would have their most effective impact on patients who were financially least well-off. One of the major lessons from the Rand experiments was that cost controls aimed at patients work, but they work in a very nondiscriminating way. That is, patients deny themselves what, from a medical point of view, are both beneficial and non-beneficial health care services (and these are decisions they typically make for themselves without the benefit of medical judgment because the decision very often is whether or not to show up in a doctor's office). These sorts of self-denials of care will often be a mix of just and unjust self-denials.

Deliberative democratic conversations about health care rationing are also forms of self-denial, but this is collectively informed self-denial shaped by the specific moral norms of justice also endorsed in that process. To the extent that rationing protocols that are a product of the deliberative conversation are congruent with our constitutional principles of health care justice, they will reflect mutual respect among free and equal deliberators. That is, no one is being denied needed health care to achieve social objectives unrelated to health care justice. From the perspective of the moral integrity of physicians, their compliance with these protocols does not represent any morally objectionable compromise of their commitments to their patients. But cost-control mechanisms that somewhat indiscriminately incentivize physicians to save money by providing less care (without the specific guidance of democratically legitimated, just, rationing protocols) risk random injustices due to the essentially private way in which physicians would make these judgments.

Our seventh constitutional principle of health care justice is a principle of Liberal Neutrality. Just rationing protocols must be rationally justified through public reason. Just rationing protocols must not reflect deep religious or comprehensive views. Thus, a rationing protocol that would deny public funding for contraceptives or for various forms of assisted reproduction or for preimplantation genetic diagnosis (when there was a known prior risk of having a child with a serious genetic disorder) because such procedures would be offensive to Roman Catholics or those committed to a right-to-life perspective would be presumptively violative of our Liberal

Neutrality principle. These are not public reasons. Having said that, the reader should not instantly come to the opposite conclusion; namely, that the health care services identified above must necessarily be part of a just comprehensive package of health benefits guaranteed to all in our society. An argument based in public reason will have to be made for the inclusion of any of these services in a national health benefit package. Further, if that argument is made successfully, then the additional argument must be made that these services deserve relatively high priority in our overall scheme of beneficial health care services. Relative to protease inhibitors for HIV+ patients, or relative to these very expensive cancer drugs in patients with metastatic disease, or relative to those drugs that might stave off macular degeneration in the elderly, or relative to patients in end-stage heart failure who need an artificial heart, is it more important or less important (as a matter of health care justice) that we fund access to preimplantation genetic diagnosis for a couple at risk of having a child with a serious genetic disorder at a cost of $40,000 per successful pregnancy? For now, we only raise these questions as a way of illustrating the applicability of this principle; we address such questions in considerable depth in Chapter 12.

Our eighth constitutional principle of health care justice is a principle of Reciprocity. Reciprocity is about cooperation among free and equal citizens. Rawls writes:

> Cooperation involves the idea of fair terms of cooperation: these are terms that each participant may reasonably accept, provided that everyone else likewise accepts them. Fair terms of cooperation specify an idea of reciprocity: all who are engaged in cooperation and who do their part as the rules and procedure require, are to benefit in an appropriate way as assessed by a suitable benchmark of comparison. (1993, p. 16)

What commitment to reciprocity will mean in practice is that the same comprehensive package of health care benefits will be guaranteed to all in our society, and that the same set of rational protocols and the same priority scheme will establish just limits with respect to that health care benefit package. Because we have to give one another reasons that are mutually acceptable for including or excluding any particular health service in particular clinical circumstances, and because we ourselves will have to live with the future consequences of our choices, and because the deliberative process itself will educate us about the range and likelihood of various health vulnerabilities (so that our individual areas of ignorance are suitably corrected for), and because we all have bonds of affection and capacities for compassion that link us in complex ways to numerous others throughout society with a broad range of health problems and needs (thereby helping to correct excessive attention to our narrow health self-interests), a suitably managed deliberative process will likely yield "fair enough" terms of cooperation that are congruent with the requirements of the Reciprocity principle. If the deliberative procedures and deliberative principles outlined here are scrupulously adhered to, it is very difficult to imagine how a rationing protocol would be legitimated as fair that disadvantaged some identifiable group in our society.

EVALUATING THE DELIBERATIVE PROCESS

I have been conducting deliberative community dialogues for more than 20 years. I have identified what I would regard as a useful set of criteria for structuring those dialogues before the fact, and assessing those dialogues after the fact.

First, do individual participants in the deliberative process say that they find themselves **internally conflicted** regarding the particular range of issues under discussion regarding health care rationing or genetics, ethics, and policy? To my mind this is the single most important touchstone for a fair and effective democratic deliberative process. In recruiting participants for these community dialogue sessions, we told them what we most wanted to avoid was the bitter ideological divisiveness and intransigence and mindless inflammatory rhetoric that has characterized much of the public debate about abortion. There is certainly the potential for that happening a hundred times over with each moral and political issue that emerges that is linked to some specific rationing issue, or to our developing genetic knowledge and related technologies. The socially important difference is that the abortion issue is relatively isolated—it touches directly the lives of only relatively small numbers of people, which means that the vast majority of our population can choose to be indifferent or disengaged from the verbal battles. The rationing and genetics issues, however, will increasingly affect directly a very large portion of our population in many different ways, which means there is the potential for a manifold increase in the level of corrosive social and political friction.

What we have found in our community dialogue projects is that the single most important goal that must be accomplished is creating in the minds of deliberators this sense of internal conflict. If this can be accomplished effectively in the earliest stages of deliberation, then political or ideological straitjackets will typically be greatly loosened. Individuals will find themselves in a puzzled frame of mind that will more readily dispose them to engage in cooperative social problem-solving, rather than heated debates where there must necessarily be winners and losers. The tone and nature of the deliberative process is markedly different when a range of options are being cooperatively assessed for their strengths and weaknesses in addressing a social problem, as opposed to having groups of individuals "defend a point of view" to which they are rigidly attached. Mutual education is possible and effective in the former process, whereas in the latter process the object is to "score points" against the opposition.

This brings us to our second norm for assessing the moral and political integrity of these deliberative efforts, which can be captured in the motto "science matters." Put in question form, we ask whether dialogue participants have been given the capacity **to use available scientific knowledge honestly** to inform their ethics and policy judgments, recognizing always the fallibility of such scientific knowledge, as well as the different degrees of confidence that might be attached to one or another scientific claim. This is where expertise has an important role to play in contributing to the value and integrity of these democratic deliberative efforts (Garland, 1999). Good ethics and policy must be informed by sound science (which is still fallible science). And good ethics and policy can be very badly subverted by science badly presented in the media—sometimes initiated by scientists themselves seeking to exaggerate the significance of their research. Much of the research related to these extremely expensive cancer drugs is presented with a level of hyperbole that is extravagant (to say the least).

This brings us to our third norm for assessing the quality and integrity of these public deliberations. Are dialogue participants more consistently in the habit of **giving reasons** for their point of view in relation to one or another option under discussion? This is absolutely essential to appreciating what is distinctive about this deliberative process, and is intended to be *rational* democratic deliberation. Some critics have suggested disdainfully that this emphasis represents an academic or philosophic bias; that what we are attempting to advocate as a social ideal is the academic seminar. However, I would contend that this criticism is unfair. The process of reason-giving is an ordinary and essential part of our lives, both as members of a moral community and as members of a political community. While practices of reason-giving are manifold and complex, the critical importance of the practice is that it permits us to relate to one another in a distinctively human way—as rational beings capable of cooperating freely with one another to create and advance common goals—as opposed to having to be coerced by formal authority into participating in specific social practices. There is nothing especially esoteric or "merely academic" about such a practice.

Closely related to our third norm is our fourth norm. Have dialogue participants been able to distinguish **specific value judgments that belong in the domain of public reason** from others that have a legitimate role only in their personal lives or in much narrower social groups? Again, this has something of an esoteric ring to it. Citing Rawls' work in this regard (as I did earlier) would likely reinforce that belief. Most members of our society would struggle to understand the central points of Rawls' *Political Liberalism*. However, Rawls' central concerns in that volume are not that distant or that intrinsically unintelligible to most citizens of our society. Most of our citizens are familiar with the phrase "separation of church and state," and have at least a rough appreciation of the importance of that political commitment. We argue about the edges of that commitment, but the core is something that is very widely endorsed as central to the liberal nature of our society. We are not at all inclined to embrace the theocratic society of the Taliban. Consequently, when we must work together to shape public policy about a social problem suffused with these conflicting values (as illustrated above), and we want to achieve agreement that is sufficiently rational and reasonable to assure stability, we realize that we must be careful about the kinds of reasons we can invoke to elicit the free agreement of other citizens. I will concede to my putative critic that as a matter of fact we have only a limited number of social and political practices that exemplify this norm; consequently, considerable political education and political practice development will be necessary to make more common and feasible this deliberative model. Hopefully, this will motivate efforts to develop these deliberative capacities.

The remaining norms for assessing the integrity of these democratic deliberative efforts may be presented more succinctly. Our fifth norm is this: Are dialogue participants recognizing the **numerous values** that have a bearing on the particular problem under discussion? This norm makes explicit what Rawls would refer to as the fact of value pluralism (Rawls, 1993, chap. 4). In our personal lives we may choose to give supremacy to one value with respect to which we organize our lives; but in our lives as liberal citizens, this is a political impossibility. The flip side of this norm (and related to the public reason norm) is that we might mistakenly dismiss from the deliberative conversation a value seen as attached to a specific religious worldview. I have in mind something like "respect for human life," which might be embedded in a rich religious perspective represented by a "sanctity of life ethic." That value can be abstracted from the religious belief system in which it may be embedded for some. To the extent that is possible, it is a legitimate member of the numerous values that need to be considered in our deliberative conversations.

Sixth, do dialogue participants see the deliberative process (as a whole) as **fair and impartial**; not designed in a way aimed at manipulating participants to endorse some predetermined outcome? All will recognize that this will be a challenging norm to satisfy in practice, but there are all sorts of ways of coming close to meeting this challenge. Failure to satisfy this challenge sufficiently clearly undermines the legitimacy of any policy choices that might emerge from the deliberative process. In our actual community dialogues, both in the "Just Caring" project in Goshen and under the ELSI grants, we deliberately recruited participants associated with Right to Life, with various disability organizations, and with various religious groups. Our thought was that failure to include these voices would almost certainly undercut entirely the legitimacy of our deliberative model.

Our next three norms may be bundled together. Seventh, do dialogue participants feel comfortable because they are genuinely **speaking to one another as equals**? Eighth, do dialogue participants consistently **show respect** to one another, avoiding behaviors that others would often regard as being signals of disrespect? Ninth, is there evidence in the dialogue process that **mutual understanding** is being achieved, that individuals are truly engaged in a common task and not just serially expressing opinions? These are all process norms, but no less important for that reason. In the deliberative process, we are all there "as citizens," as equal members of this society. Social standing, wealth, levels of formal education, and so on are all irrelevant so far as democratic deliberation is concerned. Likewise, being respectful is critical to the success of the deliberative process. By definition, the process has been initiated because there are some deeply controversial issues that need to be addressed. Participants will disagree with one another, but that disagreement can be expressed in ways that are fundamentally respectful of the other. If such mutual respect can be maintained, then the likelihood of achieving mutual understanding is improved, which in turn will provide the footing for the difficult compromises and balancings of competing values that will be needed in some chosen policy option.

Our next three norms may again be bundled together. Tenth, have dialogue participants been able **to identify and express some shared values** that are relevant to the issue being discussed? Eleventh, have dialogue participants been able to identify and assess both **assumptions and consequences** associated with their point of view? Twelfth, have dialogue participants been able to identify what they regard as **public interests or common interests** that ought to be used as reference points for assessing any public policies related either to issues of health care rationing or to genetics and emerging genetic technologies? These three norms are associated with practical things that must occur to move the conversation forward. They are very much internal norms associated with specific democratic deliberations—there is a recognition that the conversation began with a diversity of points of view, but that virtually all within the conversation are experiencing the internal conflict described above. In addition, there is a shared sense (albeit diffuse) that some sort of policy response is necessary to address the problem, that it would not be good to just allow the problem to simmer unaddressed. We need answers to a specific rationing problem we are confronted with now. Further, there are multiple policy options that might be articulated, but some common reference points are needed to assess those options. Hence, one of the mediating goals of the conversation is to identify or construct or reconstruct some shared values—considered judgments of health care justice—which would assist with policy assessment. Likewise, judging the degree to which there is a shared appreciation of the likely consequences of different policy options is important. And again, what justifies the public nature of the conversation is the initial judgment that there are public interests that are at stake that somehow need to be protected or adjudicated. To accomplish that, it may be necessary to refine and further specify the nature of those public interests.

Finally, there are three more norms that we can discuss as a cluster. Thirteenth, is there evidence from the dialogue process that there has been successful **mutual civic education**, that individuals have learned what they judge to be important things from one another for making better judgments in matters of public policy related to emerging genetic knowledge and technologies? That mutual civic education is not just about scientific matters; more importantly, it is about the gradual evolution of new or more complex shared value perspectives, the sorts of commitments that build more stable reference points (what Rawls would call "considered value judgments") for addressing what will surely be a steady flow of other social policy problems related to these new medical technologies. That will have the effect of softening the intensity of future value conflicts related to these technologies as social capacities are created for addressing the problems raised. Again, what we gradually seek to achieve as each problem reaches the social agenda is what Rawls would refer to as a "social reflective equilibrium." (Daniels, 1996; Rawls, 1993, chap. 3, pp. 95–99).

Our fourteenth norm is this: Is there evidence from the dialogue process that participants have a better understanding of the **complexity of the issues** they have been discussing, and the **inherent uncertainty** that must characterize such discussions? Given the potentially far-reaching effects that many social policies (rationing policies) can have once accepted, it may be a bit unnerving to think about all the uncertainties that are inherently part of these deliberative efforts. Such uncertainty could yield timidity—an unwillingness to face at all the policy response that may be called for by a particular genetically related social problem. But timidity can have its own costs; it can hardly be seen as a morally or politically "safe" response.

Better, I would argue that the deliberative process develop within our citizens a capacity to deal fairly and intelligently with these inherent uncertainties, both with regard to the relevant scientific knowledge as well as the consequences of putting novel policies into practice.

Finally, our fifteenth norm is: Do dialogue participants see themselves as expressing **greater toleration** for choices others might make that they might not make for themselves? This is a really a critical hallmark of a liberal society, and is especially pertinent to the issues of genetics and reproductive decision making we discuss below in Chapter 10. Public policy can serve many very broad social purposes. It may be used to *prohibit* certain options, such as cloning or physician-assisted suicide. That represents a restriction of personal liberty that might be justified if certain uses of that liberty threatened substantial harm to important public interests. Public policy might also be used to *prioritize*, to regulate and balance conflicts among important public values and public interests. This is certainly true regarding the rationing issues we are addressing. And public policy might also be used to *protect and promote* certain space for the exercise of individual liberty, even when that liberty is used in ways that others might find offensive or contrary to their visions of what it means to live a good life in a decent society. Developing a public capacity to understand the political importance of mutual tolerance in those controversial areas is a very important task for democratic deliberation in a liberal society, most especially when those controversial areas are linked to very intimate aspects of our lives as persons.

OBJECTIONS AND RESPONSES

In the concluding portion of this chapter, I will briefly address some major criticisms aimed at undermining the moral utility, reliability, and viability of attempting to use rational democratic deliberation as I have outlined it here to address the problem of health care justice, especially the problem of health care rationing. Probably the most concise way of globally capturing a central criticism is that the whole process is too utopian; it is just not capable of realization, much less the realization of a more just approach to the problem of health care rationing.

One version of this global criticism is that moral disagreement in our society goes "all the way down." An unbridgeable chasm separates different moral tribes who seem capable of doing no more than yelling and screaming at one another across that chasm. What these critics most often have in mind is the social acrimony that characterizes the abortion issue in our society. I grant my critics that that same sort of acrimony *could* infect many other morally controversial issues in our society that might require some sort of public policy response, but this is not a metaphysical or political necessity. I myself have constructed and directed a number of deliberative forums over the past 30 years that have demonstrated the capacity of citizens in our society to engage in respectful and productive deliberation around a number of morally controversial policy issues. This includes the original "Just Caring" project in Goshen, Indiana (1985–1987), and two

NIH-funded projects under the ELSI program (Ethical and Social Implications of the Human Genome project). Those latter projects were from 1995–98 and 1998–2002. The first of these was titled "Genome Technology and Reproduction: Values and Public "Policy." The second was titled "Communities of Color: Genetics and Public Policy." The first of these projects involved dialogue groups of 30–50 individuals in each of seven communities who engaged in a total of 13 deliberative sessions, each around a broad range of ethical and policy issues related to genetics, ethics, reproductive decision-making, and public policy.

We deliberately recruited in each community representatives from Right to Life, various religious groups, and various disability groups.[17] We learned a number of important lessons from these projects about successful deliberative efforts. The most important of these lessons was one that I have already described; namely, that individuals may start with very diverse moral commitments and political views, but if, at the beginning of the deliberative process, individuals can internalize in themselves a certain moral conflict at the heart of a social problem, then they are in fact strongly motivated to talk and work cooperatively with one another. This will be especially true if the problem is seen as having a degree of urgency to it, and if it is seen as a real social problem. Prominent politicians may be ideologues, but the vast majority of Americans are much more pragmatic and much less ideological. Virtually all the problems of health care rationing I have introduced so far are the sorts of problems that can be readily internalized by each deliberator as a value conflict within them, as opposed to a value conflict between themselves and their neighbors. This is what disposes individuals to talk respectfully to one another and to listen attentively to one another. At the end of these longer deliberative processes, the vast majority of participants reported that their views had changed as a result of what they had learned through the deliberative process. My judgment is that it was helpful to the deliberative goals of these projects that no one was running for office or pushing some specific public policy that (it was hoped) all would be persuaded to embrace. The deliberative agenda was open and could be constructed by participants. There were genuine disagreements throughout the project, but these disagreements were consistently respectfully presented and discussed. Care was taken by project organizers to make certain all understood this expectation from the beginning of their involvement in any of these projects.

To avoid any misconceptions, I fully expect that all manner of value disagreements will persist in our society because of commitments to differing comprehensive religious and philosophic views. However, to the extent that such views are "reasonable," respectful social tolerance is possible and destructive divisiveness is avoidable. Rawls (1993) and Sunstein (1996) have two concepts that capture the phenomenon that makes this possible. Rawls speaks of an "overlapping consensus," while Sunstein speaks of "incompletely theorized agreement"—I believe both phrases refer to the same social phenomenon. Specifically, individuals who have very different comprehensive views can agree on the same considered judgments of health care justice with respect to some very specific rationing situation, and they can articulate the same rationale from the perspective of public reason for endorsing that judgment (which means there is genuine agreement there); but they might have very different "deep" reasons for endorsing that judgment that reflect their differing comprehensive views. What public reason provides is a thin, unifying framework for a liberal pluralistic society that is sufficient for ensuring the stability of that society in the face of otherwise deep disagreements about fundamental, philosophic, or religious commitments. Sunstein writes: "My particular interest here is in a third kind of phenomenon, of special interest for law: incompletely theorized agreements on particular outcomes, accompanied by agreements on the narrow or low-level principles that account for them" (p. 37). This is often sufficient to allow social and political problem-solving that is respectful in the face of deeper disagreements.[18]

But Sunstein (2001, chap. 1) has called our attention in his recent work to another phenomenon that is more socially dangerous from a deliberative perspective—he speaks of "deliberative enclaves." These are groups of individuals who are drawn to one another because they share a certain view on a certain social problem. They often come together through these "talk radio" programs or through the Internet. These programs are very socially divisive and socially destructive; they help to create very socially isolated groups. These are precisely the sort of social phenomena that need to be resisted and criticized, in part because they have the tendency to generate opinions that are more radical, less rational, and certainly less open to revision in the light of new evidence. They are the very opposite of what deliberative democratic forums aspire to. They most certainly do not represent the liberal, pluralistic, tolerant foundational values that have defined the American experiment in democracy.

For now I will consider only one other critical comment. Hall (1997) contends that the social costs of publicity and public deliberation about tragic rationing decisions are unacceptably high. He writes, "It is rational and morally defensible to not want to know, even if, once we know, we can no longer pretend we don't" (p. 97). This comment overlooks the massive (largely hidden or obscured) injustices that are part of our health care system right now. These are very high costs which a just and caring society can hardly justifiably ignore. The justified suspicion in this case is that those who would avert their gaze from these injustices are not the victims of these injustices. We have noted already, just to mention one point, that there are about 20,000 premature deaths each year that are directly linked to the fact that these individuals are without health insurance; no one calculates other kinds of unnecessary health-related suffering other uninsured individuals endure. The "tragic choice" argument is more an excuse for moral indifference and moral apathy than a reasonable explanation for regrettable injustices. These are precisely the sorts of social problems that democratic deliberation must publicly expose.

6

SETTING LIMITS FOR EFFECTIVE COSTLY THERAPIES

PROBLEM INTRODUCTION

May a just and caring society ever justifiably deny individuals access to costly, very effective, life-sustaining medical technologies simply because of the cost of those technologies? For many, that question will be seen as answering itself, especially in the context of our own wealthy society. This is why we created the 1972 ESRD amendments to the Medicare program. We were not going to let patients die of renal failure simply for lack of money when we could sustain their lives for many years. As already noted, however, that noble sentiment had a relatively brief life expectancy—once we realized that dialysis was not a unique, costly technology but only the headwaters of a torrent of such technology, we pulled back on any implied global commitment to funding all such technologies. Specifically, Congress refused to create a sort of national health insurance program for major organ transplants, even though the development of the drug cyclosporine made such transplants very effective as a life-prolonging procedure.

As we noted in an earlier chapter, Congress could be open to moral criticism for that refusal because the ESRD amendments covered the cost of kidney transplants. Patients needing heart or liver transplants can reasonably ask why their $400,000 heart or liver transplants are not receiving equal consideration. Prima facie, they are just as urgently needy, just as morally equal, and just as likely to benefit with significantly prolonged life as any dialysis patient.[1] Further, if such a commitment were made, the likely aggregate annual cost of that commitment would be no more than $2.5 billion atop the $23 billion we are currently (2006) spending on the ESRD program. However, as we also noted, the artificial heart was in the earliest stages of development in the late 1970s when Congress was faced with this issue. Though it would still be a couple decades before a sufficiently well engineered model was ready for clinical testing, Congress had every reason to believe the device would be perfected. The moral and political problem then would be how many of these devices would be funded under a kind of national health insurance program for artificial hearts. The natural limit established by patients declared brain dead who were willing to be organ donors has been for many years in the vicinity of 2,500, but computer modeling at the time suggested we could be implanting 350,000 of these devices per year. If the cost of implanting these devices were only $200,000 each (which is a very conservative cost figure), the aggregate cost would be at least $70 billion more per year in additional health costs.[2] What these devices would promise *on average* was five additional years of life expectancy. We will explore these issues more fully later in this chapter.

Our theme throughout this chapter will be "setting limits." Of course, we have been talking about that for the first five chapters. What makes this discussion distinctive is that we will be raising the question of how a just and caring society can set limits with regard to costly but efficacious life-prolonging medical technologies. Our intuitive reaction is that there is something morally distressing about this very idea. Surely, we think, there must be thousands of ways of saving money by eliminating coverage for all manner of lower-priority health care interventions before we would reduce our commitment to technologies such as the artificial heart. This would be a reasonable thought if we were talking about a few billion dollars, but we are talking about tens of billions of dollars for just *this one new medical technology*. And, we need to add, that the 350,000 annual figure for potential recipients of the artificial heart reflects only the current U.S. population and likelihood of need. The aging out of the WWII "baby boom" generation is likely to require an even higher implantation figure, unless some sort of limits are set. A reasonable guess at that number would be an additional 200,000 of these devices per year. Let me offer an example of the sort of situation we would hope to avoid.

In the United Kingdom there are about 60,000 individuals with ankylosing spondylitis (AS), a very painful and debilitating form of inflammatory arthritis striking young men. A relatively new therapy called anti-TNF can dramatically improve their overall functioning, but at a yearly cost of about $20,000 per patient. The British National Health Service (NHS) agreed to pay for Herceptin for metastatic breast cancer, but not anti-TNF therapy. My judgment is that this represents a serious moral mistake. I cannot be 100% confident of the correctness of my judgment. I am not at all certain that this judgment of mine would be endorsed in a democratic deliberative process. I do not know for a fact what factors were most decisive for the NHS in rendering this judgment. It might have been the aggregate annual cost of the two interventions. Herceptin would have an annual cost for the defined population in Britain (metastatic breast cancer) of about a half billion dollars. Those 60,000 AS patients would generate annual costs of about $1.2 billion. Given how tight NHS budgets are, this might have been the whole story. There might also have been more sympathy generated by the fact that these were women faced with premature death.

If Herceptin rescued these women from death and offered them an indefinite life expectancy, or at least five extra years of life, then I would likely have to endorse the judgment of the NHS in this case. But the facts are that Herceptin in these clinical circumstances offers an average gain of 5.5 months of life at a cost of about $70,000. Patients with AS are so crippled and in such pain that they are unable to work—judging from the descriptions I have read of this disease process, these young men would have a seriously impaired capacity to enjoy virtually any aspect of life. If anti-TNF therapy is as effective as it seems to be, then from the perspective of protecting fair and effective equality of opportunity this intervention ought to be much higher on the priority scale than Herceptin. It is tragic and unfortunate that these women who are significantly short of achieving a normal life expectancy would be denied the last six months of their life in being denied Herceptin, but the alternative would be to permit severe suffering for decades for each of these young men denied anti-TNF therapy (Kobelt et al., 2008). From the perspective of health care justice (fair equality of opportunity), this looks like the greater harm.

I will note in passing that from a utilitarian cost-effectiveness perspective, the anti-TNF therapy would also be the better buy (roughly $20,000 per year compared to $140,000 to gain a year of life). Of course, as noted already, the fact that an intervention is a lot less expensive relative to another intervention can be irrelevant from a budgetary perspective if substantially fewer of the costly interventions are needed. Statins cost "only" $1,100 per year, but if 65 million Americans "needed" them indefinitely, we would have a serious budgetary problem.

Here is a "setting limits" problem I want to use to concretize the central issue of this chapter. Assume we have to work within a very fixed budget for the national health plan, and we can fully fund access to artificial hearts (at about $70 billion). We will imagine that the cost of anti-TNF therapy for all AS patients in the U.S. is about $3 billion. If we believe that there are very strong justice obligations that require funding all 350,000 artificial hearts, then there will be no anti-TNF therapy at public expense (as in the UK). If failing to fund anti-TNF therapy is judged to be seriously morally objectionable, then we would have to reduce by 5% the number of patients who would be candidates for an artificial heart. If we were to agree to reduce the number of candidates for an artificial heart, then what criteria would be reasonable and "just enough" to accomplish that goal?

We have to raise these very same questions over a range of costly life-prolonging technologies. Hence, we need to ask what would be fair and reasonable limits to dialysis, or to factor VIII for hemophilia, or to treatments for cystic fibrosis, or to the drugs that have been successful in keeping HIV in check. What limits should we have with regard to NICU care; especially extremely low birth weight infants? We cannot expect to come up with some complete set of rationing protocols; our goal is to identify deliberative options that are "fair enough" and "reasonable enough" for public deliberation as we have characterized it. That also means we wish to identify options that are "outside" the deliberative pale, either because they would very clearly violate one of our constitutional principles of health care justice, or because they would cause such disruption in a settled reflective equilibrium that it is virtually impossible to imagine how that equilibrium could be reasonably restored, or because a particular intervention under particular circumstances cannot reasonably be seen as a matter of justice (i.e., most sorts of cosmetic surgery).

SETTING LIMITS: OPTIONS IN THE ESRD PROGRAM

We can begin our inquiry with an historical example: the ESRD program. The original idea was that all costs of dialysis and kidney transplant would be covered by the program. As program costs grew by billions beyond the original projections, demands were made to "do something" to control those costs. Efforts were made to encourage more patients to embrace home dialysis, which would reduce annual dialysis costs by 50% (but part of that cost would in reality be shifted to the home since some other person needs to be available to assist on a daily basis). Reimbursements to providers were gradually reduced to force efficiencies, but some literature suggests some adverse impacts on quality. These were very dispersed and sporadic impacts. The justice-relevant question we can raise is whether such sporadic reductions in quality were a morally tolerable outcome from efforts to reduce costs to Medicare. This is a complicated question in practice that is very sensitive to factual details. If the Medicare payments to these private providers are fair and reasonable, then Medicare is not open to justified moral criticism. If some private providers are motivated by greed to maximize profits at increased risk to patients (reusing dialysis equipment only marginally sterilized), then they are open to justified moral criticism. The problem is that those instances of sporadic bad behavior may not be sufficient to justify any policy change. Inspections would minimize such risks, but might negate the savings that had been hoped for.

A more serious justice question arises in connection with immunosuppressant medication costs. In 2005 those costs were about $27,000 per patient per year (Transplant Living, 2006). At one time the ESRD program absorbed those costs, in part as a way of encouraging dialysis patients to pursue transplantation (which would reduce future ESRD costs for that patient substantially). More recently, ESRD is committed only to paying the first three years of those costs. Is it unjust that ESRD added that limitation to the program? Are there other choices for saving money in the program that would be less morally objectionable from the perspective of health care justice?

Just to put matters in perspective, we do about 16,000 kidney transplants each year in the U.S.; that yields an annual cost per cohort of renal transplant patients of about $432 million. If the ESRD program were willing to pay indefinitely for these drugs, then the additional cost of five cohorts per year beyond the first three years would be about $2.2 billion. The one-year cost of a renal transplant is about $226,000, which is roughly four times the cost of a year of dialysis (Transplant Living, 2006). If Medicare were paying indefinitely for the immunosuppressant drugs, it would take eight years for Medicare to break even relative to simply keeping these patients on dialysis.

If we were to ask what was in the best interest of these patients (bracketing entirely the money issue), the likelihood is that the vast majority of these patients would want a transplant rather than the reduced quality of life associated with dialysis. From the perspective of the fair equality of opportunity principle, a transplant opens up a larger part of the normal opportunity range of a society. Specifically, these individuals *can* more readily rejoin the workforce. However, as things are now in the U.S. health care system, most smaller employers would be reluctant to take on these workers if that required adding them to their health plan (because they would be taking on that additional $27,000 per year cost with that worker). Actually, it is even more complicated than that.

Both transplant patients and HIV+ patients have greatly increased risks of cancer because of the compromised character of their immune systems. Recent research (Grulich et al., 2007; Vajdic et al., 2006) shows that there are 20 different cancers to which both these groups are substantially more vulnerable. Most of these cancers have a viral link, such as to HPV or HBV or EBV. In the general population, Kaposi's sarcoma is a rare cancer, but there is an increased risk of 3,640-fold if a patient has AIDS. For renal transplant patients, there is a 208-fold increase in risk for that cancer compared to the general population. The very substantial expenses associated with combating any of these cancers in immunocompromised patients becomes another obstacle to their being hired by employers whose insurance plans would have to absorb these costs. Of course these costs are at least several years into the future, and not every one of these patients will contract one of these cancers. This state of affairs is unjust. These patients seeking jobs are effectively being denied fair equality of opportunity. This is not the fault of either government or these employers—the fault lies primarily with the highly fragmented nature of our system for financing health care in the U.S. That fragmentation permits virtually everyone to deny responsibility for the financial costs associated with needed health care, as in the situation we have described here.

An alternative question we can ask ourselves is this: If we embraced some form of national health insurance in the U.S. (perhaps some form of a single-payer model), then would we cover all the health care needs of these renal patients at social expense? That is, would we allow them the choice of either dialysis or transplantation (assuming the availability of a suitable donor)? Would we avoid the use of co-pays for the immunosuppressant drugs as a way of reducing program costs? What would be the justice-relevant considerations that would speak for or against the use of co-pays in this situation? Would we limit in any way social responsibility for the health expenses associated with the cancers that would emerge in patients who chose transplantation? We can also raise a couple of additional questions with regard to "the way the world is now" for these patients. For example, is there sufficient moral justification for the requirement that renal transplant patients accept the costs of immunosuppressant drugs after three years? And, if there are very good reasons for reducing costs associated with meeting renal-based health care needs, then are there alternative rationing strategies that could be undertaken that would be more just than current cost-control efforts in the ESRD program?

Let me tentatively suggest some responses to the questions I have posed here. First, it is very difficult to justify as a matter of justice the requirement that renal transplant patients absorb the full costs of the drugs needed to prevent rejection after three years. Second, even requiring a co-pay of some sort seems difficult to justify from a health care justice perspective. There are some drugs and interventions that are clearly very costly and marginally beneficial at best; fast CT scans for asymptomatic patients would be a good example. Justice does not require that these interventions be covered as a social expense. Requiring high co-pays for name brand drugs when generic drugs are available and virtually just as effective as their name brand counterparts is clearly morally defensible. But the drugs that need to be taken by renal transplant patients are medically necessary to prevent rejection of the transplanted organ; there are no cheaper alternatives. We cannot argue that we are trying to send signals to consumers to make wiser choices to conserve resources by requiring large co-pays for drugs such as these (Bach, 2008). Nor can we argue that because a renal transplant results in a large quality of life improvement for patients that this surgery is closer to cosmetic surgery than to medically necessary surgery. These drugs are not the analogue of Botox, and the surgery is not the analogue of a tummy tuck. This surgery permits significant functional restoration for patients, and hence, it is warranted by the fair equality of opportunity principle.

If we are forced to take a very vigorous look at how dollars are spent in caring for patients with renal failure, then I would suggest we look for savings to end-of-life circumstances, where it is likely dialysis is often overused or misused in an attempt to prolong a bit longer severely debilitated lives. One rationing protocol I would recommend for the deliberative process might go like this: Dialysis will not be provided to patients with any form of end-stage dementia, nor to patients in PVS, nor to patients in irreversible multi-organ failure destined otherwise to die in the next three months, nor to patients with other end-stage disorders whose deaths are imminent and reliably predictable (i.e., various end-stage cancers and various forms of end-stage heart disease).

I will emphasize again that I am recommending this proposal be considered through the deliberative process. This means two things. First, it would not be unjust if deliberators refused to endorse the proposal and continued to provide dialysis to all of the types of patients listed above. Second, it would not be unjust if deliberators approved this rationing protocol for their future possible selves. It is not at all obvious that any major considered judgments of health care justice would be violated by such an approval. This protocol does not represent discrimination against some medically or socially disadvantaged group, nor does it represent a failure to respect fair equality of opportunity. On this latter point, the vast majority of these patients will be incompetent; that is, they will be unable to take advantage of virtually any opportunities or experiences continued life would afford them. This also means that our autonomy principle would not be violated. Some of these patients might well have the capacity to make some autonomous choices for themselves, but the capacity to make autonomous choices does not by itself give such patients a just claim to these costly medical resources. This is especially clear if this rationing protocol has been endorsed and legitimated through a fair process of rational democratic deliberation. Again, assuming no absolute scarcity of resources, such patients would have the right to cover the cost of such end-stage dialysis from private resources so long as no other patient's just claims are eroded by that decision.

Ordinarily access to dialysis for renal failure would rank very high in any priority-setting process governed by reasonable principles of health care justice. A major source of moral legitimacy for this claim is that dialysis is costworthy and offers individuals many extra years of life of reasonable quality. But that justification is precisely what is absent in the clinical circumstances alluded to in our proposed rationing protocol. Consequently, setting limits at this point seems morally preferable so far as health care justice is concerned to denying funding for antirejection drugs for patients who have renal transplants.

Another rationing protocol related to dialysis that would be suitable for democratic deliberation would be one that required a presumption of home dialysis over center dialysis, so long as social and medical circumstances warranted that option. This is a less expensive form of dialysis, and there is no inherent reduction in quality with this option. But it would be perceived by some to have a coercive quality, and it would require making social and medical judgments open to challenge by patients. Some might argue, however, that this rationing protocol would be morally preferable to our earlier proposed protocol (which at least has the appearance of "condemning someone to death before their time"). I will abstain from commenting on this last point, but I will affirm that this protocol, too, does not violate in any obvious way any considered judgment of health care justice. Hence, it is reasonable that it be an object of democratic deliberation for purposes of setting limits on access to dialysis.

Finally, though the dialysis program has created some fairness problems in our health care system that did not exist before the introduction of that program, it does have a certain moral virtue to it. Specifically, we did not "privatize" the benefit as we have done with part D of the Medicare program. There, we have substantial inequities related to the fact that the actual benefit delivered to any particular Medicare recipient varies considerably, depending upon the coverage actually provided by a specific drug plan. In the ESRD program, fundamental equality of access for all who are eligible for the program is preserved, which is why this is often referred to as national health care for dialysis patients.

SETTING LIMITS: OPTIONS FOR HIV+/AIDS PATIENTS

Do HIV+ patients have any just claims to protease inhibitors, fusion inhibitors, or any of these other extraordinarily costly drugs needed to prevent their succumbing to one or another opportunistic infection? This is really the first issue that needs to be addressed. Our second question is: Given the huge potential expenses associated with providing these drugs to as many as one million HIV+ patients in the U.S., are there any just limits that may be set with regard to access to these drugs? My short answer to our two questions is that these patients have **limited,**

presumptively just claims, which is to say the issue is not primarily a matter of social beneficence.[3] There are two sources of the justice presumption; namely, the pronounced effectiveness of these protease inhibitors and related drug types, and secondly, their ability to protect fair equality of opportunity.

First, the drugs are remarkably effective in about 70% of HIV+ patients (with some research suggesting that figure might be over 90% for patients who have not used drugs such as AZT). With the most potent of these drugs, there are average increases of CD4 counts of 250/mL and reductions in viral burden to undetectable levels.[4] The clinical implications of this are a marked reduction in vulnerability to deadly and debilitating opportunistic infections for these patients. In addition, there have been widespread reports of dramatic improvements in the overall quality of the lives of these patients (i.e., ability to return to work and to enjoy all the other pursuits of normal life).[5] Ordinarily, results like this would warrant inclusion of these drugs in insurance packages as part of the standard of care. That is, it would be presumptively unjust to fail to include coverage for this therapy.

Second, the capacity to protect fair equality of opportunity is an essential element of our understanding of the demands of health care justice. Given the demonstrated effectiveness of these protease inhibitors, it would seem that affected individuals would have a strong presumptive just claim to them on the grounds that they protect fair equality of opportunity by restoring them to normal species functioning. We must also take note of the fact that the vast majority of these patients are relatively young; on average they will be significantly younger than dialysis patients.

We do need to stress the fact that this is a **presumptive** claim; it is defeatable. We do need to set limits in order to protect fair access for other expensive and effective life-prolonging medical interventions. Protease inhibitors are very expensive, not simply on a one-time basis, but repeatedly—for every added year of life, we were looking at costs of about $20,000 per person in 1996. Since then, we have had to create other classes of drugs that blocked or disabled the capacity of HIV to attack the immune system. This includes fusion inhibitors which are priced at $20,000 per person per year, which need to be combined with darunivir at $10,000 per patient per year and Norvir at $7,800 per patient per year. Another new AIDS drug that can be used in combination with these drugs is etravirine, priced at $8,000 per patient per year (PR Newswire, 2008). The result is that for the vast majority of HIV+ patients in the U.S. (slightly more than one million), they now need to be on combinations of drugs costing $35,000–$40,000 per patient per year (PR Newswire, 2008)—that puts the aggregated annual costs of these drugs in the U.S. in the vicinity of $35 billion. That brings us back to our central problem: Dollars directed to meet some health needs are not available to meet other needs. Priorities must be established among health needs. Not all health needs are created equal, morally speaking; some make stronger claims on limited resources than others. How strong, relatively speaking, are the claims of these protease inhibitors and related classes of drugs?

No one believes that protease inhibitors represent a cure for AIDS. Therefore, they will not be ranked in the uppermost tier of health priorities. However, from the perspective of cost-effectiveness and restoration of normal functioning at a reasonable enough cost, they would clearly rank significantly above autologous bone marrow transplants for either breast or testicular cancer (which essentially were no better than other available therapies, but cost four times as much). What we might fairly say is that they are squarely in the middle of the mass of half-way medical interventions that define early 21st-century medicine. Pessimists in the late 1990s argued that these protease inhibitors would be maximally effective for only two or three years, then they would lose their potency as the HIV virus mutated and defeated them. Optimists, on the other hand, argued that the then current generation of inhibitors might have only limited potency, but that the next generation of inhibitors (including fusion inhibitors) would tame the virus so that AIDS became a chronic disorder. The "optimal result" they expected was that patients would become long-term non-progressors.

The scare quotes are necessary for the thought that this might be an optimal result, since that outcome has proven to be quite problematic so far as health care justice is concerned. If we use cost-per-quality-adjusted-life-year-saved as a factor in assigning priority to protease inhibitors for health plan funding, then they might be roughly in the same category as major organ transplants, where we would have costs of about $40,000 per QALY. As a unit cost, that does not seem to be unreasonable, but the aggregating effects are potentially very troublesome. Apart from kidneys, we do about 8,000 major organ transplants each year in the U.S.—that represents about $3 billion in aggregated costs. The limit we are faced with is the availability of transplantable organs. But there are a bit more than one million HIV+ individuals in the U.S. If all of them have full access to protease inhibitors, there would be the potential for adding $35 billion to the cost of health care in the U.S. per year. Further, we have to assume those numbers would continue to increase for the foreseeable future.

Again, if we were successful in achieving "optimal results"(say, 20-year survival with protease inhibitors), then we would be looking at $700,000 costs per life prolonged, plus end-of-life costs, plus the usual range of other health care costs that anyone else in our society might incur. Actually, the last part of the prior sentence needs qualification. Many of these protease inhibitors can have very deleterious and costly side effects—coronary artery disease would be one. Individuals on these drugs for many years find themselves having to deal with serious heart disease and all the costs associated with responding to those health needs. We also saw above (Grulich et al., 2007) that many of these AIDS patients are vulnerable to many cancers (especially those that have a viral relationship) because of the compromised nature of their immune systems. Treating those cancers adds substantially to total care costs for these patients.

The medical reason why cancers develop at a high rate in these patients is that they are typically offered protease inhibitors when their CD4 counts fall below 350 (compared to a normal level of 1100). It might take eight years after initial infection to sink to this level. These patients would be less vulnerable to these cancers if their immune systems were sustained at a much higher level; maybe the 800 level. But then there would be extra years of costs associated with providing these drugs earlier in the disease process. This might be a morally and economically reasonable choice if virtually all HIV+ individuals were vulnerable to these cancers, but only some fraction is vulnerable in this way, and we do not seem to have any clinical tools for reliably identifying who they are. Is it still the case that HIV+ individuals in our society have a presumptively just claim to these protease inhibitors at social expense? If we are inclined to give an affirmative answer to this first question, then must we also affirm their having a just claim to these drugs at an earlier stage in the disease process? And who should have primary moral responsibility for making the relevant policy decisions in these matters within managed care plans (as things are now) or within a future national health plan, especially in a very competitive, cost-conscious health care system?

I will still defend the view that there are just claims to these protease inhibitors, but the claims are limited. If we imagine a comprehensive form of national health insurance for the U.S. in the future, then protease inhibitors would have to be part of that package for the justice-relevant considerations I listed above. But some limits would have to be established, and these should be determined through a process of rational democratic deliberation (as we discuss below). If we have to take our health care system as it is now, but we are committed to bringing about a more just and caring managed care plan in our region, then responsibility for determining those limits should fall primarily to the board of a managed care plan in conjunction with representatives of the medical staff of that plan and the managed care ethics committee for that plan.[6] The role of the ethics committee is to make "uncontaminated" policy recommendations with respect to cost containment, rationing, and priority-setting within the plan. "Uncontaminated" does not mean that their recommendations are utopian. Almost always, as we shall see below, their recommendations will reflect non-ideal judgments of health care justice (as is true for the public deliberative processes we describe). What their judgments should not be contaminated by or distorted by are strategic business considerations.

Similarly, plan physicians have at stake their own medical and moral integrity. They will ultimately have responsibility for implementing policies of the Board in their practice in the plan. It would be morally irresponsible if physicians were mere tools in the hands of the Board; hence, they must communicate to the Board what features of any options being considered would be deeply violative of their medical moral responsibilities as physicians. The analogous responsibility for the ethics committee would be to communicate to the Board the features of any option being considered that would be deeply violative of health care justice. The ethics committee should convey to the Board their judgment regarding which option, among several morally permissible options, might be most morally preferable, if in fact the ethics committee can come to something close to consensus on this matter. Beyond that, the Board may choose a morally acceptable but suboptimal option that reflects socially responsible strategic business considerations, and that seem to be an integral part of our health care system now.

With all that as preface, let us now turn to assessing some specific policy options for our managed care plan with respect to protease inhibitors. We can begin by quickly sweeping some options off the table as badly flawed so far as health care justice is concerned. We can also imagine ourselves in 1997 when these protease inhibitors are first introduced and there is considerable uncertainty as to what a reasonable coverage response might be, especially as we try to imagine how long individuals might need to be on these drugs, how long these drugs will be effective, whether there might be costly medical side effects, et cetera.[7]

Option 1: Postpone making any decision for a year. The main argument that might be deployed in support of this option is that we do not want to waste money on very expensive drugs that might offer no more than short-term false hopes. The fact is that the first protease inhibitors were approved with less than a year of clinical trials. Who knows, the argument goes, what awful surprises might emerge a little later? However, the trials were cut short because the early results were so dramatically positive. Even when we correct for considerable political and commercial pressures associated with these drugs, the results remain morally weighty—the cost of postponing a decision for a year would be the unnecessary loss of some number of relatively young lives within our managed care plan. Speculative fears about side effects cannot be given that much moral weight in these circumstances. Further, if our real concern is costly bad outcomes, then, to give just one example, moral consistency would require that we first put in place a policy of not funding aggressive life-sustaining care in the case of infants born under 750 grams/25 weeks gestation where there is already substantial evidence of very bad outcomes (death or permanent serious disabilities) in a significant majority of cases. In my judgment, Option 1 fails the minimal justice test.

Option 2: Fund protease inhibitors only to the extent that competing managed care plans fund them. There are clearly corporate self-interest considerations that speak in favor of this option. If there are several very large corporations in an area, and if they all offer options with all the managed care plans in the area (which means the option of switching on an annual basis), then there would be a risk that the first managed care plan to offer coverage of protease inhibitors would attract a disproportionate share of HIV+ individuals. Further, the argument might be made that an outcome such as this would be unfair; consequently, managed care plans are not morally obligated to accept such unfair burdens.

But Option 2 has some serious, unredeemable moral flaws. First, there are some empirical issues that would have to be addressed. How likely would it be that there would be a large influx of HIV+ individuals into our plan from competing plans? If there were a very real risk (not just the product of a fevered imagination) of economic failure of the plan as a whole from such an influx, this might justify reluctantly choosing Option 2. If the only morally defensible policy option were unlimited funding for protease inhibitors for all HIV+ plan members, then, given such costs, economic failure might be a real-world possibility. But, as I argue below, there are less costly, still "just enough" options, which reduce the plausibility of the economic failure/hard moral choice scenario.

Second, there is something morally unsavory about judging what is right and wrong on the basis of what others do. At the very least, that would reduce our moral commitments to the lowest common denominator. One might argue that, in the world of business, that is precisely how moral commitments get defined. However, that assumes that the issue we are faced with is primarily a matter of business ethics (an assumption with which I would strongly disagree), and that business ethics is adequately characterized in terms of lowest common denominator commitments among competitors (also an assumption I reject). On the latter point, there are matters of corporate beneficence where matching what competitors do (and no more) is morally permissible. However, with respect to matters of justice and strong rights claims, that kind of competitive strategy is not morally defensible, unless business ethics is reduced to corporate self-interest. That brings us to our third point.

Some might argue that access to protease inhibitors is only a matter of beneficence. This might be a plausible perspective if protease inhibitors represented marginally beneficial, non-costworthy care. But our earlier arguments showed the benefits are substantial, though fairly costly. Still, there is a presumptive just claim to them. On a priority scale for health care they are somewhere above the middle, but not near the top. That means there will be a substantial number of other medical interventions now covered by our plan that are less beneficial and less costworthy—fairness would require reducing our commitment to these other interventions before we would be justified in refusing to cover protease inhibitors. At the very least, a compelling moral argument would have to be given for refusing to include protease inhibitors as a covered benefit. Competitive economic pressures would not count as such an argument.[8]

Option 3: Let plan members themselves decide what the policy ought to be, by something like a direct vote. This may have the appearance of rational democratic deliberation, but there are good reasons for thinking this option falls far short of being a reasonable approximation of a fair deliberative process. The moral virtue of rational democratic deliberation is that it is supposed to provide a mechanism for a community to make public, self-imposed rationing decisions. It is supposed to provide a moral antidote to our typical practice of making rationing decisions invisibly and aresponsibly; it is also supposed to prevent healthy majorities from imposing unjust rationing decisions on sick and vulnerable minorities. The moral space of rational democratic deliberation is delimited by a number of what I have referred to metaphorically as constitutional principles of health care justice, one of which would be a principle of nondiscrimination. It is that boundary that is violated by Option 3. It is much too likely that ongoing patterns of discrimination against HIV+ individuals would result in an unjust rationing decision in this case (i.e., complete denial of funding or grossly inadequate funding). Further, I would contend that a Board that endorsed Option 3 would itself be open to the moral criticism that it was abdicating its own moral responsibility. Finally, as we shall see below, there are options available here that would justifiably employ rational democratic deliberation, but the creation of those options will require some responsible decision-making by the Board first.

Option 4: Let plan physicians make the relevant moral and clinical decisions for individual patients on the basis of their best professional judgment. Like the prior option, this one also allows the Board to escape responsibility for making these difficult decisions. The basic moral argument in favor of this option is that it is responsive to the complexities of clinical practice.[9] No one doubts the wisdom of a broad measure of respect for clinical autonomy, but unlimited clinical autonomy means the potential for both unlimited costs and unlimited inequities. Individual physicians might be too compassionate or too readily responsive to the demands of patients before them, at the expense of the legitimate interests of other patients not before them. Given the widely disseminated hype that protease inhibitors have received, numerous such demands are likely. If enough physicians give in to those demands by patients in the early stages of HIV infection (who are anxious about their future possible vulnerability to cancers related to a compromised immune system), then there is a good likelihood that plan resources will be squandered on non-costworthy marginal benefits. That risks the plan failing to meet some higher-priority, more just health claims.

An alternative approach is to use economic incentives to shape and constrain clinical autonomy, such as capitation attached to drugs and testing. Here too, however, there is the potential for serious injustices. The first of these would be the problem of invisible rationing. Since there would be no formal rules governing access to protease inhibitors, patients would not know if their physician was being excessively strict in providing access to protease inhibitors, thereby denying them significant and costworthy clinical benefits for reasons of economic self-interest.[10]

Second, under capitation, patients with essentially the same clinical status in the same managed care plan might be treated very differently for reasons which are neither their reasons nor for their benefit. The threat of malpractice will protect patients from the most egregious forms of under-treatment, but there is a large enough, gray enough area with respect to protease inhibitors that legal protections would not reliably prevent unjust denials. That gray area exists because of considerable clinical uncertainty regarding optimal initiation of therapy. There are also significant side effects that might give asymptomatic HIV+ patients pause regarding the initiation of therapy. But under capitation, patients are unlikely to be invited to be part of this decision-making process. Just rationing protocols ought to be rationally self-imposed, but capitation essentially hands decisional authority to physicians. For these reasons, I would reject Option 4 as seriously unjust.

Option 5: Let companies that have contracts with our managed care plan decide whether or not they want protease inhibitor coverage for their employees; then, price coverage to these plans experientially. This option is akin in many respects to Option 3. It is, for example, primarily a way of shifting moral responsibility away from the Board to others whose self-interest is likely to generate a less than just result. Libertarians, of course, will not see it this way—on the contrary, they are likely to see this as the optimal option because each payer decides for themselves what is or is not costworthy care. No one is forced to pay for care they do not want. I have addressed elsewhere what I see as the deep moral flaws of libertarianism as a conception of health care justice, so I will not repeat those arguments here.[11] Instead, I will simply point out some of the unseemly consequences specific to this proposal. For one thing, if some companies fund protease inhibitors for their employees but most others do not, then physicians in the same managed care plan will find themselves able to treat some of their HIV+ patients in a maximally appropriate way, while having to allow others to suffer and die prematurely. Outcomes like that can be tolerated as tragic and regrettable when there are absolute shortages of a life-saving drug. Similarly, if a drug is very expensive and yields only marginal benefits, then we find it morally tolerable that only those with personal ability to pay will have access to it. But neither of these conditions obtains with respect to protease inhibitors. At the very least, an outcome like this will prove to be morally and psychologically troubling for physicians who find themselves in these circumstances.

Any kind of gatekeeping can be psychologically troubling for physicians, but gatekeeping in the service of a more just distribution of limited resources should not be morally troubling. That, however, is precisely what is not true here. Physicians could initiate appeals on behalf of their unfunded HIV+ patients. But if the managed care plan responds positively to those appeals, then it sends a signal to the companies who have paid for that coverage that they need not pay for it, which could potentially worsen care for all HIV+ patients in the plan. Apart from that potential consequence, if the plan responded positively to some appeals on the basis of some moral norm, then the question would be why such a norm did not govern a minimal HIV benefit option that would be part of all their contracts. And, of course, if positive responses were elicited in a rather random or arbitrary nonmoral fashion, then those not similarly favored would have cause for just complaint.

Option 6: Fund protease inhibitors for all HIV+ individuals who believe it is in their best interest that they start on protease inhibitors immediately. This would obviously be the potentially most expensive option a managed care plan could consider. Is a just and caring managed care plan morally obligated to choose this option? I will argue that this is not a morally obligatory option, but it may be a morally permissible option.

The primary consideration that speaks against seeing this option as morally obligatory is that we have little evidence of dramatic medical effectiveness for protease inhibitors in the early stages of infection. They may make a difference for some in the mid-stages of infection (if the immune system can be sustained at a higher level, and if that is sufficient to overcome the vulnerability to some cancers in some individuals). Hence, it would be fair to conclude that in the early stages of HIV infection, protease inhibitors are an experimental form of therapy. The moral implication of that is that plan members who were HIV+ would have no just claim to protease inhibitors at plan expense. Dr. Ho's theory proved incorrect, in fact; though we remain today faced with the question of whether these drugs ought to be given earlier to protect a stronger immune system. The question that needs to be addressed here is whether individuals in the early stages of HIV infection have stronger just claims to those additional resources than any other patients in the plan with other unfunded health needs? It is very far from obvious that they do—we need a much clearer picture of the medical facts, whatever they might be.

Option 7: Fund protease inhibitors for those HIV+ individuals whom best current medical evidence suggests are most likely to benefit significantly. This will involve some set of clinical protocols that will take into account both viral load and CD4 counts below 350/mL. If we move into the future and imagine some sort of national health plan, then numerous considerations of health care justice would require funding for these drugs, even if we are talking about drug combinations with costs of about $35,000 per patient per year. These drugs yield more life-years of higher quality than either dialysis or an artificial heart. But we clearly judge that we are morally obligated to provide access to dialysis for all with the relevant need at $57,000 per person per year. And we are increasingly saving life-years with dialysis for individuals in the eighth and ninth decade of life, compared to individuals in the third or fourth decade of life with HIV. Further, if we simply focus on the present again, most managed care plans are funding these extraordinarily costly cancer drugs that generally yield only extra months of life at costs of $50,000–100,000 per case. It is difficult to imagine what justice-relevant considerations would warrant funding those drugs and refusing to cover these protease inhibitors and other such AIDS-related drugs.[12] That is, it does not seem that a decision to refuse funding these AIDS drugs while funding these cancer drugs would yield a morally possible reflective equilibrium.

As noted earlier, what Option 7 represents is a limited, non-ideal, just enough option. It is limited and non-ideal because some unknown number of HIV+ individuals in earlier stages of infection might be faced with serious health problems (cancers) that might have been averted if they had had access to protease inhibitors earlier in the disease process. But it is still a "just enough" option because we will be protecting the greatest range of fair equality of opportunity at the lowest feasible cost by choosing this option. That is, "merely" being HIV+ for the first several years after initial infection does not seem to trigger any diminishment in functional capacities; individuals can live lives that are quite normal for them from a functional perspective. Later, however, when individuals become vulnerable to serious opportunistic infections, there is a real threat of premature death and substantial loss of functional capacity. Since protease inhibitors can prevent or forestall that decline for years, that generates a strong just claim to those resources at that time, not before. The argument could be made (at least as a thought experiment) that Dr. Ho's theories will prove to be correct; that protease inhibitors given within months of initial infection defeat the virus entirely so that individuals can look forward to a normal life expectancy, but that delay in therapy will likely mean premature death for HIV+ individuals, even if they gain 10 to 20 extra years of life that otherwise would not have been available to them. If this proved to be true, it would be unfortunate that we had committed ourselves to Option 7 now, *but those premature deaths would not be unjust*. This is a point that must be emphasized. We could prevent those premature deaths only by allocating resources in a way that would almost certainly generate serious and real injustices now on the basis of *speculative* scientific evidence. Further, that strategy could be justified only if it were generalized; but if it were generalized, that would undermine almost entirely any rational foundation for setting health care priorities in a world of changing and uncertain scientific information. That sort of approach, for example, would have justified full-scale investment in autologous bone marrow transplants for women with metastatic breast cancer at $150,000 per case (44,000 women per year) in the early 1990s when there was great enthusiasm for this intervention—a provocative theory, but little solid scientific evidence. There was little evidence, of course, because we eventually learned (10 years later) that the treatment was no better than the less expensive conventional treatments already available. Worse still, a significant number of women died even sooner than necessary as a result of the treatment itself because they were entirely immunodeficient.

What I take to be a substantial virtue of Option 7 is that it avoids the moral errors associated with our creation of the End-Stage Renal Disease program under Medicare. In that program, we pay for dialysis and kidney transplants for all who have the relevant need—whether they can benefit very substantially from the therapy or only very marginally—in either case at significant expense to limited public resources. We pay for kidney transplants at public expense but generally not for other major organ transplants. These look like arbitrary distinctions that are seriously unjust. We cannot afford to make that same mistake with AIDS patients, or with others who have comparable serious illnesses. Again, this pertains to another important lesson to be learned from the Oregon approach to health care rationing; namely, that rationing decisions made in an isolated, nonsystematic fashion are more likely to be unjust, or less likely to be explicable publicly and rationally.

Finally, if Option 7 could be rationally and autonomously endorsed by HIV+ individuals in our managed care plan (or a future national health plan), as well as by the membership of the plan as a whole (or all our citizens), that would add substantially to the presumptive justness of this option. A mere thought experiment would not be very satisfactory. Still, if the argument I have made above is reasonable, then I would imagine a rational democratic deliberative process would quickly endorse funding for these protease inhibitors and related drugs. However, there is another option that ought to be considered through the deliberative process which would likely require sustained deliberation. We could permit liberalized and individualized access to protease inhibitors at social expense (Option 7a). We might permit individuals with CD4 counts below 750/mL the option of accessing protease inhibitors to prevent any further decline in their immune system. This could have very substantial additional costs to the plan, so individuals who chose this option would have to agree to a trade-off. They would have to be willing to give up aggressive and expensive life-prolonging care in the very end stages of disease, when, for example, there was less than a 25% chance they would survive another year. In effect, they decide for themselves which risks are worth taking and which benefits are costworthy enough from their point of view. Several years ago, last-year-of-life costs for AIDS patients was put at about $127,000 per patient. This would represent substantial savings for the plan as a whole, and would help to justify the very open-ended commitment to future AIDS drugs that might extend high-quality life for these patients far beyond what we presently believe is possible.

In order to protect overall fairness, and in order to make sure such an option did not support any form of invidious discrimination, this option would have to be framed so that any disease that had a similar enough clinical and cost profile would also be covered. This would be required by our constitutional principle of Equality. It may be the case, for example, that some new, very expensive, potentially very effective cancer drugs are being introduced that are not likely to cure a cancer but are likely to yield several good years of remission (very much like the protease inhibitors). They too might need to be taken on a regular basis for years, with some uncertainty as to when it would be most cost-effective to begin therapy. They too would have this rationing option, which could be described in most general terms as permission for all patients to trade expensive marginal benefits very late in life for expensive benefits (sometimes marginal) earlier in life. This is increasingly looking like a very real scenario in a number of areas of medicine (as opposed to interesting moral speculation).

Numerous costly, effective interventions are possible today for various forms of heart disease, for multiple sclerosis, for cystic fibrosis, for hemophilia, and so on. That these interventions are very effective in providing additional life years of reasonable quality for individuals makes assuring access to these interventions an imperative of justice. But we need to have limits, as well. If it is the case that these interventions generate end-of-life scenarios analogous to what AIDS patients face (very high-cost, life-prolonging interventions that generate only marginal gains in length of life of greatly diminished quality), then it is not obviously unreasonable or unjust to propose this sort of rationing protocol for democratic deliberation. We would not be rationally or morally obligated to embrace this protocol. However, assuming hard financial limits that we had to respect for our health plan, and assuming the reasonableness and justness of funding very effective life-prolonging interventions, we would have to identify somewhere other marginally beneficial health interventions we would deny our future possible selves in order to offset these costs.

One of the apparent moral strengths of this protocol is that it is an intra-individual life-rationing protocol. Individuals gain access to costly and effective life-prolonging interventions at earlier stages in their life (HIV+ patients who *might* be at risk of various cancers if they allow their immune systems to become too compromised) in exchange for giving up a costly last year of life of marginal quality. Putting in place such a protocol would be a product of democratic deliberation. I remind the reader that these deliberators are, for the most part, behind a health-related veil of ignorance, but this particular protocol would allow individuals as individuals to either accept or reject it. Some HIV+ patients might be emotionally averse to giving up their last year of life; consequently, they would postpone accessing protease inhibitors until somewhat later in the disease process. They might not see this as an imprudent choice because we may not have medically reliable markers for identifying patients who were more vulnerable to these cancers. So they might want the certainty of knowing they have access to medical interventions that will protect that last year of life for them.

As with most other rationing protocols we discuss, wealthier individuals will have the option of buying out that last year of life; that is, they would have the right to pay those medical costs privately for that last year of life which they otherwise would have been denied. Again, this is not obviously unjust. No one is made worse off as far as health care justice is concerned by their making such a choice. And, if we are talking about a national health plan, then many wealthy individuals would have contributed to supporting this plan and these rationing protocols who will never be in the clinical circumstances that would allow them to "take advantage" of bypassing this rationing protocol.

SETTING LIMITS: THE CASE OF ARTIFICIAL HEARTS

The take-home message from the earlier part of this chapter is that health care justice (in the context of the U.S. health care system) requires that effective, life-prolonging technologies be funded, even if they are extraordinarily expensive. The technologies we have discussed so far are largely directed toward individuals who are in the relatively early to middle stages of life. The implicit considered judgment of health care justice we strongly endorse is that all in our society ought to have the opportunity to achieve a normal life expectancy if that is medically possible. Further, no one should be denied that opportunity simply because they do not have the resources to pay for those medical interventions. But our other take-home message is that there must be limits. Again, implicit in those earlier considered judgments is the claim that as the effectiveness of these interventions diminishes, and as the quality of life of individuals diminishes substantially (because of comorbidities or because of the debilitating side effects of these interventions with prolonged dependency), and as these interventions successfully propel individuals significantly beyond a normal life expectancy, so also the just claims to these interventions diminishes for these individuals. The artificial heart provides us with a good test case for operationalizing through the democratic deliberative process some practical guidelines for the considered judgment of health care justice contained in that last sentence.

We need to begin with a statistical picture, the edges of which are quite fuzzy. Projections for the use of the artificial heart from 20 years ago (when only a badly flawed model existed) estimated that 350,000 individuals annually would be recipients of this device. Many surgeons regarded this figure as being exaggerated because individuals with advanced heart disease would be too debilitated to withstand the surgery required for implantation. However, a more reasonable assumption is that individuals who were diagnosed with end-stage heart failure (currently more than 500,000 per year in the U.S.) would give serious consideration to an artificial heart while they were in the early stages of heart failure when the surgery would be much better tolerated and likely to be successful (because there had been minimal damage to other vital organs). For the most part, serious heart disease is associated with somewhat advanced age (over 55 years old). That means that our 500,000 figure does not yet reflect much of the aging out of the WWII "baby boom" generation. By the year 2030 we will see a doubling (at least) of the population over age 65—rising from about 39 million to about 78 million; going from 13% of the population to about 21% of the population.

If these are reliable predictions, then the potential annual demand for this device could be in the 500,000–600,000 range. We have given costs earlier of about $200,000 for each implantation; that is likely much too conservative a figure. The artificial heart itself (even mass-produced) will cost about $50,000 each. Heart transplant surgery is now priced at about $400,000 per case for all care for a period of a year. If we use a figure of $300,000 per implantation and assume a potential of 500,000 per year, we would be looking at $150 billion per year in additional health care costs (constant dollars). Original expectations for this device were that it would yield on average five extra years of life for a recipient. That would yield a cost per life-year saved of about $60,000. This is very close to what we are currently spending to save a year of life for a patient on dialysis.

Our critical moral question is this: How many artificial hearts is a just and caring society, with limited resources to meet virtually unlimited needs, morally obligated to provide its citizens at social expense? Again, we might wish to consider two scenarios in this regard. As things are now, we do have national health insurance for the elderly in the form of the Medicare program. Would it be unjust for the Medicare program to refuse to fund access to any of these devices at public expense? For the future, we can imagine our having a national health insurance program with a very comprehensive package of benefits. Would such a program have to include coverage of the artificial heart? If it did include some coverage for the artificial heart, could we justly set an age limit beyond which individuals would not be candidates for this device at social expense? Or are there other criteria we might employ for purposes of drastically reducing the number of these devices we would fund (in order not to skew unjustly our overall commitment to a just set of health care priorities)?

If we start with the Medicare program, we are again confronted with serious injustices related to the fragmented method we have for financing access to health care in the U.S. If we assume there is an objective annual need for these devices of about 500,000, then about 380,000 of those devices would be for individuals who were over the age of 65 (eligible for Medicare). That would add $110 billion per year to the cost of the Medicare program (which was at about $420 billion in 2007). The morally relevant point is that such a choice would permit individuals who had already achieved a normal life expectancy to achieve a supra-normal life expectancy at social expense, while at the same time we were entirely indifferent to the fate of uninsured and underinsured non-elderly working individuals with end-stage heart disease who would die before they achieved age 65 because they could not afford an artificial heart. What we would be doing in effect is making those who were already well-off even better off at the expense of those who were less well-off and younger. It is again very hard to imagine that, from behind a health-related veil of ignorance, reasonable and fair-minded individuals would endorse such an arrangement. Of course, the fact of the matter is that this is the way things are right now. That does not make the present arrangement just. Adding a $110-billion benefit for the artificial heart would only exacerbate the injustice. Under those circumstances the least unjust choice that could be made would be to allow the elderly to purchase with private funds (no tax subsidies) access to an artificial heart.[13]

Let us turn our attention instead to a future possible national health insurance program. Do considerations of justice require that the artificial heart be a covered benefit? If so, what limits, if any, would be justice-warranted? Of a range of possible options, which ones would we regard as being "just enough"—that is, morally legitimate options for democratic deliberation?

Option 1: Fund artificial hearts for everyone willing to undergo the surgery that has the relevant medical need, which we will define as significant risk of death in the next two years from heart failure. On the surface, this proposal might be judged to have the most plausible moral appeal. It has a strong egalitarian glow: no one is discriminated against because of age or quality of life or disability or diminished degree of effectiveness. But this is more moral illusion than moral reality. As we noted above, the vast majority of these artificial hearts would go to individuals over age 65. This makes artificial hearts morally different from either dialysis or protease inhibitors for HIV. If there really are no limits for access to these devices (other than capacity to survive the surgery), then the implication would be that 50,000 or more individuals over age 80 would be potential candidates for these devices. From the perspective of a health care system committed to protecting fair equality of opportunity, this would look like we were committed to protecting "enhanced opportunity" for those who were already genetically favored to achieve old age.

Funding artificial hearts for those over age 80 would be less of a problem, morally speaking, if we could honestly claim that all other health needs related to protecting fair equality of opportunity for those below age 70 had been satisfactorily assured. Maybe this could be accomplished, but a skeptical attitude would be justified. If we have to live with hard budgets (defined as the current 16.5% of GDP for health care), and we have to provide a comprehensive package of health benefits for all the currently uninsured and underinsured, then it is difficult to imagine where we would generate the $150 billion that might be needed annually to fund such an extensive and costly benefit. It would clearly be morally objectionable if we were to follow the British lead (with Herceptin) and deny funding for anti-TNF therapy for ankylosing spondylitis ($3 billion) in order to generate additional funds for costly life-prolonging technologies for the hyper-elderly. The same would be true if we were to reduce funding for costly drugs that were effective in significantly reducing the pain of arthritis in the elderly in order to fund these artificial hearts.

We need also to note that Medicare Part "D" raised to about 50% the social coverage for the costs of drugs for the elderly (Medicare coverage plus coverage for retirees by former employers). That was $41 billion in 2006 for Medicare "D" (Catlin et al., 2008). To fully cover the prescription drug needs of the elderly, a national health insurance program would require another $40 billion per year (in constant dollars that would themselves increase to reflect increased prescription drug use). If we were to have a democratic deliberative conversation among the elderly regarding health care priorities, I would be very confident that for both egalitarian and utilitarian justice-based considerations funding prescription drugs would rank higher for the elderly than being able to provide artificial hearts for their future possible selves beyond age 80.

Finally, we have noted that the artificial heart (in perfected form) is estimated to provide *on average* five additional years of life expectancy. That works out to about $60,000 per life-year saved. That is a reasonable number to use in judging the costworthiness of this or other expensive life-prolonging measures. However, if we take Option 1 seriously, then someone who desperately wants to live (but is fearful of dying of heart disease in the next six months) who also has a terminal cancer likely to cause his death in two years, would still have a just claim to an artificial heart, though the cost per life-year saved then would be at least $150,000. Again, relative to other health care priorities, this looks like a bad buy and an unjust buy. I can imagine two versions of this last scenario: one in which this patient is 78 years old; the other in which the patient is 58 years old. I can imagine the latter scenario as a legitimate option to consider in a deliberative process because that individual will fall far short of achieving a normal life expectancy. I cannot imagine the first scenario as having prima facie moral credibility sufficient to warrant a deliberative effort.

Option 2: Fund no artificial hearts through a national health insurance program. This seems to have the support of libertarian, egalitarian, and utilitarian considerations of health care justice. Everyone decides for themselves whether the artificial heart is worth it to them (libertarianism; let the delinquent grand kids go into debt if they want to go to college). Everyone is treated the same from a social perspective (egalitarianism; financial and genetic luck will determine outcomes; Congress is not ripping a respirator from Granny's throat). Society makes a more efficient use of limited resources (utilitarianism; why should society subsidize post-septuagenarian sex with Viagra and an artificial heart?). However, my judgment is that this option also is a nonstarter so far as just democratic deliberation is concerned. I realize that this option represents a very clean, very bright line—that will be seen as a prudential political advantage; no squabbling about including or excluding this or that group. From a moral perspective, this would reflect the worst sort of moral timidity. There could be as many as 100,000 patients per year below age 70 who would be faced with death from heart failure if they had no access to an artificial heart. We might not be especially morally troubled by individuals in their late 60s, but there will be individuals in their 20s, 30s, and 40s faced with this problem—maybe as a result of bad genes, maybe as a result of bad luck (cardiomyopathy resulting from infection of the heart muscle).

If one of our fundamental principles of health care justice is protecting fair equality of opportunity, and if this device would give these younger individuals 10 to 20 extra years of life they would otherwise be denied, and if the cost per extra life-year saved were in the $30,000–$60,000 range, it would again be hard to imagine what justice-based argument would speak against funding this intervention. The justification for funding would be essentially the same as with dialysis or HIV or Gaucher's or hemophilia or other such costly disorders that affect relatively young individuals. What is clear is that it would not be morally sufficient to argue that addressing the "ragged edge" problem created by the artificial heart would be too difficult or too potentially socially divisive. So we need to consider another option.

Option 3: Fund access to the artificial heart for all who have the relevant medical need below age 70 as part of a national health insurance plan. This might be in the vicinity of 100,000 individuals per year at a cost of about $30 billion per year. The implication of this proposal is that individuals over age 70 would have access to the artificial heart only if they had the private resources that gave them that access (which, in theory, would include purchasing some form of private insurance for this purpose). We could add the proviso that individuals between age 65 and 70 would have access to this device only if their physicians were medically confident they were likely to survive three years. In other words, life-threatening, comorbid conditions could override any such individual's right to this device. The justification for such a limitation is that the benefits would be too marginal (morally speaking), and individuals would be very close to having achieved a normal life expectancy.

The obvious objection to this proposal is that it represents a clear case of age-based rationing. I address that particular problem fully in a later chapter; hence, at this point I will offer only a brief comment. I remind the reader that I am not arguing that any justice-relevant considerations would obligate us to adopt this option. All I am saying is that this option has enough prima facie moral legitimacy that it can be reasonably and legitimately taken up for democratic deliberation. Further, if it were approved, then it would be "just enough." It would be a morally permissible option even if we did not regard it as a morally ideal option. Again, if this option were embraced at the end of a deliberative process, then individuals would be accepting this limitation on access to the artificial heart for their own future possible selves. They would not be seeking to impose this rationing protocol on some group of sick and vulnerable elderly individuals with advanced heart disease. So there is no violation of "equal respect" considerations; there is no invidious discrimination. Further, what we have to imagine is that a suitably informed deliberative group would have a very detailed sense of the range of health needs characteristic of an elderly population—they could quite reasonably judge that many other health needs for the elderly deserved higher priority than access to an artificial heart. If this were the outcome of the deliberative process, then I cannot see a strong moral argument for rejecting it as not being "just enough."

One possible objection might go like this: Imagine an otherwise vigorous 68-year-old individual, Adam, with end-stage heart disease. He receives an artificial heart that permits him to live another 10 years. His 72-year-old neighbor, Ben, has equally advanced heart disease, but he is denied an artificial heart and dies a year later. Some may judge that it is unfair that we would have provided the resources to Adam that allowed him to live all those extra years while denying the same resources to Ben who might have lived another five years (so that they both died at roughly the same age). However, the clear practical implication of this objection is that we would have to drop the age limit. That would take us back to Option 1. Someone could suggest raising the age limit to 80, but that does not speak to the objection. It just moves the objection 10 years later. The need for limits in this case is inescapable unless we could come up with good reasons that would justify the huge distortions in health care priorities that would be created by limitless access to the artificial heart.

Another objection can be raised that needs to be taken more seriously. What we might call the "libertarian permission" that allows individuals to use private resources to purchase an artificial heart beyond age 70 is seen as being morally tolerable because no one is made worse off; the just claims of others to needed health care are not diminished by this permission. However, these individuals are still going to die of something; five, 10, or 15 years later. This is likely to be an expensive, chronic degenerative condition which could be quite costly (some form of cancer, a debilitating stroke, Alzheimer's, etc.). But for their having access to the artificial heart through their private expenditures, these additional expenditures would never have been necessary. Readers should be reminded that we are not talking about a few thousand extra dollars in health care costs, but potentially several hundred thousand dollars per individual (i.e., four years in a nursing home with Alzheimer's would easily exceed $200,000). Would it be unjust if through the deliberative process we approved a rationing protocol that said all medical expenses incurred after receiving an artificial heart through private funding would be the responsibility of the individual?

The justice issue would seem to be this: If individuals are capable of achieving age 80 through good luck and good genetics, and then experience any of the costly chronic degenerative conditions we alluded to above, they would clearly be entitled to that coverage for those degenerative conditions. So, the argument goes, it looks like we are denying the wealthy fair and equal treatment by denying them access at social expense to the same health services we cover for the non-wealthy elderly. On the other hand, if we do cover those "excess health services," then it looks as if we are providing a significant social subsidy to those who have the financial capacity to purchase an artificial heart (and, use of social resources in that way does represent taking those resources away from what might otherwise be the just claims of those who forego any opportunity to seek health care outside the national plan).

Again, my goal is not to offer some definitive resolution of this challenge. I will venture the judgment that it would not be unjust to allow the deliberative process to settle the matter one way or the other. That means I do not believe any constitutional principle of health care justice would be violated by a protocol requiring private funding for all health care after an individual received an artificial heart through private funding. The argument could be made that if such individuals had decided against the artificial heart, then endured a terminal course over a period of a year or two (incurring very substantial health care costs along the way), all those costs would usually be covered by the national health plan—they would have a just claim to those resources. This suggests they are effectively denied this "end of life" social benefit if they purchase an artificial heart; this is unfair. This is a reasonable claim. What if some individuals with a privately purchased artificial heart endure multiple costly chronic illnesses before death? They would clearly use an "excess" degree of social resources relative to what they would have been provided under the national health plan. We need administrative simplicity to preserve justice. A compromise proposal would be that patients purchasing an artificial heart privately would be responsible for 50% of their health costs after implantation. That seems to strike a reasonable balance among competing considerations of equitable treatment.

Let me very briefly consider several other options for limiting access to the artificial heart at social expense. Option 4 could cover the artificial heart for all those below the age of 80. My own judgment is that this comes very close to Option 1 in practice because the decade between age 70 and 80 is where the greatest predictable likelihood of need would occur. Hence, many of the same objections could be raised here that we raised in connection with Option 1, but Option 4 would be a very fact-sensitive option. Hence, I would not judge this option to be beyond just or responsible deliberation; I would permit the deliberative process to go forward and deliver a judgment.

A variation on Option 4 would be Option 5. It would permit funding for an artificial heart at the 50% level for those between age 70 and 80 if private funding covered the other 50% and individuals had a minimum predicted life expectancy of three years with the artificial heart. This would also require 50–50 funding for health care needs after receiving the artificial heart. This also looks like a very fact-sensitive rationing protocol. How many more people would be able to afford access to the artificial heart under this scenario? The honest answer is, likely "very few." That raises the question of whether there was any moral justification for providing this subsidy to individuals who were already very well-off (likely the top 5% of income earners in the U.S.). Someone might suggest addressing that concern by adjusting the matching ratio to be proportional to some mix of wealth and income. This becomes administratively complex, and fails to answer the question of what would be the morally defensible objective we were trying to achieve. If we were seeking to increase access to the artificial heart for the elderly, we would also be risking serious, unjust skewing of our overall health care priorities. It is difficult to see how this brings about greater fairness in our health care system. Still, rather than putting this option off the table a priori, I am inclined to trust the deliberative process to find this proposal insufficiently just.

Option 6: Fund the artificial heart for those who have the relevant medical need up to age 70 (with the three-year predicted life expectancy proviso). In addition, deny the artificial heart to individuals whose bad health habits were likely the primary cause of their heart disease—we can refer to this as the "personal responsibility for health" proviso. This has considerable attractiveness for many individuals; it brings into the discussion the issue of distinguishing deserving from undeserving individuals in ill health. A simple way of capturing the core argument is this question: Why should we (healthy, sinless individuals) have to pay for the consequences of your unhealthy irresponsible (sinful) behavioral choices to smoke, to drink alcohol in excess, to eat unhealthy foods in excess, or to have sex in excess (more than me)? No one put a gun to your head to make you eat three Quarter Pounders with Cheese and a super-sized container of French fries at a single meal. No one threatened to trample your mother's grave if you did not smoke two packs of cigarettes per day for years. You have no just claim to expensive, life-prolonging medical care for your heart disease that I have to pay for; you brought your heart disease on yourself.

I have written these last few sentences with as much self-assured arrogance as I could muster in the hopes of eliciting disgust from most of my readers. Unfortunately, what I know from talking about these issues with many audiences is that it is unlikely I achieved that objective. Often I equip an audience with these audience-response devices, and ask them to respond to the following statement on a five-point scale from "strongly agree" to "strongly disagree": "If someone has heart disease or cancer as a result of very poor health habits, such as smoking or a very bad diet, then they should be denied expensive life-saving or life-prolonging medical care in my managed care plan at plan expense." Typically, I have gotten 70–80% of any audience to agree with this statement. I would strongly disagree with this statement. This is one area in which the deliberative process could yield some badly misguided public judgments without attention to a number of morally important details. Here are some of the critical points I try to make by way of educating an audience on this issue.

First, what do we imagine the criteria should be for judging that someone has made irresponsible choices that have compromised their health? Is there a certain weight level or cholesterol level or number of cigarettes per day or number of drinks per day that would reliably and justifiably allow us to conclude that this person was responsible for their heart disease or cancer, et cetera? Over what period of time would that criterion have to be consistently met in order to justify denying an individual costly life-prolonging care at plan expense? And what would we do when individuals rise or fall substantially above or below that level over a period of years as they try to lose weight or quit smoking or exercise more, and so forth? From a moral point of view (assigning just deserts), should we think of such individuals as persistent penitents (deserving compassion) or pusillanimous sinners (deserving condemnation)? There is enormous opportunity for arbitrary judgments in this regard.

Second, who would we expect to be tracking and assessing this information? Would it be personal physicians? What if an individual had no personal physician? Is there any moral issue here with whether the professional role of physician should include being a deputy health prosecutor? Would patients have health-related Fifth Amendment rights? Think about the range of attitudes different physicians might have in making such judgments: as a result of their religious or cultural background, as a result of their political leanings, or a result of idiosyncratic personal features. Again, arbitrary and unjust judgments would be rampant and unchecked.

Third, how expansive would we imagine the range of behaviors might be that would trigger the denial of health care at social expense? Some individuals who have very type "A" personalities engage in exercise routines that cause repeated damage to their health in their quest to become healthier. Should we be just as strict in denying them health care at plan expense, even life-prolonging health care? Stress, and all the consequences of stress, is often associated with type "A" personalities. These might be extraordinarily productive individuals upon whom many social rewards are lavished. If denying such individuals health care at social expense for stress-related health problems might be seen as "sending the wrong message" (rewarding the slacker), then is the alternative message we send (only sinful, unhealthy behavior will be punished) very much contrary to our commitment to liberal neutrality? That is, is there a kind of religious message we would be seeking to enforce through public policy? Again, we are faced with multiple opportunities for arbitrary and unjust decisions.

Finally, causal relationships and moral agency can be very complexly intertwined in many of these situations such that it is virtually impossible to make a confident judgment that someone is justly blameworthy for their bad health state. Think of the smoking habits that are acquired by early adolescents who are very far from being mature and who are strongly influenced by peer pressure. We can insist that the immaturity be outgrown. However, smoking is addictive; it is obviously a very difficult habit to break once it has been entrenched. Individual genotypes may also predispose individuals much more readily to adverse health outcomes for what most would regard as relatively minor bad health choices. Some individuals are destined by genotype to have dangerously high cholesterol levels with related health consequences. Then there are also all the arguments in the medical literature about the relative safety or dangerousness of different foods. Do we deny individuals life-sustaining care because the weight of the medical debate (judging from this week's JAMA) leans in the direction of saying these individuals in these medical circumstances made bad choices? Again, the opportunity for arbitrary and unjust judgment is pervasive and unmanageable in practice.[14]

Going back to Option 6, this option is deeply flawed from the perspective of health care justice. In practice, it would be discriminatory and arbitrary in its application. However, I would not just sweep this option off the table. It ought to be the focus of intense, careful, social education through the deliberative process. Most individuals are capable of appreciating the force of the arguments above. "Winning" an artificial heart at social expense or protease inhibitors at social expense is not like the winning of the lottery—considerable pain and misery are among the side effects of "winning" such interventions. Protecting the integrity of your own health is its own reward.

SETTING LIMITS: CONCLUDING COMMENTS

If dialysis were the only significant expensive life-prolonging technology, there would be no need to "set limits" with regard to its fair use—as a society, we could afford even costly marginal uses of that technology. But the fact is that medicine today offers at least hundreds, if not thousands, of medical interventions that are costly and effective to some degree in prolonging life. Not all of those technologies, and not all of the clinical circumstances in which they might be used, are equally worthy of social funding.

The primary lessons from this chapter might be summarized as follows:

(1) Clinical circumstances matter. Some costly interventions significantly prolong human life in a wide range of cases; but not all cases, not all clinical circumstances. As those benefits diminish and as the cost of achieving very marginal benefits increases, the claims of justice diminish. This general rule suggests reasonable limits for the use of dialysis, protease inhibitors, and other comparable medical technologies.

(2) Protecting fair equality of opportunity will create a bias in favor funding expensive life-prolonging interventions that favor the young as opposed to the very old, as long as those technologies are very effective in sustaining an acceptable quality of life. Thus, a just and caring society ought to pay for imiglucerase for Gaucher's at $300,000 per person per year as well as costly factor VIII for hemophilia as well as the costly treatments for patients with cystic fibrosis as well as costly cancer interventions for children as well as costly interventions to save the lives of extremely premature neonates. The artificial heart should also be available to those

who have not achieved age 70. We should be certain that all of those life-saving or life-prolonging needs for younger members of society are met before we would commit to funding at social expense artificial hearts for those beyond age 70, given the extraordinarily high costs associated with widespread dissemination of that device, and the concomitant distortion of just health care priorities that would likely be brought about. Again, limits will be necessary, even for very young members of society. Premature infants below 500 grams and below 25 weeks gestation have a grim prognosis; the rare success story is not sufficient to justify the distortions this would cause in the just allocation of health care resources. Compassion for the fate of such unfortunate infants would also seem to be on the side of justice in such cases.

(3) We need to rely extensively upon the democratic deliberative process to fashion more finely limit-setting options and the considered judgments of health care justice that would justify those choices to all of us. Through that process we strengthen public reason and our collective capacities for public reasoning necessary to protect the liberal pluralistic foundations of our society and our shared sense of justice.

7

LAST-CHANCE THERAPIES

INTRODUCTION: SCOPE OF THE PROBLEM

What does it mean to be a just and caring society (or a just and caring hospital or managed care plan) when we have only limited resources to meet virtually unlimited health care needs, and the need before us now is a person faced with death in the near future unless he or she has access to a very expensive medical intervention that offers only a relatively small chance of a relatively small gain in life expectancy? Such medical interventions are what Daniels and Sabin (1998a) refer to as "last-chance therapies" because patients who need them have no other medical options to forestall death in the foreseeable future. It is difficult to imagine a more psychologically and morally burdensome decision than whether to offer a last-chance therapy.

Here are some examples of the sort of cases we have in mind under the rubric "last-chance therapies." Patients in end-stage COPD would have the option of lung reduction surgery. This surgery reduces the size of the lung in order to increase lung pressure, costs about $70,000, and might offer some recipients an extra six months to one year of life. There is actually a "ragged edge" problem here because it was a small subset of patients in the national trial who were the beneficiaries of some increased gain in life expectancy; others gained in terms of quality of life. The surgery itself carried a mortality risk of 6–10%. For all participants in this trial, the cost–effectiveness ratio at three years after surgery was $190,000 per QALY gained.

For the most responsive subgroup, the cost–effectiveness ratio at three years was $98,000 per QALY. There are two million patients in the U.S. today with COPD.

Though we have talked about the artificial heart as a future therapeutic option, it is at present in very restricted clinical trials.[1] This means several hundred thousand patients per year will die of their heart disease since an artificial heart is not an option today. However, we do have the left ventricular assist device (LVAD)—this device, with surgery and hospital expenses, costs about $200,000 per case. It was originally used as a "bridge to transplant" to sustain a patient until a natural heart was available for transplant. We need to pass over in silence the justice questions raised by that use of the device. Today, it is often used as "destination therapy." This device bolsters the pumping capacity of a failing heart. In theory, if the funds were available and if surgery were done early enough in end-stage heart failure, we could do 200,000 of these procedures per year at a cost of $40 billion per year. On average, this device will offer one to two years of additional life. Is a just and caring society morally obligated to provide access to this device for all who might achieve this level of benefit?

There are at least a couple dozen cancer drugs that can be thought of as "last-chance therapies" because they are typically given after all other therapeutic regimens have failed. I will list just a representative sampling of those that have drawn public and professional critical attention: bevacizumab (Avastin), cetuximab (Erbitux), trastuzumab (Herceptin), rituximab (Rituxan), gemtuzumab (Mylotarg), imatinib (Gleevec), erlotinib (Tarceva), gefitinib (Iressa). These drugs generally have costs of $50,000–$100,000 for a course of treatment, and offer anywhere from a couple weeks, to several months to a year in additional life expectancy. None of these drugs cure a cancer or save lives as such.[2] Again, if we were talking about a few thousand patients, nothing would morally justify our failure to offer these drugs to these patients for these marginal gains in life expectancy. But we are talking about 600,000 cancer deaths each year in the U.S. The vast majority of these patients would be candidates for one or another (sometimes more than one) of these drugs, so the potential costs in the aggregate will again be in the tens of billions of dollars.

To give just one example, we have already introduced a discussion of Herceptin. This drug is used for breast cancers that are HER2+—about 25% of women with breast cancer will be positive for HER2 receptors, which will result in a more aggressive cancer. Each year in the U.S. about 184,000 women are diagnosed with breast cancer, and 44,000 of these women will die from their cancer. Herceptin was originally used with women with metastatic disease; this yielded an average gain in life expectancy of about 5.5 months. It is now being used in conjunction with other chemotherapeutic agents earlier in the disease process in the hopes that it will be more effective. This expanded use means a much larger cohort of women each year will be given this drug (about 45,000 per year), and that they might receive more than one course of therapy (which would double the cost of treatment). The most recent medical reports indicate that this approach might buy an extra year of life for these women.

One other example of last-chance therapies would be providing total parenteral nutrition (TPN) to very premature infants who do not have a functioning gut. This intervention can sustain the lives of these infants for about four years, at a cost of about $200,000 per patient per year. As we noted in an earlier chapter, this therapy will actually destroy a child's liver. At that point, death can be averted only with a liver transplant ($400,000) and two more years of TPN before the transplanted liver is destroyed. About 4,000 such infants are born each year in the U.S. Could a just and caring society endorse a rationing protocol that would deny TPN to these infants at birth, provide comfort care only, and allow them to die (unless parents or charitable sources were willing to underwrite these costs)?

The defining features of last-chance therapies would seem to be the following: (1) Particular individuals are at imminent risk of death if they are denied access to one of these last-chance therapies (that is, they have a serious life-threatening medical problem and no alternative medical interventions that might prolong their life); (2) the intervention these individuals need and want is very costly, will not alter the terminal outcome, and will yield only a marginal gain in life expectancy and/or quality of life; (3) relatively large numbers of individuals would be seen as candidates for this intervention, thus generating very large aggregate costs for society; (4) though the *average* gain in life expectancy might be judged as marginal, there might be a wide variation around that average, which will add to the moral complexity as we try to come to a fair and reasonable decision about any rationing protocol. The reader will note that I have not included protease inhibitors or renal dialysis or artificial hearts among last-chance therapies, though individuals needing any of these interventions will clearly be faced with imminent death if they are denied them. Further, these are costly interventions, but they are generally very effective. They are all capable of prolonging reasonable quality of life for many years. This is precisely what is not true of last-chance therapies, which is a major reason why they are placed in a distinct moral category.

WHY LAST-CHANCE THERAPIES? WEAK MORAL ARGUMENTS

What morally relevant considerations seem to push in the direction of requiring a just and caring society to fund these last-chance therapies? The phrase that will be invoked most often is that we have a "duty to rescue." It is not as if we are short of a transplantable organ or an ICU bed. The rescue technology is available in ample supply, and it will work. The social question is whether we ought to make the dollars available necessary to underwrite the cost of the rescue. This again brings us back to the issue of pricing human life. All of us are familiar with stories of dramatic rescues that have gotten considerable media coverage: the little girl trapped in the well, stranded individuals in a snowstorm on a mountain, a physician with pancreatitis trapped at a base in Antarctica; these rescues cost millions of dollars. But no one ever turns to an economist and asks: "Is it really worth it to spend six million dollars to rescue that doctor in Antarctica? We do not have a doctor shortage; we can afford to lose a few here and there." If anyone ever deliberately asked such a question or offered such a comment in the midst of a rescue effort, they would be excommunicated from the human race. The rest of the argument is that these rescues are often dangerous and costly, but we would have to be completely lacking in compassion if we refused to undertake them. In the case of "medical rescues" of the sort we have in mind with these last-chance therapies, the claim is that these rescues are "easy"—no one has to risk life or limb to provide the needed medical services; both the technologies and the patients are right at hand.

However, the analogy and the moral conclusion are not as plain and simple as the above line of argument would suggest. While some of the persons we would hope to rescue in these more dramatic efforts may perish before rescue or shortly after rescue (because we could not get to them quickly enough), the expected outcome (and the typical outcome) is that rescued individuals go on to enjoy a normal life expectancy. But in the case of last-chance therapies, what we know before any rescue effort is initiated is that these patients are doomed to die despite our best rescue efforts. A "successful" medical rescue cannot realistically hope to offer more than a marginal gain in life expectancy or quality of life.

Other moral arguments might be deployed at this point, aimed at showing that we are still morally obligated to make that rescue effort, but I want to pass over those arguments for a moment. Instead, I want to call attention to the fact that these dramatic rescues tend to be very rare events. This is a major reason why they draw media attention. If there were tens of thousands of such efforts required every day, none of them would garner any media attention. But that is precisely the situation with medical rescues. About 10,000 people die each day in the U.S., each of whom is a very likely candidate for a medical rescue. We might describe all of these rescues as "easy" rescues, but that is not sufficient to justify the claim that there is a moral obligation to effect all these rescues. Each of these rescues would be extraordinarily costly, and, in the aggregate, would unjustly skew the distribution of health care resources. That is, we would find that in order to provide resources for all these health rescues, we would have to take away substantial resources from other health needs that did not represent imminent threats to life. The consequence would be a large increase in preventable human suffering, which would be neither just nor compassionate. This is a morally relevant consequence of unlimited expenditures for last-chance therapies. This is not the sort of consequence that we typically associate with those dramatic media rescues.

We should also raise the question of how many medical rescues an individual has a just claim to. It would be extraordinarily rare for the same individual to have been rescued more than once in one of these media rescues. But in the vast majority of cases where we talk about last-chance therapies, individuals have already been the beneficiaries of one or more prior expensive medical rescues. AIDS patients will have received hundreds of thousands of dollars of care in the form of protease inhibitors. Cardiac patients will have had bypass surgery ($65,000) or balloon angioplasty ($40,000) and/or very expensive drug regimens and/or cardiac defibrillators implanted ($40,000) before they become candidates for an LVAD. Cancer patients will have had expensive surgeries and/or chemotherapeutic regimens before they are offered these targeted cancer drugs with costs of $50,000–$100,000 for a course of treatment. If we did have some form of national health insurance that provided assured access to these earlier more effective medical interventions before we needed to talk about last-chance therapies, then this looks a lot less like patient abandonment or a heartless denial of care at the end of life, just for economic reasons. The moral analogy to "easy rescue" loses much of the force it might otherwise have outside a health care context.

One of the other factors appealed to in this discussion as having moral weight is the fact that we are dealing with "identified individuals" who are in peril and at risk of imminent death. Again, this is something that tugs at the heart in the case of those dramatic media rescues. The argument is that this same factor is relevant in last-chance therapy situations. We cannot literally look someone in the eye and tell them that we have the capacity to rescue them from imminent death but we are simply going to let them die because it would cost too much to save them. By way of contrast, the argument goes, it is less morally problematic when we are unable to fund some preventive health or safety program with the result that there will be a loss of life that would otherwise have been preventable. But the lives lost there are merely "statistical lives" that have neither names nor faces. Statistical lives do not evoke compassion. *But they should!* The psychological reason statistical lives do not evoke compassion is that it is easy to imagine that the loss of these lives was unfortunate because it was not the direct result of any decision we made to deny that person life-sustaining care. If we do not have enough money to pay for reflectors along a highway and someone misses a curve and dies, then we can easily tell ourselves that they were probably driving too fast, or they were distracted by a cell phone conversation, or they were too sleepy to drive, and so on. And, of course, some of the time some of these rationalizations are in fact correct. But it is impossible to determine when that is true and when it is just a bad excuse that provides ready salve to our conscience.

If we are more reflective about the matter, however, then I would argue that from the perspective of health care justice, statistical lives are just as morally important as identifiable lives. The reader will recall the work of David Eddy (1996) discussed earlier. Recall the women factory workers at risk of breast cancer. They can spend their insurance resources on paying for autologous bone marrow transplants for women with metastatic disease, and they "might" save an identified life for three extra years. Or they can invest those same dollars in a screening mammogram program and save seven "statistical lives." Those will be real lives that will be saved, but it will typically be practically impossible to know who the women were whose lives were directly saved through that program, since 29 other women (out of the thousand in the cohort) will still die from their breast cancer. From the perspective of health care justice and reflective compassion, those statistical lives ought to matter and count more heavily than the one identified life that might be saved for three years. If resources spent on last-chance therapies are taken away from any number of preventive health care programs (safe sex programs, antismoking programs, regular Pap smears, etc.), and if that results in a loss of "merely" statistical lives, then that is a prima facie serious injustice.

Finally, another argument deployed to defend a social moral obligation to fund these last-chance therapies is that these therapies are for the benefit of those who are "least well-off." This is a phrase introduced into the literature of political philosophy by John Rawls (1971). Rawls is a moderate egalitarian so far as his theory of justice is concerned. He is willing to countenance as "just enough" reasonable differences in income and wealth throughout society. A major part of the justification for the deviation from a strong egalitarian position is that choosing an economic system and public policies that permit such inequalities in wealth and income allows those who are least well-off in our society to be better off than they otherwise would have been in any other society that is feasible and reasonable. In other words, if income and wealth were distributed very close to evenly, and if the consequence of that was little capital available for taking risks and building large wealth-producing enterprises, then virtually everyone in such a society would be a lot less well-off than virtually everyone in our society.[3]

More recent political philosophers who have embraced assorted versions of this view call themselves "prioritarians." A central motivating idea for them is that any increment of welfare for the least well-off will mean a lot more to them than that same increment of welfare for someone who is already very well-off. Arneson (2000) writes, "The root idea of prioritarianism is that one ought as a matter of justice to aid the unfortunate, and the more badly off someone is, the more urgent is the moral appeal to aid." Thus, if I give $1,000 to someone whose annual income is $10,000, they are 10% better off. They regard this as a major improvement in their welfare. If I give that same $1,000 to someone with an income of a million dollars annually he is 0.1% better off, which would be a very insignificant increase in his welfare.

Now, none of these philosophers in explicating their views have much to say about health or health care, but it is easy enough to make the analogy. If an 80-year-old patient with advanced cancer will be dead in two weeks from that cancer (but I can spend $100,000 to give him six extra months of life), that represents a 1,200% increase in health-welfare for him. Imagine that I could take the same $100,000, and with some exquisite medical manipulation of the bone marrow of a very healthy 20-year-old, I could give that individual six extra months of life *after he achieves his predicted life expectancy of 80*. That represents a gain in life expectancy of less than 1%. If we think this prioritarian view is a reasonable moral perspective, then it would seem that last-chance therapies should be very near the top of our priority list when it comes to the just distribution of health care dollars. I will reject this conclusion.

I am sympathetic to the core prioritarian idea that those who are least well-off (in broad welfare terms) ought to have priority in constructing social policies that will have differential distributive effects. That is, justice requires that such policies be designed to improve substantially the welfare prospects of those who are least well-off. But this commitment cannot be translated so easily into the world of medicine and health care without consequences which are adverse for a reasonable pluralistic conception of health care justice.

The key claims I will defend are the following: (1) Patients who are medically least well-off have a *presumptive but defeasible claim* to high priority for needed health care resources. (2) Not all those patients who are correctly included in the category of those who are medically least well-off are *equally* entitled to needed health care resources. In other words, priorities regarding resource allocation for those who are medically least well-off can be justly determined; there is nothing intrinsically unjust about assigning highly differentiated priority for different patients who are judged to be among the medically least well-off. Some of those patients may be justly assigned very low priority for expensive life-prolonging medical resources, either through the deliberative process or as a result of careful moral argument and analysis. (3) Virtually everyone among those characterized as being among the medically least well-off would be a person with disabilities. I take it this point would be strongly affirmed by organizations whose mission is to be advocates for persons with disabilities. My claim is that prioritization within this category *does not necessarily represent discrimination in some morally objectionable sense.* Not all disabilities requiring medical resources are on an equal plane so far as the just distribution of health resources is concerned. The defense of this last claim needs to be postponed to the next chapter.

The question we need to start with is the question of who the medically least well-off are. What we shall find is that they are an extraordinarily heterogeneous lot; it is not as if there is some clear and simple criterion that readily allows us to identify who belongs in this category. If we keep our focus on "last-chance therapy" patients, then we might be inclined to say "being faced with imminent death" would surely be the prime criterion for identifying those who are medically least well-off. However, the medical circumstances of at least some of those faced with imminent death will be such that medicine will be able to do nothing to alter that terminal trajectory. Others will have the option of last-chance therapies. This might suggest that we put aside that first set, and just focus on those for whom last-chance therapies are an option. But that might be a morally precipitous conclusion.

It is true that medicine can do nothing to alter *the terminal outcome or its arrival* for that first set of patients, but medicine can improve (through the use of hospice services) the quality of life for those individuals faced with imminent death. This will require resources, so there is a justice issue to be addressed. From the perspective of health care justice, is it more important to fund these hospice services or to fund the demand for last-chance therapies? For the time being, we can put this question on hold.

There are dozens, if not hundreds, of last-chance therapies that offer some prolongation of life, usually at extraordinary expense. From the perspective of health care justice, are they all of equal priority since they are all directed to aiding individuals faced with imminent death whom we have identified for now as being among the medically least well-off? Again, I remind the reader that we have only limited resources to meet virtually unlimited health care needs—if we endorsed something like an unlimited just claim to these last-chance therapies, then we would again be affirming the thesis that human life is priceless. We have already shown that powerful considerations of justice, prudence, and compassion all speak against the thesis. In the present context, the practical implication of affirming this thesis is that we would provide no funding for hospice services, since that represented "only" a quality improvement at the end of life.

But it also seems unreasonable and unjust that we would make no differential judgments of priority among all these last-chance therapies. They have very different effects in terms of life prolongation and very different cost–effectiveness ratios.

Thus, erlotinib (Tarceva) will increase survival for some lung cancer patients by no more than two months at a cost of about $32,000 (Tigue et al., 2007). Bortezomib (Velcade) used to treat multiple myeloma will provide about one year of prolonged survival for 23% of those treated at a cost of $45,000 per case (Tigue, 2007). The left ventricular assist device may yield on average about 18 extra months of life expectancy at a cost of about $200,000. What I report here are generally average cost and survival figures; in a clinical content, it may well be determinable that various subcategories of patients are either very unlikely to come anywhere close to that average, or else they will substantially exceed that average. Are we morally obligated to ignore all this differentiating data? Is it morally sufficient that all the patients needing these last-chance therapies are among the medically least well-off? I want to claim that ignoring such information is neither fair nor reasonable.

Imagine the following scenario: We have two individuals whose heart failure is such that they each will be dead in the next two months if they receive no life-sustaining medical intervention. We can provide each with an artificial heart at $300,000. One individual is 20 years old and is likely to survive 50 years with the artificial heart; the other individual is 90 and will only survive a year because of other medical problems. From the perspective of health care justice, would we want to argue that they are equally entitled to an artificial heart? Or would we have good reason for believing that the 20-year-old had a clearly superior moral claim to that artificial heart, even though there is no shortage of the devices?

Certainly from the perspective of protecting fair equality of opportunity, the 20-year-old will have the stronger just claim. And I have to believe that the same conclusion would be endorsed through the deliberative process for multiple morally relevant reasons, such as the fact that the 20-year-old will get 50 extra years of life. But if these seem like reasonable moral judgments, then the implication of that is that being among the medically least well-off is not by itself determinative of having a just claim to any expensive life-prolonging resources. This also illustrates the point that two individuals can have the same terminal medical condition and the same terminal prognosis, but have very different just claims to expensive life-prolonging medical care.

Some prioritarians may be puzzled by this result or wish to resist this conclusion; however, an easy explanation is at hand. These prioritarians usually assert their central thesis in a very abstract context. Certainly this is true for Rawls (1971). What Rawls wants to assert is that the least well-off are those whose welfare is at the lowest end of the social welfare scale because they have the least in the way of "primary goods," especially income and wealth. Primary goods also include basic rights and liberties, opportunities to achieve positions of prominence in society, and the social bases of respect. Primary goods are "all-purpose means" for individuals being able to achieve what they judge to be a satisfactory life. What a society can do to be responsive to the unmet needs of those who are least well-off is to put in place social welfare policies that are fundamentally redistributive. If properly designed, they will have the desired effect of improving the welfare of those who are least well-off. What defeats this same strategy being applied in the domain of health care is the heterogeneity of health needs.

There are no "primary health goods" that, if distributed equally to the medically least well-off, will have the effect of making them all more or less equally better off. If we distributed $20,000 annually to the medically least well-off, the result would likely be that very few of those individuals could benefit very much at all from those resources—in fact, most of them would not benefit at all. If a heart patient needs an LVAD or an artificial heart for $200,000 or $300,000, a sum of $20,000 will do no good whatsoever. The same is true if someone needs a course of these expensive cancer drugs that costs $70,000. As Norman Daniels says (1985), these interventions are "lumpy." It is all or nothing. No one can buy 10% of an LVAD, nor are there short-term lease options for LVADs. Apart from heterogeneity of medical problems and heterogeneity of costs, there is also heterogeneity of effectiveness for different medical interventions, or the same intervention in different patients. There is also heterogeneity of quality of life prior to any of these medical interventions, as well as subsequent to any of these medical interventions. All of this heterogeneity defeats any simple application of welfare prioritarianism and its concern for the least well-off to the health care context.

We have to return to our question regarding the identity of those who are medically least well-off. Our first suggestion was that those faced with imminent death should be regarded as being the medically least well-off. Of course, the term "imminent" has some elasticity. It could mean a life expectancy of less than three months, or less than six months, or less than a year. But we can also say that any individual given a terminal diagnosis is very substantially less well-off than others whose life expectancy is open-ended. I am using the phrase "terminal diagnosis" broadly. If a physician tells a patient they have a disease process that will end in their death unless something else causes their death first, they have been given a terminal diagnosis. Patients in complete renal failure have a terminal diagnosis, even if they have a life expectancy of 10 years. Cancer patients with metastatic disease are faced with a terminal prognosis, as are many heart patients whose heart disease has a well-known downhill trajectory. Here, we run into a morally interesting problem.

If all these individuals exist side-by-side with last-chance therapy patients among the medically least well-off, and if we have successfully argued above that there ought to be priorities established so far as just claims to needed health care are concerned among those who are least well-off, then which large set of the medically least well-off ought to be thought of as having priority regarding their health needs? This is a very practical problem, not simply a philosophical puzzle. What we have to imagine in this scenario is that the group of patients I just introduced into the least well-off category are in the relatively early stages of their terminal illness. Often, numerous costly medical interventions are options for them that will have the desirable effect of sustaining their lives for significantly longer periods and at a higher quality level than would have been the case without these interventions.

Again, the whole foundation of our discussion is that we have only limited resources to meet unlimited needs; priorities must be established among these needs and interventions that reflect our shared sense of justice. But, if we were to allow what we might call our untutored sympathies to determine how we think about this matter, then those sympathies might well incline us to believe that those who were *really least well-off* were those who were faced with very imminent death; consequently, we ought to make available to them anything medical science can offer that would give them the additional life they would otherwise be denied. But the consequence of that would very likely be a shortage of dollars to underwrite the costs of aggressive and effective life-prolonging care at earlier stages of these terminal disease processes. Is it really the case that those who have the strongest just claims to life-prolonging resources (because they are the medically least well-off) are those who are closest to death but for whom some medical intervention can offer a short gain in life expectancy? What would happen if this entire issue were proposed for rational democratic deliberation?

Ordinarily, I know I have no right to make predictions about the outcomes of democratic deliberations; any number of creative resolutions to complex moral problems might emerge from that process. In this case, however, I am quite confident that deliberative individuals who were ignorant of their future possible medical circumstances would want as many resources as possible devoted to maintaining length and quality of life in those earlier stages of a terminal illness. They would understand that they were making such a choice for their future possible selves, and what they would judge is that such a choice was both just and prudent. If anything, they would insist that all costly, more than marginally effective interventions aimed at those earlier disease states be funded first, even if there were no resources available for funding last-chance therapies of the sort we described at the beginning of this chapter. Those earlier interventions would yield more high-quality life-years at a lower cost than later last-chance therapy interventions. Further, our deliberators would likely also be inclined to fund the kind of care that characterizes hospice programs before they would be inclined to spend very much on these last-chance therapies. Again, considerations of justice and compassion would warrant this conclusion. If these are correct conclusions, then the implication of this is that those who are *most often described as being the medically least well-off* because they are so close to dying would not (and should not) have moral priority for expensive life-prolonging medical care simply on the basis of those descriptors. There are limits to the scope of the prioritarian thesis. This is another version of one of the prime lessons from the last chapter.[4]

We return again to our question of who should be included among those who are medically least well-off. What we can imagine is a very diverse array of patients who may be suffering from a complex mix of medical problems, none of which would be thought of as having a fatal outcome, but all of which together profoundly diminish the quality of life for such individuals, as well as their capacity to function in carrying out their normal daily responsibilities. What we also have to imagine is that some array of moderately expensive but reasonably effective medical interventions are capable of ameliorating most of the debilitating symptoms associated with these medical problems.

We could use multiple sclerosis (MS) as one example of the sort of patients we have in mind. There are about 400,000 such patients in the U.S. (2007), each with one of four variants of the disease of which can be graded as mild, moderate or severe. Drug costs for these patients per year will average $25,000–$30,000 per patient, with additional health costs related to the disease bringing annual costs above $50,000 (*MS Network*, 2007). The drugs used for these patients are effective in slowing disease progression, minimizing the functional effects of symptoms, and restoring individuals to baseline after an exacerbation. In this regard you could say that these patients are *potentially* among those who are medically least well-off. That is, most of them would be in this category if they did not have secure access to the therapeutic interventions that prevent that level of decline. The question we would pose for the deliberative process would be the following: Should MS (and comparable kinds of medical disorders) have higher priority for funding than any of the last-chance therapies we have listed? The answer to this question (and the reasoning that would justify that answer) seem obvious. From behind a veil of ignorance regarding our future health problems, we would certainly give much higher priority to funding effective medical interventions for MS (and other such disorders) before we would provide funding for last-chance therapies. Protecting fair and effective equality of opportunity would likely be the dominant moral justification for this conclusion. These therapeutic interventions provide many years of life of reasonable quality at a reasonable social cost. Our last-chance therapies provide only marginal gains in life expectancy at extraordinarily high cost for the benefits gained. We also note that neither prudence nor compassion would warrant giving higher priority to these last-chance therapies relative to the therapies needed for MS or comparable medical problems.

We can consider another case scenario. Individuals who have suffered severe spinal cord injuries that will leave them as vent-dependent quadriplegics will have first-year medical costs and rehabilitation costs of about $800,000. If they are about 25 years old, they will have lifetime medical costs of about $2.4 million—that same amount of money would pay for lung reduction surgery for about 30 individuals in end-stage COPD. From the perspective of health care justice, which intervention should have the higher priority? One sort of follow-up question might be this: Should all those resources go to one person to give that person 30 extra years of life, or should those resources go to 30 individuals to give them each one extra year of life? Prioritarians think of themselves as egalitarians. But this particular comparison does raise some puzzles. To allow 30 individuals to each lose a year of potential life (their last year of life) in order to award all those years to one individual looks very anti-egalitarian (considered abstractly). But real-world details make a difference. Virtually all those COPD patients are likely to be above age 60, while our SCI patient is only 25 years old. All those COPD patients have had an opportunity to achieve something close to a normal life expectancy, but our SCI patient will come close to that same life expectancy only with the $2.4 million investment in rehabilitation therapy. Brock (2002) asks the critical question: What exactly is it that needs to be equalized from the perspective of prioritarianism in a health care context? Is it resources or outcomes or opportunities? If it is resources, then it certainly looks inegalitarian to award all $2.4 million to our SCI patient and nothing in the way of life-prolonging resources to our 30 COPD patients. But if it is opportunities (to achieve a normal life expectancy), then it looks like the fair egalitarian choice is to award all those funds to our SCI patient. For now, we do not have to resolve this debate; it is sufficient for our purposes that these questions again illustrate the moral complexity attached to the category of those who are medically least well-off.

I will offer as a brief afterthought the following question: What if we chose a different category of patients than those with COPD? Women with metastatic breast cancer who are HER-2 positive can have access to Herceptin (trastuzumab) at a cost of about $70,000 for a course of therapy that will yield an average gain in life expectancy of about 5.5 months. Should we use $2.4 million for our SCI patient or for 30 women with metastatic breast cancer? One reason this question might be a bit harder than our prior question is that these 30 women will likely range in age from 25 to 50. That is, many of them will have had no more an opportunity to achieve a normal life expectancy than our SCI patient. How should we judge that issue from a prioritarian perspective?

Some readers will view this last question with suspicion because it has all the marks of an airy, philosophic thought experiment. But I do have a real-world analogue for this question. In the United Kingdom, NICE recently approved Herceptin for coverage under the National Health Service (after considerable "grass roots" pressure orchestrated and funded by the makers of Herceptin). But the NHS did not add anything to "Trust" budgets to reflect the increased costs that would be generated by the approval of this drug. The Norfolk and Norwich University Hospital Trust estimated that over the next year, 75 women would be candidates for Herceptin at a cost to the Trust of about 2.3 million British pounds (roughly $4.6 million). Where would the money come from to provide this coverage? The authors (Barrett et al., 2006) of an article titled "How Much Will Herceptin Really Cost?" write: "So we could fund Herceptin if we did not treat 355 patients receiving adjuvant treatment (16 of whom would be cured) or 208 patients receiving palliative chemotherapy" (p. 1118). The palliative chemotherapy will not prolong the lives of any of these patients; it will "merely" relieve substantial suffering they would otherwise suffer in the last weeks and months of life. Herceptin will (on average) give each of those 75 women an extra half-year of life. Is it obvious that providing Herceptin is the morally preferable choice because it would provide some life prolongation for each of those women? Is this the choice we would endorse as rational democratic deliberators from behind a veil of ignorance as being the more just and caring choice?

There are three different cohorts of patients who are being talked about in the quoted passage. All can be plausibly described as bring among the medically least well-off. What is not obvious is that all should be *equally regarded* as being among the medically least well-off, especially for purposes of making just resource allocation decisions in the face of limited resources. And if, as a practical matter, these three cohorts cannot be regarded as having equal just claims to this one pot of money, then what criteria should be used for determining who should have priority? Should the fact that Herceptin represents a last-chance therapy be absolutely determinative in this matter?[5]

We again return to our base question of who should be included among those who are medically least well-off. A case could certainly be made for saying (descriptively) that patients in a persistent vegetative state (PVS) or in the advanced stages of dementia are among the medically least well-off. It is easy enough to think of dementia patients in this way because they are faced with an irreversible terminal outcome. PVS patients, however, will often have very open-ended life expectancies, so they cannot be thought of as being among the medically least well-off for that reason. But they have no capacity to function or experience in any meaningful way within their environment, and it might be for that reason we might think of them as being among the medically least well-off. So, if we think of these patients in this way, does that mean that they ought to have something close to topmost priority for expensive life-prolonging medical resources if one or another medical crisis would threaten to cause a "premature" death? Would justice require that we provide such patients with an artificial heart or an LVAD or these expensive cancer drugs or an implantable cardiac defibrillator if any of these patients were faced with medical circumstances that would ordinarily require these interventions (if patients with these problems were not grossly demented or in PVS)?

I do not think I am alone in believing these questions are morally unreasonable. It is easy enough to accept our categorizing these patients among the medically least well-off, but it is extraordinarily difficult to think that status would justify providing to these patients expensive life-prolonging care as a high priority from the perspective of health care justice. No doubt, all the life-prolonging technologies I mentioned could be successfully deployed to prolong the lives of these patients, but it would be wasteful and unjust to do that. Again, one of our core distributional principles is a commitment to protecting fair and effective equality of opportunity. The opportunity referenced here is opportunity to access "the normal opportunity range" of our society. But in the case of these two sorts of patients there are no such effective opportunities. Their medical problems cannot be reversed or ameliorated; consequently, prolonging their lives will do nothing in the way of restoring or expanding access to the normal opportunity range.

We could argue that there are some minimal sorts of positively valued experiences that some end-stage dementia patients under some circumstances could have access to if they were provided with one or another of the life-prolonging technologies we mentioned. But if we insist on that point, we surely cannot also insist that providing such expensive life-sustaining care ought to be a very high priority as a matter of justice relative to all the other unmet health care needs in our society. Consider, for example, that we had some very expensive drug for rheumatoid arthritis that was also very effective. It might cost $13,000 per year, and it would have to be taken indefinitely. Two such drugs would be infliximab (Remicade) and etanercept (Enbrel). We will say that either of these drugs is so effective that it lifts a patient from judging that their quality of life is .2 to saying their quality of life is .8; they are still experiencing some discomfort, but a huge world of functioning and experience is reopened to them as a result of this drug. We could provide this drug to 20 individuals for a year at a cost of $260,000, or we could provide an LVAD to a patient in end-stage dementia and give them 18 extra months of life.[6] The arthritis drug does nothing so far as prolonging life expectancy is concerned. What should we do?

This is what we have to ask ourselves (individually and collectively): If we are behind a veil of ignorance regarding our future possible health needs, would we give higher priority as a matter of either justice or prudence to prolonging the lives of end-stage dementia patients with an LVAD, as opposed to using those same resources to relieve the suffering of those patients with rheumatoid arthritis as well as restoring very significant functional opportunities? The answer to this question seems self-evident. There might be ideological reasons for offering a different answer, but from the perspective of public reason it seems only one answer could be given. What this example reaffirms is that merely being categorized among the medically least well-off does not generate automatically a high priority for expensive life-prolonging resources. Numerous other morally relevant considerations must be employed for determining the just claims to life-prolonging resources for those who are medically least well-off.

LAST-CHANCE THERAPIES AND RATIONAL DEMOCRATIC DELIBERATION

The central practical conclusion of this last section was that there are no powerful moral arguments that support the general claim that patients have just claims to last-chance therapies, most especially those that are very expensive and only marginally beneficial. We have to add immediately that this does not imply that it would be unjust (necessarily) if society were to pay for access to these therapies from social resources; rather, the issue is open for democratic deliberation. We can collectively determine how high or low a priority funding for these last-chance therapies ought to have. As in the prior chapter, we can consider this issue from either the present perspective of the structure of the U.S. health care system or from the future perspective of a society that would wish to provide to all assured access to a comprehensive benefit package.

As things are now, some serious injustices are associated with coverage of many of these last-chance therapies in either the private or the public sector. Probably the most serious injustice is that the insured middle-class receive large tax benefits from the fact that they have health insurance as an employment benefit. This means that no taxes are paid by employers or employees on the economic value of that insurance plan. This amounts to a governmental subsidy in the vicinity of 40–45% of the value of that plan for the typical middle-class individual. This is what economists refer to as a tax expenditure. It is currently estimated (2007) that the value of that benefit is about $200 billion—this is the amount of money that states and the federal government would have collected as taxes from businesses and individuals if this were treated as ordinary income or not permitted as a tax deduction.

The reason this is morally problematic from the perspective of health care justice is that this subsidy motivates employees to constantly accept upgraded health insurance packages. That is, these packages tend to pay for these very expensive last-chance therapies, especially if the federal government has approved them for Medicare funding. And the federal government (Medicare) is permitted (by law) only to assess the effectiveness of these new therapies, not whether they are costworthy. Consequently, private insurers provide similar coverage. As the cost of these insurance packages increases each year, employers who are at the economic margin drop all health insurance as an employee benefit or, alternatively, increase co-pays and deductibles to levels that are onerous for their workers (which causes these workers to make rationing decisions for themselves that are unwise, and likely unjust as well). In either case, we see major annual increases in the number of uninsured or underinsured in our society *who will then have to pay for whatever health care they need and can afford with after-tax dollars* rather than the tax-free dollars the well-insured get to use.

These less well-off individuals will most certainly not be able to afford these last-chance therapies. That by itself is not intrinsically unjust, especially if there are no strong considerations of health care justice that would require coverage for such therapies. But we are subsidizing with public dollars access to these therapies for those who are well-insured. There is no moral justification for that subsidy from the perspective of health care justice, especially if a consequence of that subsidy is an increase in the pool of the uninsured who will find themselves often unable to afford what all might regard as very effective costly therapies, which considerations of justice would endorse as well. Justice is not compromised if we allow those who are financially well-off to purchase these last-chance therapies with their private resources *as long as no one is made worse off as a result of such private purchases.* As things are now, however, those who are less well-off are made even worse off when government subsidizes what from a moral point of view are extravagant health care purchases (even if those purchases are aimed at satisfying what all would agree are health care needs).

The reader will recall my mentioning earlier the common description of Medicare as national health insurance for the elderly. This was a true description of the program during its early years; it reflected a sense of equality and social solidarity among the elderly. That is much less true today as we see creeping privatization erode those more ideal commitments of the Medicare program. Medicare Part D, the prescription drug benefit, has contributed very substantially to that trend because there are literally hundreds of private drug plans with an infinitely complex mix of drugs that are covered (or not covered) that the elderly must choose among. This may not have much practical significance for elderly patients on only one or two prescription drugs, but for patients who are on eight or ten or more prescription drugs, the confusion and consequences and expense can be staggering.

The drug sutinib (Sutent) is used to treat gastrointestinal stromal tumors as well as metastatic renal cell carcinoma. This is a last-chance therapy; it offers a cure to no one. The best that can be hoped for is an objective response rate of 26% to 37%. Some Medicare patients will pay only $827 for this drug, while others could pay as much as $90,000 for that drug, all depending upon Byzantine features of these drug plans that Medicare patients themselves have no control over. As noted in an earlier chapter, these sorts of differences are a product of pharmaceutical company lobbying efforts aimed at making certain that Medicare could not bargain as a single entity for discounts from pharmaceutical companies. Consequently, individuals who are medically similarly situated with similar medical needs might have radically different coverage under what is supposed to be the same government program. Again, it looks as if government is subsidizing access for some to these last-chance therapies (which is prima facie unjust), while other elderly individuals will still struggle to pay for somewhat expensive (but very effective) medications under "the same" Medicare program. The key conclusion I would draw at this point is that it is virtually impossible to achieve even rough justice with respect to these last-chance therapies in the current U.S. health care system.

So, if we imagine a future possible universal health care system in the U.S., what sort of policies ought we adopt with regard to these last-chance therapies? We can begin with these very expensive cancer therapies. As always, judgments in regard to some of these very complex medical matters must be sensitive to the medical facts and their morally relevant implications. What we call facts must reflect our best scientific judgment, and must be presented to the public (and the deliberative process) in ways that are congruent with that scientific judgment, rather than the judgment of an advertising executive seeking to maximize sales for a drug or device company.

Media writers sometimes contribute to providing an excessively optimistic picture of these drugs. In the *New York Times*, for example, Pollack (2007a) writes, "A new drug looks poised to become the first effective treatment for liver cancer." That drug is sorafenib (Nexavar). That drug costs $50,000 per year, and in a clinical trial increased survival (compared to placebo) from 7.9 months to 10.7 months. This is described in the article as less than three months, or a 44% increase in life expectancy. The percentage figure looks impressive, but the absolute gain is minimal. Late in the article it is noted that patients in the trial had relatively healthy livers, and hence, these results might not be expected for patients with advanced disease.

Another article discussed the drug bevacizumab (Avastin) in connection with breast cancer. Bevacizumab was actually approved by the FDA for use in connection with colorectal cancer. But the makers of the drug (Genentech) believed the drug could be effective against metastatic breast cancer as well. Two trials were conducted to test this use. Before the trials were concluded, Genentech was announcing how effective the drug was: women receiving this drug went a median of 11.3 months without disease progression compared to 5.8 months for women on paclitaxel (Taxol) alone. Laypeople might see this forestalling of disease progression as translating into greater life expectancy. But in point of fact, nothing requires that correlation to hold. There was only a seven-week difference in median survival time between the two groups, and five patients died as a result of their taking Avastin (Pollack, 2007b). Allen (2007a) comments on the same general problem: "For decades, promising cancer treatments have fizzled and leaders have used sometimes misleading statistics to make the case that the war is going well." He goes on to mention how five-year survival rates for cancer have improved markedly, and this is what many cancer organizations trumpet as clear success. But, he quickly adds, this is very likely a statistical artifact linked to increased use of screening tests and earlier detection, which means *patients live longer with their tumors* without any actual extension of life. Again, this sort of statistical manipulation subverts the deliberative process.

To return to our question, if we were to have some form of national health insurance, what sort of inclusions or exclusions regarding these cancer drugs would be "just enough" and "caring enough"? Option 1: Make access to these drugs entirely a matter of individual ability to pay. This might be the least morally problematic option so far as health care justice is concerned. As noted already, we would have to insist that no one is made worse off as a result of choosing this policy option. That means there could be no tax subsidies for these health care expenditures. The likelihood is that only financially well-off individuals could afford this option; but so long as the gains are very marginal (additional weeks or months of life of diminished quality) and the cost–effectiveness ratios unreasonable, no one is treated unjustly. If an alternative to this option is unlimited funding for these drugs for all cancer patients as a last-chance therapy, then the potential costs would be several tens of billions of dollars per year for very marginal gains in life expectancy. From a prudential perspective, as well as the perspective of health care justice, this would appear to be a very unwise use of resources. That money would be better spent in preventive efforts, early diagnostic efforts, and improvement in the effectiveness of cancer therapies before a metastatic process has set in.

Option 2: Many will argue that these very expensive cancer drugs would be substantially more effective if they were used much earlier in the disease process in combination with some current cancer therapies. This is what we noted above in connection with the use of Avastin for breast cancer along with paclitaxel. But we also saw those particular trials resulted again only in very marginal gains. We cannot say *a priori* that this same minimal result would be true for all of these cancer drugs in combination with other cancer drugs. Again, however, it would be unjust and imprudent to provide unlimited funding for anyone who wanted to try these novel combination therapies—we would be gambling tens of billions of dollars each year. What we could do instead is publicly fund this research and the necessary clinical trials so long as there is sound scientific research that would support the likely success of specific drug combinations for specific cancers. That means there would be no social funding for these drugs apart from clinical trials that were carefully constructed and supervised under NIH. This would avoid repetition of the mistakes (moral and scientific) associated with autologous bone marrow transplants for breast cancer in the 1990s. One potential justice-relevant concern that could be raised is this: Clinical trials must be very careful about which patients with specific medical conditions are admitted into a trial. An individual might have the right cancer at the right stage to be admitted to a trial, but they might also have some comorbid condition that would potentially confound trial data and its interpretation. To prevent that, such individuals would be excluded from the trial. Have they been treated unjustly? Has society facilitated this injustice through Option 2? This is one of those matters that should be the focus of the deliberative process. In many respects, access to these trials has much of the moral quality of a lottery; to be more precise, this is a two-edged lottery. We might be inclined to think that individuals accepted into the experimental arm of the trial are "lucky." But that assumes precisely what we do not know. There might well be a worse outcome rather than a better outcome for those in the experimental arm—the five women who died in the Avastin trial for breast cancer were not lucky. From behind a deliberative veil of ignorance, when we are all healthy enough it is easy to imagine that we could rationally and justly endorse Option 2 as a way of obtaining reliable clinical knowledge, and providing some level of access to these drugs that might prove to be relatively beneficial.

Option 3: Assume what could prove to be true at some point in the future; namely, that some subgroups of individuals with various cancers will prove to be very positive responders to some of these very expensive cancer drugs. That is, these drugs are able to provide these fortunate individuals with three or five or seven extra years of life expectancy with their cancers. This might require that they use these drugs during this entire extended period of time. If these drugs cost $50,000 per year for five years, then achieving this benefit could cost $250,000. Avastin is priced at $100,000 per year, so the cost of our five-year survival would be $500,000. Assume also that these drugs would yield a reasonably high quality of life with manageable side effects; this would make these drugs for these fortunate individuals analogous to protease inhibitors. Would a just and caring society be morally obligated to underwrite the costs of these drugs for these fortunate individuals? (For a recent real world example of this problem, see Karapetis et al, 2008.) I am inclined to think this decision would have to be left to the deliberative process. Briefly, here are some considerations that might speak for or against this option.

We could say that it is morally and politically awkward that some citizens with the right genetic endowment would receive a substantial social benefit, while others without that fortunate genetic endowment would be denied it. There is a disanalogy here with the protease inhibitors. For the vast majority of AIDS patients, some combination of protease inhibitors (and other comparable drugs) will work to keep their HIV in check and prevent further compromise of their immune systems; so, no subset of AIDS patients would be favored by our funding of these drugs. But that is what would be happening in this scenario. We could think of this with the lottery analogy in mind. It is not as if someone manipulated medical research or the deliberative process to gain special favors for their genotype; it was just dumb luck. So, we deliberators could all approve this lottery from behind the veil of ignorance. After all, we would likely approve the lottery in Option 2. Of course, a morally distinctive feature of Option 2 is that there is social gain in the form of more secure medical knowledge. In Option 3, the benefit accrues only to individuals; the costs accrue to society. But then the argument might be that moral consistency would require funding these drugs because they were roughly just as effective for these fortunate cancer patients as the protease inhibitors have been for AIDS patients.

Still other factors could be brought to deliberative attention. If the vast majority of these more fortunate cancer patients were non-elderly, then protecting fair equality of opportunity to achieve a normal life expectancy would speak in favor of funding this option. But if the vast majority of these patients were very close to a normal life expectancy (or had already achieved it), then that might speak against social funding for this option. Finally, we have to expect that the "ragged edge" problem would be unavoidable. It is most likely that a relatively wide age range might be represented by patients with the fortunate genotype relative to this cancer. Would we want to choose an age beyond which social funding would not be available for this option, even if an individual had the favored genotype? These all strike me as choices that can be left to the deliberative process and our acceptance of non-ideally just outcomes.

More needs to be said with regard to these cancer drugs, but we should first consider our options for LVADs and lung reduction as last-chance therapies. If we are in this futuristic mode with a comprehensive national health plan, it is very difficult for me to see how either of these interventions would be funded at social expense for all with the relevant need. In both cases we are talking about very costly interventions that would predominantly benefit older individuals who had achieved something close to or beyond a normal life expectancy. Both technologies yield only marginal gains in life expectancy. In any reasonable prioritization process, both these interventions would be very low on a priority scale for public funding. Even if we imagined a prioritization process regarding only the health care needs of the elderly, both these interventions would have to receive low priority. A strong and reasonable utilitarian argument would be made for saying a much more complete prescription drug benefit would have to be provided to the elderly before either of these interventions was funded. Many more of the elderly with a much broader range of medical problems would benefit from such funding. We could reasonably expect that this is what elderly deliberators would choose for their future possible selves.

Elderly deliberators might also reasonably prefer much more extensive and supportive home care services (as opposed to long-term care) to funding for these life-prolonging technologies. Also, any number of ameliorable sensory deficits (hearing or sight) or ameliorable functional impairments (hips and knees) would likely be seen as representing a better buy than these life-prolonging interventions, simply because they would represent desirable improvements in quality of life for the elderly. What would be "just enough" would be allowing elderly individuals who were financially well-off the option of buying these interventions unsubsidized entirely with their own private resources. This would include their having to pay for costly complications that might be associated with taking advantage of these technologies. Again, no one who is unable to purchase these last-chance therapies is made worse off. Further, from a global perspective, we can say that the vast majority of those unable to purchase these last-chance therapies that will then die "prematurely" will nevertheless have been better off (both in terms of length and quality of life) than they would have been under the current U.S. health care system. They would also have been treated more justly and more compassionately because they would have made these choices for their own future possible selves, as opposed to having these choices imposed upon them by insurance companies or random acts of unkindness by the market.

We now turn to the NICU and ask what a just and caring society owes to neonates without a functioning gut who need TPN for survival. Our intuitions get pulled in multiple directions by these sorts of cases. A reasonable case can be made for saying these infants should not be thought of under the "last-chance therapy" rubric—that is, they are in the same situation as patients in kidney failure. Some number of extra years of life can be obtained with TPN. Granted TPN annual costs are much higher than dialysis (roughly $200,000 versus $57,000). But we cannot characterize the use of this technology as yielding no more than a marginal benefit, which is clearly a fair characterization of the very expensive cancer drugs discussed above. Further, we might object that the $200,000 per year cost is excessive. However, I made the case earlier for saying that a just and caring society ought to underwrite the $300,000 per patient per year costs of imiglucerase for Gaucher's; the implication being that other drugs and interventions that are comparably costly and comparably effective in sustaining a reasonable quality of life ought also be funded as a matter of justice. What we must concede is that these children will have a reasonable quality of life for at least four years. In that respect, these are not children with devastating congenital deficiencies for which medicine can do little. To be clear to the reader, the sort of medical circumstances I have in mind are gross brain malformations. The circumstances are tragic; the medical devastation is irreparable. If protecting fair and effective equality of opportunity is a central element of our conception of health care justice, then there will be little in the way of just claims that can be made on behalf of these infants. Care and compassion is what we are obligated to offer, as opposed to aggressive efforts to sustain life medically.

In the case of infants with necrotic small bowel syndrome, medicine can effectively sustain their lives—there is opportunity for them to have a life, though it will be an extremely truncated life that will not permit them to achieve anything close to full human flourishing. This is not the same situation that parents find themselves in when a six-year-old child is diagnosed with a cancer that may prove fatal. The fate of these children with cancer is not something that was known within days of birth. Can we confidently judge that it would be unjust for society to sustain the lives of these infants without a functioning gut at an aggregated social cost of several billion dollars per year? I cannot find sufficiently weighty considerations of health care justice that would warrant this conclusion, especially from the perspective of a liberal and pluralistic conception of public reason. Different parents with different religious or cultural perspectives might judge very differently the value of that truncated life for that child. Respect for those differences across the board (in this very specific context) is not incongruent with public reason or health care justice. Parents need to clearly understand what the ultimate prospects are for this child: this child will have an acceptable quality of life for the next four years, but if a liver transplant is authorized and available, then the quality of this child's life for the rest of its life will be significantly diminished. Some parents will refuse TPN from the very beginning; this, too, is a decision that ought to be respected in a liberal pluralistic society. That these latter parents are willing to endorse social funding that makes possible the choices of the former parents is indicative of the sort of mutual moral respect a liberal pluralistic society needs to encourage.

I want to be careful not to leave the impression that any and all parental or medical choices ought to be respected and supported with public funding if the life of an infant or fetus is in jeopardy. Public financial support for some choices would be unjust. One case brought to my attention involved a couple whose fetus was diagnosed with bilateral renal agenesis at about six months into the pregnancy. Both the parents and their physician were strongly committed to a right-to-life perspective. Ordinarily infants in these circumstances will either die in utero (lack of amniotic fluid for lung development) or they will die shortly after birth. This physician had a plan for partially replacing the amniotic fluid—at birth, he would place the infant on dialysis for a year or so, then do a kidney transplant. While this might seem plausible to many readers, this in fact was entirely experimental. Nothing in the medical literature would suggest that this would work; what literature did exist suggested this course of action was doomed to failure.

This infant did survive for seven months in the NICU with one complication after another before dying. The medical residents who brought this case to me felt that their own consciences had been hijacked, that they were engaged in inhumane medical treatment motivated by religious conviction more than the best interests of that infant. We have to pass over that concern. Their other concern was the use of hospital resources, charitable resources, as well as their own medical talent (required by other infants); a reasonable guess might be $700,000. These are resources to which these parents and this physician had no just claim, primarily because the probabilities of success were so remote. The religious aspects of the case add another layer of complexity, but the very same judgment would have to be rendered if these parents had been atheists and were psychologically incapable of accepting the death of their baby. Finally, a very specific injustice can be identified because of the use of those charitable dollars. But if we had a national health plan, a rescue effort of this sort would have to have the lowest possible priority, given all the other health needs that infants and children have that are currently unmet. Both very low birth weight infants and infants without a functioning gut would have much stronger just claims to the social resources needed to underwrite their medical care.

FUTILITY AND LAST-CHANCE THERAPIES

Finally, we return to the inner sanctum of last-chance therapies, the ICU. A major debate in the bioethics literature over the past fifteen years has been around the topic of futility.[7] In theory, we ought to be able to say something definitive about issues of justice and futility in the space of about one sentence: No one has any just claim to care that is medically futile. In practice, the world is more complicated than that one sentence would acknowledge. I cannot get into the definitional and conceptual debates regarding futility; instead, I will assert that for purposes of addressing end-of-life justice issues "futility" ought to be construed in the strictest possible sense. Thus, once death has been determined on the basis of neurological criteria (brain death), a patient no longer has any just claim to medical care and medical resources. There are no last-chance therapies for the dead; there is no palliative care for the dead. On rare occasions, compassion may require keeping a body medically oxygenated to permit relatives to come to terms with (often) an unexpected death. But compassion and justice ought not to be confused. The Theresa Hamilton case involved a 13-year-old girl whose body was medically oxygenated for three months after death was pronounced on the basis of neurological criteria—neither justice nor compassion required that response.[8] On the contrary, justice would forbid that response, especially if the just claims of another patient to life-sustaining resources were threatened by that decision.

The more common problem is that physicians are caring for patients in the ICU who could be sustained in a near-death state for several weeks with aggressive care. The judgment of these physicians is that this patient will not survive this ICU stay, but the family is insisting that everything be done (sometimes to satisfy their emotional needs; sometimes because they correctly believe that is what the patient would have wanted). These physicians may also believe (correctly) that the care being provided is inhumane, but they also believe family members will not accept that judgment or the implication that life-sustaining care be withdrawn. Physicians may also see the care being provided as a waste of resources since there is no reasonable hope for recovery of any kind. All that is realistic is a prolonging of the process of dying at great expense. So physicians convey to the family the global judgment that additional care is futile and that life-sustaining care needs to be withdrawn. The intended effect is to use medical authority to short-circuit otherwise prolonged and painful discussions with family. This practice is clearly morally objectionable because it is larded with disingenuousness. The invocation of futility represents unlicensed linguistic gerrymandering usually reserved for use by pharmaceutical representatives.

Physicians in these circumstances may often be correct in their judgment that demands by either patients or their families for improbably effective life-prolonging care are unjust, but such judgments might also reflect their somewhat idiosyncratic sense of what is a reasonable use of medical resources for this ("difficult, demanding, deluded") patient or family. This is another place where rational democratic deliberation is useful and necessary. The question we need to put to ourselves is this: What are we willing to deny to our future possible selves under near-death ICU circumstances in the way of expensive, marginally beneficial, life-prolonging care in order to protect the availability of these resources for more effective (and more just) use at earlier stages in the life of each of us? This is the real question that needs to be addressed, not definitional arguments about futility, but this is a very difficult question to answer with confidence at present.

Many physicians who work in the ICU will tell us that they are often quite confident that a particular patient will not survive this hospital stay, but in fact they do. They may not survive for that long after discharge, but that will be another issue. As things are now, these predictions regarding survival depend to a very large extent upon medical judgment in very complex circumstances. There is enormous moral risk associated with relying upon such judgment, fraught as it is with uncertainty and individual variability (not to mention bias), as the primary evidential basis for last-chance, end-of-life rationing protocols that would have to be imposed with reasonable consistency across a national population. So the morally safe course of action would be to avoid such choices. However, if it is the case that 28% of Medicare dollars are spent for the last six months of life, and if that figure in 2007 was about $120 billion, then that represents a very substantial sum that might be used more fairly and more wisely to meet other health care needs of the elderly. This represents a competing moral consideration that cannot be ignored. Being realistic, we have to assume some portion of that $120 billion is spent in medically and morally justified ways. But even if as little as 33% represented questionably justified care, we would have good reason for trying to capture and redirect those dollars. The other figure often given is that 13% of the Medicare budget is spent on the cluster of patients in the last two months of life—that figure would be about $60 billion in 2007.

The practical problem we are faced with is the complexity of medicine and the medical problems patients bring to the ICU, the constant changes that are occurring in the practice of medicine, and the limits of our ability to predict outcomes (mortality) with respect to individual patients. Over the past 20 years, considerable effort has gone into the development of predictive instruments in an ICU context. The primary goal of these instruments was to provide appropriate care for patients with complex and uncertain prognoses. In theory, we could avoid the need for such instruments by simply building many more ICU beds, but that would be an extraordinarily expensive decision that could not possibly be justified as either wise or just. So we only need ICU beds in sufficient numbers so that all who are likely to benefit sufficiently have the opportunity to achieve that benefit.

The critical phrase here is "benefit sufficiently." Patients may benefit "too little" for polar opposite reasons. Some patients will be reasonably medically stable and most likely to have a successful hospitalization outcome if they are placed in a hospital room outside the ICU. That is, the ICU might reduce the already low risk of a bad outcome (death or serious irreversible medical injury) even further, but the cost of buying that extra margin of safety would be very costly. So the argument is that they do not *need* in a strong enough sense that ICU bed (though there will be the relatively rare case when something very bad happens to such a patient that in theory might have been prevented or quickly reversed if they had been in the ICU). The patients at the other end of the spectrum are those whose prognosis is so grim that it is very unlikely anything the ICU has to offer will alter that outcome (death in the near future). Those patients, too, can be denied admission (justifiably) to the ICU because they also will benefit too little from what the ICU can offer.

Some very experienced and intuitive physicians can make these prognostic judgments with considerable accuracy. But they may be too few in number for all the ICUs in the U.S., and they may not be able to explain with sufficient clarity and logic and evidence how they get to the judgments they offer. These predictive scoring systems are meant to correct for that by being tested over more than 100,000 ICU admissions, and by relying upon medically objective variables as the data used to generate predictions. Probably the best known of these predictive devices is the APACHE (Acute Physiology and Chronic Health Evaluation) system developed by William Knaus. APACHE II generated predictions on the basis of 28 physiologic variables. APACHE III was introduced in 1991 (Knaus et al., 1991). APACHE IV is less than five years old and includes 142 variables in the mortality equation, 115 of which are disease groups (Zimmerman et al., 2006). In some cases, APACHE is capable of identifying patients who have a 95% chance of *not surviving* this hospitalization (Berge et al., 2005). In one cluster of 248 such patients, APACHE got it wrong 23% of the time—that is, these patients survived to be discharged from the hospital. But only 10% of that group survived for more than one year beyond discharge. For this entire cohort that survived their ICU stay, patient functionality was very poor.

This is the practical question we must address through the deliberative process: If we imagine a future version of APACHE—APACHE V—that was even better at predicting which patients were not going to survive this ICU stay (such that it was wrong only 10% of the time), should a just and caring society adopt through the deliberative process an APACHE V rationing protocol? What this would mean in practice is that APACHE physiologic variables would be measured for the first three days of the ICU stay, after which they would be plugged into the APACHE algorithm. If APACHE predicted that this patient was 95% certain not to leave the ICU alive, then the patient would be transferred to a palliative care or hospice bed and aggressive life-sustaining care would be withdrawn or withheld. Because APACHE V would have been rigorously tested before being deployed, we would know before considering this rationing protocol through the deliberative process that it would "get it wrong" 10% of the time. However, we would also know that the vast majority of patients who "proved APACHE wrong" would still die during the next 12 months, and their functioning during that period would be severely compromised. Given this, would there be anything strongly morally objectionable about approving such a protocol deliberatively?

My own view is that such a protocol would not be intrinsically morally objectionable. We can imagine that such a protocol could yield $30 billion in savings annually to Medicare (50% of the dollars now spent on patients in the last two months of life under Medicare). We must also imagine that those dollars would be recaptured and redirected to higher-priority health care needs of the elderly. We (democratic deliberators) would be making this choice for our future possible selves. Those future possible selves could be sacrificing the last two months of life (if APACHE V is applied), though those would be a much debilitated two months. But those future possible selves could also be the beneficiaries of those redirected health care resources, perhaps in the form of expanded and improved home health services. The virtue of APACHE V is that it is as objective as anything can be in medicine. All the data is public and testable. APACHE V could include an "appeals option." The attending could appeal to a three-physician panel if she believed there were unique clinical circumstances that APACHE failed to capture and properly weigh. But the burden of proof in this appeal process would be on the attending who would have to offer objective clinical evidence to justify overriding an (adverse) APACHE predictive outcome.[9]

One critical question that could be raised is this: Is it possible that APACHE would *really* get it wrong, that someone would be removed from an ICU who otherwise would have survived in reasonable health for several years? The honest answer to that question must be affirmative. But before thinking that a good reason to reject the APACHE protocol as intrinsically morally flawed, we should recall that the same outcome is possible with regard to any rationing protocol that could have life-or-death consequences. Thus, use of the implantable cardiac defibrillator (used to reverse an otherwise fatal cardiac arrhythmia) could be restricted through the use of the T-wave alternans test to save $3 billion per year. That test will correctly predict 98.8% of the time who is unlikely to suffer a potentially fatal arrhythmia over the next two years—if use of that test prevents the implantation of 60,000 ICDs per year, then about 700 individuals will die that otherwise would have lived had they had the device implanted.

If any risk of loss of life would incline us to reject both the ICD and APACHE rationing protocols as intrinsically morally flawed, then we are again embracing the pricelessness of human life thesis. That is, we are saying we are morally obligated to spend unlimited funds whenever a human life is medically at risk and medically salvageable. That either fails to take seriously the issue of health care cost control, or else risks taking funds from areas of medicine where life is not at stake but where individuals would be forced to endure severe pain for lack of needed medical care (such as our rheumatoid arthritis patients). Neither of those options is morally defensible. We should also note that, *given limited resources and unlimited health needs,* last-chance therapies will often represent an unwise and an unjust buy. That is, if such resources saved are properly redeployed to what we judge are higher-priority health needs, then we might well often save more life-years of higher quality than we sacrifice through a particular rationing protocol—that outcome should be seen as being respectful of human life. Again, we need to remind ourselves that there is no "natural order" (much less a divinely ordained order) for the distribution of ICDs, or artificial hearts, or these extraordinarily expensive cancer drugs, or access to the ICU. These are all human constructions and human choices that should reflect reciprocally endorsed just and caring rational democratic choices.

8

RATIONING, CATASTROPHIC ILLNESS, AND DISABLED PATIENTS

INTRODUCTION: THE SCOPE OF THE PROBLEM

In 2001, the 5% of Medicare patients who were the sickest patients consumed more than 43% of the total Medicare budget that year (Congressional Budget Office, 2005). The average cost for each of these patients then was more than $63,000. Mr. Diaz from our first chapter would be a perfect example of one sort of patient who would generate these results—he spent more than 140 days in the ICU. He entered the ICU as a patient with advanced dementia and a bleeding problem of unknown origin that precipitated that hospitalization; the cost of his care was about $240,000. We should also call to mind the case of Dr. Michael DeBakey who suffered a dissecting aortic aneurysm at age 97. He spent eight months in the hospital as a result of complications associated with his surgery, his age, and his overall medical condition. The cost of his care exceeded one million dollars (though this was apparently paid for by private funds). Dr. DeBakey went into that surgery cognitively intact, and ultimately was able to return to his prior state of health (unlike Mr. Diaz Dr. DeBakey did die slightly more than a year after the surgery.).

Another sort of patient we introduced earlier was Mr. Van Houten, who at age 45 was described as "catastrophically and hopelessly ill." He had in 1991 used more than a million dollars worth of hospital care in connection with as many as 10 chronic degenerative conditions, any one of which was likely to cause his death in the near future. He is described by some writers as a medical "bottomless pit," capable of absorbing unlimited health care resources. We also earlier called attention to Mr. Dawson who, at age 61, incurred a hospitalization that cost almost $2.5 million (more than one million dollars beyond his insurance limit). He had somehow acquired a staph infection (that he likely lived with for many months) that caused symptoms that had been dismissed by several physicians. When he was forced into the hospital, that staph infection had caused him to become septic and go into organ failure; he was hospitalized for almost four months. Among other things, a pacemaker had to be removed but a lead broke off and remained embedded in his right ventricle. He also had an infected aortic valve that needed replacement, and he required an ICD as well. In the end, Mr. Dawson was restored to good health.

Then there is the case of Leslie Burke, which has been adjudicated all the way to the highest court in England. Leslie is 45 years old and in the later stages of a degenerative condition known as spinocerebella ataxia; he was first afflicted with this disorder at age 23. There is no cure for this disorder. He is currently paralyzed from the neck down, but paralysis will soon be complete. At that point, he would no longer be able to eat or speak; artificial nutrition and hydration would be needed to sustain his life. He would retain full cognitive capacity up until very close to his death. The case was in court because Leslie was insisting that everything medically possible be done to sustain his life, especially after he had become incompetent. He was fearful that his physicians would withdraw the artificial feeding and hydration needed to sustain his life then in order to save health care resources for those who would be able to benefit more (Cruz, 2007). This fear was not the product of an overanxious mind. His physicians had told him that they could not accede to his request for two reasons: (1) continuing to provide care beyond some point could be inhumane (i.e., induce suffering in him that he could not communicate about), (2) require the use of resources to which he had no just claim because they would do so little good and simply prolong an unalterable process of dying. The British court sided with the physicians.

The large questions raised by these cases (which represent the focal point of this chapter) are the following: (1) How much in the way of expensive health care resources are the chronically ill and catastrophically ill entitled to as a matter of justice, when we have only limited resources to meet virtually unlimited health care needs? (2) To what extent should it matter, morally speaking, that various interventions required by these individuals are very effective or only marginally effective? (3) Is it morally permissible to consider the quality of life of a patient that is saved or sustained as being morally relevant to determining whether or not a patient has a just claim to those resources? (4) If quality of life is taken into account in making these allocation judgments, does this represent discrimination against persons with disabilities? (5) Is it the case that all five of the individuals described above should be thought of as persons with disabilities (i.e., persons entitled to special moral and legal protections)?

NEEDS ARE NOT ENOUGH; EFFECTIVENESS MUST MATTER

Roughly 78% of all health care dollars spent in the U.S. today are spent on chronic illness (Anderson and Horvath, 2004). This can be seen as a reflection of both the successes and failures of medicine for the last half of the 20th century. Prior to the middle of the 20th century, individuals with heart disease or cancer or diabetes or various lung diseases or liver diseases (and so on) lived much shorter lives after the onset of these diseases. Medicine today can do much to ameliorate the symptoms of these chronic diseases, and to slow dramatically the degenerative trend associated with these diseases. This permits individuals to enjoy longer lives than they otherwise would have had and to function effectively in their life roles for much longer periods of time than their disease would have permitted in the past. These are the triumphs of medicine. But the discouraging facts are that medicine has been unsuccessful in curing any of these degenerative conditions, which has meant that the total burden for society of chronic illness has grown steadily over the past few decades, along with the costs of medically managing that burden.[1] This is because managing these chronic illnesses requires constant and costly medical intervention, as illustrated by all the drugs used to control heart disease or AIDS or schizophrenia or Parkinson's disease; or alternatively, the interventions are more episodic, as exemplified by repeated hospitalizations for exacerbations of diabetes or emphysema or hemophilia (and so forth). Lives are saved and prolonged and improved through these interventions, all of which is congruent with what a just and caring society ought to be. But without these medical triumphs, there would have been no problem of health care rationing and cost control to address today. How, then, should rationing and prioritization decisions be made with regard to all the medical interventions presently available for addressing these chronic health needs?

We can begin to answer this question by noting the obvious: In our five introductory cases, and in all the types of chronic illness to which we are now alluding, we are always talking about health *needs*. That is, all these medical conditions make presumptive just claims on us. We might regard the language of needs as representing an entry ticket to the domain of health care justice—that language is not more helpful than that. Of course, we can make some distinctions among these needs. Some health needs resolve themselves with time, a change of environment, or a change of activity. If playing tennis causes joint pain, then maybe an individual will have to give up tennis rather than demand expensive orthopedic interventions at social expense. Exercise is important, but other forms of exercise are less stressful on joints. Other health needs may have an *urgent* quality to them. If those needs are not met, then an individual may be at risk of death or serious permanent disability. We imagine a 45-year-old individual having a major heart attack due to a coronary vessel blockage that requires either bypass surgery or angioplasty. We might also imagine at the same time a 97-year-old individual with a dissecting aortic aneurysm requiring surgical repair. These cases are both correctly thought of as being *medically urgent*; but are they equally *morally urgent*? Do they make equally strong just claims to be met (when there is no shortage of surgeons or ICU beds, but there are the challenges of fiscal scarcity)? If we had some form of national health insurance in the future, would justice require our regarding these cases as having equal priority for resources?

It seems obvious to me that this last question deserves a strong negative answer. A critic might make the point that these patients deserve equal moral respect or have an equal right to life. I can readily agree with both those claims, but ask what that might have to do with the issue of health care justice. Equal moral respect does not mean that patients faced with imminent death have a moral claim to all the health care resources that might diminish or stave off that risk, no matter how great the cost, no matter how little the benefit. If equal moral respect did require something like that, then last-chance therapies would consume virtually all the health care resources our society could generate. We have already amply explained why both justice and prudence would speak against that priority. We have to make justice-warranted priority judgments—both among last-chance therapies and between last-chance therapies, and all other health care needs in our society. Equal moral respect can be a justice-relevant consideration when two individuals have the same health problem (both need bypass surgery to the same degree for the same reason), but one of them is HIV+ (not end-stage AIDS) and is denied access to the health care that they need. But that is not the issue we are talking about here.

We can make our point in yet another way. Imagine our rational democratic deliberative process. We are again behind the proverbial veil of ignorance. Our future possible self might be the 45-year-old or the 97-year-old. Would we want to say, given limited resources and virtually unlimited health care needs, that the health needs in both these cases deserved equal priority? What seems obvious is that, if protecting fair equality of opportunity is one central strand in our overall conception of health care justice, then the 45-year-old's urgent health needs deserve higher priority over the equally urgent health needs of the 97-year-old. There is also an age-relevant argument that could be invoked here, but I postpone that discussion until the next chapter.

Two other justice-relevant considerations must be teased out from this comparison: Effectiveness matters; cost matters. These are considerations that will often be relevant for purposes of prioritizing among health needs in general, or urgent health needs more specifically. Cost and effectiveness are not all that matter in making just rationing or prioritizing decisions—reasonable democratic deliberators will quickly endorse this conclusion. In the case of our 97-year-old patient, however, these considerations would be decisive. The reader will notice that I have not identified our 97-year-old patient as Dr. DeBakey. This was deliberate. Several surgical teams refused to do the surgery on him because the likelihood of success was small for someone of his very advanced age (even in reasonably good health for that age). The fact that Dr. DeBakey survived without any permanent cognitive deficits (which he rightly feared) is not morally relevant. What cannot be ignored, however, is that more than a million dollars worth of hospital and medical care (eight months in the hospital) was necessary in order to save his life and restore him to his prior state of health. It is impossible to imagine our rational democratic deliberators, mindful of the enormity of unmet health care need among younger members of our society, endorsing a comparable level of life-sustaining care for everyone in our society below the age of 100—that would again practically amount to an endorsement of the idea that human life is priceless, that society is morally obligated to spend any available sums of money to save or prolong a human life faced with a risk of death.

What we are casting about for are considerations of health care justice that would permit us to make rationing and prioritization judgments with respect to a broad range of patient circumstances that involve chronic and catastrophic illness. In 2006 we spent about $23 billion to sustain the lives of about 410,000 patients in kidney failure through the ESRD program under Medicare. We spent a roughly equal sum from public and private resources to sustain the lives of about 700,000 AIDS patients; individuals whose immune system had been severely compromised by HIV but had now been partially restored through various combinations of expensive drugs (such as the protease inhibitors and fusion inhibitors). We have also seen that the average hemophilia patient will require $150,000 worth of care per year, mostly connected to the need for factor VIII, and that severe hemophilia patients can easily require more than a million dollars worth of care in the first couple years of life and several million dollars worth of care over the course of their lives. What is it that justifies the claims of these patients to all these health care resources? What makes them so much more worthy of care compared to our 97-year-old with the dissecting aortic aneurysm, or Leslie Burke? Did the British court get it wrong in denying Burke access to all the life-sustaining care he would need and that he desperately wanted? And what should we think about Mr. Diaz? Did he in fact have a just claim to $240,000 worth of health care and 140 days in the hospital?

Here we want to tease out another morally relevant factor that we must not ignore; this has to do with disability and quality of life. The core question is this: To what extent is it just and justified to regard certain profoundly diminished quality of life states to be morally relevant in making rationing and prioritizing decisions? Or is it always the case that allowing such factors to be considered in making rationing decisions is intrinsically unjust because it will represent a form of invidious discrimination against persons with disabilities? In the Burke case, physician testimony indicated their belief that he would not have a life worth living in the end stages of his disease; he would be completely paralyzed and incompetent, incapable of either purposeful functioning or meaningful experience. This is the sort of language that elicits great concern from advocates for persons with disabilities. They fear that persons with disabilities will be discarded by our health care system, and by the larger society. To be fair, we need to add regarding the Burke case that physicians were also acting out of a genuine sense of compassion. Their fear was that in a completely paralyzed state, Burke could be suffering horribly and be unable to communicate that fact to anyone. (Many readers will be familiar with this phenomenon from recent news accounts of patients in surgery who have been given a paralytic drug and then inadequately anesthetized. They experienced the full pain of the surgery. We know their experience because they emerged from the surgery; this would not be true for Burke.) Still, the bottom line in the Burke case was that requiring physicians to sustain his life indefinitely in that debilitated state represented an inappropriate and unjust allocation of limited and costly health care resources. Is that a fair judgment?

Advocates for persons with disabilities are clearly correct in believing that there are widespread misconceptions about the quality of life of persons with a broad range of disabilities. Further, those misconceptions are not just false beliefs safely locked in the heads of some individuals; rather, they often get translated into discriminatory social practices and social policy. If we were to ask many Americans how they would assess the quality of their lives if they were suddenly struck blind as a result of disease or accident, most of them will say that their quality of life will have been reduced by half or more. Some of them will go so far as to say that they would wish to be dead then. But if we ask individuals who have had this happen to them after they have had some period of time to adapt, they will often report that their quality of life is at 100% (unless they are having a bad day). Some researchers who work with various quality of life assessment tools are befuddled by these reports, and will insist that these individuals cannot possibly be correct in their self-assessments—they will insist these individuals are putting a bright face on a sad situation as a coping mechanism. I am not inclined to accept that conclusion; I will accept the reports of those individuals at face value. Still, what sorts of quality of life reports can be given by Mr. Diaz or Terri Schiavo or the future Leslie Burke in the end stages of his disease? This is an important question that deserves a thoughtful answer, especially in connection with issues of health care rationing and prioritization.

Some advocacy groups representing persons with disabilities are very strongly opposed to all forms of health care rationing as a threat to persons with disabilities; Not Dead Yet would be one of the more prominent such groups. Given prevailing social prejudices and misconceptions, their wariness is warranted. However, the view I will defend in the remainder of this chapter is that some rationing decisions will justly and necessarily apply to persons with disabilities. That is, it is reasonable and just to establish priorities among the health care needs of persons with disabilities. Persons with disabilities will at times have the need for very expensive, marginally beneficial life-prolonging therapies in specific clinical circumstances. If we have come to social agreement through the democratic deliberative process that those interventions in those clinical circumstances deserve very low priority (which will mean, in practice, that we are denying those interventions to our future possible selves), then persons with disabilities will be denied those interventions as well in those clinical circumstances *and there will be no obvious injustice in that denial.* That is, this denial cannot be properly construed as representing discrimination against persons with disabilities. While I believe this is a reasonable and just position, we shall quickly see that it is more difficult to defend this position than this paragraph might suggest.

THE OREGON PLAN AND THE DISABILITY CRITIQUE

Readers will recall that in the late 1980s and early 1990s Oregon undertook an effort to rationalize and render more just their health care system. The president of the

Oregon Senate at the time was John Kitzhaber, an emergency room physician, who took the initiative in organizing what is generally known as the Oregon priority-setting process. Critics accused Kitzhaber of seeking to ration health care to the poor and vulnerable, as if the poor and vulnerable were going to be deprived of something they thought they securely had. This criticism was really disingenuous—the poor and vulnerable in Oregon (and everywhere else in the U.S.) had been denied access to needed health care for decades. This was accomplished in ways that were essentially hidden from public scrutiny. Individual physicians or individual hospitals or individual insurers would refuse to provide access to care for those unable to pay for the care they needed. These are all private, discrete transactions that often enough had devastating consequences for patients, but these were not the sorts of outcomes that would garner media attention.

Kitzhaber's advocating that rationing decisions be made publicly and visibly threatened to reveal that dirty little secret. Of course, there was no secret for Kitzhaber; he saw first-hand every day in his emergency room the consequences of these hidden practices of rationing. He accepted the fact that the need for health care rationing is inescapable, but he contended that it could be done more fairly and more rationally. He wanted to find a way to provide an adequate package of health care benefits for the uninsured poor and uninsured working poor in Oregon. Many in the U.S. believe that Medicaid at least covers the health care needs of the poor. That is no more than a very partial truth. The fraction of the poor covered by Medicaid varies from state to state. When Kitzhaber pushed his proposals, Oregon was covering 58% of the poor, which was better than the average of about 45% (with some states as low as 20% of the poor). What Kitzhaber found to be both unfair and irrational was that someone could get a job, earn just enough so that they were above that 58% mark (in Oregon), then find themselves without any assured access to needed health care. Kitzhaber also objected to the fact that Medicaid paid for many medical interventions that were very costly and that yielded little benefit in specific circumstances—he regarded that too as irrational and unjust.

Kitzhaber wanted some way of preventing marginally beneficial interventions from being funded, so that the dollars saved could be redirected to health care services that were clearly effective and costworthy for the then uninsured patients. He created a special commission to establish a prioritization scheme. They came up with a list of about 720 condition–treatment pairs, which they ranked from top to bottom after some significant public input; it was then up to the state legislature to determine how much they would fund health care for the poor and uninsured. Kitzhaber's hope (which was partially realized) was that legislators would be shamed into increasing funding when they saw how many health care interventions would not be covered with a stingy appropriation.[2]

There were two major repeated criticisms of the Oregon plan. One was that the well-off insured in society were imposing this rationing plan on the poor and uninsured. The other criticism was that this plan systematically discriminated against persons with disabilities because the prioritization process incorporated judgments about quality of life in its rankings. This latter criticism is the one most pertinent to the concerns of this chapter, but addressing the first criticism will prove helpful in addressing the latter.

Did the Oregon plan unjustly compromise the health care interests of the poor and uninsured in order to reduce the tax burden on the middle class? Were the poor and uninsured "victims" of a rationing scheme that was imposed upon them? The answer to both questions is a strong "No"! One result of the Oregon plan was that 100% of those below the federal poverty level would have Medicaid coverage, rather than just the 58% who were covered prior to this plan. This represented a very substantial increase in Medicaid funding in Oregon. This avoided the problem of "punishing" the poor (by taking away all their assured access to health care) because they obtained a job that paid too little to get them above the poverty level. But, the critic contends, the Medicaid services the poor received were reduced to item number 587 on the prioritization list; items below that were not covered by Medicaid—"This is unjust rationing!" they argued. This is where I ask the reader to recall our earlier discussion of moral meliorism and non-ideal justice.

Are the poor better off or worse off as a result of the Oregon plan? It seems they are clearly better off because the services they are denied are those that have been fairly and reasonably judged to yield too little benefit at too high a cost. It is not as if the prioritization process was designed to identify costly and effective services, which would then be denied to the uninsured poor; those are the services that are ranked high, and judged to yield the most health good for the poor (or anyone else with comparable medical needs). In this regard, the general health welfare of the poor has been significantly improved in Oregon.

Would there be individuals, however, who were less well-off under the Oregon plan as opposed to the old system? Yes, there would be such individuals, but this outcome would be properly described (morally speaking) as unfortunate rather than unjust. They might well feel aggrieved, but they have no right to be aggrieved. Again, a fair way to think about this situation is from behind a veil of ignorance. At an earlier point in time, this individual would have been ignorant of his future possible health needs. He could have had an expensive health need for which there was an effective medical intervention, but he would have been denied it if he had been in the upper 42% of the poor (not eligible for any Medicaid coverage)—he could suffer premature death or serious irreversible injury as a result of that. This is the sort of outcome that is foreclosed in the Oregon plan (and that obviously happened repeatedly but invisibly under the old plan). As a rational poor person aware of the various possible outcomes under either arrangement, he would freely choose the Oregon plan for his future possible selves as a fairer arrangement that best protected his long-term health interests. More generally, this is the choice that the poor would collectively make for their future possible selves. In that sense they would be freely imposing this rationing plan upon themselves, as opposed to having it imposed upon them by stingy taxpayers or legislators. This might not be "ideally just," but it is a significant moral improvement over the prior state of affairs. That gives moral legitimacy to this outcome.[3]

We now need to turn our attention to the other major criticism of the Oregon plan, that it legitimized discrimination against persons with disabilities because quality of life judgments were built into the methodology that helped to generate the rankings. This is what caused both the Bush and Clinton Administrations to fight the implementation of the Oregon plan in court. A quick illustration of the sort of sticking point that precipitated these challenges would be the fate of 600-gram premature infants of less than 24 weeks gestation. They may have been ranked around number 660. Under the Oregon plan, these infants would be given comfort care and allowed to die. Why would such a choice be made? What would be the moral arguments that might justify such a choice?

Two kinds of arguments could be given in response to our questions. One would be that this is what would be in the best interests of such infants (i.e., the suffering induced in these infants is too great relative to the benefits reasonably expected). The other argument is that those infants who survive the NICU will survive with an intolerable quality of life.

The vast majority of these infants will die in the NICU even though they were born "intact" (not like infants born with serious congenital defects). The two most common medical problems likely to beset them in the first several weeks in the NICU are "brain bleeds" and an assortment of lung problems; both problems are linked to aggressive efforts to sustain the lives of these infants. These aggressive efforts cause considerable pain and suffering for these infants, which would be morally bearable if we were highly confident of a good outcome at the end. However, the vast majority of these infants die in spite of these heroic efforts, which precipitates deep feelings of regret in health professionals who feel they have inflicted pointless suffering on these infants.

If 100% of these infants were doomed to die in spite of these efforts, we would have unequivocally good reason not to undertake such efforts to begin with, *and it would be unlikely that such a practice would raise objections from persons with disabilities*. However, at this gestational age/weight, it is likely there would be a survival cohort of about 20%. Most of these infants would survive with moderate to severe degrees of impairment related primarily to the brain bleeds. This is what elicits from some health professionals the judgment that this is too diminished a quality of life, that these infants would be better off dead. And this is precisely what elicits criticism from advocates for persons with disabilities.

The critical moral issue disability advocates raise is this: What gives anyone the right to declare that another individual has such a low quality of life that they would be better off dead, which is then followed by either the withdrawal of life-sustaining care or the denial of resources needed to provide life-sustaining care? In either case, that individual ends up dead for reasons that are not their reasons. This is viewed by advocates of persons with disabilities as an imperialism of the abled over the disabled.

We can effectively illustrate this last point with another example. Many individuals with Down's syndrome will have life-threatening heart defects. Most often these are surgically correctable defects. This is not simple surgery, but in the vast majority of cases it is successful. If someone argues that such surgery should not be done, that the quality of life experienced by these individuals is too low to justify the social costs of doing the surgery, or that these resources would be better allocated to some higher-priority health need that would yield higher quality-adjusted life-years, then this is precisely the kind of judgment that disability advocates justifiably regard as being discriminatory in the worst possible sense. That sort of judgment does disvalue the lives of persons with disabilities unjustly. The "test" that is usually recommended for purposes of making perfectly clear that objectionable discrimination is occurring is the question of whether we would do the cardiac surgery for a heart defect in someone who was otherwise of normal intelligence. Of course, an affirmative answer will be given to that question, which means that the primary reason we would deny the surgery to an individual with Down's Syndrome is that they have Down's.

The next question we have to ask ourselves is how our intuitions in this case apply to our cases of 600-gram, extremely premature infants. There are some morally distinctive features here we cannot readily ignore. In the Down's case, it is easy to treat each individual as an individual. The surgery will almost certainly be successful in all the cases. We have no concerns that some of these Down's patients will suffer miserably in order to maximize the likelihood of saving a few of these Down's patients, but we do have that concern with these 600-gram premature infants. We have no reliable method of separating likely survivors from likely non-survivors before we embark upon very aggressive life-sustaining efforts. And we know the vast majority will be non-survivors. Many of these infants will experience grade IV brain bleeds (the worst), and many of these infants will die as a result of that. But others will survive with serious impairments due to the bleed. A tiny number will survive practically unscathed for reasons we do not understand. From the perspective of disability advocates, would we ever be morally justified in withdrawing or withholding life-sustaining care from any of these infants prior to medical events that foreshadowed certain death?

We might be able to judge with confidence that some of these life-prolonging medical interventions approach being inhumane, but the practical implication of earlier withdrawal would be the "sacrifice" of the lives of infants that would otherwise have survived with serious disabilities. If disability advocates object to this trade-off, we need to remind them there is an equally morally distressing trade-off in the other direction, where care intended to be life-prolonging has the practical effect of prolonging a miserable dying process. We also want to recall the other major moral focal point of this discussion—the issue of justice and resource allocation. In 2003 in the U.S., the cost of providing NICU care to very low birth weight infants from 500 to 750 grams and 25 weeks gestation was more than $4 billion. Was this a wise and just use of these limited resources? Is this something deserving high priority? Oregon obviously judged that low priority was warranted because the costs were too high and the benefits too low. Is this judgment morally flawed because it represents discriminations against infants with disabilities?

HEALTH CARE JUSTICE AND THE DISABILITY CRITIQUE

We bracket these questions for a moment to recall again the case of Baby K, born anencephalic. The Virginia Supreme Court upheld the right of the mother in this case to demand everything medically possible in the way of life-sustaining care, no matter what the cost to the state. How should we think about this case? If the court had ruled differently, would the court be open to the charge that it was giving legitimacy to discriminatory attitudes against persons with disabilities? Given our earlier analysis, it appears a case could be made for concluding just that.

Why would we *not* do everything medically possible to sustain the life of Baby K? The honest answer is that this baby is missing most of its brain. This baby has no capacity to experience anything other than the rawest of sensations. This baby has no capacity to achieve any kind of functional status whatsoever. The life of this baby is completely devoid of distinctively human quality. All of these statements look like assessments of the quality of life (actual or possible) for this baby; all of these statements are supposed to support the judgment that it is not worth it (so far as medical resources are concerned) to apply maximal effort to supporting this life because it is of such extraordinarily low quality. These judgments look like the same sort of judgment that we critically assessed as unjust with regard to persons with Down's syndrome. However, affirming the judgment in that last sentence seems to generate more in the way of moral and cognitive dissonance than rejecting it. It seems like only blind ideology could affirm that judgment. How could it possibly be just or reasonable to spend more than a million and a half dollars to sustain the life of an infant with no cognitive capacity? How could persons with disabilities or their advocates affirm this judgment when persons with disabilities have so many other unmet health needs that could clearly be addressed with those same million and half dollars?

These very same questions can be raised in connection with patients who are in a persistent vegetative state, in the end-stages of dementia, or other comparably devastating medical disorders. I have already expressed my view on such cases—I would contend that such patients have no just claim to implantable defibrillators or LVADs or artificial hearts or any other costly life-prolonging medical care. The most salient consideration supportive of this claim is that there is no longer any fair equality of opportunity to be protected or enhanced for these patients. They have lost the capacity for any sort of meaningful human functioning or meaningful human experience. In offering this rationale, it seems clear that I am making a judgment about the quality of the lives of these individuals. If we go back to the discriminatory disability "test" introduced earlier, I would fail that test. That is, if we have a PVS patient or advanced dementia patient in whom medical examination reveals a cardiac disturbance that would warrant the implantation of a cardiac defibrillator to prevent a fatal arrhythmia, and if we refuse to implant such a device for $40,000 "because this is a PVS patient," but we would have implanted such a device for virtually any other patient who had a similar cardiac disturbance, then we have made a morally objectionable, discriminatory judgment from the perspective of disability activists. We would have said this was a quality of life not worth saving from a premature death.

Mehlman et al. (1997) would endorse the conclusion at the end of the prior paragraph. Or, to be more precise, they would say that I had reached the conclusion that seemed to be required by current law. But I want to argue that that application of the law is unreasonable and unfair, *and that advocates for persons with disabilities ought to endorse my conclusion instead.* Justifying this claim will be the task of the remainder of this chapter.

Mehlman et al. (1997) provide us with a very informative overview of disability law as it has been applied to resource allocation issues in health care. It is helpful to be reminded that these laws were originally designed to protect the employment rights of individuals with some range of impairments or disabilities against unfair discrimination. Only with the emergence of the Oregon plan did these laws get applied to resource allocation issues. It is relevant that no one has ever argued that individuals in PVS or the advanced stages of dementia had to be given due consideration when others applied on their behalf for a position as university president or chief of the medical staff. What disability law assumes is that persons with disabilities applying for specific positions have the skills and abilities needed for adequately fulfilling the responsibilities of that position, though such individuals might need "reasonable accommodation related to their disability" in order to carry out the responsibilities of that position. This is perfectly fair and right; it directly serves the goal of protecting fair equality of opportunity. But the point I want to emphasize is that these persons with disabilities clearly have functional capacities that permit them to take advantage of opportunities in their environment (so long as social prejudices are not allowed free reign). This is exactly what patients in PVS or the end stages of dementia do not have. There are no social prejudices that prevent these patients from taking advantage of some portion of the normal opportunity range in their society—no portion of that range is open to them, because they lack the capacity to access any portion of that range. This is why it seems so unreasonable that disability law would require that vast sums of health resources be used to sustain lives so completely debilitated. The counterargument is going to be that we are making a quality-of-life judgment, and that all such judgments are subjective (which means there is great risk for arbitrary discrimination). My response is that lacking the capacity to access any portion of the normal opportunity range of our society seems reasonably objective.

Mehlman et al. (1997) point out that two major circumstances permit withdrawing or withholding life-sustaining care from persons with disabilities. If a person with some disability autonomously refuses life-sustaining care for all the sorts of reasons in all the sorts of circumstances that non-disabled persons in similar medical circumstances refuse life-sustaining care, then such choices ought to be respected. And such respect does not represent any form of unjust discrimination. Likewise, if the life-sustaining medical care needed by someone with disabilities is such that it would cause objectively more harm to the patient than it would do good for the patient, then withdrawing or withholding that care is morally permissible, and does not represent any sort of discrimination against persons with disabilities. Again, the key point is that these choices are seen as being morally legitimate when made for other patients in comparable medical circumstances who would not be regarded as being a person with disabilities.

These points would seem to suggest a strategy for thinking about issues of health care justice in relation to rationing and persons with disabilities. We can again invoke processes of rational democratic deliberation to generate rationing protocols that the deliberators would be willing to impose autonomously on their future possible selves. In this case, however, we would need to consider two possible sets of deliberators: those who already have some specific disability, and those who are in good health now but are as vulnerable as anyone to being disabled in the future.

For the deliberators who are already disabled (various sensory or mobility deficits), the question we might pose to them is whether they would be willing to give up all forms of aggressive life-sustaining care for their future possible selves if those future possible selves were either in PVS or the end stages of dementia. We immediately add that the money saved by foregoing such care in those circumstances would be used to meet what they would judge to be other higher-priority health needs that would yield substantially more health benefits for some other version of their future possible selves. The reader might imagine spending these reallocated funds on some expensive arthritic medications that were very effective in relieving the symptoms of that disorder for the future possible selves of some of these persons with disabilities.

If such a conversation occurred and these individuals collectively denied themselves what they judged to be excessively costly and minimally beneficial care to prolong life in a totally demented state, then it seems that such a decision would be fair and reasonable. Most importantly, it does not look like this could be regarded as some form of invidious discrimination. This is not a matter of ignorant and biased abled persons imposing rationing protocols on persons with disabilities in order to minimize taxes and premiums they would otherwise have to pay for such care to be provided. This is a matter of self-imposed rationing protocols by persons with disabilities.

How might we imagine current disability law would regard such an outcome? It surely seems that these individuals have made a quality of life judgment about their future possible selves. If they can make a quality of life judgment such as that, and it is accepted as a legitimate judgment, then it seems like that judgment has some degree of objectivity; maybe intersubjective agreement is sufficiently objective in this context. Some persons with disabilities are likely to dissent from this agreement. But the rationing protocol would apply to them in the sense that they would be denied access to social resources to support their demand for an ICD or LVAD in a future possible end-stage demented state. Clearly, it would not be fair for the dissenters to be potential beneficiaries of the reallocated funds generated by other persons with disabilities giving up access to these last-chance therapies for their future possible demented selves. The dissenters would be free to purchase such care for themselves with their own private funds, since no one else would be made worse off by such purchases. But they could not justifiably claim that they had been treated unjustly by having such a protocol put in place.

Nevertheless, some advocates for persons with disabilities will remain discomfited by this possibility. It may still appear to them that such choices, even by persons with disabilities, represent a devaluing of these future possible lives with other disabilities. This judgment is not unfair, nor is it simply the product of irrational ideology. The deliberative process is a prioritization process—individuals are saying that it is more important to them to sustain some future possible versions of themselves that they judge as yielding more value than other future possible versions of themselves they judge as having greatly diminished value. This need not be regarded as devaluing *persons* with dementia. It is a devaluing of the dementia relative to other health states that these persons with disabilities judge to be more valuable. Nothing affirmed here would justify loss of basic moral respect for persons with dementia, but demands for basic moral respect and for just access to needed health care only partially overlap. When just rationing decisions have been made autonomously through the deliberative process, then the necessary denial of care to some individuals implied by that rationing decision does not represent a diminishment of basic moral respect for that individual.

One other objection needs to be addressed. This ultimately comes from the Missouri Supreme Court in the Cruzan case. The court would not allow Nancy Cruzan's parents to withdraw the feeding tubes that were sustaining her life for several years in PVS because they did not have "clear and convincing evidence" that this is what she herself wanted. Advocates for persons with disabilities were very strongly supportive of the court in this case. However, what was disturbing about that judgment is that virtually nothing Nancy Cruzan could have done before her accident would have met the expectations of the court for clear and convincing evidence. She could have videotaped a statement saying that if she ever ended up in PVS as a result of an auto accident, nothing should be done to sustain her life once that medical judgment had been made. But the argument the court apparently found persuasive is that Nancy could not make an informed choice about such a matter prior to being in PVS—she would have to be in the state, then emerge from it and announce to the world she had made a thoughtful determination that nothing of value existed in that state, and consequently, society should not waste resources to sustain her in that pointless state of bare existence. This is an obvious impossibility.

But if these views of the Missouri court are taken seriously, then the deliberative process I described above is entirely eviscerated since none of the deliberators would have experienced PVS. Hence, none would be able to describe or assess it knowledgeably. This line of reasoning makes sense in the disability context when we are talking about someone who becomes blind as a result of accident or disease. They may believe they would have been better off dead rather than to have to live the rest of their life as a blind person. However, we realize that with proper counseling and rehabilitation, such individuals will (usually) be able to adapt to being blind and find their lives worth living again. There are no such functional restoration possibilities for persons in PVS or the ultimate stages of dementia. We can imagine some sort of rich and interesting mental life somehow magically continues in these individuals, completely hidden from scientific recognition. But this is an *imagining*. When decisions need to be made about the fair allocation of limited health care resources, we need to rely upon the best objective scientific evidence available, not speculative imaginings. That, too, is what a commitment to public reason in a liberal pluralistic society requires of all of us.[4]

DEFINING THE DISABLED: ETHICAL IMPLICATIONS

There is a key question which, up to this point, we have completely overlooked. This is the question of who should be counted among persons with disabilities. I will frankly admit that I am very much puzzled when anencephalic infants and patients in PVS are included among persons with disabilities (where the intent is to extend certain legal and moral rights to persons within that category). This strikes me as more a product of ideological gerrymandering than careful moral argument and analysis. Proponents of such definitional expansiveness may fear some sort of slippery slope: If anyone with any degree of functional incapacity is "removed" from the fold of persons with disabilities, then all in the fold may fear they could be next. But I am going to pass over this point for now to draw attention to a larger point.

The entire cohort of "persons with disabilities deserving special legal protections" is much larger and more diverse than most Americans likely realize. The number cited most often as the cohort of disabled persons in the U.S. is 65 million. This is a number that surprises most people. Most people think of persons with disabilities as those with mobility limitations (paraplegics or quadriplegics) or sensory deprivations (loss of sight and hearing). But the Americans with Disability Act (ADA) will include everyone whose health status is such that they have (or are perceived as having) a functional limitation that results in their being denied normal opportunities for jobs or housing or other social goods. Tens of millions of individuals with heart disease or cancer or renal failure or emphysema or AIDS/HIV or multiple sclerosis or hemophilia (et cetera) will all come under the protection of ADA. I want to affirm the reasonableness of this as social policy. At the same time, I want to raise concerns about the reasonableness or fairness of the expansion of these protections into the field of health care.

My fundamental concern is that a mindless expansion of ADA protections into health care will require massive expenditures for very marginally beneficial, non-costworthy health care under the guise of protecting the fundamental rights of persons with disabilities against discrimination. Mehlman et al. (1997, p. 1392) provide a perfect example of what I have in mind in the case of *Henderson v. Bodine Aluminum* (1995). In that case, the Eighth Circuit Court of Appeals ruled that Blue Cross/Blue Shield would have to underwrite the costs of an autologous bone marrow transplant with high-dose chemotherapy for a woman with metastatic breast cancer *because they covered the cost of that intervention for other cancers*; the implication being that it would be unjust discrimination against this person with the disabling condition of advanced breast cancer.

We discussed this procedure earlier in connection with the work of David Eddy (1996). This procedure had costs then (1995) of about $150,000. It was initially believed this intervention might offer a 10% chance of three-year survival—in fact, it was no better than current therapy at the time that cost only a fraction of this procedure. But we can pretend for the sake of argument that there was this incremental gain. Would that have justified the court requiring that this procedure be covered for these women? About 44,000 women die of breast cancer each year in the U.S. If any of them were eligible for this treatment, then all would be eligible (as long as they were insured by a company that covered some sort of treatment medically comparable to this). In 2007 dollars, the aggregate cost of such treatment would be about $10 billion.

It is unseemly that the court attempted to practice medicine in this decision. Autologous bone marrow transplants are medically effective and cost-effective in the case of some other cancers (blood-borne cancers), but there was very little evidence that this would be true for metastatic breast cancer. Worse still, the court effectively interrupted the capacity of medicine to do the research that would yield a scientifically reliable assessment of this therapy. The court gave this woman (and any woman in similar medical circumstances) access to this therapy outside a double-blinded clinical study, which meant that it took extra years to recruit sufficient numbers of women into the trials that eventually showed this therapy was no better than the much less costly current therapy. That represented an unnecessary waste of life-prolonging medical resources that should have been available for some more effective therapy.

We should also take note of the justice-relevant consequences of the limits of this court opinion. The court did not affirm that *every* woman with metastatic breast cancer (and now considered as a person with disabilities, as well) had a just claim to access this last-chance therapy. It was only women who were well-insured who could make this claim with the support of the court; these were generally women who were socially and financially advantaged. The court, in effect, granted them even more of an advantage relative to their poorer, uninsured, equally cancer-afflicted sisters. We grant that the courts do not have the authority to require that insurance coverage be made available to poor, uninsured women. But the court could at least have refrained from making an already unjust situation even more unjust by legitimating the demands of better off insured citizens in our society for unfettered access to these marginally beneficial, non-costworthy, last-chance treatments that drive up insurance costs for all (and drive out of the market small businesses, thereby increasing the number of uninsured persons in our society).

But the most serious criticism of this court opinion has to do with its very broad implications for all last-chance therapies, and for all costly medical interventions that are intended to prolong life. If the pool of protected individuals under the ADA for health care purposes is as expansive and inclusive as many advocates for persons with disabilities assert, then there are no effective limits to what persons with health-related disabilities might demand in the way of very marginally beneficial, non-costworthy health care.[5]

All health care rationing and priority setting with regard to any health care interventions for any of these clinical circumstances would be regarded as unjustly discriminatory. That means that all individuals with end-stage cancers would have a just claim to all of those extraordinarily expensive cancer drugs that promised extra weeks to extra months of life. That means Mr. Diaz gets his life sustained in the hospital for all 140 days; that Dr. DeBakey gets his eight months in the hospital; that Leslie Burke gets his life prolonged to whatever extent is medically possible; that all anencephalic infants get maximal life-sustaining care (perhaps against the wishes of parents); and that all premature infants get maximal life-sustaining care.

That means, with the perfection of the artificial heart (and some form of national health insurance), we would have to be prepared to implant more than 350,000 of these artificial hearts per year at a social cost of more than $100 billion because all of these patients in end-stage heart failure would be in the protected class of persons with disabilities.[6]

I will remind the reader that the figure of 350,000 of these devices per year was based on the assumption that individual recipients would on average have a five-year additional life expectancy with the help of this device. That kind of assumption is necessary to justify the cost of the device. However, if we take seriously the full implications of this court decision, we could not deny this device to individuals who would only gain one or two extra years of life because they had a cancer likely to cause their death in that timeframe in addition to their end-stage heart disease. In brief, if we take seriously this court decision, then we would have to discard entirely everything we said about rationing decisions and priority setting with regard to all these last-chance therapies. From the perspective of the court, we would have no nondiscriminatory basis for making any kind of rationing decision with regard to these patients, because some sort of quality-of-life judgment was being made that would adversely affect the health interests of persons with disabilities.[7]

Mehlman et al. (1997, p. 1399) offer this example: Could a surgeon justifiably deny coronary bypass surgery to an individual who is diabetic with renal failure and unstable angina? Many surgeons would be motivated to give an affirmative answer to this question because the likelihood of long-term success would be substantially diminished in these medical circumstances. They do not offer any number, but the reader is free to pick any number between 10% and 30% to reflect likelihood of long-term success. Mehlman et al. believe such a denial would be objectionably discriminatory in the eyes of a court applying the ADA. Again, the practical implication of such a decision is that the relative effectiveness of different medical interventions in various clinical circumstances would be "out of bounds" legally speaking, though this seems like a reasonably objective basis for making rationing or priority-setting decisions.

We can all agree that a surgeon who denied a blind individual a coronary bypass because they were blind would be open to justified moral and legal criticism—that is the kind of quality-of-life judgment the courts rightfully protect persons with disabilities against. But judgments about likely clinical effectiveness seem to be in a different category, morally speaking; at least as long as there is consistency of application. Thus, if we were to agree through a rational, democratic, deliberative process to deny an artificial heart to our future possible selves if our overall medical circumstances were such that we would not survive two years with that heart, then this very same protocol ought to apply to individuals who are in end-stage heart disease who are blind or quadriplegic with other medical problems that will make it very unlikely they would survive two years with an artificial heart. Consistent denial such as this does not appear to be unjustly discriminatory, unless we accept the premise that all persons in end-stage heart disease must be thought of as persons with disabilities, deserving special protection in the form of unlimited access to life-prolonging medical care.[8]

We need to reflect critically on the implications of this last sentence. Mehlman et al write: "The issue [for the courts] is whether a patient can be lawfully denied treatment on the basis of another person's judgment about the value of different disabled states" (1997, p. 1397). Apropos to this quote we can ask this question: Should persons with disabilities enthusiastically embrace what seem to be the practical implications of the *Henderson v. Bodine* decision, namely, that they would have unlimited access to all last-chance therapies, no matter how cost-ineffective, no matter how marginally beneficial? Is this a triumph of justice, or a triumph of ideology?

The reader will recall our magical money wand from the first chapter. We have to imagine giving this wand to advocates for persons with disabilities. They can use that wand to move money quickly and efficiently to wherever they judge it is best used within the health care system. But, as noted already, the money wand has only limited magical powers; it cannot create money from nothing. We imagine that these advocates for persons with disabilities are committed to liberal democratic principles and practices. Consequently, they would not unilaterally make allocation decisions with the money wand. Instead, they would invite the persons with disabilities whom they represent to engage in democratic deliberations aimed at articulating fair and reasonable allocation decisions with the money wand. We realize that these democratic deliberations will not include non-disabled persons, but one good reason for that exclusion is that such individuals may have a distorted sense of what life might be like with various disabilities and they might not realize how such ignorance could distort the quality and legitimacy of the conversation.

The directors of this conversation will quickly find that they have some rather cold hard facts to deal with. The money wand cannot create money. Resources are genuinely limited. If the money wand is used to redirect unlimited resources to last-chance therapies, some other sort of health care intervention will not be covered. What should that be? We might imagine that the easiest pot to raid for money would be all manner of preventive health care services. After all, these deliberators already have their emphysema, their cancer, their heart disease, their sensory deficits, their mobility deficits etc. But we also have to imagine they have children and grandchildren, that they would have bonds of affection with these individuals, and they would want to protect these individuals as much as reasonable from the health risks that have already been actualized for these persons with disabilities. These thoughts would likely prevent too precipitous a use of the money wand.

But it is worth noting that even among all the deliberators with disabilities there are enormous differences with regard to their disabilities and what they regard as their health needs. Thus, at least some of these deliberators with disabilities would benefit from access to various cost-effective forms of preventive health care. Would they want to? Or would they want to save those resources in order to have assured access to those last-chance therapies? Of course it is reasonable for these deliberators to ask themselves why they would want *assured access* to these last-chance therapies. Does this mean they would want these last-chance therapies to have top priority with respect to the use of health care resources? A little reflection, however, will show that this might not be the most prudent choice. After all, if the money wand were used to allocate too little money to earlier health care interventions in a chronic degenerative disease process that were very effective in stabilizing the disease process for an extended period of time, then individuals would arrive "too soon" at the end-stages of that disease process so that they could "take advantage" of these last-chance therapies. This does not look like the sort of choice that prudent deliberators with limited resources would want to make. Why hasten toward death with the intent of spending lots of money then in a futile effort to resist death?

Of course, these are chronic degenerative disorders that do involve an individual facing imminent death. If we use the magic wand to direct more resources to these earlier stages in the disease process where life with the disorder is much more tolerable (and where medicine may offer more interventions that are more effective in prolonging those tolerable stages), then the consequence will be a severe shortage of resources for last-chance therapies in those lower quality, less tolerable end stages of the disease process. What needs to be noted is that we (deliberators with disabilities) are making a quality of life judgment about these later stages in the chronic degenerative disease process. We are making that judgment with rational confidence. We are not denouncing one another for arbitrarily de-valuing one or another end-stage disease process. We see such assessments as reasonable, and, presumably, we would affirm that reallocating resources to earlier disease states where they would do more good for less money is not unjust, though the clear consequence of such decisions is that persons in the end stages of these diseases will die "prematurely" (relative to the extra weeks or months that might have been obtained with the last-chance therapies).

We have endorsed the moral legitimacy of these reallocations (based on quality of life judgments and judgments about the cost-effectiveness of various interventions at various disease stages) because we say that this is self-imposed rationing, that I am making a judgment for my future possible self, as opposed to imposing a rationing decision on someone else. What I need to emphasize now is that this last point is *sometimes* true in the deliberative process among persons with disabilities. But in the strict sense it will not always be true.

Imagine, for example, that I have heart disease but that with excellent cardiac care in the early and middle stages I can look forward to about ten extra years of life. That will carry me to age eighty, so I have endorsed giving up access to an artificial heart for my future possible self. Unfortunately, in the fifth year I develop a very aggressive brain cancer for which I have at most a six-month life expectancy. There is one last-chance drug that might give me three extra months of life for $100,000. Unfortunately (again), a huge claque of my fellow disability deliberators with a variety of cancers agreed like me to invest lots of health care dollars in earlier cancer interventions that could do more medical good and preserve longer a higher quality of life for themselves in exchange for giving up socially funded access to these very expensive last-chance cancer therapies. Consequently, I am being denied access to that $100,000 brain cancer drug that might have given me that extra three months of life I now desperately desire. May I raise my voice in protest claiming that these cancer deliberators had no right to impose this rationing decision upon me? My answer to this plaintive query is a strong negative.

I would remind our cardiac deliberator that he might have failed to be quite imaginative enough in thinking about the heterogeneity of his future possible selves. He was too focused on his cardiac problems because they took up so much of his field of thought. One of the rational advantages of being a currently abled person is that I have to consider an enormous range of future possible debilitated or disabled health states in which my future possible self might be. In making rationing and prioritizing decisions for my future possible self with my fellow currently abled deliberators, I need to carefully assess the relative value of this entire range of future possible health states and what I regard as effective enough, costworthy enough medical interventions aimed at curing or ameliorating or stabilizing those health states. This is an impossible task for any one individual, which is why I welcome the opportunity to learn from my fellow democratic deliberators who are struggling just like me to make reasonable and fair decisions for all these future possible selves I might be. I welcome especially my fellow deliberators with disabilities who will prevent me from making especially egregious rationing and prioritization choices based upon faulty conceptions I might have of various states of disability.

CONCLUSIONS

Let me summarize what I take to be the primary lessons to be learned from the above line of argument.

(1) The perspectives of both abled and disabled deliberators can be flawed, though in different ways. The abled might greatly undervalue the quality of life available to persons with disabilities (and make unjust rationing or prioritization decisions). But deliberators with disabilities are biased in their own way, just by virtue of the fact that they have some serious illness or limiting medical condition that defines a substantial portion of their life. It is more difficult for them to imagine allocating fairly resources for other medical conditions that are now very unlikely to afflict them.

(2) Disability advocates place a strong emphasis on the equal value of all lives; no one has less value as a person or second-class rights because they are a person with disabilities. All are entitled to the same standard of care. No one should be denied access to needed health care because someone else judges their quality of life is too low to preserve through life-prolonging medical interventions. I endorse all these propositions, but then I need to add that these propositions are insufficient when it comes to addressing the problem of health care justice/health care rationing and priority setting. Unless advocates for persons with disabilities believe that human life is priceless, and that a just society must allocate unlimited sums of money to sustain any life we are medically capable of sustaining (which I showed in our second chapter is an unreasonable and unjust view), these advocates will have to cope in some fair and reasonable fashion with the problem of health care rationing in relation to persons with disabilities.

(3) Rationing decisions that are self-imposed through an open, transparent, rational democratic deliberative process are more likely to yield just rationing and prioritization protocols than any alternative approach to making such decisions. Though advocates for persons with disabilities have supported the ADA and court decisions that would outlaw for rationing or priority-setting purposes using quality-of-life judgments or judgments about what is or is not costworthy and effective enough in dealing with the medical needs of persons with disabilities, the fact of the matter is that a deliberative process limited to persons with disabilities would make rationing and prioritization judgments with precisely these criteria.

The assumption that has to be accepted to get the conversation off the ground is that resources are limited. (This is why the magic wand cannot create money to solve any problem.) Once that assumption is accepted, then we find our deliberators with disabilities making rationing and prioritization decisions that are very much like comparable decisions made by abled persons. That is, someone with cardiac problems can easily imagine themselves as a person with PVS. This, in fact, is what happened in the Wanglie case in Minnesota. She had suffered a massive heart attack that caused anoxic injury to her brain. Unlike Wanglie, the individual we have in mind would want resources spent on sustaining a future possible version of herself in PVS reallocated to earlier stages in her cardiac disease, where more good could be done for her in maintaining a quality of life she found to be more valuable than being in PVS. This is a fair and reasonable judgment that can be collectively made and legitimated by millions of deliberators who are all regarded as disabled as a result of a broad range of chronic degenerative medical conditions.

These very same deliberators can make exactly the same judgment in rejecting as "not good enough" a future prolonged existence requiring surgery for an aortic aneurysm just like Dr. DeBakey. And they can make the same judgment with regard to aggressive medical efforts to prolong their lives in the advanced stages of dementia or in the end stages of the disease that afflicted Leslie Burke. But, one argues, how can one justly ignore the demands of Leslie Burke for additional life-sustaining care? The short answer is that we do not ignore those demands, but we provide compassionate care and counseling rather than the marginally beneficial, excessively expensive care to which he has no just claim.

What we would have to point out was that considerable amounts of health care were provided to Burke for more than 20 years, starting with the earliest stages of his disease. Everything medically possible was done to provide him with a tolerable life he would find worth living. The resources he is demanding to prolong a kind of barren life he would be incapable of appreciating would, in effect, have to be denied to another person like him in an earlier stage of the disease process where much more good could be accomplished and appreciated. The core idea behind health care justice is reciprocity. There were others who preceded Leslie Burke who made comparable sacrifices so that he could have as good a life as possible, in spite of his medical problems. So long as that same basic perspective governs all rationing and priority-setting processes that might affect persons with disabilities, persons with disabilities will be treated fairly in a world where rationing and priority setting are inescapable.

One final point needs to be made regarding persons with disabilities and the legislation that was enacted to protect their rights and interests. Genuine opportunities existed for these individuals, which they were denied even though they possessed the capacities needed to access these opportunities. This, of course, ties in with our discussion of health care justice and its relation to protecting fair equality of opportunity (very broadly construed). It is unfortunate that some babies are born entirely lacking the physiological structures necessary to appreciate even minimally having a human life; health care can do nothing to alter that sad fact. Consequently, given limited resources, those resources should not be used to prolong that unfortunate existence when other children are born damaged who will require substantial medical resources to achieve some access to the normal opportunity range of our society.

At the other end of life, the same will hold true for patients in PVS, end-stage dementia, or other comparably devastating brain injury. No amount of life-prolonging resources will restore to any of these individuals a capacity to access any portion of the normal opportunity range of our society. Again, there are many people who are relatively young and who suffer a devastating injury that leaves them severely disabled. We have the capacity today with all manner of supplemental medical technology to provide artificial capacities for these individuals that will permit them to access a substantial portion of the opportunity range of our society that would have been closed to them in an earlier medical past. Redirecting life-prolonging resources away from the functionless to better provide for those whose function is restorable is both just and respectful of all persons with disabilities.

9

IS AGE-BASED RATIONING
EVER "JUST ENOUGH"?

DEFINING THE PROBLEM: CAN WE ACCEPT
NATURAL LIMITS TO LIFE?

It is not an exaggeration to say that Daniel Callahan (1987) set off a firestorm when he published his book *Setting Limits: Medical Goals in an Aging Society*. The central question he raises in that volume is: What should be the proper goal of medicine for those who have lived out a natural life span? The natural life span Callahan has in mind is somewhere between 75 and 80 years old. But he emphasizes that he does not want to invest a lot of effort in defending any specific number.[1] Rather, he takes a natural life span to be a period of time sufficient for an individual to live a complete biographical life (i.e., achieves success in whatever line of work she chooses, have children, see her grandchildren, enjoy some peaceful years of retirement). So, to answer his question, Callahan would regard a proper goal of medicine beyond a natural life span would be to relieve the suffering of the elderly, provide various kinds of supportive services for the elderly who have experienced functional loss, and to provide appropriate care at the end of life aimed at achieving a peaceful death. What he rejects as a reasonable goal of medicine are aggressive efforts to prolong human life by any medical means possible for as long as possible.

We should note that the argument Callahan is offering for his view might be characterized as being a *moral and humanistic* argument, as opposed to an argument rooted in some conception of justice. His overall concern (a core theme in his writing for more than 30 years) is that technology (medical technology, in this case) is often reshaping human life for the worse. Callahan is no Luddite. He gladly embraces all the health good that medicine offers, especially in earlier stages in life, especially to the extent that medicine makes it possible for more people to achieve a normal life span. But there are no natural limits to how medicine is applied. The consequence is that the boundaries of medicine are pushed further and further out in all directions. More of human life becomes medicalized (when other social practices might provide more appropriate responses to certain sorts of life problems).

Callahan's concern in this volume is the medicalization of aging—each health problem that afflicts an aging body becomes another challenge to medicine. The consequence of this tendency is a series of social conflicts that are reflected again and again in the lives of individual members of society. Callahan opines that older individuals fear abandonment or neglect if they are faced with critical illness. So they welcome the care and attention offered by medicine, along with the hope of curing or ameliorating their immediate medical problems. Older individuals are no more comfortable with the prospect of their death than younger individuals. They generally want to live a high-quality life for as long as possible. But the old also fear medical overtreatment, either in the form of a painful and prolonged process of dying over which they can exercise little control (because they are incompetent), or in the form of a prolonged, degenerative, dementing process in a nursing home over which they will be able to exercise little control. There is an obvious resolution to this problem: The old (those who have achieved a normal life span) should just say "no" to all the life-prolonging technologies that medicine might offer them. This is easier said than done.

Imagine Mr. Caplan who is 77 years old with end-stage heart disease and a life expectancy measurable in months. His death from heart disease could be relatively quick and painless, a fitting end to a fulfilling life. But he is offered an artificial heart and a very good chance at five extra years of life expectancy with a higher quality than he now enjoys—this is not an offer many of us would refuse. But two years later, a gastrointestinal cancer is detected. The cancer cannot be defeated but it can be kept at bay with some surgery and aggressive chemotherapy. The quality of Mr. Caplan's life is diminished again, though there will be a rebound after the chemotherapy. He is happy to be alive. But then two years later, he suffers a severe stroke that leaves him severely impaired. His family struggles to care for him, but they need to place him in a nursing home. They feel badly about that, so they commit themselves to making sure he has the "best medical care" possible. When his kidneys fail they demand dialysis for him. When his capacity to take food by mouth fails they insist that feeding tubes are placed. With these life-prolonging interventions he survives an additional two miserable years in the nursing home with his supremely fine-tuned artificial heart beating away flawlessly. This is the nightmare Mr. Caplan feared, but it appeared to him as the proverbial "dream come true" when the artificial heart was offered to him. What can be done?

Callahan is wary of any liberal individualist efforts to resolve this problem; what he sees as the only workable remedy is a cultural sea change. Collectively we have to come to the realization that the fate of Mr. Caplan is the fate that will await the vast majority of us unless we craft and accept an alternate set of cultural norms that reflect a more prudent, cautious, restrained use of medicine that aims at improving the quality but not the length of our golden years. After someone has achieved a natural life span, Callahan says, medicine should no longer be used to resist death. Callahan has no specific policy proposals attached to this last directive. Instead, he seems to think of it as a cultural conversion experience. As far as political philosophy is concerned, Callahan is usually thought of as a communitarian. Individuals would not need rationing protocols to make certain they did not deliberately seek life-prolonging care in old age; they would just know how indecent it was to be even tempted by such a thought. But it seems as if there are other moral issues here that ought to be addressed.

A more recent provocative essay by Shim et al. (2006) further reinforces everything Callahan has been saying. They call attention to the medical risks associated with a number of medical and surgical interventions in old age. Those risks were seen by patients and physicians as major barriers to indiscriminate use of these interventions in late life. Consequently, physicians were reluctant to present the option of something like bypass surgery to individuals over age 80 unless that option were presented with grave warnings about the likely consequences of that intervention. But that has changed dramatically in the past 10 years. Shim et al. write: "At the same time, the risks of morbidity and mortality associated with the use of medical procedures, even in very late life, have decreased dramatically in recent decades, and that reduction of risk fuels the desire for intervention" (p. 480).

Their focus in this essay is on cardiac procedures obviously related to the leading cause of death in our society. They write: "Individuals in their eighth, ninth, and even tenth decades of life are becoming routine recipients of life-prolonging cardiac treatments. The growing normalization of cardiac care for the very old is facilitated by the decreasing risks of the medical procedures (Peterson at al., 2004) themselves" (Shim et al., 2006, p. 482). Because these risks have been reduced so dramatically (through improvement in surgical technique and in features of the devices themselves) "older individuals, their families and physicians feel able to justify their use *even when they believe the benefit to be gained may be negligible*" (p. 483, my italics). It is easier (psychologically for all parties) to forego these interventions in advanced age if the risks and suffering are substantial and the likely gains small, but that equation changes dramatically when the risks and suffering become reasonable and low. The moral consequence, however, is that it is easier to expect and demand these very expensive marginally beneficial interventions, no matter what the consequences for protecting the overall justness of our health care system.

These changes in medicine are also bringing about a shift in our social understanding of what should count as "normal" senescence. And this is a shift in a direction that is exactly opposite to what Callahan would want to endorse. This is the sort of shift that would make both *more painful and more necessary* the adoption of some form of age-based rationing if we are going to be concerned about protecting health care justice across the life span. Shim et al. quote a number of cardiac surgeons who say essentially the same thing today: "For bypass surgery, probably to about age 95, it's considered standard therapy" (p. 485). Judgments of this sort have gotten us to the point where we are doing 1.2 million angioplasties in the U.S. each year at a cost of about $40,000 each. And these same judgments will motivate and justify our moving from implanting 200,000 ICDs per year to doing 600,000 per year at a cost of $40,000 each. And these social changes should cause us to take seriously the thought that we could be doing 500,000 artificial heart transplants per year at a cost of about $300,000 each.

Again, what Shim et al. note is that, as the risks associated with the technology itself diminish, the social and medical perception of risk shifts to the risks of death *and diminishing those risks by whatever means necessary*. Thus, interventions such as the ICDs, which were used sparingly up to 2003 for very stringent medical indications linked to threatening cardiac events, are now seen as having a more "preventive" function aimed at reducing the risk of a heart attack or sudden death (no matter what the age of the patient). Consequently, the clinical indications for use of the device are minimal, meaning that patients will be regarded as candidates for the device for what are regarded as small risks. The authors quote one cardiac surgeon in this regard who says, "Do I end up implanting defibrillators in people that might not need it? And the answer is yes. But my sense is, as long as the patient and the family feel comfortable with it, I don't mind having a safety net in place and never using it" (p. 490). But that is a hugely expensive safety net at the aggregate level—$24 billion per year if we were to do 600,000 ICDs per year. And "safety net" is the correct description, since *right now* 81% of these devices will never fire over a five-year period of time.

What this discussion illustrates again is Callahan's notion of the "ragged edge." Shim et al. use another phrase, "technological incrementalism," by which they mean that "the use of one treatment along the continuum makes additional procedures conceivable, possible and ethically necessary" (p. 491). They are not asserting that in fact going to the end of this continuum is "ethically necessary." Rather, they are making the sociological observation that this is how it is taken by both patients and physicians. So how should a just and caring society with only limited resources and unlimited health care needs judge what is in fact *ethically necessary* in the way of cardiac care for older patients?

JUSTICE AND AGE-BASED RATIONING: FAIR INNINGS

Imagine that a good friend of our department were to deliver to us a box of chocolates for Valentine's Day. There are 10 of us here. I eat half the box before anyone else has a chance to have any. My behavior is insensitive and indecent, but those moral criticisms seem to be a little short of the mark—what I did was *unjust*. Granted, we do not have some formal posted rule that says "It is unjust to take more than 10% of food left here to be shared by all." But I would have to be morally obtuse if I thought that taking half the chocolates would be unobjectionable. However, this too is part of what has brought the age-based rationing issue in health care to public attention.

The basic statistics that limn the problem are these: Roughly 13% of the current population in the U.S. is over age 65, but they use 35% of all the health care dollars spent in any given year—in 2007, that would be about $820 billion worth of health care. This looks like our box of chocolates problem. Currently (2007) about 47 million Americans are without health insurance, without assured access to that box of chocolates when they really "need" a chocolate fix. We noted earlier that it is estimated about 20,000 premature deaths occur each year that are linked to an individual's insurance status.[2] A statistic such as this does provoke the obvious question: What justifies such disproportionate health care resources being lavished upon those who have already lived a full life, while tens of millions of younger citizens in our society are denied assured access to needed *and effective* health care that can prevent premature death or avoidable permanent disability? Should not *something* be done to redirect some resources from the elderly to meet the health care needs of younger members of society?

One answer can be given to our first question. The elderly have a presumptively just claim to what appear to be "excessive" health care resources because they have excessive health care *needs*. It is not as if the elderly are spending tens of billions of dollars to satisfy narcissistic desires for rejuvenation; they have serious health needs that if unmet would result in reduced length of life or quality of life. But then Callahan (1990) again chimes in, and calls our attention to the very tight connection between what we identify as "health needs" and the forward edge of emerging medical technology. Thus, in the year 2000 none of the elderly needed an artificial heart—this was only because the device had not yet been perfected. In 2008 the device has been approved for large clinical trials, and at some point in the future there will be a "need" for 350,000 of these devices annually at $300,000 each. About 70% of these devices would go to individuals over age 65 who (as things are now) would have assured access to these devices because they have Medicare coverage; younger individuals would be entirely dependent upon the vagaries of private insurance to determine their coverage. The artificial heart is only one example of the problem which we are describing. All of the expensive cancer drugs we discussed in Chapter 7 would also be available to the elderly, plus any number of other very expensive medications for arthritis or macular degeneration or Parkinson's or Alzheimer's or multiple sclerosis, or diabetes, and so on. Again, access for younger patients to all these interventions would be tied to the vagaries of private insurance, or the effects of the business cycle on private industry, or bad luck.

That brings us to our second question: What should be done about this state of affairs? We could establish a policy within Medicare that artificial hearts, these very expensive cancer drugs, and other such expensive life-prolonging interventions will no longer be a Medicare-covered benefit. But this raises even more critical questions. What would be the moral justification for such a draconian denial of needed health care to the elderly? After all, they have genuine health needs and these interventions are effective in addressing those needs (even if the degree of effectiveness is reduced from what it might be among younger patients). Further, these older patients want the same access to the normal opportunity range of our society as younger patients. It certainly appears that what is being proposed here is some form of ageism; unjust discrimination against the old on a moral par with racism and sexism. Of course, what Daniels (1988) and others have pointed out is that ageism is not the same as racism or sexism—we cannot change our racial background or gender (aside from sex change surgery), so those kinds of discrimination are especially objectionable. But under normal circumstances, we will all pass through the normal stages of life.

John Harris (1985) has offered one sort of moral defense of age-based rationing as described here. He refers to it as the "fair innings" argument. It starts with the premise that there is some span of life we might all regard as a reasonable life span; this is what should be thought of as our "fair innings." Age 70 seems like a reasonable number to pick. Someone who dies before achieving that age will be sadly regarded as having died *prematurely*. But it would sound odd to speak of someone dying at age 80 of heart failure as dying prematurely. They have had their fair innings.

Medicine today is often effective in prolonging life and improving the quality of life in the face of diseases that in the past would have overmastered us. But medical resources may be scarce relative to serious health needs, and that scarcity might be either absolute or fiscal. In either case, when there is such scarcity, Harris's view is that limited resources ought first to go to those who have not had their fair innings, in order to maximize their likelihood of achieving that goal if it is medically possible—this is a matter of justice. Excess resources beyond that may be distributed to those who have had their fair innings. But it is wrongheaded (as far as Harris is concerned) to believe that giving preferential access to younger members of society for needed life-prolonging medical care represents discrimination against older members of society. Older members of society are older either because they have already benefited from medicine's life-prolonging interventions or because they have had great good fortune in the natural genetic lottery. In either case, it is hard to imagine a persuasive argument for the claim that they are owed even more as a matter of justice in the way of life-prolongation, especially if it is the case that they purchase those additional life-years at the expense of younger members of society who will die prematurely.

We might imagine some sort of egalitarian argument being mounted at this point, to the effect that we are all (young and old) entitled to equal moral respect and an equal opportunity to avoid an imminent death. Hence, the fair thing to do would be to conduct a lottery for life-prolonging resources that included both the young and the old. However, this situation looks too much like a situation in which the government has a $10 billion surplus—someone proposes having a lottery to distribute the surplus in $10,000 bundles. The lottery includes both the rich and the poor, "to be fair." Both the rich and the poor should have an equal right to vote, but that sense of equality seems neither apt nor reasonable in the context of this lottery proposal.

The 800-pound statistic peering over the horizon is the aging out of the WWII "baby boom" generation; this is what gives great urgency and saliency to the "fair innings" argument. By 2030 the number of individuals over age 65 in the U.S. will be about 78 million, who will represent then about 21% of the population.

It boggles the mind to imagine what this generation might expect or demand in the way of medical care through the Medicare program; the numbers alone are alarming. But we also need to keep in mind that medicine will advance between now and then, and that there will be even more in the way of costly medical interventions that will be options for the elderly at that time.[3]

What is likely to be even worse is what we might call the total burden of chronic illness. A number of cancer researchers have given up on the idea of curing cancer by defeating it entirely with some drug or other medical intervention. This is because of what has come to be appreciated as the complexity and diversity of cancer as a medical phenomenon (Allen, 2007b; Polyak, 2007; Sadun et al., 2007; Thomas et al., 2007). Consequently, they would regard as "medical success" being able to control cancer as a chronic disorder, just like AIDS. These researchers have in mind concocting a mix of drugs that would disrupt the capacity of new cancer cells to continue multiplying. What the reader has to imagine is that some cancer cells might be able to find hiding places in the body in which they can continue to duplicate themselves, but the daughter cells sent off would be vulnerable to attack by these drugs. Individuals would have to take these drugs for life to keep to a harmless level the number of cancer cells active in their bodies. This is cancer as a chronic, manageable disease.

We have no reason to believe that the costs of these cancer drugs would be $10 per week—a more realistic guess would be $50,000 per patient per year. This is less than the cost of a year of dialysis, and a little more than the cost of current AIDS drugs. And, unlike the current cancer drugs that have costs of $50,000–$100,000 and yield only weeks or months of additional life, these drugs would promise many extra years of life. But the aggregate costs would quickly become staggering. If there were a cohort of 500,000 cancer patients on these drugs in Year 1, that cost would be $25 billion. If a new cohort of that size were added every year for ten years (unlike AIDS where new cases are modest in size), then the result would be annual costs of $250 billion (in 2008 dollars).[4]

We should pause for a moment to reflect on the ethical implications of this last example in the light of the fair innings argument. The question of how one might operationalize the ethical intent of the fair innings argument in the context of the actual practice of contemporary medicine is quite challenging. One has had one's fair innings at age 70. Suppose Mr. A is diagnosed with his serious cancer at age 66, so he is placed on the mix of cancer drugs I described above. They will keep him going for at least 10 years (barring other catastrophic health problems). Could we have a rationing protocol that denied these drugs to someone whose need arose after age 70? We would certainly not take away these drugs from Mr. A on his seventieth birthday. But we would not offer these drugs to Mr. B at social cost at age 72 when his cancer would otherwise have been treated with these drugs. It is easy to understand how Mr. B would feel aggrieved under these circumstances. He would have the same cancer as Mr. A, but Mr. A still had an open-ended life expectancy with the help of taxpayer dollars paying for the drugs he needed. We could increase the cutoff age to 75, but that does nothing to alter the nature of the problem; it just emerges a bit later.

If we generate enough examples like the one above, our thought might be that we should abandon the whole idea of age-based rationing. But this, too, is easier said than done. The implicit suggestion (given that the need for health care rationing is inescapable) is that we ought to find some other morally acceptable basis for making these rationing decisions than age. A reasonable thought might be that we ought to maximize the number of quality-adjusted life-years (QALYs) we purchase for every million dollars we invest in purchasing health services to address health care needs. Needless to say, we will have taken note of the fact that 62% of those over age 65 have at least two chronic illnesses that will diminish to some degree the quality of their life. Likewise, 20% of those over age 65 will have five or more chronic illnesses that presumably will affect to an even greater degree their quality of life. Knowing these things will allow us to save at least tens of billions of dollars per year through using rationing protocols that say nothing at all about age but which would reduce dramatically the disproportionate share of dollars now devoted to meeting the health care needs of the elderly, because their QALYs would be (in general) a much less efficient investment of social resources than alternative health care investments in a younger portion of the population.[5]

However, this line of reasoning sounds suspiciously like the disingenuous strategies advocated by Calabresi and Bobbitt (1978) for hiding from public scrutiny rationing procedures judged to threaten important public values. Instead of picking some age as a bright line beyond which elderly individuals would not have socially funded access to life-prolonging care, this strategy creates the appearance that these rationing protocols are age-blind or age-indifferent when their actual (and intended) effect is to diminish health resources that are less "productive" for meeting the health needs of the elderly. We might regard this as "soft" or "diffuse" age-based rationing, but it is age-based rationing and requires a moral justification for what otherwise would appear to be objectionably discriminatory outcomes. The discrimination comes in because those health resources might be "as effective" or "as beneficial" as when they are used to meet comparable health needs in the young, but they might not be "as productive" of high-quality life-years because of various comorbidities often linked to being older.

One response to this last line of argument might be the following: The real moral problem associated with mid-level rationing protocols intended to have a disproportionate effect aimed at limited access to expensive health care by the elderly is that these protocols are *too indiscriminate* in their effects. For any given rationing protocol that encompasses some cluster of the elderly, some of them would likely derive only very marginal benefits from the health resources they are being denied, and so it is reasonable and not unjust that they should be denied those marginal benefits. But others in that same cluster would have derived substantial benefits from the resources they are denied, and this is what seems neither reasonable nor just. The solution to this problem is what happens in Britain in many of the Primary Care Trusts.

About 30% of the physicians in those Trusts will openly admit they make medical judgments that might be regarded as being ageist (Rivlin, 2000). That is, they take a much harder medical look at older patients who seem to need substantial resources to address a specific health problem; if their judgment is those patients are likely to benefit too little, that particular intervention will not be offered to them. In this way, there is a reasonable connection between use of resources and likely benefit. There is not coarse and indiscriminate rationing; the rationing decision, they would contend, is appropriately discriminating and reasonable. However, the fact that such medical judgments are reasonable does not mean that they are just enough. As we noted in Chapter 2, the practice described here represents invisible rationing. There is no assessment or critical oversight of such decisions from the perspective of health care justice. Patients are not in a position to object because they do not know a rationing decision has been made. Further, these judgments are made by individual physicians whose judgments might be subjective or insufficiently clinically astute or insufficiently rooted in clinical evidence. In addition, there have been no conversations among all these physicians aimed at articulating a reasonable or "just enough" set of guidelines or criteria for making these rationing judgments. Consequently, there is no assurance of consistency across Trusts in the making of these judgments—older patients in the same clinical circumstances might be treated very differently so far as access to needed health resources is concerned.

At this point the reader might feel that the road to age-based rationing is filled with too many moral potholes. But perhaps we ought to travel a bit further before we consider turning back. Why do these British primary care physicians take these moral risks? The short answer is that they are faced with moral and economic necessity. They have very real, very hard budgets that they must live within. Consequently, they feel they have to husband resources in a way that maximizes the health good they can achieve. If older patients can benefit significantly from some health resources, they will receive them. But if likely benefits are marginal for an older patient, they are likely to be denied that resource, even though a younger patient with the same prospects might receive that resource. Maybe it is the case in Britain that the cultural sea change Callahan would hope to see in the U.S. has taken hold. One British writer, Alan Williams (1997), offers the following comment in support of age-based rationing: "This attempt to wring the last drop of medical benefit out of the system, no matter what the human and material costs, is not the hallmark of a humane society. In each of our lives there has to come a time when we accept the inevitability of death, and when we also accept that a reasonable limit has to be set on the demands we can properly make on our fellow citizens in order to keep us going a bit longer" (p. 821). If Williams' comments are indeed reflective of a widely endorsed attitude among the older British patient population, then the practice of these British primary care physicians might be less morally worrisome. Still, it is reasonable to wonder if a fundamental degree of fairness is being adequately protected.

We may again be tempted at this point to give up the whole idea of age-based rationing; however, the problem might be that it is often presented in too blunt and too coarse a fashion. We might imagine an ICU in which there are large red STOP signs on the beds of older patients. When alarm bells go off at those beds, the doctors and nurses continue playing video poker (unfazed and unfeeling). If that is our image of age-based rationing, then that approach to cost control ought to be abandoned. However, we should call to mind again the case of Dr. DeBakey—he has surgery for a dissecting aortic aneurysm at age 97 with an eight-month period of hospitalization costing more than one million dollars. This would pay the salary of 20 home health nurses for a year who would save no lives during that year but who would improve considerably the quality of life for the remaining years of the patients they served.[6] Very often it is family members who are the fiercest, most demanding advocates for these patients (often for reasons other than the best interests of those patients). When we call to mind these sorts of circumstances, age-based rationing in the form of some firm public judgments seems less obviously morally objectionable.

It is also noteworthy that we accept age limits on suitability for major organ transplantation; usually age 65. Dr. Thomas Starzl from Pittsburgh challenged this limitation by doing a liver transplant on a 77-year-old woman about 20 years ago. This created something of a public stir. He was not praised for being a champion of the medical rights of the elderly because in the minds of many observers, a younger person was effectively denied access to that transplant and the extra years of life; transplantable organs are clearly an absolutely scarce medical good. In this context, it would seem the public at least implicitly endorses the fair innings argument as being morally legitimate. What these last couple of points suggest is that age-based rationing might be more easily defended on moral grounds when we have very specific rationing protocols limited to very precise clinical circumstances. We will also argue in the remainder of this chapter that these rationing protocols should be constructed and legitimated through a process of rational democratic deliberation. The cultural changes for which Callahan is a strong champion might usefully facilitate and motivate those public deliberations, but those cultural changes are not an adequate substitute for the deliberative process itself.

THE PRUDENTIAL LIFE SPAN ACCOUNT

The fair innings argument may be regarded as a useful argument for initiating cultural change with respect to a reasonable life span. It is a helpful stimulus to a deliberative process that has age-based rationing as its focus, but it is not especially helpful in providing practical, concrete guidance to that conversation. If we call to mind the very large variety of expensive life-prolonging technologies that might be used to prolong the lives of older persons, which ones should be the focus of restricted access? And what might that restricted access look like? And how will we know whether or not such restricted access in specific clinical circumstances is "just enough," all things considered? The fair innings argument offers nothing that could assist us in answering any of these questions.

Norman Daniels (1988) offers us a more helpful perspective for thinking about the age-based rationing problem, which he refers to as the "prudential life span" account. His account assumes we have thought through a certain account of health care justice which we see as reasonable; this is his "fair equality of opportunity" account. Following Rawls, Daniels puts us behind a partial veil of ignorance. We do not know our current age, nor do we know anything about our health status or health vulnerabilities (past, present or future). We do not know our health insurance status; that is, we do not know whether we are now insured or uninsured, or what our future status might be in that regard. We are familiar with current health insurance options in the U.S. (though one of the things we might hope to learn through this mental experiment is what the direction of future efforts at health reform ought to look like). We do, however, have a very rich understanding of contemporary medicine, though we have to accept the uncertainty in multiple respects that is part of contemporary medicine as well. We also know how disproportionate health spending is beyond age 65 relative to earlier stages in life. And we also know that these disproportionate levels of health spending are related both to greater health needs for those over age 65 as well as greater access to funding that will help to satisfy those needs (the Medicare program).

Under these circumstances, Daniels believes a prudent deliberator would survey her entire possible life span and the range of opportunities that might be offered to her. She would be mindful (as things are now in the U.S.) that tens of millions of individuals end up being among the uninsured for longer or shorter periods of time for reasons that are entirely beyond their control. She would also be mindful of the premature and excess death and disability that are associated with being uninsured. She would also be aware of the secure and generous health care benefits she would have once she reached age 65. But it is hardly comforting to know that there is this health care oasis far down the road, if one is very close to dying of thirst a hundred miles from that oasis. It is also discomforting to know that oasis is a risk-filled reservoir of deadly and disabling disease. As a prudent individual, I would want to purchase affordable protective gear that would allow me to enjoy the oasis without having to worry about all the risks it might pose. But if I try to buy too much protective gear for that oasis, then I will not have sufficient funds to buy protective gear for the risks that are along the road to that oasis—I might not get to that oasis.

So what Daniels imagines is that we (prudent deliberators) would reallocate some resources now being used to provide us with expensive health care in old age to earlier stages in life in order to maximize the likelihood of our reaching old age if that is medically possible. The reader will note that we must now speak in the plural. These are not choices that individuals as individuals can make; these are social choices. If we want to maximize the likelihood of our reaching old age, then we must commit ourselves to some form of universal health insurance. It will also have to be a fairly comprehensive package of health benefits we would want to assure to all. But it cannot be affordable (or represent a prudent investment) if we literally tried to cover every conceivable medical option no matter how much it cost, no matter how small the likelihood of life-prolonging benefit. That option is just another version of a commitment to the pricelessness of human life. That option would be neither fair nor reasonable.

We have to be prepared to accept the risk of premature death as *unfortunate* for some versions of our future possible self in order to maximize the likelihood that a different future possible self would reach old age and have available the medical resources necessary to have a satisfactory old age. This also means, relative to all the life-prolonging medical options available to older persons and the length of life they would offer theoretically to any individual, that we would give up some of them for our future possible self. That means we would accept a "premature" death as an older person as an unfortunate outcome of the choices we had made, rather than as an unjust outcome. That is, we would recognize the fact that we had autonomously made these choices for our future possible self as part of a prudent social effort to maximize the likelihood of achieving old age. This is not something that would have been imposed upon us by unjust or uncaring "others." This is not a concession coerced from us by a younger generation. It is a choice we would have made for ourselves behind this veil of ignorance.

Daniels presents his prudential life span account as a somewhat idealized thought experiment. He expresses great concern about the consequences of trying to implement this thought experiment in the current U.S. health care system. What he fears is using this account to justify rationing and cost-containment efforts that would simply target the elderly, without any effort to redirect those resources to younger individuals in our society. This is a legitimate fear. Unlike the British NHS (a unitary system that makes no age or employment or financial distinctions), Medicare exists in isolation from the rest of our health care system. There are no policy structures that would redirect any savings achieved through rationing decisions in Medicare to younger uninsured portions of our population. In the NHS, resources can be deployed (in theory) fairly across the entire population; there are no structural barriers that prevent that. Still, Daniels' approach can have practical applicability in the U.S. today without some of the moral risks he fears.

I have in mind deliberative conversations among the roughly 78 million individuals who make up the "baby boom" generation that threatens a fiscal and moral crisis as they age out; I am at the leading edge of that generation. We can start with the premise that we have no moral or political right to impose the huge health costs we are likely to generate on the generation behind us, which is much smaller than our own generation. We may look to the generation ahead of us and contend that we are bearing some portion of the excess burden of health costs for them, so we have the right to expect the generation behind us to do the same. However, because our generation is so large, the cost borne by any one of us is much less than half the cost that will have to be borne by the generation after us. In principle, a simple economic tool can fix the matter. My generation simply has to agree to pick up all those excess costs.

We realize that picking up these costs would be a practically difficult choice to make if we were to collect these funds from individuals in my generation who were retired. Our incomes would be diminished from what they are now in our working lives. And it would be all the more difficult to have the disinterested conversations about health care justice behind the veil of ignorance when many of us would be very mindful of our health care needs at the time. But the vast majority of us right now are still in practice behind that veil of ignorance with regard to our future health needs; we have the financial resources that would allow us to cover the excess future health expenses we are likely to incur. Still, the political and psychological reality is that we would be very reluctant to deny our present selves the enjoyments that income might represent to us now, in order to fulfill our obligations of health care justice to our future possible self.

To make this as concrete as possible, I once did one of those calculations on the back of a paper napkin; it may have been ten years ago. At that time, my generation would have to have begun saving roughly 8% of their gross income in order to fully fund the likely health care needs we would have under Medicare from roughly 2010 until about 2050. I tried to make some allowances for growth of future medical technology and demand for it; that would include things such as the artificial heart, a new generation of expensive cancer drugs, all manner of prosthetic devices for replacing knees, hips, and other joints, plus long-term care costs associated with dramatic increases in projected numbers of elderly individuals with dementia-related illness.[7] This is what generated that 8% figure. This represents roughly half of what is regarded as the discretionary income of the average worker in America.

Now what I need to emphasize is that we are not under any moral obligation to spend this entire 8%; we can collectively reduce that to any degree we wish. But in order to satisfy what are our obligations of justice (not to pass on to the next generation more health costs than we are bearing for the current generation of the elderly), we are going to have to agree to deny our future possible selves types of health services in specified clinical circumstances that will generate savings equal to whatever the reduced figure is we choose. This would be age-based, autonomous, collectively self-imposed rationing. It would be discriminating (because we would be making fine-grained judgments about costly health interventions we would forego in specific clinical circumstances because they yielded too little good at too high a cost), but it would not be discriminatory. It is not as if any of these decisions would reflect bias or prejudice against some type of patients. The judgment would represent a rejection of future possible health states for ourselves that yielded too little human value and satisfaction relative to other health states we would prefer to see prolonged through our health care allocations. We would be making these decisions behind a practical veil of ignorance.

The vast majority of members of the "baby boom" generation have no idea at all of their most likely health risks over the next 20 to 40 years. A critic might ask how we can possibly make informed choices about future possible health care interventions that have not even been invented as yet. The short answer is that we cannot make informed judgments regarding the technical aspects of those interventions, but we can make judgments about the health circumstances and health consequences of those interventions, whatever they might turn out to be. Thus, if I were in the end-stages of some type of dementia, I would not want anything at all done to sustain my life. If I were unable to take food by mouth, I would not want any feeding tubes used to sustain my life in that greatly diminished state. Feeding tubes are a simple and cheap technology, but a couple extras years in that state in a nursing home might represent costs of $120,000. I would also reject for that version of my future possible self an LVAD, dialysis, an ICD, and any medications that might contribute sustaining my life indefinitely in that state. The point is that the specific characteristics of a technology that would sustain me in this greatly diminished state are irrelevant; it is *that state* that I judge not worth prolonging, both from a resource use perspective and from a personal psychological perspective (likely widely shared).

One of my fears about such a state is that I might exhibit extreme psychotic behavior. Would I alter any of my prior judgments if I could be given a drug that reduced to zero my chances of exhibiting such behavior? We could imagine that I was in a blissfully Buddhist-like state as a result of the effects of that drug. That is, I had no sense of self or others; I was just a focal point for sensory experiences. This would be a less fearful state, but it would have no value for me. This approach would likely permit us collectively to make suitably informed judgments about what we would deny our future possible selves without having to know too many specifics about any particular health technology. This is essentially congruent with Daniels' account of our wishing to protect fair equality of opportunity. There is a broad range of human functionings that we value. We value conversations with friends and family. We value the experience of a sunset that calls up romantic memories. We value reading. We value cooking. We value being helpful to others. We value the work we do. We value *Saturday Night Live* (some do). All of these things are part of the normal opportunity range that can be effectively closed off to us in its entirety by a range of disease processes. A devastating stroke can have this effect; some number of other disease processes may yield similar results. Again, the precise disease process may not be that relevant to the deliberative conversations if the outcome of that process is an extremely debilitated state from which there is no reasonable medical prospect of recovery.

The health care costs associated with the indefinite prolongation of such states through some application of medical technology is what we are agreeing to give up now, because we want to protect current income for what we judge to be more valued uses. Might we collectively make some seriously wrongheaded judgments about the undesirability of some of these future possible states, perhaps as a result of prevailing social stereotypes? This would be a reason why persons with disabilities or their advocates need to be part of these deliberations. This is where social education would be critical. There can be significant functional recovery from some strokes and other forms of traumatic brain injury, but this will generally be truer for relatively younger individuals as opposed to older individuals.

I am reasonably confident that the deliberative process among members of the "baby boom" generation would yield wide and deep agreement regarding many of these debilitated states, and our collective unwillingness to spend substantial sums to prolong such states. What would be more difficult to predict would be the sort of judgments we might make regarding interventions such as the artificial heart. The device and the surgery are very expensive, but it is likely this will prove to be a very effective intervention for patients who otherwise might die within a year or so of heart failure. The critical issue for deliberation would be whether we would pick a specific age beyond which individuals would not be candidates for one of these devices. The virtue of age is that it is a clean bright line; the vice of age as a criterion is that it is absolutely insensitive to individual patient differences.

If we wanted criteria that were much more sensitive to individual patient differences that we regarded as being justice-relevant differences, then application of these criteria would require some significant clinical judgment. This would introduce considerable fuzziness with regard to the actual fairness of the criteria in practice—it is easy to imagine endless legal challenges. This is the "ragged edge" problem to which Callahan has called our attention. We see this now with regard to renal dialysis. The federal ESRD program was established with the thought of saving the lives of patients in middle age with renal failure. But the fastest growing segment of the dialysis population today is the cohort of patients over age 75. We could accept this consequence with regard to artificial hearts, meaning that we would be accepting implanting as many as 500,000 of these devices per year at the peak of the postretirement "baby boom" generation. But then we would also have to commit to paying for those devices for our future possible selves now, or else finding very substantial savings from other sorts of health care we would deny our future possible older selves.

There is another broad type of rationing option that would have to be a focus of deliberation among "baby boomers." This would have to do with many sorts of interventions that might be regarded as life-prolonging, but around which there was considerable uncertainty with regard to outcomes; certainly at the level of individual patients. We already discussed implantable cardiac defibrillators (ICDs). We noted that 81% of the time they fail to fire for five years in patients whose lives are supposed to be saved by these devices. To be clear, they fail to fire because they have no reason to fire; the device does not detect any heart irregularities that would prompt a firing to prevent a fatal arrhythmia. But another problem for these devices (from the perspective of a wise and just use of these devices) is that when these devices do fire because a dangerous arrhythmia has been detected, half of those patients are dead within a year after that firing—that means half the time we save less than one year of life. In such cases (when you do the math), the incremental cost-effectiveness ratio (ICER) of those devices is $400,000 per life-year saved (Stevenson, 2006). But the point that is most germane to this chapter is that the older a patient is when this device is implanted (more than 75 years old), the greater is the probability that patient will die in less than a year after that device fires (Stevenson, 2006). Should we "baby boomers" agree to an age-based rationing protocol regarding ICDs (age 75)—even if we are medically eligible for the device—because we are only likely to gain less than an extra year of life if it fires to "prevent sudden death"?

AGE-BASED RATIONING: MAJOR OBJECTIONS

Baruch Brody (1988) is a critic of age-based rationing as advocated by Daniels, Harris, and Callahan. He does not find any of their approaches to be morally permissible because he does not believe any could be morally implemented. He writes:

> It is one thing to agree in advance that certain care be rationed. It is another thing to accept the rationing when one or one's family is ill and is having care rationed. The difficulty of obtaining patient and family acceptance *at that point* is what drives providers to deceit or at least to minimize awareness. (p. 214)

We need to emphasize that Brody is not saying anything here about human nature and weakness of will in the face of death. Rather, his point is that we have no principled basis for making such decisions *at the level of the individual patient.* As far as he is concerned, a course-of-life conception of health care justice has no moral relevance to *this patient* at *this* point in time. In other words, Brody is appealing to a commonly accepted moral intuition that a patient does not have a diminished right to expensive life-prolonging health care today simply because he might have used a million dollars worth of health care at an earlier stage in his life. That past use of the health care system is morally irrelevant to assessing the justness of his claim to needed health care today.[8] Another way to make the point is that he rejects the aptness of the fair innings analogy, as if everyone were entitled to the same amount of health care over the course of a life—health needs vary enormously from one individual to another, from one part of life to another part of life.

A second reason why Brody rejects such age-based rationing attempts is that they constitute a violation of our society's fundamental commitment to the value of human life, most especially an *identifiable human life.* The miner trapped in the coal mine or the stranded mountain climber have no claim in justice to the resources needed to save them, but we will still spend millions of dollars to save either; we seem to believe it would be very wrong to fail to make that effort, no matter how non-costworthy some flinty-eyed economist believes the effort to be.

We can put on the table another consideration pertinent to this discussion, which we saw raised by Levinsky (1984) in Chapter 1. Physicians who make (carry out) rationing decisions at the bedside are really acting as double agents. They are pretending to be loyal advocates for the best interests of this patient, while going along with the cost-control preferences of some third party. They are seeing a patient who clearly wants and needs life-prolonging medical care, but they are supposed to ignore that fact and avoid providing the patient with that care. The easiest way to accomplish this (i.e., avoid a rancorous scene) is to be deceitful with the patient and family, which is hardly a practice worthy of moral commendation.

Maxwell Mehlman (1985) argues for essentially the same conclusions as Brody, though he argues from a legal and policy perspective. His basic claim is that there are formidable transaction costs associated with rationing expensive life-prolonging medical treatments at the micro-allocation level. Those transaction costs are not just economic, but legal, administrative, moral, and psychological. Like Brody, Mehlman sees the generative source of these costs the fact that *identifiable* individuals would be denied these lifesaving therapies. This is in contrast to the "merely statistical" lives that are affected when rationing decisions are made at the level of public policy; those lives have no names, no faces, no voice and no attorney.

AGE-BASED RATIONING: RESPONSES TO OBJECTIONS

In responding to these criticisms, I want to consider briefly three possible strategies for avoiding the problem of having identifiable individuals as the objects of a rationing scheme. I will show that these strategies are unsuccessful because they are morally objectionable. One way of avoiding the Brody/Mehlman criticisms is to adopt any of a variety of invisible rationing strategies. If patients do not know rationing decisions are being imposed upon them by being quietly denied access to some health service that might benefit them, then they can hardly complain. But all such strategies violate the "publicity condition," which is absolutely central to our shared conception of justice.

A second way of avoiding having identifiable individual patients as the object of a rationing scheme would be to attempt to devise policies through which all rationing could be accomplished at the macro-allocation level. This is something that it is very difficult to imagine in practice. We could have a rationing protocol that said we would not fund any artificial hearts with social resources (assuming we had some sort of national health insurance program). The virtue of that approach is that no one could be accused of age-based rationing because no one would be entitled to one of these devices. But it would still be the case that the device existed, and that relatively young individuals were faced with heart failure and death that could be saved from that fate if they had access to an artificial heart.

These are individuals who could get many extra years of life from such a device—they might not be able to achieve a normal life expectancy, but there would be considerations of justice that would support their having access to this device. Consequently, it would still be the case that a physician would have to say to such a patient, "There is the artificial heart that could save your life, but it is not covered under the national health plan." The obvious response from a knowledgeable patient would be, "But hospitals have charity care dollars; surely you would not condemn me to death at the age of 40 by failing to finance my access to that device." If the hospital refuses to underwrite those costs, then a rationing decision has been made at the level of this identifiable patient. If the hospital agrees to provide this device to this individual, they will have later in the year a very vigorous 50-year-old and 60-year-old and 70-year-old who will all be making the same request. The bottom line, as Haavi Morreim (1991) points out, is that virtually all efforts at making rationing (allocation) decisions at the macro-level will have to be implemented at the micro-level; at the bedside of patients. The architects of the macro-level policies will not see this because they are distant from patients, so their consciences will not be pricked. But caregivers who will have to implement these policies will see these patients and would be able to minimize psychological pain for those patients only by hiding these decisions from these patients.

A third approach to avoiding the problem of making life-diminishing rationing decisions for identifiable individuals would be to let patients make their own decisions. This is the libertarian strategy endorsed by Brody. This assumes that such patients have the financial resources needed to make such a choice for themselves. This option, however, can be criticized for being based upon a less than adequate conception of health care justice. The libertarian conception of health care justice starts with the premise that no one has a just claim to any health care unless they have the ability to pay for it or someone else freely gives them that as an act of charity. But that premise is flawed because it ignores how our health care system came to be as it is today—namely, through huge public investments in medical research, training, and facility construction. Those dollars came from virtually all our citizens as support for what is regarded as a *public interest* (not a private interest) because this is not the sort of interest that could be adequately constructed or sustained if reliance were entirely a matter of individual choice. This does not mean that everything that is in any way medically beneficial must be funded by our society; there are limits. The precise location of those limits must be determined by all who are part of our society who could potentially be affected by our marking out of those limits. And those limits must be determined in accord with our considered judgments of health care justice as determined through thoughtful and legitimate processes of democratic deliberation (as opposed to random economic events or organizational choices imposed on vulnerable and largely powerless patients).

There is another way of construing what Brody has in mind here in terms of respect for individual choice: It is the idea that terminally ill patients will gladly give up a lot of these efforts at life prolongation that have been foisted upon them by physicians who are excessively paternalistic (or excessively obsequious to family pressures) and (for either reason) unwilling to respect their patients' pleas for a more benign death. All physicians have to do is present these patients with the option of treatment refusal (or respect clear advance directives that might be in place). Patients would then be making rationing decisions for themselves, and there would be nothing morally problematic about such decisions—on the contrary, patient autonomy would be respected (rather than trampled), and society would achieve its cost-containment objectives at no moral cost.

No doubt there are many such cases in the real world; these cases have been thoroughly discussed with medical students. What is doubtful is that there are enough of these cases to achieve cost-containment goals without the need for rationing. There are terminal situations that are "really terminal" in the strong sense; nothing is going to turn the situation around for those patients, nothing medical will even slow appreciably the train of events that have been set in motion. But the more common and more problematic medical circumstance is one in which the terminal diagnosis is more open-ended or ambiguous or related to the state of medical technology at a certain point in time. There is a sense in which all dialysis patients are terminal or all patients in heart failure are terminal. But very few patients in either kidney failure or heart failure will refuse dialysis or all cardiac interventions aimed at sustaining a reasonable quality of life for an indefinite period of time. If we think on it a bit, it is difficult to imagine patients approaching end-stage heart failure with the option of the artificial heart available to them simply turning it away, especially if they are not afflicted with other life-threatening or quality-of-life diminishing ailments beyond effective medical amelioration, and if the artificial heart proves no more burdensome (medically speaking) than having bypass surgery. These are precisely the sorts of medical advances that people seem to want, and that are the primary source of upward pressure on health care costs. Brody's belief regarding human psychology in these circumstances seems to be off the mark. Few of us are prepared to "go gently into that good night" unless the rest of our life looks like it will be wracked with un-relievable pain and misery.[9]

AGE-BASED RATIONING AND THE DUTY TO RESCUE

I now want to critically assess more directly the central analogy that both Brody and Mehlman appeal to in their rejection of any form of age-based rationing. This is the analogy with the rescue of some identifiable individual. Some individual has managed to get himself into a perilous situation, perhaps as a result of his own carelessness or ineptitude or foolish adventuresome spirit. We likely all agree that such an individual has no moral right to be rescued. We (potential societal rescuers) would do nothing unjust if we were simply to ignore his plight. Still, it seems it would be morally wrong, inhumane, indecent, simply to ignore that individual, even though it would take considerable societal effort and resources to save that individual.

I shall argue that this analogy has no moral relevance in the circumstances that I envision with regard to the issue of age-based rationing. There are five disanalogies that we need to consider. First, rescue efforts of the sort envisioned by Brody and Mehlman are relatively infrequent affairs, whereas the vast majority of us can expect to be rescued by medicine in old age, not just once, but many times given continued advances in life-prolonging medical research. The sheer quantity of opportunities for rescue in medicine does have moral relevance, especially if there are resource limitations we must respect for either moral or prudential reasons. The reader will recall the story of Mr. Caplan above. He was rescued from death several times; sometimes by his choice, sometimes by the choices of his family members. Our question is how many times are we (his fellow citizens) morally obligated (as a matter of either justice or compassion) to underwrite the cost of his care and rescue him from death? The fact is that each time we are faced with this question we are faced with an identifiable individual. Moreover, if we answer our question by saying that we are morally obligated to rescue as long as we have the capacity to rescue, then that would mean end-of-life, life-prolonging technology would have the potential for hijacking the bulk of our health care budget. It is far from clear that this would be a morally acceptable outcome, much less something that is morally obligatory (especially if we think about somewhat expensive quality-of-life-maintaining medical interventions such as drugs for arthritis relief or new knees and new hips for the elderly).

As Callahan (1987) points out, medical need is not at all like the need for rescue:

> Medical need is not a fixed concept but a function of technological possibility and regnant social expectations. If this is true of medical care in general, it seems all the more true of health care for the aged: it is a new medical frontier, and the possibilities for improvement are open, beckoning, and flexible. (p. 134)

Callahan wrote those words more than 20 years ago, and the truth of that claim has become more evident with each passing year. Again, costly rescues of a few thousand people each year are quite fiscally manageable by our society. But when those numbers are in the hundreds of thousands each year or a couple million each year, the costs of managing that magnitude of a rescue effort are prohibitive (and distort other important societal spending priorities). The reader will recall the surgeon we quoted who recalled that last year-of-life costs for someone with intestinal cancer in 1990 were about $500; today those costs are about $250,000. Are we a more just and caring society for making such expenditures?

Second, in assessing the moral relevance of the rescue analogy to rationing access to health care for the elderly, it would be morally ludicrous to encourage those stranded on a mountain to think about accepting death rather than hoping to be rescued. This is because these individuals are typically in good health except for the fact that they have gotten themselves into life-threatening circumstances. But this is not true for the much debilitated, chronically ill hyper-elderly who would be denied certain expensive life-prolonging medical resources by Daniels and Callahan and our democratic deliberators—it is not at all inappropriate to ask that they prepare themselves for death. This is where I believe Callahan's discussion of a "natural life span" is most helpful. There is fuzziness and indeterminacy about this concept that could be morally problematic at the level of individual decision-making, but the alternative seems to be commitment to an indefinitely prolonged life span that is a very definite threat to the just distribution of health resources in our society. Here, we call to mind Dr. DeBakey or Mr. Diaz.

Third, the rescue analogy is very much a black-and-white affair—there are no trade-offs for the person needing rescue. It is rescue or death. But there are important trade-off options for the elderly. Very often these trade-off options will be more congruent with their overall long-term welfare (though current highly fragmented methods for financing health care in the United States often prevent the implementation of these options). The Medicare program has largely been shaped by the desire to be responsive to the acute health care needs of the elderly or acute exacerbations of chronic health needs. But the dominant health care needs of the elderly may be for more nonmedical chronic needs, the sort of needs that can be satisfied by long-term care or supportive care in the community. These programs are not inexpensive, but they are clearly less expensive than much of what we call "rescue medicine" that is doomed from the beginning not to "rescue" anyone. (I have in mind especially those very expensive cancer drugs that add only weeks or months to life at extraordinary expense.)

One of the other things we should note is that the rescue analogy may have badly skewed our thinking about these matters in the past; perhaps to the point of our thinking that there was no choice to be made. That is, we might have wrongly believed that what we were *really* morally obligated to do was to prolong ("save") the lives of the elderly. We might have thought that improving the quality of their lives was something morally optional. Perhaps "we" should have allowed the elderly themselves to make these judgments for themselves. If the elderly were to prefer quality-of-life improvements over prolonged life in a demented or debilitated state, then is this not a choice that should be respected if we care about the autonomy of the elderly? If we did respect such choices, then the elderly who would die "prematurely" would have made that choice for themselves in exchange for other health goods they valued more highly. Social policies and programs that respected those choices could hardly be fairly accused of failing to carry out a duty to rescue. The current Medicare generation might not have a feasible option for making such choices for themselves, but the near-elderly generation of "baby boomers" clearly has this as a deliberative possibility.

Our fourth point regarding dis-analogies between age-based rationing and a duty to rescue is that the need to be rescued is typically a sporadic, episodic, unexpected affair, whereas aging and becoming chronically ill with a disease that will bring about one's death is common, predictable, and ultimately unavoidable. We all confidently expect to grow old, whereas few of us expect to be in circumstances that will require a dramatic rescue. That means we do have the opportunity to plan with regard to our health needs when we are old. More strongly, we are morally obligated to engage in such planning efforts so as to reduce the likelihood that either we or our surrogates would make unjust demands on the health resources of society. In theory, we can engage in those planning efforts as individuals. In practice, such individual efforts will do little or nothing to address effectively the cost-control issue with regard to the elderly. What we need are widespread, clear, public agreements regarding what we collectively are willing to deny our future possible debilitated selves. That creates the necessary social understanding and social pressure for conformity with those agreements, and also helps to assure the fairness of the agreements.

Our fifth point regarding rescue situations relates to the symbolic value that is attached to the saving of identifiable lives. Economists readily observe that these dramatic rescue efforts are rarely cost-effective. But the rest of us hardly think that ought to be our highest social value. Being able to save a human life, being able to convey the message that each and every individual is worthy of maximal effort by society to save his life—that is what many regard as a powerful symbolic value that is affirmed when large-scale rescue efforts are undertaken to save a single individual. Such symbolism, however, sometimes serves to blunt or blind our moral sensibilities to serious injustices.

Here we must call attention to the fact that in health care, our rescue efforts are more selective than the non-health rescue efforts that command media attention. We are most likely to do the most by way of trying to save the life of an elderly person when that person is *well-insured*. If our everyday rescue efforts were like this, we would expect the stranded folks on the mountain to pull out their *platinum credit cards* and wave them at the helicopter pilots before they could be rescued. This fact takes a little bit of the moral luster off many of these health rescues.[10] But there is another dimension to this problem. The Medicare program is entirely separate in operational terms from all other health care funding streams; nevertheless, it can affect those funding streams through political and organizational pressures. The Medicare program is like the *platinum credit card* for the elderly. It allows them to buy lots of very expensive, marginally beneficial, rescue-like health care. Medicare does not operate with any real budget. Congress takes a guess at what Medicare expenditures might be at the beginning of a fiscal year. If Medicare expenditures greatly exceed projections, then pressure may be placed on reducing costs in other federally funded health programs, most often programs aimed at meeting the health needs of poorer members of society. This is where a serious justice issue exists. These very costly marginal benefits are being funded for the elderly on the backs of those who are least well-off in society. The bright lights are on the great good we are doing in rescuing the elderly from "premature death," and the great value and respect we have for each of those lives while budget reductions deprive poorer individuals of more basic and more effective health care outside the range of media attention. These are losses that will be largely invisible to the larger society.

Identifiable lives elicit a normal range of emotions; we cannot be empathic with a statistical life. This is what creates the illusion that identifiable lives are more valuable than statistical lives. But the lives saved or lost in both cases are real lives; these are not just "paper lives." Charles Fried (1970) calls attention to the fact that we can have relations of love and friendship with identifiable persons; this is clearly relevant to the relations that exist between doctors and patients. However, the critical point Fried makes is that

> love and friendship do not justify disregarding obligations of justice and fairness, the beneficiaries of which, after all, are real persons too. The generosity of love and friendship is based on giving up what is one's own, not in depriving a third person of his just and fair entitlements. (p. 226)[11]

What physicians need to be reminded of is that they are distributing *social resources* to which are attached obligations of justice. Our system of health care financing might obscure that fact. It creates the illusion through private insurance policies that these health resources are private entitlements of insured patients, obscuring to a large extent the fact that our health care system is a product of huge *social* investments. The recent efforts by the Bush administration to convert as much as possible of the Medicare program to these private Health Savings Accounts would only make this problem that much worse.

Next, we need to respond to Mehlman's practical concerns about high transaction costs associated with trying to put in place any age-based rationing protocols. His concerns would be legitimate if we imagined Congress imposing such protocols as part of a political response to some fiscal crisis. But that is precisely what we are *not* advocating in recommending a democratic deliberative process that at least encompasses all the members of the "baby boom" generation. This is the sort of public conversation that creates public understanding, and brings about the change in public attitude Callahan would like to see. If my generation is capable of making such wise and just choices for our future possible selves, then it is doubtful courts would have good reason to intervene to reverse the results of a democratically legitimate conversation. Further, it is not as if the results of the conversation would be that individuals had life-prolonging medical care ripped away from them so that they would die; there would always be trade-offs. We would collectively give up some forms of expensive, marginally beneficial life-prolonging medical care in exchange for care that would yield more good for us, that was more relevant to our needs as older patients. Patients who had had the opportunity to benefit from such exchanges would hardly be in a strong legal position to claim a right now to renege on that bargain, even if that meant they were faced with what they regarded as a "premature death."

There is an obvious objection to this conclusion; namely, that we could hardly expect universal endorsement of any age-based rationing protocols. Some number of individuals would feel aggrieved; they would want to protect their right to take advantage of every possible medical opportunity to protect their life in the face of a terminal illness. However, these individuals would generally have the right to do just this under the proposal I am defending—they could purchase virtually anything they regarded as medically beneficial to them, but they could not claim a right to do so with social resources. We understand that few individuals could afford to pay $300,000 for an artificial heart at age 80. Obviously, the key to circumventing that obstacle would be some form of private insurance that individuals could purchase (assuming we would have in place some form of national health insurance). It is difficult to know whether such an insurance product would have a market, or that it would be affordable. After all, what an individual is asking for is open-ended, unlimited coverage for everything medicine has to offer, that might yield some desirable life-prolongation no matter what the cost. An insurance product such as that would attract exactly the sort of patient/client most insurance companies are wary of embracing. Individuals would have no just complaint if such a product did not fail to materialize in the market, nor would individuals have a just complaint against government for failing to create a program that would offer such coverage.

There is one last type of objection to age-based rationing we need to address, which we will call the "healthy Granny" objection; several variants of this objection might come to mind. Imagine an individual who has been extraordinarily healthy their entire life; they have used not much more than $1,000 worth of health care over an 80-year period, and they have paid health insurance premiums for that entire period of time. They are now faced with a colorectal cancer that was identified late (metastases to the liver and beyond). They want access to Avastin at a cost of $100,000 so that their predicted life expectancy would be increased from two years to two and a half years. They claim that justice would require they have such access at social expense because they have hardly cost society anything for health care their entire life. However, as others have observed (Williams, 1997), health insurance is not a personal savings account; we are sharing with others coverage for financial risk due to costly health needs. This individual has been extraordinarily fortunate for their entire life so far as health is concerned. No one would regard someone who has needed and used more than a million dollars worth of health care for some illness as being a "very lucky person," as if they had won the lottery. That is a massive amount of misery they likely endured. If our collective social judgment is that Avastin is not worth it for colorectal cancer, and we agreed at an earlier point in life to deny this therapy to our future possible elderly selves, then this individual has no more a just claim to this intervention than anyone else. There is nothing unfair or discriminatory about this conclusion.

Dan Brock (1993) raises another sort of case. He asks us to imagine a very vigorous 82-year-old writer "who continues to be actively engaged in several writing projects, has a full and satisfying family life, pursues a number of community activities for the benefit of others, and greatly enjoys periodic travels" (p. 404). She develops pneumonia and requires hospitalization for treatment. A reasonable medical expectation is that she will recover fully and likely live another decade.

Could we justifiably deny her this hospitalization which might cost $30,000? Brock is writing a review of Callahan's work, and is assuming that Callahan would seek to deny the elderly all life-prolonging care beyond their late seventies. Callahan does say things that would warrant this inference. But if we had adopted instead Daniels' prudential life span account and a commitment to protecting fair equality of opportunity to a normal opportunity range, then I doubt our democratic deliberators would have put in place a rationing protocol that would deny this woman her treatment for pneumonia. In general, as I have argued above, we are likely to refrain, in most types of cases, from invoking any strict age criterion by itself for denying our future possible selves access to expensive life-prolonging medical care.

What we can do is a variation on Brock's example. We can imagine this woman is diagnosed with a dissecting aortic aneurysm, just like Dr. DeBakey's aneurysm. Here, medical details will make a difference. If we imagine she is extraordinarily vigorous for her age, that the surgery will likely go well, and that she will experience something close to a full recovery, then we would have no clear consideration of health care justice that would warrant denying her this care, even if the cost were $200,000. But if her medical condition were typical for her age, and if the risks of surgery and complications were high with a very uncertain long-term prognosis, and if total costs were likely to be more than half a million dollars, then this looks much more like the sort of intervention we would deny our future possible elderly selves for reasons of prudence and fairness.

CONCLUSIONS

I offer two quick concluding points. These reflect a response to the practical concerns both Callahan and Daniels have about putting any age-based rationing system in place in our current health care system. In brief, their concerns are that the elderly would be less well-off, and that the health care system as a whole would be less just. My first point is that these risks would be minimized if we had some seamless form of national health insurance. This is what is needed to assure that the savings achieved by denying our future possible elderly selves marginally beneficial health care are redeployed either to earlier stages in life to maximize the likelihood of all having an opportunity to achieve a normal life span, or to other health needs of the elderly not related to expensive life-prolonging medical care. My second point is that any rationing or cost-containment policy that targets the elderly must be coupled with equally effective policies that reduce the wasteful use of health resources by the non-elderly. It would certainly be unfair to impose penny-pinching on the elderly, while permitting wasteful excess by the insured non-elderly. This is another reason for having a seamless form of national health insurance. Thus, numerous forms of very marginally beneficial health care ought to be the focus of rationing protocols developed through the deliberative process. Those protocols should generally apply to both the elderly and non-elderly.

10

DO FUTURE POSSIBLE CHILDREN HAVE A JUST CLAIM TO A SUFFICIENTLY HEALTHY GENOME?

The work that has been done in genetics over the past two decades is raising numerous questions related to health care justice. Certainly Rawls (1971) took as a fixed starting point the genetic endowment of each individual—individuals could be fortunate or unfortunate so far as their health prospects were concerned in relation to their genetic endowment, but there were no relevant matters of justice to be discussed. That is clearly no longer true today. Here is a sampling of the kinds of issues we are face with today.

Most people bristle at the thought that health insurance companies could require individuals to have genetic tests that might result either in their being denied health insurance altogether or having to pay exorbitant premiums for coverage. This strikes most individuals as plainly unfair because individuals have no control over their genetic endowment. It is not as if some individuals made irresponsible choices of aspects of their genetic endowment that will now impose significant health costs on the rest of society. The way to solve this problem is to initiate a major push for some form of single-payer national health insurance. Then our genetic endowment would be entirely irrelevant so far as access to needed health care was concerned. However, life is not that simple.

Government is supposed to treat all of us equally, fairly, in a nondiscriminating manner. But fairness for all might require some degree of genetic discrimination. What we are quickly discovering is that our genetic endowment does not just predispose us from some diseases or protect us from others. Our genetic endowment will often determine the degree to which we will or will not be responsive to some medical intervention, such as a specific cancer drug, a very expensive cancer drug. How should a just and caring society with limited resources and virtually unlimited health care needs deal with that genetic fact? Small differences in response rates would not warrant any special moral attention. But if having one genotype meant there was no more than a 5% chance of a positive response to an expensive cancer drug that could promise five extra years of life, while another genotype represented a 60% chance of a positive response, would a just and caring society have a moral right to require that individuals reveal their genotype in order to be eligible for such a drug at social expense? A commitment to national health insurance does not yield an easy and obvious answer to this question.

As things are now, there is virtually nothing we can do to alter our genetic endowment; that is not true with regard to our future possible children. At this point, I do not have in mind micromanipulation of the genetic endowment of an eight-cell embryo. Rather, if parents know or suspect they are at risk of having a child with a serious genetic deficiency, should a national health insurance program pay for the genetic tests that would allow them to make a more informed and more responsible choice as to whether they would have children or how they ought to have children? The "how" issue pertains to use of some alternative reproductive technology. In both cases there would be significant costs associated with pursuing either of these options; these costs might be affordable for Americans in the upper middle class, but they might pose a substantial barrier to others who were not as financially well-off. Is that unjust?

Should the costs of genetic testing in connection with minimizing health risks to future possible children be borne by society as a whole through a national health insurance program as part of our commitment to having a just and caring society? But there is a complicating factor here. Some significant portion of our population will have deep religious or philosophic objections to the very idea of seeking to shape (even somewhat indirectly) the genetic endowment of future possible children. They may accept the fact that they live in a liberal pluralistic society, and consequently, they have no right to interfere in the making of such choices by others who do not share their beliefs. However, they might more seriously object to their contributing to making these choices possible by paying taxes or premiums for a national health insurance program that would cover such services; they would see this as social disrespect for their own deeply held conscientious beliefs. Does this concern require that we not cover such interventions as part of a national health insurance program? We turn now to a more focused discussion of that question.

The defining theme of Philip Kitcher's book, *The Lives to Come,* is that we are beyond the age of genetic innocence and that we have entered irrevocably the age of genetic responsibility (1996, p. 204). He very much wants us to avoid the excesses and moral wrongs associated with the eugenics movement in the early part of the twentieth century. He is himself an advocate for what he terms "utopian eugenics." He writes,

> Utopian eugenics would use reliable genetic information in prenatal tests that would be available equally to all citizens. Although there would be widespread public discussion of values and of the social consequences of individual

decisions, there would be no socially imposed restrictions on reproductive choices—citizens would be educated but not coerced. (p. 202)

There seem to be three key ideas that are the core of Kitcher's utopian eugenics: (1) respect for the procreative liberty of all, (2) equal access (no financial barriers) to the genetic technologies necessary for *effective* procreative liberty, and (3) a responsible social commitment to preventing "deep human suffering" (p. 192) associated with one's genetic endowment to the extent that medicine provides us with the tools needed to achieve that objective.

The primary question that will define this chapter springs from the second and third of those key ideas. If we take Norman Daniels' fair equality of opportunity account of health care justice (1985) as providing us with an essential principle of health care justice (as opposed to a full account), then what does health care justice require of us, as a society, when it comes to determining the genetic endowment of future possible children? Buchanan et al. (2000) address this question from the perspective of a future possible capacity to do germ line genetic engineering of eight-cell embryos, either repairing or enhancing that genetic endowment through the replacement of some genes in those embryos (with either normal or enhanced versions of those genes). However, I will put aside that set of issues, only for the reason that that represents a future possible capacity of medicine. More relevant current capacities of medicine now raise serious issues of health care justice which we ought to address. More specifically, I have in mind our capacity to do preimplantation genetic diagnosis (PGD) of eight-cell embryos.

For couples who know they are at risk of having a child with a serious genetic disorder (such as cystic fibrosis) which will very adversely affect both the length of life and quality of life of a child, PGD is a godsend. It means that they can avoid two choices that they might find morally and psychologically unpalatable: (1) aborting an affected fetus at 16 weeks identified through prenatal testing, and (2) taking a 25% chance that a child will be born with cystic fibrosis. With PGD, a woman would be given drugs that would cause her to hyper-ovulate. Multiple conceptions would occur *in vitro*, perhaps 12–15. They would be grown to the eight-cell stage, and a cell would be removed from each for genetic analysis. Embryos that had no copies of the gene associated with cystic fibrosis (or only one copy of the gene) would be candidates for implantation. The cost of achieving a successful pregnancy via PGD is about $40,000. This is a sum that those who were not securely in the middle class could not afford. Consequently, if nothing is done to equalize access to this technology (and associated forms of genetic testing needed to identify at-risk potential parents) for members of all socioeconomic classes, the result will be the disproportionate birth of children with serious genetic disorders for parents who are relatively less well-off in our society.

How should we judge (from a moral point of view) that outcome? By the disproportionate aspect of that outcome, or just the fact that a substantial number of children were born with these life-diminishing genetic disorders whose births could have been avoided with access to PGD? Can we confidently judge that it would merely be an "unfortunate" outcome (which would certainly be a correct judgment in a world without PGD)? That is, is this the sort of bad outcome for which no one is morally blameworthy? Or would we have to say that in this emerging world with PGD, that sort of outcome would be presumptively unjust? That is, does this represent a moral wrong which we, citizens of a society that aspires to be both just and caring, are morally obligated to remedy as a matter of justice?

FRAMING THE ISSUE

Much more needs to be done by way of framing more precisely the moral issues that are our focus. Certainly we need to consider what the scope of application of PGD might be; we have used cystic fibrosis as a placeholder on this point. Our preliminary suggestion for generalizing from this would be that PGD should be an option for any couple that knows from prior genetic testing (triggered by family history) that they are at risk for having a child with a serious genetic disorder that would adversely affect either the length of life or quality of life of that child from the early stages of life on. In addition to cystic fibrosis, we would include Duchenne's muscular dystrophy, Canavan's disease, fragile X syndrome (most common form of mental retardation), hemophilia (and other such X-linked disorders), juvenile diabetes, Tay Sachs, autism (assuming a solid genetic link), neurofibromatosis, Lesch-Nyhan syndrome, and so on. There are any number of other medical disorders with strong genetic links that emerge in midlife or later that also very adversely affect length of life or quality of life, including breast cancer linked to the BRCA1 gene, or somewhat earlier onset forms on Alzheimer's disease linked to APOE, or Huntington's, or various forms of cancer or heart disease, and so forth. However, for purposes of initially framing our discussion, we will say that there are no just claims for access to PGD for any of these later-in-life disorders to which potential parents may know their future possible children might be vulnerable. The implication of this is that potential parents who were financially more well-off would be free to access at their own expense PGD for these later-in-life disorders that might surface in the future lives of their children. Further, if some of these parents chose not to purchase PGD, their children could not justifiably claim that they had been treated unjustly, either by their parents or by the larger society. The correct moral description of their circumstances would be that they were unfortunate.

There are a number of morally relevant considerations that would justify our making the moral distinction we are proposing with regard to PGD. First, for the disorders we listed in the early stages of life, the causal connections for the children are "tight" and the consequences seriously harmful to their welfare and opportunities. In contrast, the causal connections for the later-in-life disorders are much looser and less certain. With the exception of the Huntington's example, all the other disorders listed require for their manifestation as actual disease complex environmental cofactors that are poorly understood at best.

Second, appealing in part to Daniels' fair equality of opportunity account of health care justice, children who are born with the disorders we have listed are largely deprived of the opportunity to experience anything approaching a normal human life; their lives are severely compromised for the most part. But with later onset disorders, individuals will have had the opportunity to live (and take advantage of) most of the opportunities that define a human life. It is also morally relevant that over a 40-year period of time (since few of these disorders will manifest themselves before then), given very rapid developments in medicine there may well be either cures or very effective life-prolonging therapies for many of these disorders. (We recognize that there are no guarantees in this regard, as the 40-year "war against cancer" declared by President Nixon continues with no end in sight.) As for the children born with the disorders we have listed, no realistic hope of cure exists for any of these disorders in the short term.

Third, aggregate costs are a morally relevant consideration when we have only limited resources to meet virtually unlimited health care needs for all in our society. If we restrict socially funded access to PGD for the very limited range of disorders we have listed (or implicitly included by analogy), approximately 200,000 children might be born each year in the U.S. through the use of PGD—the direct cost of that would be about $8 billion per year. But there are about four million children born each year in the U.S., virtually all of whom will carry a gene for a serious medical disorder that will diminish life expectancy and/or substantially compromise their quality of life for some number of years. If all of those births were to come about through PGD, the result would be an addition of $160 billion per year to the cost of health care in the United States. An increase in health care costs of that magnitude (or even half that magnitude) cannot be justified on either moral or economic grounds, even when we recognize that total health spending in the U.S. for 2007 was about $2.3 trillion. The argument here can be fleshed out just a bit further.

The dollars spent to make PGD available as an option for the parents of future possible children at risk for childhood genetic disorders would be more than offset by the savings achieved through not having to provide very expensive medical and social interventions for children afflicted with cystic fibrosis (or muscular dystrophy or hemophilia or fragile X syndrome). The children who would be born without these disorders would have a normal life expectancy, and would be vulnerable to the whole range of other medical problems to which the rest of the population would be vulnerable. But before most of these vulnerabilities would be actualized, most of these individuals would have enjoyed many decades of very healthy life. By way of contrast, if we sought to use PGD to eliminate various forms of earlier onset Alzheimer's, or cancers with a strong genetic association, or forms of heart disease with a strong genetic association, the result would be very high front-end social costs, with very little in the way of offsetting health care savings.

For the sake of argument we will assume that this expansive use of PGD is maximally successful, that we do eliminate thereby what would otherwise be a cause of premature death and disability for that individual. However, we need to recall that we are mostly speaking of causes of premature death that will be occurring in the later part of life. We also need to remember that none of these disorders can be properly characterized as "the" cause of the future death of an individual. Instead, the more proper characterization would be that we would have eliminated what might otherwise have been the "first" cause of their death and/or significant disability. (We do need to say "might" have been the first cause of their death or disability because there are no metaphysical guarantees that the targeted gene in a family, whose presence will trigger the rejection of one or another eight-cell embryo, might not result in choosing an embryo with an unrecognized predisposition to a medical problem that would bring about an even earlier death or serious disability.)

Again, because we are speaking of medical disorders that will manifest themselves later in life, it would be reasonable to assume that a second potential cause of death or significant disability will be lurking in the not-very-distant future for each of those individuals. That means they will gain on average a few extra years of good-quality life. However, relative to the decades of life gained per embryo for our first use of PGD, the gain for our second use of PGD can be correctly described as being only "marginally beneficial." Morally speaking, these additional years of life do not have that much moral weight when it comes to establishing just health claims. Further, though the health care system as a whole would initially achieve savings by eliminating these potential "first causes" of death or disability, the savings would prove to be ephemeral since roughly the same health costs would be incurred by these individuals for the "second causes" of their death or disability; so the costs would only have been postponed a few years. The conclusion we would draw from this analysis is that our society would not be unjust to refuse to fund publicly this expansive use of PGD.

As a liberal society we would have to permit the wealthy to purchase PGD for these more expansive uses; no one is made worse off by permitting this purchase, nor are any of the less well-off treated unjustly. The wealthy are purchasing what at best is a very marginal and very uncertain benefit for their future possible children, and they are using only their own resources. Further, it seems relatively easy to make the case that those who are less well-off in our society (the middle class and below) would rationally and autonomously reject wanting to access this expansive use of PGD for themselves and their future possible children. They would be able to identify readily numerous other currently unmet health needs for themselves or their future possible children that would deserve higher priority for public funding than this expansive use of PGD. The prescription drug benefit for the Medicare elderly, which was the focus of a major political debate, would be one clear example of such a higher-priority health need, with an estimated price tag of $800 billion over the next 10 years (which represents about 65% public funding for those costs). Even if we follow Norman Daniels' Prudential Lifespan Account (1988, chap. 4), which is aimed at showing why it would be both rational and just for each of us to allocate resources away from the latest stages in life to earlier stages in order to maximize the likelihood that each of us would reach old age, it seems impossible to imagine the logic in that argument that would yield either a rational or just allocation of resources for an expansive use of PGD.

Finally, it would be clearly disingenuous to claim that this expansive use of PGD was aimed at meeting either the best interests or the just interests of children as children. The interests that would be met would be the interests of the older adults that these future possible children would become. By way of contrast, the more limited use of PGD we recommend would obviously be aimed at improving the health prospects of children as children, since the medical disorders we would seek to eliminate would be disorders that directly affected children. However, we still need to recognize that we have not as yet provided sufficient argument to support the claim that justice requires such social support for this intervention. We turn to that task next.

PREIMPLANTATION GENETIC DIAGNOSIS (PGD): A HISTORICAL SIDE NOTE

For a seven-year period (1995–2002) I was the coprincipal investigator of an NIH-funded project through the ELSI program (Ethical, Legal, and Social Implications of the Human Genome Project). The title of this project for its first three years (1995–98) was "Genome Technology and Reproduction: Values and Public Policy." The broad goal of this project has been to test a certain model of rational democratic deliberation, a more constructive approach to shaping public policy when deeply controversial moral and social values are at stake than we have seen exhibited in the so-called "abortion debates." There was a total of 13 two-hour sessions in each of seven Michigan communities, with 30 to 50 individuals in each dialogue group. One of these sessions involved spending most of our time discussing preimplantation genetic diagnosis.

At the beginning of each cluster of six dialogues we had done a survey. Items expressed either a moral or policy judgment; responses were on a five-point Likert scale from "strongly agree" to "strongly disagree." The survey was repeated at the end of each cluster to determine whether or not views had changed significantly over the course of the six dialogues. One such item started with the stem that a genetically responsible society ought to help underwrite the costs of accessing PGD for parents who know they are at risk for having a child with a serious genetic disorder. More specifically, the item said, government should mandate that 80% of the costs of accessing PGD should be paid either by private insurance or state Medicaid programs (Fleck, 1996, 1997). This item produced what for me was a quite unexpected response.

The aggregate response from the seven communities was 21% agreement with the statement and 70% disagreement. This was at the end of the dialogue process, which reflected a slight increase in the level of disagreement from the beginning of the dialogue process (Fleck, 1997, p. 32–33). I found this result remarkable since I would have predicted ahead of time a 50–60% level of agreement, which I would also have predicted would increase as a result of sustained discussion. I should also mention that our dialogue groups were broadly representative of each of their communities, at least so far as diversity of viewpoint was concerned. In other respects they were not so representative; for example, 80% of our participants had college degrees or better. I must also mention, out of honesty, that I have used this same item in a couple dozen other audiences of varying sizes; and it is rare that I will elicit more than 25% agreement with the item. This suggests considerable social prevalence in this judgment, at least at present. That is, this is not a judgment that was peculiar to our dialogue groups.

I do not want to convey the impression that I have attempted to engage in any rigorous survey research here. I have not. My primary objective was to come up with policy judgments and moral judgments relating to emerging genetic technologies that would engage participants, spark discussion, and give the discussion focus. My primary reason for believing that this proposal would elicit a fairly high level of initial agreement was that it was aimed at saving babies considerable suffering and greatly abbreviated lives in many cases. I believed that this would connect up with very strong intuitions of justice and strong feelings of compassion. This was generally true for the 21% who agreed with this proposal, but as I learned from the discussion, there was considerable diversity among the those who disagreed regarding their reasons for disagreeing.

I had expected that those supportive of a right-to life perspective would disagree because PGD necessarily involves discarding numerous excess embryos. I expected many advocates for disability groups to be among those who disagreed because the embryos that would be especially singled out for being discarded would be those that would otherwise be born with serious disabilities. I expected political conservatives to be among those who disagreed because this was a government "mandated" program, and the mandate would be directed at private insurance companies. But I was surprised that a number of social liberals were among those who disagreed. The most common reason they gave for their disagreement was that there were stronger just claims associated with other unmet health needs in our society that would have to be satisfied before this PGD proposal could be justly funded. Most often they cited the fact that we had 43 million people (1996–97) without health insurance, whose health needs are undiagnosed and unmet to a large extent.

I was also surprised by what I will refer to as the "appeal to personal freedom" argument; variants of this argument came from individuals who were both political liberals and political conservatives. I had taken procreative liberty to be a background condition that had little in the way of moral salience for this argument. However, critics attributed considerable salience to this assumption of procreative liberty for purposes of thinking through the justice issues.

One version of their argument went like this: At the very least, a health care justice argument must start with health care needs. But there are no needs involved in this situation—potential parents *wish* to have a child. They know there is either a 25% or 50% chance that they will have a child with a serious genetic disorder. They do not *wish* to have a child with that disorder; they *wish* instead that their child will be born with at least a normal degree of health. Such wishes are quite understandable, but such wishes do not generate health needs, much less any just claims to access PGD at public expense. These parents have options. They do not need to have children. They can have a very satisfying life without children. If they want children, they have the option of adopting children. They also have the less expensive alternate reproductive option of using sperm or ova from donors whose gametes are very unlikely to result in the conception of a child who will be born with a serious genetic disorder. They may want to have a child that is genetically their own; but again, this is a want, not a need. Further, it should not go unnoticed that we are talking about couples that have the capacity to have children of their own. That is, they have effective freedom in this regard. But there are the 15% of couples in the United States who are infertile, who do not have the capacity to have children of their own without some form of outside assistance. It would seem that if anyone has a moral right to have satisfied the desire to have children, those infertile couples would have a stronger prior right than the couples seeking publicly funded access to PGD. Prima facie, this is a persuasive line of argument against the claim that anyone has a just claim to PGD.

DOES JUSTICE REQUIRE PUBLIC FUNDING FOR LIMITED PGD?

Before responding to the objections raised above regarding public funding for some limited access to PGD, we need to do a bit more by way of framing our issue. In the item used with the dialogue groups, we referred to private insurance companies being "mandated" to cover access to limited PGD. There are considerations of justice that make that proposal problematic. Specifically, if this increases the cost of employer-sponsored insurance enough for small, marginal firms, they may choose to drop health insurance for their employees, thereby increasing the pool of uninsured. So we can imagine two alternate ways of asking our question: (1) Can a justice-based argument be made for saying that limited access to PGD ought to be considered part of a comprehensive package of health benefits that a just and caring society ought to guarantee to all its citizens?

(2) Given the highly fragmented way in which we currently finance health care, and given the unlikelihood of a system of national health insurance in the U.S. in the foreseeable future, does justice require creating a separate federal program for funding a limited PGD benefit (something akin to the End-Stage Renal Disease Program, which will pay for kidney dialysis or kidney transplant for all who are in renal failure), no matter what their financial, employment, age, or insurance status might be?

Next, there is what some might regard as a metaphysically odd feature to this alleged problem of health care justice. Ordinarily, we have a person who is suffering, or at risk of suffering, a very serious health problem which can only be addressed by a very expensive, experimental, or uncertain health intervention. We want to know whether *that person*, and others similarly situated, has a just claim to that health intervention. But in the case of PGD, the object of our inquiry is a *future possible person*, not an actual person with unequivocal moral standing. Moreover, the real issue is not whether we will provide to that future possible person some life-saving or quality-of-life protecting intervention. Rather, the real issue is whether one future possible person who is at risk of being afflicted with a serious genetic disorder will be replaced by a different future possible person whom we know to be free of that disorder.[1]

A critic might reasonably ask what the justice-relevant issue is in that situation. A strong critic might argue that there is a justice issue, but it is not what we originally suggested. The problem instead is that we are proposing using social resources to bring one possible person into existence instead of another who is disfavored because of the disabilities with which they will be afflicted. The argument continues that we might have to accept reluctantly the right of potential parents to make such a choice as part of procreative liberty. But it would be clearly unjust for social resources to be used to favor for existence one person rather than another, when all members of a society are entitled to equal treatment—respect for parental procreative liberty does not require that sort of social support.

This objection rests upon one very flawed premise. It implicitly assumes that "future possible persons," as represented by some number of embryos in a Petri dish, have some sort of strong moral or political right to become actual persons. But there is no persuasive argument that can sustain that claim. Future possible persons have no actual interests, and hence, have no actual rights. There are scenarios that can be imagined that might cause us to qualify this last claim a bit, but we may ignore those scenarios for our present purposes. If multiple embryos have been brought into existence for a morally permissible purpose, such as avoiding the actual birth of children with serious genetic disorders that would adversely affect both the length and quality of their lives, then both the parents and the larger society are morally free to choose which of those embryos will have an opportunity to become actual persons. Embryos as embryos in this situation can be neither harmed nor discriminated against; this should be regarded as much a conceptual claim as a moral claim. The further implication of this claim is that it is presumptively morally permissible to use social resources to assist potential parents in achieving their objective of having children born with normal health. That is, it is *not unjust* to use social resources in this way, unless additional arguments can be adduced to demonstrate an injustice. But we must also concede at this point that we have not yet shown that justice *requires* providing social support for this purpose. In other words, a society such as our own could not be rightly judged to have acted unjustly by failing to provide social resources to support parents in these circumstances.

Advocates for the rights of individuals with disabilities have attempted to adduce arguments aimed at showing that injustices would result from social funding of our limited PGD proposal. One such objection is what is often referred to as the "expressivist objection." In brief, it is the claim that genetic interventions aimed at eliminating disabilities represent a profound devaluing of the lives of people with those disabilities. That is, the social message expressed by such interventions is that we do not want people "like that" in our society; our society is better off without them.

Buchanan (1995; et al. 2000) has provided an effective response to this line of argument which we will not repeat here. But we will make one large point, which will also serve to blunt the force of this line of argument. It is (as many will say) that it is the disabilities themselves that are disfavored, not the people who must live with those disabilities. Our society clearly has strong obligations of health care justice with respect to meeting the needs of individuals with a broad range of disabilities. Most often, the moral basis for this obligation is in something like Daniels' fair equality of opportunity account of health care justice. For individuals with spinal cord injuries, a just and caring society must provide the wheelchair assistance they need to move about in our society. And we must modify buildings so that they are readily accessible for individuals with those disabilities. And for individuals who are blind, there are now computers that can give them effective access to an extremely broad range of informational sources necessary for their accessing the range of opportunities those with sight take for granted. That, too, represents a requirement of justice.

Still, a little reflection will show that all these interventions are nothing more than "second best" interventions. They provide partial restoration of function, but not full and effective function. However, there are always new and extremely promising medical strategies on the horizon. With respect to the two examples just provided, there is the hope associated with human embryonic stem cell research. This is research that hopes to use embryonic stem cells to create any of 200 other types of cells, including nerve cells that could restore nearly full functioning to severed spinal cords, or to the nerve tissue associated with sight. If such technologies were maximally successful in their therapeutic intent and in the range of expensive but affordable medical technologies in our society, then we would undoubtedly be morally obligated as a matter of justice to provide such technologies at social expense for individuals with the relevant disabilities.

Some persons with these disabilities might reject these interventions, but it is easy to imagine that the vast majority of such individuals would embrace them. The net result would be that individuals *with these types of disabilities* would largely cease to be, as a result of their own free choice. Such a result undercuts the force of the expressivist objection, since it is a clear embodiment of the claim that it is the disability itself that is disfavored, not the person with the disability. That is, a real distinction exists between the person with the disability and the disability itself; this would be recognized by members of the disability community itself.[2] Further, it should not go unnoticed with respect to this intervention that the source of the cells for the regenerative tissue are human embryos left over from in vitro fertilization, otherwise to be discarded.

We now return to the question of whether there are considerations of health care justice which would either warrant or require public funding for access to PGD in the limited circumstances we identified. To be clear, we will defend the view that such funding would be *warranted* by considerations of health care justice, but not required. We believe this somewhat modest claim is all that can be justified at present, for reasons given more fully below. In brief, the deep theoretical reason for this conclusion is that the moral terrain of health care justice is exceptionally complex. There is no single principle of health care justice that provides us with clear criteria for concluding in all, or even most, instances of health care need that a particular health care intervention must be provided as a matter of justice.

The moral reality is that our socially shared conception of health care justice is pluralistic to its core (Rhodes, 2005). There are times when the fair-equality-of-opportunity strand of health care justice provides the surest guide to what is morally required of us; but there are other occasions when the utilitarian strand provides that guidance, or the strong egalitarian strand, or the libertarian strand, or urgency of need considerations, or considerations of personal responsibility, and so on. Further, when we step back and take a global view of the entire expanding universe of health needs with all the heterogeneity of that universe of needs (protease inhibitors for HIV positive patients, prescriptions drugs for the elderly, left ventricular assist devices for patients in congestive heart failure, dialysis for patients in kidney failure, neonatal intensive care units for extremely premature infants, various forms of rehabilitation for victims of devastating disease or accidents, etc.), we realize that there are some considerations of justice (one or another of our strands) that would provide moral support for meeting any one of these needs. But it will rarely be the case for the sorts of health needs listed here that that support will be decisive and uncontroversial.

As noted already, we cannot escape the need for health care rationing.; we have only limited resources that can be reasonably devoted to meeting health needs. So we really need to establish priorities among all these competing health needs. But our various strands of health care justice will not just logically yield such a list of justice-authorized health care priorities. Especially in the very broad middle range of any such list, reasonable people will be able to reasonably disagree with one another. But justice as fair treatment will require that we not just accede to random and arbitrary judgments in this middle range. Instead, as we have argued here and elsewhere (Fleck, 1992, 1994a, 1999; see also Daniels and Sabin, 1997; 1998a), we appeal to processes of rational democratic deliberation to achieve a reasonable ordering among our health care priorities, an ordering that can only be "just enough," given that we must make such judgments in nonideal circumstances under what Rawls (1993) refers to as "the burdens of judgment." It is for these reasons essentially that we are limited to saying that funding PGD for the circumstances we identified may be *warranted* by considerations of health care justice, but may not be required. If, for example, a fair deliberative process results in the judgment that there are many other health care needs that are judged to be of higher priority for the resources available, then we may in fact not be able to provide social resources for PGD, even though there are some considerations of social justice that would support so doing.

What are the considerations of health care justice that would warrant social funding for at least limited access to PGD? First, there are several considerations that might come under the rubric of protecting or restoring fair equality of opportunity. We noted earlier that there are strong considerations of justice that require we provide access to effective rehabilitative services for individuals who have become disabled; we might be tempted to think that this same response should be required for children born with serious genetic disabilities instead of providing funds for PGD. However, several morally relevant considerations distinguish the situations of the respective groups.

Individuals who acquire disabilities later in life as a result of disease or accident, or individuals who have these disabilities from near birth on as a result of disease or accident beyond our ability to predict or control, are individuals whose initial circumstances are unfortunate, but not unjust. No one could effectively alter their fate. However, given the existence of PGD, we cannot make that same claim in the case of children born with predictable genetic disorders. We cannot be morally indifferent or blameless with respect to their fate. Today, as Kitcher (1996) contends, we cannot escape responsibility for their fate.

Next, we need to emphasize that we are speaking of children whose lives will be seriously impaired and dramatically shortened. For many of these children, no rehabilitative efforts can make more than the merest marginal difference to either the quality or the length of their lives—this will certainly be true for disorders such as Tay Sachs or Canavan's or Lesch-Nyhan or muscular dystrophy. Adults who become disabled may have the psychological resources needed to cope with their radically altered life circumstances. But in the case of the children we have in mind, especially if they are afflicted with both mental and physical disabilities, no such internal resources will be available to them. They will not have the opportunity to develop those capacities because the very roots of those capacities are irrevocably damaged. That is, the potential for restoring for them even a small portion of what Daniels calls the "normal opportunity range" is just not there. Hence, for the sake of protecting fair equality of opportunity for children to the extent that it can be protected, we ought to provide the resources needed for PGD in the circumstances we identified.

We should emphasize again that this entire discussion is based upon respect for the procreative liberty of potential parents; recognizing this provides an important second step in our argument. What we are saying is that potential parents may know they are at risk for having a child with cystic fibrosis or fragile X syndrome. They may also know that PGD is a socially available option. We will even say that there is a socially funded program in place that makes this option readily accessible to them. But they may nevertheless reject that option for, perhaps, deeply religious reasons. They may believe they are religiously obligated to accept whatever children God provides to them, even if these children are born with serious genetic disabilities. They may also have prepared themselves for this possibility, knowing that the demands of parenting were going to be much more rigorous for them than other parents. If this is the case, then these parents are not open to any obvious moral criticism (see Andre et al, 2000). That is, they cannot be rightly accused of harming their future possible children.

More importantly, in a liberal pluralistic society the choices of such parents ought to be respected. This means both that social resources should be in place to support their efforts to care for their child, and that no social policy should legally require them to use PGD or to refrain from having children. This liberal commitment is, in fact, an important part of our justice argument, for one of the implications of society extending this sort of respect and support to these individuals is that these individuals should extend a similar degree of support and respect to those potential parents who would choose to avail themselves of PGD to avoid having a child with a serious genetic disorder. This would seem to be a reasonable, practical construal of what fair terms of cooperation might mean in these circumstances. In other words, social resources ought to be available to sustain the choices of couples who would either use or refuse PGD. We emphasize that this is not a choice that emerges from political bargaining; rather, it is a choice that emerges from a political society in which there is mutual respect for diverse, reasonable conceptions of what it means to lead a good life.

The above line of reasoning provides us with resources for responding to the objection raised in the community dialogues; namely, that access to PGD is about parental wishes and wants regarding possible children, not needs that would generate just claims. This same line of argument can be applied to the religious couple above. They choose to have children in the normal way, perhaps in keeping with their religious beliefs, the potential consequence being that children will be born with serious genetic disorders. Their religion might proscribe the use of artificial contraceptives, but few religions proscribe sexual abstinence. Hence, if they choose to engage in sexual relations, then they risk having children with serious health needs. In spite of the fact that these health needs came about because of their choice, few would deny that health care justice requires that the health needs of these children be met to the extent feasible. In the case of parents who would need to avail themselves of PGD in order to avoid having a child with a serious genetic disorder, there is a health need that is likely to be there if they are unable to access PGD. Their choice to have children is on a moral and political par with the choice of the religious couple. But for them, the health need is best addressed through a preventive choice rather than a therapeutic choice (which is not a real option); namely, the choice of a different embryo, a different future possible child. This analysis leaves open the question of whether social funding for PGD requires a comparable degree of social funding for infertile couples as a matter of social justice.

There is a somewhat more general justice argument that might be made in support of our proposal. Buchanan et al. (2000, pp. 81–82) suggest that, in the future, a just and caring society ought to do what is in its power to assure each child that is born a "genetic decent minimum." The context for that suggestion is a world in which we have the capacity to do germ line genetic engineering, including genetic enhancement. He rejects the idea of pursuing genetic equality. The general idea behind a genetic decent minimum is that every child ought to have the capacities to access the normal opportunity range of their society; and, to the extent that those capacities require a sufficiently intact genome, society is obligated to assure each child that intact genome to the extent its medical capacities permit. We do not have the capacity to do germ line genetic engineering, but we do have the capacity to create multiple embryos for couples at risk of having children with serious genetic disorders, and then allowing them to choose which of those embryos should have the opportunity to be born. We may not be able to give a perfectly precise account of what is or is not included in the genetic decent minimum, but we do not need that level of precision for our purposes. All of the genetic disorders we have identified (or implicitly have in mind) would clearly involve serious genetic deficiencies that would deprive the bearers of those genomes effective access to large portions of the opportunity range of our society with no compensating advantages. Hence, this would be another consideration of justice in support of our proposal.

There remains the morally troubling objection noted earlier, that it seems unjust that we fund access to PGD while permitting about 47 million individuals to remain uninsured (i.e., without secure access to needed health care). Surely, the argument goes, there are numerous health needs that go unmet there which ought to be awarded higher moral priority for health funding than PGD. For the sake of argument, we will accept that stipulation. However, it will not necessarily follow that justice would obligate us to meet those needs before funding the limited PGD program we propose. Here, empirical facts (whatever they might turn out to be) will be morally relevant, perhaps determinative. For example, we noted above that the approximate cost of funding access to PGD for 200,000 children would be $8 billion. We believe that these costs would be fully offset by the savings achieved from not providing to the children who will not be born very substantial health care and social support services. In fact, the likelihood is that those front-end costs would be more than offset. *If that is true*, then no social resources will have been taken away from the meeting of other health care needs. That is, no one will have been made worse off as a result of this transfer of resources; no one will find themselves denied health resources to which they had a stronger just claim. An outcome such as this might fall short of moral approval from the perspective of some "ideally just" health care system. But the world we inhabit is a world in which nonideal justice is the most we can reasonably expect to achieve, as we have argued elsewhere (Fleck, 1987). From that perspective, the outcome we portray here can be fairly characterized as being "just enough."

In concluding, we return to the point made earlier—namely, that providing public funding for limited access to PGD is justice-warranted for multiple reasons, but may not necessarily be justice-demanded. The practical moral challenge will be to determine, through a fair process of rational democratic deliberation, how high a moral priority such a program ought to be given, relative to all the other health needs that are part of our health care system. It is important to emphasize that even though our major conclusion is modest, it is not without moral force and significance. What this conclusion says is that for the relevant population of potential parents who may be at risk of having a child with a serious genetic disorder, they have a justice-warranted claim to access PGD at social expense. So a society would not be morally justified in treating the issue of such access as merely a matter of social beneficence, something that can be given or withheld as a matter of social charity without being open to moral criticism. Instead, if our conclusion is correct, a society would be morally justified in withholding socially funded access to PGD only if that society could show, given limited resources, that there was a considerable number of other higher priority health needs that justly commanded those resources. Moreover, it would not be sufficient simply to assert that there were these higher priority health needs; the reasons and arguments would have to be given in accordance with the publicity condition of health care justice (Daniels and Sabin, 1997; 1998a; Gutmann and Thompson, 1996).

A skeptic might be inclined to think that, in this sort of situation, reasons could never be given that were persuasive enough and forceful enough to compel most members of a society to accept some particular ordering of health care priorities.

We have already conceded that there will be many circumstances where that will be true, that this is connected to the fact that we cannot escape what Rawls refers to as the burdens of judgment, and that this is what motivates and justifies an appeal to fair democratic deliberative processes when we need a socially legitimated result. However, there are also many circumstances where it would be difficult to imagine the moral justifiability of a specific ordering of health care priorities. For example, if someone claimed that it was preferable from the perspective of health care justice that we fund as part of the Medicare program access to the left ventricular assist device for patients in end-stage congestive heart failure rather than funding access to the limited PGD program we have proposed, it would be exceedingly difficult to imagine what the justice-relevant considerations were that yielded this ordering of priorities. Each of those left ventricular assist devices has costs of about $200,000. There would be about 200,000 patients each year in the U.S. who would potentially need that device; that device would give them no more than an extra year or two of life at most. The annual aggregate cost of such a device could be $30 billion. It would seem that neither a utilitarian strand of health care justice, nor a strong egalitarian strand, nor a libertarian strand, nor a fair equality-of-opportunity strand, nor cost-effectiveness considerations would provide moral support for such an ordering of health priorities. The resources of public reason in this regard are much richer and internally strong than philosophic skeptics are inclined to recognize.

Finally, we need to address what Daniel Callahan (1990) refers to as the "ragged edge" problem with respect to our limited PGD program. In brief, it is that there is no bright line that sharply distinguishes why some individuals with a specific health need have a just claim to health care resources, while other individuals who have very nearly the same need are denied access to those resources. Earlier in this chapter, we pretended that there was some sort of sharp distinction between those later-in-life genetic disorders that children could be born with, and those genetic disorders that children would be born with that would manifest themselves from the very beginning of their lives. We suggested that there were considerations of justice that warranted funding the latter but not the former. The biological and medical realities are that there is a continuum in these matters—there are genetic disorders that will manifest themselves in the late part of the first decade of life, or the second decade, or the third decade. What would justify our denying potential parents access to PGD at public expense so that they, too, could choose to have different children not at risk for the disorders they fear? The short answer to this question, especially as we get closer to the first decade of life, is that there are no morally compelling considerations that unequivocally justify drawing the line in one place rather than another. The best we can do is seek to achieve democratic deliberative agreement about such matters, taking into account a very broad range of factors, including predicted cost data for a more expansive benefit, judgments about how much is gained in length or quality of life, medical alternatives on the horizon (such as gene therapy), competing health care needs, et cetera. The result we get will necessarily be nonideal, but it will be "just enough" and "rational enough," and it will have sufficient legitimacy that it ought to be respected by reasonable persons in a liberal, morally pluralistic society.

CONCLUDING COMMENTS: JUSTICE AND GENETIC ENHANCEMENT

In concluding this chapter, we can only mention in passing what is likely to be another major issue of health care justice related to genetics and reproductive decision-making—the issue of genetic enhancement. The concerns of some are that if such technology were available in a reproductive context, and if access to the technology were determined entirely by ability to pay, the result would be that the rich could use such a technology to enhance their children and create a permanent upper class—"entitled" to such status because of their superior merits and ability; a sort of genetic aristocracy (Annas, 2000; Fukuyama, 2002). This would obviously be a threat to a central element of our shared understanding of justice; namely, our commitment to protecting fair equality of opportunity. Others see the essential moral danger in an unwarranted tampering with human nature, especially if we see a broad range of behavioral traits as being the focus of enhancement efforts (President's Council on Bioethics, 2003).

However, we seem to have an equally strong commitment to respect for procreative liberty; it is unlikely that we could use the powers of government to intrude into the privacy rights or liberty rights of the rich with regard to their reproductive choices. One obvious alternative is to provide public funding to all to avail themselves of access to these genetic enhancement technologies. The enormous cost of such support would be very difficult to justify, especially if it created major distortions in our health care funding priorities; and there would be no obvious quick offsetting savings. The public interest justification for such a policy would be a very complex mix of benefits and risks. From an economic perspective, this looks like a wasteful "defensive expenditure" that merely adds to social costs for purposes of maintaining stability with regard to relative social advantage. Harris (1998) suggests the use of a lottery to distribute a right to genetic enhancements, though it is difficult to imagine in practice how such regulatory constraint would actually work without threatening the procreative liberties of potential parents.

The basic issues that need to be addressed would seem to be the following:

(1) How should we conceptualize what we will count as an "enhancement" (Juengst, 1998)? If we imagine having the capacity to bolster the effectiveness of the immune system through some sort of genetic manipulation of an eight-cell embryo, should that be regarded as an "enhancement" or as good "preventive care"? I think we are confident that numerous sorts of preventive care are appropriately thought of as matters of justice, but we are much less certain what the norms and criteria ought to be for regarding one or another enhancement as a suitable matter of justice.

(2) Should we follow Buchanan et al. (2000) in accepting as "just enough" a genetic decent minimum? And what exactly should be the criteria for judging what that decent minimum ought to look like, especially when we think about the enormous range of genetic choices that might be

possible? Or should stronger prioritarian norms of health care justice shape the allocations of genetic enhancements (Farrelly, 2002, 2004, 2005; Mehlman, 2000), meaning that those who were genetically "least well-off" would have to be the prime beneficiaries of these enhancement technologies? Again, there will be conceptual issues in getting sufficient clarity regarding who the genetically least well-off are. Or we could contend that only those genetic enhancements would be just enough that increased the ability of individuals to acquire Rawlsian primary goods (Allhoff, 2005).

(3) Others have argued that this discussion is much too premature (Lindsay, 2005), that there is too little concrete specificity regarding the genetic futures that are realistically possible, and consequently, it is theoretically impossible to formulate relevant or thoughtful norms for assessing those possibilities. Lindsay writes,

> But when the 'concrete' case is based largely on conjecture and is connected only tenuously to any recognizable social setting, it will do little to advance ethical understanding. In other words, one encounters a serious problem of indeterminacy when one extrapolates from considered judgments of justice that have been developed in, and designed to apply to, familiar settings. (p. 5)

Still, the recognition is that we are talking about germ line genetic interventions; consequently, the risks seem to be enormous. It is one thing to risk harm to an individual embryo (with the best of therapeutic intentions), but it seems to be quite another matter that those potential harms could also befall most of the descendants of that individual. These are all extraordinarily complex ethical and policy questions which will have to be the subject of a future treatise.

11

ORGAN TRANSPLANTATION
When is Enough Enough?

SCOPE OF THE ISSUE

In exploring the ethical issues associated with organ procurement we start with the recognition that: (1) organ transplantation represents a successful medical technology (nonexperimental, high probability of significant prolongation of life); but (2) it is an expensive technology (in a society obviously concerned about escalating health costs and a broad range of competing unmet health needs), and (3) there is a shortage of actually procured organs (relative to the pool of potentially procurable organs and need for these organs), which means that thousands of individuals die each year *who could have been saved if we had been more aggressive in procuring these organs.* This last phrase is suggestive of a certain moral urgency such that some might argue that failure to increase the supply of transplantable organs is morally blameworthy. But is this true? To what extent are we morally obligated as a society, or as health professionals in the transplant community, to maximize the supply of transplantable organs once we have reasonably successful transplant capacities? This is the fundamental moral question that will shape this chapter. Other questions of justice in organ transplantation that deserve our attention include retransplantation and multi-organ transplants. In both these cases, the perception is that individuals are getting "more than their fair share" of an absolutely scarce good. How should democratic deliberators think through that issue?

In the first part of this chapter we will tease out the implications of maximizing the supply of transplantable organs. While such efforts would in many cases likely result in saving more lives, which is a morally worthy goal of social policy or professional commitment, we shall nevertheless conclude that there are some morally compelling counter-considerations which would counsel against such efforts. Specifically, we shall argue that there are three other competing moral obligations which should be given moral priority with respect to transplant policy; they are: obligations of justice with respect to access to needed health care in a resource-constrained system, obligations to protect public trust (which is absolutely essential to sustaining the current altruistically-based approach to organ procurement), and obligations to protect the best interests of patients who are potential organ donors. This last obligation may be a bit obscure if we imagine that most transplantable organs will come from individuals who have been declared dead on the basis of neurological criteria. However, the University of Pittsburgh has promulgated a protocol for the use of non-heart-beating cadavers as organ donors (University of Pittsburgh, 1992). As we shall see, this protocol does represent a potential threat to the interests of patients not yet dead.

In the second part of this chapter we will address the issue of using financial incentives to increase the supply of transplantable organs. Such incentives are seen by many as a threat to the altruistic aspects of organ donation, while proponents see them as a way of enhancing the voluntaristic aspects, saving lives, and respecting individual liberty in these matters. We shall argue that there is nothing *intrinsically* morally objectionable about the use of such incentives, but that on balance there are competing moral considerations that would usually speak against the use of such incentives to increase organ procurement.

In the third part of this chapter we shall address the question of whether all of us are morally obligated to be organ donors (should we end up by chance in the medically relevant circumstances), the argument being that the vast majority of us probably would hope to have our lives saved by organ transplantation (were we to have the relevant medical need). If this line of argument were to prove morally sound, then this would undercut the strong altruistic conception we have of organ donation. Still, what would be left unanswered would be the question of whether, in a liberal democratic society, such an argument provided adequate grounds for a social policy of presumed consent. From a moral and political point of view, such a policy undercuts voluntarism. The ultimate question is whether loss of the value of voluntarism is worth it, morally speaking, if a policy of presumed consent increased the number of transplantable organs (and lives saved).

In the fourth part of this chapter we address the justice questions raised by the need for either multi-organ transplants or retransplantation. Given the very large organ shortage and the thousands of people who die each year awaiting a transplant, the obvious question is how can anyone have a just claim to either multiple organs or retransplantation when the cost of that will be the death of someone else on the transplant list.

THE MAXIMIZATION ARGUMENT: A CRITICAL MORAL ANALYSIS

The question of whether our society is morally obligated (as a matter of justice) to maximize the supply of transplantable organs is substantially more complex, more conceptually and morally "elastic" than may at first appear. As we shall see below, it is very difficult to come up with even very crude judgments of what the level of unmet need for transplantable organs is. What would seem to be an empirically determinable statistic is in fact deeply dependent upon complex moral norms and societal commitment to developing new transplant modalities, such as artificial organs or xenografts.

There is also considerable moral and conceptual elasticity with respect to our conceptions of death and voluntariness. If these concepts had very firm and very sharp edges, that would establish very fixed limits with respect to legitimate opportunities for procuring transplantable organs. The so-called "dead donor rule," for example, is seen as a moral absolute (Arnold and Youngner, 1993)—transplant surgeons may not harvest organs in such a way as to cause the death of the donor. Donors of hearts and livers and lungs must already be dead. But the criteria for determining what counts as "being dead" are obviously open to adjustment and interpretation, which is what happened in 1968 with the introduction of neurological criteria for determining death (Ad Hoc Committee of the Harvard Medical School, 1968). Clearly, the current level of transplantation surgery would not be possible without those criteria, which now have the force of law behind them as well as broad public support. More recently, there have been proposals for neocortical criteria of death, what is sometimes called "higher brain" death as opposed to "whole brain" death (Veatch, 1993). And there is the Pittsburgh protocol for non-heart-beating cadavers. Both proposals have the potential for expanding substantially the pool of transplantable organs, but both proposals also have substantial potential for increasing public distrust in the whole transplant enterprise. Certainly it may appear to the public that the criteria of death are being manipulated in order to advance the professional interests of transplant surgeons. Still, such criteriological adjustment might be morally justified if in fact there is a moral obligation to maximize the supply of transplantable organs.

As for public distrust, that can be assuaged by reemphasizing the *voluntary* character of organ donation. Individuals themselves, or their surrogates, must consent to donating organs, no matter what criteria of death might be operative. Transplant surgeons cannot simply take organs because of the good they would hope to accomplish. However, a number of advocates in the transplant community are pushing for the adoption of "presumed consent" policies, with the right of individuals to "opt out" (Caplan, 1983; Cohen, 1992). The basic argument is that numerous public surveys indicate a level of willingness to donate that is many times greater than the actual number of individuals who sign donor cards or the back of their driver's license. For now, we can avoid the intricacies of this argument—our point is that the concept of voluntariness has clearly been stretched by this line of argument. Presumed consent is less voluntary than *actual* informed consent, but more voluntary than manipulated consent. Maybe such stretching is morally warranted because it will expand the "donor" pool. No doubt that is, generally speaking, a good thing to do. But are we, as a society or as transplant professionals, *morally obligated* to do that? Would we be guilty of a serious moral wrong if we failed to embrace a policy of presumed consent?

On the face of it, maximizing the supply of transplantable organs seems like a morally good social policy (Robertson, 1993). Some will put the matter more strongly and argue that we have a "collective responsibility for maximizing lifesaving organ recovery" (Peters, 1991). But our discussion so far suggests that there are conflicting moral considerations that would warrant conflicting moral recommendations on this matter. If we probe a little further, we will discover yet more tangled moral thickets. We start with considerations of justice—the fair distribution of limited resources for meeting virtually unlimited health needs—which first speak against the maximization obligation. Some rough statistics will add several other moral dimensions to our problem.

In 2007, 20,211 organs were procured for transplant from cadaveric donors; another 5,816 were procured from living donors. There were 6,411 individuals who died on transplant lists waiting for a transplant. About 7,412 individuals were the source of those cadaveric organs, while another 5,667 served as living donors. There may be an additional 7,000 individuals who could have served as cadaveric organ donors, but did not for numerous reasons. At the end of 2007, there were 98,061 (Organ Procurement and Transplant Network, 2008) individuals on transplant waiting lists, while at the end of 1994 that number was only 37,609. These statistics should give the reader a good sense of the official growth in demand, as well as a sense of the gap between supply and demand. Some will see this gap as being modest; they have the belief that incremental efforts with current policies and practices ought to be able to close that gap entirely. Horton and Horton (1993), for example, have suggested that there are major misconceptions and information deficits in the public at large that greatly decrease the likelihood of successful organ procurement. In their survey, 82% of the adults did not know how to obtain an organ donation card; more than 45% did not know that almost all Western religions support organ donation; hospital literature on organ donation is written at the eleventh-grade level, which makes it inaccessible to many; half the respondents believed that the same physician could be responsible for providing medical care to both the organ donor and organ recipient, which could certainly be cause for distrust; and so on. If all this is true, the moral problems alluded to so far would dissolve, or at least diminish very substantially. That, however, would be a hasty conclusion.

Measuring the "true level" of need for transplantable solid organs is itself a substantial ethical problem. There are about 60,000 individuals in the U.S. (2007) with end-stage liver disease; the vast majority of them would gain at least one extra year of life if they had access to a liver transplant. But in fact, only about 6,050 liver transplants were done in 2007, and about 2000 individuals died on a list awaiting a liver transplant (out of about 18,000 individuals on that list). The criteria for getting on the list are quite stringent. Many physicians (and society at large) might like to believe that the criteria are purely medical, and hence, very objective. But the debates about whether alcoholics should be eligible for liver transplants and how long they must be alcohol-free (one year, usually) suggest that social and ethical value judgments shape much of this decision-making (Cohen and Benjamin, 1991; Moss and Siegler, 1991). Again, as we noted in Chapter 9, Dr. Starzl (1992) shocked the transplant world when he did a liver transplant on a vigorous 76-year-old woman.

Many critics would argue that that liver taken by Starzl should have gone to a younger individual who had a higher probability of gaining more high-quality life-years. Certainly that seems like a reasonable ethical judgment, which I would endorse. However, our concern at the moment is whether this woman's name should have been excluded from the transplant list for some compelling medical or ethical reason *when our objective is simply to establish the level of medical need for liver transplants.* There is no obvious reason for that exclusion. Similarly (and more troublingly), thousands of individuals each year will be denied inclusion on the transplant list because they have no ability to pay for the transplant. Finally, it should be noted that the potential demand for heart transplants is many times greater than anyone would care to acknowledge. In 2007 we did 2337 heart transplants, but there were 350,000 individuals who could have been candidates for the procedure (from the roughly 725,000 individuals who died of heart disease that year). And there are more 400,000 patients on dialysis (2007) who, in theory, would be candidates for a kidney transplant.

From a psychological perspective, it is understandable why the gap between supply and legitimate demand (the list) for transplant organs would be kept modest. It would be socially and professionally disheartening to have tens of thousands (or hundreds of thousands) of individuals dying in a very visible way that suggested society should have been doing more to expand the supply of transplantable organs. It is easier to maintain the social illusion that these deaths are wholly "natural" when these individual names are not on a transplant list.[1] Further, it would be cruel (at the level of individual patients) to include them on a list where there was no reasonable hope they would receive a transplant because priority criteria would have put them so far down. However, for our purposes, in answering the question of whether we are socially obligated to maximize the supply of transplantable organs, moral honesty requires we acknowledge this substantially greater level of need. What, then, are the moral consequences of this recognition?

One obvious consequence is that merely increasing the level of effort or efficiency of current policies will fall very far short of meeting the need for transplantable organs. More public education, more religious motivation, more efficient and aggressive required request will not make a substantial enough difference. Even if organs were procured from all 12,000 individuals who are potential dead donors (by current criteria), that would only address a small fraction of the need. But if we really did accomplish *that much*, would we not have realistically maximized the supply of transplantable organs? Would we not have satisfied our moral obligation (if, in fact, it is an obligation)? No. There are additional options, though these options are morally problematic. There are two which we should briefly identify and analyze: (1) completing the development of artificial organs, and (2) expanding operational criteria for the determination of death.

Are we morally obligated to develop artificial organs? Our first option for maximizing the supply of transplantable organs would be completion of the development of artificial organs: artificial livers and hearts. We may be very close to having a working model of an artificial liver (Mashberg, 2006; University of Chicago, 1999), and the artificial heart is now moving into expanded clinical trials. The artificial liver would be based on the dialysis model (though some research is being done on an implantable version [Roush, 2007]), but the artificial heart would be totally implanted. The moral virtue and the moral vice of these devices is that they could be produced in limitless quantities; this would mean that potentially hundreds of thousands of patients per year could be spared death and given extra years of life. The moral agony of prioritizing patients on a transplant list, thereby deciding who lived and who died, would be a thing of the past. But the morally vicious side of this possibility is the potential for serious injustices; that is, drawing huge amounts of money away from what should be higher priority, ethically more compelling health needs. We already called attention to this problem in considerable detail in Chapters 6 and 9.

As for the artificial liver, the current uses being tested are as a "bridge to transplant." This raises a number of other justice questions at both the macro- and micro-levels. When this device is used in this bridging function, it is sustaining the life of a person who otherwise would have died—their death would mean that someone else on the transplant list would move up and be available for the next matching organ. But if the person ahead of them gets that liver, then they might be the one who died who should have been saved. As things are now, the transplant list has something of the virtue of a lottery (as far as justice is concerned). Some number of random events (good match, geographic distance, degree of urgency) determines who gets that next liver. Introducing the artificial liver as a bridge adds a human intervention that corrupts the fairness of a modified lottery. At the macro-level, the artificial liver as a bridge to transplant adds to the overall cost of the transplant without saving any additional lives. That, too, may be rightly criticized from the perspective of health care justice.

The left ventricular assist device (LVAD) was also introduced as a "bridge to transplant." It was open to the same moral criticisms as the artificial liver used in this way: it adds to social costs and does nothing to save additional lives. It does shift the burden of dying to someone else a little further down on the transplant list. When that death occurs, it will appear to be natural and unfortunate; but a good case can be made for saying it is an injustice—both to the individual who died and to society at large, which has wasted health resources for no net gain. What motivates such irrational and morally problematic behavior is that we are gaining in fact some additional weeks of life for some individuals, though at very great expense. This same logic is what threatens to drive us to provide artificial hearts to individuals who may gain no more than an extra year of life.

Most recently, the LVAD is being used independently as a device to prolong life rather than as a bridge to transplant. Dr. Oz, a transplant surgeon at Columbia–Presbyterian Medical Center in New York, is quoted as saying that older patients with failing hearts ought to get the LVAD so that heart transplants can be reserved for relatively younger patients. The assumption is that the LVAD will improve both quality of life and length of life for these older patients, maybe two extra years, but certainly not for as long as a heart transplant. The first year cost of implanting this device is still estimated at $200,000 per case, and there is the potential for doing 200,000 of these procedures per year if the financing is there to cover these costs. In the face of congressional demands for $270 billion in cost savings from Medicare over the next seven years, this represents a very difficult moral and political problem.

The conclusion of our first line of argument is that commitment to strong maximization of the supply of transplantable organs through the development of artificial organs will lead to serious injustices. The counterargument will be that tens of thousands of lives will be lost that could have been saved, to which we respond that this is a moral dodge. No doubt, saving lives that we have the emerging technological capacity to save is a morally good thing to do. But when we have only limited resources to meet virtually unlimited health needs, including virtually unlimited needs for life-saving/life-prolonging medical interventions, then it is far from obvious that either considerations of justice or economics would give highest priority to saving/prolonging lives through the development/dissemination of artificial organs.

THE PITTSBURGH PROTOCOL: HOW DEAD MUST DONORS BE?

We next need to consider what I will label a "weak" commitment to maximizing transplantable organs. What I have in mind by a weak commitment is that we would do all in our power (professionally and as a society) to increase the supply of transplantable organs up to some arbitrarily defined limit, such as covering all whose names show up on a transplant list. This is where the Pittsburgh protocol has relevance. According to some analysts, a nationalization of this protocol could increase transplantable organs by 20–25% (Arnold and Youngner, 1993). Our question is this: Would we, professionally or socially, be morally culpable for failing to endorse nationally such a protocol, especially if, for example, 3,000 additional lives might be saved each year? I shall argue, all things considered, this would not be a morally culpable failure. A related moral issue (decidedly weaker in import) is whether centers like Pittsburgh should be permitted to try experimentally such a protocol, assuming certain moral safeguards have been incorporated into the protocol. Given the actual content of the protocol, it is probably safe enough to permit such an experiment.[2]

The Pittsburgh protocol is intended to apply to patients who are very near to death, on life support, who themselves (or their surrogates) request removal of life support, and then request that viable organs be removed after death has been determined by cardiac criteria. There were four requests of this sort from 1989–91 at Pittsburgh that precipitated the formulation of the protocol itself (DeVita and Snyder, 1993). No doubt what motivated these requests was the hope of obtaining some good from what were otherwise tragic circumstances. Still, some staff members associated with these requests were morally troubled by what they were being asked to do. Perhaps most troubling was that these patients would be taken to the OR for the removal of life support, the place where the most aggressive efforts were made to save lives.

Several principles were incorporated into the protocol itself to minimize these moral concerns. First, the decision to withdraw life support had to made prior to and independent of any discussion of organ donation. Second, such patients, who had chosen "comfort measures only," could be considered for organ donation only if they or their surrogates had *initiated* discussion of organ donation. Third, the process of removing life support had to "be done primarily to promote patient comfort and respect patient autonomy" (University of Pittsburg, 1993); interest in procuring organs was not to interfere with optimal patient management. Fourth, medications were to be used *only* for patient comfort, not to hasten death or to preserve more usable organs. Fifth, the attending physician responsible for patient management was to have no professional or financial connections to the transplantation team. Sixth, no organs could be procured until death had been certified. Death would be certified if the patient was pulseless, unresponsive to verbal stimuli, and experienced two minutes of ventricular fibrillation or electrical asystole or electromechanical dissociation.

Though the above principles spell out fairly stringent criteria for preventing moral problems in procuring organs from non-heart-beating cadaver donors, there remain noteworthy concerns that may not be satisfactorily addressed. First, as already suggested, there is the issue of the dead donor rule—patients must already be dead before their organs can be harvested. This means, among other things, that the state of being dead must be irreversible. But Lynn (1993) points out that we do not really *know* (in the strong sense) that a patient is irreversibly dead after only two minutes, as described by the Pittsburgh protocol; there simply have been no clinical experiments to establish this fact beyond reasonable doubt. One might respond, as Tomlinson (1993) does, that from a moral point of view nothing of significance hangs on this fact, since the patient (or their surrogate) has freely said that they would not want to be resuscitated. But Tomlinson goes on to point out that there is still an important conceptual point; namely, that two minutes of pulselessness is not the conceptual equivalent of "whole-brain death." Rather, this represents an expansion or loosening of the criteria of death. There is really a blurring of the distinction between death and near death. This is not a small point, since considerable philosophic effort went into establishing the equivalence of death as determined by traditional criteria and by neurological criteria. In part, this was necessary to build public trust that care of the dying would not be compromised by organ retrieval objectives. That trust, however, is clearly threatened by blurring the distinction between death and near death.

A second objection to the Pittsburgh protocol is the "divided loyalties" objection. The protocol itself establishes absolutely clear distinctions between clinical staff charged with the care of dying patients, and clinical staff responsible for procuring organs and transplantation. It would seem there should be no concern about conflicts of interest. However, Shaw (1993) contends that, in actual practice, such sharp distinctions may be psychologically impossible. He asks whether the loyalties of staff "may be contaminated by the slightest glimmer of sympathy for the plight of patients in need of high-quality donor organs." After all, the clinical reality is that the patients they are caring for have hopeless prognoses, while the patients awaiting organ transplants are hopeful and desperately want to live. Further, once a patient (or surrogate) has chosen withdrawal of life-sustaining care and organ donation, they are taken to the OR where the actual withdrawal of life-sustaining care will take place. In that environment, there is a very unstable and awkward mixing of clinical objectives and personnel as some individuals are charged with managing the process of dying while others are charged with preparing the body for rapid and efficient organ preservation and retrieval. More specifically, the patient is supposed to be kept as comfortable as possible, while at the same time great care is taken not to give excessive doses of any medications so that it appears death was caused by those drugs; and at the same, time the process of dying must not be drawn out to such a length that the quality of the organs to be procured might be compromised. In such a setting there is enormous potential for massive moral self-deception. Weisbard observes that the Pittsburgh protocol:

> seeks to re-characterize a coherent, carefully worked out chain of events, leading inexorably to a foreseen, desired and planned result—death and utilization of organs for transplant—as a series of isolated links, each to be understood solely as directed to the patient's needs of the moment, each entirely disconnected from all surrounding context, including the very purpose of the exercise. (1993)

Another concern with the Pittsburgh protocol is its relation to "required request." The goal of required request laws is to increase the supply of transplantable organs, as is the goal of the Pittsburgh protocol. At that level they seem compatible. However, according to the protocol the request to donate organs must be "initiated" by the patient (or surrogate), which would speak against required request. This is to make sure that the decision to withdraw life-sustaining care is not contaminated by the hope of procuring organs. Apparently, patients (or their surrogates) initiated such a request in the four cases that precipitated the idea of the Pittsburgh protocol. It would be easy enough to simply make an exception to the required request laws in these circumstances, but the likely result is that the Pittsburgh protocol might have rare applicability in practice, which would defeat its intent. The alternative is to provide suitable patients (or their surrogates) who have decided to withdraw life-sustaining care with an organ donation brochure aimed at educating and encouraging them to initiate a donation. Such a procedure is not obviously immoral (manipulative or coercive), but this is an expanded sense of what will count as a "patient-initiated" request.

What should we conclude from our assessment of the Pittsburgh protocol? A generous reading would say that the protocol attempts to push further out the boundaries of what is morally permissible. This is not necessarily a bad or dangerous thing to do, especially in the face of changing social and technological circumstances. Fost (1983), for one, believes that the dead donor rule itself is the problem, and that the rule ought to be replaced by a broader moral commitment to "violate no patient interest." A case can certainly be made that the Pittsburgh protocol would be true to this commitment. Further, the goal of the protocol itself is the morally worthy goal of saving lives through organ transplantation that would otherwise be prematurely lost. However, Caplan (1993) reminds us that that goal is not as morally pure and untainted by institutional and professional self-interest as we might like to believe.

As more transplant surgeons have been trained and more transplant programs opened, there is increasing pressure for organs. Manufacturers of immunosuppressive drugs see this as a lucrative market; hospital boards see such programs as lucrative and prestigious. As long as such pressures are addressed within the framework of current public policy, there may be little cause for moral or political concern. But, as Caplan notes, when changes in public policy are proposed, then the perception of motives will play a crucial role in the public's willingness to accept those changes. Expanding the donor pool by, for example, giving up the dead donor rule, may appear to the public "unseemly, ghoulish, or even immoral if other factors such as professional self-interest, competition, and profit are at work but are swept under the rug" (Caplan, 1993). Robertson (1993) will make a similar point. If the public comes to believe that they might be subject to abuse or exploitation in order to advance the goals of transplant programs, then there will be a substantial loss of trust and, ultimately, a net reduction in organ donations. This is essentially why family consent is sought for organ donation, even when an individual has a signed donor card (which would be legally and morally sufficient for donation).

The troubling consequences we have identified in connection with the Pittsburgh protocol are speculative, but not at all improbable. As such, they are not sufficient to justify moral condemnation of the protocol. Further, so long as the protocol itself is not intrinsically morally flawed, an experiment with the protocol may be permitted at a very small number of transplant centers; more than that would be imprudent. *This is a morally reasonable compromise because there is, in fact, no moral obligation to maximize, or even increase substantially the supply of transplantable organs, if the moral cost of so doing would involve violations of justice in determining which lives to save through medical innovations, or significant threats to public trust or professional integrity in this enterprise.*

ORGAN PROCUREMENT AND FINANCIAL INCENTIVES: A CRITICAL ASSESSMENT

The moral language that has characterized transplantation discussions is the language of altruism or charity—things that are freely given. While it is widely agreed among moral philosophers that there are *obligations* of charity, it is also agreed that these are minimal, nonspecific obligations. Thus, we can pitch all the Christmas solicitations we receive for donations, and not be open to moral censure. But if we are the proverbial lone walker on the beach and see someone drowning a hundred yards from shore and we are excellent at swimming, then we are morally obligated to make that rescue attempt. Failure to do so is clearly just grounds for moral censure. The moral argument is that life itself is at stake, and the cost to me of saving that life is relatively minor.

The comparable moral argument with respect to organ procurement is that thousands of lives are needlessly lost because we rely entirely on a *voluntary charitable* response for procuring transplantable organs. Granted, that respect for individual freedom and an altruistic response are very important moral values; they are not so important that they cannot be overridden or compromised in order to achieve our lifesaving goals. After all, the organs have no value at all to someone who is already dead; hence, it is not as if society is requiring heroic sacrifice of anyone to save these additional lives. Blumstein (1989), for one, concludes, "The organ transplantation enterprise has indulged in an excess of romanticism, mandating altruism and communitarianism possibly at the expense of saving lives." This is clearly a harsh criticism, ultimately unwarranted in my judgment. Still, we need to show that it is unwarranted by rational argument and analysis, as opposed to uncritical dismissal.

We need to note that there are really two morally relevant dimensions to the charitable response: altruism and voluntariness. Blumstein is only asking that the altruistic element be compromised. Specifically, what he advocates is that financial incentives and other market mechanisms be used to enhance the supply of transplantable organs. The virtue of this approach, from Blumstein's perspective, is that voluntariness is preserved. That is, no one is morally or legally obligated to make their organs available, because financial incentives can simply be increased until they elicit the supply of organs to match the need. However, the medical and policy communities (and public opinion) have very strongly resisted this proposal.

As things are now, economic incentives for organ donation are illegal. In addition, for many there are strong moral considerations that would speak against such a proposal (Childress, 1989). Two of the more powerful of these considerations would be: (1) the commodification of the human body (i.e., selling something that intrinsically ought not be for sale, such as babies), and (2) the potential for coercive economic incentives that undercut the claim that markets are inherently protective of individual freedom. The very specific concern on this latter point is that the poor, desperately in need of money for basic life needs, will be motivated to sell one of their kidneys, thereby exposing themselves to all the risk that that entails.

A quick preliminary response to both these concerns will help to advance the argument. To the latter concern it can be fairly argued that the actual risk associated with selling one's kidney is relatively small. (This may be a debatable point, but it would seem the risk must be reasonable enough, given our encouragement of the practice of using living-related donors for kidney transplantation.) That is, a liberal society allows individuals to take much greater risks for much more trivial reasons, such as skiing remote mountains by jumping out of a helicopter. If a poor individual wants to sell a kidney to raise capital to start a business, the argument goes, a free society should allow them that choice. As for the commodification argument, this concern seems to be rooted in a religious or philosophic vision that a liberal society ought to respect, but ought not make the basis for public policy because that would violate the "neutrality constraint," which many see as an essential feature of democratic liberalism. Certainly we ought not permit baby-selling, but that is because babies are persons, and selling them would be violative of both their rights and well-being. By way of contrast, arranging for the future sale of one's cadaveric organs for transplantation purposes (should one end up in the medically relevant circumstances), or the cadaveric organs of one's relative (who has not specifically objected while alive), does not obviously violate the rights or the welfare of the possessor of those organs. In fact, what Blumstein (1992) sees as one of the great moral deficiencies of our current altruistic practices is that relatives can override the freely expressed choice of an individual to donate (who has signed a donor card), thereby violating that individual's liberty and welfare rights, not to mention contributing to the death of individuals who would have survived if they had had access to those organs.

Blumstein, as a libertarian, is a strong advocate of the use of financial incentives to increase the supply of transplantable organs. He is very critical of federal policy in this matter, which would regard donated organs as a "national resource," a "scarce public resource," whose distribution would be governed "by criteria based on need, effectiveness, and fairness that are publicly stated and publicly defended" (1992). Blumstein's view is that organs are fundamentally a private resource which individuals (or their surrogates) should be free to dispose of as they please. Many individuals might be motivated by altruism to donate their organs, but others might be motivated to provide their organs for transplantation only with financial incentives. For Blumstein, there is no compelling reason why organs can be transferred only one way—through giving. But there is a compelling reason for permitting financial incentives—saving more lives with more organs.

Blumstein takes note of the fact that critics of markets put transplantable organs in a morally distinct category, distinct at least from the general run of consumer goods. These critics argue that these organs should be distributed in accord with medical criteria, not financial considerations. Blumstein agrees regarding the relevance of medical criteria, but adds that his critics fail to attend to the fact that medical care in general in our society is distributed in accord with ability to pay, including other life-saving medical technologies. Still, if there is broad societal concern about wealth-based inequalities in access to life-sustaining medical care, then he believes two adjustments can be made with respect to organ transplants. First, we can separate the supply and demand sides of the market, and permit market incentives to operate only on the supply side. Second, we can provide public subsidies for those whose inadequate wealth denies them access to transplantable organs. The specific proposal Blumstein endorses is a forward contract, such as proposed by Schwindt and Vining (1986). The general idea is that individuals would be offered a sum of money by a broker (maybe an insurance company) for the right to use one's organs for transplantation, should the relevant medical circumstances occur. This would be a contract which a competent individual would have executed, which could not be negated by relatives at the time of donation—a definite moral advantage, according to Blumstein.

Given Blumstein's analysis, why should we not immediately introduce market incentives to increase the organ supply? There are several critical arguments that undercut his analysis. First, there is a morally defensible sense in which organs ought to be regarded as a public resource. We concede that it would be wrong for government simply to seize cadaveric organs for transplantation. Individuals or their surrogates must consent, or at least not opt out of, a specific scheme for procuring organs, as required by respect for individual autonomy. But then we need to realize that huge public investments are what made organ transplantation possible, both with respect to research and the training of necessary personnel; those organs would have no value at all without that investment. It would be unjust to exploit this public investment for personal profit.

In fairness to Blumstein, we must acknowledge that he does not advocate wholly unregulated markets for cadaveric organs. Still, the ultimate norm for him in assessing his proposal would be success in increasing the supply of transplantable organs. This is largely an empirical question that cannot be answered by speculative argument alone. However, there are some empirical facts that would seem to speak against feasibility in this case. How do we imagine this forward contract working? If a broker offers an individual an incentive of, say, $1,000 for the future right to procure his organs for transplantation, then literally millions or tens of millions of individuals would have to take this deal in order to create a large enough pool of potential organ donors (since the vast majority of individuals will never be in the relevant circumstances to be donors). From an economic point of view, this would be a very risky and inefficient way to obtain these organs since it would be a scattershot approach. Further, whoever the brokers would be, they would have to recoup their investment plus a reasonable rate of return, which would add very substantially to the total cost of transplantation—if this were to happen, this would have an even greater exclusionary effect on those who were uninsured, underinsured, or otherwise financially unable to cover the costs of transplants. On the face of it, this appears unjust. Blumstein is willing to entertain the idea of government subsidies to the poor and uninsured as a way of correcting such injustices. However, such subsidies would really be paid by the middle class in the form of higher taxes or insurance premiums. The political perception by the middle class would be that they were subsidizing the poor so that the poor could compete for life-saving transplants, which the middle class had already paid for once; this would undermine the stability of such a system. The virtue of the present system, where donated organs are considered a public resource, is that this sort of political perception is unlikely to be generated.

We also need to note that Blumstein's decoupling of the supply and demand sides of the market may be less possible in practice than in theory. Again, the brokers in a future market would have made a very substantial up-front investment. Their willingness to take that risk would be greatly diminished if there were social controls on opportunity to profit. Their best opportunity to profit would be to hold a sort of auction for these organs among individuals who were reasonably well-matched (medically) for the organs and somewhere on the waiting list. This would clearly not be received well by Americans of average economic means. Again, a virtue of our current system is that organs are treated as a public resource to be distributed in accord with medical need/medical effectiveness criteria, not criteria linked to socioeconomic status. This may not give everyone a reason for wanting to be an organ donor, but at least it avoids giving anyone a reason for not wanting to donate.

In conclusion, Blumstein's proposal is open to serious criticism on grounds of feasibility, fairness, and efficiency. Will this be true with all financial incentives that might be used to increase the supply of transplantable organs? Some types of incentives might be morally unobjectionable. There is the notion of "rewarded gifting" (Daar, 1992). If we can get beyond the linguistic oddity of the phrase, we will see a morally plausible proposal. The general idea is that a relatively modest fixed sum ($1,000–$5,000) for funeral expenses would be paid a family for donating the organs of a loved one. In order to avoid wronging the dead donor, the assumption would have to be that that individual either had a signed donor card, or at least had not objected to organ donation. To determine fairly whether this person had serious objections, we would have to have a simple and feasible public mechanism for registering that objection, such as an alternate box on a driver's license. Another alternative, recently endorsed by the AMA and others, would be mandated choice (Council on Ethical and Judicial Affairs, 1994; Murray and Younger, 1994). This would involve a state requirement that individuals express a choice with respect to their willingness to donate organs. The expression of that choice would be repeated at regular intervals by using income tax forms or drivers' licenses. This is a compromise of voluntariness in its clearest sense, but it seems to be a very slight compromise. Both of these approaches might increase the supply of transplantable organs without violating rights, undermining trust, seriously compromising the altruistic aspects of donation, or adding substantially to the cost of transplantation. The results would likely be modest, but the argument of this chapter has been that this should not be cause for moral regret since we do not have a strong moral obligation to maximize the supply of transplantable organs.

PRESUMED CONSENT/DUTY TO DONATE: CRITICAL REMARKS

We turn now to two morally grounded strategies for increasing the supply of transplantable organs. These are commonly referred to as "presumed consent" and "duty to donate" strategies. Both strategies have been proposed in response to what are judged the inadequacies of pure voluntarism (consent explicitly given) in organ donation. Pure voluntarism, the argument goes, may be morally ideal, but it is failing to generate organs needed to save lives. A modified voluntarism may be less than ideal, but it is still respectful of individual autonomy, and may result in saving more lives.

Cohen (1992) is one strong advocate of presumed consent. He starts with the empirical fact that a significant majority of Americans indicate to survey researchers that they are willing to donate their organs at the time of death. But only a small fraction of Americans authoritatively express that preference by marking the back of their driver's license. What seems to get in the way of so marking our licenses are vague fears and anxieties that most of us are vulnerable to, if we need to think about our own death. If this true, then it is really the nonrational aspects of our selves that are interfering with effecting the real choice that our rational autonomous self would otherwise make. Morally speaking, it is only this latter self that commands respect. If this is true, then to presume consent for organ donation from the newly dead will have two morally commendable features: (1) it will maximize benefits for all concerned, since if we would hope to have our lives saved by organ transplant we must also hope individuals will overcome their irrational reluctance to donate; and (2) it will best protect the autonomy of decedents, since this is what they really wanted to do anyway. Further, the system we have now is, in practice, actually less respectful of the autonomous choices of now dead individuals because family members can refuse to approve organ donation when that individual has given explicit consent, or when a reasonable presumption might be made that that individual would have been disposed to donate.

An obvious objection to presumed consent is that some individuals will have their organs taken who, in fact, had strong objections; this is clearly violative of their autonomy. To address this, Cohen and other proponents of presumed consent offer easy "opting out"—individuals remain free to choose not to donate for any reason at all, or no reason at all. But the burden of conveying that objection would be with them, though fairness would require that expressing this objection be as simple and accessible as checking a box on the back of one's driver's license. A second objection considered by Cohen is that the spirit of voluntarism is undermined by presumed consent. A reasonable response is that when relatively few individuals give explicit consent ahead of time, then a presumption will have to be made one way or the other. Cohen's suggestion is that the presumption should favor what the majority would have done, if their anxieties had not gotten in the way of carrying out that choice. An alternative, as already noted, is mandated choice. The virtue there is that individuals themselves have made a choice, as opposed to presuming what they likely would have chosen.

Menzel (1992c) takes a stronger position in that he wants to defend a duty to donate—he clearly rejects the idea that altruism should be thought of as a moral root of organ donation. His basic contention is that organ donation is a duty of easy rescue, not a matter of charity. For Menzel, three conditions must be met for something to be a moral duty: (1) The behavior must involve great harm or significant benefit for someone else; (2) The behavior must not be too difficult to carry out (i.e., behavior only saints or heroes are capable of); and (3) There must be a special relationship with the person to whom we owe the duty. The first two conditions would seem to be easily met by organ donation. The third condition may be a little obscure because it will usually be strangers who are the recipients of donated cadaveric organs. But Menzel contends that this is an "easy rescue" situation in which "we confront an implicit, mutual, rationally self-interested, contractual relationship among human beings." All would agree, for example, that any of us are morally obligated to utter a word of warning to a blind person about to step into traffic. We can easily imagine that if we were blind, we would expect that from anyone in our vicinity because this is something required by basic human decency. Donating organs at the time of our death represents a comparable matter of easy rescue, which we all expect from one another.

Up to this point Menzel has a compelling argument, but then he adds a morally and conceptually odd qualifier. Like Cohen, he permits opting out if "we seriously object." This sounds like the sort of exception we justifiably grant to conscientious objectors to military service. Many Orthodox Jews object on religious grounds to organ donation; their objections should certainly be respected. But Menzel follows Cohen in permitting individuals to opt out for any reason, or no reason. This is morally incoherent. If, in fact, organ donation is a duty of easy rescue, then that duty can be justifiably overridden only if there are equally weighty, competing moral considerations which would justify or excuse our fulfilling that duty. Thus, if it was morally indefensible to fail to warn the blind person because "I just didn't feel like it," then the same statement with regard to donating my organs would be equally indefensible.

A second objection that needs to be considered with respect to both presumed consent and duty to donate arguments is that there is an assumption of mutual obligation and mutual likelihood of benefit, were any of us to find ourselves in the relevant circumstances as organ donors or recipients. This assumption may not fit the real world. If individuals who are poor or uninsured or underinsured have only a small chance, proportionately speaking, of being organ recipients, that takes away much of the moral force of Cohen's and Menzel's arguments. Then it can be justifiably argued that these moral arguments provide only a moral veneer for what is substantially exploitative. If this is correct, then the morally safer course is to rely exclusively on pure altruism and pure voluntarism, at least for purposes of securing organs from individuals who would never have a reasonable hope of receiving a life-saving organ transplant. All of this assumes our present system for health care financing. If we were able to put in place some form of single-payer national health insurance, then those who were financially less well-off would have equal access to organ transplantation (assuming other social factors did not create additional obstacles). Beyond that, we could invoke the deliberative process to determine whether we wanted to continue to rely upon complete voluntariness as a source of donated organs, or legitimate a policy of presumed consent. The deliberative conversation would necessarily include discussion of the likely costs of a very successful policy of presumed consent. The central question would be whether other health care priorities were at risk of inadequate funding in order to pay the costs of expanded organ transplantation.

JUSTICE AND MULTI-ORGAN TRANSPLANTS OR RETRANSPLANTS

The most painful issues of health care justice occur at the clinical level; the issue of multi-organ transplants and retransplantation are perfect illustrations of this claim.

The vast majority of us embrace strong egalitarian intuitions in a clinical context (as opposed to an economic or political–philosophical context). Patients are entitled to equal concern and respect by their caregivers, which means that socioeconomic status and all other personal accidental features of a patient should be deemed irrelevant in a clinical context. In the context of major organ transplantation, these egalitarian intuitions mean that all patients who are deemed medically suitable ought to have a fair chance to obtain an organ transplant to avoid the otherwise certain premature death. Good doctors must be responsive to the medical needs of each patient.

Sometimes, however, patients need simultaneous transplantation of two to six organs; a range of medical circumstances may bring about this extraordinary level of demand. Our egalitarian intuitions say such patients are as entitled to organ transplantation as patients who only need a single organ. These intuitions could be satisfied if transplantable organs were abundant, but they are not, as we have already documented. This is where competing utilitarian intuitions come into play. If five or six organs are given to a single individual, then three or more other individuals will lose their opportunity for a life-saving organ transplant. We will likely never know with certainty who those individuals were whose lives were lost under these circumstances. They are (in the minds of some) "merely statistical lives" as opposed to the identifiable life that is in front of the transplant team right now. But we have argued earlier that this is a moral mistake. Given the shortage of organs, there will always be thousands of individuals who die without having access to an organ transplant—those deaths will largely be correctly thought of as being unfortunate rather than unjust. But if we are going to give a disproportionate number of organs to a single individual that a larger number of individuals could have benefited from, it seems there is an issue of justice that needs to be addressed. We cannot so readily dismiss the deaths of the other "statistical individuals" as being merely unfortunate. We need to invoke some considered judgments of health care justice that are widely enough shared to justify such a distribution. The alternative, of course, is to say that we are not going to provide a disproportionate number of organs to any individual. In this case, that means this individual has *no opportunity* for a transplant. From an egalitarian perspective, that too seems to require a justice-based justification. Veatch (2000) will defend a strong egalitarian view and contend that at least some of these patients have a just claim to multiple organs. Russell (2002) will take the opposite view and contend that these patients are not treated unfairly if they are denied the multiple organs they need.

The very same issue arises with regard to retransplantation. An individual receives a heart or liver transplant that fails (for lots of reasons) within a few months of the transplant (when we would have expected a 70% chance of five-year survival). It seems so "unfair" that this would have happened; consequently, many wish to argue that this individual has a just claim to be on the transplant list again and receive another organ. Others will argue that the correct moral description is that the outcome was unfortunate, and that the real unfairness would occur if such an individual is given another organ transplant since that will almost always mean that some other "statistical life" was lost on the transplant list. Again, we might "feel" more obligated to the patient in front of us with a failing organ transplant, but that feeling is not morally defensible from an egalitarian perspective since that other person who died never had a first chance at a transplant.

Let us go back to our multi-organ transplant scenario. What would be the strongest justice-based argument that might be made to justify providing such transplants? Taurek (1977) has provided an argument in a very widely cited paper, titled "Should the Numbers Count?" He is not writing about organ transplants as such, but he is addressing the sort of problem Thomson raised with the trolley problem in our very first chapter. The difference, however, is this: The trolley problem is about the distribution of harm; our problem is about the distribution of benefit. Thomson (1976) does provide us with another vivid analogy—it is the "Health Pebble." I am about a hundred yards from shore and this amazing "health pebble" comes floating toward me. I do not need it because I am perfectly healthy. But I am roughly equidistant from these two small islands. I can see one desperately ill person on one island and five desperately ill people on the other island. Both sets of islanders need the health pebble to survive. I also know that the single person will need the entire health pebble to survive, while on the other island each individual will survive with just one-fifth of the pebble.

As a just and caring person, what should I do with the pebble? Am I morally obligated to deliver it to one island rather than the other? Or would it be morally permissible for me not to direct the health pebble one way rather than the other? That is, could I just let the current carry it one way rather than the other? Would that be the fairest choice to make? Taurek would favor this latter choice. His answer to the question posed in the title of his paper is that the numbers should not count in this situation. He wants to defend a strong egalitarian view. All six individuals equally want to live—*that is all that matters, morally speaking*. That five lives would be saved if I were to direct the pebble toward the island with the five individuals is not as weighty a moral consideration as the fact that each person has an equal right to be saved. This line of argument has some significant plausibility, especially if it is the case that the health pebble is unowned and no one on either island has any special moral claim to it (i.e., it was not won by one or another person in a lottery or in a competition, nor was it created by anyone on either island and accidentally carried out to sea).

How should we think of these transplantable organs? Most would contend that we should think of them as a "public resource" when they enter the transplant system. They certainly do not "belong" to the local hospital where some patient was declared brain dead (with a signed organ donation card). The whole idea of creating a transplant network is that the organs would go where they would do the most good (be the best match for the person who has waited the longest, needs them most urgently, and is likely to have a good outcome). But if part of the idea of doing the "most good" is saving the most lives, then it seems like we certainly ought to give five organs to five people who need them, rather than just one person. That suggests the transplant network ought not "let the currents take the organs wherever." Instead, they ought to be directed toward saving five lives. Is it wrong not to give any chance at all for survival to the person needing two or more organs?

This may be another situation where the moral arguments are not sufficient to yield a clear and decisive reason to choose one option rather than the other.

This would seem to be another situation in which we could justifiably invoke the democratic deliberative process to craft a policy that the vast majority of individuals judged to be reasonable and just enough. Virtually all of us are behind a proverbial veil of ignorance with regard to whether we will ever need an organ transplant. We have the right to make a collective decision because transplantable organs are a social resource. A number of policy options are available to us, including using a six-sided die to make an allocation that gives the individual needing five organs "a chance." We would want to take account of the medical evidence. One thing we know is that multi-organ transplants remain more experimental than not. Results are not nearly as good as single-organ transplants. That fact might be decisive in the minds of most people. If our policy were that we would do no multi-organ transplants, that policy would not be unjust, in part because it was arrived at impartially, in part because no one has some sort of prior just claim to five organs just because they need a five-organ transplant to survive.

Ubel, Arnold and Caplan (1993) raise the issue of retransplantation of organs after there has been a failure of a first transplant. As things are now, retransplant candidates are treated in accord with the same priority criteria for positioning on a transplant list as primary candidates for transplant. They find this to be morally troubling because there is an absolute scarcity of transplantable organs. Specifically, if 20% of the transplants that are done each year for hearts and livers are really retransplants, then that means an equivalent number of individuals died awaiting a transplant who never had the opportunity for a first transplant (who would have had that opportunity had retransplant candidates been banned from the list). Ubel et al., however, do not conclude that there is something absolutely unjust about allowing individuals an opportunity for retransplantation. Instead, they point to a number of studies (Radovancevic et al., 2003) that indicate that the efficacy of retransplants, as measured by one-year survival, are significantly less than is the case for primary transplants.[3] Their morally more modest conclusion is that "we should no longer allow them [retransplant candidates] to vie for scarce organs on an equal basis with those who have never received a transplant and whose chances of benefiting from transplant are much greater."

The key question we wish to raise is whether Ubel et al. have reached too modest a conclusion. Earlier in their essay they raise the question of whether transplant surgeons had a stronger moral obligation to do retransplants rather than primary transplants, the argument being that considerations of loyalty might require such preferential treatment of retransplant candidates. But they reject that line of moral reasoning. They also inquire whether considerations of fairness might require giving lower priority to retransplant candidates over primary candidates. But they reject this line of moral reasoning as well. This, we believe, was too hasty a conclusion. In the remainder of this essay we will reconsider the argument of fairness with respect to retransplantation.

Ubel et al. write that "if re-transplant were as likely to succeed as primary transplant, then theories of justice or ideas about what is a fair slice of the health care pie could not be used to favor primary candidates over those needing re-transplantation." They ask us to imagine two individuals, whom we will name Primo and Secundo, who have an equally dire need of a liver for survival. They are the same age, have an equal prognosis with transplant, are on the same list, and will have an equally good match with an available organ. The only difference between the two is that Secundo has already had one transplant. Would it be fair to allow a lottery to determine who receives the organ this time? Though the moral intuitions of many would not support a lottery in these circumstances because Secundo has already had his chance for prolonged life, Ubel et al. support the lottery as being congruent with fairness. Their claim is that it is just not morally relevant that one individual has already had one transplant. The obvious response, as Ubel et al. note, is that we ought not be giving scarce pieces of the pie to some who have already had a piece if there are others who are waiting for their first piece. However, they reject this line of reasoning as being based on too narrow a notion of what counts as the pie. That is, the objector in this case assumes the pie is transplantable organs, whereas Ubel et al. want to consider the pie as access to health care as a whole. They can then imagine a scenario in which Primo has grown up with all of life's advantages so far as access to health care is concerned (income, education, access to primary care), while Secundo has had to struggle to overcome poverty, absent parents, and inadequate access to health care. Fair treatment, from a course-of-life perspective, would seem to warrant a lottery.

There is an alternate scenario, however, which might evoke a different moral judgment. Imagine that it is Primo who has had all of life's advantages as well as the initial organ transplant. Is Secundo then treated fairly if he has only a 50% chance of receiving his first liver transplant? If a course-of-life conception of health care justice is what should shape our moral judgment in these cases, then it seems Secundo deserves that liver transplant without having to compete for it in a lottery. If this is a correct conclusion, then Ubel et al. are wrong in thinking that considerations of fairness would not, at least in some circumstances, speak against giving equal access to transplant organs for those who have already had one transplant.

We should note in passing that Ubel et al. do not really use the notion of a "course-of-life" conception of justice, though this seems to be a reasonable interpretation of their example. If so, there seems to be a consistency problem in their analysis since their original example derives its moral plausibility from the fact that they are focusing on a "slice-of-time" distributional problem. That is, Primo and Secundo are exactly alike in all morally relevant respects except for the fact that Secundo has had a prior transplant that is now failing. We are then asked to assess the legitimacy of their respective claims to a liver transplant from what is really a biographically isolated perspective; that is, a perspective in which we are entirely ignorant of how these two individuals came to be in liver failure. But this is exactly the framework that Ubel et al. reject in their second scenario.

This entire example has an artificiality about it that may be dear to analytic philosophers (and lawyers), but it is probably quite annoying to most clinicians. An example with more practical relevance might look like this. A significant number of transplant failures occur in the first 30–90 days. There are lots of reasons why this happens, which may have nothing at all to do with the probability of long-term transplant success under slightly more favorable conditions (which are not very likely to be obtained if a second transplant is attempted). Under these circumstances, a reasonable and morally compelling argument might be made that these individuals have not really had a fair chance at a first transplant; consequently, they ought to go back on the list and be treated as if this were their first transplant. To use the language of John Harris (1985), they have not had their "fair innings." Indeed, a baseball analogy is helpful in that a game that has been rained out in the third inning is not a game at all. It has to be replayed as an entirely new game, which means that if one team scored 15 runs in the first inning, it was all for naught.

By way of contrast to our first example, we can imagine that an individual has had three or four extra years of life with a liver transplant. Now, however, the transplant is failing for the usual assortment of reasons. Should they, too, have an equal claim to a spot on the transplant list, especially if we were to assume that they had as good a chance for extra life-years from a second transplant as the average person on the transplant list at the time? In considering this case, we ought to be mindful of the fact that 50% of liver transplant recipients will survive for more than five years. But even when we take that into account, our suspicion is that most people would conclude that this second individual has had their "fair innings," and consequently, they have no just claim to an equal chance for a second transplant. That is, it would be unfair to deny someone their first transplant in order to give this individual a 50% chance of a second transplant.

Our moral judgments in this matter are not absolutely secure. The circumstances we have described are very abstract; there are details that can be filled in that might tug our judgment in one direction or another. Suppose that in our first case the individual who received the transplant was 52 years old, and the transplant is now failing at 45 days. If the person who would otherwise receive the second liver is 26 years old, we might think it fairer to allow him to have a few extra years of life, compared to the 52-year-old who has had less than a full life, but twice as much as the 26-year-old. In our second example, we can imagine just the reverse. That is, the 26-year-old has had a liver transplant for three years which is now failing. The next person on the list who would be a very good match for the available liver is the 52-year-old. Are we now as confident that the fairest choice is to deny the 26-year-old a second transplant and automatically award it to the 52-year-old who has not had a transplant?

Our intuitive moral judgments in these matters are just not very secure at all. Ubel et al. ask what rational planners behind a veil of ignorance might choose in some of these retransplant cases. Their conclusion is that veil of ignorance experiments with respect to most retransplant cases fail to yield a determinate response to the question of what would be fair. To be precise, their conclusion is stronger than that—they conclude that such mental experiments could result in coming to contradictory conclusions, depending upon what sorts of assumptions might be made behind that veil. As noted already, their stronger conclusion is that there are no fairness arguments that tell us what is just with respect to retransplant cases. Where we can make morally justifiable distinctions are in circumstances where we know that the efficacy of retransplants is significantly lower than the efficacy of primary transplants.

I am not satisfied with their conclusion because there is at least one approach to making judgments of health care justice that they have not considered, but that seems to be morally relevant to this issue. Again, it is our model of rational democratic deliberation. Among the virtues of this approach are the fact that it is an *actual deliberative process* (rather than being imagined or hypothetical) that will yield actual results that the deliberators themselves will have to live or die with, because the prioritization scheme is one that would govern their own access to transplants should they find themselves in the relevant medical circumstances in the future. Part of what I wish to emphasize is that this is conceived of as a broadly democratic process of priority setting, as opposed to relying upon "the transplant community" to make these choices. No doubt this broadly democratic, deliberative body would need considerable expert advice from the transplant community. But the ultimate decisions that need to be made are moral and political in character, not medical; consequently, these are decisions more appropriately made by this democratic deliberative body.

I take it that what I need to justify is the claim that the results of this deliberative democratic process are "just," or at least "just enough." What I need to speak to are two potential objections: (1) this is merely a political process that has no moral legitimacy whatsoever; and (2) the results of the process might very well be unjust, which would mean one of two things: (a) either there is an external substantive moral perspective from which we can judge the justness of the results of the process (which would then seem to make the process itself otiose), or (b) this is in fact a matter of pure procedural justness, which would mean an intuitively unjust result would nevertheless have to be considered just.

As we have already seen, this is how we need to think about the domain of rational democratic deliberation. This domain is framed by a number of principles of health care justice, which might be thought of as being analogous to constitutional principles. What that means is that there is no morally authoritative or legitimate result from this deliberative process if one of these principles is violated (just as a legislatively enacted law is not a law if it is found to be unconstitutional, though it may be able to masquerade as a law for some period of time).

There are three conditions that must be met to invoke the model of rational democratic deliberation. Condition 1 is that we must have an authoritative moral/public policy decision because an important moral or public interest is at stake. In the case of retransplantation, there are clear considerations of justice that need to be attended to. We cannot justify complete indifference, morally or politically, with respect to whether retransplants will be permitted, who will receive them, and where on a transplant list such candidates might be placed relative to primary transplant patients.

Condition 2 is that we cannot simply allow individual liberty to operate with respect to how this social problem is resolved in specific circumstances. If we did permit total medical or administrative or consumer discretion with respect to retransplantation, the result would be arbitrary, potentially discriminatory results so far as the fair distribution of transplantable organs was concerned. We noted earlier that these transplantable organs must be thought of as a social resource, given the social practices and policies we have put in place to maximize the fair and efficient use of this life-saving resource.

Condition 3 is that there are plural choice possibilities in this decision sphere, all of which have prima facie moral and political legitimacy, but none of which are unequivocally superior from a moral, political, or rational perspective. A point that Norman Daniels (1985) has made (and other philosophers, too) with respect to any particular conception of health care justice is that it will be indeterminate very often when we get down to the level of making micro-allocation or micro-prioritization choices. That seems to be the result that we ended up with earlier in this chapter so far as several of our examples were concerned. That is, there are legitimate considerations of justice that would support the case of some individuals for retransplant, and there would also be other considerations of justice that would support the case for a primary transplant candidate being given priority over this specific retransplant candidate. We could go to a lottery, but it is far from obvious that this would be the most just way of resolving this conflict. Instead, what we imagine happening is that our actual rational democratic deliberators would consider all the moral arguments that might be made with respect to choosing one or another set of rules to govern prioritizing access to transplants for both primary and retransplant candidates in a range of clinical circumstances, and they would also consider some number of rationally relevant non-moral consequences that might be connected with one or another decision, then come to a judgment about a reasonable policy to adopt in these circumstances.

I will remind the reader that these rational democratic deliberators are adopting policies for their future possible selves and those they care about who might have the relevant medical need. They are not behind a hypothetical Rawlsian veil of ignorance, but they are, for the most part, ignorant of considerations that might cause their choices to be biased in a morally objectionable sense. That is, it is relatively easy for these deliberators to be suitably impartial. The decisions they ultimately reach will mean, in practice, that some individuals will be denied transplants or retransplants who will be able to invoke a moral argument suggesting that they have a just claim to that transplant. But that claim has now been justly adjudicated through this democratic process; it is, in fact, an alternate allocation scheme that has been accorded moral and political legitimacy. Under such circumstances, and assuming that the framing principles of justice have not been violated, the results of that democratic process are morally authoritative, which is to say that the individual before us now has no just claim to the transplant he desires.

What does this analysis mean so far as Primo and Secundo are concerned? What might we reasonably expect from a rational democratic deliberative process of the sort that I envision? I have no way of confidently predicting what the outcome of such a process might be like. As noted earlier, it is easy to imagine that for most people, if Secundo has had three years of a successful transplant that is now failing, he has had his fair innings; consequently, they would judge that it would be unfair to give him a 50% chance of another transplant against someone who has yet to have a first transplant. The "fair piece of the pie" argument does have moral bite in the minds of very many people, though perhaps some carefully shaped exceptions to that moral argument could be carved out, and our democratic deliberators could be persuaded to legitimate those exceptions. Maybe there is a range of circumstances in which morally relevant considerations are so complex and confusing and ultimately indeterminate that rational democratic deliberators would go with a lottery for this range of cases as the most reasonable and fairest method of resolution (given our ultimately limited moral capacities and our need to have a determinate decision procedure). But, and this is our concluding point, this will be the result of a fair, rational, deliberative democratic process. This approach to fairness in the matter of retransplantation is on sounder moral and political footing than what Ubel et al. have to offer.

CONCLUDING COMMENTS

This chapter has had modest objectives. We want to argue that the traditional moral bases for our organ donation practices (the dead donor rule, voluntarism, and altruism) are, in fact, worthy of continued moral respect. That moral respect includes considerations of justice. We recognize that there are substantial pressures for increasing the pool of transplantable organs. Some of those pressures are morally compelling: knowing that more lives could be saved with more organs. Others, candor requires us to admit, are more self-serving: institutional prestige, professional rewards. With respect to the moral pressures, we have argued that they are not of overriding moral urgency; that is, there is no moral duty to maximize the supply of transplantable organs. More strongly, there are powerful considerations of justice in the allocation of limited health resources that would speak directly against any such goal.

No doubt it is morally desirable to expand the supply of transplantable organs so long as we do not violate or significantly undermine other weighty moral values, especially those that have undergirded our reasonably successful efforts at organ procurement thus far. There are quite a few strategies for increasing the supply of transplantable organs that are clearly within bounds, morally speaking. We are morally obligated to pursue those strategies vigorously before we start pushing on the moral boundaries themselves. Testing the dead donor rule with the Pittsburgh protocol, introducing markets and financial incentives as an alternative to altruism, adopting presumed consent policies in place of pure voluntarism—all are properly described as morally risky at best, significantly flawed at worst. That they all promise to save more lives has some moral weight, but nowhere near the moral weight proponents of these changes have imagined. We have tried to show there are competing moral considerations, and they must be duly weighed as well.

12

THE LIBERALISM PROBLEM

JUSTICE, HEALTH CARE NEEDS, AND MORALLY CONTROVERSIAL INTERVENTIONS

In 1993, some residents in obstetrics brought me a case that they found troubling; it involved a 26-year-old woman with an ectopic pregnancy (Fleck, 1995). She was a Jehovah's Witness patient. She made it unequivocally clear to the attending surgeon that she was not to be transfused, no matter what happened in the surgery. She understood she was at risk of death. During the surgery she did in fact bleed excessively, to the point that her life was clearly at risk. The surgeon administered a paralytic drug and gave her high doses of Epogen in order to save her life without a transfusion; the intervention was successful. But it did require that the patient be hospitalized in the ICU for a period of two weeks. The cost of saving her life was about $100,000. She had no health insurance. The cost of saving her life was "covered" as charity care from the hospital budget. The residents were conflicted about the case because they felt she had no just claim to those resources. This hospital served an area that a very large number of poor and uninsured patients—they felt that those patients had a stronger just claim to those resources. What also bothered them, however, was the fact that these resources were provided to her in order to accommodate her religious commitments.

Now it should be clear from the case description that this patient made no demand for this treatment. The attending surgeon made this commitment, presumably because he or she might not have been morally or psychologically comfortable with the thought of allowing this woman to die when there was a medical alternative available to save her life. But I want to pass over any discussion of this personal moral choice. The larger question would seem to be this: If other members of that religious community were to become aware of how her life was saved without a transfusion, could they justifiably demand comparable treatment when undergoing surgery with risk of substantial blood loss? Could they make this demand as a way of both living in accord with their religious commitments and not dying prematurely? Would a just and caring, liberal, pluralistic society (respectful of a broad range of belief systems) be morally obligated to accede to this demand?

To put this case in a slightly more contemporary context, the drug that would likely be used today in this situation for rapid blood clotting would be NovoSeven; it is also referred to as recombinant Factor VIIa (rFVIIa). It is most often used in the treatment of patients with hemophilia. This is another extraordinarily expensive drug—in those hemophilia cases, the average cost of providing this drug for a single episode is about $50,000 (Ratko et al., 2004). This is the figure we can use for our purposes. We should imagine a case like this in two contexts: an uninsured Jehovah's Witness patient today, or the same patient in a single-payer national health insurance system in the future. The question in today's context is whether a hospital could justly refuse to honor a request from such a patient for rFVIIa when they clearly had no ability to pay for this drug. Could the hospital justifiably refuse to honor this patient's request on the grounds that they *did not need this drug for pure medical reasons, but only for medical–religious reasons*? Likewise, essentially the same question can be raised in the context of creating a national health insurance program. Would we be morally obligated, as a matter of justice, to cover the cost of the drug in these circumstances? As a *liberal* society, would refusal to provide such coverage be rightly seen as offensive to our liberal commitments? Or would such a refusal be *required* in order to be true to the requirements of liberal neutrality in matters of health care justice? This is the beginning of what we will refer to as "the liberalism problem."

The larger problem we need to address is the increasingly large range of medical interventions that are morally controversial for one or another segment of our society. To be more precise, we are talking about interventions that others would find deeply morally troubling if they were somehow required to be supportive of those interventions. The context we have in mind is a future possible single-payer national health program. Such a program would have to be funded by taxes, or compulsory premiums of one sort or another. This would mean that various members of society who found some range of procedures profoundly morally objectionable would be paying their money to support access for others. Here is a sampling of the sort of interventions we would see generating this problem.

Should a national health insurance (NHI) program pay for prenatal screening, either chorionic villus sampling or amniocentesis, when the *possible* intent of the intervention would be abortion of an affected fetus? Some parents might only want this information so that they were better prepared for the challenges they might face as parents. It would be hard to imagine in practice how one would fund this intervention in some cases but not others, in order to avoid collecting taxes from religious objectors to this service. Both these prenatal testing interventions carry some risk with regard to the pregnancy itself. However, we are seeing the rapid development of noninvasive methods of acquiring this information regarding fetal status (Newson, 2008)—this will likely generate a greater demand for use of this technology.

Should NHI pay for genetic testing when the testing is being done for purposes of making reproductive decisions (as opposed to genetic testing that is part of some therapeutic intervention)? We worded this question in as open-ended a way as possible, because some individuals might choose to have no children, or to adopt, or to avail themselves of some alternative reproductive method. For couples that have difficulty conceiving, should NHI pay for any attempts at using IVF? Here, of course, we would again be faced with the question of whether "wanting to have a baby" should be regarded as a medical need. For some, the answer to that question will be obvious. But there is a flip side to that question which we cannot ignore: we do pay for childbirth expenses under many health insurance plans now, and we pay for those birthing costs no matter how many children couples *choose* to have. That observation does not settle the question of whether NHI ought to pay for the means a couple might need to become pregnant, but it does make clear that some nonmedically necessary health expenses are covered by insurance.

Brain tissue from aborted fetuses has been injected into the brains of individuals with Parkinson's as a way of relieving some of the associated symptoms. Insurance would be expected (normally) to pay for an indefinitely large range of brain surgeries done for therapeutic purposes. Could we justify excluding this brain surgery from a NHI package to be sensitive to the objections raised by advocates of a right-to-life position?

As I write, we are in the middle of debates about the use of embryonic stem cells for a range of potential medically therapeutic purposes. For research purposes, these cells are derived from embryos that will otherwise be discarded by fertility clinics. But the therapeutic uses most often mentioned in press releases include repairing spinal cord injuries, regenerating heart tissue that otherwise would have been irreversibly damaged from a heart attack, curing diabetes by creating pancreatic islet cells, and repairing brain damage from injury or some range of brain disorders. These uses would likely require embryonic stem cells derived from the person who would have the medical need, to avoid potential rejection problems. That means these cells would be created by a process of cloning that would start with one of the cells from that individual that had been enucleated to create an embryonic genetic twin of that person. Would any therapeutic medical interventions rooted in this technology have to be excluded from a NHI benefit package in order to avoid violating the ethical sensibilities of right-to-life advocates?

One of the politically interesting things that have happened in this regard is that there has been a split among right-to-life advocates. Some see this research and its projected therapeutic outcomes as life-affirming; consequently, they support public funding for the research (and presumably would support inclusion of coverage in a NHI benefit package for these therapeutic outcomes). Others among right-to-life advocates continue to reject it. Under these circumstances, what would considerations of justice and respect for diverse religious perspectives permit or require with regard to these elements in a NHI benefit package?

I have used the right-to-life perspective to frame several issues, because that would be one of the more prominent such perspectives in our society. But obviously there are others which could generate comparable objections. I have not actually heard of Jehovah's Witness adherents objecting to paying for blood transfusions for others who are not adherents of their faith; still, it seems they would have as much a right to raise that objection as anyone else. Would we have to exclude blood transfusions from NHI in order to avoid giving offense to them? Some in the deaf community object to cochlear implants for deaf children; they see that as a threat to the viability of their deaf culture. Are these objections sufficient to require that cochlear implants not be included in a NHI package? We can easily imagine comparable issues arising in connection with other groups of persons with disabilities. There are things we might learn from neuroscientists that will permit substantial restoration of sight to individuals who have suffered damage we believed at one time was irreparable. If there were a movement among persons who were blind to think of themselves as a distinct culture threatened with extinction by emerging medical technologies aimed at curing or substantially ameliorating blindness, would those concerns be sufficient to justify not including coverage for those technologies in a NHI package? Again, what we have to imagine is that some from this group might embrace this technology, while others might reject it.

One of the more famous cases in medical ethics is the Ayala case (Silver, 1997 pp. 110–15). This family had a 17-year-old daughter who needed a bone marrow transplant in order to save her from a likely fatal leukemia. She was going to be very difficult to match. The father had a vasectomy reversed in order to conceive another child who would provide the needed bone marrow. The mother took drugs that allowed her to hyper-ovulate in order to produce egg cells that her husband could inseminate. It may have taken genetic analysis of 34 eight-cell embryos before one was identified as a perfect match for the young woman. This young woman's life was saved. This has now been accomplished a number of times for different disorders. Should the costs associated with this procedure by covered under NHI as a therapeutic intervention?[1]

We have provided multiple examples here of somewhat costly alternative reproductive options that some in our society would choose to access. Could any liberally justifiable public policies be put in place that would outlaw access to these technologies? Political liberals of virtually all stripes would answer this question negatively. What about covering these interventions as part of a national health insurance package? John Robertson (at the libertarian end of that spectrum) would argue that procreative liberty is almost entirely a negative right, a right of noninterference (1994, chap. 2). No one has the right to put in place laws that would prohibit individuals from accessing these technologies unless we could justifiably show that persons (such as the children resulting from these technologies) were at excessive risk of serious harm. Society, however, has no obligation to facilitate access to these technologies by supporting those costs in any way. For Robertson, no one is treated unjustly if no public funding supports such access.

At this point we need to call to mind another very different controversial bioethics case, the Wanglie case in Minnesota. Helga Wanglie was 85 years old when she suffered a massive heart attack that left her anoxic for 15 minutes or longer. She was left in a vent-dependent PVS state. After several months, her physician tried to persuade the family that care should be withdrawn and she should be allowed to die because this care was "inappropriate." Her husband and two children were utterly opposed to this proposal because they were firmly committed to a right-to-life perspective; being alive in any way at all was better than being dead. They were clear that this was Helga Wanglie's view, as well. Her life was sustained in this state for a period of 14 months at a cost (in 1990) of about $800,000—many of those dollars were Medicare dollars. Would taxpayers have the right to object that they should not be coerced into paying for her care, since religious reasons were the root cause of that demand? Though I refer to a single case here, the larger issue I would raise again is the whole issue of last-chance therapies. Can individuals claim, on the basis of their religious commitments, unlimited access to costly life-prolonging medical technologies at the expense of others? Would our society be illiberal if we had a national health insurance plan that severely limited access to last-chance therapies, contrary to the commitments of specific religious groups, in order to provide sufficient resources for what were collectively judged to be higher-priority health care needs?

Loren Lomasky (1980), a libertarian, considers this question (and versions of many of the controversial examples given above), and quickly concludes that this represents an irrefutable argument against any form of national health insurance that would impose a single set of health benefits upon all. In his ideal society, he would want individuals to be free to choose health insurance that was congruent with their deepest personal values. I would assume that Lomasky would be favorably disposed to the Health Savings Accounts concept that the last Bush Administration had been pushing, since that would seem to yield something close to the highly individualized form of health insurance Lomasky sees as being politically desirable. Unfortunately, as I will argue in the concluding chapter of this volume, that approach will not yield a "just enough" health care system; on the contrary, the most serious injustices in our current health care system would likely be magnified even further.

Ezekiel Emanuel (1991) takes a different approach to this problem. He wants to protect something close to a moderate egalitarian conception of health care justice, while at the same time protecting the moral or religious integrity of groups of individuals who would strongly object to their paying for some health services they judged to be deeply offensive. He believes there is something fundamentally incoherent about a *liberal* conception of *health care justice*, which the range of examples introduced above perfectly illustrate. He will advocate for what he calls a liberal communitarian approach to addressing this problem.

LIBERAL COMMUNITARIANISM: IS IT JUST ENOUGH? IS IT LIBERAL ENOUGH?

I now want to turn to a critical assessment of the vision of liberal managed care presented by Emanuel. I begin by noting that there are some significant agreements between Emanuel and myself. We would both agree that there are some very serious injustices in our current system of health care financing and health care rationing. We would both also recognize the need for something like a managed care mechanism (hard budgets/integrated delivery systems) to come about for addressing these injustices, especially the problem of health care rationing/health care cost containment/health care priority setting. We would also both endorse the need for a federal health care policy that would assure all in our society access to a fairly comprehensive package of health care benefits. We would both reject the idea that managed care plans should be simply organizational shells for health-related economic transactions. We both want instead managed care plans that have a communal character to them, and that encourage democratic deliberation among plan members regarding the goals and policies of those plans. Beyond this point, we seem to go in separate directions.

Emanuel wants to permit (maybe encourage) managed care plans to be defined in terms of some sort of comprehensive vision of a health good. What he most strongly rejects in the liberalism of Rawls and Dworkin and their philosophic brethren is the notion of liberal neutrality—he sees this as something of a sham. That is, liberalism itself represents a fairly definite set of value commitments, which may be congenial to many comprehensive visions of the good to which individuals would commit themselves, but it is also uncongenial to others—very often religiously based comprehensive visions. Maybe some writers would say it is too genteel to speak of liberalism merely being uncongenial to some religious visions; they would find it more honest to say that liberalism represents a threat to the survival of some sorts of religious communities. Emanuel would seem to endorse the idea that there is something fundamentally wrong with a political society that would force an individual to choose between being a good liberal citizen and being a good Catholic or a good Amish person or a good Orthodox Jew. Thus, if we were to have some sort of national health insurance, and if abortion services or physician-assisted suicide or embryonic genetic analysis and selection were funded benefits, then some individuals who were deeply opposed on moral/religious grounds to any or all of these practices would be contributing tax/premium dollars to support these practices. This seems illiberal and dishonest, because liberalism claims to be neutral with respect to competing comprehensive visions, but is (by these policies supporting social practices) deeply violative of some comprehensive visions.

Emanuel sees the managed care movement as a way of escaping these problems that is both protective of our liberal political traditions (minus the neutrality commitment) and protective of the integrity of these distinctive religious/philosophic communities. He sees managed care plans as possibly forming around lots of differing organizational perspectives, including religious commitments. He would give each family or citizen of our society a voucher for health care benefits that would have a precise economic value that would be sufficient to purchase a very good package of health care benefits. Individuals could use those vouchers to join whichever managed care plan they found most congenial to them in terms of a comprehensive vision of some sort. This would mean (at the national level) that there would be no specified health care benefits/services that would be nationally required. Instead, it would be the right of the members of each plan to decide among themselves the precise content of their benefit package, up to whatever limit was allowed by the value of the vouchers that members brought to the plan, plus whatever private resources they were willing to add to a common pool of resources for purchasing health care services. At first glance, such an approach might seem to be both liberal enough and just enough; I, however, will argue that Emanuel's proposal is flawed in both these respects.

Emanuel seems to be committed to some deeper set of liberal civil rights that should not be violated by these managed care plans. Thus, he says that he would not allow any of these managed care plans to discriminate against individuals on the basis of preexisting medical conditions. No managed care plan would be allowed to say "We will not treat people who are HIV+." But it would seem that a managed care plan could get away with saying (under Emanuel's approach), "We choose to invest our health resources in preventive health care, childhood illnesses, et cetera; we choose not to cover any of the more expensive therapies associated with HIV. Part of our reasoning is that the vast majority of individuals who are HIV+ are gay or IV drug abusers, and we strongly feel that this is God's punishment for their excesses. It would be wrong of us to undercut the will of God." A "liberal" response is to say, as Emanuel does at several places, that gay individuals are free to form gay managed care plans—that is, managed care plans can be organized in terms of sexual orientation just as readily as in terms of religious commitment. However, a managed care plan with a very high number of HIV+ individuals (which would likely be the case in one organized by sexual orientation) would have only average value vouchers to meet very far above average health care costs, which seems presumptively unjust since there would likely be large numbers of health needs in that plan that would go unmet.

Emanuel does suggest at some places that the specific value of the vouchers might be "graded" in some fashion, increased in value to reflect the likely health needs of individuals with those vouchers so as to minimize any risk of economic discrimination against older or chronically ill individuals. This would seem to address the justice problem noted above. However, we would then need at the national level some sort of decision-making mechanism that would do the grading. That is, someone would need to decide which medical problems with what degree of severity, with what likelihood of being responsive to various more or less costly medical technologies, ought to be considered for purposes of assigning a value to a particular voucher for a particular individual. If you "cap" health care spending at the national level (which is central to the whole rationale for moving toward managed care in the first place), then to accommodate the needs of these very ill individuals, you would have to reduce the average value of the voucher that everyone else received. "Everyone else" means all those individuals from all those diverse managed care plans with those diverse comprehensive visions. *Whose vision of the good would be operative at the national level for purposes of setting the value of the vouchers by judging which therapies would be covered for which medical problems under which circumstances?* This is supposedly the problem that prompted Emanuel to devise his proposal in the first place. But it looks like he still has that problem—at least if he remains committed to protecting the overall justness of the system. Could those religious, anti-gay managed care plans object that they do not want their tax dollars spent, or the value of their own personal health vouchers reduced, to accommodate the perverse health needs of that HIV+ population (just as many object to the use of federal money for the funding of abortions)? If the federal government was responsive positively to this challenge, then it seems you would end up with de facto discriminatory outcomes that certainly seem both illiberal and unjust.

We should also point out that the same problem arises for Emanuel with respect to the problem of funding medical research. Emanuel suggests (1991, p. 186) that something like 5% of all federal funds ought to be set aside for funding medical research, because there would otherwise be a free rider problem. That is, each managed care plan would expect other managed care plans to fund such research. But Emanuel also says that individual managed care plans could fund research that was congruent with their vision of the good. But then again, we are going to be faced with the question of someone having to decide what medical research projects deserved to be funded, without at the same time violating someone's comprehensive vision (i.e., embryo research, genetic research aimed at germ line engineering, research on HIV, etc.). To make this very vivid, we note that 5% of $2.3 trillion is $120 billion; not a small sum. Again, this is a problem that Emanuel's proposal was supposed to get us away from. We are then either stuck with the same problem, or else at risk of adopting a strategy for addressing it that would prove to be either illiberal or unjust. We might also note in passing that this same problem arises in connection with medical education. Whose vision of what a good doctor ought to be should shape the contours of medical education? My response will be that a Rawlsian-like liberalism is more likely to yield a less morally problematic response to this question than the liberal communitarianism endorsed by Emanuel.

There are times when Emanuel suggests that managed care plans might be organized on geographic lines, perhaps groups of 20,000 individuals in relatively close proximity to one another. At one place he suggests that it might be ideal if managed care plans were coextensive with local government. Here, it strikes me that Emanuel in his search for community and solidarity in meeting health care needs may have too romantic a vision of what local government and local decision-making are all about. At one point (1991, p. 202), Emanuel is discussing the dialysis problem from the late '60s–early '70s. He expresses regret at the local loss of control and funding for those dialysis centers. He seems to think it truly regrettable that the federal government created this single national benefit, and that this represents a loss of communal solidarity. (I will note in passing that from the point of view of health care justice, there are some serious moral criticisms that can be directed against the ESRD program. But those criticisms emerge from the current context of a highly fragmented system for health care funding wherein virtually any effort to redress one inequity generates others.) But, going back to Emanuel's concerns about loss of solidarity, he needs to read more carefully much of the history that surrounded those centers; for clearly, one of the more morally problematic features of those dialysis centers (and the boards that ran them) was the arbitrary and discriminatory way in which they judged the "worthiness" of individuals who would be granted access to dialysis at community expense. This was all too frequently the middle class protecting other like-minded members of the middle class (Alexander, 1962). There is something very illiberal about this kind of social solidarity.

Emanuel says in many places that he is committed to the democratic deliberative quality of these managed care plans. In fact, he says at one place that government might reward deliberative managed care plans with more funding and penalize nondeliberative managed care plans by reducing their funding. However, this does not seem entirely congruent with his vision of liberal *communitarianism*. It is easy enough to imagine, for example, that some managed care plans would be organized around some set of religious commitments, which would include unwavering respect for sometimes dogmatic religious authority (represented in the person of bishops or rabbis or a mullah). From the point of view of such authorities, government encouragement of democratic deliberation would represent a threat to their authority; perhaps to the whole way of life represented by that religious organization. Democratic deliberation will be seen by them as the seedbed of heresy and confused thinking that might threaten the integrity of their religious traditions. But if Emanuel is responsive to this concern, then it seems he would have surrendered the core of any worthy liberalism. If he is not responsive to this concern, then his liberal commitments will look more Rawlsian-like and less communitarian.

How does this discussion of Emanuel's views fit the issues we raise in connection with "last-chance therapies"? I take it that the central idea behind communitarianism is that communities ought to be organized around some conception of the good, a common good, which is to say a good for each and all. This good (or these goods) are what provide the essential glue of that community. Right and wrong (in a moral sense) will be determined by reference to that common good; hence, for communitarians, we would say that the good precedes the right. The claim of liberals, such as Rawls, is that the right ought to precede the good, at least if we judge it is important to protect our pluralistic commitments morally and politically. The primary concern of liberals will be governmental institutions because these are the institutions that set the rules that all members of our society must live by; in addition, government alone has the coercive power and authority to deprive individuals of life and liberty if they violate the rules of that society badly enough. If protecting pluralism is important, which means in political terms protecting the right of individuals to form many kinds of communities around many conceptions of the good, then a liberal government will have to be "neutral" among these different (sometimes competing) conceptions of the good. That neutrality will be in the "justificatory" mode rather than the "consequentialist" mode. In other words, in justifying any particular law or policy, a liberal government will have to show that policy is justified by appeal to "thin" values and interests that can be reasonably construed as being supportive of the general good of liberal citizens as liberal citizens in a liberal society (as opposed to some more specific good, reflective of a comprehensive philosophic view). That is, these are interests that transcend (but are also necessary to support) the much thicker and more specific conceptions of values that define the multiplicity of communities that comprise our society as a whole. Our conception of justice, as Rawls articulates, is intended to be the most important value embraced by a liberal society—in part, as a way of protecting the stability and peacefulness of our society. It is important to note that Rawls is a moral and political constructivist: the conception of justice (or any other basic social value) is not just "out there" to be discovered; rather, it is constructed through rational, democratic deliberative processes as we struggle with constantly emerging social problems (such as the problem of health care rationing).

Let us now translate this general framework into something more specific to the "last-chance therapy" problem. Imagine that we have either Emanuel-like managed care plans organized around a core value such as the "sanctity of life" or "maximum healthy living," or imagine that we have groups of like-minded individuals in generic managed care plans of the sort we are all familiar with organized around each of these basic values. Those who are committed to the sanctity of life ethic will want everything medically possible done to sustain their own lives or the lives of their loved ones, so they will want access to Herceptin or LVADs or TIAHs or TPN, all at plan expense. By way of contrast, those who are committed to the ideal of maximal healthy living adhere to the belief that most of the chronic illness characteristic of contemporary Western society is due to very bad lifestyle choices that weak-willed individuals in our society make. They want nothing to do with paying for the medical costs of the weak-willed misbehavior of those who failed to organize their lives around the ideal of maximal commitment to making healthy choices. What they want funded with their health care dollars is an indefinitely large array of health-promoting practices (herbal supplements, say). What I am suggesting with these descriptions is that both sets of these individuals define their sense of what should count as strong morally legitimate health needs from the perspective of their comprehensive visions of the good.

How can individuals with such radically different visions of what should count as a health need coexist in the same health plan? This is what generates Zeke Emanuel's vision of separating out into distinct managed care plans adherents of all these different comprehensive visions. However, this does not really solve any moral or practical problems. As noted above, if there is some sort of national commitment to "necessary health care for all," and if that is expressed through giving health vouchers to all, some economic value will have to be attached to that voucher, and that value cannot be fairly or reasonably determined by reference to what adherents of those different comprehensive visions judge to be *their* health needs. To address that problem, we will need some thin conception of health care justice that can be the focal point of an overlapping consensus.

A more telling point, however, is that *this very same problem would exist in each of these philosophically distinctive managed care plans we have postulated.* This is because there are, as a psychological and sociological fact, indefinite degrees of commitment to the core vision of the good that would define any of these plans by individual members of these plans. Some will be ultra-health enthusiasts (and demand health resources to achieve their ultra-health goals) whereas others will be only "excellent" or "very good" or "near average" health enthusiasts (still a couple standard deviations beyond the minimal level of commitment to health promotion of the average American). And the same will be true in the "sanctity of life" managed care plan where some will enthusiastically endorse sustaining at all cost the life of Helga Wanglie and others in a persistent vegetative state, while other plan members would see that as a wasteful and inappropriate use of limited plan resources that ought to be directed to more support for "last-chance therapies." To resolve such possible conflicts within any of these plans, appeal would have to be made to some conception of health care justice (and method for justifying that conception) that was "independent of" the more radical and less radical commitments of plan members to their central value conception. If such a conception and method can be worked out within these plans (to prevent destabilizing, fractious bickering within these plans), then the same conception and method can be appealed to for purposes of resolving conflicts among these plans with respect to how (at the national level) we ought to determine the value of these "health vouchers" that would be given to all. And if it is possible to achieve that (to a sufficient degree), then there is no need to try to organize health plans around differing comprehensive visions, for we would then have the resources that allowed individuals with very different deep comprehensive visions of the good (health-related or not) to function fairly and respectfully in relation to one another within the bounds of liberal, generic managed care plans. My contention is that something akin to Rawls' liberal conception of justice, something akin to the version of rational democratic deliberation I described in Chapter 5, is what is necessary to achieve these objectives, *while at the same time preserving the value of community and solidarity to the limited functional extent that is possible.*

RESOLVING THE LIBERALISM PROBLEM: PUBLIC REASON AND PUBLIC INTERESTS

Imagine a situation in which a 40-year-old man is talking with his psychiatrist about his own gender identity issues. He feels more like a woman, and is giving serious thought to having gender reassignment surgery. As he is explaining his internal psychological conflicts, his psychiatrist interrupts him to say, "I need to inform you that the substance of this conversation is deeply offensive to more conservative religious sects in our society. Consequently, this session will not be covered by our insurance program." This scenario has an obviously absurd quality to it. We cannot imagine a legitimate reason why someone would have a "need to know" the content of a psychiatric conversation in order to determine whether or not that therapeutic session would be reimbursed through an insurance plan. On the contrary, all we need to know is that an individual's psychological equilibrium was sufficiently disturbed that their ability to function in their various social roles was significantly compromised. This is a judgment we leave to a referring physician; beyond that, we respect the privacy rights of the patient.

We can think about the rationale behind this respect in two ways. First, no public interest is threatened or compromised by our failing to know the details of these counseling sessions; on the contrary, the public interest is that these privacy rights be respected. As individuals, we are not well positioned to protect our own privacy rights against powerful corporations. This is why we invoke the coercive authority of government to assure effective protections of these rights against others who would use intrusive information-gathering technologies to cause harm to the welfare of individuals.

Second, no *public reason* can be invoked that would justify differential reimbursement for counseling depending upon whether specific content was offensive or not to some religious or social group in the U.S. Imagine that the Catholic Church objected to having a national health insurance plan paying for any counseling session in which abortion was discussed as an option regarding a tentative pregnancy. If we agreed to such a proposal, we would be using the coercive powers of government to enforce some specific religious commitment against those who did not embrace that faith (or even for those who were Roman Catholic, but might have personal differences with orthodox beliefs and expectations). This would fail the *public reason* test. We could not say to someone, "You will need to pay the full cost of that counseling session because you discussed abortion as an option, and that is offensive to the Roman Catholic Church."

In theory, what we could say is that no counseling sessions of any sort would be funded under our national health plan; that statement by itself would not be intrinsically objectionable. But obviously we would have to give some reasons why we refused to fund all counseling sessions. If we could pull up reams of empirical studies that showed virtually no benefit from such counseling sessions (psychological problems were not resolved or ameliorated, effective coping skills were not acquired), we would then be justified from the perspective of public reason (and health care justice) in refusing to provide public funding for such services. We have no moral obligation to fund ineffective therapies. However, if the exact opposite were true, if large numbers of patients did benefit significantly from such counseling sessions in terms of their capacity to cope better with many sorts of adversities in life, we could not justify refusing to cover such interventions with public funding because too many different religious or social groups objected to too many different sorts of things that might be discussed in those counseling sessions. That too would fail the *public reason* test, even though no particular religious faith was having its behavioral expectations enforced by the state.

What we are addressing here is what we have called "the liberalism problem." This first example is supposed to be easy and obvious. If we needed an even more obvious one, we would have to abolish all public funding of health care and health care research if we were going to avoid giving offense to Christian Scientists. This would undermine a public interest (that even Christian Scientists have) in having secure access to needed and effective health care, as judged by the best science we have available.[2] We do not force adult Christian Scientists to accept health care. In that regard, we do respect their religious beliefs and their liberty right to make that choice for themselves. But if we did have a national health plan of some sort, Christian Scientists would be justly compelled to pay the same taxes or premiums in support of that plan as everyone else in our society; this would be for essentially the same reasons that we collect taxes to support the police and military from individuals who have armed themselves to the teeth claiming they are capable of defending themselves. We would otherwise have the risk of a "free rider" problem. In the case of Christian Scientists, the risk would be that they would have a "conversion experience" when faced with cancer or some other life-threatening problem. Then we (liberal citizens) would be faced with two morally problematic options: turn them away from the health care system to suffer and die (uncaring), or take them in and absorb the costs (unjust).[3]

We can now turn to some of the more controversial examples we introduced earlier. Would we be liberally justified in including some range of morally controversial reproductive services as part of a national health plan? We can start with some services intended to respond to problems of infertility, such as artificial insemination by donor and in vitro fertilization. Roughly 15% of couples in the U.S. would be unable to conceive and have children of their own without some form of assisted reproduction—does this represent a health care *need* or a health care *desire*? I do not doubt that couples faced with infertility experience this as a strong need. However, that psychological experience is not sufficient to justify from a moral point of view invoking the language of need. The most honest description would say that it is a very intense and very reasonable desire, but it is also correctly describable as a deviation from normal biological functioning. It does represent a regrettable deficiency in what is seen as normal species functioning. This points us in the direction of protecting fair equality of opportunity and related considerations of health care justice.

Burley (1998) and Warren (2002) suggest a line of thought that might be helpful. Following a Rawlsian strategy, Warren asks us to imagine ourselves behind a Rawlsian veil of ignorance. We do not know whether we will be able to have children of our own or not. But we do understand how intense and normal a desire that is, and we understand how having children can be an intensely satisfying life experience. We also understand the frustration and sense of loss experienced by those who find themselves unable to have children. Under these circumstances, Warren imagines that the vast majority of us would want to be assured the opportunity to have children, if that is something medically possible. That is, we would regard including some range of fertility services in the health care benefit package that might be established as national health insurance. We would see this as something a just and caring society ought to do.

Having said this much, we would still have to address the issue of limits and priorities. Each cycle of IVF has costs today in the range of $10,000–$12,000. The likelihood of achieving pregnancy during any one IVF cycle at the best facilities is no better than 30%, so we have to assume on average that three cycles might be necessary to achieve a successful pregnancy. At this point, several other morally relevant considerations come into play. Some clinics have been in the habit of implanting multiple embryos (four or more) in the hopes of maximizing the likelihood of achieving pregnancy on any given round of IVF; this is regarded as serving the interests of both the clinic and the parents. But this practice often resulted in multiple gestations, which generated some potentially costly risks. The whole pregnancy might be lost, especially if we are talking about quadruplets. Or parents would have to consider the risks (and moral/psychological costs of pregnancy reduction). Or parents might deliver these babies very prematurely, which will generate NICU costs in addition to the risk of lifelong disabilities for some or all of the babies. In response to these concerns, professional medical societies have strongly recommended implanting no more than two embryos during any one cycle. This is seen as being in the best interest of those future possible children, as well as the best interests of the parents (all things considered).

Taking this recommendation seriously, however, will have justice-relevant consequences. It might mean that more cycles of IVF will have to be undergone in order to achieve a successful pregnancy. If this is medically accurate, this would suggest that a just and caring society ought to be willing to underwrite some number of cycles of IVF. This is again the point at which we would have to invoke rational democratic deliberation to determine limits, and the place of this intervention in an overall set of health care priorities. I cannot go into all the medical details associated with all the kinds of medical circumstances that might interfere with the ability of a particular couple to achieve pregnancy; it is likely the case that no reasonable, democratic deliberative process could manage those details, either. There are just too many medical factors that, in any individual case, could create a barrier to a successful pregnancy. A wide range of costs might be associated with an equally wide range of medical interventions.

Another question that would have to be considered would be how many children a couple struggling with fertility issues had a right to conceive at social expense. I can imagine one practical "just enough" resolution. We could pick a dollar amount which we might call the "assisted reproduction benefit" that would be available to all in our society. The first number I would propose is $100,000. There is nothing morally sacred about that number—it could be lower; it is hard to imagine it being much higher. By picking a number we avoid mucking around in a very complex area of medicine.

The message our society would be giving to infertile individuals would be essentially this: "We want to provide you with a reasonable opportunity to have children of your own. If you were very fortunate and your infertility problem not too complex, then you might be able to have as many as three children with this benefit. You might be less fortunate. It might take considerable medical effort to identify and remedy the various medical factors interfering with your efforts to become pregnant. You might have to use the entire benefit to achieve a single pregnancy. If that is the case and you wish to have more children, then these additional costs are costs you will have to bear yourself. We have only limited health care resources, and there are many other higher-priority health needs for which those dollars must be reserved; that includes your own future possible health needs. It might also be the case that you are very unfortunate, that multiple medical efforts to address your fertility problems fail to achieve the pregnancy you seek, even though you have exhausted a substantial social benefit. Our best judgment is that the chances of your achieving a pregnancy with the investment of more resources and more effort are remote at best. As a society, we must regrettably acknowledge such limits. In many other circumstances, we have had to make equally painful judgments, some of which have resulted in death that we could no longer afford to forestall. You are free to continue to pursue any other medical options you believe might help you achieve your objective, but this pursuit will have to be funded by your own private resources."

In the deliberative process, we would have to ask ourselves where in the priority scheme this assisted reproduction benefit belonged so far as justice was concerned. I can imagine the sort of questions we would have to ask ourselves. To make things as concrete as possible, let us assume that the total annual cost of this benefit would be $5 billion. We presently spend about $8 billion per year on implantable cardiac defibrillators. If we could purchase $5 billion more of these per year (keeping in mind our earlier discussion of ICDs), would considerations of justice require that benefit, before we spent $5 billion on infertility services? If we could purchase $5 billion worth of artificial hearts for those between age 75 and 80, would considerations of justice require that we do that before we spent $5 billion on infertility services? If we could purchase $5 billion worth of those extraordinarily expensive anti-cancer drugs (Erbitux, Tarceva, Avastin, Herceptin, etc.) that would yield extra weeks or months of life for these patients, would considerations of justice require that we do that before we spent $5 billion on infertility services? From the perspective of health care justice, would it be more important to spend $5 billion on Factor VIIa for hemophiliacs or imiglucerase for patients with Gaucher's (at $300,000 per person per year), or spend that same $5 billion on infertility services? There are dozens of comparable questions that can be raised that are likely to be useful in establishing a reasonably just place in a prioritization scheme for these infertility services at $5 billion per year.[4]

We now have to return to the liberalism issue. If access to this range of infertility services is rightly construed as a matter of justice, then this takes away much of the force of the objections that might be raised by various religious or social groups to funding this benefit as part of a national health insurance scheme. That is, we would not be justified in refusing to fund blood transfusions because Jehovah's Witnesses were religiously opposed to this intervention. Likewise, if some religious group objected to funding protease inhibitors and comparable life-prolonging interventions for individuals who were HIV+ because AIDS was "just punishment from God," we would rightly ignore such objections as representing invidious discrimination under the cover of religious commitment. A just liberal society could hardly violate the basic rights of some citizens in order to satisfy the religious beliefs of others.

Critics of this line of argument above would have to show that the assisted reproductive benefit was not a matter of justice, or that this benefit caused unjust harm to them. They would have to justify these claims through public reason, not through any premises that were specifically tied to their religious commitments. One possible argument might be that it is unfair that they should have to pay for health care benefits that they would never use because those interventions are entirely contrary to their religious beliefs. This argument has prima facie plausibility. But then, some individuals choose a life of celibacy for either religious or nonreligious reasons—they can legitimately ask why they should have to pay the health care costs associated with giving birth or caring for children when they will never have children. But then, why should men have to pay for health care services that affect only women? And why should women have to pay for health care services that affect only men? If we carry that line of argument far enough, we dissolve the whole idea of an insurance pool. That outcome would be both unjust and imprudent. If a justice argument is going to be made, it will have to be made on stronger grounds than that.

Can critics of this liberal assisted reproductive benefit claim that their consciences are grievously harmed by their being forced to contribute money to the national insurance program that provides this benefit? Here, I believe we need to distinguish "offense" to the religious sensibilities of another as opposed to something approximating "invidious psychological harm" to another. Muslims might claim that their consciences are violated by seeing women in skimpy bikinis on public beaches, but this is more properly characterized as being offensive to them. A liberal society could not justifiably require women to be completely clothed at the beach to avoid the risk of giving offense to Muslims in the vicinity. Muslims are free to find more remote beaches or install swimming pools in their backyards. By way of contrast, many Muslims will refuse to eat pork for serious religious reasons. If the U.S. required Muslims in the U.S. to consume pork at least once a month to prove their loyalty to America and its liberal political system, this would represent "invidious psychological harm." This would be the moral equivalent of requiring a right-to-life health professional to perform an abortion as a requirement for keeping their job. Paying into a health insurance fund that underwrites a huge range of health care services, some of which are objectionable to some individuals with specific religious commitments, strikes me as being much closer to my example of Muslims on the beach as opposed to Muslims forced to eat pork.

I am obligated to pay taxes that support the war in Iraq, though I am certain it is an unjust war. I do not see myself as guilty of being a supporter of that war just by virtue of paying those taxes, especially if I speak out against it at every opportunity I might have. The necessary links for assigning moral responsibility are simply not there. It seems to me the same is true for individuals who object on moral or religious grounds to specific health services being included in a national health plan. They may object that my "sense of moral responsibility" is too lax. But I can respond that my judgment in this case reflects widely understood and accepted practices of assigning moral responsibility in our society. Further, if they wish to make more rigorous those assignments of responsibility, then they will have to offer public reasons (detached from any specific religious commitments) for their specific recommendations. Otherwise, public policy would have to reflect the most guilt-ridden religious psychopathies expressed by some religious group.

Here is another example that makes the same point from another perspective. Some deeply committed environmentalists have grave concerns about the effects of overpopulation on the fate of the earth's ability to sustain these populations. They imagine tens of millions of lives being lost as a result of famine or disease related to the fact that we have exceeded the carrying capacity of the earth. They would be especially outraged by religious individuals who choose to have six, seven, or eight children, thereby making the problem even worse. They, too, might claim that their consciences as environmentalists are grievously harmed by their paying into a national health insurance program that pays the birthing costs of all these children; they might want the national health insurance program to pay for no more than two births in a family. Again, however, though I myself would agree with the legitimacy of their concerns, I would not endorse the conclusion they want all to embrace. The limitation they propose would be illiberal. While we should be attentive to controlling the overall population of the earth for environmental reasons, those reasons are not strong enough to require limiting funds for births as a solution to that challenge. Other alternatives are available that will not violate our liberal commitments.

I said nothing about who could take advantage of this assisted reproductive benefit that could be part of a national health insurance program. The reader might have assumed that I had heterosexual couples in mind. But from a liberal pluralistic perspective committed to public reason for making public policy choices, limiting that benefit to couples would not be justified. Gay couples or single individuals would be eligible to take advantage of that benefit so long as there were no clear reasons for believing some particular couple or individual were incapable of being reasonably competent parents. If someone wishes to reject this expanded right to parenthood, the burden would be on them to provide reasons that were congruent with the requirements of public reason for this rejection.

This same line of argument can be deployed with regard to some of the objections that feminists might raise to having as part of a national health plan this assisted reproduction benefit. Feminists might see this as reinforcing traditional male stereotypical expectations that women had to be mothers. I can see the point of their argument. I would not want some overbearing male to force his wife to seek fertility services to gratify his ego need for children. However, I would have to count on competent counselors to assist in preventing this sort of unfortunate outcome from coming about. This represents a liberally reasonable approach to protecting the rights of women as persons to decide whether or not they wish to bear children, without taking away that option (wrongfully) from women who very much autonomously wish to have children of their own but would be unable to do that for reasons related to infertility.

One further point needs comment. I deliberately referred to the "assisted reproduction benefit" in as generic and aggregated a way as I could conceive. Some readers might have assumed that every service covered by that phrase would have elicited strong objections from one religious group or another. However, that would not be true. orthodox Roman Catholics might not take advantage of IVF, but they could certainly take a drug such as Clomid which can be effective in helping to increase the probability of becoming pregnant in a way that orthodox Catholics would not reject. I should also call attention again to the fact that there are degrees of Catholicism, just as there are degrees of liberalism or conservatism or environmentalism, et cetera. I might be excommunicated by the Pope for saying that, but it is at least a sociological truth. More than 85% of adult American Roman Catholics use some form of birth control, contrary to the official teaching of the Catholic Church. Also, roughly half of Catholics see abortion as a morally legitimate choice under some range of circumstances. They might see it as an unfortunate choice, but they do not condemn women who see this as a necessary option for themselves. Likewise, some fraction of Roman Catholics who are faced with infertility will wish to avail themselves of IVF or some comparable form of assisted reproduction that might be rejected by official church teaching. I mention these things because if we are going to make public policy in ways crafted not to offend this or that religious group, then we should be honest enough to recognize that few religious or social or political groups are homogeneous enough that all members of the group affirm precisely the same moral commitments. If we eliminated the reproductive assistance benefit entirely from a national health plan to avoid giving offense to the most conservative of Catholics, then we would have effectively imposed those limitations on more liberal Catholics, as well as numerous non-Catholics. That is more properly characterized as illiberal, especially if considerations of health care justice would support such a benefit and it were legitimated through a reasonable process of democratic deliberation.

CONCLUDING REFLECTIONS

Public reasons linked to public interests and our shared sense of health care justice (as constructed through well-ordered, rational, democratic deliberative processes) are what are necessary to justify the inclusion or exclusion of any particular health service in a national health care benefit package. As long as this general guideline is followed, what we have referred to as the "liberalism problem" is dissolved. That is, no one is forced to violate or abandon their reasonable religious commitments in order to have full and secure access to the broad range of health care services that we would guarantee to all in our society as a matter of justice.[5] If such individuals object to some medical services in a national benefit package, they always have the liberty right to avoid using those services. They also have the right to use the normal processes of democratic deliberation to seek to effect changes in the content of the national benefit package, but they can hardly expect to receive a sympathetic hearing if they are unable to offer public reasons in support of their requests for change. Likewise, such religious individuals may advocate for an expanded benefit package, or they might advocate for abandoning one or another future rationing protocol that might be part of the national benefit package. But they will again have to offer public reasons to support that for which they advocate. Let me give some brief concluding examples to illustrate my major points. Some religious individuals (as in the Wanglie case) might want unrelenting, aggressive, life-sustaining efforts to be made in the case of patients in PVS or in the case of anencephalic infants, though what I am imagining for the sake of this example is that we have a rationing protocol in the future that would provide comfort care only to such patients once a diagnosis was confidently established. Advocates for rejecting this rationing protocol might insist these patients are alive, and therefore, a just and caring society must sustain those lives. This is a public reason, but it is not a public reason with which anyone in our society will disagree. These patients are alive in only the most minimal sense imaginable, and nothing that medicine has to offer today can improve their status an iota. Their lives are not correctly described as being of "low quality." They are lives of no quality; no capacity to experience anything at all. The potential billions of dollars per year that would be needed to sustain such lives indefinitely are more justly used to protect the lives and quality of lives of patients whom medicine can substantially benefit.

What does this last conclusion mean with respect to the Jehovah's Witness patient who will bleed out and die without access to Factor VIIa? There is a full life that can be completely saved by contemporary medicine. This is not a PVS patient. The problem is, however, that it would cost $100,000 to save that life *because of the very specific religious demands associated with that religious commitment*. We can save that life for less than 1% of that cost but for those religious commitments. If we agreed to pay those costs through a national health insurance program, we would be providing public support for that religious commitment, which would be unjust and illiberal. The logic of that support would force us to accept the legitimacy of the claim that human life is priceless, and all the practical implications attached to that view; this is the view we rejected in Chapter 2. We emphasize again that we are not condemning such patients to death. We have to rely upon members of that faith community to make appropriate, prudent, collective decisions about how to respond to such medical risks. If they wish to assure themselves access to Factor VIIa in the relevant medical circumstances, they will have to find an insurance plan or create an insurance plan that would provide those resources to its members when needed. This is not a broader responsibility of the larger society.

An objection might be raised along these lines. Some religious groups engage in snake handling with the risk of snake bites; other religious groups might engage in various forms of self-mutilation that will require medical attention. Are we going to deny these individuals medical attention because these medical needs were attached to religious practices? The obvious answer is that we will not deny them the care they need. However, this would not represent public support for the religious practices that generated these injuries. Individuals may imprudently wander over areas of vegetation infested with snakes in spite of clear signs warning of such danger; we treat those individuals without inquiring in any detail how they acquired those injuries. All snake bites get treated the same way, whether religiously or irreligiously acquired. All episodes of bleeding out get treated the same way. The problem arises when someone requests $100,000 worth of special care to accommodate their religious beliefs when $1,000 worth of the usual care would have addressed the medical problem. We (liberal citizens and health professionals) do adjust normal medical practices to reflect respect for particular religious or cultural commitments. But such adjustments may never be at the expense of the rights or just claims of other patients.

Finally, there is a current case in Canada that has garnered substantial media attention. This is the Golubchuk case (Blackwell, 2007). In 2003, this gentleman fell and hit his head; he was severely brain damaged as a result. He was unable to speak or communicate in any way. He was unable to take food by mouth or breathe on his own, so he was on feeding tubes and a ventilator. Some additional medical problems forced him into a hospital on November 11, 2007. He had 45 liters of excess water in his body. He was so swollen that his skin was near to bursting. He was suffering horribly. But his family (as Orthodox Jews) insisted that everything medically possible be done to sustain his life. It is irrelevant to them that he is suffering greatly; his son insisted it would be "a sin to do anything to hasten death." There is a justice issue here (especially in Canada where hospitals must work with global budgets). But I am going to pass over that issue. The physicians in this case believe everything they are doing is the moral equivalent of torture. They are using their medical skills to inflict a prolonged and painful death on this individual, contrary to what they see as the central values of the medical profession. They feel that they have been conscripted into the service of this religion, that they are mere tools in the hands of this family, and that their own consciences are deeply violated by having to work so hard to only prolong a process of dying. I believe in this case that their moral judgments are correct. This is not a situation that a liberal society is forced to tolerate out of respect for this religious tradition. The core commitment of a liberal society is to mutual respect—that is precisely what is lacking in this case.

13

THE ETHICAL CHALLENGES OF PRIORITY SETTING IN PUBLIC HEALTH

DEFINING THE PROBLEM

"Explicating the demands of justice in allocating public health resources and in setting priorities for public health policies, or in determining whom they should target, remains among the most daunting challenges in public health ethics" (Childress et al., 2002). This is the primary challenge taken on in this chapter. Our key question is as follows: What does it mean to be a just and caring society so far as meeting public health care needs is concerned when we have only limited resources to meet virtually unlimited health care needs of all sorts? This is a complex question, so our first task will be to sort out this complexity.

Three working assumptions lie behind our key question. First, we assume that issues of justice need to be addressed with respect to meeting public health needs, that these decisions are not simply a matter of social beneficence (freely given or withheld for any reason at all), and that these decisions also ought not be determined through the morally arbitrary use of political power. The basis for this first working assumption is that we are talking about public health *needs*, which, if a society fails to address them, will have morally objectionable consequences so far as protecting fair equality of opportunity is concerned. Daniels (1985) has argued that we are not morally obligated as a society to pursue "equal health for all," an impossible ideal. But we are obligated as a matter of health care justice to provide access to needed and effective health care for all whose normal opportunity range has been significantly constrained by ill health. Public health, just like expansive public education, has the morally desirable feature of protecting fair equality of opportunity for all. (Again, we regard Daniels' conception of health care justice as a reasonable perspective but not the only perspective for justified judgments of health care justice.) Further, for reasons we explain in the following text, the public nature of these needs means that individuals as individuals will lack the capacity to meet these needs effectively.

Second, the needs we have in mind are truly endless. Hence, we assume that health care rationing and priority setting are inescapable. Efforts to get rid of waste and inefficiency in the health care system will not magically generate resources that will obviate the need for rationing (Ubel, 2000). Third, public health needs will have to compete with individualized medical needs for resources; that is, as a moral and practical political matter, public health needs cannot be segregated from the rationing issues that we have seen are ubiquitous in medicine. Part of the reason for this competition is the current controversy around the legitimate scope of public health.

Many opinion and editorial writers today tell us that we are faced with an "epidemic of obesity" (Lichtarowicz, 2004). That language is intended to suggest that we are faced with a public health crisis and that the government needs to intervene to somehow contain this threat to public health. Others (Epstein, 2003), however, would see this as a massive abrogation of personal responsibility, which personal physicians and their overweight patients need to acknowledge and then effectively address. We will also find in both medical journals (Hogan, 1999) and the popular press references to an "epidemic of violence," followed by a long recitation of statistics documenting a multitude of modes of mayhem, such as the 29,000 firearm deaths in the United States in 2003. Often the follow-up commentary will conclude with a call for public health officials to do something. Over the past few years, multiple studies have documented racial and economic disparities in health and access to health care, often denouncing the injustice represented by these disparities (Kawachi and Kennedy, 1999; Kawachi, Kennedy, and Wilkinson, 1999; Daniels, 2002). Again, these moral judgments are very often accompanied by a call for public health officials to become engaged in and to find ways of reducing or eliminating these disparities (Mann, 1997; Kass, 2001).

No doubt obesity, violence, poverty, and racial discrimination all represent threats to the health of the population. They represent unnecessary morbidity and mortality that in principle could be reduced or eliminated. And if we think of the mission of public health as the reduction or control of threats to the health of the public, then we might well conclude that it is the responsibility of public health officials to do something about obesity, violence, poverty, and racial discrimination. However, this conclusion yields a very unwieldy, very expansive conception of what ought to come under the rubric of public health. The task of the second part of this chapter is to establish some reasonable boundaries around the conception of public health, without which issues of public health justice are impossible to address.

Public health expenditures are typically contrasted with medical expenditures for individual health. In 2007 in the United States we spent about $2.3 trillion on health care, roughly 16.3 percent of our GDP. Only 3 percent of that total expenditure is attributed to public health. We could argue about whether such relatively small expenditures for public health were prudent or imprudent. But that is not our focus. Our concern is whether such limited expenditures represent an injustice, an unfair distribution of either the benefits of our very advanced health care system or the burdens (death/disability) associated with preventable or ameliorable illness and injury. We might concretize the issue as follows: If there are disproportionate rates of premature death and avoidable disability among identifiable social groups (i.e., the poor, racial or ethnic minorities, or other groups that are the targets of discriminatory social attitudes), and if these health disadvantages are properly judged to be matters of injustice, then will considerations of justice require that resources be reallocated from medical interventions to public health interventions instead? Or, alternatively, would justice be equally well satisfied if medical resources were simply redistributed from the relatively healthy and advantaged (de-funding expensive, marginally beneficial interventions) to the disproportionately unhealthy (and in other ways socially disadvantaged), funding other *medical* interventions that were typically effective and cost worthy? In other words, there would be no increase in public health spending to achieve this goal because reallocation within the domain of medicine would have been sufficient. This issue is the focus of the third part of this chapter.

In the fourth part we will address the question of priority setting within public health. Our core question is as follows: Are there considerations of health care justice that ought to dictate to some extent what our public health priorities ought to be? If so, what precisely are those considerations of justice? Should the dominant consideration be the Rawlsian concern for the least well off? If so, what criteria should we use for identifying who the least well off are from a public health perspective? Assuming we can provide a satisfactory answer to the previous question, is it in fact possible to target the relevant public health interventions *that precisely*, which we seem to do regularly and easily in medicine generally? Alternatively, should public health priorities be determined mostly or entirely by utilitarian considerations? If so, what is it that we are seeking to maximize across the spectrum of public health needs? Are we, for example, seeking to maximize the number of life-years saved through various public health interventions? If so, does this imply that we are morally obligated to award higher priority to each and every public health intervention that has the promise of saving lives or life-years over any public health intervention that would merely result in the prevention of injury or disability? Further, is this an implication we ought to endorse as a matter of health care justice? Finally, should either cost-effectiveness or quality-of-life considerations be regarded as morally relevant in determining priorities among public health needs? One recent essay strongly recommends that improving the quality of end-of-life care should be a high-priority focus for public health (Rao et al., 2002). Is this a conclusion that ought to be endorsed from the perspective of health care justice?

THE SCOPE OF PUBLIC HEALTH: CHALLENGES AND CHOICES

Considerable controversy exists over what the scope of public health ought to be. To simplify matters, we will distinguish the *traditionalists* from the *expansionists*. The traditional tasks of public health include (1) prevention and control of infectious diseases, such as acquired immunodeficiency syndrome (AIDS), severe acute respiratory syndrome (SARS), West Nile virus, tuberculosis, Legionnaires' disease, various sexually transmitted diseases, and so on; (2) prevention and control of food-borne illness, which involves recommending and enforcing regulations aimed at protecting the food supply at all stages of production and distribution; (3) monitoring the quality of the environment and enforcing environmental regulations to protect the public's health from contaminated air or water, or hazardous waste, or a broad range of other environmental threats; (4) health education and health promotion activities aimed at discouraging behavioral activities that represent serious threats to health, such as antismoking campaigns; (5) epidemiological research aimed at generating an accurate assessment of the magnitude and relative risk associated with various threats to public health. What unifies these otherwise apparently disparate activities is that (1) they are all aimed at efficiently and effectively preventing injury, disability, or premature death; (2) the specific activities are seen as protecting what are primarily the *public interests* rather than the health interests of individuals; and (3) the coercive powers of the government are legitimately employed to achieve these ends.

Some (Epstein, 2003) will argue that health promotion and health education should not be regarded as part of traditional public health. The thought of "obesity police," hanging around doughnut shops only for purposes of apprehending the criminally obese, is frightening. However, neither I nor others (Gostin and Bloche, 2003) have anything like that in mind. To the extent that health promotion and health education are analogous in practice to "public education" they can be fitted under the traditional public health rubric. Our society makes formal public education "freely available" because there is a strong public interest in having a well-educated citizenry capable of contributing to our economic advancement (as well as their own personal well-being). Less well-off citizens would not be able to avail themselves of these educational opportunities if they were not "free at the point of service." In theory, individuals can "educate themselves" either in the formal general sense or about health matters. But in practice we might have a less healthy citizenry if we left health education entirely to private and personal initiative and expense. As for the coercion part, our society cannot endorse coercing individuals to shed pounds (given our liberal political commitments), but we can use the coercive powers of the government to require all manner of food labeling in order to educate the public about the nutritional value or nutritional risks posed by various foods. This is entirely congruent with our liberal political values. The fact that genuine *public interests* are at stake is most central to what public health is about (as opposed to the more expansive notion of the *social determinants of health*).

A reasonable definition of public interests would say that they are interests that each and every citizen has but that citizens as individuals (or even as organized private groups of individuals) would be unable to maintain or protect adequately without the organizational and coercive powers of the government. Clean air, clean water, and a safe food supply are all readily seen as satisfying this definition in our contemporary world. Powerful corporations motivated by profit maximization have no reason to pay anything at all to protect air or water quality from being fouled by their activities, nor do individuals have either the power or the interest to compel corporations to behave in a more socially responsible manner. Though each of us would rationally not wish to see our lives shortened by polluted air or water, none of us would spend most of our resources to achieve such an objective since everyone else would benefit from our efforts without having contributed to underwriting those costs. This is the classic "free rider" problem. The government can use its powers to collect taxes from all to put in place policies and regulations that will compel a level of corporate compliance that could never be achieved by individual effort. Likewise, few of us individually have the expertise needed to ensure the safety of the food we consume. And none of us can really protect ourselves through our own efforts alone from infectious diseases. Typically we would have no way of knowing in a timely enough way as to who might be infected with a serious disease before we ourselves would have been exposed to the infection and put at risk. This is what *traditional* public health is about. Then there are the expansionists.

The expansionists build on the core elements that have justified traditional public health activities. Public health regulates and discourages the use of tobacco products because of the inherent dangers of tobacco to health (thought of on the model of food), with manufacturers emphasizing the pleasures of smoking and denying for a very long time its dangers (which few individuals could assess on their own). But someone will point out that smoking is a "voluntary" activity, the point being that public health authorities are not legitimate regulators of the activity since individuals have "chosen" to assume this risk themselves. However, smoking puts at risk third parties who have not volunteered to assume those risks and who are unjustly harmed by the choices of smokers. That restores the (apparent) legitimacy of the public interest claim. I will stipulate for the sake of argument that this is a reasonable claim. However, this line of reasoning launches the expansionist project.

The use or abuse of alcohol represents an individual choice. This fact would hardly warrant public health attention. But the social consequences of alcohol abuse are massive, as represented by drunk driving or excess health costs associated with alcohol-related diseases that are borne by taxpayers or insurance premium payers. And, while alcoholism stretches across all income tiers, poverty or dead-end jobs or a host of other social determinants (corporate performance pressures) create an environment that motivates and supports alcohol abuse. All of this is again intended to suggest both that a public health response is legitimate and necessary and that an individualized medical response is misguided and ineffective because such individualized responses fail to address the deep social determinants associated with alcohol abuse. This very same line of reasoning can be deployed with respect to illegal recreational drugs. Likewise, with some moderate factual adjustments, this line of reasoning will (apparently) justify a public health effort to address the "epidemic of obesity" or the "epidemic of violence."

Note that the language of "epidemic" is deliberate and that the public health expansionists who invoke this notion do not intend this as just a bit of rhetorical excess. The relevant argument might go like this: In the case of the 1918–1919 influenza pandemic or in the case of AIDS there is a biological infectious agent that is the immediate cause of illness or death in individuals. But it would be very wrongheaded to believe that that the infectious agent was the sole cause or the whole cause of the morbidity and mortality in either epidemic. Complex social factors (e.g., ease of worldwide travel, bath houses, discrimination against gays that drives them into a hidden subculture, denial of access to the stability of marriage) are also integral in explaining the magnitude and the precise form of a particular epidemic (and, by implication, the complex social response that will be needed to contain or abort that epidemic). The infectious agent is just one of the causal factors in a multidimensional causal schema that results in a particular pattern of morbidity and mortality.

Sometimes no infectious agent is needed to trigger a very complex social process that results in unnecessary morbidity and mortality, as would be the case with obesity or violence or alcohol abuse or a very steep income gradient in a particular society. What is most salient (and warrants a public health response from the perspective of the expansionists) is that there are these persistent social determinants that precipitate and sustain the ill health effects associated with obesity or violence (e.g., a fast-paced culture that demands cheap fast food, easy access to cheap guns, a cultural belief system that encourages gun ownership), and these social determinants (and their ill health effects) remain largely unaffected so long as the primary health response involves no more than the medical treatment of affected individuals. What is really needed to substantially reduce the "epidemic" nature of the ill health effects is a comprehensive public health response aimed at those deep social determinants of violence or obesity or alcoholism.

Both Rothstein (2002) and Gostin (2001) are critics of this expansionist version of public health, and I am strongly inclined to agree with them. None of us reject the rightness or legitimacy of the social goals that these expansionists would like to see achieved. For example, I agree with Daniels (2002) that the steepness of the gradient between the rich and the poor in our society is a serious social injustice, which ought to be remedied. But I do not agree with those expansionists who would see this as a responsibility that ought to fall under the rubric of public health. Gostin (2001, p. 123) provides us with three reasons for this conclusion that I find persuasive. First, this expansivist view would make public health limitless in scope. Virtually every social problem that has any adverse consequences for health would become a matter of public health. Such limitless responsibility would ultimately be counterproductive. This can be readily seen when we consider his second point, which is that public health officials would have to acquire expertise in virtually every major academic discipline available in order to fulfill such a wide-ranging view of their role. And third, what the expansivist project would require is economic redistribution and social restructuring on a massive scale by officials representing public health. In other words, public health officials would have to take on (to use one example) the task of major tax reform for purposes of improving social justice. This would be a very politically controversial task, far removed from the more traditional, more mundane, largely noncontroversial tasks associated with public health.

I would put the matter as follows: There are numerous domains or dimensions to social justice, that is, social institutions and practices that might fall far short of the requirements of justice. We have no good reason to believe that a social justice czar should have the responsibility for remedying these deficiencies, much less a public health czar. Rather, as a moral and a practical matter the social and political leaders in those social domains should have that responsibility. This implies an acceptance of nonideal incremental sectoral approaches to bring about a more just state of affairs so far as health care is concerned (Fleck, 1987, pp. 165–176). This may well be all that is morally reasonable and politically possible. Gostin and Bloche (2003) make a useful distinction between public health research, which can be legitimately more expansive, and public health practice, which needs to be more constrained in its ambitions. This is a reasonable distinction.

HEALTH CARE JUSTICE AND PUBLIC HEALTH: WHEN IS ENOUGH ENOUGH?

Daniel Callahan writes: "The best prescription for a healthy population is a good public health system, decent jobs and education, and a prudent lifestyle" (1998, p. 173). He goes on to say that in the future priority for resource allocation ought to go to public health rather than individual health and that this is the key to a "sustainable medicine." This latter phrase is a term of art referring to the extraordinary and unsustainable pace at which medical care costs have increased over the past 40 years. Roughly, we have seen more than a tripling of the fraction of GDP allocated to health care in the period from 1960 to 2007, from 5.2 percent of GDP to 16.3 percent. Further, the projections to 2017 are that we will be spending $4.3 trillion on health care then, roughly 19.5 percent of GDP (Keehan et al., 2008). The majority of those health cost increases are tied to an explosion in life-preserving medical technologies during that period, virtually all of which are aimed at meeting *individual* health needs as opposed to population health needs. Callahan sees this as a moral and political failure. He calls our attention to scientific research emphasizing the "behavioral causes of many illnesses and disabilities" (1998, p. 175) and concludes that our society must demand much more from its citizens in terms of personal responsibility for illness. The appropriate social response to such failure for him is increased investment in public health efforts aimed at disease prevention and health promotion. He also wants to see dramatically increased recognition by individuals "that their personal behavior will significantly determine their lifetime health prospects and that they have a social obligation to take care of themselves for their own sake as well as that of their neighbor" (p. 176).

Callahan wants to see a significant decrease in expenditures on "rescue medicine." From his perspective, the bulk of rescue medicine is aimed at rescuing people from their own bad choices (over the course of a lifetime). Rescue medicine tends to be very costly and the benefits tend to be marginal in the aggregate. Callahan attaches moral primacy to the value of social solidarity, which he sees in a health care context as being best satisfied by substantial investments in public health. He writes: "Communal sufficiency will include an effort to help the majority of citizens avoid premature death, and to protect them from epidemics, contaminated food and water, correctable environmental hazards, and the like. Technologies for this purpose should have the highest priority" (p. 204).

Though Callahan does not explicitly make this next point, we could add that this pronounced emphasis on rescue medicine has unacceptable social justice consequences. The prime beneficiaries of rescue medicine are those who are already financially well off and well insured. What we have seen over the last 20 years are rapid increases in the number of uninsured in the United States (about 47 million in 2007), mostly attributable to escalating health costs that prompt employers to drop health insurance as a benefit. These are largely smaller employers and employees who are financially less well off, who will also be less well off health-wise due to their inability to pay for costly health care if they have serious health problems. The implicit argument here is that a shift of resources to public health investments will result in a more equal sharing by all who enjoy the benefits of those investments. The background belief in this argument is that public health expenditures have the morally virtuous outcome of benefiting virtually everyone more or less equally. If we improve sanitation or environmental quality, then everyone enjoys that benefit; no one can be arbitrarily excluded for morally dubious reasons, as with our private health insurance system. And, therefore, putting more money into public health represents a clear moral imperative. It is this last claim that needs some critical moral assessment.

Friends of public health routinely cite the huge population health gains that have been achieved as a result of investments in public health over the last century. These have included childhood vaccination programs, motor-vehicle safety, safer workplaces, control of infectious diseases, safer and healthier foods, healthier mothers and babies (90 percent decrease in infant mortality, 99 percent decrease in maternal mortality), fluoridation of drinking water, and a 51 percent decrease in deaths from stroke and coronary heart disease since 1972 (Centers for Disease Control and Prevention, 1999). Further, these enormous health gains were achieved with relatively modest investments in public health. In comparison, rescue medicine today benefits far fewer individuals to a much smaller degree at very much higher costs. The implicit moral conclusion is that this state of affairs is fundamentally unjust.

I am not so confident that that moral judgment is unequivocally true. I take as a fundamental moral premise that health care ought to be distributed by a just society in accord with health care need. I am cognizant of the fact that this is only the beginning of a moral argument. Not all health needs are morally equal; priorities need to be established among health needs. Health needs can become unsustainably expansive if they are closely linked to advancing medical technologies (Callahan, 1990, chapter 2). The health needs that make just claims on us must somehow be linked to the costs of meeting those needs and the effectiveness of available therapeutic interventions. Meeting health needs ought not to be linked either to the ability to pay by individuals who have those needs or to the arbitrary beneficent inclinations of employers, both of which are amply represented in the current U.S. health care system. The virtue of a commitment to universal health care is that *everyone* has a significant portion of his or her health needs met without having to be concerned about denial of care due to personal inability to pay or other arbitrary factors. Public health is seen as having this very same virtue. If infectious diseases are well controlled and if the water supply is fluoridated, then *everyone* benefits and no one is denied those benefits on morally arbitrary grounds. This suggests the moral conclusion embraced by Callahan that a truly just society ought to be investing a lot more in public health and a lot less in meeting the health needs of individuals as individuals. However, that conclusion might have been drawn too quickly.

A number of morally relevant distinctions need to be made among the types of public health interventions. To begin with, many public health interventions may have relatively significant upfront costs and very low maintenance costs. Once sanitation systems are put in place or factories are retrofitted to protect air quality, the environmental quality gains are sustained for decades at very low annual costs. This intervention has the very desirable effect of reducing to almost insignificant levels the cost per unit of benefit (contrary to much of medicine where the cost of a heart transplant is $300,000 whether we do one thousand or a hundred thousand of them). Further, these interventions may be very effective in terms of dramatic reductions in mortality and morbidity. However, it might also be the case that we are dealing with the proverbial "low-hanging fruit" phenomenon.

Future public health interventions might not be able to come anywhere close to achieving these outcomes. Public health interventions will reach the economist's flat of the curve just as readily as other medical interventions. That maternal mortality was reduced by 99 percent over the course of a century (due to excellent infection control) is clearly morally commendable. But the cost of eliminating that final 1 percent might be exorbitant. Reducing carcinogenic effluents in air or water another one or two parts per billion by controlling factory emissions, thereby preventing 10 more cancer deaths per year nationally at an amortized cost per year of $10 million likely represents an excessively costly marginal benefit, especially if we can identify alternative ways of saving a greater number of lives at a lower cost with those same dollars. Given any number of presently unmet health needs of women, even needs that have nothing to do with mortality reduction, those needs might make stronger claims on resources from the perspective of justice than additional maternal mortality reduction or marginal improvements in air or water quality.

The work of Louise Russell is quite salient at this point. She calls our attention to a number of public health interventions that are very inexpensive at the level of individual screening and that appear eminently worthy of funding in terms of the desirability of the goals being sought, for example, reduction of uterine cancer by

93 percent through annual Pap smears for women older than 40, but that might have a very low payoff from the perspective of cost-effectiveness analysis. The cost of such a program is more than $2.3 million per life-year saved. However, if that same screening program is carried out at 3-year intervals, then we will still save 91 percent of the potential life-years to be saved and the cost will be approximately $84,500 per life-year saved (Russell, 2000). A similar story can be told with regard to screening mammograms for women 50–69 years old, which we imagine is a free public screening program aimed at an at-risk group. Screening can be done either annually or biennially. Only a very slight gain in lives saved is achieved through an annual program, again at a very high cost-per-life-year-saved (Russell, 2000). But Russell also points out that false-positive results are a significant problem with screening mammograms. One study found that over a 10-year period, 31.7 percent of women who received biennial mammograms experienced at least one false-positive result, with all the additional expense, suffering, and anxiety attached to such results.

The above examples suggest the following reasonable conclusion: No wholesale transfer of resources from the medical side of the ledger to the public health side is warranted if the motivating belief is that this will result in a more just distribution of health care in our society. All manner of public health investments are as vulnerable to being marginally beneficial and non–cost worthy as anything that is part of medicine (see Cohen et al., 2008). If, with Callahan, we are inclined to judge that very expensive marginal benefits associated with high-tech medicine generate no just claims, then we ought to affirm the same judgment with respect to public health interventions that yield similar expensive marginally beneficial results.

One book by Louise Russell has the provocative title: *Is Prevention Better Than Cure?* (1985). Our common sense intuition might be to give a quick affirmative answer to this question. Why, we ask ourselves rhetorically, should anyone have to suffer disease or injury if we have the capacity to prevent that from happening? And, if the costs of prevention were very low, and if our preventive efforts were extraordinarily effective, then the answer to our question would be easy and obvious. However, the world is more complex than that. Hundreds of screening tests could in theory be put in place for public health purposes. But it is certain that not all these tests would be worthy of being funded. About 33 percent of HIV-infected individuals in the United States do not know they are HIV positive. We would like to prevent them from unknowingly infecting others. We could identify virtually all those individuals if we tested everyone. Do we have any reason to believe, however, that this would be a wise or just or cost-effective use of limited health care resources? Would we have any guarantee that individuals informed of their HIV-positive status would refrain from any behavior that could result in the infection of others? Uncertainty in this regard would clearly diminish the utility of this test. Further, if this screening test cost only $25, universal screening in the United States would cost more than $7 billion per round of testing. Given new infections with each passing day, screening twice per year would be necessary. That would be $14 billion per year. What health care should we give up in order to fund that screening program? Should we give up the $5 billion we discussed in the previous chapter for an assisted reproduction benefit as part of a national health insurance program? We currently spend about $14 billion per year for the complex drug regimen used to protect the lives of HIV-positive individuals whose immune systems have been seriously compromised. Would it be just to take away all these funds from that sort of "rescue medicine" in order to fund this public health intervention? Further, apart from the money issue and justice issue, could we justify the privacy rights violations that would be required by such a screening program? We run into a similar problem today with regard to the proposal in some states that we make human papillomavirus (HPV) vaccination mandatory (Gostin and DeAngelis, 2007). The public health objectives are clearly meritorious, but they might be better achieved (all things considered) through a more voluntary public education effort.

Other screening programs for public health purposes would raise other issues. Some screening programs could identify individuals in the earliest stages of a disease process for which we had no effective therapeutic intervention. Depending upon the nature of the disease process and its health implications, such knowledge might still be somewhat beneficial to some individuals, perhaps for life planning purposes. But, depending upon the cost of such screening and the trade-offs that would have to be made to fund the screening, it might be unjust to offer such a program for such limited and personal benefits. Further, with other screening programs there will be complex causal networks that introduce substantial uncertainty into the practical significance of positive test results. This is very likely to be true in the case of most genetic tests, which will reveal at most increased susceptibility to a certain disease process for individuals with a specific genotype. A particular genotype may be associated with an increased risk for various forms of cancer or heart disease, but additional complexly related causal factors (epigenetic or environmental) may be necessary in order to trigger an actual disease process in any individual. From a practical point of view, positive test results will have little or no utility, either at the individual or at the social level. Hence, what would be the justification for the reallocation of social resources for that sort of screening program?

Other potential screening programs undertaken as a public health measure could raise more directly problems of health care justice. Recent medical research (Ehrenstein et al., 2005; Ridker et al., 2005) suggests that it might be desirable to reduce both low-density lipoprotein (LDL) levels and C-reactive protein (CRP) levels (associated with arterial inflammation) for purposes of reducing heart attacks and stroke. Both can be measured with simple, inexpensive ($55 for the CRP test) blood tests. In this case a therapeutic response exists for elevated levels of either LDL or CRP. Specifically, individuals would begin taking statins. But these drugs can easily cost in excess of $1,200 per year, and they would need to be taken for years and years. Well-insured individuals could readily afford to do this; others who were uninsured or less well off economically could not. If such a testing program were deployed as a public health screening program, the net result, morally speaking, would be a net increase in the maldistribution of health care resources. (Noteworthy is the fact that in 2007 in the United States we spent $15 billion on statins.) The already well off would be made better off while the less well off would be no better off. The point again is that investments in public health efforts are no guarantee of a fairer or more equitable distribution of health care in our society. Some public health expenditures can yield more unjust outcomes.

The key question we need to answer is whether we ought to be reallocating health resources from medicine aimed at meeting individual needs to public health aimed at meeting the needs of all. For the moment we need to consider that question in the context of the actual organizational features of our health care system. The proverbial 800-pound fact that confronts us is that those who are working at "good jobs" all have private health insurance. But we have no practical way of transferring resources expended on marginally beneficial noncostworthy health care in the private sector to the public sector.

Someone might suggest a 10 percent tax on private insurance premiums to be used for public health purposes. That, however, is not a transfer of resources from private health care; it simply represents an addition to overall health costs. This is not morally objectionable intrinsically, but a likely result is that these added costs would prompt employers providing health insurance at the margins to drop health insurance altogether as a benefit, thereby adding to the pool of the uninsured. Apart from that, public health care would need to be paid with public resources.

Assuming we are not free to rob other nonhealth budget areas, increasing public health expenditures means resources would need to be transferred from health care, Medicare and Medicaid. The problem, of course, is that both these programs serve largely vulnerable populations that are less well off health-wise and wealth-wise. From the perspective of health care justice it looks like we would be taking resources from the less well off and least well off in order to fund broad public health purposes. This is not an outcome that commands moral approbation. Also, it is not unreasonable to ask whether the poor and the elderly who are the beneficiaries of Medicare and Medicaid would (or should) endorse such a transfer of resources. Just so the reader knows in concrete terms what we are asking here, I would note that if we only wanted to raise public health expenditures from 3 to 5 percent of total health expenditures, those two percentage points equal $46 billion in 2007.

We could argue that we intended to cull those resources from marginally beneficial noncostworthy health services currently provided to the elderly and the poor, which they ought to rationally and morally forgo. However, they could then reasonably respond that those recaptured dollars ought to be redirected to what they judged as higher priority health needs for themselves rather than public health needs. This response might not be well received by Callahan and his communitarian allies because it would reflect the individualistic biases of contemporary medicine. But in these circumstances it is not obvious that these biases are open to justified moral criticism.

A case could be made more readily for a shift in resources toward public health objectives and away from expensive marginally beneficial health care if all in our society were part of the same health plan, and hence, more or less equally likely to lose access to health services judged too expensive for the marginal benefits achieved. In that scenario, given wise public health investments, virtually all in our society would be beneficiaries of those public health investments and also at risk to a small degree of being denied those expensive marginal benefits. Some of those denied these marginal benefits would be among the "least well off," but this would not be morally consequential so long as they were not disproportionately vulnerable to those losses, which is precisely the moral problem with any reallocation of resources away from Medicare and Medicaid.

Perhaps we ought to take another critical observation by Callahan as our reference point for justifying a transfer of resources from medical care to public health. Callahan contends that a very large proportion of what we regard as health needs in our society is a product of irresponsible health choices by individuals (e.g., smoking, unhealthy diets, excess use of alcohol, and so on). I will grant for the sake of argument that this claim is largely true. What, practically and morally, ought to follow from that? Should society, for example, devise a system for "punishing" such individuals by denying them access to expensive lifesaving or life-prolonging medical resources, thereby generating the savings that would be redirected to public health?

Imagine this scenario: An individual has been in a serious auto accident and is bleeding badly. There is a strong smell of alcohol on his breath. A quick blood alcohol test is done to establish that his levels are over twice the legal limit. Would we be morally justified in allowing him to bleed to death right there because he had made an irresponsible choice? And if he has a passenger in his car, equally inebriated and equally injured, do we treat that person as an unfortunate victim (and therefore save that life), or do we treat the passenger as an irresponsible co-conspirator (subject to the same denial of care)? If either of these individuals was able to pay for the lifesaving care they needed from their own personal resources, should the care then be provided to them? Under any of these options, would we see such social choices as reflecting a morally defensible conception of what a just and caring society ought to be?

The virtue of this first scenario is that there are relatively tight causal connections between the behavior and the outcome that seem to support strong personal responsibility judgments. But fair judging gets a lot more complicated if we consider smoking and lung cancer or heart disease or emphysema. Perhaps reliable judgments of responsibility can be made for the individual with a 40-year two-pack-a-day history. But how should we judge the individual who starts with a 10-year two-pack history, quits for a year, then relapses, quits again, and relapses again for varying lengths of time over 30 years, faced now with advanced heart disease? Should we judge such a person a recalcitrant sinner (duly denied lifesaving health care) or a persevering penitent (deserving the life-sustaining care)? Would even Dworkin's Hercules (1986, chapter 7) have the rational capacities and moral discernment needed to make a fair judgment regarding this individual's fate? One public health researcher concludes in this regard, "The considerable attention paid to identifying plausible justifications for restricting individual autonomy to change unhealthy behaviors is largely misguided" (Buchanan, 2008). He believes public health needs to have other priorities rooted in a conception of social justice articulated through a democratic deliberative process.

Then there are all the truly complicated scenarios associated (I suspect) with the vast majority of chronic illness in our society, all the personal failings mixed in inextricably complex ways with family histories and psychological vulnerabilities and genetic happenstance and innumerable social behavioral determinants, cultural and economic, largely beyond individual control or responsibility. Who could fairly judge in each and every individual case whether the person's ill health was due to a culpable failure of personal responsibility? How would we imagine gathering evidence to support such judgments? Would personal physicians have this responsibility? If so, what would that do to the nature and quality of the doctor–patient relationship? Finally, can we imagine any of these proposals as being congruent with the defining values of a liberal society, even the more constrained forms of liberalism endorsed by most communitarians (Wikler, 1987)?

I am certain Callahan would not endorse any of the scenarios I have laid out here. But he does need to get beyond vague admonitions to individuals to take more responsibility for their personal health especially since his other major concern is with the social determinants of health, which presumably are beyond the control of individuals. Again, there will be critical issues associated with protecting the integrity of our liberal political commitments. It is relatively easy to justify as a public health measure banning cigarette smoking in restaurants or the workplace or various public facilities. These are very low cost initiatives that at least have the just effect of preventing harmful second-hand smoke from adversely affecting the health of nonsmokers who have no choice but to be where they are (i.e., their jobs) or who clearly have a right not to be driven by smokers from places in which they have a right to be and a desire to be (i.e., restaurants). These sorts of policies minimally restrict the rightful freedom of smokers who are typically free to smoke outdoors, where no one else's health is threatened. However, the health gains achieved through these policies, as measured by mortality and morbidity reductions, are likely very modest. Very significant gains might be achievable (in theory) through public policies that banned entirely the sale or manufacture of cigarettes (or alcohol or foods high in cholesterol or other health-compromising substances), but such policies would require a virtually complete repudiation of our liberal political traditions. I cannot imagine a reasonable argument outside the most dictatorial regime that would justify such policies. Our society would have to embrace "maximal healthiness" as some sort of supreme political value, again very much contrary to the value pluralism integral to our political traditions.

In conclusion, I cannot imagine any successful arguments that would warrant any wholesale reallocation of health care resources from medical care to public health. There are considerations of justice, cost-effectiveness, privacy, and respect for our most fundamental liberal and pluralistic commitments that all speak against any such wholesale transfer. The most that we can reasonably hope to justify would be retail judgments of justice regarding public health priorities within public health as it is generally currently understood.

SETTING PUBLIC HEALTH PRIORITIES JUSTLY: THE LIMITS OF MORAL THEORY

How should public health priorities be justly established? I would give two answers to this question. First, we need to distinguish national public health priorities from local public health priorities. Second, at both levels there will need to be a predominant role for a certain conception of rational democratic deliberation in the priority-setting process as opposed to any one theory of health care justice.

Some public health needs are necessarily national in scope. Most problems related to infectious disease, such as AIDS or SARS, cannot be safely relegated to local public health bodies. Effective responses require national commitment and coordination and resources. Many environmental matters of public health will be like this as well, though not all. Clean air and clean water require a national commitment and national resources. Polluted air and water tend to cover numerous political boundaries, thereby creating an opportunity for diffusion of responsibility to the detriment of all. National laws and standards effectively prevent locally powerful polluters (i.e., factories and jobs) from being used to blackmail local governments with threats of moving elsewhere in the country. Threats such as this can represent significant threats to public health. These are potential injustices that require high priority at the national level. But there may not be that many strong obligations of health care justice that determine public health priorities at the national level. That is, there can be lots of possible orderings of public health priorities at the national level that will not justifiably elicit moral criticism from the perspective of health care justice. In most cases there will simply be too many morally relevant considerations and justice-relevant considerations too complexly interrelated and too dependent upon probabilistic predictive judgments to warrant a single "most just" ordering of public health priorities. Rawls (1993) refers to this complex mix of morally relevant factors that are beyond both our rational and our moral capacities for confident, fine-grained balancing judgments as "the burdens of judgment." This is the social space within which there can be reasonable disagreement. However, if we need a socially acceptable policy or course of action, which is to say persistent disagreement is not socially desirable, then we need to turn to fair processes of rational democratic deliberation to achieve some "just enough" and legitimate set of public health priorities. The practical moral challenge is then to establish morally reasonable deliberative forums.

My suspicion is, relatively speaking, that there will not be that many opportunities at the national level to make grossly unjust choices so far as public health priorities are concerned. If, for example, in the early years of the AIDS epidemic, public health authorities at the national level caved in to discriminatory public prejudices and allocated minimal resources to AIDS prevention and education because AIDS was concentrated among homosexuals and black and Hispanic IV drug abusers, then strong considerations of health care justice would rightly condemn that minimalism. At the very least Rawlsian and egalitarian requirements of respect for the least well off would be violated. But if we consider the broad spectrum of public health needs at the national level, we may not find that many comparable instances or opportunities for gross injustices of that kind. If we are not quite as diligent and committed to certain levels of air or water quality at the national level, then elevated rates of cancer or emphysema or other health problems are likely to affect more or less equally all income groups, all racial and ethnic groups, and any other grouping of citizens we might imagine. To the extent that the health risks are that widely and indiscriminately dispersed, concerns about health care justice in those specific respects will be minimized.

There are some obvious exceptions to this last generalization. If refineries or smelting plants or power plants represent significant health threats (elevated cancer rates) to those within a 2-mile radius of one of these plants, and if those living in that circle are primarily poor and socially disadvantaged and politically powerless, then there will be an obvious injustice that may well require a national policy to remedy (or better, to prevent in the first place). A national policy might be needed because local economic interests may ignore too readily the health risks to those about whom they care little in order to bring the jobs and economic gains to those who matter more (politically).

By way of contrast to the national level, at the local level of public health needs, there may be more frequent opportunities for moral criticism of public health priorities. Lead paint abatement would provide a good example. The number of white middle-class children at risk of health problems due to lead-based paint is negligible to nonexistent. This is an environmental problem very much concentrated in older housing in poorer neighborhoods mostly occupied by racial and ethnic minorities. Assigning a very low local priority to this sort of public health problem would be open to serious moral criticism as an injustice because, again, those least well off (already with greater than average health problems), those with the least political power, those who are most vulnerable and least able to defend their rights (children), and those already targets of deep-seated discriminatory attitudes are having their basic welfare further reduced by such a choice.

The general point I am making here is that at the local level there may be much more need for retail moral vigilance in the setting of public health priorities. I am also saying that this points up the limits of rational democratic deliberative processes for public health priority setting. Some public health needs will have attached to them a sort of moral necessity such that failure to address those needs adequately will justly elicit moral criticism. Most often this will be related to the seriousness of the harm, the nature of the harm, the massiveness of the harm, and the social target of the harm (already seriously disadvantaged members of society). No democratic deliberative process can legitimate wrongs such as that.

I have described in Chapter 5 what I believe a just and legitimate democratic deliberative process ought to look like for purposes of health care priority setting. Among other things, I called attention to what I refer to as "constitutional principles of health care justice" that define the boundaries of the space within which these deliberative conversations must occur. Any democratic deliberative judgment about priority setting that violated those boundaries would lose its legitimacy as a just outcome. This is a major needed constraint on the deliberative process (Gutmann and Thompson, 2004). Beyond that, one of the most critical requirements will be that these deliberative groups be broadly representative of all those who will be affected by the priority-setting process, especially those social groups that are least well off and most often excluded from effective participation in democratic politics. This is a very demanding requirement but it is a matter of absolute necessity (Young, 2000). This would be the prime lesson we learned from the Communities of Color dialogue project funded under the National Institutes of Health Ethical, Legal, and Social Implications of the Human Genome Project program 1999–2003 (Fleck, 2001).

Finally, in this chapter I have been critical of a number of assertions that Daniel Callahan has made with respect to public health priorities. But there is at least one point on which I believe he is certainly correct. We have likely over-invested in medical rescue and treatment of medical disease because the lives that we save there are visible and individually identifiable. The lives at risk when we consider public health priorities are largely invisible, nameless, and statistical. They have an abstractness about them that can cause a serious distortion in our capacity to make sound moral judgments in the setting of social health priorities. But when public health failures occur, the deaths and injuries and illness will be attached to very visible individuals. The deliberative process provides a place where public education can occur, where those sorts of common distortions can be corrected so that we collectively make better judgments about health care priorities overall. That is an enterprise worthy of significant social investment.

14

FINANCING HEALTH CARE FAIRLY

WHY NATIONAL HEALTH INSURANCE?

One of the saddest pictures I have ever seen in my life is that of a 75-year-old man, William Hart, in a wheelchair in San Diego who was caught robbing a bank of $70 that he needed to pay for his heart medications (Associated Press, 1991). This is not someone without health insurance; he was covered by Medicare. But Medicare covers only about half the health expenses of the average elderly person in the U.S., which is why about 35% of the elderly have and need MediGap coverage (the other 65% need the coverage but cannot afford it). The really unfortunate (and unjust) thing today (given the extraordinarily high cost of many prescription drugs) is that Mr. Hart would have to rob a bank vault (a much more challenging task for the elderly) because bank tellers would not have enough in their cash drawers to meet his prescription drug needs!

In 1993, I was one of the 500 or so experts brought to Washington by the Clinton Administration to craft some form of national health insurance; I was part of Working Group #17 charged with articulating the ethical foundations of the new health care system. The primary results of our work were published in *JAMA* by Brock and Daniels (1994). That reform effort failed. This was a surprise to many because the polling done at the beginning of this effort suggested that more than 80% of Americans believed that "fundamental reform of the U.S. health care system was necessary." With such strong support for reform, how could *all* the reform proposals fail? Some will blame the evil minds that created the "Harry and Louise" commercials. Others will blame greedy, selfish, special interests (medical specialists and insurers and small businesses). Political scientists will blame "arrogant experts" who forgot about the need for incrementalism in American politics. Political pundits accused the Clinton Administration of political ineptitude by engaging in a "secret" process that excluded members of Congress from the crafting of their plan.[1] My view is that these are all distracting and disingenuous excuses for a failure by all of us to "look within."

What everyone involved in any of the health reform efforts realized was that the need for "sacrifice" was inescapable. If the goal of any health reform effort was going to be to provide *secure access for all to a comprehensive range of needed health services at reasonable cost*, then very serious efforts to control health care costs were absolutely imperative. Here, I remind the reader of Reinhardt's "Great Equation"— Cost Control = Income Control (1982). There are no costs in health care that do not represent income to someone. If we control costs, then we are imposing income sacrifices on someone. Of course, only a fraction of the American work force is involved in health care (roughly 15%). But then there is the other Great Equation: Cost Control = Care Control. In order to control health care costs, we have to reduce the amount of health care that is delivered to patients. In a broad sense, this is health care rationing—this second Great Equation affects all of us as future possible patients.

All the health reform proposals failed in 1993 because all attempted to impose the "sacrifices" that were necessary on "others." Those "others" resisted mightily, which is why no reform proposal could garner more than 30% support within Congress (or within the public). The message from this failed effort should be clear (though we may not wish to hear or heed it): If we genuinely want health reform that has its central purpose assuring universal access to a comprehensive range of needed health services that are affordable, we will all have to accept some degree of sacrifice that we freely and collectively agree is fair. If we are unwilling to engage in a national democratic deliberative conversation that has as its primary goal articulating the considered judgments of health care justice that will determine the kinds of sacrifices we all must be prepared to make, there will be no morally significant health reform.

Earlier in this volume I called attention to a moral argument by Allen Buchanan (1998) that I believed had great practical, persuasive power. He wrote this paper at the peak of the managed care revolution in the late 1990s; at the time, complaints by individuals within managed care plans were loud and ubiquitous. The complaints were about all the care these patients wanted but were being denied "in order to save the managed care plan money." What Buchanan called attention to was the frequency with which these patients invoked the language of justice. They were outraged because they were being treated so unfairly. The challenge Buchanan issued to all these patients was, in effect (my words, my snideness), this: "Tell me more precisely how it is that you believe you are being treated unfairly. Tell me what the conception of justice is to which all members of the plan agree and that is the basis for your complaint of unfairness. Is this something you have talked about with one another? Is this something that the managers of the plan also endorse? Or are you only telling me about some personal psychological moral fantasy you have conjured up in your mind to justify your sense of outrage?"

The goal of Buchanan's essay was to get those who were very securely and comprehensively insured to take seriously the plight of the uninsured. His point was that if there were widely understood norms of justice that these outraged patients in these managed care plans were appealing to as justification for their complaints, then those same norms required their equally vociferous advocacy (and willingness to put up more tax dollars) to assure the same standard of health care for the 47 million uninsured in our society. If they were unwilling to see themselves in solidarity with the uninsured, then there was no reason for anyone else to come to their rescue and advocate on their behalf for the health care services they felt they were unjustly denied. A similar point can be made with a variation of Buchanan's scenario. When managers of a health plan deny some specific health service to a now outraged plan member, the managers can claim that they are acting on behalf of all the other plan members' claims of fairness. That is, they can accuse the aggrieved plan member of being greedy and seeking to take more than their fair share from the "commons" of the plan.

All these scenarios, however, are just fantasies. Buchanan's ultimate point is that we have failed to articulate in our society a shared sense of health care justice, which means *everyone* is vulnerable to the way in which plan managers or insurance executives choose to wield their market power or administrative authority in allocating health resources under their control. This same failure blocks any realistic hopes for health reform if the need for sacrifice is inescapable. All will too readily contend that their "personal sense of justice" requires that others make the sacrifices from which they are exempted. This thought ought to motivate us to have those deliberative conversations.

The vast majority of health policy analysts agree that health care costs must be controlled, and that this is an essential part of any health reform effort worth the name. But some writers believe such cost control can be achieved painlessly, without the need for sacrifice, simply by finding ways to achieve health care goals more efficiently. Bodenheimer and Grumbach (2005) are among those who advocate for this view. If we just find ways to deliver health services more efficiently (better care for less money), then we can avoid difficult moral conversations about health care justice and painful rationing decisions that involve denying patients care they want. The most frequently invoked analogy in this context is with the computer industry. Look at what computers cost 20 years ago and how little they could do then compared to the cost and performance of computers today. Unfortunately, nothing in health care fits nicely that analogy. Someone might argue that radiological technology today has spared millions of patients risky and costly exploratory surgery, thereby saving billions of dollars per year. This is true as far as it goes, but the rest of the story is that the ease of the technology and its noninvasive character has increased exponentially the use of this technology for a much broader range of medical indications (many of which might be of very marginal benefit). Thus, a technology that cost a few billion dollars per year in the 1980s is now costing more than $120 billion per year, and growing at a rate of 15–20% per year (Knaub, 2007; Pesavento, 2001). This sort of "efficiency" is rampant throughout the health care system.[2]

Another example of "painless" cost control and health reform is offered by Himmelstein, Woolhandler, and Wolfe (2004). They have argued since the early 1990s that the U.S. has huge, excessive administrative costs in its health care system compared to other advanced countries in the world. If European countries in general have administrative costs in the 10–12% range of total health care costs, then the U.S. might have administrative costs in the range of 22% of total health care costs. These excess costs are tied to the 1,500 or so health plans in the U.S., and all the permutations of coverage and cost-sharing that require armies of clerks and accountants to sort out in every hospital and doctor's office. The for-profit aspects of some of these plans also add to overall excess administrative costs. These costs are regarded as "excessive" because those costs could be avoided if we embraced a single-payer universal system for financing health care. Those costs are also "excessive" from a moral point of view, since those dollars provide no health care. If those excess administrative costs are represented by ten percentage points of total health spending, that would be more than $200 billion per year—this would be sufficient to underwrite the costs of a decent package of health benefits for all the currently uninsured. With one fell swoop we would achieve both a more just and a more efficient health care system.

I will state outright that I am in essential agreement with both the analysis and recommendations of Himmelstein et al. However, embracing their recommendations will not yield painless cost control or obviate the need to make more painful rationing decisions beyond a year or two; all such efficiency schemes yield one-time gains in efficiency and cost control. This does nothing to control all the other forces in our health care system, most especially all those related to emerging medical technologies, that are the most pervasive and persistent drivers of increasing health costs. Once we add 47 million individuals to the pool of insured individuals in our society, we increase by 18% the number of individuals who can rightfully demand access to the same radiological services as all other insured individuals, the same angioplasties, the same very expensive cancer drugs, the same LVADs, the same ICDs, et cetera.

If there is no reciprocal sacrifice, there is no cost control. Decisions have to be made about the range of services that will be covered by a national benefit package, as well as limitations on access to those services in specific clinical circumstances. In both these cases, we are talking about rationing and priority-setting decisions. In both respects we would have to have achieved some sort of shared understanding regarding the very specific considerations of health care justice that would shape those decisions; the assumption being that we would want a *stable* health care system with rationing and cost control protocols accepted by all as being "just enough." As things are now, we have an extraordinarily fragmented system for financing health care that permits all manner of cost-shifting and all manner of avoiding responsibility for meeting the health care needs of very high-cost patients. If we see this as a serious moral deficiency, then we need a universal health care system with fair and effective financing and cost-control mechanisms.

WHY HEALTH REFORM?

Let us briefly review the range of factors that seem to precipitate the call for health care reform. There are the *access* issues: 47 million individuals without health insurance, another 20 million significantly underinsured. One major consequence of this is an estimated 18,000 unnecessary deaths each year linked to being uninsured (Institute of Medicine, 2004). Also, those who are least well-off health-wise (those with the greatest health problems) are least likely to have secure access to the health care they need. Chronically ill patients are not profitable patients. That such patients are denied health insurance (or dumped from health plans when faced with serious costly illness) strikes a large majority of Americans as uncaring, or worse.

There are *access/liberty* issues. Roughly 52% of American workers who have health insurance have a "choice" of only one health plan. That means they are essentially forced to accept whatever the coverage limitations of that plan might be, and whatever groups of physicians who have contracts with the plan. If that employer believes a better deal can be had with another insurer or managed care plan, then all those employees may be forced to sever ties with their physicians, thereby sacrificing some continuity of care. If that employer makes some bad business decisions or market forces conspire against that employer who is forced into bankruptcy, workers lose their jobs and their health insurance. An unfortunate statistical fact is that unemployed workers have more health problems than employed workers, often related to the stresses of being unemployed. Linking health insurance to a particular employer seems imprudent, certainly in the context of a global economy.

There are the *uncontrolled, escalating health costs* issues. New medical technologies seem to be the primary driver of this 40-year trend. However, many will argue that the health insurance mechanism provides the financial fuel needed to heat up the technology market—no hospitals or medical groups could afford many of these technologies if there were not steady revenue streams supporting those purchases. Opportunities for profit or for competitive advantage among non-profit hospitals add more fuel to that fire. New technologies are also linked (culturally) to the belief that this represents "higher quality" health care. Investors have also been drawn into health care because of the promise of above-average profits, again supported by revenue from insurers. All of this raises the very challenging question of where precisely reform efforts ought to be targeted.

There are all the *inefficiency* issues in health care. These include the excess administrative costs identified by Himmelstein et al. linked to the highly fragmented insurance mechanism we use to finance health care. These also include the "small area variations" research of Wennberg (1973; 2004) and colleagues that demonstrates large variations in the use of specific health services from one area of the country to another that seem to have no link with objective health need but may be linked instead with excess numbers of specific types of practitioners in an area. There are also the inefficiencies associated with excess dissemination of new technologies, such as MRI scanners or PET scanners or other procedure-focused technologies. Demand always seems to rise to meet the available supply.

There are *medical integrity* issues that need to be addressed. Of the $2.3 trillion spent on health care in the U.S. in 2007, roughly 80% of those dollars were allocated as a result of physician decisions. What this statistic says to policymakers who must design mechanisms to control costs is that regulatory controls or financial incentives need to be used to "better shape" physician behavior with regard to resource use on behalf of patients. As we saw in the late 1990s, some managed care plans put as much as 30% of a physician's income "at risk" if they failed to meet cost-control targets set for them by the plan. This represents a very powerful incentive to compromise the best interests of the patients a physician is supposed to care for loyally.

There are *security* issues that must be part of a reformed health care system; this was one of the key points of emphasis for the Clinton Administration. If health care is merely thought of as a "benefit," then it can be just as freely withdrawn as it can be given. Health care insurance contracts are typically written for a year at a time. For individuals insured as individuals who are unfortunate enough to have diagnosed a serious illness in one year, the likely result is that they will be dropped by a private insurer for the next year, or charged a premium ($30,000) that will make it impossible for them to renew the plan. Small employers at the economic margins routinely drop insurance as a benefit to stay afloat. Other employers are requiring larger and larger co-payments and deductibles by their workers as a "disincentive" to overuse of the health care system. This poses the same risks to these workers as if they were uninsured (i.e., timely primary care is avoided until a medical problem becomes more serious). Many employers have promised supplemental Medicare coverage to their retired employees. This benefit has disappeared for about two-thirds of workers who originally thought they had it; courts have upheld the right of companies to renege on these promises. Economic downturns can result in hundreds of thousands of workers finding themselves without health insurance.

Finally, there are *basic justice* issues that need to be considered. In calling attention to this point I do not have in mind more fine-grained disputes related to health care justice; I have in mind larger system features. Thus, it looks seriously unjust that the insured, secure middle class should get very generous tax benefits in relation to their health insurance (it is a tax-free benefit), while the less financially well-off uninsured would have to try to purchase health insurance with after-tax dollars. It will also strike many as unjust that three patients will be in a physician's office, all with the same medical problem, all with very different health plans, and they will receive three very different levels of care, ranging from "barely adequate" to "excellent," all depending upon the details of these health plans. This is likely a threat to medical integrity, as well. More generally, if a health care system does not have a mechanism for identifying and remedying injustices, injustices will persist.

ASSESSING COMPETING PROPOSALS FOR HEALTH REFORM

We can take the discussion above as giving us seven criteria (counting *access/liberty* as two of those criteria) for assessing health reform efforts. We have these seven criteria because these are seven respects in which our health care system is seriously deficient.[3] It would take another book to assess properly, from a moral point of view, all the health proposals that are regarded as representing serious efforts at health care reform. For our purposes, I need to make two simplifying assumptions: (1) Health reform proposals that are essentially incremental in character and attempt to build on the current employment based system can yield no more than marginal, temporary improvement that will likely give way in the near future to the justice-threatening trends deeply embedded in our current system. (2) Health reform proposals that fail to take seriously the "Just Caring" problem as I have articulated it here will also fail to achieve any significant or lasting reform of our health care system. The "Just Caring" problem is the largest and most persistent source of injustices in our health care system. There is no health reform from a moral point of view if that problem is not addressed in all its complexity.

The biggest failings of an employer-based system for financing health care are its enormous fragmentation and its voluntary character. The overall fragmentation of the system means that no one is responsible for making sure that all workers have assured access to needed and effective health care. Individuals can (and are) denied jobs by potential employers because they represent future costly health risks. If health insurance is "only a benefit," it can be just as freely taken away as it is given; no one would have a moral right to object to the partial or full loss of that "benefit." Employers have the right to control virtually any and all aspects of the insurance contract beyond what is required by law; no one with employer-based health insurance can rationally feel that they have secure access to that benefit. Consequently, if the seven criteria we have proposed here for assessing health reform proposals are taken seriously, then all incremental reforms of our employer-based health care financing system will still result in a seriously deficient financing system (with unacceptable consequences for access, equity, cost-control, administrative efficiency, and medical integrity).

Three other broad approaches to very serious health reform deserve consideration. These include the Health Savings Accounts (HSAs) advocated by the recent Bush Administration, vouchers advocated by Emanuel and Fuchs (2005) and Kotlikoff (2007), and some version of a Canadian-style, single-payer health plan. We can think of these three approaches as being on a continuum from libertarian to a mixed libertarian/egalitarian to a strong egalitarian approach.

HEALTH SAVINGS ACCOUNTS: A CRITICAL ASSESSMENT

HSAs (as the name implies) involves the creation of a savings account dedicated to spending for health care needs. These accounts are like 401K accounts in that they are granted tax-exempt status. Strictly speaking, HSAs are not linked to employment; though in practice, that link is usually there. HSAs are an option only for individuals who have in place a high-deductible health plan—what is usually known as catastrophic health insurance. If an individual has that (either as an individual or through an employer), that individual or their employer can contribute up to $2,500 to that HSA, which is tax-exempt. The deductible for the catastrophic health plan will be $2,000–$5,000 for an individual; up to $10,000 for a family. The cost of the catastrophic plan will vary depending upon how large a deductible an individual is willing to accept. The money in the HSA itself can be rolled over from one year to the next, accumulating indefinitely. Though an employer may put $2,500 per year into that account for some number of years, the account belongs to the individual who can take that money to another place of employment. However, if that future employer does not offer health insurance as a benefit, that individual would need to purchase from their own pocket that catastrophic health insurance plan in order to continue putting tax-exempt money into the HSA.

The primary virtue of these accounts is that they are supposed to maximize the ability of individuals to control their own health costs, by their judging whether or not specific health products or services are "worth it to them." Individuals also have more "liberty" to spend HSA funds on a range of health services and products (such as nonprescription drugs) that are usually not covered by insurance plans. Individuals are also "freed" from the obligation to assist in covering the costs of other plan members who are chronically ill. To illustrate, if the university pays $9,000 per year for my health plan and I am perfectly healthy for 10 years, then $90,000 will have "disappeared" to underwrite the health care costs of others at the university. I have nothing to show for my good luck or good health or good choices. Under an HSA scheme, I would have $25,000 in my health account that I could use to buy an implantable cardiac defibrillator if Medicare said I was at too low a risk to justify their paying for it (or else I could buy a really large supply of Viagra).

How should we assess HSAs from the perspective of our seven criteria? First, HSAs do nothing to address the basic access issue. If you are without health insurance altogether, you do not have the option of a tax-exempt HSA. If in theory you can afford the cost of catastrophic insurance with a $5,000 deductible, then you enter the market *as an individual*, which means the insurance company can readily reject you if they believe you might have a catastrophic illness in the coming year. If you have several perfect years of health, you are still completely vulnerable to being dumped at the end of any insured period if you have a major health problem (heart attack or cancer, etc.). This speaks against the idea that your access to needed health care would be *secure*. Also, a tie remains for most individuals to employment. A company that went bankrupt (followed by sudden job loss for all and loss of health insurance) would represent a threat to secure access to needed health care. Further, nothing requires any employer to offer even this modest level of insurance coverage; it can be taken away at any time for any reason.

Individuals who are young and very healthy will see themselves advantaged under the HSA model. This may be a gain for them in the short term, but for many it will be contrary to their long-term best interests. HSAs in this regard segregate the "likely well" from the "likely ill." Political conservatives (healthy ones) tend to see this as a desirable outcome because they are committed to the belief that individuals should "take responsibility" for their health, which means individuals should accept the "just desserts" of their bad health choices rather than imposing those costs on others. As we argued earlier, however, responsibility for ill health is rarely clearly and neatly the result of bad choices made by individuals.

Apart from that, if very large numbers of young healthy individuals embraced HSAs, the consequence would be that the chronically ill and catastrophically ill would be in traditional insurance plans of some sort that would be doomed to fail because of the extremely high premiums that would have to be charged to all. Alternatively, a government program of some sort would have to be put in place to provide access to needed health care for these costly chronically ill patients. This would require a very substantial increase in taxes. In addition, to respond to taxpayer calls for fiscal discipline, draconian rationing choices would have to be made. Any rationing decisions made in that context would be open to serious objections from the perspective of health care justice because so much money in the health savings accounts could be used for health care that satisfied wants rather than needs (i.e., all manner of cosmetic interventions).

Advocates for HSAs claim that we would see effective consumer-based cost control of the system as a whole; however, no empirical evidence supports this hope. Considerable empirical evidence speaks against this hope. Health consumers are supposed to identify and reject non-costworthy health care. But how are consumers supposed to know the price of almost anything in health care, especially if they are faced with an acute health problem? Consumers can get comparative prices on some prescription drugs, but it is virtually impossible to know the cost of seeing a physician until after services are rendered. Among other things, patients would have to have diagnosed themselves before trying to get a price for services from a physician.[4] Also noteworthy is that physicians are generally strong supporters of HSAs because HSAs do nothing to control whatever a physician wishes to charge for services. Unlike managed care plans which can bargain with physicians for discounted rates for their subscribers, the "price of freedom" to choose whatever physician a patient prefers is that they have no capacity to bargain over fees.

Patients may believe that once they exceed the limits of their deductible, the sky is the limit so far the demands they wish to make on their catastrophic health plan—but no health plan would take on that sort of unlimited risk. Those plans are free to put in place whatever limitations they wish, none of which are likely the result of justice-based reflection or the self-imposed choices of rational democratic deliberators. They will refuse to fund whatever they regard as "experimental" interventions. They may also refuse to cover those very expensive cancer drugs we discussed earlier; they may place limits on the number of hospital days per episode of illness. None of these limitations are something that consumers in practice are free to bargain over. If the catastrophic insurance is provided through an employer, then the employer will determine which single plan their employees will have to use. The net result is that employers have greater ability to control their health care costs with HSAs because they shift responsibility for this to their employees. From a social point of view, HSAs add to the overall administrative inefficiency of our health care system because so much is individualized. The plight of the uninsured is totally ignored. There are no direct controls on the dissemination of new medical technologies. Though the rhetoric emphasizes consumer choice, the reality is that patients/consumers have less control of their health care costs and options than patients under virtually all universal health plans. Nothing in these plans reflects justice-based considerations; profit and self-interest shape the behavior of virtually all actors connected to HSAs.[5]

HEALTH CARE VOUCHERS: A CRITICAL ASSESSMENT

This brings us to the voucher proposal of Emanuel/Fuchs and Kotlikoff. In both cases, the writers see themselves as satisfying both egalitarian and libertarian value considerations. The general idea is that everyone has a voucher that allows them to shop around whatever health insurance plans are available in the U.S. for a health plan they see as meeting their needs. Medicare and Medicaid would cease to exist, since everyone would have one of these vouchers. These vouchers would allow each individual to access the equivalent of a very good, middle-class health plan today. The actual value of the voucher would be risk-adjusted to reflect the likely future health needs of that patient during the coming year. In theory, this would make all patients equally attractive to all health plans. To assure that this was not just a theoretical hope, no health plan would be allowed to turn away individuals with these vouchers if individuals chose that particular plan. Employers would have absolutely nothing to do with these health plans or these vouchers. A value-added tax would be put in place that would be the primary source of funding for this universal voucher plan; food might be exempted from the tax to avoid what might otherwise be serious regressive effects. Individuals who had the income to spend disproportionately on consumer goods would also be covering disproportionately the cost of funding the health care system, which might be a roughly just approach to health care financing. I presume tax dollars that currently fund Medicare and Medicaid would continue to be provided for financing the system, even though those programs would cease to exist. A national budget for health care would be politically determined as a fixed fraction of GDP; that would be the sum of dollars available to fund the vouchers. The government would determine the content of the "basic plan," which would cover the usual sort of hospital services and medical services in addition to prescription drugs, home health care, and long-term care. All insurers would have to offer this basic plan, which they were free to enhance as they wished (paid for by consumers from their own pockets).

This voucher plan certainly looks like a nice balance between libertarian and egalitarian values. It is universal; everyone is covered. And it meets the security test; no one needs to worry about losing access to health care as a result of bad business decisions by an employer or insurer. However, a number of critical questions need to be addressed.

As far as access is concerned, how "basic" would we imagine the basic plan to be? If the basic plan were *very* basic so that the vast majority of the middle class would be strongly motivated to "buy up," then we would have a multitiered health care system, which would be a lot less egalitarian than we first imagined. When I was working with the Clinton Administration in 1993, the rule we used to determine how adequate (comprehensive) the basic plan would need to be was that no more than 10% of the population would be motivated to "buy up." The argument we have been making throughout this volume is that no one has a just claim to marginally beneficial, non-costworthy health care. This is the sort of care that I imagine consumers ought to be allowed to "buy up to," if they so desired. As long as such purchases do not interfere with the just claims of those who have access only to basic health care, no grounds for moral objection exist to such additional purchases. Hence, if I had to decide what care ought to be included in this basic but comprehensive package of health benefits, it would be all care that was effective and costworthy and necessary for protecting fair equality of opportunity. This is a relatively vague standard, but I need to leave it there for now.

Another critical question pertains to how the value of the voucher would be determined so that all patients were roughly equally attractive to all insurance plans. Kotlikoff (2007) is very clear and direct on that point: "The size of the annual voucher would be based on the participant's current medical condition. Hence, a perfectly healthy 67-year-old might get a voucher for $8,000, whereas an 85-year-old with diabetes might get a voucher for $80,000. Because those in the worst medical shape would have the largest vouchers, insurance carriers would be just as happy to have them as customers as their healthy contemporaries" (p. 77). I need to confess that this was one of the more astounding statements I came across in my research—I had to wonder what the implications of this were for controlling overall health care costs.

Actually, two critical points need to be made here. One pertains to what we have to imagine would be the administrative costs associated with determining the value of the voucher for each individual person. The other would pertain to the overall mechanisms in the health care system for controlling costs at the local level. Determining the value of the voucher for a chronically ill person with heart disease or cancer or diabetes could be an extraordinarily complicated task. Would that number be determined by looking backward to what was spent last year for that person? Was that an especially bad year as far as disease exacerbation was concerned, or an especially good year? Or would that number be determined by looking forward? If we looked forward, what would be the basis for making one prediction rather than another? Would we just take an "average" diabetic patient or "average" cardiac or cancer patient? What in the world would "average" mean under these circumstances when we consider a range of comorbid conditions that often are a part of more complicated chronic illnesses?[6]

Here are some additional questions to further complicate matters. Has that patient been religiously compliant with their medication and dietary requirements, or irreligiously noncompliant? Which physicians managed the care of this patient, and who determined that? Were they all medical specialists, or were specialists used only on rare occasions? Who controlled the number of days this patient spent in the hospital? Who determined which medications this patient needed? If this patient is a cardiac patient, and if there continues to be a large and medically controversial area around the question of who ought to be a candidate for a $40,000 implantable cardiac defibrillator, and if this patient's cardiac symptoms fall into this controversial gray area, then who gets to determine whether or not he gets an ICD when he very much wants to have one implanted? If a patient is terminally ill in that somewhat more expansive sense (might have another two years to live), may they insist that everything medically possible be done to sustain their lives (within the limits of basic comprehensive coverage) and that the value of their voucher be determined so that it is certain their wishes will be respected? Think about the aggressive life-sustaining care provided in the Wanglie case. Or think about the costs of providing Factor VIIa to Jehovah's Witness patients who did not want to bleed out. Is it just that these expenses be absorbed by all others in the system? Would patients have a right to appeal if they believed the value of their voucher was inadequate?

These are all very complicated questions tied up with ethical commitments and religious/cultural practices and complex controversial medical evidence and economic value, not to mention matters of personal behavior—all of which would have consequences for determining the cost of the medical care needed by this patient during the coming year. It is easy to imagine that this would add very substantially to the administrative costs of the program. Those administrative costs are part of total health care costs, which means that much less health care would be delivered in order to cover those administrative costs. This is what makes excess administrative costs a moral issue and not just a business issue.

The potential value of the voucher must also be limited by the national budget for the voucher program, which would be some specific fraction of projected GDP. But if the value of vouchers is being calculated individually, then all those values would have to added together to get a grand total. If that grand total were 10% larger than the amount allocated as a fraction of GDP, then do we imagine that the value of each voucher would be slashed by 10% to eliminate that potential deficit? That is clearly the administratively most efficient solution. But we would have to ask whether that would have any justice-relevant consequences requiring critical attention. The alternative would be to look for likely wasteful projected expenditures connected to individual patient vouchers, which would add another costly layer of administrative costs to the effort.

What is unclear from what proponents of the voucher proposal say is exactly how costs would be controlled in the overall health care system, especially when we consider all the pressures we have been discussing related to emerging medical technologies. The voucher is a prospective payment mechanism, and it is payment in full so far as the patient is concerned; the patient would not have to worry about co-payments or deductibles. The burden of controlling costs would fall upon the insurer. That insurer could be a traditional indemnity-type plan, but it is difficult to imagine how that would be practically workable. The insurer would have to have some capacity to control physician fees and hospital costs and drug costs and diagnostic testing costs and all the other things a physician might order in the course of trying to provide very good care to that patient. That suggests that virtually all insurers in the future would have to be very large, managed care plans, Kaiser Permanente-like plans, that controlled (at least contractually) large numbers of hospitals and large numbers of physicians who were either salaried or linked contractually to the managed care plan in a way that rigorously controlled plan costs. I will remind the reader that physician income represents no more than 20% of total health care costs in the U.S—this means that controlling physician income has only marginal effects on overall health care costs. What needs to be controlled is physician behavior; that is, tests ordered, prescriptions written, hospital days, surgical procedures, and so on.

Emanuel (2008) is a critic of single-payer plans because they provide few incentives for organizational innovation. That is, every health care delivery organization that is part of the health care system now will continue to get paid under a single-payer plan, so there is no incentive for very small groups of dispersed physicians to organize into much larger, more integrated, and more efficient group practices. What this suggests, however, is (to my mind) the naïve hope that cost control will be sufficiently attained through innovative organizational efficiencies. This is the painless cost control that Bodenheimer and Grumbach (2005) also hope will solve our cost control problems. As I have said before, some genuine savings can be achieved in this way without compromising the just claims of anyone to needed health care. But we need to be honest with ourselves and with patients about this.

If we employ DRG-like mechanisms to determine how much a hospital will be paid for a particular episode of illness, then that creates incentives for moving patients out of the hospital sooner rather than later. The vast majority of the time, this will have no bad consequences for these patients; but on occasion, the result will be a bad outcome that in theory could have been averted with a longer stay. This is more correctly characterized as a form of rationing (denying patients noncostworthy marginal benefits). Patients ought to have the opportunity to endorse explicitly these sorts of efforts to control health care costs. Otherwise, what we have are invisible forms of rationing that are presumptively unjust simply because they are hidden from patient scrutiny.[7]

In the Clinton Administration health reform plan, we imagined that many tasks now performed by primary care physicians would be carried out by nurse practitioners and physician assistants. We imagined that primary care physicians would, in turn, become quasi-specialists in the more routine areas of cardiac care or care of diabetic patients or other specialized patient groups. What we call our medical specialists now would become fewer in number and handle the more difficult, nonroutine patients in their areas of specialization, so that their talents were put to their best use. All of this can be presented as a way of making better use of highly trained medical talent, but it would pose some small risks that something would be missed by one or another of these practitioners that would not have been missed had the patient been seen by the next provider higher up on the specialization ladder. This, too, would represent a form of rationing; not intrinsically morally objectionable, but something that should be clearly explained to the public and endorsed by that public.

A very large cost-control question not addressed by advocates for vouchers (as nearly as I can judge from my reading) is how the most painful sorts of rationing decisions would be made. I have in mind the question of whether anyone would have access at public expense to the artificial heart, or the left ventricular assist device (Heart Disease Weekly editors, 2003), or these extremely expensive cancer medications (Dowling et al., 2003). I also have in mind the question of whether we would implant 50,000 cardiac defibrillators per year or 600,000, and the question of how aggressively we were obligated to sustain the lives of patients in PVS or patients with end-stage Alzheimer's. Yet another question would be whether preimplantation genetic diagnosis would be a covered benefit (factored into the value of a voucher) for couples who knew they were at risk of having a child with a genetic disorder that would very adversely affect the length of life or quality of life of that future possible child. Neither Kotlikoff nor Emanuel/Fuchs explicitly addressed any of these questions.

What I speculated on earlier was that many of these very expensive, marginally beneficial interventions would be relegated to a second tier where it would be up to individuals to decide whether or not they wanted to pay from their own pocket for these benefits under some type of insurance mechanism. It is very difficult to imagine that all these new technologies would simply be included as part of the comprehensive basic benefit package. There would be no effective cost control under those circumstances. But it is equally difficult to imagine what proponents of vouchers might have in mind if these interventions were part of some upper tier of health benefits.

The first difficult question would be who would determine what technologies in what clinical circumstances were going to be placed in this top tier. What would assure that such decisions were "just enough"? Would there be a rational, democratic deliberative process that would answer these questions so that we could confidently judge that these decisions would be public, visible, publicly legitimated, and "just enough"? We need to keep in mind that some very painful and difficult decisions would need to be made along the way. It is hard to imagine, for example, that we would quickly agree that the artificial heart was going to be accessible only in this upper tier. It might be easier to get this agreement if we said that no one over age 75 would have access to an artificial heart at public expense. But there could be at least 50,000 individuals per year below age 60 who will die before age 60 of their heart disease without access to an artificial heart. My suspicion is that most Americans might not be morally comfortable with that thought if access to the artificial heart for those individuals depended upon their having purchased that second-tier coverage.

In the United Kingdom, the British National Health Service (NHS) engages the services of the National Institute of Clinical Excellence (NICE) to assist in making these decisions. NICE is entirely independent of the British government, and supposedly immune to political pressure. NICE relies upon the most reliable medical research and a somewhat engaged public outreach effort to make its recommendations to the NHS. But many of its more recent recommendations, especially in relation to these very expensive, marginally beneficial cancer drugs, as well as several Alzheimer's drugs, have precipitated angry public reactions (often fomented by cleverly disguised pharmaceutical company interventions) (Fleck, 2006; Harris, 2005; Raftery, 2006; Rawlins, 2004). I call this to the reader's attention because these decisions have to be made somehow. Proponents of vouchers must make clearer how they imagine this occurring relative to the process of determining the value of the voucher in general, or for specific individuals.

A second difficult question proponents of vouchers must address is what rules will govern purchase of insurance for whatever medical interventions were part of that upper tier. The vouchers are such that individuals would have the right each year to move to another health plan if they were dissatisfied with the plan they were in this year. In any given year, the vast majority of individuals would have no reason to take on the added expense of buying into the upper tier. But if I were to have a heart attack and find myself over the next three years in progressive heart failure, and if I were 55 years old, then I would buy into that second tier in order to have assured access to an artificial heart. This is what insurance companies refer to as moral hazard (because I am in effect cheating other members of the plan by buying insurance at the proverbial last minute). If they charged me $30,000 to buy that second tier policy this year, that would be a great buy since I would be getting a $300,000 benefit for a tiny fraction of its value. But it would be impossible for me to afford that benefit if I had to pay the full $300,000 cost.

This same problem can be repeated in a large number of other medical circumstances. I would have no reason to purchase this second tier insurance to cover these very expensive cancer drugs until I had been diagnosed with a cancer likely to require access to these drugs in later stages of the disease process. Kotlikoff does speak directly to this issue. He would not allow insurance plans to discriminate against individuals, at least in the case of individuals who used their voucher with a specific plan in the primary tier. That plan could not refuse that individual when they wanted to purchase a second-tier policy from them (Kotlikoff, p. 80). Kotlikoff is silent on the question of what an insurer would be allowed to charge for that second-tier plan, especially if the insured individual had the option of taking advantage of such insurance at the last minute. What I would have to imagine is that a prudent insurer would choose not to offer the option at all. The consequence of that would be that there would be no insurance available for much of what our society chose to relegate to this second tier. Individual ability to pay would be the prime determinant of whether any individual had access to those second tier services.

What is a virtue of these vouchers as well as single-payer plans is that any savings achieved through rationing protocols aimed at the elderly can be easily redeployed to meet higher-priority health needs among the non-elderly. In a fragmented health care system where, for example, Medicare is its own program, this sort of reallocation of resources is not readily accomplished. Having said that, however, another critical point needs to be made with regard to the vouchers.

From one perspective, the vouchers are remarkably egalitarian; they seem to reflect very accurately the different levels of health needs that different individuals have. We would typically regard this as an admirable virtue. But in our discussion of the just claims to needed health care by the elderly, we noted those needs (as measured by dollars) are three times greater than the health care needs of the non-elderly. If we believe unfiltered health needs ought to represent the dominant criterion for determining what counts as a just allocation of health care resources, then vouchers as described here will satisfy that criterion best. Vouchers are invulnerable to the charge of discrimination against the elderly. But Callahan (1987) and Daniels (1988) and I would all ask whether this represents a "just enough" allocation of health resources across the lifespan.

We recall again Kotlikoff's comment about an $80,000 voucher for an 85-year-old individual. We can imagine a couple different outcomes, neither of which appears especially morally desirable. On the one hand, we might imagine that the $80,000 is thought of as "last-year-of-life costs." If Patient A is very demanding of aggressive life-prolonging medical care, that patient might successfully get a "second" "last-year-of-life" voucher for that same amount or greater. On the other hand, if Patient B (same medical circumstances as Patient A) is identified as likely being in his "last year of life," and Patient B is a timid patient who timidly goes to the grave for $30,000, that generates a profit of $50,000 for the managed care plan. Prima facie, this does not appear to be a just outcome.

Physicians need clinical flexibility in responding to patients, even patients that are in "the same" clinical circumstances. And we need to respect autonomous choices that patients make with regard to their care. But respect for patient autonomy should not extend to respecting any and all demands for care, no matter how marginal the benefits, no matter what the outcomes are so far as health care justice is concerned. What Patient A represents is the risk that excessive resources might continue to go toward meeting the health care needs of elderly patients—the voucher system (certainly as described by Kotlikoff) does nothing to alter that. If anything, it would permanently put in place that misallocation of resources. What would be needed to correct such a misallocation would be an inclusive, democratic deliberative process that articulated a set of rationing protocols for our future possible elderly selves. Somehow these protocols would have to be used in determining the value of these vouchers for our future elderly selves. This would assure some consistency across all managed care in making fair rationing decisions that might affect elderly patients disproportionately.

SINGLE-PAYER REFORM: A CONSTRUCTIVE PROPOSAL

We turn next to the task of assessing a single-payer system from the perspective of our seven criteria, and the degree to which this system could be constructed to be responsive to the "Just Caring" problem. To be as concrete as possible, we should imagine some version of the Canadian single-payer system—this means everyone is covered with a reasonably comprehensive package of health care benefits. This is clearly *secure* coverage; the government cannot turn anyone away because they have a preexisting condition. The moral virtue of this system is that the "least well-off" health-wise would have secure access to the health care that they needed. This would be a seamless system: no Medicare, no Medicaid, and no special programs for veterans or children with costly disorders—all of that represents costly and unnecessary fragmentation of the health care financing and delivery system. Also, there would generally be no co-payments or deductibles that are currently used as barriers to the use of the system. Patients who were relatively poor would not have to rely upon their own judgment (or that of a Web-addicted neighbor who obsessively scanned medical Web pages) regarding whether or not they needed to be medically assessed.

All physicians who delivered the same care to patients with the same medical problems would receive the same level of reimbursement. That is, no physician would have an economic incentive for refusing to see Medicare or Medicaid patients because reimbursement rates were lower than for privately insured patients. There would be no privately insured patients, at least with regard to the package of health care benefits guaranteed to all. Patients would be free to choose among primary care physicians who had room in their practice to take on additional patients; that is, patients would not be locked in to some limited set of physicians. But patients would not have the right to self-refer to specialists. This would be a reasonable way of assuring appropriate use of specialty care.

As in Canada, the government would negotiate with types of physician groups for standard fees within the group. Physicians could not bill patients for anything more than these negotiated fees. The moral virtue of this approach is that it assures something close to "equal treatment" for all patients; no patients will be more "economically valuable" than any other patient. What has come to be called "boutique medicine" would not be an option under this version of a single-payer system.

Physicians would likely vigorously object to "negotiating" with government over their fees because government would have the power to effectively dictate their fees. But for their complaints to be taken seriously, they would have to show that the outcomes were clearly unjust. As things are now, this is a challenge physicians would be unlikely to meet. The vast majority of our physicians have disproportionately high incomes compared to their European or Canadian counterparts; this is especially true for our medical specialists. This has largely been a product of market power and favorable market anomalies fostered by the U.S. insurance system that have precipitated this outcome. There is very little connection to merit or desert or fair compensation for effort or risk. Government ultimately must be responsible to its citizens (future possible patients) who want high-quality care at an affordable price. What this suggests is that concerns about government dictatorially setting fees are overblown. Government would have to set fees high enough to continue to attract bright, compassionate students to the practice of medicine. Government would want a socially appropriate distribution of physicians across all the medical specialties. There are objective enough methodologies (Relative Value Units) for determining the degree of effort and training and skill associated with a broad range of medical procedures; these procedures can yield reasonable formulas for determining relative fees among areas of specialization (Maxwell et al., 2007).

Hospitals would be paid with global budgets, though ideally it would be desirable for there to be some incentive for the creation of vertically integrated health care systems (i.e., Kaiser Permanente-like entities) that integrated into a single system home health programs, long-term care facilities, and rehabilitation services. The general idea is to keep payment mechanisms as neutral as possible with regard to the places where patients would receive care so that the care provided to patients was both cost-effective and appropriate to their medical circumstances. Investor-owned hospitals could not be part of this future health care system. The general idea is that all dollars in this system ought to be "care dollars," and the minimal number of dollars needed to administer the system efficiently and effectively. As we will see, many decisions have to be made in any health care system that will represent health care rationing. The moral legitimacy of these decisions is less open to question if the dollars saved by denying patients marginally beneficial care cannot "leak out" of the care-providing system into the pockets of investors (or others who would be in a position to enrich themselves by making such decisions).[8]

How precisely would health care dollars be used wisely and justly in the system as a whole? How would health care costs be constrained? How would priorities be set? It is at this point that advocates for a single-payer system get too optimistic and invoke too freely the magic of efficiency (DeGrazia, 2008). We concede that there is a huge gap between what we currently spend in the U.S. on health care as a fraction of GDP, and what Canada and Europe generally spend. The high end of the European range is 10–11% of GDP, whereas we are currently at about 16.5% of GDP. European nations have high-quality health care for that much smaller fraction of GDP. This is what assures advocates of a single-payer system that we can easily provide high-quality universal health care within current GDP limits. No doubt there are hundreds of billions of dollars of wiggle room here that would be generated from administrative savings, downward pressure on physician incomes, and hard bargaining by the federal government with pharmaceutical companies so that U.S. patients got the same discounts as their European counterparts.[9] But it is a pipedream to think this would be sufficient to keep escalating health care costs under control.

If the dissemination and promiscuous use of new medical technologies cannot be controlled effectively, then health care costs will continue to take a greater and greater share of GDP (and crowd out other desirable social uses for those dollars). Somehow, decisions have to be made whether we will implant 50,000 or 500,000 implantable defibrillators next year. Decisions have to be made whether we will pay for 100,000 artificial hearts per year or 400,000. Decisions have to be made regarding what degree of access at public expense cancer patients should have to this rapidly growing array of extremely expensive anti-cancer drugs that yield only marginal prolongations of life. Then there are all the other "Just Caring" problems we have dissected and analyzed throughout this volume. This is where we need to invoke a rational, democratic deliberative process.

If we are all part of the same health care system having to live within the constraints of a budget we collectively decide, then we are in the best position possible to decide fairly for our future possible selves what health care interventions in what specific clinical circumstances we would deny our future possible selves because the benefits were too small relative to the costs. If rationing protocols can be successfully endorsed through this deliberative process that are "just enough," this would assure reasonable consistency and reasonable shared sacrifice across the country as a whole. In some range of circumstances, the very well-off would have the opportunity to buy their way out of compliance with these rationing protocols. As we have stressed throughout, however, what they are buying is what we collectively agreed was marginally beneficial, non-costworthy health care. As long as no one else is made worse off by those purchases, as long as the just claims of others to needed health care are not adversely affected by such purchases, we have no basis for denying individuals the right to use their personal resources in this way.

Participating in these deliberative conversations should be seen as a civic responsibility (though I do not think I would advocate calling up citizens for "deliberative duty," comparable to the way we call up citizens for "jury duty"); I would want the deliberative process to be as inclusive as possible. Ideally, I would want major rationing decisions to reflect the considered judgment of roughly 100,000 citizens who would have participated in local deliberative forums. If information necessary for the deliberative process is properly prepared (relevant information presented in as clear, succinct, and neutral a way as possible) and made available ahead of time, deliberations can be efficient and productive. I will emphasize again that the deliberative process is a *constructive* process; it is not just an opportunity to aggregate preformed judgments. That is what distinguishes it from survey research or focus group research. If we imagine this as a somewhat formalized process, then deliberators would serve for a year or two at a time, maybe one evening a week for three hours. This sort of commitment is necessary to build trust, knowledge, and consistency of judgment.

No one could reasonably expect that 100,000 citizens would come to the same considered judgment of health care justice with respect to any particular rationing problem, so we would imagine that these are advisory judgments that would be fed into a National Priority-Setting Commission. Here we would follow scrupulously several key practices embraced by Oregon in its priority-setting efforts (see Garland, 1992). This Commission would have to have maximal political insulation from the agendas of different political parties, as well as all manner of special interest groups in the health care system. The Oregon state legislature could not alter the prioritization list created by the Commission there; the same would have to be true for Congress. Congress would have the right to set a national health care budget, perhaps as a percentage of GDP. Congress could then see what the consequences of that budget would be so far as health care limits were concerned.

We have to imagine that the rationing protocols that emerged from the deliberative process would be priority-ordered in accord with what seemed reasonably just to the Commission. Congress would have no right to tinker with that order. If Congress appropriated more money for the national health plan, items in that order established by the Commission would be added to the health plan. Congress would have to keep in mind that some items that would be the object of specific rationing protocols would be one-time expenditures (such as the artificial heart). Others would involve a multiyear commitment (until death) because these interventions were repeatedly required for a chronic condition (i.e., dialysis in the case of kidney failure). It would strike most people as unkind (maybe cruel) if funding for life-prolonging care would be withdrawn by Congress for some intervention because of a budget shortfall in a particular year (thereby bringing about the "premature" deaths of those individuals as a result of that decision). Congress could choose instead the next year that no "new" candidates for that intervention would be covered. This might violate our sense of "fair and equal treatment." It will not seem right to most of our citizens that whether an individual lived or died as a result of a chronic degenerative disorder depended upon the vagaries of Congress and the economy. This might have the felicitous (and just) effect of minimizing any motivation by Congress to interfere with the benefit package or rationing protocols for the national health plan.

Part of our national health care system would be a scrupulously objective and transparent process for assessing new medical technologies (again, fully insulated from political winds and political whining). This would be a way of sending clear signals to manufacturers and pharmaceutical companies (and their investors) that new medical technologies would have to be significantly more effective and cost-worthy (compared to what is already in the market) if these new interventions were going to be incorporated into the national benefit package. As things are now, Medicare is forbidden from taking cost into account in judging whether a new drug or other medical intervention will be eligible for Medicare reimbursement (Davis, 2008). As long as a drug is effective (even if only marginally so) and has tolerable side effects, it will be approved by Medicare (and other insurers that key off Medicare). Given the highly fragmented nature of our system for financing health care, this usually opens the floodgates for wide and rapid dissemination of that technology. The necessary corrective for this might be publicly financed clinical trials of new drugs and other such interventions.

Patients (clinically suitable for a specific trial conducted in a rigorously objective manner) would only have access to these drugs or interventions through a trial, so that there was a gain in public knowledge from this public investment. Given resource limits, this is a reasonably just approach for providing access to experimental technologies. Some patients with a medical condition relevant to a specific trial might be excluded because of comorbid conditions that could undermine the reliability of data that would be derived from the trial. This is unfortunate, but not unjust. Such a patient could have access to that drug or device outside the trial as a "compassionate use" exception. However, the cost of taking advantage of that compassionate option would have to be borne privately, either by the patient or charitable resources accessible to that patient.

We have said little up to this point about protecting medical integrity in health care systems where the need for health care rationing was inescapable. There are two positions on this matter that I would quickly reject. First, some physicians would say that they came into medicine to practice; *that* was what they were going to do. Whatever rationing or cost-control decisions needed to be made would have to be made by managers or administrators or policymakers; these matters were entirely external to the role of physicians. They would practice medicine in accord with whatever the rules of the system were. If those rules had bad consequences for patients, then those who made those rules would have to accept that responsibility. This position represents a complete and morally criticizable surrender of medical integrity. In effect, such physicians would be allowing themselves and their medical skills to be used as agents of cost control; sometimes just, sometimes unjust. Some forms of rationing and cost control are clearly unjust—physicians have a moral obligation as physicians to resist rules and practices of that sort.

The opposite perspective is that advocated by Levinsky (1984); namely, that physicians are to be absolutely loyal advocates of the best interests of their patients, no matter what the cost to society or some specific organization. This position has a prima facie aura of nobility about it, but that is more phantasm than fact. There are limits to the just claims of any individual patient to the common resources of the health care system. If we imagine that there are all manner of clever, evil bureaucrats (the CEO version of Descartes' evil genius) seeking to profit from the medical misery of defenseless patients, then there is a role for the wise and loyal physician who rescues patients from the miserly claws of these corporate vultures. Sometimes physicians need to fill this role; sometimes patients need a strong advocate because they are being denied health care to which they have a just claim. But if a physician can see *clearly and distinctly* the just claims of *her* patients to needed health care, then she ought to be able to see equally clearly and distinctly the just claims of *other patients* in the health care system. And if that is so, she ought not to use her medical power and authority to obtain resources for her patients to which they have no just claim. Moreover, if she cannot see such things clearly and distinctly, then she needs to be part of the democratic deliberations aimed at achieving the clarity necessary for having a health care system that is both just and caring. David Eddy (1996, p. 108) writes insightfully in this regard:

> After Mother Nature completes all the bookkeeping, the result is that well-intentioned attempts to maximize the care of individual patients can harm other people. The sense of harm is lessened by depersonalizing these other people as society and seeing them only through statistics. But in reality, they are just as real as the individual patients we see face to face; what is society or a statistic to one physician is another's patient.

The view for which I have been advocating is that physicians need to be loyal advocates of the just interests of their patients; no more, no less. If we have had these rational, inclusive, fair, democratic deliberations that have resulted in the articulation of a set of rationing protocols that deliberators intend to accept as "just enough" for their future possible selves, then physicians have no moral right to ignore those just constraints and become coconspirators with their patients in subverting those just limits.

SUMMARY AND REFLECTIVE CONCLUSIONS

Let me conclude with what I regard as the major lessons I would hope the reader would take home concerning the "Just Caring" problem and how best to address it.

LESSON ONE: Rationing decisions made in a piecemeal, uncoordinated fashion are very likely to be arbitrary and unjust. Fair rationing decisions must be a product of comprehensive, systematic, rational deliberation. This is the main lesson we draw from our analysis of the Coby Howard case at the beginning of this volume. Rationing decisions always imply trade-offs. Health resources will be denied to some health needs because there are other health needs that have a stronger just claim to those resources. When rationing is done systematically and explicitly, then we know precisely what the trade-offs are that we have endorsed, and those trade-offs are open to rational and moral assessment.

LESSON TWO: Rationing decisions made publicly are open to critical assessment and correction, and are more likely to be just. It should be obvious to everyone that Oregon was not the first state to permit the denial of life-sustaining medical care to a Medicaid patient. This is surely a routine occurrence in Medicaid programs throughout the United States, and for patients who are without health insurance (Hadley et al., 1991). But the denials are effected subtly and in ways that are essentially hidden from public scrutiny, as well as scrutiny by the patient, which is to say there is ample opportunity for invidious discrimination.

LESSON THREE: The whole process of health reform and health care rationing must be guided primarily by explicit moral considerations—especially considerations of health care justice—and only secondarily by economic or managerial or organizational considerations. There are thousands of children and adults in the United States just like Coby Howard or Mr. Diaz whose lives are threatened by a deadly illness and whose lives could be prolonged if they had access to some expensive life-prolonging medical technology (such as a bone marrow transplant). Whether they have a just claim to that technology will not be settled primarily by an appeal to an economic equation or organizational theory or more clinical data. We need to address that issue directly as a moral problem.

LESSON FOUR: Fair rationing decisions ought to be a product of processes of rational democratic deliberation that include all who will be affected by the decision.

LESSON FIVE: If all who will be affected by rationing decisions have a fair opportunity to participate in these democratic deliberative processes, then these rationing decisions will be freely self-imposed, which is an essential feature of just rationing decisions.

LESSON SIX: Stable community membership over the course of a life is essential to preserving the overall fairness of the rationing process. Individuals cannot have the option of enjoying the benefits of health reform in a given community only to exit the community when the burdens of rationing fall upon them. A single-payer system of the sort described above addresses this concern.

LESSON SEVEN: Justice requires that there are limits that health care makes on total societal resources, and that these limits are expressed in the form of hard budgets. The moral virtue of hard budgets is that they make clear and visible the trade-offs that must be made among competing health needs and services.

LESSON EIGHT: Hard budgets give structure and coherence to a process of prioritizing health needs and services; a process of prioritizing (and actual priorities) that are explicit, rationally determined, and freely agreed to protects fairness against special pleading by individuals or health interest groups.

LESSON NINE: Those who are least well-off health-wise have presumptively stronger moral claims to needed health resources so long as they are able to benefit sufficiently from those resources, and so long as their health needs are fairly judged as being of sufficiently high priority from the larger social perspective embodied in the prioritization process. No individual has a right to unlimited health care; no individual has a moral right to have their health needs met at the expense of the more just (higher-priority) health claims of others.

LESSON TEN: Physicians and other health professionals are more likely to protect their own moral integrity as loyal advocates of their patients' just interests and as fair rationers of societal resources if they make their rationing decisions within the framework of a fixed global budget and a system of health priorities that have been freely agreed to by all (representatively) who are part of that health care system. This is the perspective that allows physicians to be just and compassionate to patients over the course of their life, rather than simply at the point in time when they are in their office.

LESSON ELEVEN: Equity and efficiency must be achieved together. We will not have fair or effective or affordable or stable health reform if we attempt to maximize either of these social values at the expense of the other. Equity without efficiency is unaffordable; efficiency without equity is iniquitous.

In conclusion (and as I said in the preface), my goal in writing has been to initiate a certain kind of conversation; an inclusive, democratic, deliberative process aimed at addressing the "Just Caring" problem. I regard this as the most profoundly challenging moral problem within the field of health care policy, because the two values that are the very soul of medicine are at risk of being set against one another by ideologues, entrepreneurs, and assorted zealots. We dare not allow the "Just Caring" problem to become more political space where the culture wars that have characterized the abortion controversies get fought out. Some writers (Sabik and Lie, 2008) have become less hopeful about our capacity for (and commitment to) democratic deliberation as the preferred social response to the problems of health care rationing and priority setting. They want to invoke the authority of experts in addressing the "Just Caring" problem. Experts, however, have not resolved the abortion problem as a social policy issue, nor will they resolve the "Just Caring" problem. Nor will it be resolved by individuals turning within, struggling in the privacy of their own consciences.

Kant was struck with awe by the starry sky above him and the moral law within him. In a liberal pluralistic society, the moral law (our sense of justice) must be without, in public space, reflected in our public conversation, etched in our democratic practices. It is public reason that is most worthy of awe and respect. It is through public reason that we must forge the health care policies that best reflect our shared social understandings and shared social aspirations to be a just and caring society.

NOTES

Chapter 1   Just Caring: An Introduction

1. We must pass over in silence a sad irony in this case. The first five weeks of Mr. Schmidt's hospital care cost $272,000. His total bill for those seven months was in excess of a million dollars. Still, the reader should know that if state bureaucrats could have had near certainty that there would be this outcome, they would still find themselves compelled to cut the state prescription drug program for the uninsured poor since they would still save many more millions of dollars. The logic behind this outcome reflects the extremely fragmented way in which we finance health care in the U.S. The newspaper account does not tell us how his care was actually paid for. It might have been covered by the "charity care budget" of the hospital, which really means that charges to insured patients were inflated to cover costs such as this. Or Medicaid might have paid, which means state and federal financing. In this case, the federal government would have absorbed roughly 60% of those charges.
2. There are some truly challenging clinical ethics issues raised by this case, and reported in great detail by Altman. However, for our purposes we have to avoid getting tangled in that thicket.
3. Canada, France, and Germany are all spending in the vicinity of 9–11% of their GDP on health care—and these are universal systems. (Anderson et al, 2006).
4. Puritanical analysts have noted that we spend more than $8 billion per year in the U.S. on potato chips, the implication being that that money ought to be spent on needed health care instead. However, this is another limitation of our magic wand. There are liberal democratic political barriers (rights) that prevent our using that wand to move

money from outside health care to inside health care without the free and informed permission of those who rightfully possess that money. So the beer industry and the candy industry are also safe from renegade wand-wavers.
5. It is worth reminding younger readers who may be puzzled over the prescription drug debate in Medicare why prescription drugs were not included as part of Medicare. The simple reason is that drugs in 1965 were very inexpensive and there were not that many of them. No one at the time would have judged the failure to include prescription drugs as a moral or political failure, or as a form of negligent indifference to the elderly.
6. It can be readily argued that expenditures such as that for a single drug will never happen; I am certain that is true. But the reason that it will not happen is that a social judgment will be made, likely at multiple points in our health system now, that it is not "worth it" to spend such large sums for what are likely to be only marginal gains. This is, as we argue below, a rationing decision, though it is very likely this will be mostly an invisible rationing decision.
7. Aaron Wildavsky (1977) is the first to speak of a Great Equation in Health Care. His version was: Medical Care = Health. He denies that this is a general truth. Uwe Reinhardt is the source of the Great Equation: Cost Control = Income Control. Anytime we seek to "save money" we are always doing so by denying someone else "their income." When government seeks to do that we typically are faced with a political problem of some sort. The Clinton Administration faced that problem in 1993 during their health reform effort as they sought to control health costs by encouraging the shift of more medical care to primary care providers, thereby threatening the incomes of subspecialist physicians who strongly resisted these reform efforts.
8. For a fuller discussion of this point see Peter Ubel's (2000) second chapter, which is perfectly titled: "The Politics of Health Care Rationing."
9. In this introductory discussion the reader should take me as suggesting that perhaps justice would require some special priority rules in regard to those who were least well-off—at least health-wise, maybe wealth-wise as well. We take up an analysis and defense of this claim later.
10. This is what is known in the literature as "the problem of statistical lives." The tempting (but I would argue wrongheaded) moral intuition is that we are always morally obligated to devote resources to save the life of an actual person before us now no matter how many "merely" statistical lives could have been saved if those resources were reserved for that purpose. There are numerous permutations of this problem in the real world, each of which requires a very specific considered moral judgment (I claim), as opposed to a blanket general moral principle that says an actual life at risk always trumps any number of statistical lives at risk. For further discussion see Ackerman and Heinzerling (2002), Bayles (1987), Calabresi and Bobbitt (1978, pp. 20–21), Heinzerling (1999), Hope (2001), McKie and Richardson (2003), Menzel (1983, pp. 159–63).
11. This example is a variation of an example proposed by David Eddy (1996, chaps. 14–15).
12. It would take us too far afield just now to discuss what a fair percentage of income might be for funding a reasonably fair package of health care benefits. We would probably not get a fair enough result if that percentage were flat across all income categories. What I would judge to be fairer would be a progressive rate that represented roughly the same utility at different income levels.
13. This point is discussed at some length by Casarett and Lantos (1998). Casarett and Lantos are critics of "AIDS exceptionalism," not because they see these expensive drugs as a waste of resources, but because it further fragments our health care financing system and results in increased levels of unfairness. They themselves favor a comprehensive system

of national health insurance within which fairer and more reasonable judgments could be made about expensive new medications, such as the protease inhibitors. Further, the reasoning behind those judgments would be visible to the affected public.

14. Some benighted postmodernists might object to these conversational constraints on the grounds that some entrenched political interests will use a very self-serving appeal to "deep moral values" as a justification for conversational constraints aimed at protecting those entrenched interests. But postmodernists are typically inclined to question the legitimacy of the moral enterprise as a whole. That debate is too large to engage here. What I have in mind as a conversational constraint are things that virtually any reflective moral agent would accept as reasonable. Imagine, for example, a group of political advisors around a candidate, all concerned about limiting expenditures. Someone suggests that tens of millions of dollars could be saved by not buying political attack ads if $10,000 was spent to hire a hit man to kill their political opponent. I assume all my readers agree that such an option has no place in a democratic deliberative process. There are considerations of justice that can be just as clear as that in rightly excluding options from the deliberative process.

15. For the record we will note that three million CT scans were done in the U.S. in 1980. That number had risen to 67 million in 2006. The aggregate cost of this level of use of the procedure is a problem. The very marginal benefits from these CT scans is another concern so far as health care justice goes. The radiation exposure and increased risk of cancer is yet another concern that requires public and professional attention (Stein, 2008).

Chapter 2 *The Ethical Challenges of Health Care Rationing*

1. Thomas (1993, pp. 60–91) provides a useful summary of both the emergence of the Medicaid program and the problems it has had to face in connection with escalating health care costs. Most notably, it was the intent of the authors of that legislation that 100% of those below the federal poverty level would be eligible for Medicaid coverage of health needs. However, that figure declined to an average of 40% across the states by the end of the 1980s as state budgets were squeezed by competing demands for resources. Oregon is often accused of being the first state to do Medicaid rationing. This is not a fair criticism—the history of Medicaid makes clear that all the states were already doing rationing. Oregon saw itself as trying to do this more rationally and more fairly than any other state (Kitzhaber, 1993).

2. There is considerable debate over precisely how the term 'rationing' ought to be defined. Space does not permit an extensive discussion of that debate. I follow Uwe Reinhardt (1996)—and the vast majority of other economists—in embracing a broad definition of rationing. Briefly, rationing involves using any mechanism, price or non-price, to deny individuals (or groups of individuals) access to beneficial health care. By way of contrast, when discussing what will count as health care rationing, political conservatives tend to maintain that rationing requires withholding a health care good or service from someone even though they have the money to pay for that good or service. This suggests coerciveness, a presumptive violation of individual liberty rights. For conservatives, if there is a shortage of some health care good or service, then allowing individuals to bid up the price of that good or service is *the* fair and liberty-respecting way of determining who should have access to that good or service. Ability to pay then determines access.

Because ability to pay is seen as a liberty-preserving distributional mechanism, it is claimed that it cannot be described as "rationing," since rationing necessarily involves the use of some form of coercive authority. To my mind, this is a bit of elegant rhetorical gymnastics intended to protect ideology from needed moral argument and analysis. The deep moral and political question is whether health care must be regarded as a "morally special" social good to be distributed in accord with norms other than market norms (Daniels, 1985; Ubel, 2000, chap. 2).

3. Uwe Reinhardt notes that over the past four decades health care expenditures have grown annually on average by 2.5% above overall GDP growth in the economy. This is what has led from health care taking 5.2% of GDP in 1960 to 16.5% in 2006, with projections of 20% for 2015. If those projections are pushed to 2050, health care will take 37% of GDP. Reinhardt then comforts us with the mathematical truth that health care spending can never actually reach 100% of GDP; it can only approach that figure asymptotically during this millennium. There will always be money for most of us to buy a Quarter Pounder with Cheese.

4. Some readers might be inclined to think of Medicaid administrators as being stingy or villainous. Perhaps we think a majority of Americans have these defects for their tepid support of Medicaid, somehow concluding that the Coby Howard case would not have occurred but for these moral deficiencies. That, however, is a path we should avoid. Rationing has nothing to do with heroes and villains; rather, it has to do with limited resources and virtually endless health needs. I would call attention to a British case from 1995 that is almost a perfect analogue of the Coby Howard case: the case of Jaymee Bowen, known in court records and the press as Child B. She was ten years old at the time. She had been diagnosed with non-Hodgkin's lymphoma in 1990, and was given two rounds of chemotherapy initially. In 1993 she was diagnosed with a second cancer, acute myeloid leukemia. In 1994 a bone marrow transplant was performed, all at the expense of the British National Health Service (NHS). But she suffered a relapse in January of 1995. Her only chance of prolonged life was a second transplant and more chemotherapy, but the Health Authority denied her that, and the courts upheld that decision in spite of her father's pleas. This occasioned the same public outrage as the Coby Howard case. In her case, however, a private benefactor did put up the equivalent $100,000 for the treatment. What she actually received was an experimental treatment known as a donor lymphocyte infusion. She died anyway in May of 1996, as her original physicians had predicted. Her father had been a very aggressive advocate for her, going so far as to secure the opinion of two California pediatricians who contended that that there was a 20% chance of achieving remission. Interestingly, her father believed he was vindicated by events since his daughter gained several extra months of life she otherwise would have been denied. For these case details see Ham (1999); for critical commentary on this case see Entwistle et al. (1996), Ham (1999), Light (1997), and Price (1996). The critical question I pose to readers is this: Is a just and caring society morally obligated to provide $100,000 for the experimental treatment that gained Jaymee Bowen several extra months of life? That is, could we be rightly criticized for being either unjust or uncaring for failing to provide these resources? Readers should know that money alone did not dictate the outcome in the Bowen case. As Ham (1999) notes, the same health authority that denied Bowen experimental therapy approved spending almost $300,000 for a boy with hemophilia, the argument being that this latter intervention was much more likely to be successful in yielding many years of additional life.

5. The Institute of Medicine (2002) estimates that as many as 18,000 Americans each year die prematurely as a result of being uninsured or underinsured (and denied access to

timely diagnostic and curative care). Of course "uninsurance" is never listed as a cause of death, which is why these deaths are effectively hidden from public scrutiny. For a number of painful personal stories that speak to this point, see Mahar (2006, chap. 6).

6. Details of the methodology of the Oregon priority-setting process are clearly and concisely explained in Garland (1992).
7. We will simply note in passing that little of moral significance could be attached to medicine prior to the beginning of scientific medicine in the early part of the twentieth century. No rational person at the end of the nineteenth century would want to claim a "moral right" to health care interventions that had an equal chance of making him better or worse.
8. "Today dueling institutions spend millions on the latest diagnostic tools—even while admitting that they are merely duplicating services that other hospitals in their community already offer" (Mahar, 2006, p. 188). The phrase most often used to describe this phenomenon is the "medical arms race."

> While not universal, the arms race is being seen from coast to coast, both in areas where the population is increasing and in cities where growth remains flat. Researcher Devers says that 44% of 43 hospitals surveyed…are building specialty care centers, such as units dedicated to cancer, bone care, or weight loss. By far, the most heated race is to add cardiac surgery centers. No hospital wants to be left behind in the race to grab the prestigious and lucrative cardiac business. (Appleby, 2002)

9. Again, as a matter of intellectual honesty, we must note that overuse of these technologies is not uniformly beneficial. On the contrary, overuse of CT and MRI scans can result in detecting "suspicious findings," which then require more complicated invasive diagnostic procedure (perhaps a biopsy, perhaps a more serious surgical intervention), which can have adverse health consequences for someone when in fact there was no actual health problem from the beginning. This is the "false positive" problem which, our critic will contend, is resolved by a more efficient use of these technologies. But that merely generates the "false negative" problem; we can err in either direction. Our conclusion is that we have a *moral* problem either way, which ought to be addressed as such. See Hunink and Gazelle (2003) as well as Beinfeld et al. (2005). The latter authors note that nonsymptomatic whole-body CT screening of 50-year-old men would yield six extra days of life expectancy with an incremental cost–effectiveness ratio of $151,000 per life-year gained. Further, they note that most patients (91%) would have at least one positive finding, but only 2% would have disease. See also Grann and Neugut (2003) and Waugh et al. (2006).
10. Wright and Katz write, "Many patients who meet the criterion for hospice care—having less than six months to live—still opt for palliation from oral chemotherapies, radiation, antiemetics, or blood transfusions. But these treatments can cost more than $10,000 per month" (2007, p. 325).
11. At the time that the ESRD program was created it was expected that some form of national health insurance would very quickly follow. Obviously, that proved to be a mistaken belief (Nissenson and Rettig, 1999, p. 162).
12. In the original legislation, an age 65 limit was included. A 1978 amendment removed any reference to age (Nissenson and Rettig, 1999, p. 162).
13. We do recognize the fact that there are significant (and costly) side effects associated with transplantation, in part as a result of a compromised immune system due to the need for antirejection medications. Only in a few cases would those costs approach the cost of continued dialysis.

NOTES

14. This question captures as succinctly as possible what distinguishes libertarian from more egalitarian conceptions of health care justice.
15. In 2006 there were approximately 65,000 individuals on the transplant waiting list who were in need of kidneys. This is a number that will grow substantially over the next 30–50 years due to the aging out of the post–WWII "baby boom" generation and even more rapid growth in the incidence of type 2 diabetes, which is linked to both heart disease and kidney failure.
16. Kurella et al. (2007) note that more than a third of the octogenarians and nonagenarians initiating dialysis from 1996–2003 had four or more comorbid conditions, such as congestive heart failure, diabetes, COPD, cerebrovascular disease, cancer, et cetera. This explains why median survival was only one year. More noteworthy, those starting dialysis in these cohorts had a higher glomerular infiltration rate than would be typical for dialysis initiation, which raises the question of *how medically necessary* starting dialysis was. In other words, dialysis initiation might have added to end-of-life costs without affecting mortality outcomes.
17. Kurella et al. (2007) noted median survival of only one year from the initiation of dialysis for octogenarians and nonagenarians. However, that median data masks a very wide survival range that went out as far as 52 months.
18. Hamel et al. (1997) reported in this study that the overall cost per quality-adjusted life-year saved as a result of initiating dialysis in these seriously ill patients was $128,200. For the 103 patients in the worst prognostic category the estimated cost per quality-adjusted life-year was $274,100. For the 94 patients in the best prognostic category the cost per QALY was $61,900. The authors report that there were a few patients who survived, and for them their clinical outcomes "were fairly good." Otherwise, median survival was 32 days. Only 27% were alive at five months from an initial cohort of 490. This is another nice illustration of the ragged edge problem. For those few "fairly good" survivors are we morally obligated to accept the very high costs associated with providing dialysis to the entire cohort?
19. In the referenced document, the 2006 statistics were projections that proved to be accurate.
20. On the meaning and use of cost-effectiveness in a clinical context, see the collections of essays by David Eddy (1996) that were originally published in *JAMA* from 1991–95.
21. A real-world example of this point would be the Lakeberg conjoined twins case. Amy and Angela were born sharing a single six-chambered heart. Their predicted survival (if nothing were done) was slightly more than a year. Surgery to reconstruct the heart and attempt to save the life of one twin (while allowing the other to die) was estimated to have less than a 1% chance of success. The cost of attempting this extraordinarily complicated surgery was more than one million dollars. Loyola University of Chicago refused to perform the surgery, in part because a substantial portion of those costs would come from charity care dollars to which the uninsured poor in their area had a more just claim. In addition, the very low probability of success spoke against that surgery as well, both for reasons of justice and compassion. The surgery was done in Philadelphia. Amy survived for 11 months in the hospital dealing with one surgical complication after another.
22. Quite a stir was created by the publication of an article in the *British Medical Journal* in June of 2003 (Wald and Law, 2003). They proposed the creation of what they called a "polypill." This pill would be a combination of six drugs shown to be effective in reducing heart disease: aspirin, a statin, folic acid, and three drugs that reduced blood pressure. They contended that if such a pill were created and were taken by everyone over age 55,

no matter what their risk profile for heart disease, the result would be an 80% reduction in the incidence of cardiovascular disease. The authors contended that about one third of those taking this pill would gain on average 11 extra years of life free from either heart attack or stroke. The editors of the journal (Rodgers, 2003) gushed over the ingenuity of this proposal, but an enormous number of letters from medical readers reflected a very different perspective. The paper itself by Wald and Law was based only on a literature review and mathematical analysis, which prompted one letter writer (Powlson, 2003) to remark acidly, "Indeed, why bother with new trials if one can find such apparently definitive answers so conveniently from existing data?" Others (Trewby and Trewby, 2003) contended that the way in which data was presented was misleading; absolute risk reduction numbers were to be preferred over relative risk reduction numbers. Thus, they note that if a healthy 55-year-old were to take the polypill for ten years "the chance of benefit will be less than 1% per year." They also point out that if the polypill were as effective as the authors contend, there would be a large increase in deaths that were a product of cancer, trauma, and degenerative brain disease—all of which would have substantial costs attached to them, which would somehow have to be calculated and considered. Still others call attention to a number of studies on the cost-effectiveness of statins, which yield an extremely wide range of data, prompting the authors to conclude that rigorous data are needed "before one can propose an indiscriminate use of statins in people aged 55 years and older" (Messori et al., 2003).

23. To add one more layer of complexity to this chapter, Hreybe et al. (2007) report that patients on hemodialysis, despite having an ICD, have approximately a three-fold increase in total mortality compared to their non-hemodialysis counterparts. This diminished benefit for these patients leads the authors to conclude that "if duplicated in larger randomized trials, these results may demonstrate the futility of implanting defibrillators in HD [hemodialysis] patients" (p. 1091). To my mind, this is another example analogous to the T-wave alternans test. What is noteworthy about the quoted passage is the invocation of the language of futility, as opposed to the language of rationing or priority-setting. As noted earlier, this has the effect of being a conversation-stopper—from this perspective, there is no need to offer any further justification for this conclusion.

Chapter 3 *Pricing Human Life: Getting Beyond Tragic Choices*

1. To avoid confusion in the reader's mind, I should make clear that the actual institutional ethics committee in this case did not have the alternative option of directing the funds to 150 AIDS patients. What they did know, however, is that demands from various insurers for discounts for hospital services had severely eroded the capacity of this hospital (and every hospital) to provide charity care. Still, I want the reader to appreciate the reality of this situation. In Massachusetts recently (Smith, 2004), there was the headline "Rationing Feared as Many Flock to HIV Drug Program." The story noted that enrollment in the HIV Drug Assistance Program had soared by 70% in the past year. For the coming fiscal year this was going to produce a funding shortage of at least $6.6 million, perhaps as much as $12 million—all of this related to the costs of these newer AIDS medications. One AIDS activist, Rebecca Haag, is quoted as saying, "There are people in places like North Carolina and West Virginia who are on wait lists for drugs, and they die while waiting.... Is that what we want in Massachusetts?" What is noteworthy in this story for our purposes is that there is no mention of the needs of hemophiliacs for extraordinarily expensive medications, nor are any other unmet expensive health needs mentioned. In

409

other words, the reader would have no inkling that there was a trolley-like problem lurking in the background. On the contrary, the headline suggests the opposite. The headline suggests that rationing would be avoided if the Massachusetts legislature appropriated these additional funds, which is simply not true. Instead, the need for rationing would be redirected down a spur less visible to media scrutiny.

2. This is the principle that was apparently violated by the ethics committee at Swedish Covenant Hospital in Seattle in the 1960s when they used "social worth" criteria to determine who would or would not be awarded a dialysis slot. This was brought to public attention by Shana Alexander in a *Life* magazine article (1962). Women who identified their social roles as being "models" were among those whose social worth was judged to be minimal. This same principle was at risk of being violated by some preventive health care research being done in the 1960s that relied upon what is known as the "human capital" method for allocating resources. The goal of the research was to determine the best way to invest dollars for saving lives with the greatest return. In one case, a program to get motorcycle riders to wear helmets was compared to a program aimed at getting women to have regular Pap smears. Both programs had about the same costs when looked at from the perspective of what it would cost to save a life that would otherwise be lost to cancer or to an accident. But from a human capital perspective, the motorcycle helmet intervention was clearly the better investment because it was young men with the highest earning potential ahead of them who were most at risk of losing their lives from a motorcycle accident, whereas the Pap smear program was aimed at middle-aged women who had only low earning potential or no earning potential—consequently, their lives represented a very poor investment. Needless to say, research such as this would anger feminists who now saw being underpaid relative to men as having life and death social consequences.

3. Gaucher's is a rare (1 in 50,000) inherited metabolic disorder. It is medically complicated because there are so many variants (more than 200 mutations have been identified), the consequence of which is that the natural history of the disease is mostly unknown. "The severity of symptoms and rate of progression vary considerably from patient to patient, and range from asymptomatic to severe with early death" (Connock et al., 2006). Gaucher's is one of forty metabolic disorders that can be detected at birth with a readily available test. Ideally, treatment would begin then to prevent bone and organ damage. However, some will not become symptomatic, and others may become mildly symptomatic but not progress to the point where imiglucerase would be medically necessary (Beutler, 2006). This means physicians need to wait until some damage has been done before initiating therapy. If imiglucerase cost only ten cents per dose, that delay would be unwarranted. But the extremely high cost of the drug, along with the fact that some patients with some specific mutation may never need the drug, justifies permitting this harm as "not unjust." Finally, the $300,000 figure is an average of sorts for symptomatic patients, the range being from $50,000–$800,000 per year, mostly depending upon the dose needed (Clarke et al., 2001; Wraith, 2006).

4. The actual case was litigated in Virginia under EMTALA, the Emergency Medical Treatment and Labor Act, a federal law intended to prevent poor and uninsured individuals from being turned away from hospital emergency rooms in life-threatening circumstances because they were unable to pay for the care they needed. There is no doubt in my mind as to the moral utility of this act, given the nature of the U.S. health care system. However, I will contend that health care justice does not require its application in the case of anencephalic infants. In re Baby K, 832 F. Supp. 1022 (E.D. Va. 1993), 16 F. 3d 590 (4th Cir. 1994).

5. We discuss more fully below the nature and implications of the publicity condition with regard to the challenge of articulating fair rationing policies and practices.
6. It is not easy to express precisely the point I want to make here without sounding morally lax (i.e., being too willing to tolerate injustices). I am essentially in agreement with Rawls' (1971) view that the first virtue of society must be justice (p. 3), but justice is not the only virtue. We may have to be relatively uncompromising with respect to the justness of the basic structure of society, which is Rawls' primary goal. But when we get down to the level of micro-justice issues, we will often have to settle for non-ideally just outcomes (as Rawls himself concedes) because of (among other things) the "burdens of judgment," the limits of our capacity to take in and fairly interpret all the factors that might have a bearing on a particular matter of justice (i.e., who has the strongest claim to the last bed in the ICU or to a limited supply of antivirals during a pandemic. We are certain that neither antivirals nor ICU beds can be justly allocated on the basis of ability to pay, which would favor the rich. But we could reasonably argue about whether or not it was unjust to give priority for antivirals to parents of minor children over couples who were childless or whose children were now adults.
7. The defining feature of "aresponsible agencies" is that they produce judgments without having to elaborate on or explain the reasons for those judgments.
8. We will note in passing that the term "fair" here will satisfy libertarian, utilitarian, egalitarian, and fair equality of opportunity accounts of health care justice. That is, proponents of any of these accounts will have no reason for objecting to this agreement as being unfair from their preferred perspective.
9. What would we imagine the moral argument would be that would justify either physicians or administrators giving themselves bonuses through the stingiest possible administration of DRGs, even if what is denied patients under these DRGs is what all would agree was marginally beneficial health care? If justice in its most minimal sense is a matter of fair agreements among free and equal persons, then what would motivate older patients freely to deny themselves marginally beneficial care in order to enhance the incomes of physicians or administrators?

Chapter 4   Elements of Health Care Justice

1. I readily acknowledge that there are features of our health care system that might be described fairly as being essentially unjust. The practical challenge there is to engage in the political and economic reform efforts needed to change those features. However, many other justice-challenging features of our health care system are features of every other health care system in every other advanced economy in the world. I have in mind especially the rationing issues generated by advances in all forms of medical technology. In that respect, the "Just Caring" problem is as real a problem in Britain or France or Germany or Holland as in the United States.
2. What I do need to acknowledge is that there is often a relationship between access to transplantable organs and ability to pay. Most often it is the case that individuals will not be listed for a transplant unless they can prove they have the ability to cover at least half the costs up front. The critical reader might ask, "If we have this supposed social understanding that access to needed lifesaving medical interventions should not depend on ability to pay, then why do we tolerate this practice?" I can only give a very brief answer to that critical question: It might be a matter of "local justice" forced on local institutions by a larger health care system that does not permit a more just response. That is, these situations might be morally analogous to the Lakeberg conjoined twin

case already discussed. Funds would have to come from somewhere to cover the costs of transplants ($200,000+) that individuals had no ability to pay for. If those funds were taken from hospital charity care dollars, then many hundreds or thousands of health needs for poor, uninsured patients around the hospital would go unmet. That might be judged to be the greater injustice (as Loyola Medical center concluded); consequently, the vast majority of transplant patients must be able to pay for that care themselves. To avoid this sort of problem, we would need to have a form of national health insurance that gave everyone equal financial access to an organ transplant (if they were medically suitable candidates).

3. We are in fact deficient in this regard in many respects, but this is not a topic I can address.
4. This phrase might be taken in a way that would give offense. It is not intended to do that. It simply refers to the fact that these patients have extraordinarily costly, complicated, seemingly never-ending medical needs.
5. Segall herself concedes that most of the time physicians only know what the last six months of a person's life is after the fact. Consequently, in the real world there is no opportunity to save Medicare $130 billion. For purposes of responding to her objection, we will bracket this fact.
6. What moral pluralists wish to reject are both moral absolutism and moral fanaticism. Both these perspectives can be shown to be unreasonable, as we tried to show in our discussion above of the principle of the pricelessness of human life.
7. This is a contractualist argument that Scanlon makes and that I endorse as being central to my understanding of what rational democratic deliberation must be about. Contractualism is about mutual justification, the equal respect we owe each other as moral agents in a single moral community. Thinking about right and wrong, thinking about what is just or unjust, is thinking about what we do in terms that could be justified to others and that they could not reasonably reject.
8. We are not talking about Katrina-like desperate circumstances in a New Orleans hospital where some number of patients may have been euthanized because the hospital had to be abandoned by health professionals due to rising flood waters, loss of all electricity, marauding gangs, no food, and inability to transport the most desperately ill patients who were doomed to die by their illness.
9. Space limitations prevent some fine-grained qualifications that are desirable. I speak of the Medicare program in general and the elderly in general benefiting enormously from the existence of this program. But that is only a half-truth. Though the Medicare program is thought of as providing "the same benefit package" and "equal access to covered health care services" for all the elderly, there is considerable differential access depending upon the financial status of each older individual. This is painfully evident in the case of the Medicare Part "D" prescription benefit.
10. A concrete example of what I have in mind are the for-profit specialized hospitals that have opened in a number of parts of the U.S. These are typically 30-bed hospitals that care for only cardiac patients or only cancer patients or only orthopedic patients. Groups of physicians are the investors who create and staff these hospitals. They provide no charity care; they accept as patients only those who are likely to be most profitable. They effectively remove these profitable patients from community hospitals that used those profits to underwrite the costs of charity care, thereby rendering these hospitals less able to meet the health needs of the uninsured working poor. These physician investors will have been earning $300,000 or more per year at these community hospitals, hardly what can be described as economic exploitation, but they would hope to double their incomes through these ventures. These are the consequences of libertarianism in practice.

11. Readers familiar with the history of philosophy will recall David Hume who is a critic of Cartesian radical skepticism. His quick critique is captured in this sentence: "Nature is always too strong for principle." We wonder if the floor below us is just an illusion. Do we know *for certain* that is not true? Then we take a step because we are hungry for dinner. The theoretical doubt disappears in the face of pragmatic need. The argument I offer here is in that mode. The libertarian is absolutely committed to respecting the liberty of all, so long as there is no fraud or violence—the position has a kind of theoretical elegance and simplicity. But the practical consequences of having a social world designed in accord with that theory would be intolerable. We need a shared sense of justice to contain the excesses of liberty.
12. I have already argued that it is essential for any just rationing scheme that it be self-imposed. The difference between my view and that of a libertarian is that a just rationing scheme must necessarily be part of a just package of health care benefits guaranteed to all—that means that the choices to be made (inclusions and exclusions for the health care benefit package) must be a product of collective deliberations, the outcomes of which are self-imposed. Libertarians may not be satisfied with this approach because they see individual choice as being too attenuated. However, the virtue of this deliberative model is that deliberators are free and equal, which means that the outcome of the deliberative process will be nonexploitative. In the libertarian model, exploitative bargains among individuals is a recurrent risk because of wealth and power imbalances that reduces the liberties of poorer individuals to merely theoretical liberties.
13. I will argue later that (1) the need to make such quality of life judgments for rationing purposes is inescapable, but (2) this is something that can be accomplished in a fair-minded, nondiscriminatory way.
14. If space permitted, a very long string of examples could be used to further reinforce my point that there are multiple strands necessary for an overall satisfactory pluralistic conception of health care justice. These strands are not bound to one another through some elegant set of theoretical considerations. The problem of justice in health care is too complex in its multiple manifestations to be adequately addressed by any single concept of justice. Further discussion of this point (containing many more interesting examples) may be found in a recent essay by Rosamond Rhodes (2005). She writes that,

> we should avoid both the allure of a single simple ideal conception of justice and the temptation to shoehorn distinctly different principles into the scope of our cardinal ideological commitment. The just allocation of medical resources is and should be governed by a variety of considerations that reasonable people endorse for their saliency. Several principles have a legitimate place in medical and public health allocation. They include: *the anti-free rider principle, avoid undue burdens, avoid the worst outcome, the difference principle, efficacy, maximin, provide public goods, the vital and constant importance to well-being.* (pp. 23–24, her italics)

Chapter 5 Rational Democratic Deliberation: Scope and Structure

1. After a careful effort to analyze the results of major market-based efforts to reform health care by controlling health care costs, Wells, Ross, and Detsky (2007) affirm the conclusion I offer here. They write in their conclusion:

> Perhaps it is time to wave the white flag and admit that it is impossible to develop policy initiatives that correct market distortions and produce a truly efficient health care market, in which value received per dollar spent is maximized and the distribution of services is both fair and equitable for the population. (p. 2787)

2. This article reports the story of Lisa Jardine (a patient with breast cancer), who was annoyed by Roche's persistent efforts to recruit her for what were really their marketing operations. This same phenomenon may be found in the U.S., though on a grander but more subtle scale. See Healy (2007), who reports that drug makers "richly support the nation's proliferating patient-advocacy groups." She also reports that the Colorectal Cancer Coalition got 81% of its funding from drug makers.
3. In the Medicare program the 5% of beneficiaries who are the sickest account for $43.1% of Medicare expenditures, while the top 10% account for 61.5% of Medicare expenditures.
4. John Dewey is the philosopher who deserves credit for this insight. If any one philosopher deserves to be credited as the grandfather of rational democratic deliberation, it is John Dewey, starting with his volume *Democracy and Education*. The phrase Dewey uses is "social intelligence," which is the rough counterpart to Rawls' "public reason."
5. As a side note, we should keep in mind that only about 2,500 livers per year in the U.S. are available for transplant purposes. There are no artificial livers. If a liver were given to this girl to sustain her life in PVS, that would mean some other patient died who could have lived a fully cognizant life. That outcome does not appear to be either just or compassionate.
6. "UnitedHealthcare and a few other payers offered to cover bone marrow transplants if patients would enroll in a clinical trial. We had one patient take us up on the offer, while approximately 500 other patients were covered off-trial using litigation and market pressure. It took a long time to learn that bone marrow transplantation is often not a useful therapeutic approach. Quite the contrary." (Culliton, 2008c, p. W47).
7. As Rawls would say, in a liberal pluralistic society one of our two highest interests would be an interest in altering our most fundamental life commitments. That means a liberal pluralistic society would be committed to protecting the right of Roman Catholics to convert to being Baptists or Buddhists, the right of Republicans to become Social Democrats, and the right of meat lovers to become vegetarians.
8. This is what Joshua Cohen refers to as the "reasonable consensus test." For a fuller explanation and justification of the point I am making in this sentence, see Cohen's essay, "Moral pluralism and political consensus" (1993).
9. A recent illustration of the point I am making here has to do with public funding for embryonic stem cell research that would use "excess embryos" from fertility clinics as sources of these embryonic stem cells. A number of prominent advocates for a strict right-to-life perspective have endorsed these policy proposals as being congruent with a "pro-life" position. Senator Orrin Hatch (R–Utah) would be one such example. The research offers the hope of cures for Alzheimer's disease, spinal cord injuries, and other medically devastating disorders that severely diminish either length of life or quality of life. These individuals see such policies as being "fully justified" at both the levels of their own comprehensive doctrines and at the level of a liberal, pluralistic, overlapping consensus. Other right-to-life advocates would not see such policies as being congruent with their own comprehensive doctrines, but they do respect the deliberative process and the values integral to that process that generated those policies (since that same process has generated significant restrictions on public funding for Medicaid-related abortions).
10. To be clear, the Alice/Betty case is deliberately simplified for illustrative purposes from more complicated real-world scenarios. In the real world, if it were believed that Alice and Betty each had two months to live without a transplant, and if Alice suddenly developed a complication that would cause her death in the next week, and if a liver

became available that was a good match for either, then an *urgency* criterion would kick in and Alice would receive the liver (assuming her medical condition had not deteriorated to the point that the liver was very likely to fail). The hope would be that another liver would become available for Betty. This urgency criterion is widely accepted as morally reasonable (not unjust), though there is some debate about its use because of an increase in the risk of transplant failure due to broader medical vulnerabilities in the patient. What it means in practice is the loss of many more otherwise salvageable life-years in patients who will not receive a liver transplant (i.e., patients who are better medical candidates for a transplant, but less urgent candidates at a point in time).

11. I use the word "imagine" here because I am presenting a simplified hypothetical scenario. But what provoked this imaginative thought experiment is the real world where researchers are quickly discovering that patients with different genomes (or different mutations in their genomes) respond more or less positively to these so-called "targeted" cancer therapies that carry these very expensive price tags. See Culliton, 2008a, 2008b, 2008c. Roberts, an oncologist, being interviewed by Culliton (2008b) says, "Up to 80% of the patients with the mutation will experience a response to Iressa, compared to 20% for an unselected lung cancer population" (p. W38).

12. The proponents of this priority-setting process recognized clearly their own limitations in doing these rankings. Shortly after coming up with their list of 709 condition–treatment pairs, they came up with seventeen "mega-categories" that were much more intuitively manageable and practically capable of being discussed by a broad public and then operationalized. The top category would include medical conditions that were life-threatening but that could be effectively treated at reasonable cost. The bottom category included all these medical interventions that were very costly and yielded only very marginal benefits, either from a life-prolonging perspective or a quality-of-life sustaining perspective.

13. We see this same sort of phenomenon in the practice of science. Scientists make some observations that are inconsistent with current scientific theory and that are resistant to being "explained away," so we might be forced to revise our theories. In 1970 it was proposed that the continents actually move about the earth. This was greeted with great skepticism at first because it seems so "obvious" that the continents are immoveable. However, the theory of plate tectonics explained how that would happen, and that theory gradually became fully corroborated as scientists were now directed by that theory to make other observations that further confirmed that theory. Initially, this theory was "unsettling," but explanation and evidence could eventually be offered to support its validity.

14. The vast majority of us on reflection might be very reluctant to hold an individual accountable for bad health choices in the past that have resulted in a costly medical crisis in the present. That is, we would be morally reluctant to deny them access to necessary life-saving or life-prolonging medical care at social expense. But if an individual is duly warned at that time that future medical crises due to those same choices would result in denial of that care at social expense (or might require a very substantial copay), there might be less reluctance to see this as a "just enough" judgment. The rubric sometimes used to categorize these patients is RHSDs (repeated hospitalizations for the same disease). Medical problems associated with alcoholism will often come under this rubric (which will raise additional moral issues regarding personal responsibility because of the nature of addiction); so also will the repeated hospitalizations associated with poor diabetes management. Of course, a legitimate question to raise will be the extent to which poor diabetes control is like or unlike the addictive behavior associated with

alcoholism. See in this connection a recent discussion by Feiring (2008) who writes in connection with the health care rationing issue, "It seems that while a backward looking interpretation of individual responsibility cannot be relevant as a criterion of priority setting, a forward-looking conception of responsibility may be approved" (p. 33).
15. A very embarrassing report recently surfaced regarding one of these cholesterol medications, Zetia. One physician described the results as "shocking." This clinical trial showed Zetia did nothing to improve mortality or morbidity. On the contrary, plaques in the coronary arteries grew somewhat faster, especially when Zetia was combined with Zocor. This actually raised the risk of potential heart attacks for these patients (Berenson, 2008).
16. This point is nicely and concretely delineated in a recent essay by Buchanan (2008) on public health ethics.
17. Interested readers may write to me at Michigan State University for copies of final reports from any of these projects.
18. Sunstein actually distinguishes three types of incompletely theorized agreements, depending upon where the disagreement might be located. Sometimes we agree on a high-level abstraction without being able to agree on the legitimacy of a specific concrete application. Other times we agree on the appropriate response but disagree on the deep reasons for a judgment. Sunstein writes:

> Incompletely specified agreements thus have important social uses. Many of their advantages are practical. They allow people to develop frameworks for decision and judgment despite large-scale disagreements. At the same time, they help produce a degree of social solidarity and shared commitment. People who are able to agree on political abstractions—freedom of speech, freedom from unreasonable searches and seizures—can also agree they are embarking on shared projects. (p. 36)

Chapter 6   Setting Limits for Effective Costly Therapies

1. Someone might choose to respond to this objection by saying that the dialysis program was an act of social beneficence or social charity. The implication of that claim is that this benefit is freely offered, and consequently, can just as freely be limited in whatever way Congress might choose. However, this is not a morally or politically defensible claim. These are public dollars that are being spent, not private dollars. We are clearly free as individuals to distribute our charitable largesse as we wish. The same is not true of government. Whether we regard the ESRD program as a matter of justice or social beneficence there will be obligations of fairness governing access to the program and related benefits. Thus, there is a prima facie problem of fairness in underwriting the cost of kidney transplants but not heart transplants. This is not an easily dismissed problem.
2. The actual average charges for a heart transplant in 2005 were about $507,000 per case; that included procurement costs and immunosuppressant medications for a year. If an artificial heart cost "only" $50,000, the cost for each artificial heart transplant would be about $450,000. No medications would be needed to head off immune system rejection, but all the other costs would be necessary, including careful and costly monitoring for a year after surgery (Transplant Living, 2006).
3. Actual practice in the U.S. today (2008) would suggest that we think of access to these drugs as merely a matter of social beneficence. Less than 40% of HIV+ individuals needing these drugs have health insurance that will cover most of the cost of these drugs. A number of federal, state and local programs have been created to underwrite the costs of these drugs, and there are a number of private charities that help with these costs. This

is an obvious patchwork of support that can easily unravel in the face of a weak economy or other pressing demands for charitable support. The medical difficulty is that patients cannot stop and start these drugs in accord with their access to charitable resources, since that kind of sporadic access will only worsen their medical circumstances.
4. John Bartlett, "Protease Inhibitors for HIV Infection," *Annals of Internal Medicine*, 124 (June 1996), 1086–88. This is an early article announcing the astounding effectiveness of these drugs in clinical trials that had to be interrupted because the interim results were so dramatic. In the 10 years since, we have seen HIV mutate around these drugs, but we have also seen more than 20 versions of these drugs developed that in ever-changing combinations with one another have managed to contain HIV for the vast majority of these patients.
5. "The End of AIDS?" *Newsweek* (December 2, 1996), 64–73; David Dunlap, "Hype, Hope, and Hurt on the AIDS Front Lines," *The New York Times* (February 2, 1997), p. E3. This prior article was excessively optimistic in expecting that AIDS would be eradicated. One of the hallmarks of contemporary medicine is that we have been extraordinarily successful in containing numerous chronic illnesses, but we have very few examples of our literally defeating any of the more prevalent chronic illnesses in our society. AIDS is very much following this pattern, which is central to the problem of escalating health care costs. If we are imaginative enough (and persuasive enough for investors) we will always find "one more thing (costly)" that we can do in response to a chronic medical problem. AIDS again illustrates this pattern.
6. I realize that only a minority of managed care plans currently have an ethics committee that would be attentive to the sorts of justice issues we are discussing. So my recommendation is that all managed care plans ought to have such a committee.
7. Some readers might not see the point of trying to put ourselves in this past situation. However, the very next example we introduce in this chapter is the artificial heart and the issue of whether or not just and caring managed care plans are morally obligated to provide coverage for that device. In that regard, we are in precisely the same position as managed care plans in the 1990s. Among other things, if individuals have some degree of freedom to change managed care plans, we would be afraid of attracting excess number of patients with serious heart disease if we were to offer coverage for this device.
8. For a fuller discussion of these issues, see Wendy Mariner (1995).
9. For this line of argument, see David Mechanic (1992).
10. For a discussion of the problem of invisible rationing in a managed care context, see Leonard M. Fleck (1990b).
11. Tristram Engelhardt's libertarianism is the direct object of my criticisms in my paper, "Just Health Care(I): Is Beneficence Enough?" (Fleck, 1989).
12. One potential rationale will be an appeal to the fact that these are "last-chance" therapies. However, we will argue in Chapter 7 that that characterization of these interventions carries very little moral weight for the most part.
13. We will note in passing that when Medicare was created in 1965, a very definite actual and potential injustice was remedied: the elderly were assured secure access to much of the health care they would need. Workplace insurance was much more common and health care was much less expensive, so the injustice for younger workers was a relatively minor injustice. Also, life-prolonging medical technologies were rare. The ICU was just being introduced in the 1960s, along with respirators. Dialysis was only in early clinical testing stages. There were no organ transplants or extraordinarily expensive drugs.
14. For a much more extensive and philosophically elegant version of the argument I have been making here, see Wikler (1987).

NOTES

Chapter 7   Last-Chance Therapies

1. A recent press release from the Centers for Medicare and Medicaid indicates that they are seeking public comment regarding a future funding decision regarding the artificial heart. Their apparent intent is to issue a final coverage decision regarding the artificial heart sometime in May of 2008. The press release was in *US Fed News* (Feb. 1, 2008). Apparently the intent is that access to artificial hearts will be restricted to patients in FDA approved trials.
2. A very nice table of all the drugs I am alluding to, their uses, degree of effectiveness, and costs can be found in the article, "The Value of Innovation: The Economics of Targeted Drugs for Cancer." (Tigue and Fizner, 2007).
3. We need to be careful to emphasize that Rawls is not a defender of "trickle down" economics: If the rich get even richer, then they can throw a few crumbs to the exploited poor to make them "better off." Rawls wants the welfare of those who are least well-off maximized to the greatest extent possible, given the desirability of having an expanding economy.
4. An alternate conclusion someone might be motivated to draw is that we placed the wrong individuals in the category of those who were least well-off. The implication is that if we placed the right type of individuals there, we would again have congruence between the prioritarian thesis and those who ought to be the beneficiaries of that thesis. However, in order to achieve that objective, we would likely have to use some moral criteria to identify the "right individuals," which would be obviously circular. We have to have nonmoral criteria for identifying those who are medically least well-off.
5. There are two things that bother the authors of this article. One is that the NHS mandated the coverage of Herceptin without providing the necessary resources to fulfill that mandate. The reader is free to speculate on the reasons why such a decision would have been made (politically speaking). The other item that bothered the authors was that no serious effort was made to inform the public of the need for trade-offs if Herceptin was approved for NHS funding. The makers of the drug were successful in keeping the public focused on the fact that this drug provided some additional life that morally required NHS coverage. This is precisely the sort of public manipulation that processes of rational democratic deliberation are supposed to correct for.
6. It might be helpful to have some additional statistics for this context. There are about three million individuals in the U.S. with rheumatoid arthritis. This represents a very large sum of human suffering that is ameliorable if these patients have access to the costly therapies that are available. There are about one million individuals in the U.S. at any point in time who are in the end stages of dementia. In 2007 there are about 4.5 million individuals with diagnosed dementia at all stages of the disease process.
7. A nice overview of this debate can be found in Schneiderman and Jecker (1995). A nice collection of essays fairly representing diverse views on the issue of futility may be found in Zucker and Zucker (1997). A more recent collection of essays maybe found in the journal *HEC Forum*, Issue 1 (2007). See the essays in that volume by Jecker, (2007), Rubin (2007), Tomlinson (2007), and Tonelli, (2007).
8. Ellen Wright Clayton writes in connection with both the Baby K case and the Theresa Hamilton case, "Among other things that people should not be able to demand are high technology interventions for patients who have no chance of ever (re)gaining consciousness" (1995, p. 14). An opposite view is advocated by Ellen Flannery who writes, "Can Congress enact laws that deny lifesaving treatment to certain classes of sick or disabled individuals in order to assure adequate resources for preventive care for healthy babies and adults" (1995, p. 12)? I respond to the challenge in this question in the next

chapter when we address the concerns of disability advocacy groups regarding various health care rationing proposals.
9. Many attendings have strong reservations on the use of APACHE or other such prognostic systems as a basis for making "ultimate" decisions. Mendez-Tellez (2005) would reflect that view, which is why I have proposed this physician panel appeals option.

Chapter 8   Rationing, Catastrophic Illness, and Disabled Patients

1. At present (2008) about 133 million Americans have one or more chronic illnesses. Among Americans over age 65, 75% will have two or more chronic illnesses, and 20% will have five or more chronic conditions. These figures also make clear that the most concentrated burden of chronic illness is among the elderly. We will also note in passing that the U.S. has more centenarians on a per capita-adjusted basis than any other country in the world. The U.S. currently has 55,000 centenarians, but the projections are that we will have 800,000 by the year 2050 (Hall, 2008; Terry et al., 2008).
2. Interested readers who want a range of perspectives on the multiple issues raised by the Oregon plan should consult Strosberg et al. (1992).
3. This is a compression of an argument I made more fully at the time the Oregon plan was the focus of a national debate. See Fleck (1990a)
4. If anyone is tempted to give moral weight to these imaginings, I will call to mind the wild fears and imaginings regarding the transmissibility of HIV that grabbed the public mind in the late 1980s. There were demands that all health professionals undergo regular HIV testing, as well as restaurant workers and virtually anyone whose job involved contact with the public, even though it was scientifically certain then that the basic modes of transmission were very limited. If those fears and imaginings had been taken seriously as the foundation for changes in public policy, the result would have been clear injustices—precisely the sort of injustices the ADA was designed to prevent.
5. This is an issue that is taken up by Peters (1995). The basic value conflict he sees there is a conflict between reasonable utilitarian considerations (limited resources and unlimited needs) and equally legitimate concerns about protecting our deep egalitarian commitments. He sees courts (so far) as leaning in the direction of protecting those egalitarian considerations, which yields cases such as that of Baby K.
6. We will comment in passing that for those who contend that universal access to a comprehensive package of health care services is a matter of justice, achieving that outcome in the U.S. would be all the more politically difficult if we must take seriously the implications of the Eighth Circuit Court opinion we have been discussing. Since the court seemed to affirm these health care claims only for those who had the proper insurance, the surest way to prevent these claims from becoming more expansive would be to prevent any form of universal health insurance from coming to be. Private insurers are clever enough that they would be able to craft policies that would avoid the requirements of this court, either through policy limits or through refusing to cover at all individuals likely to have disability protections.
7. The work of Anita Silvers (2003) is quite helpful on this point. She is an advocate for a "neutral" conception of disability. Not all disabilities or impairments represent some form of ill health deserving of special moral treatment. She writes, "Health care should be allocated to persons in ill health, a category that often intersects with, but should not be conflated with, the disability category" (p. 479). She wants to resist in particular the thought that persons with disabilities ought to be regarded as being among "the

medically least well-off," and consequently, would be entitled to distributional priority as a result of being so categorized. She gives the following example to illustrate her point: Imagine six individuals with really terrible headaches. Four of them are individuals with various sorts of disabilities (the reader is free to imagine whatever they wish); the other two are otherwise healthy individuals. Only four doses of a drug are available that will dramatically alleviate the headaches of any of these individuals. Who should get those four doses? If we assign disabled persons to the "medically least well-off" category, then we might be tempted to think our four persons with disabilities have a strong just claim to those four doses. However, that is the view she rejects. A headache is a headache is a headache; it is the same in all six individuals. It has no relation to their status as persons with disabilities. Consequently, a lottery or other equality-preserving device should be used to make the allocation.

8. This is again a point that I believe Anita Silvers would endorse (2003). I can offer another example to reinforce this point: We can imagine ten patients in an ICU who have all gone septic. Five of them are persons with serious disabilities (however the reader would choose to imagine those disabilities); the other five are individuals who were in improving health in the ICU, but unfortunately a raging infection has now taken over their bodies. There are currently intense medical debates (and economic debates) about the use of drotrecogin alfa (Xigris) in response to septic shock—this drug costs about $7,000 per dose. About 750,000 Americans need to be treated for septic shock each year (Huang et al., 2007). Septic shock adds dramatically to the costs of hospitalization (Laupland et al., 2006). Mortality associated with sepsis is in the 18% to 30% range. The best research suggests that only very marginal benefits are associated with Xigris, and that is with a segment of patients who have APACHE scores above 25 (Abraham et al., 2008). There might be a 6% improvement in mortality for that group. We could imagine that, through a democratic deliberative process, we would judge that gain to be too little relative to total costs (the potential cost of giving all such patients Xigris would be several billion dollars per year). Consequently, we would agree to a rationing protocol denying Xigris to our future possible septic selves. If so, then all 10 of our patients above are justly denied Xigris. The fact that some might have various disabling conditions adds no relevant moral weight to their claims to this drug in these circumstances.

Chapter 9   Is Age-Based Rationing Ever "Just Enough"?

1. Some might wish to argue that the human genetic endowment is such that the maximum achievable life span for an individual under ideal circumstances is about 120 years old. That would suggest to some that a reasonable goal of medicine would be to identify everything at the cellular level that defeats our achieving that goal and correct those cellular deficiencies through new medical interventions. That is the conclusion Callahan would strongly reject.
2. A very comprehensive study on this point linking insurance status and cancer was recently published in the journal *Lancet Oncology*. The main conclusion of the study was that individuals who are uninsured or covered by Medicaid are more likely to receive a late diagnosis of cancer compared to those with private insurance, thus diminishing survival chances. This study was described in the *New York Times* (Sack, 2008).
3. Some will argue that all the emphasis on cost control will generate technological advancements that will be much more efficient and cost-effective than anything in medicine today. But this argument has been used for the past 30 years to justify all manner of new medical interventions. Often these claims are true in a narrow sense. The

invention of laparoscopic surgery has dramatically reduced the number of in-hospital days for surgery for many procedures. We imagine this yields aggregated cost savings. But in practice, surgery becomes a "more attractive" option for some range of medical problems over more conservative strategies because the surgery involves a shorter recovery time. The result is that the total volume of surgery and the aggregate costs of these surgeries has increased, with the result that there is a net increase in total health costs. The efficiencies are "phantom efficiencies" unless the comparison is to the cost of all these additional surgeries done as non-laparoscopic surgeries.

4. These projections are likely on the conservative side as we move toward 2030. I picked the number 500,000 per year because that is slightly below the annual number of cancer deaths in the U.S. Cancer is largely a disease of older persons. If the absolute size of the cohort over age 65 doubles by 2030, then we should expect more than a million cancer deaths per year, or a million patients per year who would be on these drugs aimed at controlling cancer as a chronic condition. Again, in 2007 there were about 1.4 million new cancers diagnosed. That number ,too, could double by 2030. For a very complete statistical picture of cancer in the U.S., go to the American Cancer Society, Cancer Statistics 2007, online at http://caonline.amcancersoc.org/cgi/content/full/57/1/43?maxtoshow=&HITS=10&hits=10&RESULTFORMAT=&searchid=1&FIRSTINDEX=0&minscore=5000&resourcetype=HWCIT

5. There is a very large literature that has grown up around the topic of QALYs. Some of that literature represents a strong defense of the virtue of QALYs and one or another methodology used to construct them. Other literature critically attacks the whole notion as grossly prejudicial to the just claims for needed health care of those who are medically least well-off. I cannot review that literature here. Advocates for persons with disabilities are almost certainly correct that the QALY methodology greatly undervalues how persons with disabilities view the quality of their own lives. In other cases, I would contend that we can fairly and reliably judge that the quality of certain sorts of lives is miserable and largely devoid of meaning and purpose. I have in mind PVS patients, end-stage Alzheimer's, and a broad range of other physically and cognitively devastating medical disorders. I do not see QALY methodology as adding anything more than false precision to these judgments. Harris (1987) and Hope (1996) are strong critics of QALYs because they have unacceptably ageist discriminatory implications. McKie et al. (1998) will defend QALYs as yielding ethically defensible outcomes in a range of circumstances. Specifically, they reject the claim that QALYs are ageist in a morally objectionable sense. "Since the elderly as a group experience many more health problems than the young, they also stand to gain more in the form of QALYs from health care expenditure. Thus, while their fewer remaining life years are a disadvantage when it comes to calculating their QALY score, their greater susceptibility to illness and disease and thus greater potential to benefit from health care expenditure are an advantage" (p. 48). McKie et al. see QALYs as satisfying both egalitarian and utilitarian considerations of health care justice. For additional critical discussion of several philosophic theories linking QALYs and ageism, see Tsuchiya (2000).

6. To avoid the risk of tarnishing Dr. DeBakey's reputation, published reports made clear that those around him (family and professionals) were insisting on this care, as opposed to Dr. DeBakey himself.

7. The projections for dementia in 2050 are that about four million individuals will be in the advanced stages of dementia (needing long-term care, either in a nursing home or round-the-clock coverage by family). A total of 16 million individuals will have some degree of dementia at that time.

NOTES

8. Brody is likely not talking about health care goods that are absolutely scarce, such as a transplantable heart. Given the scarcity of natural hearts, it would not be unjust if an individual were denied another heart transplant because he had a heart transplant five years ago that is now failing. Too many others would have a stronger just claim to that heart because they had not already had an opportunity for those five extra years of life. What Brody is talking about is fiscal scarcity, a situation in which an individual would be denied some health intervention because it was judged not to be costworthy from some larger societal perspective.
9. The reader will recall our introduction of Wildavsky's characterization of our health care system: we are "doing better and feeling worse." This is another area where this is painfully true. Hospice programs were conceived as a humane way to yield a kinder death as an alternative to overly aggressive death-prolonging medicine. Part of what became a defining feature of hospice programs was extraordinary skill in providing palliative care, and incidentally, saving society substantial sums of money. However, success in palliative care has resulted in patients expecting more in the way of aggressive life-prolonging medical care because the side effects of that care that made it so awful can now be effectively managed. The result has been very large increases in the cost of end-of-life "hospice care."
10. Lest the reader think the remark about a *platinum credit card* being needed for medical rescue was just something cute to write, we have a painfully real example from the news. A woman named Patsy Bates was in the middle of breast cancer treatment when her insurer, HealthNet of California, pulled her insurance. This is awful, but the rest of the story is worse. "She said she had undergone surgery to remove a tumor and had received her first two chemotherapy treatments *when doctors stopped treating her because her bills were going unpaid*" (Associated Press, 2008). These are my italics to emphasize why readers better keep that *platinum credit card* handy if they expect medical rescue.
11. Charles Fried is politically conservative, and likely has in mind a libertarian conception of justice in this passage. His likely intent is to denounce political liberals who would "seize through taxation" the assets of the wealthy in order to fund welfare programs for those less well-off. Still, the considered moral judgment expressed by the passage remains true when we read it from the perspective of a more liberal egalitarian conception of justice.

Chapter 10 Do Future Possible Children Have a Just Claim to a Sufficiently Healthy Genome?

1. If we did have the capacity to do germ line genetic engineering of eight-cell embryos, the issue raised here would not arise. In that case we could delete from that embryo the faulty gene and replace it with a normal copy of the gene that is supposed to be there. This sort of intervention may be described as the ultimate in transplant microsurgery. That is, it seems to fit the standard model of the practice of medicine and the justice issues raised by that model.
2. See also Silvers (2001) and Silvers and Satz (2000).

Chapter 11 Organ Transplantation: When Is Enough Enough?

1. Readers should again call to mind Calabresi and Bobbitt (1978); this is yet another way in which rationing decisions are rendered invisible so far as a broader public is concerned.

2. A recent case calls attention to the risks associated with the Pittsburgh protocol. In this story, a transplant surgeon is accused of having "rushed a patient to death" in order to gain quicker access to his organs (McKinley, 2008).
3. I have inserted into the text a more recent study than that cited by Ubel et al. This is the work of Radovancevic et al, 2003. Their key conclusion is: "The results of re-transplantation for acute rejection and early graft failure are poor enough to suggest that this option is not advisable."

Chapter 12   *The Liberalism Problem*

1. This issue is what has come to be known in the literature as "savior siblings." It is seen by some as being morally problematic because the child that is conceived to save an older sibling is thought to be a mere means to achieving the good of that older sibling. That is, the Kantian principle that forbids using persons as mere things is thought to be violated. This is a moral risk. However, if that savior sibling is cherished as much as any other child in the family (as was true in the *Ayala* case), and if the biological sacrifice made by the savior sibling poses no more than normal risk to that child, the Kantian principle has not been violated. Still, the other part of the moral problem is that numerous excess embryos are necessarily created as part of this intervention—they are generally going to be discarded once a suitable baby has been born. That, too, will generate opposition to funding this intervention as part of a national health insurance plan. For further discussion, see Bennett and Harris (2006).
2. Some might object that Christian Scientists could not possibly have an interest in having secure access to needed health care. However, as Rawls (1993) notes, part of what a liberal society is designed to protect is the right of individuals to have a radical change of mind about their most fundamental beliefs. This is a matter of rational self-interest. The most recent studies in the U.S. indicate that about 25% of adults change their religious commitments from the faith tradition (or non-faith tradition) in which they were raised as children. Committed Christian Scientists at the moment may not have an interest in having secure access to needed health care, but their future possible "other denominational" selves would have that interest. That is the public interest we are protecting.
3. To offer another example, vegetarians must pay taxes to support FDA efforts at meat inspection, even though they may never have another bite of meat for the rest of their lives. Again, there is a public interest at stake. In this case, fruits and vegetables must also be inspected by the FDA. In the case of Christian Scientists, their children will be assured access to obligatory needed health care for the same reasons that we will transfuse the children of parents who are Jehovah's Witnesses. Parents do not have a moral or political right to make martyrs of their children for beliefs those children are incapable of rationally endorsing.
4. Rather than keep the reader guessing as to the specific judgments I would make, I would support with $5 billion annually the alternative reproduction benefit before I would provide funding for more ICDs, or artificial hearts for those over age 75, or left ventricular assist devices for those with end-stage heart failure, or any of these very expensive cancer drugs that yield only small gains in life expectancy. In all these cases, too little opportunity is being protected at too great a cost. The vast majority of individuals who would have the relevant health needs above would either already have had the opportunity to lead a "full life" (as Callahan would understand that phrase) or else they are beyond the capacity of medicine to avert a terminal outcome in the near future. These are unfortunate facts, but they do not represent injustices. Giving individuals the opportunity to have children who

would otherwise not be able to have children without medical and financial support is a very significant part of what most would regard as a "full life." That statement can be endorsed as a matter of public reason; it is not tied to any particular comprehensive vision of the good or religious tradition. Still, offering our assisted reproduction benefit will not be a topmost health priority in our society. What would clearly have higher priority would be a broad range of costworthy public health benefits, as well as any number of very costly but very effective life-prolonging interventions (such as Factor VIIa or imiglucerase), as well as a broad range of non-curative medical interventions that protected the quality of life of individuals with various chronic disorders (such as various drugs that effectively diminished discomforts associated with arthritis, or effectively managed symptoms associated with MS, or technologies that yielded effective functional substitutes as part of a rehabilitation program). In theory, given a limited budget, we could run out of funds before we got far enough down our priority list to fund this assisted reproduction benefit. In practice, this might be a remote likelihood in the U.S., given what appear to be a very large number of high-cost, low-benefit interventions—part of the usual medical armamentarium today that would deserve low-priority status in the future.

5. Someone may wonder what will count as a "reasonable" religious commitment. I want that term understood in a very minimalist sense to mean: (1) no violation of the basic rights of others (child abuse cannot be tolerated because some religious group endorses it); (2) no violation of public interests (no despoiling the environment because God commanded us to subdue the earth); (3) no violation of just laws and social policies (practices of polygamy).

Chapter 14   *Financing Health Care Fairly*

1. For the record, the "accusation" of secrecy always struck me as the most unfair criticism of the process. We did do our work "in secret," but this was not in order to subvert any part of the democratic process. Rather, the secrecy assured all of us that we could be utterly candid in proposing ideas. We did not have to fear being ridiculed in the press the next morning. The secrecy also protected us from lobbyists for various special interests who would seek to corrupt our thinking in order to protect their current advantages in the health care system. The secrecy also protected us from "political strategists" who would also threaten the moral integrity of the plan by pushing for changes that would gain political advantage or protect against political loss. We had no power to impose anything upon the American public; once we completed our work, our proposal would be vetted through the normal legislative and democratic processes. So far as I know, no lobbyist was ever denied the opportunity to buy the favor of any member of Congress as a result of our work. What could be fairer?
2. I discussed this earlier in connection with the work of Shim et al. (2006). They called attention to the large increase in major cardiac procedures being done on patients in their eighties and nineties because the risk and misery to such patients has been dramatically reduced. This same phenomenon can be seen with regard to the increase of surgical procedures done laparoscopically. The surgery saves money for any individual case by reducing the number of days required in the hospital, but the aggregate use of the surgery has increased total costs to society. Improvements in doing hip and knee replacements in the elderly have generated comparable increases in total volume and total costs. This phenomenon gets repeated across many areas of medicine.
3. Additional criteria could be used to make more fine-grained assessments of various proposals for health reform. Daniels, Light, and Caplan (1996) offered 10 criteria for

assessing health reform proposals. Working Group #17 (Brock and Daniels, 1994) offered 14 criteria. Levine et al. (2007) provide just four major criteria, with a number of very specific operational directives. Their work comes from the *Ethical Force Program* of the AMA. Their goal is not to advocate for any specific reform proposal but to set forth the most important criteria that would have to be met by any changes worthy of being judged as "reform" from a moral point of view. DeGrazia (2008) also provides only four criteria for assessing reform proposals. He is a strong advocate for a single-payer system, which he sees as being the only type of reform effort that will successfully meet his criteria. All four of these criteria sets present assessments from a moral point of view. In all these cases, when so many values are being used for assessment purposes, trade-offs will be unavoidable. What we need to be clear about are the boundaries for trade-offs that are clearly morally objectionable. This again (for me) is the role of the constitutional principles of health care justice I articulated in Chapter 5.

4. This again raises the RAND problem. Half the time, patients will make the "wise choice" and refrain from seeing a physician for what is essentially a minor, self-limiting problem; the other half of the time, patients will make a very unwise choice (driven by their desire to minimize expenditures from that health account) that has serious (sometimes irreversible) health consequences that could have been avoided with timely medical advice (Lohr et al., 1986). Middle-class individuals will not usually make these mistakes because they have the additional income needed to underwrite these costs. The result (in practice) is differential access to needed and effective health care, mostly related to ability to pay. This is presumptively unjust.

5. Kuttner (2008) summarizes well the major failings of any private system for financing access to health care:

> The private insurance system's main techniques for holding down costs are practicing risk selection, limiting the services covered, constraining payments to providers, and shifting costs to patients. But given the system's fragmentation and perverse incentives, much cost-effective care is squeezed out, resources are increasingly allocated to profit opportunities rather than medical need, many attainable efficiencies are not achieved, unnecessary medical care is provided for profit, administrative expenses are high, and enormous sums are squandered to game the system. (p. 549–50).

6. What Kotlikoff actually writes in this regard is the following:

> Each and every factor relevant to a participant's expected healthcare costs would be used in determining each participant's voucher, including the participant's preexisting conditions, region (since health care costs differ regionally), age, sex, current medication regime, latest medical tests, current diagnoses, past medical history, and family medical history. (p. 78)

> How one would acquire much of this medical information in a timely manner is worth pondering. Privacy issues would also be a concern for many.

7. What Hall (1997) advocates in this connection is what he refers to as "global informed consent" to health care rationing. That is, when an individual chooses a specific managed care plan, she would be told that the plan is committed to providing health care services that are costworthy in as efficient a way as possible. She might be given a booklet that described the different sorts of rules and incentives and other cost-saving mechanisms that managed care employed in order to achieve these objectives. If the plan employed capitation with regard to primary care physicians, that concept would be explained in that booklet. The ultimate implication of this approach is that patients consent in this

"global" way to the "kinds" of cost-control and rationing mechanisms employed by that plan. They are not told at the time they are receiving care in the plan all the specific decisions being made to limit the costs of care being provided to them at that time. If a physician judges that a specific medical test is somewhat costly and unlikely to yield that much clinically useful medical information, then the test will not be done. The patient would not be told explicitly that the physician had considered the test but rejected it for these reasons. In that respect, patient-specific rationing decisions would be invisible to the patient. Hall has in mind what we might call garden-variety cost-control decisions.

To be fair, Hall also says that rationing decisions that could have major consequences for the patient would be brought to the attention of the patient, but at that point an interesting moral challenge is faced. What do we imagine is the source of a specific rationing decision with these larger consequences? Is this something that has been specifically excluded from the comprehensive basic benefit package covered by the value of the voucher? If so, and if that exclusion is the product of broad public deliberation, then there would be nothing especially objectionable from the perspective of health care justice. If, on the contrary, this limitation emerged from within that plan as a result of an administrative decision, such decisions could vary from health plan to health plan. That would alter the real value of the voucher that patient held. And at that point in time, that patient would have little capacity or power to argue about the decision. (Again, this is where Buchanan's (1998) point comes in—if there is not a shared sense of justice among plan members, then individual plan members have no basis for claiming they have been treated unjustly beyond their "personal feelings" of injustice.) If this was how things would work out with vouchers, this would be a potentially serious justice issue that required explicit attention. It would be too much to expect perfect consistency in the making of all rationing decisions across the plans (especially if some encouragement was being given to organizational innovation), but rough justice would have to exist *and would have to be known to exist*. At the very least, what would have to be known with confidence by plan members and the architects of the health care system as a whole was that cost savings were not achieved through organizational innovation in any particular plan requiring unjust denials of needed and effective health care.

8. In the National Health Service in Great Britain, patients are organized into geographic areas of care. Primary Care Trusts are given a global budget to provide all the primary care needed by these patients over the course of a year. Roughly 50–100 physicians might comprise the medical staff for one of these Primary Care Trusts. They are paid by salary. They are motivated to deliver care as efficiently as possible in order to maximize the collective health good of their patient population. If they have a "profit" at the end of the year, they are free to invest it in whatever they judge to be useful services or equipment for their practice; but they may not pay themselves a bonus. This is the sort of "leakproof" system in which rationing decisions can be made in good conscience.

9. It is no secret that European countries can extract discounts of 50–70% from major drug companies if those companies want their drugs available as part of a national formulary. And this is the reason why pharmaceutical companies lobbied so vigorously to prevent the federal government from doing the same thing on behalf of Medicare beneficiaries in connection with the Medicare Part D benefit. It may take very intense grassroots pressure to reverse this sad and unjust state of affairs, but it can be accomplished. The most likely consequence of such an effort is that a more level playing field would be established regarding the cost of prescription drugs between the two continents.

REFERENCES

Aaron, H.J., and Schwartz, W.B. 1984. *The Painful Prescription: Rationing Hospital Care.* Washington, D.C.: The Brookings Institution.
Aaron, H.J., Schwartz, W.B., Cox, M. 2005. *Can We Say No? The Challenge of Rationing Health Care.* Washington, D.C.: Brookings.
Abraham, E., Laterre, P., Garg, R., Levy, H. et al. 2008. "Drotrecogin Alfa (Activated) for Adults with Severe Sepsis and a Low Risk of Death." *New England Journal of Medicine* 353: pp. 1332–41.
Ackerman, F., and Heinzerling L. 2002. "Pricing the Priceless: Cost–Benefit Analysis Of Environmental Protection." *University of Pennsylvania Law Review* 150: pp. 1553–84.
Ad Hoc Committee of the Harvard Medical School to Examine the Definition of Brain Death. 1968. "A Definition of Irreversible Coma." *JAMA* 205: pp. 337–40.
Alexander, S. 1962. "They Decide Who Lives, Who Dies: Medical Miracle Puts Moral Burden on Small Committee." *Life Magazine* 53: pp. 102–25.
Al-Khatib, S. et al. 2005. "Clinical and Economic Implications of the Multicenter Automatic Defibrillator Implantation Trial-II." *Annals of Internal Medicine* 142: pp. 593–600.
Allen, S. 2007a. "Critics Blast Slow Progress on Cancer: Say Costly Drugs Do Little to Extend Lives." *Boston Globe* (December 2): Nation section.
Allen, S. 2007b. "Researchers Detail Cancer DNA Damage—Work Paves the Way To Map Disease." *Boston Globe* (November 5): A1 Health section.
Allhoff, F. 2005. "Germ-Line Genetic Enhancement and Rawlsian Primary Goods." *Kennedy Institute of Ethics Journal* 15: pp. 39–56.
Altman, L. 2006. "The Man on the Table Was 97, but He Devised the Surgery." *New York Times* (December 25): A1.

REFERENCES

American Heart Association. 2007. *Heart Disease and Stroke Statistics—2007 Update.* Dallas, TX: American Heart Association.

Anand, Geeta. 2003. "Who Gets Health Care? Rationing in an Age of Rising Costs." *Wall Street Journal* (September 12): A1.

Anderson, G., and Horvath, J. 2004. "The Growing Burden of Chronic Disease in America." *Public Health Reports* 119: pp. 263–70.

Andre, J., Fleck, L., and Tomlinson, T. 2000. "On Being Genetically 'Irresponsible.'" *Kennedy Institute of Ethics Journal* 10: pp. 129–46.

Annas, G.J. 1994. "Asking the Courts to Set the Standard of Emergency Care—The Case of Baby K." *New England Journal of Medicine* 350: pp. 1542–45.

Annas, G.J. 2000. "The Man on the Moon, Immortality, and Other Millennial Myths: The Prospects and Perils of Human Genetic Engineering." *Emory Law Journal* 49: pp. 753–82.

Appleby, J. 2002. "Hospitals Fight for Turf in Medical Arms Race." *USA Today* (February 19): national news section.

Arneson, R. 2000. "Luck, Egalitarianism and Prioritarianism." *Ethics* 110: pp. 339–49.

Arnold, R., and Youngner, S. 1993. "The Dead Donor Rule: Should We Stretch It, Bend It, or Abandon It?" *Kennedy Institute of Ethics Journal* 3: pp. 263–78.

Associated Press. 1991. "Bank Robber in Wheelchair Has an Alibi: Costly Medicine." *New York Times* (January 18): A15.

Associated Press. 2003. "Oregon Judge Rejects Life Support Request." *New York Times* (November 18): National section.

Associated Press. 2008. "Insurer That Cut Client's Care Fined $9M." *New York Times* (February 23): Health section.

Bach, P. 2008. "Cost Sharing for Health Care–Whose Skin? Which Game?" *New England Journal of Medicine* 358: pp. 411–13.

Bachetta, M., Ko, W., Girardi, L., Mack, C. et al. 2003. "Outcomes of Cardiac Surgery in Nonagenarians: A 10-Year Experience." *Annals of Thoracic Surgery* 75: pp. 1215–20.

Baker, R. 1992. "The Inevitability of Health Care Rationing: A Case Study of Rationing in the British National Health Service." In M. Strosberg et al. (eds), *Rationing America's Medical Care: The Oregon Plan and Beyond.* Washington, D.C.: Brookings, pp. 208–229.

Barrett, A., Roques, T., Small, M., and Smith R. 2006. "How Much Will Herceptin Really Cost?" *British Medical Journal* 333 (November 25): pp. 1118–20.

Bartlett, J. 1997. "Infectious Diseases." *Journal of the American Medical Association* 277: pp. 1865–66.

Bayles, M. 1987. "The Value of Life." In D. VanDeVeer and T. Regan (eds), *Health Care Ethics.* Philadelphia: Temple University Press.

BBC News. December 14, 2007. "U-Turn Over Sight-Saving Drugs." Accessed on December 15, 2007 at http://news.bbc.co.uk/go/pr/fr/-/hi/health/7142167.stm

Beinfeld, M., Wittenberg, E., and Gazelle, G. 2005. "Cost-Effectiveness of Whole-Body CT Screening." *Radiology* 234: pp. 415–22.

Benjamin, M. 1990. *Splitting the Difference: Compromise and Integrity in Ethics and Politics.* Lawrence, KS: University Press of Kansas.

Benjamin, M. 2001. "Between Subway and Spaceship: Practical Ethics at the Outset of The Twenty-First Century." *Hastings Center Report* 31 (4): pp. 24–31.

Bennett, R., and Harris, J. 2006. "Reproductive Choice." In R. Rhodes, L. Francis, and A. Silvers (eds.) *The Blackwell Guide to Medical Ethics.* London: Blackwell Publishing: pp. 201–219.

Berenson, A. 2006. "A Cancer Drug Shows Promise at a Price That Many Can't Pay." *New York Times* (February 15): Health section.
Berenson, A. 2008. "Drug Has No Benefit in Trial, Makers Say." *New York Times* (January 14):, Business section.
Berge, K., Maiers, D., Schreiner, D., Jewell, S. et al. 2005. "Resource Utilization and Outcome in Gravely Ill Intensive Care Unit Patients with Predicted In-Hospital Mortality Rates of 95% or Higher by APACHE III Scores: The Relationship with Physician and Family Expectations." *Mayo Clinic Proceedings* 80 (2): pp. 166–73.
Berk, M., and Monheit, A. 2001. "The Concentration of Health Care Expenditures, Revisited." *Health Affairs* 20 (2): pp. 9–18.
Beutler, E. 2006. "Lysosomal Storage Diseases: Natural History and Ethical and Economic Aspects." *Molecular Genetics and Metabolism* 88: pp. 208–15.
Blackwell, T. 2007. "Family Fights Hospital Over Father's Care: Lack of Treatment Violates Jewish Faith, Court Told." *The Financial Post* (Canada) (December 11): A14.
Bloomfield, D.M. et al. 2006. "Micro-Volt T-Wave Alternans and the Risk of Death or Sustained Ventricular Arrhythmias in Patients with Left Ventricular Dysfunction." *Journal of the American College of Cardiology* 47: pp. 456–63.
Blumstein, J. 1983. "Rationing Medical Resources: A Constitutional, Legal, and Policy Analysis." In *Securing Access to Health Care*, Vol. III, Report of the President's Commission for the Study of Ethical Problems in Medicine and Biomedical and Behavioral Research. Washington, D.C.: Government Printing Office: pp. 349–394.
Blumstein, J. 1989. "Government's Role in Organ Transplantation Policy." *Journal of Health Politics, Policy, and Law* 14: pp. 5–39.
Blumstein, J. 1992. "The Case for Commerce in Organ Transplantation." *Transplantation Proceedings* 24: pp. 2190–97.
Bodenheimer, T., and Grumbach, K. 2005. *Understanding Health Policy: A Clinical Approach* (4th Ed). New York: McGraw-Hill.
Bohman, J. 1996. *Public Deliberation: Pluralism, Complexity, and Democracy*. Cambridge, MA: MIT Press.
Borger, C., Smith, S., Truffer, C., Keehan, S., Sisko, A., Poisal, J. et al. 2006. "Health Spending Projections Through 2015: Changes on the Horizon." *Health Affairs* 25: pp. w61–73.
Boseley, S. 2006. "The Selling of a Wonder Drug." *The Guardian* (London) (March 29).
Boseley, S. 2007. "Medical Advance: Woman With the Golden Arm that Points to a Surgical Breakthrough." *The Guardian* (London) (February 2): p. 9.
Bradley, C., Clement, J., and Lin C. 2008. "Absence of Cancer Diagnosis and Treatment In Elderly Medicaid-Insured Nursing Home Residents." *Journal of the National Cancer Institute* 100 (1): pp. 21–30.
Brennan, T. 1993. "An Ethical Perspective on Health Care Insurance Reform." *American Journal of Law and Medicine* 19: pp. 37–74.
Brock, D. 1993. *Life and Death: Philosophical Essays in Biomedical Ethics*. Cambridge: Cambridge University Press.
Brock, D. 1995a. "Justice and the ADA: Does Prioritizing and Rationing Health Care Discriminate Against the Disabled?" *Social Philosophy and Policy* 12 (Summer): pp. 159–85.
Brock, D. 1995b. "Some Unresolved Ethical Issues in Priority-Setting of Mental Health Services." In P. Boyle and D. Callahan (eds), *What Price Mental Health? The Ethics and Politics of Setting Priorities*. Washington, D.C.: Georgetown University Press, pp. 216–33.

REFERENCES

Brock, D. 2000. "Enhancements of Human Function: Distinctions for Policymaykers." In E. Parens (ed.) *Enhancing Human Traits: Ethical and Social Implications.* Washington, D.C.: Georgetown University Press, pp. 48–69.

Brock, D. 2002. "Priority to the Worse Off in Health-Care Resource Prioritization." In R. Rhodes, M. Battin and A. Silvers (eds), *Medicine and Social Justice.* Oxford: Oxford University Press, pp. 362–72.

Brock, D., and Daniels, N. 1994. "Ethical Foundations of the Clinton Administration's Proposed Health Care System." *Journal of the American Medical Association* 271: pp. 1189–96.

Brody, B. 1988. "The Macro-Allocation of Health Care Resources." In H.M. Sass and R. Massey (eds), *Health Care Systems: Moral conflicts in European and American Public Policy.* Dordrecht: Kluwer Academic Publishers, pp. 213–36.

Buchanan, A. 1995. "Equal Opportunity and Genetic Intervention." *Social Philosophy And Policy* 12: pp. 105–135.

Buchanan, A. 1998. "Managed Care: Rationing Without Justice, But Not Unjustly." *Journal of Health Politics, Policy, and Law*, 23: pp. 617–34.

Buchanan, A., Brock, D., Daniels, N., and Wikler, D. 2000. *From Chance to Choice: Genetics and Justice.* Cambridge: Cambridge University Press.

Buchanan, D. 2008. "Autonomy, Paternalism, and Justice: Ethical Priorities in Public Health." *American Journal of Public Health* 98 (1): pp. 15–21.

Burley, J. 1998. "The Price of Eggs: Who Should Bear the Costs of Fertility Treatments?" In J. Harris and S. Holm (eds.) *The Future of Human Reproduction: Ethics, Choice and Regulation.* New York: Oxford University Press, pp. 127–49.

Butler, J. 1999. *The Ethics of Health Care Rationing: Principles and Practices.* London: Cassell.

Calabresi, G., and Bobbitt, P. 1978. *Tragic Choices: The Conflicts Society Confronts in the Allocation of Tragically Scarce Resources.* New York: W.W. Norton.

Callahan, D. 1987. Setting Limits: Medical Goals in an Aging Society. New York: Simon and Schuster.

Callahan, D. 1990. *What Kind of Life: The Limits of Medical Progress.* New York: Simon and Schuster.

Callahan, D. 1995. "Setting Mental Health Priorities: Problems and Possibilities." In P. Boyle and D. Callahan (eds) *What Price Mental Health: The Ethics and Politics of Setting Priorities.* Washington, D.C.: Georgetown University Press, pp. 175–92.

Callahan, D. 1998. *False Hopes: Why America's Quest for Perfect Health is a Recipe For Disaster.* New York: Simon and Schuster.

Callahan, D. 2003. *What Price Better Health? Hazards of the Research Imperative.* Berkeley: University of California Press.

Callahan, D., and Wasunna, A. 2006. *Medicine and the Market: Equity v. Choice.* Baltimore: Johns Hopkins University Press.

Caplan, A. 1983. "Organ Transplants: The Costs of Success." *Hastings Center Report* 13 (6): pp. 23–32.

Caplan, A. 1993. "The Telltale Heart: Public Policy and the Utilization of Non-Heart-Beating Donors." *Kennedy Institute of Ethics Journal* 3: pp. 251–62.

Carreyrou, J. 2007. "Maxed Out: As Medical Costs Soar, the Insured Face Huge Tab." *Wall Street Journal* (November 29): A1.

Casarett, D., and Lantos, J. 1998. "Have We Treated AIDS Too Well? Rationing and the Future of AIDS Exceptionalism." *Annals of Internal Medicine* 128: pp. 756–59.

Catlin, A., Cowan. C., Heffler, S., and Washington, B. 2007. "National Health Spending in 2005: The Slowdown Continues." *Health Affairs* 26: pp. 142–53.

Catlin, A., Cowan, C., Hartman, M., and Heffler S. 2008. "National Health Spending in 2006: A Year of Change for Prescription Drugs." *Health Affairs* 27: pp. 14–29.

Centers for Disease Control and Prevention. 1999. "Ten Great Public Health Achievements: United States, 1900–1999." *Morbidity and Mortality Weekly Report* 48: pp. 143–46.

Centers for Medicare and Medicaid Services, Office of the Actuary. 2004. *"National Health Care Expenditures Projections: 2005–2015."* pp. 1–18.

Cervia, J., and Smith, M. 2003. "Enfuvirtide (T-20): A Novel Human Immunodeficiency Virus Type 1 Fusion inhibitor." *Clinics of Infectious Disease* 37: pp. 1102–06.

Chadwick, A. 2003. "Advances in Xenotransplantation," transcript from radio program *Day to Day, National Public Radio* (August 5).

Childress, J. 1989. "Ethical Criteria for Procuring and Distributing Organs for Transplantation." *Journal of Health Politics, Policy, and Law* 14: pp. 87–113.

Childress, J., Faden, R., Gaare, R. et al. 2002. "Public Health Ethics: Mapping the Terrain." *Journal of Law, Medicine, and Ethics* 30: pp. 170–78.

Clayton, E. 1995. "Commentary: What is Really at Stake in Baby K? A Response to Ellen Flannery." *The Journal of Law, Medicine, and Ethics* 23: pp. 13–14.

Cohen, C. 1992. "The Case for Presumed Consent to Transplant Human Organs After Death." *Transplantation Proceedings* 24 (5): pp. 2168–72.

Cohen, C., and Benjamin, M. 1991. "Alcoholics and Liver Transplantation." *JAMA* 265: pp. 1299–1301.

Cohen, J. 1993. "Moral Pluralism and Political Consensus." In D. Copp, J. Hampton, and J. Roemer (eds.) *The Idea of Democracy*, Cambridge: Cambridge University Press, pp. 270–91.

Cohen, J., Neumann, P., and Weinstein, M. 2008. "Does Preventive Care Save Money? Health Economics and the Presidential Candidates." *New England Journal of Medicine* 358: pp. 661–63.

Colburn, D. 2003. "Man Dies After Being Taken Off Life Support." *The Oregonian* (November 19): p. A1.

Congressional Budget Office. 2005. "High-Cost Medicare Beneficiaries." Prepared by Julie Lee and Todd Anderson, Health and Human Resources Division, CBO. Accessed on January 28, 2008 at http://www.cbo.gov

Connock, M., Burls, A., Frew, E. et al. 2006. "The Clinical Effectiveness and Cost-Effectiveness of Enzyme Replacement Therapy for Gaucher's Disease: A Systematic Review." *Health Technology Assessment* 10: no. 24.

Cooper, D. 2003. "Clinical Xenotransplantation—How Close Are We?" *Lancet* 362: pp. 557–59.

Council on Ethical and Judicial Affairs. 1994. "Strategies for Cadaveric Organ Procurement: Mandated Choice and Presumed Consent." *JAMA* 272: pp. 809–12.

Cruz, P. 2007. "The *Burke* Case: The Terminally Ill Patient and the Right to Life." *The Modern Law Review* 70 (2): pp. 306–17.

Culliton, B. 2008a. "The Intersection of Basic Science and Health Policy: A Conversation with Victor Velculescu." *Health Affairs* (web) 27 (1): pp. W27–33.

Culliton, B. 2008b. "Promoting Medical Innovation While Developing Sound Social And Business Policy: A Conversation With Thomas G. Roberts." *Health Affairs* (web) 27 (1): pp. W34–40.

REFERENCES

Culliton, B. 2008c. "Insurers and 'Targeted Biologics' for Cancer: A Conversation With Lee N. Newcomer." *Health Affairs* (web) 27 (1): pp. W41–51.
Cutler, D.M. 2003. "Disability and the Future of Medicare." *New England Journal of Medicine* 349: pp. 1084–85.
Daar, A. 1992. "Rewarded Gifting." *Transplantation Proceedings* 24: pp. 2207–11.
Daniels, N. 1985. *Just Health Care*. Cambridge: Cambridge University Press.
Daniels, N. 1986. "Why Saying No to Patients in the United States is So Hard: Cost Containment, Justice, and Provider Autonomy." *New England Journal of Medicine* 314: pp. 1381–83.
Daniels, N. 1988. *Am I My Parents' Keeper: An Essay on Justice Between the Young and the Old*. New York: Oxford University Press.
Daniels, N. 1993. "Rationing Fairly: Programmatic Considerations." *Bioethics* 7: pp. 224–33.
Daniels, N. 1996. *Justice and Justification: Reflective Equilibrium in Theory and Practice*. Cambridge: Cambridge University Press.
Daniels, N. 2002. "Justice, Health, and Health Care." In R. Rhodes, M. Battin, and Silvers (eds.) *Medicine and Social Justice: Essays on the Distribution of Health Care*. New York: Oxford University Press, pp. 6–23.
Daniels, N. 2007. "Rescuing Universal Health Care." *Hastings Center Report* 37 (2): p. 3.
Daniels, N., Light, D., and Caplan, R. 1996. *Benchmarks of Fairness for Health Care Reform*. Oxford: Oxford University Press.
Daniels, N., and Sabin, J.E. 1997. Limits to Health Care: Fair Procedures, Democratic Deliberation, and the Legitimacy Problem for Insurers." *Philosophy and Public Affairs* 26 (4): pp. 303–350.
Daniels, N., and Sabin, J.E. 1998a. "Last Chance Therapies and Managed Care: Pluralism, Fair Procedures, and Legitimacy." *Hastings Center Report* 28 (2): pp. 27–41.
Daniels, N., and Sabin, J.E. 1998b. "The Ethics of Accountability and the Reform of Managed Care Organizations." *Health Affairs* 17 (5): pp. 50–69.
Daniels, N., and Sabin, J.E. 2002. *Setting Limits Fairly: Can We Learn to Share Medical Resources?* New York: Oxford University Press.
Darr, A.S. 1992. "Rewarded Gifting." *Transplantation Proceedings* 24: pp. 2207–11.
Davis, K. 2008. "Slowing the Growth of Health Care Costs—Learning From International Experience." *New England Journal of Medicine* 359: pp. 1751–55.
DeGrazia, D. 2008. "Single Payer Meets Managed Competition: The Case for Public Funding and Private Delivery." *Hastings Center Report* 38 (Jan/Feb): pp. 23–33.
DeVita, M., and Snyder, J. 1993. "Development of the University of Pittsburgh Medical Center Policy for the Care of Terminally Ill Patients Who May Become Organ Donors After Death Following Removal of Life Support." *Kennedy Institute Of Ethics Journal* 3: pp. 131–43.
Dewey, J. 1916. Democracy and Education: An Introduction to the Philosophy of Education. New York: Macmillan.
Dewey, J. 1935. Liberalism and Social Action. New York: G.P. Putnam's Sons.
Dominus, S. 2004. "Life in the Age of Old, Old Age." *New York Times Magazine* (February 22): p. 26ff.
Dorschner, J. 1991. "Life at Any Price?" *Chicago Tribune Magazine* (October 27): pp. 14–19.
Dougherty, C. 1991. "Setting Health Care Priorities: Oregon's Next Steps." *Hastings Center Report* 21 (3): pp. 1–10 (Supplement).
Dowling, R.D., Gray, L.A., Etoch, S.W. et al. 2003. "The AbioCor Implantable Replacement Heart." *Annals of Thoracic Surgery* 75 (6 Suppl): pp. S93–99.

Dworkin, R. 1986. *Law's Empire*. Cambridge, MA: Harvard University Press.
Dworkin, R. 1993. "Justice in the Distribution of Health Care." *McGill Law Journal* 38: pp. 883–98.
Dworkin, R. 2000. *Sovereign Virtue: The Theory and Practice of Equality*. Cambridge, MA: Harvard University Press.
Eddy, D.W. 1996. Clinical Decision Making: From Theory to Practice. Boston: Jones and Bartlett.
Eggers, P.W. 2000a. "Medicare's End Stage Renal Disease Program." *Health Care Financing Review* 22 (1): pp. 55–60.
Eggers, P.W. 2000b. "A Quarter Century of Medicare Expenditures for ESRD." *Seminars in Nephrology* 20 (6): pp. 516–22.
Ehrenstein, M., Jury, E., and Mauri, C. 2005. "Statins for Atherosclerosis: As Good As It Gets?" *New England Journal of Medicine* 352: pp. 73–5.
Emanuel, E. 1991. *The Ends of Human Life: Medical Ethics in a Liberal Polity*. Cambridge, MA: Harvard University Press.
Emanuel, E. 2008. "The Problem with Single-Payer Plans." *Hastings Center Report* 38 (Jan/Feb): pp. 38–41.
Emanuel, E., and Fuchs, V. 2005. "Health Care Vouchers—A Proposal for Universal Coverage." *New England Journal of Medicine* 352: pp. 1255–60.
Engelhardt, H.T. 1996. *The Foundations of Bioethics*. 2nd Ed. Oxford: Oxford University Press.
Enthoven, A., and Fuchs, V. 2006. "Employment-Based Health Insurance: Past, Present, and Freund, D and Smeeding T. 2002. "The Future Costs of Health Care in Aging Societies: Is the Glass Half Full or Half Empty?" Accessed on December 11, 2008 at http://www.sprc.unsw.edu.au/seminars/Tim%20Smeeding%20paper.pdf Future." *Health Affairs* 25: pp. 1538–47.
Enthoven, A. and Kronick, R. 1989. "A Consumer-Choice Health Plan for the 1990s." *New England Journal of Medicine* 320: pp. 29–37.
Entwistle, V.A., Watt, I.S., Bradbury, R., and Pehl, L.J. 1996. "Media Coverage of the Child B Case." *British Medical Journal* 312: pp. 1587–91.
Epstein, P. 2007. "Trials That Matter: Two Faces of Progress in the Treatment of Age-Related Macular Degeneration." *Annals of Internal Medicine* 146: pp. 532–34.
Epstein, R. 2003. "Let the Shoemaker Stick to his Last: A Defense of the Old Public Health." *Perspectives in Biology and Medicine* 12: pp. 165–96.
Farrelly, C. 2002. "Genes and Social Justice: A Rawlsian Reply to Moore." *Bioethics* 16: pp. 72–83.
Farrelly, C. 2004. "The Genetic Difference Principle." *American Journal of Bioethics* 4 (2): pp. W21–W28.
Farrelly, C. 2005. "Justice in the Genetically Transformed Society." *Kennedy Institut Of Ethics Journal* 15: pp. 91–99.
Feiring, E. 2008. "Lifestyle, Responsibility and Justice." *Journal of Medical Ethics* 34: pp. 33–36.
Fishkin, J., and Laslett, P. (eds). 2003. *Debating Deliberative Democracy*. London: Blackwell.
Flannery, E. 1995. "One Advocate's Viewpoint: Conflicts and Tensions in the Baby K Case." *The Journal of Law, Medicine, and Ethics* 23: pp. 7–12.
Fleck, L.M. 1987. "DRGs: Justice and the Invisible Rationing of Health Care Resources." *Journal of Medicine and Philosophy* 12: pp. 165–96.
Fleck, L.M. 1989. "Just Health Care: Is Beneficence Enough? (I)." *Theoretical Medicine* 10: pp. 167–82.

Fleck, L.M. 1990a. "The Oregon Medicaid Experiment: Is It Just Enough?" *Business and Professional Ethics Journal* 9 (3/4): pp. 201–17.

Fleck, L.M. 1990b. "Justice, HMOs, and the Invisible Rationing of Health Care Resources." *Bioethics* 4: pp. 97–120.

Fleck, L.M. 1992. "Just Health Care Rationing: A Democratic Decision Making Approach." *University of Pennsylvania Law Review* 140 (5): pp. 1597–1636.

Fleck, L.M. 1994a. "Just Caring: Oregon, Health Care Rationing, and Informed Democratic Deliberation." *Journal of Medicine and Philosophy* 19: pp. 367–88.

Fleck, L.M. 1994b. "Just Caring: Health Reform and Health Care Rationing." *Journal of Medicine and Philosophy* 19: pp. 435–44.

Fleck, L.M. 1995. "My Conscience, Your Money." *Hastings Center Report* 25(5): pp. 28–9.

Fleck, L.M. 1996. *Genome Technology and Reproduction: Values and Public Policy: A Report on the Fall Community Dialogues.* East Lansing: Michigan State University.

Fleck, L.M. 1997. *Genome Technology and Reproduction: Values and Public Policy: A Report on the Spring Community Dialogues.* East Lansing: Michigan State University.

Fleck, L.M. 1999. "Just Caring: Managed Care and Protease Inhibitors." In J. Arras and B. Steinbock (eds) *Ethical Issues in Modern Medicine*, 5th ed. Mountainview, CA: Mayfield Publishing, pp. 679–86.

Fleck, L.M. 2001. *Policy Reports and Recommendations: Communities of Color and Genetics Policy Project.* East Lansing and Ann Arbor, Michigan: Michigan State University. Available from the author upon request.

Fleck, L.M. 2002a "Last Chance Therapies: Can a Just and Caring Society do Health Care Rationing When Life Itself is at Stake?" *Yale Journal of Health Policy, Law, and Ethics* 2 (2): pp. 255–98.

Fleck, L.M. 2002b. "Do Future Possible Children Have a Just Claim to a Sufficiently Healthy Genome?" In R. Rhodes, M. Battin, and A. Silvers (eds) *Medicine and Social Justice: Essays on the Distribution of Health Care*. New York: Oxford University Press, pp. 446–57.

Fleck, L.M. 2006. "Just Caring: Who Pays? Who Profits? Who Panders? *Hastings Center Report* 36 (3): pp. 13–17.

Foot, P. 1967. "The Problem of Abortion and the Doctrine of Double Effect." *Oxford Review* 5: pp. 5–15.

Fost, N. 1983. "The New Body Snatchers: On Scott's *The Body as Property*." *American Bar Foundation Research Journal* 3: pp. 718–32.

Freund, D., and Smeeding, T. 2002. "The Future Costs of Health Care in Aging Societies: Is the Glass Half Full or Half Empty?" Seminar paper prepared for "Aging Societies: Responding to the Policy Challenges" University of New South Wales (April 8). Accessed on December 31, 2008 at http://www.sprc.unsw.edu.au/seminars/Tim%20smeeding%20paper.pdf.

Fried, C. 1970. *An Anatomy of Values*. Cambridge: Harvard University Press.

Fukuyama, F. 2002. *Our Posthuman Future*. New York: Farrar, Strauss and Giroux.

Galvin, R., and Delbanco, S. 2006. "Between a Rock and a Hard Place: Understanding the Employer Mind-Set." *Health Affairs* 25: pp. 1548–55.

Garland, M.J. 1992. "Rationing in Public: Oregon's Priority-Setting Methodology." In M. Strosberg, J. Wiener, and R. Baker (eds) *Rationing America's Medical Care: The Oregon Plan and Beyond*. Washington, D.C.: Brookings, pp. 37–59.

Garland, M.J. 1999. "Experts and the Public: A Needed Partnership for Genetic Policy." *Public Understanding and Science* 8: pp. 241–54.

Gehi, A., Haas, D., and Fuster, V. 2005. "Primary Prophylaxis with the Implantable Cardioverter-Defibrillator: The Need for Improved Risk Stratification." *JAMA* 294: pp. 958–60.

Gibbard, A. 1983. "The Prospective Pareto Principle and Equity of Access to Health Care." In President's Commission for the Study of Ethical Problems in Medicine And Biomedical and Behavioral Research, *Securing Access to Health Care*, Vol. II. Washington, D.C.: Government Printing Office.

Gladwell, M. 2005. "The Moral-Hazard Myth." *The New Yorker* (August 29). Accessed on January 12, 2008 at: http://www.newyorker.com/archive/2005/08/29/050829fa_fact

Gojgic, L. 2000. "A Routine Wonder: Despite Rare Mishaps, Dialysis is a Workhorse Technology that Keeps Thousands of Kidney Patients Alive." *Pittsburgh Post-Gazette* (September 26): p. F1.

Goldberger, Z., and Lampert, R. 2006. "Implantable Cardioverter-Defibrillators: Expanding Indications and Technologies," *Journal of the American Medical Association* 295: pp. 809–18.

Gordon, E. 2006. "The Ethics of Medicare Policy: Increasing Transplant Access and Survival." *DePaul Law Review* 55: pp. 1045–66.

Gostin, L. 2001. "Public Health, Ethics, and Human Rights: A Tribute to the Late Jonathan Mann." *Journal of Law, Medicine, and Ethics* 29: pp. 121–30.

Gostin, L., and Bloche, M. 2003. "The Politics of Public Health: A Response to Epstein." *Perspectives in Biology and Medicine* 46: pp. S160–75.

Gostin, L., and DeAngelis, C. 2007. "Mandatory HPV Vaccinnation: Public Health Vs. Private Wealth." *JAMA* 297: pp. 1921–23.

Grann, V., and Neugut, A. 2003. "Lung Cancer Screening at Any Price?" *Journal of the American Medical Association* 289: pp. 357–58.

Gray, B. 1991. *The Profit Motive and Patient Care: The changing Accountability of Doctors and Hospitals*. A Twentieth Century Fund Report. Cambridge, MA: Harvard University Press.

Greenland, P. 2003. "Improving Risk of Coronary Heart Disease: Can a Picture Make A Difference?" *Journal of the American Medical Association* 289: pp. 2270–2.

Grulich, A., van Leeuwen, M., Falster, and M. Vajdic, C. 2007. "Incidences of Cancers in People with HIV/AIDS Compared with Immunosuppressed Transplant Recipients: A Meta-analysis." *Lancet* 370 (July 7): pp. 59–67.

Gutmann, A., and Thompson, D. 1996. *Democracy and Disagreement*. Cambridge: Harvard University Press.

Gutmann, A., and Thompson, D. 2003. "Deliberative Democracy Beyond Process." In J. Fishkin and P. Laslett (eds) *Debating Deliberative Democracy*. London: Blackwell.

Gutmann, A., and Thompson, D. 2004. *Why Deliberative Democracy?* Princeton: Princeton University Press.

Hadley, J., Steinberg, E., and Feder, J. 1991. "Comparison of Uninsured and Privately Insured Hospital Patients: Condition on Admission, Resource Use, and Outcome." *JAMA* 265: pp. 374–79.

Hadorn, D.C. 1991. "Setting Health Care Priorities in Oregon: Cost-Effectiveness Meets the Rule of Rescue." *Journal of the American Medical Association* 265: pp. 2218–25.

Hadorn, D.C. 1992. "The Problem of Discrimination in Health Care Priority Setting." *JAMA* 268: pp. 1454–59.

Hall, M. 1997. *Making Medical Spending Decisions: The Law, Ethics, and Economics Of Rationing Mechanisms*. New York: Oxford University Press.

REFERENCES

Hall, W. 2008. "Centenarians: Metaphor Becomes Reality." *Archives of Internal Medicine* 168 (3): pp. 262–3.

Ham, C. 1999. "Tragic Choices in Health Care: Lessons from the Child B Case." *British Medical Journal* 319: pp. 1258–61.

Hamel, M.B., Phillips, R.S., Davis, R.B., Desbiens, N., Connors, A.F., Teno, J.M., Wenger, N., Lynn, H., Wu, A.W., Fulkerson, W., and Tsevat, J. 1997. "Outcomes and Cost-Effectiveness of Initiating Dialysis and Continuing Aggressive Care in Seriously Ill Hospitalized Patients." *Annals of Internal Medicine* 127: pp. 195–202.

Hardin, G. 1968. "The Tragedy of the Commons." *Science* 162 (December 13):pp. 1243–48.

Harris, J. 1985. *The Value of Life.* London: Routledge and Kegan Paul.

Harris, J. 1987. "QALYfying the Value of Human Life." *Journal of Medical Ethics* 13: pp. 117–23.

Harris, J. 1995. "Double Jeopardy and the Veil of Ignorance—A Reply." *Journal of Medical Ethics* 21: pp. 151–57.

Harris, J. 1996. "Would Aristotle Have Played Russian Roulette?" *Journal of Medical Ethics* 22: pp. 209–15.

Harris, J. 1998. *Clones, Genes, and Immortality.* New York: Oxford University Press.

Harris, J. 2005. "It's not NICE to Discriminate." *Journal of Medical Ethics* 31: pp. 373–75.

Healy, M. 2007. "Sold on Drugs; Selling the Patient." *Los Angeles Times* (August 6): p. F4.

Heart Disease Weekly editors. 2003. "Congestive Heart Failure: Price of Heart Device May Mean Rationing." *Heart Disease Weekly* (September 28).

Heffler, S., Smith, S., Keehan, S., Borger, C., Clemens, M., and Truffer, C. 2005. "U.S. Health Spending Projections for 2004–14." *Health Affairs* 24, Supplement I, W5: pp. 74–85.

Heinzerling, L. 1999. "Discounting Life." *Yale Law Journal* 108: pp. 1911–15.

Henderson v. Bodine Aluminum, Inc., 70 F.3d 958 (8th Cir. 1995).

Hennessey-Fiske, M. 2007. "Tough Calls in Transplant Case." *Los Angeles Times* (December 22): p. A1.

Heuser, S. 2006. "Medicare to Pay for Heart Test." *Boston Globe* (March 22).

Himmelstein, D., Woolhandler, S., and Wolfe, S. 2004. "Administrative Waste in the U.S. Health Care System in 2003." *International Journal of Health Services* 34 (1): pp. 79–86.

Hirsch, J. 2005. "Raising consciousness". *The Journal of Clinical Investigation.* American Society for Clinical Investigation. 115(5): p. 1102.

Hirskyj, P. 2007. "QALY: An Ethical Issue that Dare not Speak its Name." *Nursing Ethics* 14 (January): pp. 72–82.

Hope, T. 1996. "QALYs, Lotteries, and Veils: The Story So Far." *Journal of Medical Ethics* 22: pp. 195–96.

Hope, T. 2001. "Rationing and Life-Saving Treatments: Should Identifiable Patients Have Higher Priority?" *Journal of Medical Ethics* 27: pp. 179–85.

Hogan, M. 1999. "The Epidemic of Violence in America: What Can We Do About This Public Health Emergency?" *Postgraduate Medicine Online*, 105, #6. Accessed on May 22, 2005 at: http://www.postgradmed.com/issues/1999/05_15_99/guest_ed.htm

Horton, L., and Horton, P. 1993. "Improving the Current System for Supplying Organs For Transplantation." *Journal of Health Politics, Policy, and Law* 18 (1): pp. 175–88.

Hreybe, H., Razak, E., and Saba, S. 2007. "Effect of End-Stage Renal Failure and Hemodialysis on Mortality Rates in Implantable Cardioverter-Defibrillator Recipents." *PACE*: pp. 1091–95.

Huang, D., Clermont, G., Dremsizov, T., Angus, D. et al. 2007. "Implementation of Early Goal-Directed therapy for Severe Sepsis and Septic Shock: A Decision Analysis." *Critical Care Medicine* 35: pp. 2090–2100.

Hunink, M., and Gazelle, G. 2003. "CT Screening: A Trade-Off of Risks, Benefits, and Costs." *The Journal of Clinical Investigation* 111: pp. 1612–19.
Institute of Medicine Committee on the Consequences of Uninsurance. 2002. *Care Without Coverage: Too Little, Too Late.* Washington, D.C.: National Academy Press. Institute of Medicine. 2004. *Insuring America's Health: Principles and Recommendations.* Washington, D.C.: National Academies Press.
Intestinal Transplant Registry. 2003. *Final Report—2003.* Accessed on February 25, 2007 at http://www.intestinaltransplant.org
Jecker, N. 2007. "Medical Futility: A Paradigm Analysis." *HEC Forum* 19: pp. 13–32.
Jonker, D., O'Callaghan, C., Karepetis, C. et al. 2007. "Cetuximab for the Treatment of Colorectal Cancer." *New England Journal of Medicine* 357: pp. 2040–48.
Juengst, E. 1998. "The Meaning of Enhancement." In E. Parens (ed.) *Enhancing Human Traits: Ethical and Social Implications.* Washington, D.C.: Georgetown University Press, pp. 29–47.
Kant, I. 1785/1958. Groundwork of the Metaphysic of Morals. Translated by H.J. Paton. New York: Harper Torchbooks, p.102.
Karapetis, C., Khambata-Ford, S., Jonker, D. et al. 2008. "K-ras Mutations and Benefit from Cetuximab in Advanced Colorectal Cancer." *New England Journal of Medicine* 359: pp. 1757–65.
Kass, N. 2001. "An Ethics Framework for Public Health." *American Journal of Public Health* 91: pp. 1776–82.
Katz, J., and Capron, A. 1975. *Catastrophic Diseases: Who Decides What?* New York: Russell Sage Foundation.
Kawachi, I., and Kennedy, B. 1999. "Income Inequality and Health: Pathways and Mechanisms." *Health Services Research* 34: pp. 215–27.
Kawachi, I., Kennedy, B., and Wilkinson, R. 1999. *Income Inequality and Health: A Reader.* New York: The New Press.
Keehan, S., Sisko, A. Truffer, C. Smith S. et al. 2008. "Health Spending Projections Through 2017: The Baby-Boom Generation is Coming to Medicare." *Health Affairs* 27 (Web exclusive): W145–W155.
Kitcher, P. 1996. *The Lives to Come: The Genetic Revolution and Human Possibilities.* New York: Simon and Schuster.
Kitzhaber, J. 1991. "Developing an Equitable Health Policy in an Era of Limited Resources." *Seminars in Anesthesiology* 10 (3): pp. 211–19.
Kitzhaber, J. 1993. "Prioritising Health services in an Era of Limits: The Oregon Experience." *BMJ* 307: pp. 373–77.
Klevit, H.D., Bates, A.C., Castaneres, T., Kirk, E.P. et al. 1991. "Prioritization of Health Care Services: A Progress Report by the Oregon Health Services Commission." *Archives of Internal Medicine* 151 (5): pp. 912–16.
Knaub, J. 2007. "Turning Crisis into Opportunity—Challenges Facing Radiology in The 21st Century." *Radiology Today* 8 (July 30): pp. 10–12.
Knaus, W., Wagner, D., Draper, E. et al. 1991. "The APACHE III Prognostic System: Risk Prediction of Hospital Mortality for Critically Ill Hospitalized Adults." *Chest* 100: pp. 1619–36.
Kobelt, G., Sobocki, P., Mulero, J. Gratacos, J. Collantes-Estevez, and E., Braun, J. 2008. "The Cost-Effectiveness of Infliximab in the Treatment of Ankylosing Spondylitis in Spain." *Scandinavian Journal of Rheumatology* 37 (1): pp. 62–71.
Kotlikoff, L.J. 2007. The Healthcare Fix: Universal Insurance for All Americans. Cambridge, MA: The MIT Press.

Krach, C.A., and Velkoff V.A. 1999. *U.S. Bureau of the Census, Current Population Reports, Series P-23–199RV, Centenarians in the United States.* Washington, D.C.: Government Printing Office.

Krugman, P. 2007. "Prostates and Prejudice." *New York Times* (Nov. 2): A section.

Kurella, M., Covinsky, K., Collins, A., and Chertow, G. 2007. "Octogenerians and Nonagenerians Starting Dialysis in the United States." *Annals of Internal Medicine* 146: pp. 177–83.

Kurtz, S., Ong, K., Lau, E., Mowat, F., and Halpern, M. 2007. "Projections of Primary and Revision Hip and Knee Arthroplasty in the United States from 2005 to 2030." *Journal of Bone and Joint Surgery* 89: pp. 780–85.

Kuttner, R. 2008. "Market-Based Failure—A Second Opinion on U.S. Health Care Costs." *New England Journal of Medicine* 358: pp. 549–51.

Lalezeri, J., Henry, K., O'Hearn, M. et al. 2003. "Enfuvirtide: An HIV-1 Fusion Inhibitor, for Drug-Resistant HIV-Infection in North and South America." *New England Journal of Medicine* 348: pp. 2175–85.

Lantos, J. et al. 1989. "The Illusion of Futility in Clinical Practice." *American Journal Of Medicine* 87 (July): pp. 81–84.

Laupland, K., Lee, H., Gregson, and D., Manns, B. 2006. "Cost of Intensive Care Unit-Acquired Bloodstream Infections." *Journal of Hospital Infection* 63: 124–32.

Lee, J. 2007. "An Extra Hour of Halloween Daylight? Thank the Candy Lobby." *New York Times* (Oct. 31): City section.

Levine, M., Wynia, M., Schyve, P., Teagarden, R. et al. 2007. "Improving Access to Health Care: A Consensus Ethical Framework to Guide Proposals for Reform." *Hastings Center Report* 37 (Sept/Oct.): pp. 14–19.

Levinsky, N.G. 1984. "The Doctor's Master." *New England Journal of Medicine* 311: pp. 1573–75.

Levinsky, N.G. 2001. "Equity and Patient Autonomy in Dialysis." In N. Levinsky (ed) *Ethics and the Kidney*. New York: Oxford University Press, pp. 99–109.

Lichtarowicz, A. 2004. "Obesity Epidemic 'Out of Control.'" *BBC News World Edition*, Accessed on May 17, 2007 at http://news.bbc.co.uk/2/hi/africa/3969693.stm

Light, D.W. 1997. "The Real Ethics of Rationing." *British Medical Journal* 315: pp. 112–15.

Lindsay, R. 2005. "Enhancements and Justice: Problems in Determining the Requirements of Justice in a Genetically Transformed Society." *Kennedy Institute of Ethics Journal* 15: pp. 3–38.

Lohr, K., Brook, R., Kamberg, C., et al. 1986. "Use of Medical Care in the Rand Health Insurance Experiment: Diagnosis- and Service-Specific Analyses in a Randomized Control Trial." *Medical Care* 24: Supplement: pp. S1–S87.

Lomasky, L. 1980. "Medical Progress and National Health Care." *Philosophy and Public Affairs* 10: pp. 65–88.

Lowance, D.C. 1993. "Factors and Guidelines to be Considered in Offering Treatment To Patients with End-Stage Renal Disease: A Personal Opinion." *American Journal of Kidney Diseases* 21: pp. 679–83.

Lubitz, M.P., Liming, C., Kramarow, E., and Lentzner H. 2003. "Health, Life Expectancy, and Health Care Spending Among the Elderly." *New England Journal of Medicine* 349: pp. 1048–55.

Lynn, J. 1993. "Are the Patients Who Become Organ Donors Under the Pittsburgh Protocol for 'Non-Heart-Beating Donors' Really Dead?" *Kennedy Institute of Ethics Journal* 3: pp. 167–78.

REFERENCES

Mahar, M. 2006. *Money-Driven Medicine*. New York: Harper Collins. Mann, J. 1997. "Medicine and Public Health, Ethics, and Human Rights." *Hastings Center Report* 27 (May/June): pp. 6–13.

Manning, J. 2003. "For-Profit Specialty Hospitals Treat Fewer Severely Ill Patients." *Knight Ridder Tribune Business News* (October 23): p. A1.

Mariner, W. 1995. "Business vs. Medical Ethics: Conflicting Standards for Managed Care." *Journal of Law, Medicine and Ethics* 23: pp. 236–46.

Marshall, T. 2003. "Coronary Heart Disease Prevention: Insights From Modelling Incremental Cost Effectiveness." *British Medical Journal* 327: pp. 1264–68.

Mashberg, T. 2006. "A Life-Saving Liver Machine." *MIT Technology Review* (March 28). Accessed February 25, 2008 at http://www.techreview.com

Mathews, T.J. 2007. "Trends in Spina Bifida and Anencephalus in the United States, 1991–2004" National Center for Health Statistics, Division of Vital Statistics, Accessed on February 25, 2007 at http://www.cdc.gov/nchs/products/pubs/hestats/spinr_anen.htm

Matthews, R. G. 2003. "A Retired Steelworker Struggles with a Health-Insurance Crisis." *Wall Street Journal* (May 12): p. A1.

Maxwell, S., Zuckerman, S., and Berenson, R. 2007. "Use of Physicians' Services Under Medicare's Resource-Based Payments." *New England Journal of Medicine* 356: pp. 1853–61.

McGann v. H & H Music Company, 946 F.2d 401 No. 90–2672 (5th Cir. 1991).

McKie, J., Kuhse, H., Richardson, J., and Singer, P. 1996. "Another Peep Behind the Veil." *Journal of Medical Ethics* 22: pp. 216–21.

McKie, J., and Richardson, J. 2003. "The Rule of Rescue." *Social Science and Medicine* 56: pp. 2407–19.

McKie, J., Richardson, J., Singer, P. and Kuhse, H. 1998. *The Allocation of Health Care Resources: An Ethical Evaluation of the 'QALY' Approach*. Hampshire: Ashgate Publishing.

McKinley, J. 2008. "Surgeon Accused of Speeding a Death to Get Organs." *New York Times* (Feb. 27): Health section.

Mechanic, D. 1986. *From Advocacy to Allocation: The Evolving American Health Care System*. New York: The Free Press.

Mechanic, D. 1992. "Professional Judgment and the Rationing of Medical Care." *University of Pennsylvania Law Review* 140 (May): pp. 1713–54.

Mechanic, D. 1997. "Muddling Through Elegantly: Finding the Proper Balance in Rationing," *Health Affairs* 16 (no. 5): pp. 83–92.

Mechanic, D. 2006. *The Truth About Health Care: Why Reform is Not Working in America*. New Brunswick, NJ: Rutgers University Press.

Mechanic, D., and Schlesinger, M. 1996. "The Impact of Managed Care on Patients' Trust in Medical Care and Their Physicians." *Journal of the American Medical Association* 275: pp. 1693–97.

Mehlman, M. 1985. "Rationing Expensive Life-Saving Medical Treatment." *Wisconsin Law Review* 1985: pp. 239–303.

Mehlman, M. 2000. "The Law of Above Averages: Leveling the New Genetic Enhancement Playing Field." *Iowa Law Review* 85: pp. 517–93.

Mehlman, M., and Botkin, J. 1998. *Access to the Genome: The Challenge to Equality*. Washington, D.C.: Georgetown University Press.

Mehlman, M., Durchslag, M., and Neuhauser, D. 1997. "When do Health Care Decisions Discriminiate Against Persons with Disabilities?" *Journal of Health Care Politics, Policy, and Law* 22: pp. 1385–1412.

REFERENCES

Mendez-Tellez, P. 2005. "Predicting Patient Outcomes, Futility, and Resource Utilization in the Intensive Care Unit: The Role of Severity Scoring Systems and General Outcome Prediction Models." *Mayo Clinic Proceedings* 80: pp. 161–63.

Menzel, P. 1983. *Medical Costs, Moral Choices.* New Haven: Yale University Press.

Menzel, P. 1992a. "Oregon's Denial: Disabilities and Quality of Life." *Hastings Center Report* 22(6): pp. 21–5.

Menzel, P. 1992b. "Equality, Autonomy, and Efficiency: What Health Care System Should We Have?" *The Journal of Medicine and Philosophy* 17: pp. 33–58.

Menzel, P. 1992c. "The Moral Duty to Contribute and its Implications for Organ Procurement Policy." *Transplantation Proceedings* 24: pp. 2175–78.

Messori, A., Santarlasci, B., Trippoli, S., and Vaiani, M. 2003. "Cost Effectiveness of Statins for Primary Prevention of Cardiovascular Events is Questionable." (letter) *British Medical Journal* 327: pp. 808–09.

Mitka, M. 2003. "Expanding Statin Use to Help More At-Risk Patients is Causing Financial Heartburn." *Journal of the American Medical Association* 290: 2243–45.

Morreim, H. 1991. *Balancing Act: The New Medical Ethics of Medicine's New Economics.* Dordrecht, Holland: Kluwer Academic Publishers.

Moss, A.H. 1995. "To Use Dialysis Appropriately: The Emerging Consensus on Patient Selection Guidelines." *Advances in Renal Replacement Theory* 2: pp. 175–83.

Moss, A., and Siegler, M. 1991. "Should Alcoholics Compete Equally for Liver Transplantation?" *JAMA* 265: pp. 1295–98.

MS-Network 2007 at http://www.ms-network.com. Murray, T., and Youngner, S. 1994. "Organ Salvage Policies: A Need for Better Data and More Insightful Ethics." *JAMA* 272: pp. 814–15.

Nadler, E., Eckert, B., and Neumann, P. 2006. "Do Oncologists Believe New Cancer Drugs Offer Good Value?" *The Oncologist* 11: pp. 90–95.

National Heart, Lung, and Blood Institute. 2002. *Third Report of the National Cholesterol Education Program Expert Panel on Detection, Evaluation, and Treatment of High Blood Cholesterol in Adults (ATP III)*, Pub. no. 02–5215. Bethesda, MD: NHLBI.

Newson, A. 2008. "Ethical Aspects Arising from Non-Invasive Fetal Diagnosis." *Seminars in Fetal and Neonatal Medicine* 13: pp. 103–08.

Nissenson, A., and Rettig, R.A. 1999. "Medicare's End-Stage Renal Disease Program: Current Status and Future Prospects." *Health Affairs* 18 (1): pp. 161–79.

Nord, E. 1999. *Cost–Value Analysis in Health Care: Making Sense out of QALYs.* Cambridge: Cambridge University Press.

Organ Procurement and Transplant Network. 2008. Scientific Registry of Transplant Recipients. http://www.ustransplant.org/csr/current/fastfacts/datatours.aspx. Accessed March 10, 2008. Orentlicher, D. 1994. "Rationing and the Americans with Disabilities Act." *Journal of the American Medical Association* 271: pp. 308–14.

Orentlicher, D., 1996. "Destructuring Disability: Rationing of Health Care and Unfair Discrimination Against the Sick." *Harvard Civil Rights-Civil Liberties Law Review* 31: pp. 49–87.

Parens, E. (ed.). 1998. *Enhancing Human Traits: Ethical and Social Implications.* Washington, D.C.: Georgetown University Press.

Pauker, S., Ester, N., and Salem, D. 2005. "Preventing Sudden Cardiac Death: Can We Afford the Benefit?" *Annals of Internal Medicine* 142: pp. 664–66.

Pesavento, P. 2001. "A Turn of the Century Census: Current Trends and Future Projections Portray a Booming Future for Radiology." *Imaging Economics.* Accessed on March 10, 2008 at: http://www.imagingeconomics.com/issues/articles/2001-01_03.asp?

Peters, P. 1995. "Health Care Rationing and Disability Rights." *Indiana Law Journal* 70: pp. 491–547.

Peters, T. 1991. "Life or Death: The Issue of Payment in Cadaveric Organ Donation." *JAMA* 265: pp. 1302–05.

Petersen, Melody. 2003. "Heart Device to Get More U.S. Support." *New York Times* (June 7): Business section.

Pollack, A. 2000. "Two Paths to the Same Protein." *New York Times* (March 28): Section C1.

Pollack, A. 2007a. "New Liver Cancer Drug is Promising, Doctors Say." *New York Times* (June 4): Health section.

Pollack, A. 2007b. "F.D.A. Criticizes Avastin Use for Breast Cancer." *New York Times* (December 4): Business section.

Polyak, K. 2007. "Breast Cancer: Origin and Evolution." *Journal of Clinical Investigation* 117: pp. 3155–63.

Powers, M., and Faden, R. 2006. *Social Justice: The Moral Foundations of Public Health and Public Policy.* New York: Oxford University Press.

Powlson, M. 2003. "Universal Polypharmacy Goes Against Recent Beliefs in Prescribing Practice." (letter) *British Medical Journal* 327: pp. 807–08.

President's Council on Bioethics. 2003. *Beyond Therapy: Biotechnology and the Pursuit of Happiness.* Washington, D.C.: Government Printing Office.

Price, D. 1996. "Lessons for Health Care Rationing from the Case of Child B." *British Medical Journal* 312: pp. 167–69.

PR Newswire. 2008. "AHF Criticizes Tibotec over Steep Price for Newest AIDS Drug, Etravirine." (January 21). Accessed January 24, 2008 at http://www.prnewswire.com

Radovancevic, B., McGiffin, D., Kobashigawa, J. et al. 2003. "Retransplantation in 7,290 Primary Transplant Patients: A 10-Year Multi-Institutional Study." *Journal of Heart and Lung Transplantation* 22: pp. 862–68.

Raftery, J. 2006. "Review of NICE's Recommendations, 1999–2005." *British Medical Journal* 332: pp. 1266–68.

Rao, J., Anderson, L., and Smith, S. 2002. "End of Life is a Public Health Issue." *American Journal of Preventive Medicine* 23: pp. 215–20.

Ratco, T., Cummings. J., and Matuszewski, K. 2004. "Off-Label Use of Recombinant Activated Factor VII (NovoSeven)." *P&T* 29 (11): pp. 712–20.

Rawlins, M. 2004. "NICE Work—Providing Guidance to the British National Health Service." *New England Journal of Medicine* 351: pp. 1383–85.

Rawls, J. 1971. *A Theory of Justice.* Cambridge, MA: Harvard University Press.

Rawls, J. 1980. "Kantian Constructivism in Moral Theory." In Samuel Freeman (ed) *John Rawls: Collected Papers.* Cambridge, MA: Harvard University Press, 1999, pp. 303–58.

Rawls, J. 1993. *Political Liberalism.* New York: Columbia University Press.

Rawls, J. 1999. *John Rawls: Collected Papers*, edited by J. Freeman. Cambridge, MA: Harvard University Press.

Reilly, P. 2002. "Caught in the Middle." *Modern Healthcare* 32 (September): pp. 26–27+.

Reilly, P. 2003. "A Conflict of Interest." *Modern Healthcare* 33(May): pp. 7, 16.

Reinhardt, U. 1982. "Table Manners at the Health Care Feast: Regulation vs. Competition." In D. Yaggy and W.G. Anlyan (eds) *Financing Health Care: Competition vs. Regulation.* Cambridge, MA: Ballinger, pp. 13–34.

Reinhardt, U. 1996. "Rationing Health Care: What It Is, What It Is Not, and Why We Cannot Avoid It." In S. Altman and U. Reinhardt (eds) *Strategic Choices for a Changing Health Care System*. Chicago: Health Administration Press, pp. 63–99.

Rettig, R.A. 1976. "The Policy Debate on Patient Care Financing for Victims of End-Stage Renal Disease." *Law and Contemporary Problems* 40: pp. 196–230.

Rhodes, R. 2005. "Justice in Medicine and Public Health." *Cambridge Quarterly of Healthcare Ethics* 14 (Winter): pp. 13–26.

Rhodes, R., Battin, M., and Silvers, A. 2002. *Medicine and Social Justice: Essays on the Distribution of Health Care*. Oxford: Oxford University Press.

Rhodes, R., Francis, L., and Silvers, A. 2007. *The Blackwell Guide to Medical Ethics*. Oxford: Blackwell Publishing.

Ridker, P., Cannon, C., Morrow, D. et al. 2005. "C-Reactive Protein Levels and Outcomes After Statin Therapy." *New England Journal of Medicine* 352: pp. 20–28.

Rivlin, M. 2000. "Why the Fair Innings Argument Is Not Persuasive." *BMC Medical Ethics* 1 (1). Accessed February 18, 2008 at: http://www.biomedcentral.com/content/backmatter/1472-6939-1-1-b1.pdf

Robertson, J. 1993. "Policy Issues in a Non-Heart-Beating Donor Protocol." *Kennedy Institute of Ethics Journal* 3: pp. 241–50.

Robertson, J. 1994. *Children of Choice: Freedom and the New Reproductive Technologies*. Princeton, NJ: Princeton University Press.

Rodgers, A. 2003. "A Cure for Cardiovascular Disease." *British Medical Journal* 326: pp. 1407–08.

Rothstein, M. 2002. "Rethinking the Meaning of Public Health." *Journal of Law, Medicine, and Ethics* 30: pp. 144–49.

Roush, W. 2007. "BioEngine: One Step Closer to Artificial Liver Device." *Xconomy: Kendall Square* (September 20). Accessed February 25, 2008 at http://www.xconomy.com

Rubin, S. 1998. *When Doctors Say No: The Battleground of Medical Futility*. Bloomington, IN: Indiana University Press.

Rubin, S. 2007. "If We Think It's Futile, Can't We Just Say No?" *HEC Forum* 19: pp. 45–65.

Russell, L.B. 1985. *Is Prevention Better Than Cure?* Washington, D.C.: Brookings Institution.

Russell, L.B. 2000. "Cost-Effectiveness Analysis and Screening Tests for Women." *Journal of the American Medical Women's Association* 55: pp. 207–09.

Russell, B. 2002. "Fair Distribution and Patients Who Receive More Than One Organ Transplant." *Journal of Clinical Ethics* 13 (1): pp. 40–48.

Sabik, L., and Lie, R. 2008. "Priority Setting in Health Care: Lessons from the Experiences of Eight Countries." *International Journal for Equity in Health* 7 (January 21): p. 4ff. [available from BioMed Central]

Sack, K. 2008. "Study Finds Cancer Diagnosis Linked to Insurance Status." *New York Times* (February 18): Health section.

Sadun, R., Sachsman, S., Chen, X., et al. 2007. "Immune Signatures of Murine and Human Cancers Reveal Unique Mechanisms of Tumor Escape and New Targets for Cancer Immunotherapy." *Clinical Cancer Research* 13: pp. 4016–25.

Satcher, D., and Pamies, R. (eds). 2006. *Multicultural Medicine and Health Disparities*. New York: McGraw-Hill.

Scanlon, T.M. 1998. *What We Owe to Each Other*. Cambridge, MA: Harvard University Press.

Schauer, F. 1995. "Giving Reasons." *Stanford Law Review* 47: pp. 635–59.

Schmid, R. 2007. "Elderly Health Costs Growing Slowly." *Washington Post* (November 6): Health section.
Schneiderman, L., and Jecker, N. 1995. *Wrong Medicine: Doctors, Patients, and Futile Treatment*. Baltimore: Johns Hopkins University Press.
Schwindt, R., and Vining, A. 1986. "Proposal for a Future Delivery Market for Transplant Organs." *Journal of Health Politics, Policy, and Law* 11: pp. 483–500.
Segall, S. 2007 "Is Health Care (Still) Special?" *Journal of Political Philosophy* 15: pp. 342–61.
Shaw, B. 1993. "Conflict of Interest in the Procurement of Organs Following Withdrawal of Life Support." *Kennedy Institute of Ethics Journal* 3: pp. 179–87.
Shim, J., Russ, A. and Kaufman, S. 2006. "Risk, Life Extension, and the Pursuit of Medical Possibility." *Sociology of Health and Illness* 28: pp. 479–502.
Silver, L. 1997. *Remaking Eden: Cloning and Beyond in a Brave New World*. New York: Avon Books.
Silvers, A. 2001. "Normality and Functionality: A Disability Perspective." In M. Mahowald, V. McKusick, A. Scheurle, and T. Aspinwall (eds.) *Genetics in The Clinic: Clinical, Ethical, and Social Implications for Primary Care*. St. Louis: Mosby, pp. 89–100.
Silvers, A. 2003. "On the Possibility and Desirability of Constructing a Neutral Conception of Disability." *Theoretical Medicine* 24: 471–87.
Silvers, A. and Satz, A. 2000. "Disability and Biotechnology." In T. Murray and M. Mehlman (eds.) *Encyclopedia of Ethical, Legal and Policy Issues in Biotechnology*. New York: John Wiley and Sons, pp. 173–87.
Singer, P., McKie, J., Kuhse, H., and Richardson, J. 1995. "Double Jeopardy and the Use of QALYs in Health Care Allocation." *Journal of Medical Ethics* 21: pp. 144–50.
Smith, S. 2004. "Rationing Feared as Many Flock to HIV Drug Program." *Boston Globe* (May 14): local section.
Soubrane, G., Cruess, A., Lotery, A., Pauleikhoff, D., Jordi, M., Xiau, X., et al. 2007. "Burden and Health Care Resource Utilization in Neovascular Age-Related Macular Degeneration." *Archives of Ophthalmology* 125: pp. 124–54.
Sreenivasan, G. 2007. "Health Care and Equality of Opportunity." *Hastings Center Report* 37 (2): pp. 21–31.
Stanton-Ife, J. 2006. "Resource Allocation and the Duty to Give Reasons." *Health Care Analysis* 14: pp. 145–56.
Starzl, T. 1992. *The Puzzle People: Memoirs of a Transplant Surgeon*. Pittsburgh: University of Pittsburgh Press.
Stein, R. 2008. "Too Much of a Good Thing? The Growing Use of CT Scans Fuels Medical Concerns about Radiation exposure." *Washington Post* (January 15): p. HE1.
Steinbock, B., and Norcross, A. (eds). 1994. *Killing and Letting Die (2nd ed)*. New York: Fordham University Press.
Stell, L. 2002. "Responsibility for Health Status." In R. Rhodes, M. Battin, and A. Silvers (eds) *Medicine and Social Justice: Essays on the Distribution of Health Care* New York: Oxford University Press, pp. 405–25.
Stevenson, L. 2006. "Implantable Cardioverter Defibrillators for Primary Prevention of Sudden Death in Heart Failure: Are There Enough Bangs for the Bucks?" *Circulation* 114: pp. 101–03.
Strom, S. 2003. "In the Middle Class, More are Deprived of Health Insurance." *New York Times* (November 16): National section.
Strosberg, M., Weiner, J. Baker, R., and Fein, I. (eds) 1992. *Rationing America's Medical Care: The Oregon Plan and Beyond*. Washington, D.C. The Brookings Institution.

REFERENCES

Sulmasy, D. 2007. "Cancer Care, Money, and the Value of Life: Whose Justice? Which Rationality?" *Journal of Clinical Oncology* 25: pp. 217–22.

Sunstein, C. 1996. *Legal Reasoning and Political Conflict.* New York: Oxford University Press.

Sunstein, C. 2001. *Designing Democracy: What Constitutions Do.* New York: Oxford University Press.

Tai, H., Ezzelarab, M., Hara, H., Ayares, D., and Cooper, D. 2007. "Progress in Xenotransplantation Following the Introduction of Gene-Knockout Technology." *Transplant International* 20: pp. 107–17.

Taurek, J. 1977. "Should the Numbers Count?" *Philosophy and Public Affairs* 6: pp. 293–316.

Terhune, C. 2003. "Fast Growing Health Plan Has a Catch: $1,000-a-Year Cap." *Wall Street Journal* (May 14): p. A1.

Terry, D., Sebastiani, P., Andersen, S. and Perls, T. 2008. "Disentangling the Roles of Disability and Morbidity in Survival to Exceptional Old Age." *Archives of Internal Medicine* 168 (3): pp. 277–83.

Thomas, R., Baker, A., Debiasi, R., Winckler, W. et al. 2007. "High-Throughput Oncogene Mutation Profiling in Human Cancer." *Nature Genetics* 39: pp. 347–51.

Thomas, W.J. 1993. "The Oregon Medicaid Proposal: Ethical Paralysis, Tragic Democracy and the Fate of a Utilitarian Health Care Program." *Oregon Law Review* 72 (Spring): pp. 47–156.

Thomson, J. 1976. "Killing, Letting Die, and the Trolley Problem." *Monist* 59: pp. 204–17.

Thomson, J. 1986. "The Trolley Problem." In her collection *Rights, Restitution, and Risk: Essays in Moral Theory.* Cambridge, MA: Harvard University Press, pp. 94–116.

Thorne, J. 1992. "The Oregon Plan Approach to Comprehensive and Rational Health Care." In M. Strosberg, J. Wiener, and R. Baker (eds.) *Rationing America's Medical Care: The Oregon Plan and Beyond.* Washington, D. C.: Brookings, pp. 24–34.

Tigue, C., Fitzner, K., Alkhatib, M., Schmid, E., and Bennett, C. 2007. "The Value of Innovation: The Economics of Targeted Drugs for Cancer." *Targeted Oncology* 2(2): pp. 113–19.

Tomlinson, T. 1993. "The Irreversibility of Death: Reply to Cole." *Kennedy Institute of Ethics Journal* 3: pp. 157–65.

Tomlinson, T. 2007. "Futility Beyond CPR: The Case of Dialysis." *HEC Forum* 19 (1): pp. 33–43.

Tomlinson, T., and Brody, H. 1990. "Futility and the Ethics of Resuscitation." *JAMA* 264: pp. 1276–79.

Tonelli, M. 2007. "What Medical Futility Means to Clinicians." *HEC Forum* 19: pp. 83–93.

Transplant Living. 2006. "Financing a Transplant: The Costs." Accessed January 23, 2008 at: http://www.transplantliving.org/before the transplant/finance/costs.aspx

Trewby, P., and Trewby, C. 2003. "Patients Before Populations." (letter) *British Medical Journal* 327: p. 807.

Tsuchiya, A. 2000. "QALYs and Ageism: Philosophical Theories and Age Weighting." *Health Economics* 9: pp. 57–68.

Ubel, P. 2000. *Pricing Life: Why It's Time for Health Care Rationing.* Cambridge, MA: MIT Press.

Ubel, P., Arnold, R., and Caplan, A. 1993. "Rationing Failure: The Ethical Lessons of Retransplantation of Scarce Vital Organs." *JAMA* 270: pp. 2469–74.

University of Alabama–Birmingham Spinal Cord Injury. 2006. Facts and Figures at a Glance. Accessed November 15, 2007 at: http://www.spinalcord.uab.edu/show.asp?durki=21446

University of Chicago Medical Center. 1999. "Trial Begins for First Artificial Liver Device Using Human Cells." Press release (February 25). Accessed February 25, 2008 at: http://www.uchospitals.edu/news/1999/19990225-elad.html

University of Pittsburgh Medical Center. 1992. "Management of Terminally Ill Patients Who May Become Organ Donors After Death." *Policy and Procedure Manual.*

U.S. Renal Data System. 2006. USRDS 2006 Annual Data Report: Atlas of End-Stage Renal Disease in the United States, National Institutes of Health, National Institute of Diabetes and Digestive and Kidney Diseases, Bethesda, MD.

Vajdic, C., McDonald, S., McCredie, M. et al. 2006. "Cancer Incidence Before and After Kidney Transplantation." *JAMA* 296: pp. 2823–31.

Veatch, R. 1986. *The Foundations of Justice: Why the Retarded and the Rest of Us Have Claims to Equality.* New York: Oxford University Press.

Veatch, R. 1988. "Justice and the Economics of Terminal Illness." *Hastings Center Report* 18 (4): pp. 34–40.

Veatch, R. 1993. "The Impending Collapse of the Whole Brain Definition of Death." *Hastings Center Report* 23 (4): pp. 18–24.

Veatch, R. 2000. *Transplantation Ethics.* Washington, D.C.: Georgetown University Press.

Wald, N.J., and Law, M.R. (2003). "A Strategy to Reduce Cardiovascular Disease by More Than 80%." *British Medical Journal* 326: pp. 1419–25.

Warren, M.A. 2002. "Does Distributive Justice Require Universal Access to Assisted Reproduction"? In R. Rhodes, M. Battin, and A. Silvers (eds) *Medicine and Social Justice: Essays on the Distribution of Health Care.* New York: Oxford University Press.

Wasserman, D., Bickenbach, J., and Wachbroit, R. (eds). 2005. *Quality of Life and Human Difference: Genetic Testing, Health Care, and Disability.* Cambridge: Cambridge University Press.

Waugh, N., Black, C., Walker, S., Mcintyre, L., Cummins, E., and Hillis, G. 2006. "The Effectiveness and Cost-effectiveness of Computed Tomography Screening for Coronary Artery Disease: Systematic Review." *Health Technology Assessment* 10 (Oct.): pp. 1–41.

Weisbard, A. 1993. "A Polemic on Principles: Reflections on the Pittsburgh Protocol." *Kennedy Institute of Ethics Journal* 3: pp. 217–30.

Wells, D., Ross, J., Detsky, A. 2007. "What is Different About the Market for Health Care?" *JAMA* 298: pp. 2785–87.

Wennberg, J. 1973. "Small Area Variations in Health Care." *Science* 182 (December 14): pp. 1102–08.

Wennberg, J. 2004. "Practice Variation: Implications for our Health Care System." *Managed Care* 13 (9 Supplement): pp. 3–7.

Whetten-Goldstein, K., Sloan, F.A., Goldstein, L.B., and Kulas, E.D. 1998. "A Comprehensive Assessment of the Cost of Multiple Sclerosis in the United States." *Multiple Sclerosis* 4: pp. 419–25.

Wikler, D. 1983. "Philosophical Perspectives on Access to Health Care." In President's Commission for the Study of Ethical Problems in Medicine, *Securing Access to Health Care* Vol. 2. Washington, D.C.: Government Printing Office.

Wikler, D. 1987. "Personal Responsibility for Illness." In D. van DeVeer, and T. Regan (eds) *Health Care Ethics.* Philadelphia: Temple University Press, pp. 326–58.

Wildavsky, A. 1977. "Doing Better and Feeling Worse: The Political Pathology of Health Policy." In J.H. Knowles (ed.) *Doing Better and Feeling Worse: Health Care in the United States.* New York: Norton, pp. 105–23.

REFERENCES

Williams, A. 1997. "The Rationing Debate: Rationing Health Care By Age: The Case For." *BMJ:* 314: pp. 820–22.

Winslow, G. 1986. "Rationing and Publicity." In G. Agich, and C. Begley (eds) *The Price of Health*. Dordrecht: D. Reidel Publishing.

Woodward, R., Brown, M., Stewart, S., Cronin, K., and Cutler, D. 2007. "The Value of Medical Interventions for Lung Cancer in the Elderly: Results from SEER-CMHSF." *Cancer* 110 (Dec. 1): pp.2511–18.

Wraith, J.E. 2006. "Limitations of Enzyme Replacement Therapy: Current and Future." *Journal of Inherited Metabolic Disorders* 29: pp. 442–47.

Wright, A., and Katz, I. 2007. "Letting Go of the Rope—Aggressive Treatment, Hospice Care and Open Access." *New England Journal of Medicine* 357: pp. 324–27.

Yellin, E., Murphy, L., Cisternas, M., Foreman, A., Pasta, D., and Helmick, C. 2007. "Medical Care Expenditures and Earnings Losses Among Persons with Arthritis And Other Rheumatic Conditions in 2003, and Comparisons With 1997." *Arthritis and Rheumatism* 56: pp. 1397–1407.

Young, I.M. 2000. *Inclusion and Democracy*. New York: Oxford University Press.

Young, I.M. 2003. "Activist Challenges to Deliberative Democracy." In J. Fishkin, and P. Laslett (eds.) *Debating Deliberative Democracy*. London: Blackwell, pp. 102–20.

Zimmerman, J., Kramer, A., McNair, D., and Malila, F. 2006. "Acute Physiology and Chronic Health Evaluation (APACHE) IV: Hospital Mortality Assessment for Today's Critically Ill Patients." *Critical Care Medicine* 34 (5): pp. 1297–1310.

Zucker, M., and Zucker, H. 1997. *Medical Futility and the Evaluation of Life-Sustaining Interventions*. Cambridge: Cambridge University Press.

INDEX

Age-based rationing
  and the artificial heart, 223–24
  and duty to rescue, 294–97
    and frequency of rescue problem, 294
    and identifiable lives, 37–38, 57, 233, 291–94, 296–97, 234, 378
    and medical trade-offs problem, 295
    and natural life span, 295
    and predictability of aging health needs, 296
  and elderly population statistics, 280
  and "healthy Granny" objection, 298–99
  and lack of universal endorsement, 298
  and national health insurance, 299
  and Primary Care Trusts in Britain, 283–84
  and prudential life span account, 285–87
  and responses to objections, 291–93
Age-related macular degeneration (AMD), 145, 183–84, 194, 280
  and quality of life, 147–48
  and range of effectiveness, 147–48
Ageism, 124
AIDS exceptionalism, and fairness, 404n13
AIDS patients, 7, 19–20, 27, 72–73, 135–37, 142, 179, 184, 206, 215–18, 232, 246–47, 256–58, 268, 282, 356, 365, 367, 375–76, 409n1, 417n5
  and high-cost patients, 26
  and invisible rationing, 86–87
  and Levinsky, Norman, 53–54
  and McGann, John, 86–87
  and protease inhibitors, 181
  and setting limits for
    protease inhibitors/fusion inhibitors, 6, 19, 61, 136–37, 143, 179, 181–83, 194, 208, 218, 221, 227, 231, 246–47, 258, 311, 356, 417n4
Alice and Betty problem, 139, 166, 176, 414n10
  need for a consistent rule, 137
  and rational democratic deliberation role, 137–39
Alternative reproduction benefit vs. artificial hearts, 423n4

INDEX

Alzheimer's disease, 7, 16, 22, 30, 59–60, 68, 99, 101, 135, 144–45, 148, 154, 182, 224, 303–304, 392–93, *See also* Diaz
    and the artificial heart (TIAH), 144–45
    increased incidence of, 68
Anencephalic infants
    and fair equality of opportunity, 182
Anti-TNF therapy, 203–204
    vs. artificial heart, 221
Artificial hearts, allocating, 64–65. *See also* TIAH
    allocation norms
        ability to pay, 63–64
        age limits, 63–64
        aggregated lifetime costs, 61
        cost-effectiveness, 59–61
        equal value of lives, 58
        life years saved, 58–59
        personal responsibility and dessert, 64
        quality of life years saved, 59–60
        urgency of need, 61
    need for, costs of, 56–58
    priorities and probabilities, 64–65
    problem of private purchase, 223–24
    setting limits: options, 220–27
    deny TIAH to the medically irresponsible, 225–27
    fund no TIAH publicly, 222
    fund TIAH at only 50% for the elderly, 225
    fund TIAH for all with this medical need, 221–22
    fund TIAH only for those below age eighty, 224
    fund TIAH only for those below age seventy, 222–24
Autologous bone marrow transplant (ABMT), 90–93, 150, 171, 183, 210, 216, 233, 245, 268–69
    and breast cancer, 161–62
Autonomy principle defined, 186
Avastin (bevacizumab), 74, 95, 150, 167, 183–84, 230, 244–46, 298, 356,
Ayala case, 345
    and savior siblings, 423n1

"Baby boom" generation, 7, 203, 219, 281, 287–90, 296, 408n15
    and escalating health care costs, 17–18, 24, 56
    and rational democratic deliberation, 17–18
    and self-imposed rationing decisions, 17–18
Baby K case, 75, 141, 173–75, 263–64, 410n4, 418n8, 419n5
    vs. Down's syndrome, 262–63
    and pricelessness of human life, 75, 173
Benjamin, Martin
    and "integrity-preserving compromise," 112–13
Blumstein, James, 85
    as defender of financial incentives for organ procurement, 328–331
    and invisible rationing mechanisms, 87–89, 94
Bodenheimer, Thomas, 40
"Bottomless pit" patients
    defined, 25, 108–12, 255
    and least well off patients, 25
Bohman, James, 160–62
Brody, Baruch, 422n8
    as critic of age-based rationing, 290–92
    and identifiable lives problem, 291
    and loyal physician advocates, 291
    and rejection of fair innings argument, 291
    and libertarian age-based rationing, 292–93
Brody, Howard, 43
Buchanan, Allen, 374, 426n7
    and the expressivist objection, 309–10
    and genetic decent minimum, 313
    and health reform, 380–81
    and no shared conception of justice, 129, 161, 380–81
Bureaucrats, and rationing protocols, 150–51
Burke, Leslie, 255, 269, 274, 431

Callahan, Daniel, ix, 6, 28, 51, 63, 280
    and age-based rationing, 276–78, 299
    and benefits for all, 370
    and expansive health needs, 104
    and personal responsibility for illness, 374–75
    and public health, 368–69
    and "ragged edge" problem, 52–53, 58, 60, 63–64, 68, 122, 146, 222, 229, 246, 279, 290, 315, 408n18
    and rescue medicine, 369
    and social solidarity, 369

Cardiac surgery, and the very old, 278–79
  and ragged edge problem, 279
Cardiovascular disease
  and angioplasties, volume of, 67
  and bypass surgery, volume of, 67
  and life-expectancy, 67
Child B (Jaymee Bowen) case, 73, 76, 178, 406n4
Cholinesterase inhibitors, 99, 149
  and marginal benefit, 99
Chronic illness, burden of, 121, 129, 224, 255–56, 282, 351, 374, 389, 417n5, 419n1
  and AIDS, 258
  and disability, and quality of life, 258–59
  and the elderly, 123
  and hemophilia, 258
  and kidney failure, 258
Coby Howard, 35–39, 48, 73, 142, 400, 406n4
  and Oregon rationing experiment, 35–38, 48
Cohen, Carl
  defender of presumed consent for organ procurement, 331–32
Considered judgments of health care justice, x, 19, 21, 31–32, 89, 101, 103, 112, 124, 160, 164, 173–74, 177, 181, 190, 198, 200, 207, 219, 228, 293, 317, 334, 380, and justification, 164
Constitutional principles of health care justice, 19–21, 112, 184–94, 224
  defined, 184
  and health needs of children, 178–79
  and hemophilia, 178
  as justice-promoting, 19–20
  listed, 184–85
  and rational democratic deliberation, 137–38, 180–82, 204, 213, 217, 339, 377, 425n3
  role of, 102
Contractualism, defined, 412n7
Cost-effectiveness, 8, 53, 60, 69, 74, 92, 95, 136, 138, 144, 149, 153, 161, 168–69, 204, 209–10, 229, 235, 245, 269, 271–72, 296, 315, 364, 371, 375, 396, 407n9, 408n20, 420n3, 425n5
  and publicity condition, contrasted, 92
Cost-effectiveness analysis, 65–66, 290, 409n22

Course-of-life and health care justice, 26, 290-91, 337
Cruzan, Nancy, 41, 76, 267
  and cost of care, 76
CT scans, and marginal benefits, 405n15
Cyclosporine
  and ESRD program, 48

Daniels, Norman, 15, 18–19, 33, 152, 190–91, 281
  and age-based rationing, 285–87, 299
  and fair equality of opportunity, 101, 104–106, 111–12, 124, 156, 262
    compared to education, 105–106
  and health disparities, 367
  and identifying health needs, 23–24
  and "lumpy" health care distribution, 61
  and normal opportunity range, 104–105
  and normal species functioning, 104–105
  and traumatic brain injury, 134
Dawson, Jim
  and $2.3 million health problem, 154–55, 255
DeBakey, Michael, 4–5, 254, 257, 269, 274, 295, 299, 421n6
  and age-based rationing, 285
  and dissecting aortic aneurysm, 4, 274
Deliberative model
  validated by applications, 20–22
Deliberative process evaluative norms
  assess assumptions and consequences, 198
  equal respect and mutual understanding, 197
  express and capture shared values, 197–98
  fair and impartial process, 197
  greater toleration, 199
  habit of giving reasons, 196
  identifying public value judgments, 196
  internal conflict in deliberators, 195
  mutual civic education, 198
  respect for complexity, 198
  using science honestly, 195–96
  value pluralism, 197
Dementia, advanced stages, 16, 53–55, 135–36, 185, 191, 207, 241–42, 254, 264–67, 275, 288, 418n6, 421n7
  and disability challenges, 264
  and Levinsky, Norman, 53–54
Democracy problem, 18
  and Daniels, Norman, 102

INDEX

Democratic deliberative process
  and deliberative autonomy, 92
  and educative role, 160
  and giving one another reasons, 163
  and impartiality, 18
  and mutual education, 18, 117
  not adversarial, 159
  as public, visible, transparent, 15–16
  and publicity condition, 92
Dewey, John, xi, 172
  and rational democratic deliberation, 414n4
Dialysis centers, 349
  and federal reimbursement, 48–49
  as for-profit enterprises, 48
Dialysis, home
  and fairness and efficiency, 47–49
Dialysis patients, 20, 47–50, 205, 209, 293, 409n23
  and growing older, 50–52
  hyper-elderly, 408n16
Diaz, Angel, 3–4, 8–9, 14, 16–18, 30, 108, 111, 254, 259, 269
  and Alzheimer's disease (AD), 3
  and implantable cardiac defibrillator (ICD), 3
  and left ventricular assist device (LVAD), 3
Disability, persons with
  Americans with Disability Act (ADA), 268
  defining, 30
  defining scope of, 268–70
  as democratic deliberators, 272
  Henderson vs. Bodine Aluminum, 268–71
  heterogeneity of, 30
  and impartiality, 30
  and neutral conception of, 419n7
  and QALYs, 421n5
  and self-imposed rationing choices, 271–73
  and Silvers, Anita, 419n7
  and unjust care denials, 270–71
Disability challenges
  and the *Cruzan* case, 267
  and end-stage dementia, 264
  and persistent vegetative state (PVS), 264
  and protecting fair equality of opportunity, 265–67
  and quality of life judgment, 266–67, 273
  and rational democratic deliberation, 266–67
  and resource allocation issues, 265–67

Down's syndrome, 30
Duty to rescue, 9, 12–14, 103, 231, 294–96
  and Diaz, Angel, 8–9, 13–14
  and identified individuals, 232–34
Dworkin, Ronald, 15, 126, 136–37, 347, 374
  and deliberative black box, 137
  and prudent insurance approach, 136–37

Eddy, David, 15, 151–52, 233, 268, 399, 404n11, 408n20
  and autologous bone marrow transplant, 90–93
  and cost-effectiveness analysis, 92, 132
Effective costly therapies
  and ankylosing spondylitis
  and anti-TNF therapy 203–204
  and British National Health Service (NHS) 202–204
  and problem of rationing, 202–204
Egalitarianism, 15, 55, 79, 83, 88–89, 101, 105, 117, 124, 126, 129–30, 133–36, 138, 167, 176, 220–22, 234, 239, 281, 311, 316, 334–35, 346, 376, 385, 388, 393, 408n14, 411n8, 419n5, 421n5
  and limits of strict view of, 135
  moderate view of, and least well off, 135–36
  and problem of what to equalize, 133
  reasonable view of, and quadriplegia, 134
  and rejection of social worth criteria, 135
  resource perspective of, and Dworkin, 136–37
  strict view of, and equal concern and respect, 135
  strict view of, and prioritization problem, 134–35
Elderly
  and increasing use of dialysis, 50–52
  and prioritizing health needs, 24–25
  and ragged edge problem, 123–24
  and right to new medical technologies, 122–25
  and risk of ageism, 124
ELSI program
  and "Genome Technology and Reproduction: Values and Public Policy," 306–307
Emanuel, Ezekiel, 385, 388, 391–92. *See* Liberal communitarianism, 347–52
Embryonic stem cell research, 414n9
Emerging medical technologies, 6–7

450

"doing better and feeling worse", ix, 43, 47, 422n9. *See also* Wildavsky, Aaron
and escalating health costs, 6, 122
End-Stage Renal Disease (ESRD) Program of Medicare, 7, 19
  and costs, 44
  and cyclosporine, 45
  and dialysis public funding {Public Law 92–603), 44
  and Epogen costs, 47–48
  and hemophilia patients, 45
  historical background, 44–45
  and transplant funding, 7
Engelhardt, Tristram, 15, 125–28, 129–30, 417n11
  and concept of property, 126–27
  and libertarianism, 125–28
  and limits of reason, 125–28
  and minimalist state, 125–26
Equality principle
  and AIDS end-of-life rationing protocol, 217–18
  defined, 189–90
  rejection of social worth criteria, 190
Erbitux (cetuximab), 100, 230, 256
  and marginal benefit, 100
ESRD program
  compared to Medicare Part D program, 208
  and immunosuppressant medication costs, 205–207
  and setting limits, 205
Explicit rationing, 95–96. *See also* Mechanic, David
Extremely low birth weight infants, 141, 175, 178, 183, 204, 249, 263
  and justice relevance of medical facts, 183–84
  and NICU costs, 175–76

Factor VIII
  and hemophilia, 45, 72, 80, 109, 174–75, 204, 227, 258, 356, 424n4
  and Jehovah's Witness patients, 192–93
  and Mr. H, 72–73, 109–110, 114, 174
Fair and effective equality of opportunity principle
  defined, 191–92
  and genotypes problem, 191–92
Fair equality of opportunity, 15, 101, 104–12, 114, 124, 130, 133, 156, 176, 178, 182–83, 189, 204, 206–207, 209, 216, 221–22, 227, 236, 246, 257, 264–65, 275, 285, 289, 299, 302–303, 310–12, 315, 354, 362, 389, 411n8. *See also* Daniels, Norman
  and the artificial heart, 222
  and "bottomless pit" patients, 108–10
  and constitutional principle of health care justice, 111–12
  and context-dependent claim limits, 107–108
  and early onset genetic disorders, 203–204
  and Ed Van Houten, 109
  and Gaucher's disease, 110
  and rational democratic deliberation, 108–109
  and terminally-ill Medicare patients, 110–11
Fair terms of cooperation, 82, 88, 99, 164–65, 186, 194, 312
  and health care rationing, 164–65
  and mutual respect, 165
Fast CT scans, 23
Foot, Philippa, 71
Fusion inhibitors, 26, 73, 136–37, 143, 179, 182–83, 208–10, 258
  and AIDS patients, 136
Futile medical care
  and health care inefficiencies, 43
  problem of defining, 43
Futility
  vs. rationing or priority setting, 409n23
  Theresa Hamilton case, 418n8

Gaucher disease, 74–76, 110, 132, 136, 156, 176, 222, 227, 248, 256
  described, 410n3
  and imiglucerase costs, 74, 110, 132–33, 136, 156, 176, 227, 248, 356, 410n3
Genetic endowment
  and future possible children, 301
  and serious genetic deficiency, 301
Genotypes, 191
Giuliani, Rudy, 84, 86
Golubchuk, G, (Canada), 359, 361
Gostin, Larry, 365, 367–68, 372
Great Equations in health care: COST CONTROL = CARE CONTROL; COST CONTROL = INCOME CONTROL, 7, 380, 404n7. *See also* Reinhardt, Uwe
Grumbach, Kevin, 40

451

Hall, Mark
   and "bundled" informed consent, 98–99
   and publicity condition, 98
   rationing as informed consent problem, 97–99
Hamilton, Theresa, 418n8
Hardin, Garrett, "tragedy of the commons," 157–58
Harris, John, 75, 290, 316, 338, 421n5
   and fair innings argument, 281–83
   and expensive cancer drugs, 282–83
Health benefits
   problem of limits, 165–66
Health care
   and fair equality of opportunity principle, 112
   as morally special, 39–40, 103–12
Health care cost control
   and need for reciprocal sacrifice, 382
Health care justice
   Albert and Bonnie case, 51–52
   and coherence, 19
   and considered judgments of, 19
   and constitutional principles of, 19
   and democratic deliberation, 167–70
   as fair equality of opportunity, 15, 124
   and genetic endowment of future possible children, 302
   and genotypes cases, 167–70
   and justice-warranted public funding for limited PGD, 308, 311–14
   libertarian, 15
   moderately egalitarian, 15
   need for pluralistic conception of, 70, 310–11
   no widely shared conception of, 15
   and pluralism, 112, 124–25, 162, 172, 184, 197, 350, 375, 414n8
   pluralistic conception of, 15, 70, 101, 128, 185, 234, 413n14
      and moral limits of utilitarianism, 131–33
      and virtues of utilitarianism, 131–33
   and preimplantation genetic diagnosis (PGD), 302–306
      early onset genetic disorders, 303–306
      late onset genetic disorders, 303–306
   and public health, 368–70, 373–74
   and ragged edges, 62–65
   and self-imposed rationing decisions, 274–75
   strictly egalitarian, 15, 117
   utilitarian, 15
   virtues of, 101
Health care rationing
   and efficiency first approach, 40
   and getting rid of waste and inefficiency, 40–43
   and global informed consent, 435n7
   and Medicaid, 405n1
Health care system in U.S.
   as cooperative enterprise, 13
Health care vouchers
   basic description of, 388
   and cost control, 390–91
   and defining a basic health plan, 388–89
   and demanding patients, 393–94
   and determining value of voucher, 389–390, 392–93
   and DRG-like mechanisms, 391
   and egalitarian virtues, 393
   and Emanuel, E, 388, 391–92
   and high-cost technologies, 391–93
   and Kotlikoff, 388–91, 393–94
   and moral hazard, 393
   and two-tiered health care, 392–93
Health reform. *See also* Single-Payer Reform
   and access issues, 383
   and access liberty issues, 383
   and basic justice issues, 384
   and Clinton administration, 379–80
   and employer-based system for financing, 385
   and escalating health cost issues, 383
   and health savings accounts (HSAs)
      basic description of, 385–86
      and consequences for chronically ill, 386–87
      and consumer-based cost control, 387–88
      and health care justice, 388
      and security of access to care, 386
   and inefficiency issues, 383–84
   and medical integrity issues, 384, 398–400
      physicians as loyal advocates of just patient interests, 399
   and Reinhardt's Great Equation: Cost Control = Income Control, 380
   and security issues, 384
   and Working Group #17, 279
Heart transplant costs, 416n2

Hemophilia, 7, 45, 60, 72, 76, 80, 109, 113, 174–76, 192, 204, 218, 222, 227, 256, 258, 268, 303–304, 343, 356, 406n4, 409n1
   Mr. H, and severe hemophilia A, 72–73, 174
   and interstitial justice, 113
Herceptin
   and metastatic breast cancer, 150, 166, 183, 203–204, 221, 230, 240, 251, 256
   and NHS, 418n5
High spinal cord injury (C1-C4), 21, 78, 110–11, 133–35, 184, 239, 310, 344, 414n9
   and health care justice, 110
Hip arthroplasty, 7
HMOs
   and conflicting incentives for physicians, 93–95
   and prospective payment mechanisms, 93–95
Hospice, and "doing better and feeling worse," 422n9

ICU beds
   and non-ideal justice, 119
Imiglucerase, 74, 110, 132–33, 136, 156, 176, 227, 248, 356, 410n3
   and Gaucher's disease, 74–76, 110, 132, 136, 156, 176, 222, 227, 248, 256
Implantable cardiac defibrillator (ICD), 3, 6–7, 12, 17, 22, 67–68, 78, 100, 130, 147–48, 177, 189, 241, 252, 264, 290, 323, 356, 386, 389, 396. *See also* Diaz, A
   and Alzheimer's rationing, 100
   needs and costs, 68–69
   and T-wave alternans test, 69, 100, 120, 177, 189, 253, 409n23
Implicit rationing, 95–97
   defined, 95. *See also* Mechanic, David
Incompletely theorized agreement
   and Sunstein, 416n18
Interstitial justice, 119
   defined, 113
Invisible rationing, 9–10, 77, 81–89, 97–99, 145, 151, 185, 214, 284, 292, 404n6, 417n10
   and Blumstein, 85
   and publicity condition, 82
   and serious injustices, 82
   and tragic choices, 81–84

Jehovah's Witness patients, 27, 192–93, 342–43, 356, 360, 390, 423n3
   and Factor VIIa, 343, 360, 390, 424n4
Just Caring, vii, ix, xi, 5–7, 34, 39, 48, 109, 197, 199, 385, 394, 396, 399, 401, 411n1
   complexity and magnitude, 39
   and Goshen project, 197, 199
   as moral problem, 34–35
   problem definition, 5, 7, 34
   summary lessons, 400–401
Just health care rationing
   practical and pragmatic, 172–73
   and shared considered judgments of justice, 171–73
   and wide reflective equilibrium, 171–73
Just health care system
   and health reform, 32–33
   and "leak-proof" rationing, 33
   and non-ideal justice, 32–33, 102, 112, 261, 314
Justice
   and burdens of judgment, 101, 311, 315, 376, 411n6
   and HIV, 376
   and lead abatement, 376–77
   and rational democratic deliberation, 377–78
   and Medicare Part D benefit, 426n9
   and public funding for limited PGD, 308
   and public health priorities, 375–78
Justice and rationing decisions, self-imposed, 274–75
Justice and genetic enhancement, 316–17
   and genetically least well off, 317
   and risk of genetic aristocracy, 316
Justice preserving integrity
   and rational democratic deliberation, 115–21

Kant, Immanuel, 77
   and moral law within, 401
   and public reason without, 401
Kitcher, Philip
   and age of genetic innocence, 301–302
   and age of genetic responsibility, 301–302
   and Utopian eugenics, 302
Kitzhaber, John, 38
   and Down's syndrome infants, 262–63
   and persons with disabilities, 261–64
   and rights of the poor, 260–61
Knee arthroplasty, 7

INDEX

Lakeberg conjoined twins, 76, 80–81, 166, 408n21, 411n2
Laparoscopic surgery
  and health care costs, 420n3
Last-chance therapies, 24–29
  and the artificial heart [TIAH], 24
  and bevacizumab (Avastin), 244–47
    options for access: ability to pay, 245
    options for access: fund early use, 245–46
    options for access: fund preferred genotypes, 246–47
  and bilateral renal agenesis, 248–49
  defined, 24
  defining features of, 231
  and duty to rescue, 231–33
  and futility, 249–53
  and herceptin, 230
  and ICU care, 250
  and least well off
    and costs of therapies, 237
    and dementia patients, 240–42
    and fair equality of opportunity, 236
    and imminent death, 237–38
    and metastatic breast cancer, 240
    and multiple sclerosis, 238–39
    and necrotic small bowel syndrome, 247–49
    and needs of rheumatoid arthritis patients, 241
    not all medically least well off have equal claims, 234–35
    and persons with disabilities, 235
    and prioritarianism, 234
    and Rawls' primary goods, 236–37
    and severe spinal cord injuries, 239–40
  and left ventricular assist device, 230
    for the elderly, 247–48
  and lung volume reduction surgery, 229–30
    for the elderly, 246–48
  and medical judgment, 250–52
    and APACHE IV scoring system, 251–53
    and APACHE V rationing protocol, 251–53
  and Medicare Part D, 243–44
  and private insurance subsidy, 242–43
  and rational democratic deliberation, 250, 252–53
  and sutinib problem, 214
  and total parenteral nutrition (TPN), 230–31
  and ultimate needs, 24,
  and very expensive cancer drugs, 230–31
Least well off patients, 25–26, 114, 135–36
Left ventricular assist device (LVAD), 3, 6, 12, 17, 24, 67, 183, 230, 311, 315, 323, 391, 423n4
Levinsky, Norman
  and advanced dementia, 53–54
  and AIDS, 53–54
  and moral integrity of physicians, 54–55, 62
  and PVS, 52–54
  and rejection of ragged edges, 52–55
Liberal communitarianism
  communitarians vs. liberals, 350–51
  and Emanuel, E, 347–52
  and deliberative managed care plans, 350
  and diverse managed care plans, 347–52
  and health care vouchers, 348–52
  and last chance therapies, 350–52
  and medical research funding, 349
  and rejection of Rawlsian liberalism, 347
Liberal democratic societies
  and value pluralism, 162–63
Liberal neutrality, principle of, 185, 328–29, 343–44, 347, 350–51
  defined, 193–94
Liberalism problem
  and abortion, 27
  and assisted reproductive technologies, 27, 356
    and conscience objections, 357
    and feminist objections, 358
  defined, 26–28
  and embryonic stem cell research, 27
  and Jehovah's Witness patients, 27, 342–44
  and national health insurance, 343–46
    and embryonic stem cells, 344–45
    and Lomasky, 346
    and Right to Life, 344–46
  and public reason, 352–54
  and reproductive services, 354–59
    and costs of, 355–56
    and feminists, 358–59
    and relative health care priority, 356
    and religious critics, 357–59
    and veil of ignorance, 354

Libertarianism, 15, 55, 63, 79, 86, 97, 101, 105, 125–131, 144, 149, 214, 222, 292, 311, 315, 329, 345–46, 385, 388, 408*n*14, 411*n*8, 412*n*10, 413*n*11, 413*n*12, 417*n*11. *See also* Engelhardt, T
  and effective liberty problem, 129–30
  and liberalism problem, 131
  and practical consequences of, 128–29
  and wealth-related purchasing, 130
Libertarians
  vs. rational democratic deliberation, 413*n*12
Liberty principle
  defined, 188–89
  and fair equality of opportunity, 189
  and for-profit medicine, 189
Limits of reason, 125–26
Limits of state authority, 125–26
Lomasky, Loren, 27, 346
  and invisible rationing defended, 86, 89

Magic money wand, 4–5, 12, 271–72, 274, 403*n*4
McGann, John
  and H&H Music Company, 86–87
Markets, moral failure of
  failure to control health costs, 148–49
Markets, moral virtue of
  impersonal and impartial, 148
Mechanic, David
  explicit rationing, critic of, 95–97
  managed care and implicit rationing, 95–97
Medical arms race, and technology costs, 407*n*8
Medical expertise
  and rationing decisions, 149–50
  and setting health priorities, 149–50
Medical rescues
  multiple times in a life, 160–61
Medically urgent vs. morally urgent, 256–57
Medicare
  and 1972 ESRD amendments, 202–203
  and age-based rationing, 280–81
  and cost of artificial hearts, 154
  DRGs (Diagnosis-related Groupings), 41, 85–86
    and conflicting incentives for physicians, 92–95
    and discouraged deliberation, 39–40
    and invisible rationing, 85–86

  and marginal benefits, 93–94
  and Medicaid, funding issues, 123
  and medical flexibility, 94–95
  and physicians, 31–32
  and prospective payment mechanisms, 93–95
  and rationing, 31–32
  and "rough justice," 94–95
  and ESRD, 47–48
  and high-cost patients, 6–7, 14, 24, 99, 176, 218, 227–28, 239
  population increase, 68
  prescription drug benefit, 56–57
Medicare Part D, 243–44
  vs. artificial heart, 221
Meliorism
  and justice, 120
Menzel, Paul
  and duty to donate organs for transplant, 332–33
Minimalist state, 125. *See also* Engelhardt, T
Morreim, Haavi
  and disguised rationing, 292–93
Mutual respect, 164–65

National health insurance, 27–28, 65, 86, 131, 141, 143, 146, 202–203, 211, 220–22, 232, 243–44, 270, 292, 298–301, 308, 333, 343, 345–46, 353–54, 356, 358, 360, 371, 379, 405*n*13, 407*n*11, 412*n*2, 423*n*1
National Health Service (NHS), 81, 178, 240, 392, 406*n*4, 426*n*8
Necrotic small bowel syndrome, 75–76, 142, 175–76, 248
  and total parenteral nutrition (TPN), 75, 142, 230–31, 247–48, 351
NICE (National Institute for Clinical Excellence) in Britain, 146–48, 240
  and AMD, 146
  and cancer drug limits, 150–51
  and technology assessment, 392
Non-ideal justice
  and complacency, 120–21
  domain of, 102
  and instability, 120–22
  and meliorism, moral worth of, 120
  moral defense of, 112–124
  and new medical technologies, 122

Non-ideal justice (*Cont.*)
  and problem/decision sphere, 119
  and rational democratic deliberation, 102
  and rejection of utopianism, 119
Normal opportunity range, 104, 106–107, 178, 206, 241, 265, 275, 280, 289, 291, 312–13, 363
  and PVS patients, 53, 59, 76–78, 107–108, 117, 135–36, 159, 166, 173, 182, 207, 240, 264–65, 267–68, 274–75, 346, 360, 392, 421*n*5

Oregon, 3, 8, 10–11, 22–23, 35–38, 73, 171, 178, 217, 259–63, 397, 405*n*1, 407*n*6, 419*n*2, 419*n*3
  and Medicaid, 35
  and non-ideal justice, 171
  and priority setting, 23, 171
  and rationing experiment, 35. *See also* Coby Howard
Organ procurement
  and duty to donate, 332–33
    and P. Menzel, defender of, 332–33
  and financial incentives, 327–331
    and Blumstein, defender of, 328–31
  and inadequate voluntary response, 328
  and mandated choice, 331
  and presumed consent, 331–32
    and C. Cohen, defender of, 331–32
Organ transplantation
  and artificial organs, 323–24
  and dead donor rule, 320–21
  and financial incentives, 319
  multi-organ transplants
    and democratic deliberation, 336
    and egalitarian commitments, 334–36
    and fair access, 333–36
  and obligation to maximize, 318–19
  and Pittsburgh protocol
    and altered criteria for death, 324–27
    and dead donor rule, 325–26
    and required request, 326–27
  and presumed consent, 319–21
  retransplantation
    and course-of-life conception of justice, 337–38
    and fair access, 336–339
    and rational democratic deliberation, 339–41

and veil of ignorance, 338
and statistics, 321–22

Painless health cost control
  and bedside decision making, 42
  and Bodenheimer and Grumbach, 381–82
  and excessive administrative costs, 381–82
  and Himmelstein and Woolhandler, 381–82
  very rare, 41
Palliative care, escalating cost of, 43
Persistent vegetative state (PVS), 53, 59, 76–78, 107–108, 117, 135–36, 159, 166, 173, 182, 207, 240, 264–65, 267–68, 274–75, 346, 360, 392, 421*n*5
  Cruzan, Schiavo cases, 41
Phantom efficiencies, 421*n*3
Physicians
  moral integrity of, 54–55
Pluralism
  and health care justice, 124–25
  and liberal democratic societies, 162
Pluralistic conception of health care justice
  and Rhodes, R, 413*n*14
Polypill
  and preventive health care, 408*n*22
Preimplantation genetic diagnosis (PGD)
  and autism, 303
  and Canavan's disease, 303, 312
  and cost savings, 314
  and cystic fibrosis, 304, 312
  and disability advocates, 29, 307
  and Duchenne muscular dystrophy, 303, 312
  and the expressivist objection, 309–10
  and Fragile X syndrome, 303, 312
  vs. funding of left ventricular assist devices, 315
  and future possible children, 309
  and health needs vs. health desires, 307–308
  and hemophilia, 303
  and justice-warranted public funding, 310, 314
  and juvenile diabetes, 303
  and Lesch-Nyhan syndrome, 303, 312
  and neurofibromatosis, 303
  and ragged edge problem, 315
  and Right to Life, 307
  and Tay-Sachs disease, 303, 312
Pricelessness of human life, 9, 12–15, 74
  and Baby K, 75

and genetic endowment, 300
and highest liberal interests, 442n7
and ideal theory of justice, 113–14
and "least well off," 114, 236
and morally tolerable inequalities, 89
and non-ideally just outcomes, 411n6
and original position, 187
and overlapping consensus, 200–201
and publicity condition, 82, 88
and rational autonomy, 186–88
and reasonable pluralism, 184
and veil of ignorance, 91
Reason-giving
nature of, 165–66
Reciprocity, principle of
defined, 194
Reflective equilibrium, contextual, 19–21, 102–103, 128, 137–38, 171–73, 175, 177–78, 179–84, 192, 198, 204, 216
Reinhardt, Uwe, 7
and Great Equation: Cost Control = Income Control, 404n7
and health reform, 380
Renal dialysis
and end-of-life costs, 207–208
and home dialysis vs. center dialysis, 208–209
Resource allocation issues
and disability challenges, 265–67
Respect for persons principle
defined, 192–93
Rheumatoid arthritis, 418n6
Rhodes, Rosamond, 310–11, 413n14
Rough justice, 84, 94, 426n7
limits on, 114
Russell, Louise, 334, 370–71
and marginal health prevention, 371–73
and C-reactive protein screening, 372–73
and universal HIV screening, 371–72
and marginal public health benefits, 371

Sabin, James, 18
Sarkisyan, Nataline, viii, 159, 160–62
Scanlon, Thomas, 126
Schauer, F, 165
Schiavo, Terry, 41, 59, 76, 259
and cost of care, 76
Schmidt, Douglas, 3–4, 6, 8–9, 10–12, 14, 30, 403n1

and uninsured, 3
Sepsis, costs of, 155
Silvers, Anita
and ICU patients, 420n8
and neutral conception of disability, 419n7
Single-Payer Reform
basic description, 394–96
and cost control, 396
and global hospital budgets, 395–96
and Oregon priority-setting commission, 397–98
and physician payment, 395
and rational democratic deliberation, 396–97
and technology assessment, 398–99
Social justice
limits of, 131
Social worth criteria
and rationing, 410n2
Starzl, Thomas, 285
Statins
and cost-effectiveness, 65–67
expansive use and just priorities, 182–83
and marginal benefit, 99, 132
and predicted effectiveness, 67
Statistical lives, 41, 79, 81, 233, 291, 297, 334, 377, 404n10
Streptokinase, 153
and HOCA/LOCA, 97
Strict egalitarianism, 133, 135–36
and Veatch, 133
Sulmasy, Daniel, 31
Sunstein, Cass
and deliberative enclaves, 201
and incompletely theorized agreement, 200–201

Thomson, Judith Jarvis
and the "health pebble" 335
Tomlinson, Tom, 43
Totally implantable artificial heart (TIAH), 7, 24, 39
Tragic choices
Calabresi, G and Bobbitt, P, 10, 82, 85, 89, 283, 404n10, 422n1
defined, 82–83
and "an exposed inegalitarianism," 83
and pricelessness of human life, 82
as "rough justice," 84

Tragic choices (*Cont.*)
  and sense of honesty, 83
  and societal consciences, 84
  and ultimate values, 83
Transplant program
  and selling organs to highest bidder, 13–14
  "Trolley" problem, 71–73, 410*n*1
  and deliberate killing, 71
  and number of lives saved, 71–72
Tuskegee syphilis experiments, 90

Ubel, Peter, 8–9, 336–38
  and pricelessness of human life, 8–9
  and retransplantation, 336–38
Unequal health needs
  and equal resources, 105
Utilitarianism, 15, 28, 55, 57, 60, 74, 79, 92, 116–17, 130–33, 135, 138, 176, 204, 221, 247, 311, 315, 334, 364, 411*n*8, 419*n*5, 421*n*5

Van Houten, Ed, 109–10, 114, 254
Veatch, Robert, 13, 25, 133–34, 320, 334
  as strong critic of untilitarianism, 133–34
  and traumatic brain injury, 134

Wanglie case, 346, 359–60
White House Task Force on Health Care Reform, 8
Wide reflective equilibrium, 19–20, 102, 172
  comparison to our legal system, 179–81
  and medical, social, scientific facts, 181–84
  a practical, pragmatic conception of justice, 172–73
  and rational democratic deliberation, 177–81
Wikler, Daniel, 26
Wildavsky, Aaron, 47

Xenotransplantation
  and health care justice, 46
  and increasing transplantable organs, 46